AF304830

A THEORY OF MEDIATORS' ETHICS

Many aspects relating to the conduct of mediation are left to mediator choice, but mediators often lack adequate guidance on how their discretion ought to be exercised. In this book, Omer Shapira identifies the ethical norms that govern mediators' conduct. Adopting a professional ethics perspective on the basis of role-morality and applying it to a core definition of mediators' role, Shapira argues that all mediators are placed in ethical relationships with mediation parties, the mediation profession, the public, and their employers or principals that produce ethical obligations. The book goes on to explore the legitimate expectations of these groups and analyses existing codes of conduct for mediators. Shapira constructs a theory of mediators' ethics that produces a *Proposed Model Code of Conduct for Mediators* – a detailed set of norms of mediators' ethics that can be rationally justified and defended with regard to mediators at large.

OMER SHAPIRA is Senior Lecturer in the Law Faculty at Ono Academic College, Israel.

A THEORY OF MEDIATORS' ETHICS

Foundations, Rationale, and Application

OMER SHAPIRA
Senior Lecturer, Law Faculty, Ono Academic College

CAMBRIDGE
UNIVERSITY PRESS

CAMBRIDGE
UNIVERSITY PRESS

University Printing House, Cambridge CB2 8BS, United Kingdom

Cambridge University Press is part of the University of Cambridge.

It furthers the University's mission by disseminating knowledge in the pursuit of education, learning and research at the highest international levels of excellence.

www.cambridge.org
Information on this title: www.cambridge.org/9781107143043

© Omer Shapira 2016

This publication is in copyright. Subject to statutory exception and to the provisions of relevant collective licensing agreements, no reproduction of any part may take place without the written permission of Cambridge University Press.

First published 2016

Printed in the United Kingdom by Clays, St Ives plc

A catalogue record for this publication is available from the British Library

Library of Congress Cataloguing in Publication data
Shapira, Omer, author.
A theory of mediators' ethics / Omer Shapira.
New York : Cambridge University Press, 2016.
LCCN 2015042978 | ISBN 9781107143043 (hardback)
LCSH: Legal ethics. | Dispute resolution (Law) | Mediation. | BISAC: LAW / Arbitration, Negotiation, Mediation.
LCC K123 .S54 2016 | DDC 174/.3–dc23
LC record available at http://lccn.loc.gov/2015042978

ISBN 978-1-107-14304-3 Hardback

Cambridge University Press has no responsibility for the persistence or accuracy of URLs for external or third-party internet websites referred to in this publication, and does not guarantee that any content on such websites is, or will remain, accurate or appropriate.

To my wife Shirly and our children
Matan and Daniel with love

CONTENTS

List of figures *page* xix
List of tables xxi
Preface xxiii
Abbreviations of codes of conduct xxviii

PART I **A theory of professional ethics** 1

1 Fundamental concepts 3

1.1 Introduction 3

1.1.1 The meanings of ethics 3

1.1.2 Role-ethics and professional ethics 4

1.1.3 Mediators' ethics as professional ethics or role-ethics 5

1.2 Professional ethics: an integration of morality and role 8

1.2.1 Moral norms and ethics 8

1.2.1.1 A definition of moral norms 8

1.2.1.2 Distinguishing duties from aspirations: between rules, principles, values, and ideals 12

1.2.1.3 Rights and powers: permissive or power-conferring norms 19

1.2.1.4 Moral norms that are not norms of ethics 20

1.2.1.5 Ethical demands that exceed the demands of ordinary morality: unethical moral behavior? 20

1.2.1.6 Ethical demands that fall short of ordinary morality: immoral ethical behavior? 21

1.2.2 Delineating the limits of professional ethics: the element of role 22

1.2.2.1 Identifying professional roles and particular activities 23

1.2.2.2 Professional role norms 23

1.2.2.3 Ethical norms: a union of moral norms and professional norms 24
1.2.3 Ethics and law: legal norms that are both moral and professional 27
1.2.3.1 The application of law to professional activities 27
1.2.3.2 Legal norms that are norms of ethics and legal norms that are not 28
1.2.3.3 Distinguishing legal threshold from ethical threshold and ethical bar 30
1.3 Non-professional norms that complement professional ethics 32
1.3.1 Personal integrity or sense of morality 32
1.3.2 Religious belief 33
1.3.3 Other professional role norms 33
1.4 The functions of professional ethics 33
1.5 Conclusion 35
2 Ethical relationships 37
2.1 Introduction 37
2.2 Duties toward clients 38
2.2.1 Introduction 38
2.2.2 The normative basis of duties toward clients 38
2.2.3 Ethical duties toward clients 40
2.2.3.1 Competence 41
2.2.3.2 Disclosure of conflicts of interest 42
2.2.3.3 Client autonomy or self-determination 43
2.2.3.4 Professional integrity 46
2.2.3.5 Impartiality 49
2.2.3.6 Diligence 51
2.2.3.7 Respect and dignity 52
2.2.3.8 Honesty 54
2.2.3.9 Confidentiality 54
2.2.3.10 Fairness 55
2.2.4 Conclusion 56
2.3 Duties toward the profession 57
2.3.1 Introduction 57
2.3.2 The normative basis of duties toward the profession 58

2.3.3 Ethical duties toward the profession 60
2.3.3.1 A duty of fairness: following all the standards that apply to professionals 60
2.3.3.2 A duty to maintain the profession's standing 61
2.3.3.3 Helping the profession to fulfill its social role 63
2.3.4 Conclusion 64

2.4 Duties toward the public 65
2.4.1 Introduction 65
2.4.2 The normative basis of duties toward the public 66
2.4.3 Ethical duties toward the public 68
2.4.4 Conclusion 71

2.5 Duties toward employers and principals 72
2.5.1 Introduction 72
2.5.2 The normative basis of duties toward employers and principals 73
2.5.3 Ethical duties toward employers and principals 75
2.5.4 Conclusion 79

2.6 The rights of professionals 79

2.7 Conclusion 81

PART II **A theory of mediators' ethics** 83

3 Mediation, mediators' role, and mediators' ethics 85

3.1 Introduction 85

3.2 The nature of mediation and the role of mediators: a core descriptive definition 85

3.3 Shared professional ideals 95

3.4 Separate professionals ideals 97

3.5 Flexible and diverse practice 98

3.6 The shared normative features of mediators' conduct 101

3.7 From general ethics of roles to the ethics of mediators: the ethical relationships of mediators 105

3.8 The norms of mediators' ethics 114

3.9 The meaning of the norms: understanding the meaning of mediators' ethical duties and resolving tensions between duties 115

3.10 A proposed model code of conduct for mediators 121

3.11 A road map for the next chapters 122

4 Party self-determination 127

4.1 Introduction 127

4.2 The extent of party self-determination and the allocation of decision-making authority between mediators and parties 129

4.2.1 The normative sources of party self-determination 129

4.2.2 Justifying wide self-determination for mediation parties 132

4.2.3 Exercising wide self-determination through shared decision-making; Limitations on self-determination 134

4.3 The meaning of party self-determination: the elements and quality of self-determination 137

4.3.1 Distinguishing between the extent of self-determination and its elements 137

4.3.2 Competency to make decisions 138

4.3.3 Voluntariness and lack of coercion 140

4.3.4 Knowledge of relevant information 141

4.3.5 Summarizing the conditions for exercise of substantive self-determination 141

4.4 Waiver of self-determination 143

4.5 Mediators' duties regarding party self-determination 144

4.5.1 Duties regarding party competency 145

4.5.2 Duties regarding voluntariness 146

4.5.2.1 A duty to refrain from undermining voluntariness 146

4.5.2.2 A duty to prevent coerced decisions 148

4.5.3 Duties regarding the availability of relevant information 150
4.5.3.1 A duty to refrain from provision of inaccurate information 151
4.5.3.2 A duty to take measures to generate conditions for making informed decisions 151
4.6 Conclusion 159
4.7 A proposed standard of self-determination 159
5 Mediator competence 163
5.1 Introduction 163
5.2 A duty of competence to mediation parties 164
5.3 The profession's and public expectations of mediator competence: the professional and social interests in mediator competence 165
5.4 The meaning of mediator competence 166
5.4.1 Distinguishing between the expectations of particular parties and the expectations of reasonable parties 166
5.4.2 Basic competence 167
5.4.2.1 Knowledge and skills 167
5.4.2.2 A requirement for training and experience 171
5.4.2.3 The question of mediator qualities 173
5.4.3 Specific competence 174
5.4.3.1 An expectation of subject matter expertise due to role definition 174
5.4.3.2 An expectation of subject matter expertise due to case complexity and related factors 175
5.4.3.3 An expectation of subject matter expertise due to institutional rules 176
5.4.3.4 An expectation of cultural knowledge or language skills 177
5.5 Bridging competence gaps 177
5.6 Providing information regarding mediator competence 178
5.7 Maintaining competence 179
5.8 Conclusion 180

5.9 A proposed standard of mediator competence 182

6 Conflicts of interest 183

6.1 Introduction 183

6.2 The inevitability of mediator conflicts of interest 183

6.2.1 Mediator fees 184

6.2.2 Agreement as a goal 184

6.2.3 Psychological needs, prejudice, and bias 185

6.2.4 A duty to take action 185

6.3 Defining mediator conflicts of interest 186

6.4 The normative implications of mediator conflicts of interest 190

6.4.1 The legitimate expectations of parties in a conflict of interest situation 190

6.4.2 The legitimate expectations of the profession and the public in a conflict of interest situation 193

6.4.2.1 Serious conflicts of interest 194

6.4.2.2 Conflicts of interest subsequent to mediation 199

6.5 Conclusion 204

6.6 A proposed standard of conflicts of interest 204

7 Mediator impartiality 207

7.1 Introduction 207

7.2 The sources of mediators' duty of impartiality 208

7.2.1 The reasonable expectations of mediation parties 208

7.2.2 The reasonable expectations of the profession and public 208

7.2.3 A practical source 209

7.3 The meaning of the duty of impartiality 209

7.3.1 A legitimate expectation of parties of freedom from favoritism and bias 209

7.3.2 Internal and external impartiality: between ideal and duty 212

7.3.3 Avoiding perceived partiality or the appearance of it 213
7.3.4 Between impartiality and equality: substantive interpretation of impartiality 217
7.3.4.1 Legitimate expectations of parties for a fair process 218
7.3.4.2 Legitimate expectations of the profession and the public that mediators protect the process of mediation and the profession's standing 223
7.4 Refusal of cases and withdrawal 224
7.5 Criticism of impartiality 227
7.6 Conclusion 229
7.7 A proposed standard of impartiality 229
8 Professional integrity 231
8.1 Introduction 231
8.2 Mediators' duty to conduct mediation with integrity 234
8.2.1 Decision-making and the exercise of professional discretion 234
8.2.2 Separation of professional roles 236
8.2.3 Appropriateness of case to process 241
8.2.4 Prevention of process abuse or substantial defects in the process 243
8.2.4.1 Process abuse by mediators 243
8.2.4.2 Process abuse by other participants – the parties' expectations 244
8.2.4.3 Process abuse and prevention of substantial defects in the process – the professional and public aspects 245
8.3 Conclusion 252
8.4 A proposed standard of professional integrity 252
9 Diligence, respect and dignity, and honesty 255
9.1 Diligence 255
9.1.1 A duty to conduct mediation with diligence 255
9.1.2 The meaning of diligence in mediation 256

9.1.2.1 Attention to the parties and their case 256
9.1.2.2 Preparation for mediation? 256
9.1.3 Care 257
9.1.4 A proposed standard of diligence 258
9.2 Respect and dignity 258
9.2.1 Treating mediation parties with respect and dignity 258
9.2.2 Treating participants and nonparticipants with respect and dignity 260
9.2.3 Promoting respect among participants 261
9.2.4 The relationship between respect and other standards 262
9.2.5 Conclusion 263
9.2.6 A proposed standard of respect and dignity 263
9.3 Honesty 264
9.3.1 Honesty toward mediation parties 264
9.3.2 Honesty toward participants and nonparticipants 265
9.3.3 Honesty among participants 265
9.3.4 Legitimate exceptions to the norm of honesty 266
9.3.5 Conclusion 269
9.3.6 A proposed standard of honesty 270
10 Confidentiality 271
10.1 Introduction 271
10.2 Expectations of confidentiality 271
10.2.1 The parties' expectations of mediator confidentiality 271
10.2.2 The profession's and public expectations of mediator confidentiality 273
10.2.3 Participants' obligation of confidentiality 274
10.2.4 Knowledge about the scope of confidentiality 275
10.3 Defining the type of information that is subject to expectations of confidentiality 277
10.4 Justified grounds for disclosure 281
10.4.1 Disclosure with the parties' consent 283
10.4.2 Disclosure in claims between parties and mediators 285
10.4.2.1 Claims or complaints against mediators 285

10.4.2.2 A mediator claim for fees 285

10.4.3 Disclosure upon mediation program request of information relating to the appearance of parties and as to whether an agreement has been reached 286

10.4.4 Disclosure required or permitted by morality or law 288

10.4.4.1 Ethically required disclosure (a mediator duty to disclose) 288

10.4.4.2 Ethically permitted disclosure (information mediators may disclose) 290

10.4.4.3 A note on mediation privilege and court ordered disclosure 294

10.4.5 Disclosure for the purpose of research, teaching, evaluation or mediator training that protects the anonymity of parties 297

10.5 Conclusion 298

10.6 A proposed standard of confidentiality 300

11 Fairness 302

11.1 Introduction 302

11.2 Understanding the meaning of fairness in mediation 303

11.3 Mediators' duty of fairness 307

11.3.1 Fairness toward mediation parties: an expectation that mediation be conducted in accordance with its standards 307

11.3.2 Fairness toward the profession, the public, and an employer or principal: an expectation that mediation be conducted without causing harm to the institution of mediation, to important social interests, and to the standing of the employer or principal 308

11.4 Conclusion 309

11.5 A proposed standard of fairness 310

12 Maintaining the profession's standing and advancement of the profession 311

12.1 Maintaining the profession's standing 311

12.1.1 Introduction 311

12.1.2 The meaning of maintaining the standing of the profession 312

12.1.3 Implications of the duty to maintain the standing of the profession for the conduct of mediators 313

12.1.4 The duty to maintain the standing of the profession as a duty to the public 315

12.1.5 Conclusion 316

12.1.6 A proposed standard of maintaining the profession's standing 316

12.2 Advancement of the profession 317

12.2.1 The ideal of advancing the profession 317

12.2.2 The meaning of advancement of the profession 318

12.2.3 A proposed standard of advancement of the profession 319

13 Advertising, solicitation, and mediator fees 320

13.1 Introduction 320

13.2 Advertising and solicitation 321

13.2.1 The purpose of regulating mediator advertising and solicitation 321

13.2.2 The content of advertising and solicitation provisions in codes of conduct for mediators 322

13.2.3 A proposed standard of advertising and solicitation 324

13.3 Mediator fees 325

13.3.1 The purpose of regulating mediator fees and other mediation charges 325

13.3.2 The content of mediator fees standards in codes of conduct for mediators 326

13.3.3 A proposed standard of mediator fees 329

14 Obligations to employers and principals 330

14.1 Introduction 330

14.2 The obligations of court-connected mediators to the court 331

14.3 The obligations of volunteering mediators to the community mediation center 334

14.4 Conflicting duties 337

14.5 Conclusion 339

14.6 A proposed standard of obligations to employers and principals 339

PART III **Dealing with ethical problems** 341

15 Ethical decision-making 343

15.1 Introduction 343

15.2 On ethical decision-making 344

15.3 Ethical questions and ethical sensitivity 347

15.3.1 Ethical questions 347

15.3.2 Intention to take an action 348

15.3.3 Ethical sensitivity and awareness 348

15.4 Easy cases/questions 349

15.4.1 Clarifying the facts 350

15.4.2 Identifying the relevant ethical norms 350

15.4.3 Applying the norms to the facts and arriving at a conclusion 351

15.5 Hard cases/questions and dilemmas 351

15.5.1 Indeterminacy of *facts*: attempting to establish a clear set of facts where facts are unclear 351

15.5.2 Uncertainty as to the *identity* of the relevant ethical norms: attempting to identify relevant norms where multiple norms exist 352

15.5.3 Ambiguity of the norms' *content*: identifying alternative interpretations or meanings of the norms 352

15.5.4 *Conflicting* ethical norms or meanings: identifying ethical dilemmas 354

15.5.4.1 Ethical dilemmas 354

15.5.4.2 Non-ethical dilemmas 356

15.5.4.3 Dilemmas resulting from conflicting ethical and legal duties 357

15.5.5 Resolving hard cases: evaluating, ranking, and choosing between alternative courses of action 357

15.5.6 Dead-ends and creative solutions 360

15.6 Conclusion 362

16 Case illustrations 364

16.1 Introduction 364

16.2 Case illustrations 365

16.2.1 The uninformed wife: *party self-determination (informed decision-making) and mediator impartiality* 365

16.2.2 Ziba and Ahmed's Iranian-American divorce: *party self-determination and professional integrity (unacceptable mediation outcomes and separation of professional roles)* 373

16.2.3 The probing judge and the ordering court: *confidentiality and disclosure of mediation information to court* 384

16.2.4 The emotional interrupting party: *party self-determination (party incompetency) and respect and dignity* 390

16.2.5 Post-mediation psychiatric treatment: *conflict of interest* 394

Appendix I A proposed model code of conduct for mediators 397

Appendix II Model standards of conduct for mediators (2005) 412

Bibliography 420

Index 433

FIGURES

1.1 Ordinary morality and professional ethics *page* 4
1.2 Standards of professional conduct and professional ethics 5
1.3 Types of moral and ethical norms 17
1.4 Types of professional role norms (the norms of good practice) 24
1.5 Types of ethical norms 27
1.6 Law, ethical norms, and standards of professional conduct 29
1.7 Legal threshold, ethical threshold, and ethical bar 31
1.8 Professional ethics as the union of professional and moral norms 35
2.1 The normative basis of duties toward clients 40
2.2 Duties toward clients 57
2.3 The normative basis of duties toward the profession 60
2.4 The effect of the duty to maintain the profession's standing and public trust on the duties toward clients 61
2.5 Duties toward the profession 65
2.6 The normative basis of duties toward the public 69
2.7 Duties toward the public 72
2.8 The normative basis of duties toward employers and principals 75
2.9 Duties toward employers and principals 80
3.1 Core descriptive definition and shared professional ideals 97
3.2 Perspectives from below and above of mediators' ethics 106
3.3 The layers of meaning of mediator duties 118
4.1 Wide and narrow self-determination 131
4.2 The extent of party self-determination and the allocation of decision-making authority between mediators and parties 137
4.3 The elements of self-determination: between formality and substance 139
4.4 Substantive and formal self-determination 142
4.5 Voluntariness and lack of coercion 148
4.6 The element of information in the exercise of self-determination 151

5.1 Mediator competence 178
6.1 Why mediators' conflicts of interest matter to mediation parties? 188
6.2 Circumstances of mediators' conflicts of interest 190
6.3 The expectations of parties regarding a conflict of interest 192
6.4 The expectations of the mediation profession and the public regarding mediators' conflicts of interest 194
6.5 The severity of a conflict of interest and its implications 196
7.1 The meaning of mediator impartiality 225
8.1 Mediator professional integrity 234
10.1 Confidential information 279
10.2 Justified disclosure of information 284
15.1 Ethical decision-making 346

TABLES

3.1 The duties of mediators and corresponding standards *page* 123
6.1 Illustrating the severity of a conflict of interest 200

PREFACE

There is uncertainty among both mediation practitioners and theoreticians in Anglo-American countries as to the identity, content, and scope of mediation norms and the relationship between them. Mediation practice is under-regulated, and accreditation and licensing of mediators is mostly restricted to court-connected mediation programs or to voluntary grassroots initiatives. Mediation programs and voluntary associations of mediators have developed a large number of codes of conduct for mediators, and from time to time they issue ethical opinions that interpret the codes and offer guidelines for mediators' behavior. These codes and opinions vary in content. Furthermore, they formally apply only to mediators who are members of these programs and associations. In practice, however, most mediators are not subject to any written code of conduct, and those who are find the codes too abstract, general, and vague to offer them a sound guide on ethical mediation conduct. As a result, many aspects relating to the conduct of mediation are left to mediator choice, but mediators have inadequate guidance on how their discretion ought to be exercised. These issues need to be addressed for the benefit of mediators, mediation participants, mediator organizations, advisory bodies, policymakers, and teachers and students of mediation.

Rather than a textbook on mediation laws, this book is a monograph constructing *a general theory of mediators' ethics* that applies to mediators in the United States, United Kingdom, Canada, Australia, and other Anglo-American countries that share the definition of mediators' role suggested in the book. The theory identifies the *ethical* norms that govern mediators' conduct, describes their content and meaning, and explains how their meaning has been shaped. It does so by looking at the role of mediators from the perspective of *professional ethics.*

The professional ethics perspective assumes that holding a professional role comes with responsibilities, and that a theory of professional ethics can offer tools for identifying and interpreting these responsibilities. The main argument of the book is that mediators perform *a role* that has evolved and been shaped by the conduct, writings, and other public representations of mediation practitioners, mediation theorists, legislatures, and mediator organizations. The role of mediators has *a core meaning and definition* that mediators in Anglo-American countries share, notwithstanding the variety of mediator styles and types of mediation. This role places mediators in ethical relationships with mediation parties, the mediation profession, the public, and their employers or principals (when they are employed or conduct mediations on behalf of others), who expect mediators to act in accordance with their role definition. The ethical relationships of mediators produce ethical obligations, the content and meaning of which can be discovered by exploring the legitimate expectations of those who have ethical relationships with mediators and by looking into the relationships among these expectations. The inquiry produces a minimum set of detailed norms of mediators' ethics that can be rationally justified and defended with regard to mediators at large, whether they practice in California or Alabama, or in the United States or Australia, whether they are paid or not, practice in court-connected programs, community programs, or privately, and irrespective of mediation style. Mediators ought to conduct themselves in accordance with these minimal ethical norms irrespective of the *absence* of a formal code of conduct adopted by them or imposed upon them. Local laws of mediation and existing codes of conduct for mediators are used as a source for exploring the content of these norms. Where local laws or codes do exist, the professional ethics perspective and its products enable the book to expose the often implicit and unexplained rationales underlying their provisions, evaluate them, endorse their content, or suggest modifications.

Although dozens of books on mediation have been published, the volume and depth of the discussion of the ethics of mediators in these books is remarkably limited. Excellent books such as Carrie Menkel-Meadow, Lela Porter Love, and Andrea Kupfer Schneider, *Mediation: Practice, Policy and Ethics*, 2nd edn. (New York: Aspen, 2013), Kimberlee K. Kovach, *Mediation: Principles and Practice*, 3rd edn., (St. Paul, MN: Thompson West, 2004), and Christopher W. Moore, *The Mediation Process: Practical Strategies for Resolving Conflict*, 4th edn. (San Francisco: Jossey-Bass, 2014) typically assign one chapter for the discussion of some ethical issues in mediation. None of them offers a comprehensive theory of mediator ethics. In fact, there is only one book to date that is exclusively dedicated to mediation ethics, titled *Mediation Ethics: Cases and Materials* (Ellen Waldman [ed.], Jossey-Bass, 2011). The book presents thirteen illustrative ethical dilemmas that are commented upon by twenty-seven mediation experts. It provides a valuable resource for teaching mediation ethics and shows how prominent mediators handle ethical issues, but it lacks a uniform approach that is grounded in an explicit theory of mediator ethics. As a result, although the book is thought-provoking it does not offer a systematic step-by-step approach to dealing with ethical questions that arise in mediation practice. This is the case with refereed articles on mediation ethics as well. Hundreds of published articles touch upon various aspects of mediator ethics, such as neutrality, impartiality, party self-determination, and confidentiality, but none weaves them together into a single coherent theory. This book offers tools for guiding mediators' conduct in the absence of applicable codes of conduct, and for helping mediators who are subject to such codes to interpret them, fill up lacunas, criticize them, and resolve internal tensions between their provisions.

The first part of the book develops a general theory of professional ethics on the basis of which, in the second part, a theory of mediators' ethics is formulated. Chapter 1, titled 'Fundamental concepts,' presents professional ethics as an integration of morality and role; discusses the differences between duties and aspirations and between rules, principles, values, and ideals; clarifies the relationship between ethics and law; and highlights the main functions of professional ethics. Chapter 2, titled 'Ethical relationships,' discusses in detail the duties of professionals that follow from the meeting of role and morality towards their clients, their profession, the public, and their employers or principals when they have any. Part I draws upon literature on morality in general and on professional ethics in particular, and is especially influenced by the writings of Bernard Gert, Lon Fuller, Michael D. Bayles, Michael Davis, Daryl Koehn, and Michael S. Pritchard.

The second part of the book, titled 'A theory of mediators' ethics,' explores the content and meaning of the norms of mediators' ethics. Chapter 3 suggests a core definition of mediation and of the role of mediators. It then applies the theory of professional ethics that is the subject of Part I, in particular the concept of an ethical relationship, to mediators and the practice of mediation, and proposes a scheme of ethical obligations of mediators. The chapter concludes with an explanation of the method whereby the content and meaning of these obligations are to be ascertained in the remainder of Part II. Chapters 4–14 then explore mediators' duties of competence, conflict of interest, party self-determination, professional integrity, impartiality, diligence, respect and dignity, honesty, confidentiality, fairness, maintaining the profession's standing, advancement of the profession, and their duties regarding advertising and solicitation, fees, and employers and principals. Each chapter concludes with a proposed ethical standard that summarizes the preceding discussion, and together they comprise a 'Proposed Model Code of Conduct for Mediators.' Part II of the book draws heavily on major codes of conduct for mediators in the United States, Canada, and Australia, and refers to the writings of mediation experts when appropriate.

The third part of the book illustrates the application of the theory of mediators' ethics to ethical questions that come up in mediation practice. Chapter 15 presents a recommended approach to ethical decision-making that draws upon the writings of Bernard Gert, Tom Beauchamp and James Childress, Julie Macfarlane, and Daniel Statman. The chapter discusses the possibility and utility of distinguishing between ethical and professional questions; offers a typology of easy cases, hard cases, and dilemmas; and suggests an ethical decision-making process that can be followed when confronting ethical questions, hard cases, and dilemmas in the practice of mediation. Chapter 16 concludes the book by providing illustrations of ethical analysis of real stories and cases that involve mediators' conduct. The chapter draws on my experience of sitting on a mediator ethics committee and drafting ethics opinions in response to mediator queries.

Mediation practice has continuously grown in the last two decades in the United States, Canada, Europe, and Australia. Many countries have adopted mediation programs alongside their court systems, and encourage the spread of mediation as a voluntary, peaceful method for resolving disputes between individuals, businesses, and groups. Mediation is practiced by many thousands of mediators around the world, in the public sector, in private settings, and in voluntary community service. The mediation process is utilized by mediators to address a great variety of disputes, including family, business, employment, neighbor, landlord-tenant, environment, and criminal disputes. In addition, mediation is being researched and taught in numerous academic and nonacademic dispute resolution programs, and thousands of people seek mediator training every year, or take ADR and mediation classes and seminars at both the undergraduate and graduate levels.

This book is the first to develop a novel theoretical basis for discussing and evaluating mediators' ethical conduct, and to provide a comprehensive and coherent theory of mediators' ethics. It is intended for all those who have a stake in the practice and study of mediation: *mediation researchers* of all disciplines who wish to familiarize themselves with the ethics of mediators or further develop it; *mediation teachers* who wish to upgrade their teaching of mediation ethics in both academic courses and mediator training courses, and their *students; mediators* who wish to conduct mediations ethically but are unsure what that means or how that can be achieved, and mediators who feel they know what the "right thing to do" is but want to test that feeling or be able to justify it for themselves or for others; *actual and potential mediation participants* who want information with regard to the ethical rights of mediation participants and the obligations of mediators toward them; *mediation organizations, program directors and staff, and policymakers* who wish to adopt guidelines for mediators that can be ethically defended and to review existing guidelines; and *ethical advisory bodies* who want to expand their resources for drafting reasoned ethical opinions on mediators' conduct. I hope the book will attract interest within the growing ADR community and generate further discussion of mediation ethics. In particular, I hope the book's *Proposed Model Code of Conduct for Mediators* will set a new benchmark for adopting new codes of conduct for mediators and a point of reference for reforming existing codes, in particular the very influential *Model Standards of Conduct for Mediators* (2005) that needs to be updated.

This book has grown out of many years of teaching and researching mediation ethics, discussing ethical questions with practicing mediators, and conducting mediations. I am grateful to the members of the Kiryat-Ono community mediation center's ethics forum (committee), and in particular to Carmela Zilberstein, for helping me through fruitful discussions, and for their enthusiasm and support. I would like to thank my home institution, Ono Academic College, for providing the environment that made writing this book possible. In particular, my thanks go to the institution's founder, Ranan Hartman, the Rector, Professor Dudi Schwartz, and the law school Dean, Professor Amichai Cohen. I am grateful to Professor Michal Alberstein for her continuous support and faith in me over the years. I would also like to thank Ruvik Danieli for stylistic contributions to the text, and Kim Hughes, Law Editor at Cambridge University Press, for her promptness and kind support. Finally, I thank my wife, Shirly, and my children, Matan and Daniel, for their love, support, and understanding. This book is dedicated to them.

ABBREVIATIONS OF CODES OF CONDUCT

A

ADR Institute of Canada, Inc., Code of Conduct for Mediators (2011) available at www.adrcanada.ca/resources/documents/CodeOfConduct2012August30.pdf (ADR Canada Code)

Alabama Code of Ethics for Mediators (1995, amended 2013) available at www.alabamaadr.org/web/roster-documents/documents/med_2014_Mediator_Code_of_Ethics_updated.pdf (Alabama Code)

American Bar Association (ABA) Model Rules of Professional Conduct, available at www.americanbar.org/groups/professional_responsibility/publications/model_rules_of_professional_conduct.html (ABA Model Rules)

American Psychological Association (APA) Ethical Principles of Psychologists and Code of Conduct, available at www.apa.org/ethics/code/index.aspx (APA Ethical Principles and Code)

American Society of Civil Engineers (ASCE) Code of Ethics available at www.asce.org/code-of-ethics/ (ASCE Code of Ethics for Engineers)

Law Council of Australia, Ethical Guidelines for Mediators (2011) available at www.lawcouncil.asn.au/lawcouncil/images/LCA-PDF/a-z-docs/EthicalGuidelinesforMediators.pdf (Australian Ethical Guidelines)

Australian National Mediator Accreditation Standards: Practice Standards (2012) available at www.msb.org.au/sites/default/files/documents/Practice%20Standards.pdf (Australian Practice Standards)

C

California Dispute Resolution Council (CDRC) Standards of Practice for California Mediators available at www.cdrc.net/adr-practice/mediator-standards/ (California-CDRC Standards)

California Rules of Conduct for Mediators in Court-Connected Mediation Programs for Civil Cases, California Rules of Court (Revised January 1, 2015) available at www.courts.ca.gov/cms/rules/index.cfm?title=three (California Rules)

Code of Conduct for United States Judges available at www.uscourts.gov/judges-judgeships/code-conduct-united-states-judges (Code of Conduct for United States Judges)

Code of Ethics for Arbitrators in Commercial Disputes (2004) available at ethics.iit.edu/ecodes/node/4705 (Code of Ethics for Arbitrators in Commercial Disputes)

F

Family Mediation Canada Members Code of Professional Conduct available at fmc.ca/sites/default/files/sites/all/themes/fmc/images-user/Members%20Code%20of%20Professional%20Conduct_0.pdf (Family Mediation Canada Code)

Model Standards of Practice for Family and Divorce Mediation (2000) available at www.americanbar.org/content/dam/aba/migrated/family/reports/mediation.authcheckdam.pdf (Family Mediation Model Standards)

A Guide for Federal Employee Mediators (2006) available at www.adr.gov/pdf/final_manual.pdf (Federal Employee Mediators Guide)

Florida Rules for Certified and Court-Appointed Mediators (in ADR Resource Handbook January 2015) available at www.flcourts.org/core/fileparse.php/550/urlt/RuleBookletJanuary2015.pdf (Florida Rules)

G

Georgia Ethical Standards for Mediators (1994) available at www.godr.org/files/APPENDIX%20C,%20CHAP%201,%206-18-2013.pdf (Georgia Standards)

I

Mediation Council of Illinois (MCI) Professional Standards of Practice for Mediators (2009) available at www.mediationcouncilofillinois.org/sites/default/files/MCI%20Professional%20Standards%20of%20Practice.pdf (Illinois Standards)

K

Kansas Ethical Standards for Mediators Prefatory Comment, Rule 903 adopted by the Supreme Court of Kansas available at www.kscourts.org/rules/Rule-Info.asp?r1=Court+Rules+Relating+to+Mediation&r2=316 (Kansas Ethical Standards for Mediators)

L

Code of Professional Conduct for Labor Mediators, the Federal Mediation and Conciliation Service of the United States and the Association of Labor Mediation Agencies available at ethics.iit.edu/ecodes/node/3410 (Code of Labor Mediators)

M

Maryland Standards of Conduct for Mediators, Arbitrators and Other ADR Practitioners available at www.courts.state.md.us/macro/pdfs/standardsfinal.pdf (Maryland Standards)

Michigan Standards of Conduct for Mediators (2013) available at courts.mi.gov/Administration/SCAO/Resources/Documents/standards/odr/Mediator%20Standards%20of%20Conduct%202.1.13.pdf (Michigan Standards)

Model Standards of Conduct for Mediators (2005) available at www.americanbar.org/groups/dispute_resolution/policy_standards.html and in Appendix II (Model Standards)

Montana Mediation Association Code of Ethics and Standards of Practice (2014) available at mtmediation.org/wp-content/uploads/2015/04/mtma-code-of-ethics-standards-of-practice-rev-2-13-14-reviewed-by-committee.pdf (Montana Association Code)

N

National Association of Social Workers (NASW) Code of Ethics available at www.socialworkers.org/pubs/code/code.asp (NASW Code of Ethics for Social Workers)

National Society of Professional Engineers (NSPE) Code of Ethics for Engineers available at www.nspe.org/resources/ethics/code-ethics (NSPE Code of Ethics for Engineers)

Nebraska Office of Dispute Resolution Manual of Standards and Ethics for Center Mediators, Directors and Staff, available at supremecourt.nebraska.gov/5530/professional-ethics-mediators (Nebraska Standards)

Standards of Conduct for New York State Community Dispute Resolution Center Mediators available at www.nycourts.gov/ip/adr/Publications/Info_for_Programs/Standards_of_Conduct.pdf (NY-CDRC Standards)

North Carolina Revised Standards of Professional Conduct for Mediators (2011) adopted by the Supreme Court of North Carolina available at www.aoc.state.nc.us/www/public/html/pdf/SOC4_14.pdf (North Carolina Standards)

O

Ontario Association for Family Mediation Code of Professional Conduct (2013) available at www.oafm.on.ca/membership/policies/standards-of-practice (Ontario Family Mediation Code)

Oregon Mediation Association Core Standards of Mediation Practice (2005) available at www.omediate.org/pg61.cfm (Oregon Standards)

P

Proposed Model Code of Conduct for Mediators, in Appendix I (Proposed Code)

T

Tennessee Standards of Professional Conduct for Rule 31 Neutrals, Rule 31 Appendix A available at www.tsc.state.tn.us/rules/supreme-court/31 (Tennessee Standards)

Texas Ethical Guidelines for Mediators (2011) available at www.txcourts.gov/All_Archived_Documents/SupremeCourt/AdministrativeOrders/miscdocket/11/11906200.pdf (Texas Guidelines)

V

Virginia Standards of Ethics and Professional Responsibility for Certified Mediators (2011) available at www.courts.state.va.us/courtadmin/aoc/djs/programs/drs/mediation/soe.pdf (Virginia Standards)

W

Wisconsin Association of Mediators (WAM) Ethical Guidelines for the Practice of Mediation (1997) available at www.wamediators.org/publication/ethical-guidelines-practice-mediation (Wisconsin Association Guidelines)

PART I

A theory of professional ethics

1

Fundamental concepts

1.1 Introduction

1.1.1 The meanings of ethics

Ethics is a concept with multiple meanings. Some scholars treat ethics as synonymous with *morality*.[1] For them, ethics, like morality, means the moral rules that govern individual behavior and determine what is right and wrong and what the moral duties of individuals are.[2] Others believe that morality and ethics differ from each other for various reasons.[3] They understand ethics as the *discipline* or study of morality. Ethics according to this view is the philosophy of morality that deals with the big questions of human life: what is justice? What is fairness? What is right and wrong? What rights does a person have? A third approach sees ethics as a type of *particular morality*. Ethics as particular morality refers to specific standards of behavior that apply to members of a particular group because of their belonging to the group.[4] This book refers to ethics as particular morality. It explores the morality that applies to people who exercise a professional role, and focuses on the ethics of mediators.

[1] See, e.g., William H. Shaw, *Business Ethics*, 6th edn. (Boston, MA: Wadsworth, 2008), p. 5. See also Manuel G. Velasquez, *Business Ethics: Concepts and Cases*, 5th edn. (Upper Saddle River, NJ: Prentice-Hall, 2002), pp. 7–8; Donald Nicolson and Julian Webb, *Professional Legal Ethics: Critical Interrogations* (New York: Oxford University Press, 1999), p. 4.

[2] See, e.g., Shaw, *Business Ethics*, p. 5.

[3] See, e.g., Nicolson and Webb, *Professional Legal Ethics*, p. 4 at notes 30–32 (referring to such writers).

[4] See, e.g., Michael Davis, *Thinking Like an Engineer: Studies in the Ethics of a Profession* (New York: Oxford University Press, 1998), p. vii (noting that the word "ethics" "refers to those special standards of conduct that apply to members of a group just because of that membership"). See also Kevin Gibson, "The New Canon of Negotiation Ethics" (2004) 87 *Marquette Law Review* 747, 747 (noting that one meaning of the term "ethics" is "a set of rules that applies to specific activities").

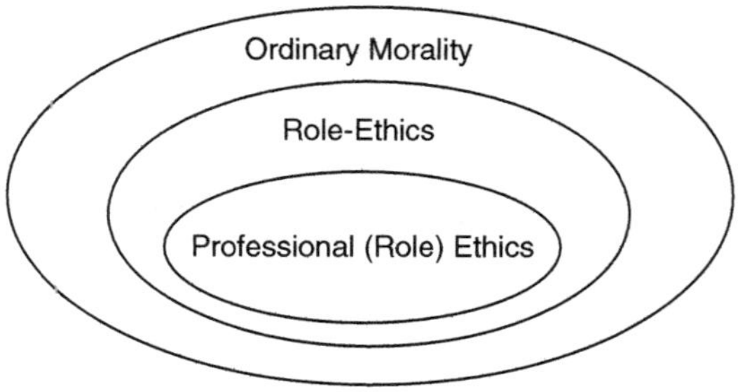

Figure 1.1: Ordinary morality and professional ethics

1.1.2 Role-ethics and professional ethics

If ethics is a type of particular morality that applies to role-holders, it must combine two essential components: morality and role, that is, norms of morality as applied to the performance of a role. Daniel E. Wueste, for example, argued that "a professional ethics is not a mere restatement of the norms of ordinary morality (i.e. norms governing human conduct generally); the norms of a professional ethic are tied to an occupation or role."[5] I use the term "ethics" for reasons of convenience. It serves to distinguish between the particular morality of role-holders (which could also have been termed "role-morality") and ordinary or common morality that applies to every person. Professional ethics is a special case of role-morality because all professionals fulfill a role but not all roles are professional. Thus, role-ethics is broader than professional ethics. Figure 1.1 describes the relationship between ordinary morality and professional ethics.

Professional ethics refers to the *moral aspects* of performing a professional role, that is, to the evaluation of professional conduct as morally appropriate or inappropriate. For example, a professional is morally bound to keep in confidence his or her clients' personal information when the information has been obtained in the course of practice. Professional ethics enables us to take a critical look at the conduct of professionals, at professional practices, and at standards formally and informally adopted by professionals, and to morally evaluate them. Thus, a theory of professional ethics describes what professionals *should* morally do or aspire to; it is not satisfied with what professionals *do* in practice or with their claims regarding the norms that allegedly apply to them. A professional may take a particular action that he or she is legally obligated to take, or fulfill his or

[5] See Daniel E. Wueste (ed.), *Professional Ethics and Social Responsibility* (Lanham, MD: Rowman and Littlefield, 1994), p. 1.

Figure 1.2: Standards of professional conduct and professional ethics

her role in accordance with some conventions of practice that are acceptable, at least in part, to the professional community to which he or she belongs. In doing so, however, he or she could be following norms of professional conduct that are not necessarily moral, and thus might be inconsistent with professional ethics. For this reason I do not use the term "norms or standards of professional conduct" and "professional ethics" as interchangeable. The standards of professional conduct include the standards of professional ethics, but some of them, notwithstanding their legal status or the fact that they reflect actual practices, may possibly be immoral and thus unethical.[6] Figure 1.2 describes the relationship between standards of professional conduct and professional ethics.

1.1.3 Mediators' ethics as professional ethics or role-ethics

Mediators' ethics is a special case of professional ethics or role-ethics. It is a case of role-ethics because it is concerned with the norms that apply to those who perform the role of mediators. It is a case of professional ethics, because the role of mediators is a professional role and mediation is a profession.

The mediation profession

There is no one acceptable definition of a profession.[7] In the past it was common to reserve this term for religion, medicine, and law, and to regard the clergy, medical doctors, and lawyers as professionals.[8] Today,

[6] See Sections 1.2.2.3 and 1.2.3.2.

[7] See, e.g., Eliot Freidson, *Professionalism Reborn: Theory, Prophecy and Policy* (Chicago: University of Chicago Press, 1994), p. 149. See also Eliot Freidson, *Professional Powers: A Study of the Institutionalization of Formal Knowledge* (Chicago: University of Chicago Press, 1986), pp. 20–38; Michael S. Pritchard, *Professional Integrity: Thinking Ethically* (Lawrence: University Press of Kansas, 2006), p. 4 (noting that "[t]here are no generally accepted definitions of 'profession' or 'professional'").

[8] See, e.g., Daryl Koehn, *The Ground of Professional Ethics* (New York: Routledge, 1994), p. 12.

the term is used more loosely in connection with other occupations such as engineering, business, teaching, nursing, and journalism.[9] In fact society nowadays tends to see every person working for a living[10] or exhibiting a high level of skills as a professional.[11]

Scholars have suggested various criteria for the existence of a profession. Among them one can find special knowledge and skills, autonomy of conduct, commitment to the public, organizational affiliation, and a code of ethics.[12] Scholars view differently the weight that each of these features has in the definition of a profession. Some claim that a profession cannot exist without a commitment to the public.[13] Others argue that the distinguishing feature between a profession and a mere occupation is the adoption of ethical standards.[14] This debate is reflected in mediation

[9] See id., p. 11. See also John Kultgen, *Ethics and Professionalism* (Philadelphia: University of Pennsylvania Press, 1988), p. 5.

[10] See, e.g., Tom L. Beauchamp and James F. Childress, *Principles of Biomedical Ethics*, 6th edn. (New York: Oxford University Press, 2009), p. 6 (noting that "... the word *profession* has come, in common use, to mean almost any occupation by which a person earns a living").

[11] See, e.g., Koehn, *The Ground of Professional Ethics*, p. 11 (noting that "sometimes the term 'professional' is applied indiscriminately to anyone who exhibits a high level of style, skill, or even cunning").

[12] See, e.g., Freidson, *Professionalism Reborn*, p. 154 (noting that "the denominators connected with various notions of professions, from least to most exclusive, are expertise, credentialism, and autonomy"). See also W. van der Burg, "The Morality of Aspiration: A Neglected Dimension of Law and Morality", in W.J. Witteveen and W. van der Burg (eds.), *Rediscovering Fuller. Essays on Implicit Law and Institutional Design* (Amsterdam: Amsterdam University Press, 1999), p. 172 (referring to three characteristics of a profession discussed in Michael Davis and Frederick A. Elliston (eds.), *Ethics and the Legal Profession* [Buffalo, NY: Prometheus Books, 1986], p. 15: a commitment to the social good, based on special skills and knowledge, with certain autonomy and self-regulation); Barry L. Padgett, *Professional Morality and Guilty Bystanding: Merton's Conjectures and the Value of Work* (Newcastle upon Tyne, UK: Cambridge Scholars, 2009), p. 2 (noting that "[f]our general criteria indicate a profession and typify the persons who occupy the roles therein: specific training, autonomy, public service, and ethical codes"); Koehn, *The Ground of Professional Ethics*, p. 56 (listing five traits of professionals); Michael D. Bayles, *Professional Ethics*, 2nd edn. (Belmont: Wadsworth, 1989), pp. 7–12, 14 (discussing various features of professions); Davis, *Thinking Like an Engineer*, p. 164 (noting that "... a profession is a number of individuals sharing an occupation voluntarily organized to earn a living by serving some moral ideal in a morally permissible way beyond what law, market, and ordinary morality require").

[13] See Koehn, *The Ground of Professional Ethics*, p. 56.

[14] See Davis, *Thinking Like an Engineer*, pp. 29, 37. But see Carrie Menkel-Meadow, "Are There Systemic Ethics Issues in Dispute System Design? And What We Should [Not] Do About it: Lessons from International and Domestic Fronts" (2009) 14 *Harvard Negotiation Law Review* 195, 196 (noting that "[w]hether a field or discipline requires ethical standards to be considered a profession remains an issue of some debate due to its

literature, which finds it hard to decide whether mediation is a profession or not, but tends to agree that it is a field that is going through a process of professionalization, on its way to being formally recognized as a profession.[15] There are good reasons to support such recognition.

A growing number of people around the world engage in the practice of mediation. Some do it for a living, others as volunteers. Mediators undergo training that provides them with the special skills and knowledge necessary for conducting an effective mediation. Some of them are members of mediator organizations or are affiliated with mediation programs that lay down criteria for training and practice, adopt a code of conduct for mediators, and sometimes enforce the code through disciplinary bodies. These organizations and programs explicitly instruct mediators to utilize their knowledge and skills for the benefit of mediation parties even at the expense of their own interests. In addition, mediation advances the public good; while lawyers are committed to an ideal of legal justice, and medical doctors to an ideal of health,[16] mediators promote mutual understanding, dialogue, and harmony.

It seems to me that a mediation profession exists, but the great variety in mediation practice among practitioners – the existence, side by side, of paid and volunteer, organized and unorganized, highly skilled, experienced mediators and amateur, sporadic mediators – does not comfortably enable us to label all mediators as professionals. Thus, theoretically, one could distinguish between professional and non-professional mediators.

Mediators' ethics as either professional ethics or role-ethics

From an ethical perspective, however, the distinction between professional and unprofessional mediators should not be overemphasized.

tendency to 'exclude' some professions or to mark them as separate from important lay expertise and service").

15 See, e.g., Menkel-Meadow, ibid, (noting that "[t]he field of conflict resolution, broadly defined, is currently at what I would describe as a 'mid-point' in this quest for formal recognition as a profession"). See also Craig McEwen, "Giving Meaning to Mediator Professionalism" (2005) 11 *Dispute Resolution Magazine* 3 (discussing the meaning of mediator professionalism and suggesting ways to promote it); Jacqueline M. Nolan-Haley, "Lawyers, Non-Lawyers and Mediation: Rethinking the Professional Monopoly from a Problem-Solving Perspective" (2002) 7 *Harvard Negotiation Law Review* 235, 243–45 (discussing professionalization of mediation); David N. Hofstein, "Ethical Guidelines for Attorney-Mediators: Are Attorneys Bound by Ethical Codes for Lawyers When Acting as Mediators?" (1997) 14 *Journal of the American Academy of Matrimonial Lawyers* 267; Jeffrey W. Stempel, "The Inevitability of the Eclectic: Liberating ADR from Ideology" (2000) *Journal of Dispute Resolution* 247.

16 See Davis, *Thinking Like an Engineer*, p. 165.

Non-professional mediators, whatever that term precisely means, who present themselves as mediators, perform the role of mediators, and are identified by the public as members of the mediation profession, should be treated as subject to the ethical standards that apply to professional mediators. This is simply because mediators' ethics is the ethics that applies to those who perform the role of a mediator. A person who performs a role that places him or her in a position of power and influence, and who conducts a process that has a social definition and purpose, is subject to norms of role-morality that apply to role-holders, whether or not they are named professionals.[17] Thus both professional and non-professional mediators are subject to the ethical standards that apply to those who conduct mediations. It is possible in principle to distinguish between the professional ethics of mediators and the role-ethics of mediators, but that would be to insist on semantics. Therefore, this book refers to mediators' ethics, mediators' professional ethics, and mediators' role-ethics as interchangeable. It treats all mediators as subject to mediators' ethics irrespective of whether they are paid or unpaid, mediating many mediations or few, are members of a mediator organization or not.

1.2 Professional ethics: an integration of morality and role

If ethical norms are moral norms that apply to the performance of a role, then understanding professional ethics requires us first to examine what norms of morality are, and second to apply these norms to the circumstances of holding a role.

1.2.1 Moral norms and ethics

1.2.1.1 A definition of moral norms

An attempt to define moral norms in simple terms is bound to fail, as there are numerous theories of morality that come up with different definitions of morality and with various criteria for moral conduct and living a moral life. For example, Immanuel Kant (1724–1804) offered a moral criterion or a categorical imperative according to which a moral

[17] See, e.g., Kevin Gibson, "Contrasting Role Morality and Professional Morality: Implications for Practice" (2003) 20 *Journal of Applied Philosophy* 17, 17, 28 (arguing that the "distinction between role morality and professional morality is over-determined" [p. 17] and that "it might be correct to think of individuals not so much as professionals in role, but rather as people who are able to manifest power" [p. 28]).

rule is a rule that rational people accept as universal, or put differently, a rule that respects people and treats them as ends rather than as means only.[18] Theories of consequentialism such as *utilitarianism* measure morality according to a cost-benefit criterion and instruct us to prefer those acts and rules that result with the greatest amount of happiness.[19] Theories of *rights* focus on the moral rights that individuals have and dictate how they ought to be treated. According to these theories, some moral rights derive from a special relationship or role, while others are fundamental human rights that all persons have; these latter rights are universal, equal, and natural, and their existence does not depend on being conferred by human institutions such as the legal system.[20] Another group of theories – theories of *virtues* – focus on the character of moral persons.[21] These theories can assist in making moral decisions by posing the question: how would a virtuous person have acted in similar circumstances?[22]

Theoretically, each of these theories could be employed to identify all moral norms, and serve to justify and interpret particular individual norms.[23] In practice, however, each has limitations that preclude the exclusive use of *one* theory alone.[24] Moreover, combining *all* the theories

[18] See, e.g., Shaw, *Business Ethics*, pp. 59–60. See also James Rachels and Stuart Rachels, *The Elements of Moral Philosophy*, 6th edn. (Singapore: McGraw-Hill, International Edition, 2010), p. 128 (quoting Kant who wrote "Act only according to that maxim by which you can at the same time will that it should become a universal law"); id., p. 137 ("Act so that you treat humanity, whether in your own person or in that of another, always as an end and never as a means only").

[19] According to the classical version of act-utilitarianism "right actions are those that produce the greatest balance of happiness over unhappiness, with each person's happiness counted as equally important" (Rachels and Rachels, *Moral Philosophy*, p. 109). According to the new version of rule-utilitarianism we ask "what rules should we follow to maximize happiness? Individual acts are then judged right or wrong according to whether they are acceptable or unacceptable by these rules" (id., p. 118).

[20] See, e.g., Shaw, *Business Ethics*, p. 66.

[21] See, e.g., Beauchamp and Childress, *Biomedical Ethics*, p. 31 (noting that "a *moral virtue* is a trait of character that is morally valuable").

[22] See, e.g., Rachels and Rachels, *Moral Philosophy*, p. 170. See also Beauchamp and Childress, *Biomedical Ethics*, pp. 45–47 (considering the connection between moral virtues and moral norms of action).

[23] See, e.g., Beauchamp and Childress, *Biomedical Ethics*, p. 103 (using the moral theories of Kant and Mill to justify and clarify a principle of respect for autonomy).

[24] See, e.g., id., pp. 336–363 (discussing various moral theories and their failure to provide a comprehensive and adequate theory of morality). See also Rachels and Rachels, *Moral Philosophy*, pp. 113–114 (noting that utilitarianism might justify an action causing harm to some individuals but increasing overall public happiness); Shaw, *Business Ethics*, p. 61.

in order to identify moral norms is problematic because they sometimes yield different and inconsistent results.[25]

This book cannot determine which of these theories is correct, yet has to adopt a workable perspective of morality to enable it to arrive at the norms of professional ethics. The perspective that will guide us rests on a consensus among theoreticians of morality that moral norms (and thus norms of ethics as well) must meet *minimum criteria of rationality and impartiality.* James Rachels and Stuart Rachels argue that most theories of morality incorporate a minimum conception of morality in one form or another.[26] According to a minimum conception of morality, "morality is, at the very least, the effort to guide one's conduct by reason – that is, to do what there are the best reasons for doing – while giving equal weight to the interests of each individual affected by one's decision."[27] David E. Cooper claims that "[i]n ethics there is a general consensus that the moral point of view from which to judge and make claims has to be a standpoint that is impartial . . . The most popular current consensus in ethics maintains that for a moral point of view to be impartial, it must (1) meet publicly acknowledged rational standards, (2) satisfy conditions of universality – that is, in principle be compatible with what all honest people could agree to after deliberation, (3) be self-critical rather than ideological, and (4) promote generalized empathy and respect among all people."[28] The philosopher Bernard Gert adds that "given agreement on the facts, a moral philosopher can show that a moral decision or judgment is mistaken if he can show that the moral decision or judgment is

[25] See, e.g., Richard Norman, "Applied Ethics: What is Applied to What?" (2000) 12 *Utilitas* 119, 131 (noting that "[i]f the resolution of moral conflicts about abortion, or euthanasia, has to await the resolution of disputes between utilitarianism, rights-based theories, and their other theoretical competitors, there is little hope of progress towards agreed answers. The alternative view of applied ethics as the clarification and articulation of the values which people actually hold may offer more scope for agreement"). See also Beauchamp and Childress, *Biomedical Ethics*, p. 334 (noting that "[w]e accept as legitimate various *aspects* of many theories advanced in the history of ethics. However, we reject both the hypothesis that all leading principles of the major moral theories can be assimilated into a coherent whole and the hypothesis that each of the theories offers an equally tenable moral framework"). But compare David E. Cooper, *Ethics for Professionals in a Multicultural World* (Upper Saddle River, NJ: Pearson Prentice Hall, 2004), p. 36 (noting that "[t]he premise of this book is that we need to adopt a combination of the principles approach [i.e. ethical egoism, utilitarianism, natural rights theory, social contract theory, Kantian duty ethics, and discourse ethics] and the virtues approach to ethics").

[26] See Rachels and Rachels, *Moral Philosophy*, p. 13. [27] Ibid.

[28] Cooper, *Ethics for Professionals*, p. 33.

incompatible with the moral decisions or judgments that would be made by any impartial rational person."[29]

The literature on morality, therefore, tells us that in order to justify a norm, behavior, or decision as moral, it must be shown to be both rational and impartial. By these terms we mean that (a) the norm, behavior, or decision is supported by good reasons, and these reasons, if made public, could be defended;[30] and (b) the norm, behavior, or decision attaches equal weight to the interests of any affected person, and applies equally to similar cases.[31]

It must be admitted that these criteria are not exact enough to dispel all doubts with regard to the identity and content of moral norms. Clearly, rational persons can disagree on the existence and meaning of moral norms. However, morality in this respect is not different from other normative orders such as law and religion that exhibit uncertainty as well. This state of uncertainty could be mitigated to some extent by reference to *fundamental social values* that are in consensus in Western developed societies and among theoreticians. These are values or norms – such as autonomy and self-determination, avoidance of causing harm, truth telling, and obedience to law – which, besides fulfilling the criteria of rationality and impartiality, we *assume* to be binding and *accept* as valid.[32] Gert, for example, has taken that route in an attempt to further clarify the meaning of morality, noting that "[t]he only feature that the descriptive and normative senses of 'morality' have in common is that they refer to guides to behavior that involve, at least in part, avoiding and preventing harm to some others."[33]

The account of morality taken by this book, like the main body of professional ethics literature, rejects *moral relativism*.[34] Moral relativism considers morality to be a descriptive concept, that is: a description of the

[29] Bernard Gert, *Common Morality: Deciding What to Do* (Oxford University Press, 2004), p. 17.

[30] See, e.g., Pritchard, *Professional Integrity*, pp. 26–27.

[31] See, e.g., id., p. 27. See also Davis, *Thinking Like an Engineer*, p. 99.

[32] See, e.g., Bayles, *Professional Ethics*, pp. 6–7, 20. See also Beauchamp and Childress, *Biomedical Ethics*, p. 3; Gert, *Common Morality*, p. 20 (listing ten moral rules of common morality).

[33] Bernard Gert, "The Definition of Morality" in *The Stanford Encyclopedia of Philosophy* (Summer 2011 Edition), Edward N. Zalta (ed.), available at plato.stanford.edu/entries/morality-definition/.

[34] See, e.g., Shaw, *Business Ethics*, pp. 15–16. See also Bayles, *Professional Ethics*, p. 18; Bernard Gert, *Morality: Its Nature and Justification*, Revised edn. (Oxford University Press, 2005), p. 10.

norms of behavior of a particular society. According to descriptive morality, moral norms describe the social conventions of societies. Therefore, morality varies between societies and reflects a variety of conceptions of the good that cannot be morally criticized.[35] H.L.A. Hart referred to this type of morality as "'positive morality', the morality actually accepted and shared by a given social group."[36] The rival approach, which dominates the professional ethics literature and is taken by this book as well, is *critical morality*. Critical morality regards norms as moral when they satisfy criteria external to individuals or to a particular society. H.L.A. Hart explained critical morality as "the general moral principles used in the criticism of actual social institutions including positive morality."[37] Moral norms, as we have seen, must be both rational and impartial, and therefore majority will and social conventions may fail to be moral.[38] According to this approach, causing harm to another person would be immoral even in a society where such an act is tolerated, unless the act can be justified on other compelling moral grounds. The rejection of moral relativism has implications for professional ethics. As Pritchard noted, "professional ethics embraces norms that are 'conventional' within the practice of the profession in question. Still, what is accepted as right is not necessarily actually right."[39] The fact that a professional group considers certain behavior to be right does not in itself make that conduct right or immunize it from ethical criticism.

1.2.1.2 Distinguishing duties from aspirations: between rules, principles, values, and ideals

(a) Morality of duty and morality of aspiration Philosophers of morality such as Lon Fuller and Bernard Gert have recognized a distinction between morality of duty or rules, and morality of aspiration or ideals.[40] While moral duties set a minimum threshold of behavior, for

[35] See, e.g., Shaw, *Business Ethics*, pp. 15–16 (discussing ethical relativism).

[36] H.L.A. Hart, *Law, Liberty, and Morality* (Stanford: Stanford University Press, 1963), p. 20.

[37] Ibid.

[38] See, e.g., Bayles, *Professional Ethics*, p. 20 (noting that " . . . as the Nazi example shows, the accepted social values might be unjustifiable"). See also Shaw, *Business Ethics*, p. 16.

[39] Pritchard, *Professional Integrity*, p. 160. See also Beauchamp and Childress, *Biomedical Ethics*, pp. 1–2 (distinguishing normative ethics from nonnormative, descriptive ethics).

[40] See Lon L. Fuller, *The Morality of Law*, Revised edn. (New Haven: Yale University Press, 1969), pp. 5–6 (distinguishing between morality of duty and morality of aspiration). See also Gert, *Common Morality*, pp. 22–23 and Bernard Gert, Charles M. Culver and K. Danner Clouser, *Bioethics: A Systematic Approach*, 2nd edn. (Oxford University Press, 2006), pp. 43–44 (distinguishing between moral rules and moral ideals).

example a prohibition on lying or on breaking promises, moral aspirations set higher levels of conduct, that is: ideals that serve as points of reference and encourage worthy conduct. For example, we recognize a moral ideal of saving the lives of others, but reject a general moral duty to save others in circumstances that jeopardize the life of the rescuer, unless he or she occupies a role that imposes on him or her such a concrete duty. Following morality, professional ethics combines duties and aspirations as well.

The *ethics of duty* determines the minimum ethical threshold that is expected of professionals and is binding on them. It differs from morality of duty in that morality of duty applies to any person, including professionals, while the ethics of duty (a) applies to professionals who perform a role, and (b) demands more of the professional than morality demands of ordinary persons. For example, a lifeguard has an ethical duty to save the life of a drowning man notwithstanding the fact that by doing so he risks his own life, while an innocent bystander is under no such duty. *Ethics of aspiration* encourages professionals to take positive actions to prevent or relieve harms in their practice,[41] strive towards excellence in performing their role,[42] and calls for *commitment* to role and *professional pride.*[43] Ethics of aspiration differs from morality of aspiration in that morality of aspiration encourages everyone to realize general moral ideals in living the "Good Life, of excellence, of the fullest realization of human powers,"[44] while ethics of aspiration encourages professionals to realize moral and professional ideals in the course of their practice. While moral ideals are relevant for every person, including professionals, ethical ideals relate to the performance of a role, and are not necessarily relevant to the non-role-holder. For example, proficiency and style in writing are ethical ideals of editors, stemming from one of the goals of their professional role to present texts in their best light. An ordinary person, writing a letter to a friend, has no such moral ideal.

(b) Rules, principles, values, and ideals The terminology that is used in professional ethics literature in describing the standards or norms of

41 See Gert, Culver and Clouser, *Bioethics*, pp. 81–82.

42 See W. van der Burg, "Morality of Aspiration", 171.

43 See, e.g., Fuller, *Morality of Law*, p. 43 (arguing when discussing the inner morality of law that the "primary appeal [of the morality of aspiration] must be to a sense of trusteeship and to the pride of the craftsman"). See also W. van der Burg, "Morality of Aspiration", 188.

44 Fuller, *Morality of Law*, p. 5.

morality and ethics is diverse and inconsistent. Bernard Gert, for example, bases moral theory on moral rules and ideals.[45] Tom Beauchamp and James Childress argue that common morality is made up of rules and principles that are norms of obligation and moral traits or virtues that are moral ideals beyond obligation (supererogation).[46] Bayles bases his theory of professional ethics on standards (of virtue), principles (of responsibility), and rules (of duty), claiming that they all express obligations,[47] and Frederic G. Reamer focuses on the place of values in professional ethics.[48] For purposes of clarity I will refer to the norms or standards of morality and ethics as being composed of rules, principles, values, and ideals. The meaning of these terms and possible distinctions between them are briefly discussed, though they do not have fixed or consensual definitions and their exact meaning is open to debate.

Rules are concrete norms that impose *duties* and dictate a particular course of action. *Moral* rules indicate moral duties that apply to all persons. For example, anybody who makes a promise has a moral duty to keep his or her promise. *Ethical* rules, in comparison, indicate ethical duties that apply to role-holders. For example, a lawyer must not disclose information that his or her client provided to him in confidence.

Principles are another type of duty-imposing norms. There is no sharp distinction between rules and principles.[49] A principle may be considered as the summary of a number of rules, which together specify the principle, or as a "super-rule." Beauchamp and Childress noted that they "draw only a loose distinction between rules and principles. Both are general norms of obligation. The difference is that rules are more specific in content and more restricted in scope than principles."[50] For example, Beauchamp and Childress argue that respect for autonomy is a moral principle that is basic to biomedical ethics.[51] And Raz pointed out that "'[p]rinciples' and 'rules' are often used interchangeably, though the

[45] See Gert, Culver and Clouser, *Bioethics*, pp. 11–12.

[46] Beauchamp and Childress, *Biomedical Ethics*, pp. 3, 12–14, 49.

[47] Bayles, *Professional Ethics*, p. 25.

[48] Frederic G. Reamer, *Social Work Values and Ethics*, 3rd edn. (Columbia University Press, 2006)

[49] See, e.g., Ronald Dworkin, *Taking Rights Seriously* (Cambridge, MA: Harvard University Press, 1978), pp. 23–27 (discussing the differences between rules and principles). See also Joseph Raz, "Legal Principles and the Limits of Law" (1972) 81 *Yale Law Journal* 823 (criticizing the rules/principles distinction).

[50] Beauchamp and Childress, *Biomedical Ethics*, p. 13. [51] See id., pp. 12, 99.

word 'principles' usually carries an implication of greater generality and greater importance than the word 'rules'."[52]

Value is another term that is used in connection with morality and ethics. Reamer, quoting Nicholas Rescher, noted that "over the years scholars have penned diverse definitions of value and values, including 'any-thing capable of being appreciated'; 'the object of any need'; 'a conception, explicit or implicit, distinctive of individual or characteristic of a group, of the desirable which influences the selection from available means and ends of action'; 'the desirable end states which act as a guide to human endeavor or the most general statements of legitimate ends which guide social action'; and 'normative standards by which human beings are influenced in their choice among the alternative courses of action which they perceive'."[53] Moral values are used in the literature to describe both norms of obligation (duties) and ideals that encourage behavior (aspirations). Fuller, for example, argued that "[t[he concept of value is congenial to a morality of aspiration. Had we chosen some other companion for it, and spoken, say, of the 'perception of value' we would have had an expression thoroughly at home in a system of thought directed toward the achievements of human excellence. But instead we coupled 'value' with the term 'judgment,' an expression which suggests not a striving toward perfection, but a conclusion about obligations."[54] The dual function of values is demonstrated by Gert, who treats moral values as moral virtues: "they are those virtues that result in people acting in morally good and morally right ways. Moral values, like goods and evils, are objective values. Honesty, dependability, and kindness are moral virtues, and all impartial rational persons want everyone to have them. Other traits of character, like courage and prudence, are virtues that all rational persons want for themselves, whether they want others to have them."[55] Gert argues that some of the moral values or virtues are norms of obligation, which can be rephrased as duty-imposing rules. For example, he claims that the values or virtues of truthfulness, dependability, fairness, and honesty correspond with the moral rules not to deceive, to keep your promises, and not to cheat, and can be rephrased as rules: do not be deceitful, undependable, unfair, or dishonest;[56] other moral virtues such as kindness are to be regarded as moral ideals that encourage behavior but do not impose obligations.[57] We should therefore remain alert to the possibility that

[52] Joseph Raz, *Practical Reasons and Norms* (Oxford University Press, 1999), p. 49.

[53] Reamer, *Social Work Values*, p. 12 quoting Nicholas Rescher, *Introduction to Value Theory* (Englewood Cliffs, NJ: Prentice-Hall, 1969), p. 2.

[54] Fuller, *Morality of Law*, p. 13. [55] Gert, *Morality*, p. 96. [56] Id., p. 283. [57] Ibid.

when the terminology of values is used a further inquiry might be required in order to ascertain whether the speaker or writer intended to make an assertion of duty or aspiration. Moreover, the distinction between values and principles, like the distinction between principles and rules, can become blurred. Raz, for example, noted that "the word 'principle' is sometimes used to assert an ultimate value or to assert that such a value is a reason for action ('the principle of the supreme value of human life' or 'the principle that human life should always be respected')."[58]

To summarize, rules, principles, and sometimes values, are terms that are used in professional ethics discourse in connection with duties, namely norms of obligation. They indicate actions that are required or prohibited. Ideals, sometimes termed values, indicate a desirable state of affairs and encourage actions. As a general observation, rules tend to be more precise than principles and values, but in practice, rules, like values,[59] are sometimes ambiguous, have more than one meaning, and allow for the exercise of discretion.[60] For example, a duty to disclose conflicts of interest may be strict, yet it is dependent on an interpretation of the meaning of a conflict of interest.[61] Ideals tend to be more abstract than norms of obligation, often allow for a variety of interpretations, and serve as "points of orientation."[62] For example, consent as a value or ideal requires elaboration. Should it be interpreted, for example, as formal or substantive (informed) consent? Should the power to give consent be restricted in some circumstances?[63] Another rough observation suggests a possible practical connection between rules, principles, values, and ideals: rules may specify principles; principles may explicate values; and norms of obligation may help realize ideals.[64] Figure 1.3 describes the types of moral and ethical norms.

[58] Raz, *Practical Reasons*, p. 49.

[59] See, e.g., Davis, *Thinking Like an Engineer*, p. 17 (arguing that "[v]alues . . . are reasons for acting, and so reasons for adopting standards of conduct, but values as such . . . do not tell us how we should act. A value as such can only demand consideration, that is, a certain weight in our deliberations").

[60] See, e.g., H.L.A. Hart, *The Concept of Law*, 2nd edn. (Oxford University Press, 1994), pp. 126–128 (discussing the open texture of language which results with indeterminacy of rules and other standards of behavior).

[61] See Chapter 6. [62] W. van der Burg, "Morality of Aspiration", 187.

[63] For a discussion of these issues see Chapter 4.

[64] See, e.g., Bayles, *Professional Ethics*, pp. 25–27 (discussing the justification and relations between standards, principles, and rules); Beauchamp and Childress, *Biomedical Ethics*, p. 13 (noting that rules specify principles); W. van der Burg, "Morality of Aspiration", 178–179 (describing the transformation of abstract ideals to concrete rules).

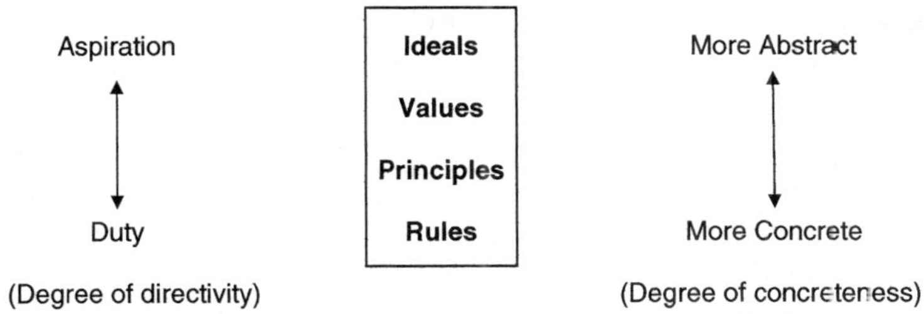

Figure 1.3: Types of moral and ethical norms

(c) Differentiating between duty and aspiration The distinction between moral or ethical duty and aspiration (and thus between norms of obligation and ideals) is not always easy to make for several reasons. First, moral and ethical duties are often not supported by *institutional enforcement* (unlike legal duties, for example).[65] As a result, those who treat duty and sanction as correlatives might mistake moral and ethical duties with aspirations, whereas in fact the normative, obligatory nature of moral and ethical norms is owing to the sheer existence of the norm, not to the existence of a sanction.[66] Second, duties and aspirations are placed on a *continuum*. It is not always clear where a duty ends and an aspiration begins, and vice versa. Fuller, for example, suggested that the relation of the moralities of duty and aspiration is of "an ascending scale . . . The lower rungs of this scale represent the morality of duty; its higher reaches, the morality of aspiration. Separating the two is a fluctuating line of division, difficult to locate precisely, yet vitally important."[67] Fuller argued that "there is an invisible pointer that marks the dividing line where the pressure of duty leaves off and the challenge of excellence begins."[68] In his view, "[d]eciding where duty ought to leave off is one of the most difficult tasks of social philosophy. Into its solution a large element of judgment must enter and individual differences of opinion are inevitable."[69] Scholars of professional ethics express similar views. Beauchamp and Childress, for example, note that "some actions do not fit neatly into [the categories of obligation and supererogation] because they

[65] However, some professions are more regulated than others and establish institutions that enforce the standards of ethics. For example, many ethical duties of *lawyers* in the United States have been translated into law and are institutionally enforced, but the argument made is more general and goes beyond legal ethics. It is certainly true for other professionals who are less regulated than lawyers, like mediators.

[66] See, e.g., Hart, *Concept of Law*, pp. 6–7, 82–83. [67] Fuller, *Morality of Law*, p. 27.

[68] Id., p. 10. [69] Id., p. 12.

fall between the two. The common morality and ethical theory are not precise enough to determine whether these actions are morally required or morally elective . . . the two 'levels' of the obligatory and supererogatory lack sharp boundaries both in the common morality and in professional ethics";[70] and Kultgen argues that "[i]deals . . . are a segment of a continuum that overlaps the segment of rules . . . "[71]

Having noted the difficulty in recognizing the point at which an aspiration turns into a duty, it is still possible to suggest some indicators of that point. First, with respect to a moral or ethical *duty*, one should be able to point to a *legitimate expectation* that an action be taken and to *reliance* on that expectation, as opposed to an aspiration that is not accompanied with legitimate expectation and reliance.[72] For example, clients reasonably expect professionals to have the competence to perform their professional role. They rely on that expectation and it can establish a duty of competence toward clients. However, clients cannot legitimately expect professionals to be leaders in their field of expertise in the absence of such representation by the professionals. Excellence is an aspiration of all professionals, but it cannot establish a duty of excellence. A related idea is that while everyone is expected to discharge (obey) duties *all the time* (though one may have an adequate justification for not doing so in a particular case), it is impossible to expect everyone to follow aspirations and ideals all the time toward everyone.[73] For example, everyone has a duty not to cause harm to others, but the ideal of preventing harm caused and suffered by others cannot be followed at all times.[74] For example, no doctor can be expected to be on call twenty-four hours a day.[75]

Second, while a breach of duty is associated with *serious criticism and punishment*, aspirations are largely associated with *praise and rewards*,

[70] Beauchamp and Childress, *Biomedical Ethics*, p. 49.

[71] Kultgen, *Ethics and Professionalism*, p. 249.

[72] See Gert, Culver and Clouser, *Bioethics*, pp. 89–91 (noting, for example, at 91 that "[i]f there are valid expectations that others have come to count on, then it is likely that a duty exists"). See also Beauchamp and Childress, *Biomedical Ethics*, p. 49 (treating strict obligations, i.e. actions which are strictly obligatory as "the core principles and rules in the common morality" to be differentiated from weaker obligations defined as "the periphery of ordinary expectations in the common morality").

[73] See Gert, *Morality*, p. 248; Gert, Culver and Clouser, *Bioethics*, pp. 43, 92–93, 115–116. See also Beauchamp and Childress, *Biomedical Ethics*, p. 101 (noting, while discussing the ethical principle of respect for autonomy that "[n]o theory of autonomy is acceptable if it presents an ideal beyond the reach of normal agents and choosers"); W. van der Burg, "Morality of Aspiration", 172.

[74] Gert, *Morality*, pp. 248–249.

[75] Gert, Culver and Clouser, *Bioethics*, p. 93.

and punishment for failure to follow them and to achieve the object of an aspiration would be inappropriate.[76] For example, charging fees in breach of formal rules of conduct would lead to criticism. On the other hand, the provision of pro-bono services, in the absence of rules demanding it, would be a reason for praise, and failure to provide them would not be followed by punishment.

And third, duties tend to be relatively *clear and precise* in order to be capable of demanding a particular conduct and incurring punishment for failure, while ideals and aspirations tend to be more abstract and flexible.[77]

The rules–principles–values distinction has been discussed in order to make readers familiar with these terms, which are often mentioned in professional ethics discourse, and identify them as belonging to the ethical discussion. However, in Parts II and III I will not distinguish between them and simply refer to standards or norms of ethics. The duty–aspiration distinction will continue to be used to remind readers that professional ethics is more than ethics of duty that sets minimum standards of conduct, and includes an ethics of aspiration that encourages professionals to take actions that are beyond the obligatory and strive for professional excellence beyond the minimum.[78]

1.2.1.3 Rights and powers: permissive or power-conferring norms

Besides imposing duties and setting aspirations, moral and ethical norms confer rights and powers. The moral right of one person usually follows from the moral duty of another. A's duty not to lie is followed by B's right

[76] See, e.g., Fuller, *Morality of Law*, p. 30; Hart, *Concept of Law*, pp. 171, 174; Gert, *Morality*, pp. 246–247; Gert, Culver and Clouser, *Bioethics*, pp. 12, 116. But see Kultgen, *Ethics and Professionalism*, p. 249 (noting that "[t]he dividing line [between rules and ideals] is not sharp, of course. Condemnation, peer pressure, ostracism, and boycott are all punishments. We certainly want to criticize people for low ideals or failure to live up to accepted ideals.").

[77] See, e.g., Fuller, *Morality of Law*, pp. 28–29 (suggesting "a certain quality of stickiness inherent in all duties" while "it is in the nature of all human aspirations . . . to be pliable and responsive to changing conditions"); Id., p. 43 (noting that "[n]o matter how desirable a direction of human effort may appear to be, if we assert there is a duty to pursue it, we shall confront the responsibility of defining at what point that duty has been violated". [Thus, if we are unable to define the duty in such manner it is] " . . . condemned to remain largely a morality of aspiration and not of duty" [ibid.]).

[78] See, e.g., David Luban, *Legal Ethics and Human Dignity* (New York: Cambridge University Press, 2007), pp. 105–107 (applying this distinction to lawyers); W. van der Burg, "Morality of Aspiration", 171 (applying this idea to doctors).

to be told the truth by A. In professional relationships, the ethical *duties* of professionals are accompanied by ethical rights of clients. For example, professionals have a duty to disclose conflicts of interest and clients have a right to receive that information. This is also true with regard to the *rights* of professionals. For example, professionals often have a right to charge fees for their services, and in these cases their clients are under a duty to remunerate them. In other issues, the rights of the professional would be better described by the term liberty, because they are not followed with duties on the part of clients.[79] For example, the professional may have the liberty (or right) to refuse to accept a certain case or a particular client, or to withhold his or her services.[80]

1.2.1.4 Moral norms that are not norms of ethics

According to a concept of ethics as particular morality, the norms of ethics are defined by the particular activity they regulate. It follows that moral norms that are not related to that activity are not norms of ethics. The ethics of professionals applies to the conduct of professionals in the performance of their role and to behavior that is sufficiently connected to that role. It does not prima facie apply to "private" actions of professionals, for example, actions they take in their capacity as parents or neighbors. This non-professional activity is supposedly regulated by the norms of morality. However, as we shall see, the distinction between norms of morality and norms of ethics can become blurred due to ethical obligations of professionals toward their profession and the public. These norms instruct professionals to maintain the standing of the profession and public trust, and as a result import the norms of morality that apply to the private conduct of professionals into professional ethics.[81]

1.2.1.5 Ethical demands that exceed the demands of ordinary morality: unethical moral behavior?

Every person must morally conduct him or herself in accordance with the norms of morality. Persons who hold a professional role generate expectations beyond the expectations of ordinary persons. Therefore, the

[79] On the meaning of right see Wesley N. Hohfeld, *Fundamental Legal Conceptions as Applied in Judicial Reasoning* (New Haven: Yale University Press, 1919). See also M.D. A. Freeman, *Lloyd's Introduction to Jurisprudence*, 8th ed. (London: Sweet & Maxwell, 2008), pp. 396–397.

[80] See, e.g., Bayles, *Professional Ethics*, p. 25. See also Kultgen, *Ethics and Professionalism*, p. 246 (noting that ethical codes sometimes have permissive clauses).

[81] See Chapter 2 Section 2.3.3.2 and 2.4.3.

norms of ethics set standards higher than ordinary morality.[82] For example, firemen must put themselves at risk in order to save the lives of strangers, while ordinary persons who are not acting in that role need not. The general moral ideal of saving human life becomes a particular ethical duty of the professional.[83] The higher expectations from the professional, informed by the definition of his or her role and the representations of his or her profession, and the reliance on these expectations, produce higher standards of conduct. It follows that conduct that is morally appropriate in the case of an ordinary person could be ethically wanting in the case of a professional.

1.2.1.6 Ethical demands that fall short of ordinary morality: immoral ethical behavior?

Sometimes professionals find themselves in situations in which following their ethical obligations would be considered immoral according to standards of ordinary morality that apply to non-professionals. For example, judges are often regarded as obligated to prefer legal norms over moral norms even when this means producing an immoral, unjust decision.[84] Similarly, lawyers are commonly viewed as if they are operating under a duty to give more weight to the interests of their clients to an extent that justifies harming non-clients' interests.[85] The view taken in this book is that since ethics as particular morality is derived from ordinary morality, conflicts between professional duties and morality are largely resolvable.[86] The way to resolve an alleged conflict between ethical and moral norms is similar to the way one handles conflicting moral norms; one must realize that moral norms are not absolute and

[82] See, e.g., Davis, *Thinking Like an Engineer*, at 112.

[83] See, e.g., Gert, Culver and Clouser, *Bioethics*, p. 92. See also Gert, *Common Morality*, p. 24.

[84] See, e.g., Alan H. Goldman, *The Moral Foundations of Professional Ethics* (Totowa, NJ: Rowman and Littlefield, 1980), p. 7.

[85] Ibid. See also Charles Fried, "The Lawyer as Friend: The Moral Foundations of the Lawyer-Client Relationship" (1976) 85 *Yale Law Journal* 1060 (describing criticism of the traditional conception of the lawyer's role which appears to authorize "tactics which procure advantages for the client at the direct expense of some identified opposing party. Examples are discrediting a nervous but probably truthful complaining witness or taking advantage of the need or ignorance of an adversary in a negotiation").

[86] Much of *legal* ethics discourse is dedicated to the discussion of possible justifications of the so-called standard conception of lawyers' role or "neutral partisanship," which arguably can sometimes excuse morally wrong conduct of lawyers in the exercise of their role. See, e.g., Nicolson and Webb, *Professional Legal Ethics*, pp. 160–247; Luban, *Legal Ethics*, pp. 19–64; W. Bradley Wendel, *Lawyers and Fidelity to Law* (Princeton University Press, 2010), pp. 20–48.

may be deviated from on the basis of objective reasons of rationality and impartiality.[87] After all, one may justifiably distract even from the fundamental moral norm "do not kill" in appropriate circumstances of self-defense. Bayles recognized the possibility of a justified role-related norm inconsistent with a universal moral norm, noting that "if role-related norms permit or require conduct that would be wrong by universal ones, they must be justified as in effect exceptions based on the predominance of the value served by the profession. They are thus justified by the special function of the profession."[88] Professionals, therefore, must be able to justify their seemingly immoral conduct by *the necessities of duty*, and when successful their conduct will be regarded as *a legitimate moral exception* to the demands of ordinary morality.

1.2.2 Delineating the limits of professional ethics: the element of role

Thus far we have examined the component of *morality* in the definition of professional ethics, that is, that professional ethics is a branch of ordinary morality. It followed that ethical norms, like moral norms, must be justified on grounds of rationality and impartiality; can be placed on a continuum of duties and aspirations; and may be roughly sorted into rules, principles, values, and ideals. The second component of professional ethics is the *particular activity* to which the norms of morality apply. Without a particular activity ethics will have no meaning, because it would merely mean ordinary morality. Therefore, the existence and meaning of the norms of professional ethics are dependent on the definition of a particular activity.

The particular activity that we are focusing on is the *performance of a professional role*. Roles create special relationships between role-holders and their environment. If we take the role out of the relationship, we are left with an "ordinary" moral relationship rather than an ethical relationship. Thus the definition of a role and the particular activity of the role-holder are *constitutive* in the definition of ethics and in the identification of the ethical norms that apply to professionals.

[87] See, e.g., Gert, Culver and Clouser, *Bioethics*, p. 91. See also Bayles, *Professional Ethics*, p. 24.

[88] Bayles, *Professional Ethics*, p. 28.

1.2.2.1 Identifying professional roles and particular activities

Identifying professional roles and the particular activities associated with those roles is essential for establishing the norms of ethics that regulate them. Professional roles have *goals and values* that they seek to realize through shared practices. They are not defined by morality or ethics. They develop and are shaped in response to various factors such as social needs that the particular activity of the professional role-holders seeks to meet (for example, provision of healthcare services); economic needs (for example, providing livelihood to the professionals); sociological needs (for example, acquiring social status); psychological needs (for example, desire for respect and self-fulfillment); and political struggles (for example, adaption to developments in other fields of activity). As a result, professional roles have *dynamic* and changing definitions. Their definitions may be ascertained by examination of (a) *legislation and codes of conduct* that regulate particular fields of activity; and (b) *professional literature* that describes the history and development of the professional role, its philosophy, the social needs it serves to meet, and conventions of practice among the professional community in that field.

1.2.2.2 Professional role norms

Professional role definitions and particular activities reflect *professional norms* that determine from a *practical* perspective how professionals should act in order to realize the goals of their role. Bayles, referring to this idea, argued that "[s]ocial roles or positions are defined by [role-defining norms]. These role-defining norms need not be ethical; they simply state the actions that people with certain characteristics may or must do. [They] specify the powers and tasks of a role or position ... Similar norms define professional roles."[89] Professional norms, like norms of morality and ethics, can be roughly sorted into rules, principles, values, and ideals along a continuum of duties and aspirations.

Professional values and ideals Roles have purposes. They are designed to achieve certain outcomes. Gert noted that "a profession treats its accepted ideals as goals, as something to be worked toward, as aspiration."[90] Professional values and ideals signal what the "good" is from a professional perspective, that is, the *goal* that professionals aspire to achieve. For example, one professional value and ideal of the medical

[89] See Bayles, *Professional Ethics*, p. 20.
[90] See Gert, Culver and Clouser, *Bioethics*, p. 93.

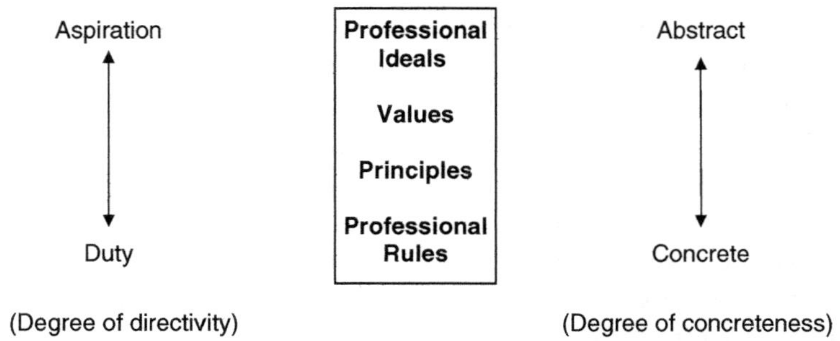

Figure 1.4: Types of professional role norms (the norms of good practice)

profession is restoring and maintaining health,[91] which medical practitioners seek to realize in their work.

Professional rules and principles Particular roles are practiced through procedures and techniques that are utilized in order to perform the role. Time, tradition, experience, and social processes affect the emergence of a professional practice, which is aimed at achieving the goals of the professional role. The practice has normative force to the extent that it reflects shared social conventions of the professional group. The norms of practice are a type of social rules that failure to follow might result in criticism by members of the group. These professional norms are not necessarily moral or legal; they simply instruct the professional role-holder how he or she should *technically, procedurally, and efficiently* fulfill his or her role. For example, professional norms could direct professionals regarding the stages of the professional process they manage, the paperwork to be done, or the clothes they should wear. Figure 1.4 describes the types of professional role norms.

1.2.2.3 Ethical norms: a union of moral norms and professional norms

The integration of moral norms with professional role norms produces norms of professional ethics. Professional ethics begins at the point that morality and the exercise of a professional role meet. This meeting produces three types of ethical norms. First are *norms of ordinary morality* that apply to professional role-holders in the execution of their role. Professionals are expected to follow the norms of ordinary morality like

[91] See, e.g., Koehn, *The Ground of Professional Ethics*, p. 70.

everyone else.[92] For example, they are expected to keep their promises, tell the truth, and refrain from harming others like any moral person. What makes these moral norms ethical is simply the fact that they apply to the particular activity of the professional. Similarly, the aspirations of ordinary morality apply to professionals in their work. The morality of aspiration, that is, the pursuit of the moral good in every activity one is involved in, guides the ethical professional to be a "good person" in his or her work as well as in his or her private life.

A second type of norms of professional ethics is *moral norms of role* that follow from the special relationships professional role-holders have with their environment.[93] The role of professionals places them in a position of power and influence over the lives and interests of others. Others rely and depend on them, and the conduct associated with the role is to a large extent determined by others. Those who might be affected by the exercise of the role legitimately expect the role-holder to behave in certain ways, and norms of ethics are partly the product of these expectations. Gert, for example, argued that "[m]ost roles have duties, more or less precise, attached to them," and referred to "actions that are a person's duty because of a special role, such as being a doctor, lawyer, parent, or teacher."[94] Pritchard, agreeing with Gert, commented that some "basic duties derive from professional roles or take on special significance because of those roles."[95] Pritchard argued that "the basic professional responsibilities are to employers, clients, the public, and fellow professionals."[96] The next chapter develops this idea and explores the content of these responsibilities. It shows that the legitimate expectations of four reference groups – clients, the profession, the public, and employers and principals – produce *general norms of professional role-ethics* that apply to all professionals because of their role-holding position. These norms include, for example, norms of competence, impartiality, honesty, professional integrity, and protection of the profession's standing.[97] They impose duties on professionals and at the same time set aspirations. For example, the norm of competence both imposes a duty on professionals to have the qualifications and skills *necessary* for conducting their role,

92 See, e.g., Bayles, *Professional Ethics*, p. 28 (noting that professional ethics includes norms which "are universal ones that apply to professionals simply because they apply to everyone").

93 See, e.g., Kultgen, *Ethics and Professionalism*, p. 227 (referring to role norms as the ethics of the profession).

94 See Gert, *Common Morality*, p. 50.

95 See Pritchard, *Professional Integrity*, p. 85.

96 Id., p. 157.

97 See Chapter 2.

and sets an ideal that professionals have the *best* qualifications and skills possible so they can provide their clients with excellent services.

The third type of norms of ethics consists of *specifications* of the general norms of professional role-ethics that apply to *particular* professionals in the practice of a particular profession. Each role encourages different expectations of conduct. For example, a doctor is expected to care for his or her patients' health, while a lawyer is expected to care for his or her clients' legal rights. However, these expectations are merely specifications of the general ethical norms that apply to all professionals, with a modification and adaptation of the *content* of the norms in light of the particular characteristics of the professional activity. For example, all ethical professionals must be competent, but the content of the demand for competence from doctors and lawyers differs. Moreover, every profession has its own practice that is manifested in its professional rules, conventions, procedures, and tactics. This practice can sometimes generate particular ethical duties. When a certain practice is largely in agreement within the professional community, and most of the professionals belonging to that group follow that practice and criticize members of the group that fail to do so, a legitimate expectation arises that every professional in that group follow that practice. It becomes an ethical duty to do so, as long as this practice is not immoral, for moral reasons of fairness, reciprocity, and promise keeping.[98] When the professional group disagrees with regard to the correct practice, several practices can coexist and be considered as legitimate by the group members. In that case, there is no professional rule regarding that particular practice and members of that profession are free to choose how to conduct themselves. In the absence of a professional rule regarding that particular practice, no ethical duty of professionals to act in that particular way is established. It is a professional norm because some professionals conduct themselves according to it, but has no obligatory force, only guiding. It is one of the standards of professional conduct, accepted and practiced at least by some professionals, but it is not part of professional ethics.

This analysis applies to the *aspirations* of particular professional role-holders as well. The definition of professional roles and the particular conduct associated with those roles, produce different professional ideals that fit the special characteristics of the professional role. For example, an ideal of saving lives is an aspiration of medical doctors, while lawyers

[98] See Chapter 2, Section 2.3.

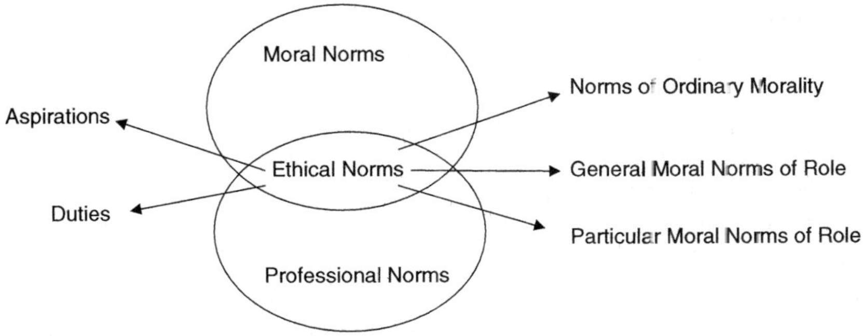

Figure 1.5: Types of ethical norms

have an ideal of defending legal rights. The integration of these professional aspirations with the morality of aspiration transforms these ideals, as long as they are not immoral, into ethical ideals as well. For example, the aspiration to save lives is not only a professional good but a moral good as well, thus an ideal for the ethical doctor. In other cases, the professional ideal might point to a goal that does not have a moral content in itself but is instrumental in achieving moral ideals. For example, effectiveness in the provision of professional services is amoral but can advance a moral ideal of client satisfaction and happiness. Thus the amoral professional ideal that furthers a moral ideal may be considered ethical. In contrast, on the rare occasion that the "professional" goal is immoral, the ideal cannot be ethical. For example, a "professional" killer is not realizing an ethical ideal by being excellent in what he or she does. His or her role and particular activity are immoral and therefore his or her "professional" goal or ideal cannot form a part of professional ethics. Figure 1.5 describes the types of ethical norms.

1.2.3 Ethics and law: legal norms that are both moral and professional

1.2.3.1 The application of law to professional activities

Law, like morality, is a normative system that instructs people how to behave. As with regard to morality, conduct in violation of the norms will likely be followed by some degree of social criticism. However, legal norms, contrary to moral norms, are enforced institutionally by state authorities and backed by sanctions. Moreover, while legal norms need not evince good reasons for the norm to be valid, and their authority may rest on *formal* criteria, such as the origin of the norm (e.g. parliament), morality requires norms to satisfy *substantive* criteria of validity, that is, be justified by rational and impartial reasons.[99]

Legal norms apply to professional activities in several ways. The first is through legal norms that address the general public. For example, the law of contracts applies to every person who is party to a contract. Thus, professionals who make contracts in the course of work must follow the legal norms of contract law. Second, professional activities may be regulated by legislation that specifically addresses them. For example, laws commonly regulate the practice of lawyers, doctors, psychologists, and social workers. And third, some professionals choose to regulate some aspects of their practice by voluntary agreements that have legal force, without the intervention of the legislature. Such agreements may be named "standards of conduct" or "code of ethics" and apply to members of professional organizations by virtue of their membership. For example, engineers who are members of the National Society of Professional Engineers agree to abide by the society's Code of Ethics for Engineers.[100] The fact that a code of ethics or standards of professional conduct have legal status does not strip them of their ethical identity.[101]

1.2.3.2 Legal norms that are norms of ethics and legal norms that are not

While legal norms may be a source of standards of professional conduct, they are not necessarily norms of professional ethics. That is because for legal norms to qualify as norms of ethics they must satisfy the dual criteria of validity of norms of ethics, that is (a) not be immoral, and (b) apply to a professional activity (see group C in Figure 1.6). If a legal norm is immoral (for example, if it orders doctors to refuse to treat patients for racist reasons),[102] or if it does not apply to a professional activity (for example, if it requires all drivers to have insurance where the activity of driving is not connected to the professional role), it cannot be considered a norm of ethics, because ethics concerns the application of moral norms to professional activities. In addressing this issue, Davis noted that "[p]rofessional rules are themselves a proper subject of moral evaluation."[103] In discussing the ethical duties of engineers, he argued that engineers' "code of ethics is what they make it – as long as the

[99] See Section 1.2.1.1. [100] See www.nspe.org/Ethics/CodeofEthics/index.html.

[101] See, e.g., Pritchard, *Professional Integrity*, p. 86.

[102] See, e.g., Koehn, *The Ground of Professional Ethics*, pp. 151–152.

[103] See Michael Davis, "Professionalism Means Putting Your Profession First", in Cohen and Davis, *Ethics and the Legal Profession*, p. 170.

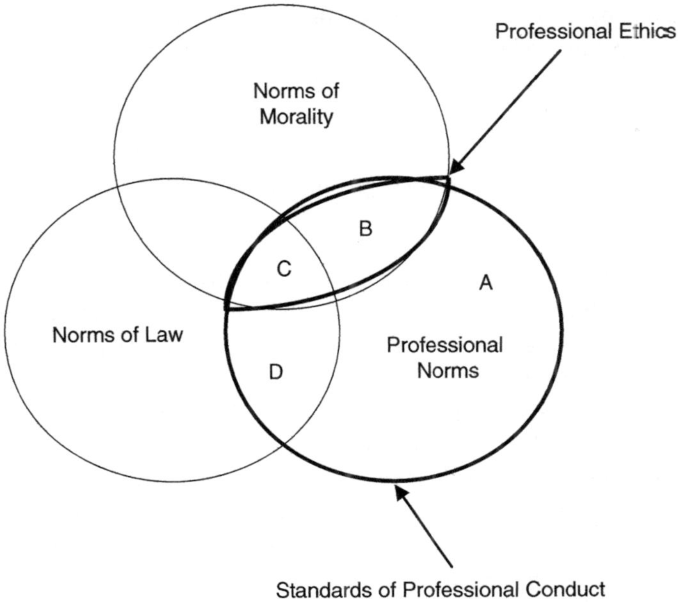

Figure 1.6: Law, ethical norms, and standards of professional conduct

standards they lay down are consistent with ordinary morality."[104] Pritchard seems to concur with that view, arguing that "[c]odes of ethics are hardly the last word in professional ethics."[105] Thus, as Shaw says, professionals "must be alert to situations in which professional standards or customary professional practice conflicts with the ordinary demands of morality."[106] They should be aware, as Beauchamp and Childress note, that their standards or code of practice might reflect an attempt "to protect the profession's interests more than to offer a broad and impartial moral viewpoint,"[107] and are thus possibly unethical notwithstanding their legal status.

It should be noted, however, that the legal adoption of a particular professional practice by the legislature or by a professional group (in a code of conduct) might confer ethical status on it despite its amoral, "technical" status. For example, the formal obligation that uniforms must be worn on duty transforms this amoral demand (which morality is

[104] See Davis, *Thinking Like an Engineer*, p. 16.
[105] See Pritchard, *Professional Integrity*, p. 87. [106] See Shaw, *Business Ethics*, p. 12.
[107] See Beauchamp and Childress, *Biomedical Ethics*, pp. 7–8. See also Kultgen, *Ethics and Professionalism*, pp. 212–216, 218.

indifferent to) into an ethical duty. This is so because the inclusion of this rule in a binding code establishes a legitimate expectation on the basis of fairness that professionals whose conduct is regulated by that code behave accordingly.[108]

Figure 1.6 illustrates and summarizes the relationship between standards of professional conduct, professional ethics (norms of ethics), and law.

A. Professional norms inconsistent with morality, and professional practices that are not in consensus within the professional community and thus have not yet acquired the status of a professional (duty-conferring) rule
B. Professional norms that have acquired ethical status because of their interaction with norms of morality
C. Professional norms that have legal force and have acquired ethical status because of their interaction with norms of morality
D. Professional norms that are imposed by law but have no ethical force because they are immoral.

1.2.3.3 Distinguishing legal threshold from ethical threshold and ethical bar

The difference between law and ethics in guiding professionals can be honed through the use of the normative terms "threshold" and "bar" (see Figure 1.7). Legal norms dictate minimum standards of behavior that no one is allowed to ignore. Any action falling short of the legal threshold is considered illegal and may be followed by legal sanctions.[109] For example, where the law protects the confidentiality of medical information, doctors must not disclose information relating to their patients without legal authorization. However, actions may be legal and yet inappropriate according to other social norms. Norms of ethics often set a higher threshold of behavior than law, so that legal conduct may be unethical, that is, in breach of ethical duties.[110] In addition, norms of ethics include aspirations that represent an ideal bar to be sought. The ethical bar is set

[108] See Chapter 2, Section 2.3.2.
[109] See, e.g., Shaw, *Business Ethics*, p. 11 (noting that "[t]he law ... is the 'floor' of moral conduct").
[110] For discussion see Asa Kasher, "Ethics, Law, and Adjudication" in Aharon Barak (ed.), *Essays in Honour of President Meir Shamgar*, Vol. II (Tel Aviv: Israel Bar Publications, 2003), pp. 434, 441–442 [Hebrew].

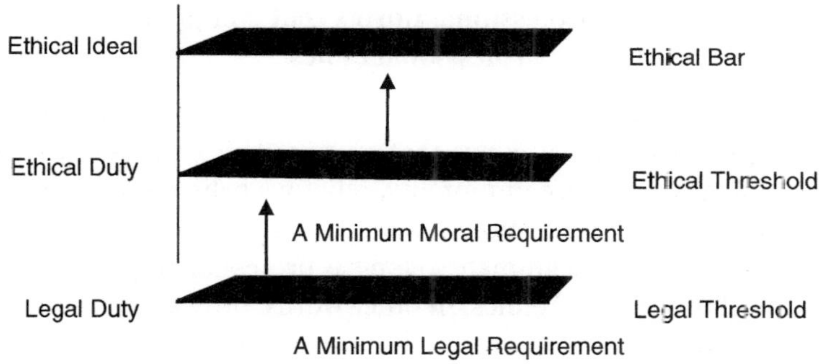

Figure 1.7: Legal threshold, ethical threshold, and ethical bar

higher than the ethical threshold, and failure to reach it does not constitute a breach of duty.

Usually the ethical threshold is set higher than the legal threshold and requires the professional to do more than his or her legal duty prescribes. However, when the law gives force to norms of ethics, the legal and moral thresholds are supposedly the same. Moreover, the legal threshold may be set higher than the moral threshold, thus instructing the professional to act unethically. For example, journalists may be ethically bound to keep in confidence their sources of information yet face a legal demand for their disclosure.[111]

The distance between the legal and ethical thresholds or between the ethical threshold and bar depends on the exact scope of each ethical duty. Since the meaning of ethical duties is not always precise, it is difficult to point to the exact location of the ethical threshold. There is therefore a gray area that may make it hard to decisively decide whether an ethical duty has been breached.[112] For professional practice, the implication is that a zone of professional discretion does exist. The gray area thus signifies the existence of several legitimate actions among which the professional may choose. We will address this issue in Chapter 15, which focuses on ethical decision-making.

[111] See, e.g., "New York Times reporter jailed" at cnn.com, available at edition.cnn.com/2005/LAW/07/06/reporters.contempt/ ("A federal judge ordered New York Times reporter Judith Miller jailed for contempt of court Wednesday for refusing to testify to a grand jury investigating the leak of a CIA operative's name").

[112] See Section 1.2.1.2(c).

1.3 Non-professional norms that complement professional ethics

Professionals may elect to be guided in their practice by norms other than the norms of professional ethics that govern their profession, such as personal integrity or sense of morality, religious belief, or ethical norms that relate to another profession. Looking for guidance in other normative systems is ethically legitimate so long as professionals give priority to the norms of professional ethics. In other words, professional ethics may be supplemented by other norms, but not replaced.

1.3.1 Personal integrity or sense of morality

Lynne McFall argued that "[p]ersonal integrity requires that an agent (1) subscribe to some consistent set of principles or commitments and (2), in the face of temptation or challenge, (3) uphold these principles or commitments, (4) for what the agent takes to be the right reasons."[113] Professionals, like every person, have their personal views, beliefs, and opinions about the world. Acting in accordance with their worldview might be very important to them. As a matter of personal integrity, they might feel it necessary to follow their personal beliefs and values. Bringing these personal norms into professional practice is inevitable and may contribute to ethical practice. Personal morality and conscience could draw red lines that professionals refuse to cross where supervision over their actions is limited, and prevent abuse of power when professionals have a high degree of discretion due to the uncertainty of the relevant ethical norms. However, professionals must be aware that their personal convictions must not replace professional ethics. If the criterion for right conduct were the personal convictions of professionals, the distinction between right and wrong conduct would be rendered meaningless, because whatever professionals thought right according to their personal convictions would have to be considered right.[114] It follows that while personal integrity may guide professionals, it must concede precedence to the norms of ethics.

[113] See Lynne McFall, "Integrity" (1987) 98 *Ethics* 5, 9.

[114] See, e.g., Davis, *Thinking Like an Engineer*, p. 97 (noting that "[i]ndividual-centered relativism thus cuts off ethical discussion as soon as it begins"). See also Pritchard, *Professional Integrity*, p. 160 (noting that "professional ethics is not an ethics for each individual professional simply to conjure up").

1.3.2 *Religious belief*

The norms of religion are considered binding in the eyes of religious persons, and continue to be considered so in the course of professional practice. Religious persons differ in their commitment to religious rules. Some see them as mandatory, while others treat them as advisory. Like a personal sense of morality, religious faith can be a source of help to the professional, or alternatively a source of confusion in the event of a clash between the norms of religion and the norms of ethics.[115] For example, a religious doctor may find it hard to reconcile his or her patient's wish to have an abortion with his or her religious belief that abortions are wrong and prohibited.

1.3.3 *Other professional role norms*

Some professionals practice more than one profession. They may be, for example, both lawyers and accountants, or both teachers and engineers. These professionals could be influenced in the practice of one profession by the standards that guide their conduct in the practice of their other profession. It is important, however, that these professionals be able to distinguish between their professional roles, because their conduct might be considered ethical under the standards of one profession yet unethical according to the standards of their other profession. For example, a lawyer who is also a mediator must not give mediation parties legal advice when he or she is acting as a mediator in their case. Offering legal advice, which is a core practice of lawyers, is ethically prohibited in the case of mediators.[116]

1.4 The functions of professional ethics

Professional ethics has several functions.

Providing information and guidance to both professionals and clients

Professional ethics sets standards of worthy conduct. These standards guide professionals in their practice. They provide them with information

[115] See, e.g., Martha Minow, "On Being Religious Professional: The Religious Turn in Professional Ethics" (2001) 150 *University of Pennsylvania Law Review* 661.

[116] See Chapter 7, Section 7.2.2.

on how they ought to behave and on their rights and duties in the course of practice, and offer guidance on dealing with complex situations. In addition, professional ethics provides *clients* with information on their rights and obligations as the recipients of professional services. It helps clients to better understand what they can expect from professionals and the limitations of the professional service.[117]

Supervision

Professionals have power that may be abused and needs to be supervised.[118] While legal supervision is largely based on punishment and deterrence, ethics focuses on personal responsibility, learning, and self-improvement. Thus, the essence of ethical monitoring and supervision is awareness-raising rather than sanctioning.

Ethical supervision is exercised through *clients* who are aware of their rights and demand that they be respected by the professionals. Ethical supervision can also take place through ethical *institutions* that publish opinions on the expected conduct of professionals, investigate complaints against professionals, and receive inquiries from both professionals and clients. When such institutions are given legal powers of enforcement and sanctioning (by statute or agreement), the supervision becomes legal or disciplinary. When professional conduct is in breach of law, for example in the case of professional negligence, legal supervision is also exercised by the *courts*.

Reputation and public confidence

Adoption of ethical standards is often viewed as a step for promoting public confidence in the profession.[119] It sends a message to the public

[117] See, e.g., Pritchard, *Professional Integrity*, p. 86 (noting that a code of ethics can be used "to resist pressure from others to engage in unethical behavior").

[118] See, e.g., Gibson, "Contrasting Role Morality", 22 (noting that professionals are in a position of power that may be abused). See also Davis, *Thinking Like an Engineer*, p. 16 (noting that ethical regulation of engineering serves to ensure "that engineering would be used for good rather than evil").

[119] See, e.g., Julie Macfarlane, "Mediating Ethically: The Limits of Codes of Conduct and the Potential of a Reflective Practice Model" (2002) 40 *Osgoode Hall Law Journal* 49, 55. See also Model Standards of Conduct for Mediators (2005) available at www.americanbar.org/groups/dispute_resolution/policy_standards.html and in Appendix II (Model Standards), Introduction (noting that one of the primary goals of the Standards is "to promote public confidence in mediation as a process for resolving disputes").

that the professionals are committed to responsible conduct.[120] Moreover, it is a sign of professionalization.

1.5 Conclusion

Professional ethics applies to the particular activity of exercising a professional role. Professional roles have definitions and objectives that yield professional norms, which are mainly norms of utility and functionality. These norms determine how a role should be executed in practice in order to achieve the purpose of the role, and set values or ideals that role-holders aspire to realize.

Professional norms become norms of ethics through their interaction with morality (see Figure 1.8). Norms of morality apply to the professional activity, and the professional's position triggers expectations of and a reliance on the professional that impose on him or her role-morality obligations. Thus professional ethics, through morality, serves as an *external limitation* on role-holders that professionals must not ignore. It is not a matter of personal choice and it does not depend on the existence of a written, formal code of conduct. Professional ethics imposes on professionals standards of conduct that are independent of the professional's will and sometimes of the will of their clients as well. The professional must meet minimum standards of conduct that stem from role-morality and can be objectively justified on the basis of rational

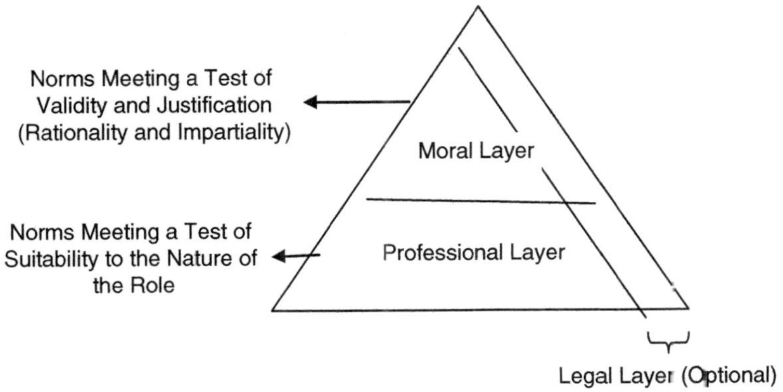

Figure 1.8: Professional ethics as the union of professional and moral norms

[120] See, e.g., Pritchard, *Professional Integrity*, p. 87.

and impartial reasons. In practice, it will often be possible to evaluate the ethical status of a particular norm in light of its compatibility with fundamental moral values that are widely agreed and assumed to be justified and valid.

Professional ethics may have legal force in the event that the professional activity is subject to norms of law. However, the norms of professional ethics are not necessarily norms of law, because for professional ethics to exist a meeting of moral norms and role-holding suffices. In addition, legal norms that regulate the professional activity are not necessarily ethical, because for legal norms to be ethical they must satisfy the criteria for moral validity.

Clearly, professionals must be aware of legal norms that apply to the execution of their role, whether they are part of professional ethics or not. This is because legal norms are normally backed by the force of the state, and their legal validity is not necessarily dependent on their being moral. Understanding the distinction between law and professional ethics is critical for professionals if they are to behave beyond the minimum standards of conduct that the law imposes on them. The distinction will also be important in the relatively rare cases in which professionals are instructed by law (for example by a court order or a code of conduct that has legal status) to take an action that is inconsistent with the norms of professional ethics. Professionals in these cases should be aware that following the law blindly does not guarantee that their actions are ethical.

The next chapter complements the discussion of the fundamental concepts of professional ethics by exploring the ethical relationships that professionals have with their environment and by establishing the general norms of ethics that govern these relationships.

2

Ethical relationships

2.1 Introduction

Chapter 1 dealt with the meaning of professional ethics as an intersection between norms of morality and norms of a role, where that role is socially perceived as a professional activity. It argued, inter alia, that this encounter creates general ethical norms that apply to all professionals. This chapter examines that argument in depth. It will establish, as part of a general theory of professional ethics, the ethical obligations of professionals toward four major groups – clients, the profession, the public, and employers or principals – that legitimately expect professionals to conduct themselves in particular ways. This theory, I argue, is suitable for any professional who occupies a trust-based role, but since the book focuses on the ethics of mediators, I intend to defend the theory only insofar as it applies to persons occupying the role of a mediator.

The reader should note that as the ethical duties of professionals are relative, it is inevitable that one duty will sometimes clash with another. For example, professionals have an ethical obligation of confidentiality to their clients, and that duty might conflict with their ethical obligation toward the public to report a client's intention to commit a crime. Professionals in such an event will have to weigh the conflicting obligations, balance them, and make a reasoned choice. This weighing and balancing will not be dealt with in the present chapter because it deals with the general ethical obligations of professionals, and cannot offer a general balancing equation that applies to all professionals in any event of conflicting duties. A balance between conflicting duties can only be struck with respect to a particular professional role, after an in-depth examination of the nature of that role. Parts II and III of the book illustrate how this balancing can be done with respect to mediators.

2.2 Duties toward clients

2.2.1 Introduction

A person performing a professional role has a special relationship with those for whose benefit he or she acts. We shall call them "clients" for convenience, and they could be, for example, the patients of a doctor or psychologist, persons who hire an engineer for engineering services, clients of a lawyer, or mediation parties. They are persons or bodies who approach the professional for a certain service and rely on his or her abilities to provide that service. They are normally expected to pay for that service, though payment is not a necessary element of a professional–client relationship. What makes that relationship special are the express and implied promises that professionals make upon taking on a case, their position of power and influence, and the reliance of clients on them.

2.2.2 The normative basis of duties toward clients

Keeping promises

When a person presents him or herself as a professional or otherwise assumes a professional role, he or she is making an explicit or implicit public declaration that he or she is "a professional" in a certain field. In doing so, he or she voluntarily commits him or herself to a role that has been defined by others, is practiced in a certain way, and is governed by standards of conduct.[1] That person can be considered to have promised to act in accordance with the accepted standards in that field and those standards which follow from the nature and definition of the professional role.[2] The clients of that person are entitled to expect that he keep his or her promises, as promise-keeping is a basic moral duty of all persons.[3]

Trust

A second feature of the professional–client relationship is the inherent inequality of power between professionals and their clients. Professionals have knowledge and expertise that their clients do not have, and clients depend on professionals to take actions that they cannot take by themselves.[4] This relationship of power on the one side and dependence on the

[1] See, e.g., Koehn, *The Ground of Professional Ethics*, p. 63.
[2] See, e.g., Pritchard, *Professional Integrity*, p. 33.
[3] See, e.g., Gert, *Common Morality*, pp. 42–43 (discussing the morality of promises).
[4] See, e.g., Pritchard, *Professional Integrity*, p. 3 quoting William F. May, "Professional Virtue and Self-Regulation", in Joan Callahan (ed.), *Ethical Issues in Professional Life*

other side establishes special duties toward clients, duties that follow from the legitimate expectation of clients that professionals do not abuse their position of power and the clients' dependence and reliance on them.

Numerous publications support the view that a position of power and influence creates ethical responsibility. Steven Lukes wrote that "[t]he point ... of locating power is to fix responsibility for consequences held to flow from the action, or inaction, of certain specifiable agents";[5] Andrew Schaap argued that "[t]o 'have' or 'exercise' power is to be morally and politically accountable for one's actions (including inactions) and their consequences on others."[6] More specifically, in discussing professional relationships, Michael Bayles argued that "[i]n a fiduciary relationship ... Because one party is in a more advantageous position, he or she has special obligations to the other. The weaker party depends on the stronger in ways in which the other does not and so must trust the stronger party,"[7] and " ... the client must rely on the professional to use his or her knowledge and ability in the client's interests. Because the client cannot check most of the work of the professional or the information supplied, the professional has special obligations to the client to ensure that the trust and reliance are justified."[8]

To summarize, the professional–client relationship is one of *trust*, and clients legitimately expect professionals to be *trustworthy*, that is, not conduct themselves in a manner that might undermine trust.[9] Note that

(New York: Oxford University Press, 1988), p. 408. See also Wueste, *Professional Ethics*, p. 13 ("The professional is seen as a source of expert advice or help. Moreover, it often happens that the need or interest that prompts the client to seek professional help can neither be fully understood nor handled without professional assistance").

5 Steven Lukes, *Power: A Radical View* (London: Macmillan, 1974), p. 56.

6 Andrew Schaap, "Power and Responsibility: Should We Spare The King's Head?" (2000) 20 *Politics* 129, 130.

7 Bayles, *Professional Ethics*, p. 78.

8 Ibid. See also George F. DeMartino, *The Economist's Oath: On the Need for and Content of Professional Economic Ethics* (New York: Oxford University Press, 2011), pp. 103–117 (noting that a position of power creates ethical responsibility); Shaw, *Business Ethics*, p. 66 (noting that some moral rights derive from special relationships and roles); Beauchamp and Childress, *Biomedical Ethics*, p. 79 (noting that moral obligations arise from professional relationships such as the patient–physician relationship).

9 See, e.g., Bayles, *Professional Ethics*, pp. 79–80 ("A professional's obligations to a client are those necessary to deserve the client's trust that these activities will be performed in a manner to promote the client's interests ... "); See also Pritchard, *Professional Integrity*, p. 32 ("Given our extensive dependence on professionals, we expect them to conduct themselves responsibly ... This expectation ... is normative, implying standards of accountability ... at a minimum, we expect professionals to be trustworthy ... i.e, worthy of our trust"); Arthur Chaykin, "Mediator Liability: A New Role for Fiduciary Duties?"

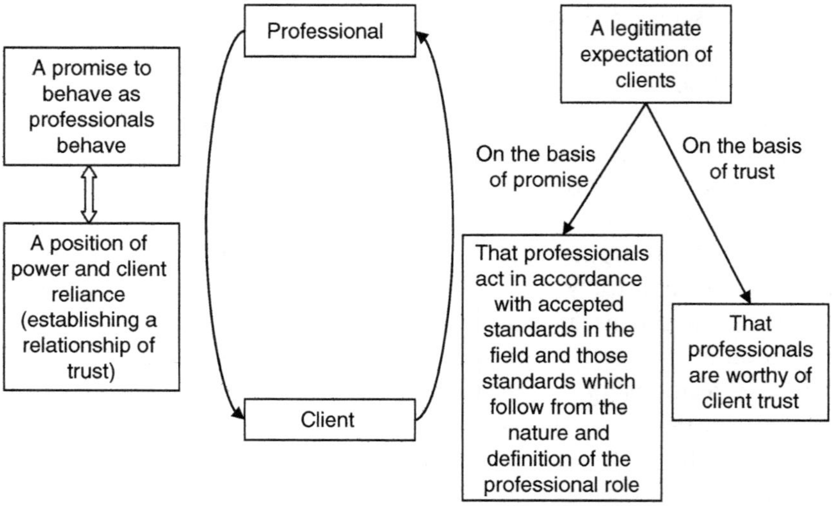

Figure 2.1: The normative basis of duties toward clients

while the existence of trust in a professional is a matter of fact, the legitimate expectation that he be trustworthy is a normative requirement that remains even where a client does not in fact trust the professional. That is because the inequality of power between clients and professionals, the dependence and reliance on professionals, and the promise professionals make to provide adequate services all remain the same in the absence of trust. Figure 2.1 describes the normative basis of duties toward clients.

2.2.3 Ethical duties toward clients

It is argued that the professional–client relationship establishes ten ethical standards: competence, disclosure of conflicts of interest, client autonomy or self-determination, professional integrity, impartiality, diligence, respect and dignity, honesty, confidentiality, and fairness. This is not necessarily an exhaustive list. Moreover, some scholars have suggested other lists of standards.[10] Yet I would argue that a robust

(1984) 53 *University of Cincinnati Law Review* 731, 750 ("The duty to be trustworthy is a basic component of fiduciary duties in general. One who is justifiably trusted by another is under an obligation to act in a manner that is consistent with the trust").

10 For different lists of standards see, e.g., Bayles, *Professional Ethics*, pp. 79–99 (arguing that there are "seven general obligations that professionals must fulfill to be deserving of client trust": honesty, candor, competence, diligence, loyalty, fairness, and discretion. Bayles writes that "[n]o hard claim is made that the obligations presented are exhaustive" and

commitment of professionals to these standards is necessary if they are to be worthy of their clients' trust and keep their promise to perform their role "as professionals." The standards are abstract and thus can be interpreted and specified according to the nature of the professional role under examination, and in Part II they will be interpreted and specified in the context of the role of mediators. These standards are primarily norms of *duty*. They set a threshold that professionals must not fall beneath for their conduct to be considered ethical. The standards have an aspect of *aspiration* as well,[11] that is, they also set ideals that professionals should aspire to but cannot be criticized for not achieving.

2.2.3.1 Competence

Clients expect professionals to have the *ability* to perform their role. When professionals take on a case, they make a representation and in effect promise that they are qualified to perform their role and are therefore worthy of trust.[12] Bayles argued that "[p]rofessionals have an ethical responsibility not to hold themselves out to do or accept work they are not competent to handle . . . if [professionals] are incompetent, they are unworthy of trust, for they cannot do well the job for which they are hired."[13] The meaning of competence is that the professional has the knowledge, expertise, and skills required to provide professional services that are suitable to the role. Several rules follow from the standard of competence:

(a) Limitations on accepting cases: professionals who do not possess the competence required to perform their role should refrain from taking on a case.
(b) Limitations on handling cases: professionals who become incompetent or aware of their incompetence must take appropriate measures such as bringing in another specialist, making a referral to another professional, or terminating the services.
(c) Maintaining competence: professionals must preserve their competence and should further develop it.

The standard of competence applies to any professional, but its content varies between roles and professions and is determined by specific rules

admits that " . . . some [obligations] (for example, honesty and candor) might be combined." See also Koehn, *The Ground of Professional Ethics*, pp. 54–56 (listing seven conditions for trustworthiness).

[11] See Chapter 1, Section 1.2.1.2. [12] See, e.g., Pritchard, *Professional Integrity*, p. 33.

[13] Bayles, *Professional Ethics*, pp. 84–85.

relevant to the occupational field. A competent doctor, for example, must have knowledge of the human body, while an engineer must have knowledge of the strength of materials.

The standard of competence, like all the standards presented in this chapter, has an aspect of aspiration. We would like professionals who provide us with services to be excellent, leaders in their field, with many years of experience, and with full command of all innovations and developments in their field. This ideal is worthy of respect but can hardly establish an obligation of competence. We cannot legitimately expect every professional to be a leader in his or her field and the reality is that professionals have different levels of competence depending on their experience, intelligence, and economic resources. The obligatory ethical threshold of competence is lower than ideal competence, though professionals should be encouraged to strive for excellence.

2.2.3.2 Disclosure of conflicts of interest

Clients legitimately expect professionals who provide them with services to act in a way that does not injure them and their interests. Since professionals have their own interests, these interests will sometimes conflict with clients' interests. Professionals are expected to *separate* their interests and the interests of clients, provide services that *meet* the interests of their clients, and *give priority* to the interests of their clients to an extent required by their role in the event of a conflict of interests.

Michael Pritchard argued that "it is important to realize that merely having a conflict of interest is not, in general, to have done anything ethically suspect or wrong."[14] He suggested that "we might think of actual, and even potential, conflicts of interest as yellow traffic lights. Caution must be taken. Depending on the available alternatives, the light may turn red or green – or it may remain yellow for the duration."[15] Thus, a conflict of interest is a warning sign that requires professionals to consider how to proceed. Bayles argued that "[a]t the very least, professionals have a duty to inform clients of their own personal interests that might affect their independence of judgment."[16] In other cases, the appropriate step would be for the professional to withdraw.

Conflicts of interest cannot be avoided entirely. For example, professionals have an interest in getting the highest fees for the smallest amount

[14] Pritchard, *Professional Integrity*, p. 65. [15] id., p. 66.

[16] Bayles, *Professional Ethics*, p. 91. See also Ken Kipnis, "Conflict of Interest and Conflict of Obligation", in Elliot D. Cohen and Michael Davis (eds.), *Ethics and the Legal Profession*, 2nd edn. (Amherst, NY: Prometheus Books, 2009), p. 271.

of work. They have an interest in reducing the scope of their work when they receive a fixed fee, and in extending the period of work when getting paid by the hour.[17] However, professionals are expected to refrain from acting in accordance with their personal interest in these situations because of the special nature of the professional–client relationship, which imposes a duty on professionals to protect the interests of their clients and give them priority over their own interests; a person who is not performing a professional role and is not in a relationship of trust and reliance with another has no obligation to protect the interests of another.[18] Sometimes, however, professionals are justified in preferring their personal interests or interests other than those of their clients. For example, if a professional is asked by his or her client to break the law or violate ethical standards, or to provide services for free, he would be justified in rejecting the client's wishes, even though doing so means preferring his or her own interests or interests other than those of the client over the client's interests.

2.2.3.3 Client autonomy or self-determination

Clients' legitimate expectation of autonomy or self-determination Every person has a moral right to make decisions for him or herself, to determine how to manage his or her affairs, and to enjoy various liberties such as freedom from injury, freedom of movement, and freedom of speech.[19] Clients have this right in their relationship with professionals as well, while the content of the right is shaped by the type of services sought.[20] Clients legitimately expect professionals to respect their

[17] See, e.g., Kipnis, "Conflict of Interest", 279–280 (referring to such conflicts as "structural or systemic; rooted in the institutional context of the professional role").

[18] See, e.g.,Michael Davis, "Introduction", in Michael Davis and Andrew Stark (eds.), *Conflict of Interest in the Professions* (New York: Oxford University Press, 2001), p. 8 (noting that a relationship of trust is required for a conflict of interest).

[19] On the moral right to autonomy see, e.g., Ruth R. Faden and Tom L. Beauchamp, *A History and Theory of Informed Consent* (New York: Oxford University Press, 1986), p. 8; F. E. McDermott (ed.), *Self-determination in Social Work: A Collection of Essays on Self-determination and Related Concepts by Philosophers and Social Work Theorists* (London; Boston: Routledge and Kegan Paul, 1975), pp. 9–10; Gerald Dworkin, *The Theory and Practice of Autonomy* (New York: Cambridge University Press, 1988).

[20] See, e.g., Beauchamp and Childress, *Biomedical Ethics*, pp. 99–140 (discussing the principle of autonomy in a doctor-patient relationship); The American Psychological Association's (APA) Ethical Principles of Psychologists and Code of Conduct, available at www.apa.org/ethics/code/index.aspx (APA Ethical Principles and Code), Principle E ("Psychologists respect . . . the right[s] of individuals to . . . self-determination"), and Standard 3.10 (Informed Consent); American Bar Association (ABA) Model Rules of Professional Conduct, available at www.americanbar.org/groups/professional_

autonomy or self-determination because professionals' involvement in their clients' lives could have an impact on clients' assets, quality of life, mental and physical health, and sometimes liberty.

Decision-making by professionals The provision of professional services requires the professional to use skills and knowledge that are not at the client's disposal, and sometimes make decisions that cannot for practical reasons be made by clients. For example, professionals cannot consult with clients on the questions to be asked, the advice to be given, or the type of professional intervention needed in unanticipated circumstances that do not permit conferring with clients. In other words, professionals must *exercise discretion and make decisions* that cannot be made together with their clients. This is an inherent and unavoidable feature of professional roles that necessarily erodes some of clients' autonomy.[21]

Sharing decision-making If clients have a right to make decisions on any topic that affects them, and professionals have an implicit authority to make decisions that are necessary for adequate performance of their role, then a crucial question in any professional–client relationship is the allocation of decision-making authority between the client and the professional, or, in other words, the extent of client autonomy or self-determination.

This question has naturally occupied many scholars.[22] In a nutshell, for many years the dominant approach adopted a *paternalistic* view of

responsibility/publications/model_rules_of_professional_conduct.html (ABA Model Rules), Rule 1.2.

21 See also Section 2.2.3.4.

22 For writing on decision-making in the lawyer–client relationship see, e.g., Douglas E. Rosenthal, *Lawyer and Client: Who's In Charge?* (New York: Russell Sage Foundation, 1974); Mark Spiegel, "Lawyering and Client Decisionmaking: Informed Consent and the Legal Profession" (1979) 128 *University of Pennsylvania Law Review* 41; Marcy Strauss, "Toward a Revised Model of Attorney-Client Relationship: The Argument for Autonomy" (1987) 65 *North Carolina Law Review* 315; Robert D. Dinerstein, "Client-Centered Counseling: Reappraisal and Refinement" (1990) 32 *Arizona Law Review* 501; Robert F. Cochran, "Legal Representation and the Next Steps Toward Client Control: Attorney Malpractice for the Failure to Allow the Client to Control Negotiation and Pursue Alternatives to Litigation" (1990) 47 *Washington and Lee Law Review* 819; Daniel Markovits, *A Modern Legal Ethics: Adversary Advocacy in a Democratic Age* (Princeton University Press, 2008), pp. 28–31. For writing on decision-making in the doctor–patient relationship see, e.g., Linda L. Emanuel and Ezekiel J. Emanuel, "Four Models of the Physician-Patient Relationship" (1992) 267 *Journal of the American Medical Association* 2221; Roger B. Dworkin, "Getting What We should from Doctors: Rethinking Patient

the professional–client relationship. According to this approach, professionals know better what is in their clients' best interest, clients are incapable of understanding the considerations that guide professionals' judgment, and therefore there is no point in seeking clients' consent to professional decisions. The paternalistic model and its assumptions have been severely criticized,[23] and these days a new model of *sharing decision-making* is gaining wide acceptance. This model places the client at the center of the relationship, is based on a theory of informed consent, and requires the professional to involve the client in the decision-making process.[24] A collaborative approach to decision-making must guide the professional on two key issues: first, on the *types* of decisions which (a) require the involvement of clients, (b) are in the exclusive jurisdiction of clients, or (c) are within the sole authority of professionals and can be made without the consent of their clients and even against their wishes; and second, on the *conditions* that must exist for clients to be able to exercise autonomy or self-determination in making decisions.

With regard to the first issue, one can find different approaches in the professional literature to the types of decisions that are within the professional's authority as opposed to decisions that clients are entitled to make. Some of the literature seems to suggest that clients should make *all* decisions.[25] Other approaches divide decision-making authority on the basis of various standards. For example, according to an *end/purpose* test, clients are responsible for determining goals while the professional has the authority to make decisions on the means for achieving these goals;[26] According to a test of *importance*, substantive decisions are to be made by clients, non-substantive decisions by the

Autonomy and the Doctor-Patient Relationship" (2003) 13 *Health Matrix* 235; Marjorie Maguire Shultz, "From Informed Consent to Patient Choice: A New Protected Interest" (1985) 95 *Yale Law Journal* 219.

[23] See, e.g., Bayles *Professional Ethics*, pp. 76–77. See also Strauss, id., 324–325, 329–330; Cochran, id., 827.

[24] See, e.g., Strauss, id., 324. See also Cochran, id., 830–835; Rosenthal, *Lawyer and Client*, pp. 7–28; Cathy Charles, Amiram Gafnia, and Tim Whelan, "Decision-making in the Physician–patient Encounter: Revisiting the Shared Treatment Decision-making Model" (1999) 49 *Social Science and Medicine* 651, 652–653.

[25] For such an approach in medical decision-making see, e.g., Simon N. Whitney, Amy L. McGuire and Laurence B. McCullough, "A Typology of Shared Decision Making, Informed Consent, and Simple Consent" (2004) 140 *Annals of Internal Medicine* 54.

[26] For the ends/means test in lawyer-client relationship see, e.g., ABA Model Rules, Rule 1.2; Strauss, "Toward a Revised Model", 318–319.

professional.[27] Regarding the second issue, the literature emphasizes three conditions for the exercise of autonomy or self-determination: the client must have the *capacity* to make a decision,[28] the client's decision must be *voluntary* and uncoerced,[29] and it must be *informed*.[30]

Limitations on autonomy or self-determination Clients' right of autonomy is not an absolute right and can sometimes be justifiably restricted. First, as we have seen, the involvement of professionals with clients' affairs necessarily limits clients' autonomy where the professional has to make a decision in circumstances in which he could not realistically share the decision-making with the client. However, it is important to emphasize that the choice of clients to receive professional services is not tantamount to a sweeping authorization for the professional to make any decision on the client's behalf. This paternalistic approach is no longer acceptable, although clients may explicitly choose to waive their right. Second, as we shall see, professionals have ethical obligations toward their profession and the public and therefore may have to refuse some of their clients' requests (for example, where following a request would break the law), or even to act against their clients' wishes (for example, when the professional is under a legal duty to act in a way that is inconsistent with his client's will).

2.2.3.4 Professional integrity

Clients expect professionals to act in accordance with the *nature and definition of their role*. I shall refer to this as an expectation of professional

[27] For a substantive/non-substantive test in mediator-parties relationship see, e.g., Florida Rules for Certified and Court-Appointed Mediators (in ADR Resource Handbook January 2015) available at www.flcourts.org/core/fileparse.php/550/urlt/RuleBookletJanuary2015.pdf (Florida Rules), Rule 10.310(a); Omer Shapira, "A Theory of Sharing Decision-Making in Mediation" (2013) 44 *McGeorge Law Review* 923, 929–930.

[28] See, e.g., Bernard Lo, "Assessing Decision-Making Capacity" (1990) 18 *Law, Medicine and Health Care* 193 (discussing the capacity of patients to make decisions about medical care). See also Beauchamp and Childress, *Biomedical Ethics*, pp. 111–117.

[29] See, e.g., William M. Altman, Patricia A. Parmelee, and Michael A. Smyer, "Autonomy, Competence, and Informed Consent in Long Term Care: Legal and Psychological Perspectives" (1992) 37 *Villanova Law Review* 1671, 1684–1685. See also Beauchamp and Childress, *Biomedical Ethics*, pp. 132–135 (discussing voluntariness as part of informed consent).

[30] See, e.g., Beauchamp and Childress, *Biomedical Ethics*, pp. 121–132 (discussing disclosure and understanding as elements of informed consent). See also Charles, Gafnia, and Whelan, "Decision-making", 654–655; Spiegel, "Lawyering and Client Decisionmaking", 44–48.

integrity. Yet professional integrity is a complicated and vague concept. Stephen Carter argued that "[a] person of integrity . . . [is] a person we feel we can trust to do right, to play by the rules, to keep commitments."[31] As for professionals, Damien Cox, Marguerite La Caze, and Michael P. Levine argued that "[p]rofessional integrity . . . is, very roughly, a matter of remaining true to the fundamental role and character of one's profession – to its principles, values, ideals, goals and standards. This requires . . . that [professionals] remain true to the role they are publicly entrusted with."[32] Thus, as Pritchard had noted, "[t]he responsibilities a professional has are not simply a matter of individual determination; they are also determined by requirements of the profession itself and the particular setting within which a professional works."[33] In other words, a professional exhibits professional integrity when in doing his job he is truly committed to the definition of his role and to the values and principles associated with that role, which have been determined by others.

Dictionaries can also help clarify the meaning of professional integrity. Dictionary meanings of integrity tend to focus on two features of that term: one is "the quality of always behaving according to the moral principles that you believe in, so that people respect and trust you," and if you are a professional – "the quality of behaving according to the rules and standards of your job or profession"; and the other is "the quality of being complete or whole, without missing a part."[34]

In this book I refer to the first feature of integrity – the adherence to standards – as fairness,[35] and to the second feature of integrity – the quality of being complete or whole – as a core element of professional integrity, which is taken to mean *remaining true or being committed to the nature and definition of the professional role and to the wholeness of the professional service provided.*

[31] See Stephen Carter, *Integrity* (New York: Basic Books, 1996), p. 7 quoted in Pritchard, *Professional Integrity*, p. 67.

[32] See Damien Cox, Marguerite La Caze, and Michael P. Levine, *Integrity and the Fragile Self* (Aldershot, UK: Ashgate, 2003), p. 103 quoted in Pritchard, *Professional Integrity*, p. 68.

[33] See Pritchard, *Professional Integrity*, p. 69.

[34] See MacMillan Dictionary, available at www.macmillandictionary.com/dictionary/british/integrity. Compare The Free Dictionary available at www.thefreedictionary.com/integrity (defining integrity as (1) Steadfast adherence to a strict moral or ethical code; (2) The state of being unimpaired; soundness; (3) The quality or condition of being whole or undivided; completeness). See also Pritchard, *Professional Integrity*, p. 67 (using words such as "wholeness," "completeness," and "remaining true to oneself" to convey the meaning of integrity).

[35] See Section 2.2.3.10.

In a professional–client relationship, professional integrity has several expressions: decision-making and exercise of professional discretion, separation of professional roles, appropriateness of case to process, and prevention of process abuse or substantial defects in the process.

Decision-making and exercise of professional discretion Making decisions and exercising discretion are core components in the performance of any professional role. It is virtually impossible to carry out a professional role without making decisions and exercising some degree of discretion, and the ethical source that authorizes professionals to do so is the standard of professional integrity, because one cannot be truly committed to the nature of his or her role without making decisions and exercising discretion.[36] Yet decision-making and exercising discretion are primarily ethical *obligations* of professionals. Professionals *must* make decisions otherwise they will not be able to carry out their job.

Moreover, in making decisions and exercising professional judgment, professionals are expected (a) to *utilize* their professional knowledge and skills (i.e. competence) and (b) to take account of *relevant considerations*. The first point draws attention to the fact that a professional may be competent but fail to use her professional knowledge and skills in the service of clients. Professionals worthy of their clients' trust use their knowledge and skills (which exceed those of an ordinary person) for the benefit of their clients. The second point focuses on the kind of considerations that guide the professional's decision-making. A professional is not free to take into account extraneous considerations such as frustration, anger, or prejudice. He or she is expected to ignore irrelevant considerations and exercise sound judgment based on considerations that are relevant to the decision in question and to the role he or she performs. If he or she fails to do so he or she is not acting in the way professionals are expected to act, in breach of the standard of professional integrity.

[36] The standard of professional integrity is a *general* source of authority and duty to make decisions and exercise discretion. However, every one of the ethical standards discussed in this chapter constitutes a *specific* source of authority and duty in its area of application. For example, the standard of competence requires professionals to consider whether or not to accept a case; the standard of impartiality guides professionals to make decisions that do not give an impression of impartiality; and the standard of confidentiality instructs professionals to consider whether certain information should be kept secret or disclosed.

Separation of professional roles Clients expect professionals to provide them with the professional services that are associated with their profession and that professionals of their kind usually supply. For example, clients that turn to psychologists expect to receive psychological services, not legal advice. Professional integrity in this context means a commitment of professionals to the nature and definition of their professional role in supplying the type of professional services that are within the definition of their role.

Appropriateness of case to process Clients expect professionals to take on their case only when the case is suitable for the type of professional service they provide. For example, the expectation of an ear, nose, and throat specialist is that he will treat patients suffering from ear, nose, or throat problems. It is a matter of professional integrity, that is, a commitment to the nature and definition of his professional role, that he or she should refuse to take on cases that are not appropriate for the type of service he or she provides.

Prevention of process abuse or substantial defects in the process Clients expect professionals to refrain from abusing professional services for their own good, and prevent substantial flaws in the process that are inconsistent with the objectives of the process and could harm clients. For example, professionals must not use information that has come to their knowledge in the course of work for personal benefit. Abuse of process and failure to prevent substantial defects in the process are inconsistent with a commitment to the professional role and to the objectives of the process, and are contrary to the standard of professional integrity.[37]

2.2.3.5 Impartiality

The philosopher Bernard Gert wrote that "impartiality is a complex concept ... Understanding what is meant by saying that a person is impartial requires knowing both toward which group the person is impartial and in what respect the person is impartial with regard to this group."[38] He illustrated this idea with an example of a teacher who "may be impartial toward all of the students in her class with respect to grading their papers, that is, she is not influenced in her grading of a paper by

[37] For further discussion see Section 2.3. [38] Gert, *Morality*, p.131.

whose paper it is; however, she may not be impartial toward her students in providing time and effort in helping them to write better papers."[39] He then summarized: "a person is impartial with regard to a group in a given respect if he does not favor any member of the group over any other member in that respect."[40]

Clients expect professionals to act *impartially* toward them with respect to members of the general public and other clients, in the sense that they do not wish to be discriminated against and receive treatment or services of a lesser quality than others would have received had they been in their position. Bayles, for example, who considered impartiality to be an aspect of fairness, argued that "professionals should not discriminate on grounds of race, religion, ethnic origin, or sex" in the provision and the quality of services.[41]

However, clients expect professionals to act with *partiality* toward them with respect to members of the general public, in the sense that they want professionals to be committed to their interests and promote them over and above the interests of others. For example, in discussing the ethical duties of lawyers, Elliot D. Cohen and Michael Davis argued that "[l]awyering seems inevitably to involve identification with the ends the client seeks and the means used to achieve it," and described this practice as "mechanical partiality."[42] The expectation of partiality is legitimate in a moral sense because impartiality is not an absolute value. As Tom Beauchamp and James Childress put it, "we are morally prohibited from causing harm to anyone. However, we are morally permitted to help or benefit those with whom we have special relationships."[43]

The meaning of impartiality changes with the role professionals perform. As opposed to lawyers, psychologists, and doctors, some professionals, such as judges, arbitrators, and mediators, serve *clients with conflicting interests* on a regular basis.[44] These clients legitimately expect the professional to be committed to their interests and at the same time

[39] Ibid. [40] Id., p. 132.

[41] Bayles, *Professional Ethics*, p. 95. See also APA Ethical Principles and Code, Standard 3.01 (unfair discrimination).

[42] Elliot D. Cohen and Michael Davis (eds.), *Ethics and the Legal Profession*, 2nd edn. (Amherst, NY: Prometheus Books, 2009), p. 107.

[43] Beauchamp and Childress, *Biomedical Ethics*, p. 199 (distinguishing rules of beneficence from rules of nonmaleficence).

[44] Representation of conflicting interests may be acceptable in some circumstances for lawyers. See, e.g., ABA Model Rules, Rule 1.7(b). See also Kipnis, "Conflict of Interest", 265–272 (discussing ethical strategies which might enable lawyers to represent several

refrain from favoring the conflicting interests of other clients. This delicate position of serving two masters at the same time requires the professional to limit his or her actions in ways that are not necessary when a professional serves clients whose interests are not in conflict.[45] While a lawyer, for example, is free to conduct himself in a manner that identifies him or her with each of his or her clients, judges,[46] arbitrators,[47] and mediators[48] are expected to exhibit impartiality among their clients.

2.2.3.6 Diligence

Bayles argued that "a responsibility of diligence clearly follows from the criterion that a professional be worthy of a client's trust. A reasonable person would not entrust his important affairs to someone he thought would not actively and carefully handle them."[49] Dictionary definitions of diligence often point to two elements in the exercise of diligence: (a) a constant and earnest effort to accomplish what is undertaken; and (b) the degree of care and caution required by the circumstances of a person.[50]

Codes of conduct of various professionals recognize a duty of diligence. *The ABA Model Rules*, for example, state that "a lawyer shall act with reasonable diligence and promptness in representing a client."[51] *The Code of Conduct for United States Judges* provides that "judges should perform the duties of their office . . . diligently."[52] Engineers,[53] public

clients with divergent interests, i.e. ways to accommodate situations in which professional obligations to one client might conflict with professional obligations to another).

45 See, e.g., Jacqueline M. Nolan-Haley, "Informed Consent in Mediation: A Guiding Principle for Truly Educated Decisionmaking" (1999) 74 *Notre Dame Law Review* 775, 825 note 236 (arguing that "the fiduciary duties owed by mediators differ from those of physicians and lawyers. The physician owes a duty only to his or her patient. The lawyer owes a duty to his or her client and the court system. The mediator however, owes an obligation to both parties to maintain the integrity of the mediation process").

46 Code of Conduct for United States Judges available at www.uscourts.gov/judges-judgeships/code-conduct-united-states-judges (Code of Conduct for United States Judges), Canon 3.

47 See, e.g., Code of Ethics for Arbitrators in Commercial Disputes (2004) available at ethics.iit.edu/ecodes/node/4705 (Code of Ethics for Arbitrators in Commercial Disputes), Canon I.B.(1), I.C, II.

48 Model Standards, Standard II.

49 Bayles, *Professional Ethics*, p. 86.

50 See, e.g., Dictionary.com available at dictionary.reference.com/browse/diligence. See also the Free Dictionary available at www.thefreedictionary.com/diligence ("1. Earnest and persistent application to an undertaking; steady effort; assiduity; 2. Attentive care; heedfulness").

51 ABA Model Rules, Rule. 1.3 (Diligence).

52 Code of Conduct for United States Judges, Canon 3.

53 See, e.g., Guidelines for Institution Codes of Conduct, UK Engineering Council available at www.engc.org.uk/ecukdocuments/internet/document%20library/UK-SPEC.pdf, p. 29.

servants,[54] bankers,[55] hospital medical staff,[56] and insurance brokers[57] are also expected to perform their roles diligently.

The meaning of exercising diligence changes with the role professionals perform. Lawyers, for example, are expected to file claims on time,[58] and to control their work load "so that each matter can be handled competently."[59] Judges should "devote adequate time to judicial duties . . . be punctual in attending court and expeditious in determining matters under submission, and . . . take reasonable measures to ensure that court personnel, litigants, and their lawyers cooperate with the judge to that end."[60]

The duty of diligence complements the duty of competence. A professional may be competent but not diligent; the duty of diligence requires the professional to make use of his or her competence in the service of his or her client.

2.2.3.7 Respect and dignity

The literature on respect and human dignity is vast and cannot be fully explored here. Professor Robin S. Dillon noted that "respect for persons is a central concept in many ethical theories; some theories treat it as the very essence of morality and the foundation of all other moral duties and obligations."[61] Gert suggested that "to treat a person with dignity is to treat her with respect, that is as a moral agent and as someone fully protected by morality. It is to regard the person as competent to engage in moral reasoning. Humility requires that a person regard all moral agents as protected by morality and as competent to engage in moral reasoning."[62] In Gert's view, "it is what Kant meant, or should have meant, by saying that persons should be treated as ends and never merely as means."[63] Legal ethicist David Luban argued that "at the very least

[54] See, e.g., Code of Conduct and Ethics, NSW Department of Community Services available at www.community.nsw.gov.au/docswr/_assets/main/documents/codeconductethics_pol.pdf, s. 2.1.

[55] Code of Conduct, Private Banking in Singapore available at www.wmi.com.sg/files/docs/programmes/abs-pbcode.pdf, s. 4.2(b).

[56] See, e.g., Code of Conduct, Children's Hospital Boston available at childrenshospital.org/about/Site1394/Documents/CodeofConduct.pdf.

[57] See, e.g., Code of Ethics and Conduct, Ace available at www.aceinsbrokers.com/sites/default/files/pdf/code-of-conduct.pdf, Value C.b).

[58] Bayles, *Professional Ethics*, p. 86. [59] ABA Model Rules, Rule 1.3 Comment 2.

[60] Code of Conduct for United States Judges, Commentary Canon 3.A(5).

[61] Robin S. Dillon, "Respect" in Stanford Encyclopedia of Philosophy available at plato.stanford.edu/entries/respect/.

[62] Gert, *Morality*, p. 409 note 6. [63] Ibid.

honoring human dignity requires not humiliating people."[64] Human dignity, according to Luban, refers to "the prestige conferred simply by being human. To violate someone's human dignity means to treat them as if they were a being of lower rank – as an animal, as a handy but disposable tool, as property, as an object, as a subhuman, as an overgrown child, as nothing at all."[65]

It seems, therefore, that respect and dignity set a minimum standard for treatment of others. All persons are entitled to expect others to treat them with dignity and respect. A person who is in a relationship of trust with another has an enhanced expectation of being treated with respect. It is not surprising, then, that many codes of professional conduct refer to a duty of the professional to treat his clients with dignity and respect. The *Code of Conduct for United States Judges*, for example, provides that "a judge should be patient, dignified, respectful, and courteous to litigants, jurors, witnesses, lawyers, and others with whom the judge deals in an official capacity."[66] Psychologists are expected to "respect the dignity and worth of all people";[67] and the American Medical Association *Code of Medical Ethics* states that "the patient has the right to courtesy, respect, [and] dignity."[68]

The meaning of a duty to respect the client can take various forms, some of which have already been mentioned in the earlier discussion of the standards. Ignoring the client's right to make his or her own decisions, for example, would violate his or her right to autonomy and self-determination, as well as his or her right to dignity and respect; discriminating against a client on the basis of sex, race, or religion would breach his or her right to impartial regard or equality, as well as exhibit disrespect. The close affinity between dignity and respect on one side and autonomy and equality on the other requires us to limit the meaning of dignity and respect for purposes of clarity and avoidance of repetition. In this book, a professional's duty to respect his or her client means an obligation to listen to what the client has to say,[69] refrain from humiliating the client,[70] and avoid discriminatory language when addressing the client or talking about the client's case with others.

64 Luban, *Legal Ethics*, p. 88. 65 Id., p. 89.
66 Code of Conduct for United States Judges, Canon 3.A(3).
67 APA Ethical Principles and Code, Principle E.
68 The American Medical Association (AMA) Code of Medical Ethics, Opinion 10.01 available at www.ama-assn.org/ama/pub/physician-resources/medical-ethics/code-medical-ethics/opinion1001.page?
69 See, e.g., Luban, *Legal Ethics*, pp. 70–71. 70 See, e.g., id., p. 88.

2.2.3.8 Honesty

Clients expect professionals to be honest with them, that is, tell them the truth and refrain from lying and deception. Pritchard noted that some professions "place special emphasis on truthfulness as an essential feature of the work that is done."[71] He argued, for example, that in journalism truthfulness "provide[s] the foundation for trust," and accountancy "is another profession whose services are essentially bound up with truthfulness."[72] Bayles, on the other hand, made a more general claim that "by definition, a dishonest professional is not worthy of a client's trust"; therefore "professionals should be honest with their clients."[73]

As clients rely on the information professionals supply them with, they trust professionals that the information be truthful. However, the obligation of honesty is not absolute. It is thought that in exceptional circumstances partial disclosure of information, temporary withdrawal of information, and even deception by a professional could be justified. Bernard Gert, Charles M. Culver, and Danner Clouser, for example, described paternalistic deception by doctors, which could be justified where (a) the deception was for a short period of time, (b) full disclosure would have resulted with significant harm to the patient while the deception caused no significant harm, and (c) a rational person would have publically allowed the deception, that is, would be willing for everyone to know about the deception.[74]

2.2.3.9 Confidentiality

In performing their roles, professionals receive information from and about their clients. This information may be sensitive and relate to private or business matters. Clients expect professionals to keep information that they have been exposed to and can adversely affect their interests in confidence. This expectation rests on several grounds. First, by disclosing information to the professional the client has become more vulnerable, and a trustworthy professional should not abuse this vulnerability;[75] and second, the provision of information and the exposure to information have been made possible to a large extent because of the client's trust, thus making an unauthorized disclosure a breach of

[71] Pritchard, *Professional Integrity*, p. 44. [72] Id., p. 45.

[73] See Bayles, *Professional Ethics*, p. 80. Bayles discusses the obligations of honesty and candor separately (id., pp. 80–84) but accepts that they might be combined (id., p. 80).

[74] Gert, Culver and Clouser, *Bioethics*, pp. 271–272.

[75] See, e.g., Koehn, *The Ground of Professional Ethics*, pp. 163–164.

trust.[76] It has been suggested that a duty of confidentiality supports the client's right to privacy,[77] his or her right to control information about him or herself (which is an aspect of his right to autonomy or self-determination),[78] and his or her right to respect.[79] A duty of confidentiality can be found in codes of conduct for lawyers,[80] psychologists,[81] medical doctors,[82] and mediators.[83] This duty is not absolute, as professionals may be justified in disclosing information, for example where their clients agree to such disclosure, when disclosure is necessary to prevent serious bodily harm, or when disclosure is required by law.[84]

2.2.3.10 Fairness

Fairness is defined by various scholars as *adherence to the rules* of a social game. Following the rules is considered fair, while a violation of the rules is considered unfair. Gert, for example, argued that "[t]o talk about a person being fair presupposes that she is participating in some practice with rules that everyone in that practice is required to follow."[85]

If we consider professional activity such as lawyering, therapy, or mediation as a kind of a game, the norm of fairness would describe the expectation of participants in the game that other participants comply with its rules. Clients expect professionals to treat them *in accordance with the standards* that regulate the professional service they provide. This is an expectation of fairness or fair treatment. Therefore, if we consider the various standards discussed thus far, such as competence, impartiality, and confidentiality, as the rules of the professional "game," their violation would be a violation of the standard of fairness and unfair treatment of clients.

Normative fairness, that is, fairness as a norm that should be followed, has another meaning that shall be called here *substantive fairness*. Following the rules to the letter may sometimes produce results that

76 See, e.g., id., p. 164. See also Bayles, *Professional Ethics*, p. 96; Pritchard, *Professional Integrity*, p. 35.
77 See, e.g., Bayles, *Professional Ethics*, p. 96.
78 See, e.g., Koehn, *The Ground of Professional Ethics*, p. 164.
79 See, e.g., Bayles, *Professional Ethics*, p. 96. 80 ABA Model Rules, Rule 1.6.
81 APA Ethical Principles and Code, Standard 4.
82 American Medical Association (AMA), Opinion 5.05 available at www.ama-assn.org/ama/pub/physician-resources/medical-ethics/code-medical-ethics/opinion505.page?.
83 See, e.g., Model Standards, Standard V.
84 See, e.g., ABA Model Rules, Rule 1.6(b); APA Ethical Principles and Code, Standard 4.05(b).
85 Gert, *Morality*, p. 196.

are inconsistent with the spirit of the game and with the objectives of the game or the rules. John A. Miller, for example, argued that "fairness cannot be achieved mechanically through the use of unbending rules,"[86] and Craig L. Carr argued that fair play "means making sure things go as they should even when the rules might work in the other direction. It seems ... that sometimes insisting upon a strict adherence to rule can actually constitute a form of unfair play."[87]

Substantive fairness means a *deep and real understanding* of the rules as opposed to a formal one, that is, an understanding designed to realize *the spirit* of the rules or the *true purpose* of the rules or the game. For example, according to a substantive fairness conception, an uninformed consent is not a realization of fairness because it is not a real consent but a formal and illusionary one.[88] Thus the standard of fairness has two layers: a formal layer, which imposes on professionals a duty to follow the standards that apply to them when they provide professional services (formal fairness), and a substantive layer that instructs them to interpret and apply these standards in a realistic manner in accordance with their spirit and purpose. And this, it is argued, is what clients legitimately expect professionals to do: not merely follow the rules, but adopt a substantive-realistic perspective as to their interpretation and implementation.

2.2.4 Conclusion

Professionals are in a relationship of trust with their clients, and in order to be worthy of their clients' trust must comply with the ethical standards that have been discussed in this chapter (see Figure 2.2). The *scope* of the duty of trustworthiness and the *content* of the ethical obligations that derive from it are context-sensitive and vary between different professional roles. In general, (a) the higher the level of trust required from clients for the professional activity to succeed, (and) (b) the more the professional solicited the clients'

[86] John A. Miller, "Indeterminacy, Complexity, and Fairness: Justifying Rule Simplification in the Law of Taxation" (1993) 68 *Washington Law Review* 1, 70. See also id., 14 (arguing that "The central fairness or unfairness of the tax is measured by whether it reaches past the form to the substance of the transaction or other taxable event.").

[87] Craig L. Carr, "Fairness and Political Obligation-Again: A Reply to Lefkowitz" (2004) 30 *Social Theory and Practice* 33, 44.

[88] See, e.g., Nolan-Haley, "Informed Consent", 778–779 (advocating a real, as opposed to illusionary, concept of consent in court-connected mediations).

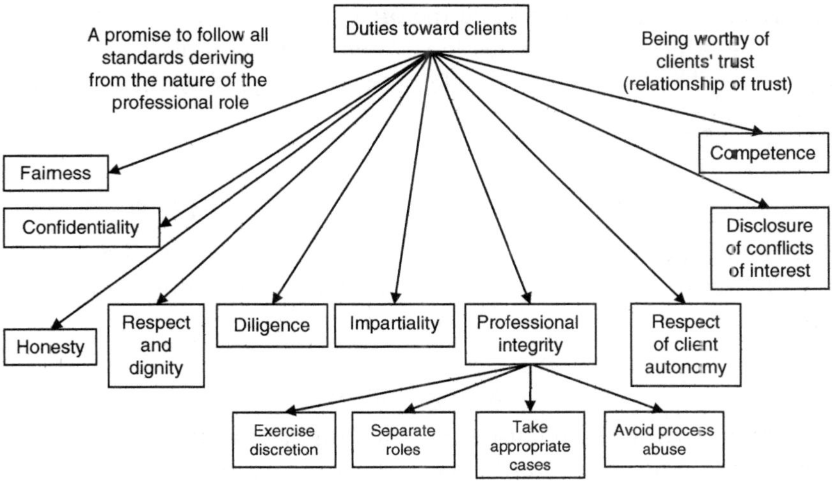

Figure 2.2: Duties toward clients

trust in the course of the provision of services, (and) (c) the greater the power disparities between the professional and his or her clients, and (d) the greater the reliance on the professional, the more demanding is the duty of the professional to be worthy of his or her clients' trust. That is why lawyers, medical doctors, and, as we shall see later, mediators[89] must be so careful to conduct themselves in a trustworthy manner.

2.3 Duties toward the profession

2.3.1 Introduction

Professionals have duties to their professions. The term "profession" as used in this book is not limited to the classic professions of law, medicine, and the clergy. It is applied to any activity that is (1) regularly conducted by persons whose role is to conduct this activity on behalf of others (to whom we shall refer as "professionals"), (2) perceived by the public as requiring special skills and knowledge, and (3) at least some of those who perform this role are doing it for a living and are organized.[90] A profession

[89] See Chapter 3.

[90] See Chapter 1, Section 1.1.3. Compare William F. May, *The Beleaguered Rulers: The Public Obligation of the Professional* (Louisville, Kentucky: Westminster John Knox Press, 2001), pp. 7–14 (discussing three "marks of the professional": intellectual (a body of knowledge

consists of the professionals and the organizations that represent them. Thus the ethical duties professionals owe to their profession are the duties they have toward their colleagues and the professional organizations that represent them.

2.3.2 The normative basis of duties toward the profession

The choice one makes to perform a professional role imposes on one, for reasons of promise keeping, fairness, and reciprocity, duties toward the profession.

Keeping promises

A person presenting themselves as a professional is distinguishing himself by doing so from ordinary persons and committing themselves to acting as a professional.[91] This is an undertaking toward the profession, not only toward clients.[92] When a profession has a formal code of practice, this person can be taken to have *promised* to conduct themselves according to that code.[93] When a profession does not have a formal code of practice, this implied promise is made with regard to the standards of conduct that professionals in that field can be expected to follow. These expectations are built upon fairness and reciprocity considerations.

Fairness and reciprocity

Gert argued that "[a] person who benefits from a practice but does not do what is required for that practice to be maintained is often regarded as acting unfairly. He is not abiding by the rules that everyone who benefits from the practice is expected to follow."[94] Professionals who follow the standards applicable to their profession restrict their freedom of action.

and experience), moral (acting on behalf of someone or some institution), and organizational (a setting of colleagues).

[91] See Section 2.2.2, Notes 1–2.

[92] See, e.g., Davis, *Thinking Like an Engineer*, p. 37 (noting that "The defense, 'I'm an engineer but I didn't promise to follow the code and therefore did nothing wrong,' is never accepted. The profession answers: 'You committed yourself to the code when you claimed to be an engineer'").

[93] See, e.g., Michael Davis, "Professionalism Means Putting Your Profession First" in Cohen and Davis, *Ethics and the Legal Profession*, pp. 171–172 (describing a contractual relationship between lawyers and between a lawyer and the profession); Davis, *Thinking Like an Engineer*, pp. 50–51 (describing a code of ethics as a contract between professionals).

[94] See Gert, *Morality*, p. 197.

For example, they do not take on cases for reasons such as incompetency and conflicts of interest. The loss of freedom comes with a benefit: by following the standards, professionals protect themselves from clients' pressures to violate professional standards, because clients know that other professionals follow the same standards of practice. Moreover, being a member of a profession entails social benefits such as status, opportunities, and potential remuneration that follow from the joint activities of professionals as a group. Michael Davis, for example, noted that "[a] profession is a cooperative undertaking. In exchange for putting herself under an obligation to do as those in her profession are doing, each member of the profession receives the benefits of being identified as a member of that profession."[95]

Thus, a professional who does not follow the standards enjoys an *unfair advantage* because (a) he or she exercises a freedom of action that his or her colleagues forego for the benefit of the group of professionals,[96] and (b) he or she enjoys free-riding social benefits that have been made available to him or her through his or her ties with the profession. It is "a form of cheating";[97] therefore, professions expect professionals to follow the standards applicable to them in their role as professionals, that is, act *fairly*.[98]

In addition, professions expect professionals to refrain from conduct that might harm legitimate interests of the profession. One such interest is the existence and survival of the profession, which depend on public trust. Pritchard argued that "for all professions, public trust is essential";[99] without public trust the profession would not survive. Any person who joins the group of professionals, otherwise called a "profession," can be considered to have undertaken not to harm the profession; he or she is expected to reciprocate the benefits arising from belonging to the profession with conduct that avoids injury to the profession; and it would be unfair of him or her to unilaterally relieve him or herself of constraints his colleagues have taken upon themselves in order to maintain public confidence in the profession. Thus professions legitimately expect professionals to conduct themselves in a manner that will not undermine public trust in the profession. Figure 2.3 describes the normative basis of duties toward the profession.

95 Davis, "Professionalism", 166. 96 Davis, *Thinking Like an Engineer*, pp. 50, 52–53.
97 Id., p. 169. 98 See, e.g., id., p. 111.
99 Pritchard, *Professional Integrity*, p. 45. See also Bayles, *Professional Ethics*, p. 180.

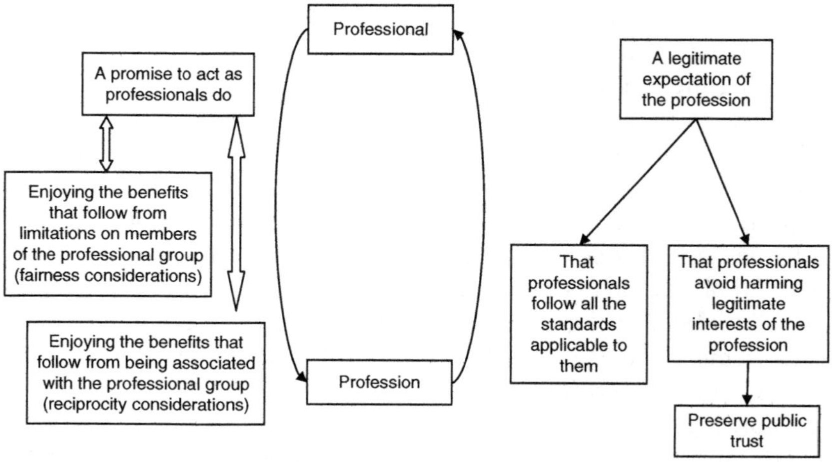

Figure 2.3: The normative basis of duties toward the profession

2.3.3 *Ethical duties toward the profession*

A professional–profession relationship establishes three general ethical standards: fairness, maintaining the profession's standing, and helping the profession to fulfill its social role.

2.3.3.1 A duty of fairness: following all the standards that apply to professionals

When a professional fails to follow any of the standards that apply to professionals of his or her kind, he or she enjoys an unfair advantage. He or she is not "playing by the rules" of the professional game.[100] Since "the rules of the game" involve duties toward clients, the public, and potentially an employer or principal, as well as duties toward the profession, it follows that a violation of any of these duties is also a breach of duty toward the profession. Thus, for example, a breach of duty of confidentiality owed to the client, or acting without professional integrity toward the client by taking a decision based on irrelevant considerations, is not only a breach of duty toward the client but a violation of the duty of fairness owed to the profession as well. The duty toward the client is in effect an indirect duty toward the profession.

[100] See Section 2.2.3.10.

2.3.3.2 A duty to maintain the profession's standing

A duty to avoid professional conduct that harms the profession and undermines public trust Professionals must conduct themselves in a manner that preserves the profession's standing in society. This means avoiding conduct that could adversely affect public confidence and trust in the profession. Bayles, for example, argued that "[r]espect [for the profession] is important so that professions can properly perform their functions and contribute to the public good."[101] The duty to maintain the profession's standing and preserve public trust applies to all of the professional's actions. This has several implications. First, professionals must consider the potential effect of *any of their decisions* on the profession's standing and public trust. Second, professionals should *interpret* their duties toward their clients and employers or principals in light of their duty to maintain the profession's standing and preserve public trust. It follows that the "private" duties of professionals toward their clients and employers have a *public aspect* as well (see Figure 2.4). For example, a professional must be competent in order to be worthy of his or her client's trust. However, if his or her level of competence is such that taking on a case could jeopardize public confidence in the profession he or

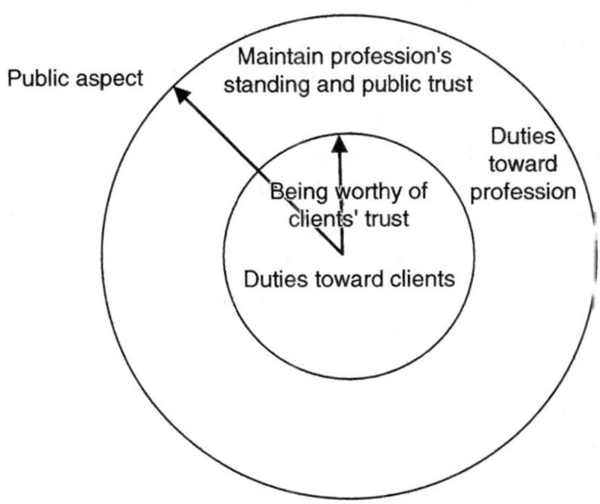

Figure 2.4: The effect of the duty to maintain the profession's standing and public trust on the duties toward clients

[101] Bayles, *Professional Ethics*, p. 180.

she must decline the case despite his or her client's wishes that he or she take it.

Third, a breach of any duty toward a client, the public, or an employer or principal might constitute a breach of the duty to maintain the profession's standing and preserve public trust if the breach is *serious* enough to undermine the public's confidence in the profession. For example, a professional must act with professional integrity and thus limit the services he or she provides to clients to services that are within the scope of the role (Separation of Professional Roles) and to cases which are appropriate to the professional service (Appropriateness of Case to Process).[102] When a professional fails to act with professional integrity in circumstances that might jeopardize public trust, he or she breaches not only his or her duty to his or her clients but his or her duty to maintain the profession's standing as well. And fourth, the duty toward the profession to maintain the profession's standing and preserve public trust establishes concrete expectations of professionals to treat colleagues, professional organizations, and other people or bodies with honesty and respect, and to avoid conduct outside the course of professional practice that may harm the profession's honor.

A duty to treat colleagues, professional organizations, and other people or bodies with honesty and respect Treating people with honesty and respect is a moral obligation of all persons. It becomes an ethical duty of professionals toward their profession because it is hard to win public confidence in a profession whose members are dishonest and disrespectful. Bayles, for example, noted that "professionals should exhibit respect for one another. Only if they respect one another can they expect the public to do so."[103] If professionals lie to or deceive colleagues, professional organizations, and other individuals and institutions with whom they engage in the course of practice, or if they behave in a discriminatory, degrading, or insulting manner, they jeopardize the profession's standing and undermine public trust in the profession.[104] They must therefore avoid such conduct.

[102] See Section 2.2.3.4. [103] See Bayles, *Professional Ethics*, p. 177.

[104] Duties of honesty and respect are owed to clients and to employers or principals as well for other reasons (see Sections 2.2.3.7 and 2.2.3.8; Section 2.5.3); however treating them with dishonesty and disrespect could also undermine public confidence in the profession.

A duty to avoid personal conduct outside the course of professional practice that may harm the profession and undermine public trust Professionals should be aware that personal conduct can affect public trust in the profession. The 1940 *Statement of Principles on Academic Freedom and Tenure*, for example, states that college and university teachers "should remember that the public may judge their profession and their institution by their utterances. Hence they should at all times be accurate, should exercise appropriate restraint, [and] should show respect for the opinions of others";[105] and the *Code of Conduct for United States Judges* provides that a judge "should act at all times in a manner that promotes public confidence in the integrity and impartiality of the judiciary,"[106] stating in a Commentary that this duty applies to both professional and personal conduct.[107] Clearly, the expectation of appropriateness in the course of professional conduct is more demanding than in respect of personal conduct, and therefore professional misconduct is likely to be judged more critically than personal misconduct. However, a serious breach of social norms, such as committing murder or rape, abusing children, or stealing, is harmful to the profession even when made in a "private capacity" and thus constitutes a breach of duty to the profession.

2.3.3.3 Helping the profession to fulfill its social role

Professions have a social role: they provide professional services to members of the public.[108] Scholars have suggested that the *profession* may owe a duty to the public to fulfill its role. Davis, for example, observed that "[t]he legal profession is committed to the ideal that those needing a lawyer's help to seek justice within the law should have the help they need,"[109] and Lon L. Fuller and John D. Randall argued that

105 The American Association of University Professors and of the Association of American Colleges (now the Association of American Colleges and Universities) 1940 *Statement of Principles on Academic Freedom and Tenure, available at* www.aaup.org/AAUP/pubsres/policydocs/contents/1940statement.htm, s. 3.

106 Code of Conduct for United States Judges, Canon 2.A.

107 Id., Commentary to Canon 2.A.

108 See, e.g., Gibson, "Contrasting Role Morality", 22 ("The essential nature of a profession is to provide service to individuals, but more importantly, to society as a whole"). See also Cohen and Davis, *Ethics and the Legal Profession*, p. 105 ("A profession is . . . a way of carrying on an occupation according to special standards designed to serve a certain moral ideal ('public service')"); Bayles, *Professional Ethics*, p. 179 (referring to "the responsibilities of a profession as a whole to further social values").

109 Davis, "Professionalism", 174.

"[t]he legal profession has … a clear moral obligation to see to it that those already handicapped do not suffer the cumulative disadvantage of being without proper legal representation."[110] If the profession has a role to fulfill, members of the profession have a duty to help the profession achieve that end for reasons of fairness. As Bayles argued, "[t]he obligations of the profession as a whole can be fulfilled only by the individual members, and each member owes it a duty of fairness to the others to do a fair share in fulfilling these obligations."[111] The content of this duty of assistance depends on the social role of a given profession and on a specific statement by the professional bodies clarifying the share of work that is expected of individual professionals. Until such statement is made (for example, on the scope of pro-bono services each professional is expected to provide), the obligation of assistance remains an ideal (or aspiration) rather than a concrete duty.[112]

2.3.4 Conclusion

A professional, like any moral person, must keep his or her promises and act fairly. The application of norms of morality to the relationship between professionals and their profession produces ethical norms that oblige professionals alone (see Figure 2.5). One general ethical norm is a *duty of fairness* toward the profession, that is, a duty of professionals to follow the standards that apply to their profession. As a result, a breach of any standard constitutes a breach of duty toward the profession. Thus, a breach of duty to a client, the public, or an employer or principal violates the duty to the profession as well.

Another general ethical norm is a *duty to maintain the profession's standing*. It is impossible to maintain high standing without public trust. Therefore, professionals must conduct themselves in a manner that avoids harm to the profession's standing and preserves public confidence

[110] Lon L. Fuller and John D. Randall, "Professional Responsibility: Report of the Joint Conference" in Cohen and Davis, *Ethics and the Legal Profession*, p. 208. See also id., p. 211 ("Every calling owes to the public a duty of leadership in those matters where its training and experience give it a special competence and insight").

[111] Bayles, *Professional Ethics*, p. 177. Compare Davis, "Professionalism", 164 ("Ordinary people, however decent, do not have any specific obligation of public service (for example, an obligation to provide free to the poor who need it the service they make their living selling). All lawyers have that obligation – because, and only because, it is part of what they profess").

[112] See, e.g., Cohen and Davis, *Ethics and the Legal Profession*, p. 395. See also Pritchard, *Professional Integrity*, pp. 106–107.

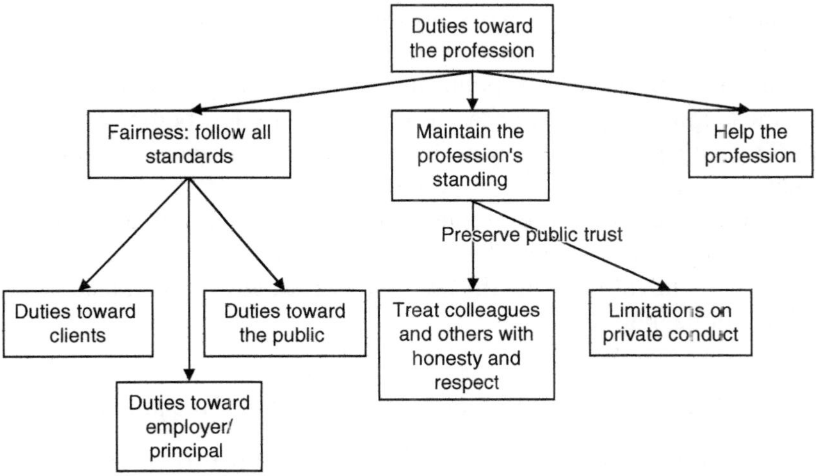

Figure 2.5: Duties toward the profession

in it. In other words, this norm instructs professionals to preserve public trust in all actions and it affects the interpretation of all of the profession's standards. In addition, a breach of any standard could be a violation of the duty to maintain the profession's standing as well, where the breach is serious enough to undermine public confidence in the profession. The duty to maintain the profession's standing can be further specified as a duty to treat colleagues, professional organizations, and other people or bodies with honesty and respect and a duty to avoid personal conduct outside the course of professional practice that may harm the profession or undermine public trust. A third general ethical norm which has been identified is a *duty to help the profession to fulfill its social role.*

2.4 Duties toward the public

2.4.1 Introduction

Every person has duties toward the public, and so do professionals.[113] The duties of professionals are enhanced in comparison to the duties of ordinary members of society because of the position of social power and

113 For literature on the duties of professionals to the public see, e.g., May, *Beleaguered Rulers*; "Symposium: The Future of Callings: An Interdisciplinary Summit on the Public Obligations of Professionals into the Next Millennium" (1999) 25 *William Mitchell Law Review* 43.

influence and the social benefits that professionals enjoy. "The public" to whom professionals owe duties is made up of individuals and bodies who are members of society. The public interests that the duties aim to protect are those interests that are shared by individuals and bodies as a community, rather than the private interests of a particular individual or body. The distinction between private and public interests, however, is not always clear-cut. For example, maintaining the rule of law is both a public and private interest. The interest of A not to be assaulted overlaps with the public interest that the law be observed and all members of the public not be injured.

2.4.2 *The normative basis of duties toward the public*

Professionals owe duties to the public for three main reasons: they are legitimately expected to keep their promises, to reciprocate the benefits they enjoy, and to responsibly use their social position of power and influence in a trustworthy manner.

Keeping promises

Professionals publicly commit themselves to the role they are performing, a role whose definition and nature have been determined by the profession and by the public expectations that the profession has generated.[114] The public expects professionals to act "like professionals," and this involves expectations of certain conduct vis-à-vis the public at large. The *specific* content of these expectations varies between professional roles in accordance with the express and implied undertakings each profession makes over time. Thus the public duties of lawyers and doctors, for example, need not be the same. However, the *general* content of public expectations from professionals remains the same: that they reciprocate the good they have been enjoying and refrain from abusing their social position.

Reciprocity

David Hume argued that "[a]ll our obligations to do good to society seem to imply something reciprocal. I receive the benefits of society, and therefore ought to promote its interests."[115] Being a part of society grants

[114] See Section 2.2.2, Notes 1–2.

[115] See, e.g., Beauchamp and Childress, *Biomedical Ethics*, p. 205 (quoting David Hume on reciprocity).

individuals benefits, some of which are most fundamental, such as institutional protection from violence and enforcement of private promises. The social benefits of professionals are greater than those enjoyed by ordinary members of society with respect to status, income, and opportunities. Moreover, some professionals have special privileges such as a monopoly on the provision of services and confidentiality protection attached to communications with their clients. In return, professionals are expected to conduct themselves in a manner that *promotes important social interests and avoids harming them.* Beauchamp and Childress, for example, argued in discussing the duties of medical doctors that "many physicians and health care professionals owe a large debt to society (e.g., for education and privileges)," and this gives rise to obligations of beneficence to society.[116] The more benefits one receives from society, the higher the expectation of one to reciprocate and be loyal to the interests of the public. Thus, the bar of expectations from professionals is set higher than for ordinary members of society and imposes enhanced duties upon them. For example, professionals are expected to strictly follow the law in circumstances that ordinary citizens might have been forgivingly excused for not doing so.

Trust

In addition, the knowledge and expertise that professionals have and the social permit to perform a professional role place them in a position of social power and influence. The permit may be a formal license to engage in the professional activity or an informal one in the form of social acquiescence to such conduct. From their position of power and influence, professionals affect the general public well beyond their clients and thus have a responsibility toward the public. Bayles, for example, described professionals as social leaders and argued that because "they make many decisions that significantly affect others, they share responsibility for the realization of ... values in society";[117] and George DeMartino claimed in discussing the ethics of economists that economists' social influence comes with accountability.[118] Thus, the social arrangements that make professionals' position of power and influence possible and the potential effect of their decisions on the public create a

[116] Beauchamp and Childress, *Biomedical Ethics*, p. 206.
[117] Bayles, *Professional Ethics*, p. 109.
[118] See Demartino, *The Economist's Oath*, pp. 103–117.

relationship of *trust* between professionals and the public and an expectation of professionals to be *worthy* of the public's trust.

The public's expectation that professionals be trustworthy in their relationship with the public has several expressions. First, there is an expectation that professionals perform their role in a manner that *promotes* public interests. Bayles, for example, argued that "[t]he granting of a license and privilege in effect creates trust for professionals to ensure that these activities are performed in a manner that preserves and promotes values in society."[119] Second, there is an expectation that professionals *refrain from abusing their position of power*, harming the public, or undermining important social interests. For example, professionals should respect the rule of law.[120] And third, there is an expectation that professionals *prevent*, if possible, the abuse *by others* of the professional services they provide in order to avoid harm to the public and to important social interests. Fuller and Randall, for example, have argued while discussing lawyers' obligations to society that "[t]he lawyer's highest loyalty ... runs, not to persons, but to procedures and institutions. The lawyer's role imposes on him a trusteeship for the integrity of those fundamental processes of government and self-government upon which the successful functioning of our society depends."[121]

The first expectation – the promotion of social interests – is too abstract to establish a duty and should be considered an *ideal* that professionals aspire to.[122] The other two expectations are concrete enough to produce obligations and are discussed in the following section. Figure 2.6 describes the normative basis of duties toward the public.

2.4.3 Ethical duties toward the public

The relationship between professionals and the public, and the expectations that professionals be trustworthy, and avoid, and in certain circumstances prevent, harm to important social interests, produce three general ethical duties toward the public: a duty to maintain the profession's standing, a duty to follow the rules of law and critical morality in the course of practice, and a duty to prevent process abuse or substantial defects in the process.

[119] Bayles, *Professional Ethics*, p. 112 [120] See Section 2.4.3.
[121] Fuller and Randall, "Professional Responsibility", 207.
[122] See, e.g., Note 112 and the text accompanying it.

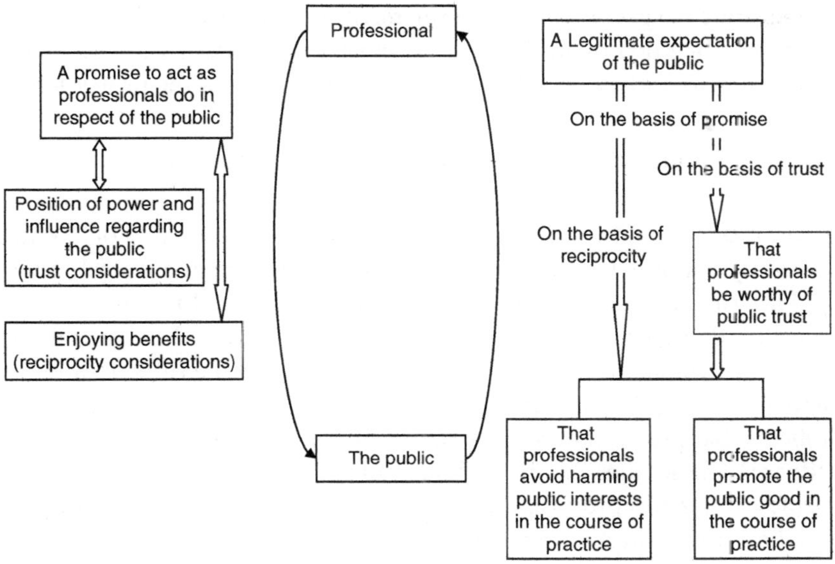

Figure 2.6: The normative basis of duties toward the public

A duty to maintain the profession's standing

Maintaining the standing of professions is a public interest as well as an interest of every profession. Professional activities cater to social needs and promote social goods, such as legal justice in the case of lawyers[123] or physical and mental health in the case of the healthcare professions. Thus society has an interest that professions function properly and are capable of providing services. As we have already noted, professions cannot properly function without public confidence. Therefore, professionals owe a duty to the public, as well as to their profession, to avoid conduct that could adversely affect public confidence in the profession. The difference between the two duties is that while the duty to the profession protects an interest of the profession (to survive and provide work for its members), the duty to the public protects a social interest (that certain social needs be met by the profession). Professional conduct that could

[123] See, e.g., Cohen and Davis, *Ethics and the Legal Profession*, p. 107 (noting that "the end the profession of law claims to serve" is "legal justice, justice within the law, or the like"). See also Fuller and Randall, "Professional Responsibility", 205–207 (arguing that the private practice of lawyers is a form of public service, for e.g., "partisan advocacy is a form of public service so long as it aids the process of adjudication" [p. 206] and "[w]here the lawyer serves as a negotiator and draftsman, he advances public interest when he facilitates the processes of voluntary self-government" [pp. 206-207]).

undermine the profession's standing might involve any conduct – illegal, immoral, or unconscionable – that radically digresses from acceptable social norms and as a result jeopardizes public trust in the profession.

A duty to follow the rules of law and critical morality in the course of practice

Professionals must conduct themselves according to the rules of law and morality not only because violation of these rules might adversely affect public trust in the profession, but also because law and morality are the most fundamental social rules of any modern society and are considered obligatory for all members of society.[124] If following the rules of morality and law is legitimately expected of any member of society, it surely follows that professionals in a relationship of trust with the public must adhere to these rules.[125] Thus, a breach of the rules of law and morality by professionals compromises important social interests, is *unworthy* of the public's trust, and must be avoided.

This rationale explains the duty of professionals not to harm *non-clients*. From a moral point of view, every person is under a duty not to harm another, and this moral rule applies to professionals as well. Bayles, for example, argued that "[t]o the extent professionals are free moral agents, they are responsible for effects on third parties and subject to obligations to them"[126] ... [one] "responsibility of a professional is nonmaleficence or not to injure third parties."[127]

124 See, e.g., M.B.E. Smith, "Is There a Prima Facie Obligation to Obey the Law" (1973) 82 *Yale Law Journal* 950 (discussing the moral duty to obey the law); Hart, *Concept of Law*, pp. 86-87, 169-70 (discussing the obligatory nature of legal and moral rules). See also Hart, *Law, Liberty, and Morality*, p. 20 (discussing the difference between critical and positive morality).

125 See, e.g., ABA Model Rules, Preamble and Scope, s. 5 ("A lawyer's conduct *should conform to the requirements of the law*, both in professional service to clients and in the lawyer's business and personal affairs") (emphasis added); s. 9 ("the basic principles underlying the Rules ... include the lawyer's obligation zealously to protect and pursue a client's legitimate interests, *within the bounds of the law*, while maintaining a professional, courteous and civil attitude toward all persons involved in the legal system." [emphasis added]). See also National Society of Professional Engineers (NSPE) Code of Ethics for Engineers available at www.nspe.org/resources/ethics/code-ethics (NSPE Code of Ethics for Engineers), s. I Canon 6.

126 Bayles, *Professional Ethics*, p. 112.

127 Id., p. 113. See also Beauchamp and Childress, *Biomedical Ethics*, pp. 150-151, 199.
The literature however recognized that sometimes causing harm to another in the service of clients could be justified. For such an argument in the context of the lawyer-client relationship, see, e.g., Deborah L. Rhode, "Ethical Perspectives on Legal Practice" (1985) 37 *Stanford Law Review* 589; Murray L. Schwartz, "The Professionalism and

The duty not to harm non-clients can be considered a duty toward the public because any member of the public is a "non-client" most of the time and might get injured when professional services are provided to others. It is therefore a public interest that professionals refrain as much as possible from harming non-clients in the course of practice. The public aspect of the duty toward non-clients is most dominant where the harm is serious and the injured party is considered weak, vulnerable, and unaware of the risk of harm.[128] The more serious the harm to an individual non-client and the more innocent and vulnerable he or she is, the greater the public interest in preventing that harm and the professional's accountability for doing so.

A duty to prevent process abuse or substantial defects in the process

Professionals are perceived by the public as responsible for the professional process they conduct, a process that is always aimed at producing some social good. Where the process is abused and used for purposes for which it has not been designed, either by the professional or by clients, and where the professional could have prevented the abuse or the defect, the professional will be perceived accountable for the abuse or defect; and his or her integrity, that is, his or her public commitment to loyally follow the definition and nature of his or her role, will suffer. Thus, in order to be *worthy* of the public's trust, and in order to maintain their profession's standing and the public's trust in it, professionals must prevent process abuse or substantial defects in the process that endangers important social interests such as the maintenance of the rule of law, critical morality, and the profession's standing. For example, professionals are expected to prevent the use of process for illegal purposes to the extent that they are aware of such intended abuse of process.

2.4.4 Conclusion

The choice one makes to become a professional carries with it both social privileges and public responsibility. The professional has to be worthy of the public's trust and avoid harming society's important interests in the course of exercising his or her professional role. Professionals must

Accountability of Lawyers" (1978) 66 *California Law Review* 669, 673; Fried, "The Lawyer as Friend."

128 See, e.g., Davis, *Thinking Like an Engineer*, p. 57 (discussing engineers' duties toward the public).

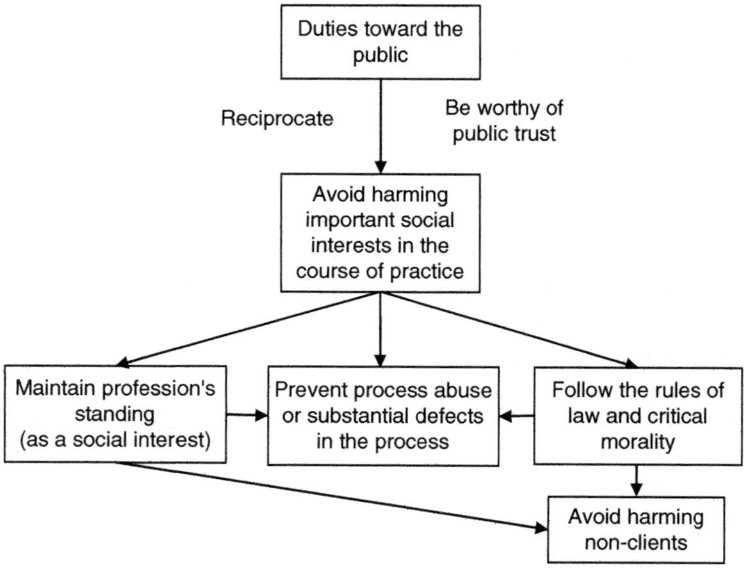

Figure 2.7: Duties toward the public

therefore perform their role in a manner that does not harm their profession's standing, in accordance with the rules of law and morality, and in line with the definition and nature of their role, that is, without abusing the professional process or allowing it to be abused by others. Figure 2.7 illustrates the professional's duties toward the public.

2.5 Duties toward employers and principals

2.5.1 Introduction

Professionals are often the employees of other professionals or bodies and provide professional services on their behalf.[129] For example, a lawyer may provide legal services to clients on behalf of a law firm that employs him or her, and a doctor may be employed by a hospital to treat patients. A key feature of a professional employer–employee relationship is that the client pays the professional's fees to the professional's employer and the professional is paid for his or her services by his or

[129] Note that an employer–employee relationship may exist between clients and professionals, for example a company may employ a lawyer as an internal legal adviser, and in that case the employer and the client are the same.

her employer rather than by the client. In addition, professionals sometimes provide services on behalf of others with whom they do not have an employer–employee relationship; instead they act as sorts of agents or representatives of individuals or bodies that will be referred to here for the sake of convenience as "principals."[130] These principals appoint professionals to provide professional services on their behalf and maintain some degree of control and supervision over their actions. For example, courts might appoint lawyers as representatives of the court to serve as receivers or guardians ad litem.[131] When professionals provide services to clients on behalf of employers or principals, they owe them duties beyond the duties they owe to their clients, the profession, and the public.

2.5.2 The normative basis of duties toward employers and principals

Keeping promises

An employer or principal who authorizes a professional to provide professional services to clients on his or her behalf expects the professional to act "like a professional," and a professional who agrees to take that role can be considered to have promised to act "like a professional." The content of the promise can be made explicit in a formal contract of employment or agency. Otherwise, in the absence of a written or detailed contract that specifies the professional's obligations, a promise to act in accordance with the purpose of the relationship may be *implied*. The main goal of the relationship will often be to provide professional services to the employer's or principal's *clients*. Thus, one feature of the promise to act "like a professional" is to *perform the role in accordance with the standards of conduct that professionals in that field can be expected to follow with respect to their clients*. This implied promise makes the duties professionals have toward their clients duties toward their employers or

[130] The terms "principal" and "agent" in this book are not used in their strict legal sense.

[131] The legal term of agency might not adequately describe the role of those appointed on behalf of the court to serve as its representative. See, e.g., Lawrence A. Frolik, "Is a Guardian the Alter Ego of the Ward?" (2007) 37 *Stetson Law Review* 53, 57 ("That the guardian's authority derives from the court's appointment does not make the guardian an agent of the court. Unlike an agent, the guardian is not merely an extension of the court; rather, the guardian acts 'for' the ward . . . a fiduciary guardian acts in the best interests of the ward, rather than in the best interests of the guardian, the court, or any third party, such as society"). See also Deborah A. DeMott, "The Lawyer as Agent" (1998) 67 *Fordham Law Review* 301, 306 ("The lawyer is not the court's agent, even metaphorically, because the lawyer's acts do not bind the court").

principals as well: the professional promises his or her employer or principal to honor his or her commitments to the clients.[132] Moreover, an employer or principal expects a professional who provides professional services on his or her behalf *to follow the employer's or principal's own rules and instructions*. This may be seen as a legitimate expectation as long as these rules and instructions are within the bounds of law and morality.

Trust

The employer or principal that authorizes the professional to provide professional services on his or her behalf places the professional in a position of power and influence in relation to both the client and him or herself. The position of power in relation to the employer or principal is established for two reasons. First, the professional provides services in circumstances where the employer or principal is unable to closely control and supervise the work of the professional. Thus the employer or principal *relies* on the professional to provide an adequate service. And second, important interests of the employer or principal are placed in the hands of the professional and may be adversely affected by the professional's conduct. The professional's conduct potentially affects clients' satisfaction, future work through returning clients and the attraction of new clients, and the maintenance of the employer's or principal's reputation and standing. It is a relationship of *trust*, and the professional is expected to perform his or her role in a manner that is *worthy* of his or her employer's or principal's trust and avoid harming their legitimate interests.[133]

Reciprocity

The circumstances of employment or agency confer on the professional benefits such as income, status, sense of self-worth, and opportunities. In return, the employer or principal expects the professional to reciprocate by promoting the employer's or principal's interests and avoid harming

[132] Compare Bayles, *Professional Ethics*, pp. 141–142 (looking at this issue from the *employer's* perspective Bayles argued that the professional's *employer* assumes the duties of the professional to the client).

[133] See, e.g., American Society of Civil Engineers (ASCE) Code of Ethics available at www.asce.org/code-of-ethics/ (ASCE Code of Ethics for Engineers), Canon 4 ("Engineers shall act in professional matters for each employer or client as faithful agents or trustees"). See also NSPE Code of Ethics for Engineers, s. II.4; Bayles, *Professional Ethics*, p. 136 (considering the professional employee–employer relationship a fiduciary one).

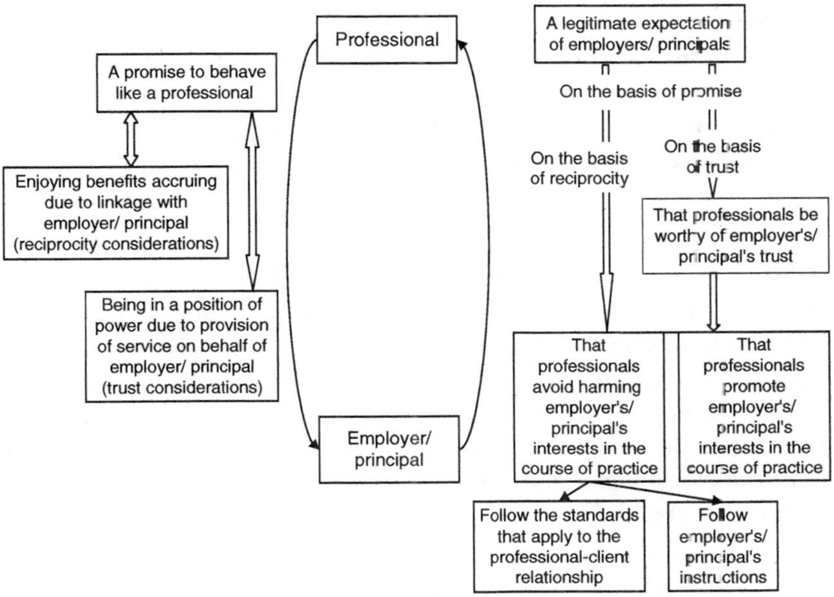

Figure 2.8: The normative basis of duties toward employers and principals

them.[134] Figure 2.8 describes the normative basis of duties toward employers and principals.

2.5.3 *Ethical duties toward employers and principals*

The duties of professionals toward their employers or principals are similar to the duties they owe their clients.[135] A trustworthy professional must be competent, disclose conflicts of interest, respect the autonomy of his or her employer or principal and obey his or her instructions, conduct themselves with professional integrity, impartiality, and diligence, treat his or her employer or principal with respect and honesty, preserve confidentiality, maintain the standing of his or her employer or principal, and act fairly. These duties are briefly discussed in the next section.

134 On reciprocity in employer–employee relationships see generally Jacqueline A-M. Coyle-Shapiro and Ian Kessler, "Exploring Reciprocity through the Lens of the Psychological Contract: Employee and Employer Perspectives" (2002) 11 *European journal of Work and Organizational Psychology* 69.

135 See, e.g., Bayles, *Professional Ethics*, p. 137.

Competence

A professional worthy of his employer's or principal's trust must be competent to fulfill his professional role. Professionals are engaged on the assumption that they are capable of performing their role[136] and are expected to refrain from providing professional services they do not have the competence to provide.

Disclosure of conflicts of interest

A trustworthy professional should avoid conflicts of interest between his or her interests and his or her employer's or principal's, or otherwise disclose conflicts of interest and receive the employer's or principal's consent before providing professional services on his or her behalf.[137] Working for a competitor and using the employer's facilities for personal purposes are examples of conflicts of interest in a professional–employer/principal context.[138]

Respect employer's or principal's autonomy and obey instructions

When a professional acts as a representative of another his freedom of action is more limited than the freedom of an independent, self-employed professional. He or she is the long arm of the employer or principal and thus should normally obey his or her instructions and respect his or her right to make decisions concerning the terms of the provision of services on his or her behalf.[139] For example, the employer or principal might determine issues such as fees and conditions of payment, the type of cases that are taken or dismissed, and circumstances that require the termination of services. The autonomy of the employer or principal is not unlimited. The professional has no ethical duty to follow instructions that are immoral, illegal, or in violation of his ethical duties toward clients or others.[140]

[136] See, e.g., ibid. [137] See, e.g., ASCE Code of Ethics for Engineers, Canon 4(a).

[138] See, e.g., ASCE Code of Ethics for Engineers, Canon 4(g) and 5(h). See also Bayles, *Professional Ethics*, p. 139.

[139] See, e.g., Wilbert E. Moore, *The Professions: Roles and Rules* (New York: Russell Sage Foundation, 1970), pp. 189, 194-195 (noting the decrease of professional autonomy in circumstances of employment).

[140] See, e.g., National Association of Social Workers (NASW) Code of Ethics available at www.socialworkers.org/pubs/code/code.asp (NASW Code of Ethics for Social Workers), s. 3.09(d) ("Social workers should not allow an employing organization's policies, procedures, regulations, or administrative orders to interfere with their ethical practice

Professional integrity

Even though employers and principals expect professionals who act on their behalf to respect their autonomy and follow instructions, they are unable and unwilling to instruct them on every detail of the work they conduct. Thus they rely on the professionals to exercise good judgment and make decisions when these are necessary for the provision of quality professional services.[141] In other words, they expect professionals to exercise professional discretion, which is a fundamental characteristic of all professional roles. The exercise of professional discretion is one aspect of professional integrity, that is, of being truly committed to the nature and definition of the professional role and to the wholeness of the professional service. The other aspects of professional integrity are separation of professional roles; appropriateness of case to process; and prevention of process abuse or substantial defects in the process.[142] Employers and principals expect the professionals they hire to manifest these features of professional integrity in their conduct for two reasons. The first is in order that the professionals, who act as their representatives, discharge their duties to the clients; and the second is in order to preserve the standing of the employer or principal, which could suffer if the professional exhibits lack of integrity.

Impartiality

A duty of impartiality toward an employer or principal might be relevant where a professional has more than one employer or principal. In that case the professional is expected to refrain from discriminating between his employers or principals or favoring one at the expense of the other.

Diligence

Employers and principals expect "a loyal performance of services"[143] from professionals who act on their behalf. As representatives, professionals should act diligently,[144] that is, with caution and without undue delays or waste of the employer's or principal's resources.[145]

of social work"). See also NSPE Code of Ethics for Engineers, s. III.2.b; Bayles, *Professional Ethics*, p. 140.

141 See, e.g., Bayles, ibid. 142 See Section 2.2.3.4.

143 See, e.g., Moore, *The Professions*, p. 202.

144 See, e.g., Bayles, *Professional Ethics*, p. 137.

145 See, e.g., NASW Code of Ethics for Social Workers, s. 3.09(g).

Respect

Employers and principals expect professionals who have a working relationship with them to treat them with respect and avoid demeaning or degrading language. This issue is hardly mentioned in the literature and in codes of conduct, probably because in practice a professional who acts on behalf of an employer or principal wishes to secure his or her position and is therefore unlikely to exhibit disrespectful behavior.

Honesty

A trustworthy professional must be honest with his or her employers or principals, tell them the truth, and avoid lying and deceit.[146]

Confidentiality

The loyalty of the professional to his or her employer or principal is also expressed in his or her keeping in confidence any sensitive information, acquired by him or her in the course of practice, whose disclosure might adversely affect the employer's or principal's interests.[147] Again, this duty is not absolute and in some circumstances disclosure might be ethically justified, for example in whistle-blowing cases.[148]

Maintaining the employer's or principal's standing

Employers and principals depend on their reputation and on the public's trust to achieve their goals, whether economic ones such as maximizing profits, or social, such as the provision of services for the benefit of the public. Professionals should be aware that their actions and statements may affect the public image of the employer or principal that they represent, and the public's trust in them. Thus, employers and principals are entitled to expect professionals who work on their behalf to avoid conduct that could undermine their standing in the eyes of those with whom they come in contact.[149]

146 See, e.g., Bayles, *Professional Ethics*, p. 137.

147 See, e.g., David Appelbaum and Sarah Verone Lawton (eds.), *Ethics and the Professions* (Englewood Cliffs, NJ: Prentice-Hall, 1990), pp. 197–198. See also ASCE Code of Ethics for Engineers, Canon 4(f); Bayles, *Professional Ethics*, p. 138.

148 See, e.g., Appelbaum and Lawton, id., pp. 198–203.

149 Of course, this obligation is not absolute. See, e.g., Bayles, *Professional Ethics*, p. 138 (noting that "Loyalty does not require faithfulness to employers no matter what. Both within and outside one's employment, freedom, especially of expression, carries weight").

Fairness

Employers and principals expect professionals who provide services on their behalf to play by the rules, that is, to follow the rules that apply to them. Thus, if professionals fail to comply with any of the abovementioned standards, for example act dishonestly or reveal sensitive information or breach their employers' or principals' legitimate instructions, they are acting unfairly. Since employers and principals expect their professionals to comply with the standards of conduct that apply to them with respect to their *clients*, the duty of fairness toward employers and principals encompasses a duty to follow their obligations toward clients. And because professionals are expected to maintain their employers' and principals' standing, they must comply – as part of their duties toward their employer or principal – with their obligations toward the *public* and the *profession* insofar as this is necessary in order to preserve their employers' and principals' standing.

2.5.4 Conclusion

Professionals do not necessarily act on behalf of an employer or principal when they provide services to clients, but when they do they owe those they represent duties (see Figure 2.9). These duties are quite similar to the duties they owe their clients and overlap where the client is the professional's employer or principal. When the client is not the employer or principal, the professional's duty toward his or her employer or principal includes an obligation to comply with his or her duties toward the client as well. A professional's duty to an employer or principal may conflict with a duty to his or her client, and such a clash will have to be handled and resolved as in cases of conflict between a duty toward the public and a duty toward a client.[150] These issues are discussed in Parts II and III with regard to mediators.

2.6 The rights of professionals

Professional ethics mainly deals with the obligations of professionals, but professionals also have rights. In general, professionals have the liberty to

150 Lawyers, for example, have a duty toward the court not to deceive the court even if it hurts the client's position (see, e.g., ABA Model Rules, Rule 3.3; Cohen and Davis, *Ethics and the Legal Profession*, p. 331). Engineers have a duty to protect public safety, health, and welfare that can sometimes clash with their duties toward their clients (See, e.g., Davis, *Thinking Like an Engineer*, pp. 55–56).

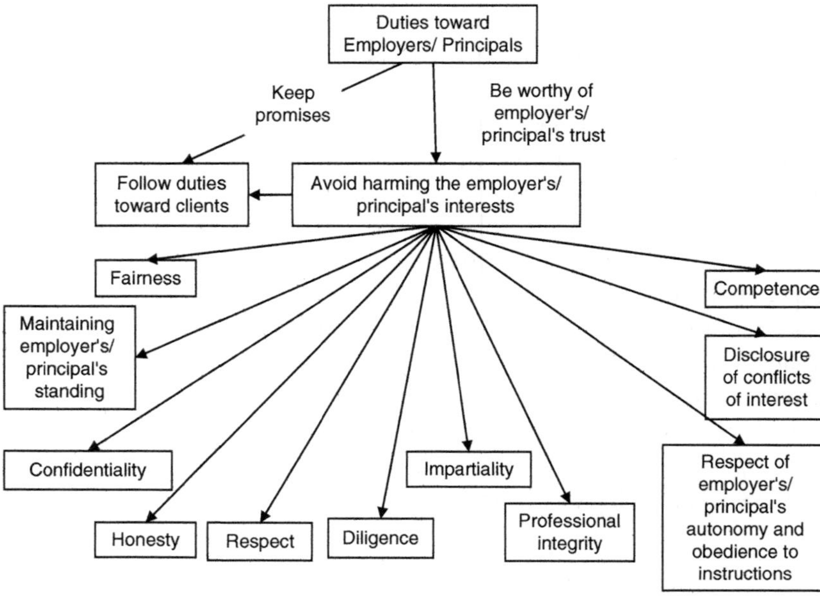

Figure 2.9: Duties toward employers and principals

conduct themselves as they wish so long as they are not in breach of one of their obligations.[151] More specifically, professionals may have various rights. For example, a professional in the private sector may *charge fees* for his or her services, and may *terminate his or her services* in the event of non-payment.[152] Such a professional may *refuse to provide his or her services* in a particular case or to a particular client, or *withdraw* his or her services for good cause. The right to withdraw services is more restricted than the right to refuse to take on a case, because once a case has been taken the client's interests could be adversely affected by the withdrawal and the need to find a new professional to take on the case and start all over again. Voluntary withdrawal of services[153] might be justified where the client does not pay the professional's fees; the professional has lost faith in the client or vice versa; the client fails to cooperate with the

[151] See, e.g., Bayles, *Professional Ethics*, p. 25.

[152] This right could sometimes be curtailed. See, e.g., Nicolson and Webb, *Professional Legal Ethics*, p. 218 (discussing limitations on lawyer withdrawal).

[153] Professionals could be under a *duty* to withdraw their services, for example when they realize they do not have the necessary competence or that they are in a conflict of interests.

professional to a degree that makes the provision of services impossible; the client behaves with disrespect or inappropriately toward the professional; or where the provision of services is inconsistent with the professional's personal integrity.

2.7 Conclusion

Part I is now concluded, leaving us with a general theory of professional ethics. Chapter 1 on "Fundamental concepts" examined what professional ethics is and how its norms are created; Chapter 2 on "Ethical relationships" detailed the ethical norms that apply to professionals in general as a result of the legitimate expectations of four interested groups: clients, the profession, the public, and employers or principals. In the next part, Part II, I will apply this professional ethics perspective to mediation and mediators to construct a theory of mediators' ethics.

PART II

A theory of mediators' ethics

3

Mediation, mediators' role, and mediators' ethics

3.1 Introduction

A general theory of professional ethics having been presented in Part I, this chapter discusses the process of mediation and the role of mediators in Anglo-American countries in order to move from the ethics of professionals in general to the ethics of mediators in particular. The chapter begins with an exploration of the nature of mediation and the role of mediators, arguing on the basis of codes of conduct for mediators and mediation literature in Anglo-American countries that despite differences in style, mediation and mediators' role have a *core descriptive definition* and *shared professional ideals*. The chapter goes on to establish on the basis of the codes and the literature a *shared set of mediation norms* that mediators are expected to follow. The product of the discussion is termed a *perspective-from-below* of mediators' ethics, because the identified set of mediation norms reflects an internal understanding of mediators' ethics from within the practice of mediation. The chapter then introduces a *perspective-from-above* of mediators' ethics that reflects the application of a theory of professional ethics derived from role-morality to the core definition of mediation and the role of mediators. This exercise culminates in the establishment of a set of mediation norms that is compatible with both perspectives of mediators' ethics and applies to mediators in Anglo-American societies regardless of style or type of case. The chapter ends with an explanation of the methods for ascertaining the *content and meaning* of these norms. These methods will be employed in the following chapters to produce a *Proposed Model Code of Conduct for Mediators* (Proposed Code).

3.2 The nature of mediation and the role of mediators: a core descriptive definition

One can learn about the nature of mediation and the role of mediators in Anglo-American societies from two main sources: *mediation laws and formal codes of conduct for mediators* that deal with mediation and define the process, its objectives, and the functions of mediators as understood by legislatures and professional organizations; and *mediation literature* that describes the evolution of the process, its philosophy, the social needs that it seeks to meet, its values, and common practices in carrying out the role of mediator. Codes of conduct for mediators and scholars offer various definitions of mediation and the role of mediators. There is no consensus on these issues,[1] and mediations are practiced in different styles (or models) in a variety of conflicts.[2] There are, however, three main mediation styles: problem-solving, transformative, and narrative mediation.[3] Problem-solving mediators see mediation as a process of assisting parties to negotiate freely in order to reach an agreement that resolves the dispute in whole or in part.[4] The problem-solving style has variations, the most famous being facilitative mediation and evaluative mediation. The facilitative mediator concentrates on easing

[1] Kimberlee K. Kovach, *Mediation: Principles and Practice*, 3rd edn., (St. Paul, MN: Thompson West, 2004), pp. 26–27; Jay Folberg and Alison Taylor, *Mediation: A Comprehensive Guide To Resolving Conflicts Without Litigation* (San Francisco: Jossey-Bass, 1984), p. 7; Laurence Boulle and Miryana Nesic, *Mediation: Principles, Process, Practice* (London: Tottel, 2001), p. 3; Michael Moffitt, "Schmediation and the Dimensions of Definition" (2005) 10 *Harvard Negotiation Law Review* 69, 78. Murray S. Levin, "The Propriety of Evaluative Mediation: Concerns About the Nature and Quality of an Evaluative Opinion" (2001) 16 *Ohio State Journal on Dispute Resolution* 267, 267.

For some examples of mediation definitions, see, e.g., Folberg and Taylor, *Mediation*, p. 7 ("process by which the participants, together with the assistance of a neutral person or persons, systematically isolate disputed issues in order to develop options, consider alternatives, and reach a consensual settlement that will accommodate their needs"); Kovach, *Mediation*, p. 26 ("a process by which a neutral third party, the mediator, assists disputing parties in reaching a mutually satisfactory resolution").

[2] See, e.g., Carrie Menkel-Meadow, Lela Porter Love, and Andrea Kupfer Schneider, *Mediation: Practice, Policy and Ethics* (New York: Aspen, 2006), pp. 113–132 (discussing different approaches to mediation); Nancy Welsh, "All in the Family: Darwin and the Evolution of Mediation" (2001) 7 *Dispute Resolution Magazine* 20 (discussing and comparing different types of mediation and mediator practices); E. Patrick McDermott and Ruth Obar, "'What's Going On' in Mediation: An Empirical Analysis of the Influence of a Mediator's Style on Party Satisfaction and Monetary Benefit" (2004) 9 *Harvard Negotiation Law Review* 75, 80–89 (identifying facilitative and evaluative techniques used in mediation).

[3] See, e.g., Michal Alberstein, "Forms of Mediation and Law: Cultures of Dispute Resolution" (2007) 22 *Ohio State Journal on Dispute Resolution* 321, 328–331; Michal Alberstein, "The Jurisprudence of Mediation: Between Formalism, Feminism and Identity Conversations" (2009) 11 *Cardozo Journal of Conflict Resolution* 1, 5–6.

[4] See, e.g., Kimberlee K. Kovach, "New Wine Requires New Wineskins: Transforming Lawyer Ethics for Effective Representation in A Non-adversarial Approach to Problem Solving Mediation" (2001) 28 *Fordham Urban Law Journal* 935, 942.

communications between parties in order to help them negotiate effectively, while the evaluative mediator focuses on evaluating the strengths and weaknesses of each party's case in order to bring them to an agreement.[5] In practice, however, as Murray S. Levin commented, "many mediators combine aspects of facilitative and evaluative mediation; thus, the philosophical and stylistic differences between the two approaches is less distinct and instead represents more of a continuum."[6] Transformative mediation focuses on the interaction between the parties and seeks to facilitate personal transformation through empowerment and mutual recognition that may enable the parties to better cope with the conflict and make decisions.[7] Lastly, narrative mediation focuses on the relationship between the parties as well, and tries to induce the parties to develop an alternative story (or narrative) of their relationship that will allow the emergence of renewed confidence and enable the resolution of the conflict if the parties wish that end.[8]

Despite the variety of mediation styles, the most common is problem-solving mediation, probably because it is viewed as more practical in its focus on reaching a mediated agreement as a central objective of the process. This book concentrates on problem-solving mediation as a prototype, but is relevant to other mediation styles as well, as will be explained in this chapter.

Scholars Laurence Boulle and Miryana Nesic argued in 2001 that "mediation has yet to develop a coherent theoretical base and an accepted

[5] See, e.g., Leonard L. Riskin, "Understanding Mediators' Orientations, Strategies, and Techniques: A Grid for the Perplexed" (1996) 1 *Harvard Negotiation Law Review* 7. See also Kimberlee K. Kovach and Lela P. Love, "Evaluative Mediation Is An Oxymoron" (1996) 14 *Alternatives to High Cost Litigation* 31; Kimberlee K. Kovach and Lela P. Love, "Mapping Mediation: The Risks of Riskin's Grid" (1998) 3 *Harvard Negotiation Law Review* 71.

[6] Levin, "The Propriety of Evaluative Mediation", 269. See also Jeffrey W. Stempel, "Identifying Real Dichotomies Underlying the False Dichotomy: Twenty-First Century Mediation in an Eclectic Regime" (2000) 2000 *Journal of Dispute Resolution* 371, 375 ("the definition of mediation according to the facilitative-evaluative dichotomy is unrealistically formalistic as well as theoretically and empirically erroneous"). McDermott and Obar, "What's Going On", pp. 87–89 (discussing "eclectic mediation"); John Lande, "Toward More Sophisticated Mediation Theory" (2000) 2000 *Journal of Dispute Resolution* 321, note 4.

[7] On transformative mediation, see Robert A. Baruch Bush and Joseph P. Folger, *The Promise of Mediation: Responding to Conflict through Empowerment and Recognition* (San Francisco: Jossey-Bass, 1994). See also Michal Alberstein, *Jurisprudence of Mediation* (Jerusalem: The Hebrew University Magnes Press, 2007), Ch. 9 [Hebrew].

[8] On narrative mediation, see John Winslade and Gerald Monk, *Narrative Mediation: A New Approach to Conflict Resolution* (San Francisco: Jossey-Bass, 2000). See also Alberstein, *Jurisprudence of Mediation*, Ch. 10 [Hebrew].

set of core features which enable it to be differentiated from rival processes."[9] Although one cannot point to a single definition of mediation in the professional literature,[10] one can find among the definitions of mediation and mediation styles a *common denominator* reflecting the nature of mediation and the role of mediators. There are, I would argue, basic features that must exist in order for a process to be considered mediation rather than negotiation, arbitration, adjudication, therapy, or any other professional process. Like Boulle and Nesic and Michael Moffitt, I distinguish between a *descriptive* definition of mediation that offers an uncritical description of mediation practice, and a *normative* definition of mediation that describes what mediation *ought to* look like in practice.[11] To identify the minimum common features of mediation, I adopt a descriptive definition of mediation that reflects the practice of mediation as described in codes of conduct for mediators and mediation literature, rather than a normative approach that reflects the desired state of affairs. A review of mediation literature and many codes of conduct for mediators from the United States, Canada, and Australia points to four features that must be present together for a mediation process to exist; the absence of one or more of them will not allow the process to be identified as mediation.[12]

(1) The existence of an actual or potential *conflict* or *dispute*.[13] Mediation comes to answer some difficulty, crisis, dissatisfaction, misunderstanding, or a particular problem. The use of mediation is designed to handle an existing situation (e.g. helping spouses make

[9] See Boulle and Nesic, *Mediation*, p. 3. [10] See Note 1.

[11] See Boulle and Nesic, *Mediation*, pp. 4–5. Michael Moffitt, "Schmediation", 79–89 (discussing prescriptive and descriptive definitions of mediation).

[12] Of course, other professional procedures may share *some* of these features with mediation.

[13] See, e.g., ADR Institute of Canada, Inc., Code of Conduct for Mediators (2011) available at www.adrcanada.ca/resources/documents/CodeOfConduct2012August30.pdf (ADR Canada Code), s.2.1(a); Australian National Mediator Accreditation Standards: Practice Standards (2012) available at www.msb.org.au/sites/default/files/documents/Practice%20Standards.pdf (Australian Practice Standards), Standard 1(1); The Mediation Council of Illinois Professional Standards of Practice for Mediators (2009) available at www.mediationcouncilofillinois.org/sites/default/files/MCI%20Professional%20Standards%20of%20Practice.pdf (Illinois Standards), Definition; Model Standards of Practice for Family and Divorce Mediation (2000) available at www.americanbar.org/content/dam/aba/migrated/family/reports/mediation.authcheckdam.pdf (Family Mediation Model Standards), Overview and Definitions. See also Christopher W. Moore, *The Mediation Process: Practical Strategies for Resolving Conflict*, 3rd ed. (San Francisco: Jossey-Bass, 2003), pp. 16–17 (noting that mediators mediate latent, emerging, and manifest conflicts).

decisions relating to a divorce) or prevent problems in the future (e.g. helping coworkers construct a working relationship at work).[14] There is no mediation without an actual or potential conflict.

(2) The conflict is between at least *two* parties.[15] Mediation focuses on intervening in conflicts between individuals, organizations, and even countries. Mediation does not engage in personal, internal conflicts between an individual and him or herself, as opposed to some types of therapy.

(3) A *third person* (referred to as mediator) is involved,[16] whose role is to assist all parties in maintaining a *dialogue* about the conflict.[17] When

[14] See, e.g., Menkel-Meadow, Love and Schneider, *Mediation*, p. 91 (defining mediation as "a process in which an impartial third party acts as a catalyst to help others constructively address and perhaps resolve a dispute, plan a transaction, or define the contours of a relationship"). See also Boulle and Nesic, *Mediation*, pp. 9–13 (discussing the many uses of mediation which include defining problems, settling disputes, managing conflicts, negotiating contracts, formulating policy, and preventing conflicts).

[15] See, e.g., Folberg and Taylor, *Mediation*, p. 19 (noting that "Mediation is primarily concerned with *interpersonal* conflict – situations that arise between individuals or groups of individuals"); David Spencer and Michael Brogan, *Mediation Law and Practice* (Cambridge University Press, 2007), p. 42. Codes of conduct for mediators typically refer to *the parties* to the dispute. See, e.g., Australian Practice Standards, s. 1(1) ("These Practice Standards apply to any mediator acting as a third party to support *two or more individuals or entities* to manage, settle or resolve disputes ... "); Oregon Mediation Association Core Standards of Mediation Practice (2005) available at www.omediate.org/pg61.cfm (Oregon Standards), Definitions (noting that mediation is "a process in which a mediator assists and facilitates *two or more parties*" (emphasis added). See also Law Council of Australia, Ethical Guidelines for Mediators (2011) available at www.lawcouncil.asn.au/lawcouncil/images/LCA-PDF/a-z-docs/EthicalGuidelinesforMediators.pdf (Australian Ethical Guidelines), s. 1; ADR Canada Code, s.2.1 (a); Alabama Code of Ethics for Mediators (1995, amended 2013) available at www.alabamaadr.org/web/roster-documents/documents/med_2014_Mediator_Code_of_Ethics_updated.pdf (Alabama Code), s. II(b); California Rules of Conduct for Mediators in Court-Connected Mediation Programs for Civil Cases, California Rules of Court (Revised January 1, 2015) available at www.courts.ca.gov/cms/rules/index.cfm?title=three (California Rules), Rule 3.852(1); Florida Rules, Rules 10.210 and 10.220; Illinois Standards, Definition; Divorce Mediation Model Standards, Overview and Definitions; Revised Standards of Professional Conduct for Mediators (2011) adopted by the Supreme Court of North Carolina available at www.aoc.state.nc.us/www/public/html/pdf/SOC4_14.pdf (North Carolina Standards), Preamble.

[16] See, e.g., Australian Practice Standards, s. 1(1) ("These Practice Standards apply to any mediator acting as a third party . . . "); ADR Canada Code, s. 2.1(a); Alabama Code, s. II(b); Florida Rules, Rule 10.210; Illinois Standards, Definition; Family Mediation Model Standards, Overview and Definitions; Model Standards, Preamble. See also Folberg and Taylor, *Mediation*, p. 7; Kovach, *Mediation*, p. 26; Spencer and Brogan, *Mediation Law*, p. 3; Boulle and Nesic, *Mediation*, p. 7; Moore, *The Mediation Process*, p. 15.

[17] See, e.g., California Rules, Rule 3.852 (1) ("[m]ediation means a process in which a neutral person or persons facilitate communication between disputants"); Australian Ethical

dialogue between parties to a conflict takes place without the involvement of a third person (a representative of either party would not be considered a third person) the process will not be considered mediation but negotiation.[18]

(4) The third person *lacks authority to force a solution* on the parties and the parties can choose an outcome acceptable to them (including an agreement that ends the conflict).[19] A process in which the third person has authority to impose a solution on the parties and does not need the parties' consent to the outcome cannot be considered mediation, but rather arbitration or adjudication.[20] However, the lack of coercive authority of the third person itself is not unique to mediators, and neutral evaluators and expert advisors do not have coercive authority as well.

Mediation has other common descriptive characteristics that can be gleaned from codes of conduct for mediators and mediation literature, but they are not necessary for the existence of a mediation process in the sense that their absence does not make the process other than mediation. For example, codes of conduct for mediators often define mediation as a process whose goal is to *reach a resolution of a dispute or an agreement*.

Guidelines, s. 1 ("A mediator facilitates communication, promotes understanding"); Alabama Code, s. II(c) and (d); California Rules, Rule 3.852(1); Florida Rules, Rule 10.220 ("The role of the mediator is to reduce obstacles to communication"); Family Mediation Model Standards, Overview and Definitions ("The family mediator assists communication"); Model Standards, Preamble ("an impartial third party facilitates communication"); North Carolina Standards, Preamble ("It is the mediator's role to facilitate communication and understanding among the parties"). See also Kovach, *Mediation*, p. 47 (noting that "mediation is quite correctly considered to be the facilitation of a negotiation"); Spencer and Brogan, *Mediation Law*, p. 42 (treating mediation as negotiation aided by a third party); Moore, *The Mediation Process*, p. 16 (noting that "[m]ediation is essentially dialogue or negotiation with the involvement of a third party").

18 See, e.g., Boulle and Nesic, *Mediation*, p. 7 (treating the assistance of "a third person, the mediator" as a core feature of mediation and commenting [at note 9] that "This may seem trite. However, many counselors and lawyers at mediation training courses claim that they have been 'practicing as mediators for years'. This may indicate a certain style of practice, but it cannot constitute mediation").

19 See, e.g., ADR Canada Code, s. 3.1; Alabama Code, s. II(b); Florida Rules, Rule 10.210; Illinois Standards, Definition at s. D; North Carolina Standards, Preamble; Texas Ethical Guidelines for Mediators (2011) available at www.txcourts.gov/All_Archived_Documents/SupremeCourt/AdministrativeOrders/miscdocket/11/11906200.pdf (Texas Guidelines), s. 1. See also Folberg and Taylor, *Mediation*, p. 10; Boulle and Nesic, *Mediation*, p. 7; Moore, *The Mediation Process*, p. 15; Menkel-Meadow, Love, and Schneider, *Mediation*, p. 92.

20 See, e.g., Menkel-Meadow, Love and Schneider, *Mediation*, p. 92.

The *Model Standards of Practice for Family and Divorce Mediation* (Family Mediation Model Standards), for example, provides that "[f] amily and divorce mediation ... is a process in which a mediator ... facilitates the resolution of family disputes ..."[21] The *Ethical Guidelines for Mediators* adopted by the Law Council of Australia (Australian Ethical Guidelines) provide that "[m]ediation is a process in which ... a mediator – facilitates the resolution of a dispute by promoting uncoerced agreement by the parties to the dispute."[22] And the *Code of Conduct for Mediators* of ADR Institution of Canada, Inc. (ADR Canada Code) provides that "'[m]ediation' means the use of an impartial third person to assist the parties to resolve a dispute".[23] These definitions sit well with the problem-solving model of mediation, especially with court-connected mediation whose objective is that disputants reach mediated agreements that render the continuation of court proceedings unnecessary. It is clear, however, that reaching an agreement is not a constitutive element in the definition of mediation because there is no way to ensure that *all* mediations end in agreements and no one is suggesting that mediation processes *must* end with agreements. Thus, a mediated agreement may be a professional ideal or aspiration for some mediators, but cannot be treated as a core descriptive element of mediation's definition.

Along with the four basic features discussed in this section, which are *descriptive* elements of mediation comprising the minimum components of a mediation process, codes of conduct and mediation literature refer to commonly shared *normative aspects* of mediation and mediators' role that reflect what code drafters and scholars believe mediation ought to look like, even where the process does not actually comply with them. Here are some examples of these normative features.

(a) A neutral or impartial third person

Codes of conduct for mediators and scholars often define mediation as a process involving a *neutral* third person,[24] *impartial* third person,[25]

[21] Family Mediation Model Standards, Overview and Definitions.

[22] Australian Ethical Guidelines, s. 1.

[23] ADR Canada Code, s. 2.1(a). See also Florida Rules, Rule 10.210; Alabama Code, s. II(b).

[24] See, e.g., Alabama Code, s. II.(b); California Rules, Rule 3.852. See also Folberg and Taylor, *Mediation*, p. 7; Kovach, *Mediation*, p. 26.

[25] See, e.g., Family Mediation Model Standards, Overview and Definitions; Texas Guidelines, s. 1; Virginia Standards of Ethics and Professional Responsibility for Certified Mediators (2011) available at www.courts.state.va.us/courtadmin/aoc/djs/programs/drs/mediation/

or both.[26] Neutrality has multiple meanings and there is no consensus among scholars on its exact meaning in mediation and whether it can ever be achieved in practice.[27] Impartiality is another vague term. Some scholars have suggested that impartiality and neutrality have the same meaning, while others claim that these terms have different meanings.[28] While I agree that neutrality and impartiality are important characteristics of both mediation and mediators, and that mediators ought to abide by these norms, I argue that they are not constitutive components of mediation. In other words, unlike the four basic features discussed in this section, their absence would not strip the process of its mediation identity. A biased mediation process is flawed but does not lose its identity as mediation. Boulle and Nesic explicitly agree with this argument regarding mediators' neutrality, noting that "[i]t is not possible to assert as a matter of definition that mediators are always neutral,"[29] but their position on impartiality is less clear. On the one hand they claim that in comparison to neutrality, impartiality "must be regarded as a core requirement in mediation, in the sense that its absence would fundamentally undermine the nature of the process,"[30] but on the other hand they do not include impartiality in their proposed definition of mediation and do not mention it as a core element of mediation when they discuss these elements in their book.[31]

I believe that Boulle and Nesic were right not to include neutrality and impartiality as core definitive features of mediation. Other professional processes such as adjudication and arbitration require the professional to exhibit neutrality and impartiality as well, and it cannot be said that a failure to do so transforms one process into another. The absence of neutrality and impartiality undermines the integrity of the process, be it mediation or otherwise, but it remains the same process though a defective one.

soe.pdf (Virginia Standards), s. B. See also Menkel-Meadow, Love, and Schneider, *Mediation*, p. 91.

26 See, e.g., Florida Rules, Rule 10.210; Georgia Ethical Standards for Mediators (1994) available at www.godr.org/files/APPENDIX%20C,%20CHAP%201,%206-18-2013.pdf (Georgia Standards), Introduction.

27 See, e.g., Boulle and Nesic, *Mediation*, p. 17 (discussing some of the meanings of neutrality).

28 Neutrality, impartiality, and conflicts of interest are discussed in Chapters 6 and 7.

29 Boulle and Nesic, *Mediation*, p. 19. 30 Id., p. 18. 31 See id., pp. 3, 7.

(b) Confidentiality

Another common characteristic of mediation is confidentiality. Codes of conduct for mediators regularly include a confidentiality provision stating that mediators must keep in confidence information that came to their knowledge during mediation,[32] and scholars treat confidentiality as a key feature.[33] The maintenance of confidentiality has practical importance because it contributes to an atmosphere of trust between the mediator and the parties, which is conducive to an effective mediation process. But like the argument with respect to neutrality and impartiality, a breach of confidence does not deny mediation its nature and identity. It would be wrong for a mediator to divulge confidential information, as would be the case with doctors, lawyers, and accountants, but the professional process would retain its name, description, and character.[34]

(c) Party consent to entry and participation

The right of mediation parties to self-determination is commonly considered to apply to the decision whether to enter mediation (giving parties a right to refuse to go to mediation) and to the decision whether to continue to participate in the process (giving parties a right to withdraw from the mediation).[35] These are important characteristics of mediation, differentiating it from other dispute resolution processes such as adjudication, where the consent of defendants is not required for the process to begin, and arbitration (and adjudication again), where participants cannot unilaterally withdraw from the process. And yet, as the case of mandatory mediation demonstrates, a temporary and limited suspension of the rights to refuse entry to mediation and to withdraw from the process does not deny the process its mediation

[32] See, e.g., Family Mediation Canada Members Code of Professional Conduct available at fmc.ca/sites/default/files/sites/all/themes/fmc/images-user/Members%20Code%20of%20Professional%20Conduct_0.pdf (Family Mediation Canada Code), Article 7; Texas Guidelines, s. 8; Family Mediation Model Standards, Standard VII; Model Standards, Standard V.A; Florida Rules, Rule 10.360(a); Illinois Standards, Standard II; North Carolina Standards, Rule III.

[33] See, e.g., Folberg and Taylor, *Mediation*, p. 264; Kovach, *Mediation*, pp. 262–266; Spencer and Brogan, *Mediation Law*, pp. 85–86; Boulle and Nesic, *Mediation*, p. 458.

[34] See also Boulle and Nesic, *Mediation*, p. 9 (describing confidentiality as one of the variable features of mediation).

[35] See, e.g., Model Standards, Standard I.A; California Rules, Rule 3.853(2); Georgia Standards, Standard I.A.6; Family Mediation Model Standards, Standard I D.

title,[36] provided that the core descriptive features of mediation mentioned above are in existence. Although some critics argue that mandatory mediation is an oxymoron, the lack of consensus on this issue among scholars and the growing use of mandatory mediation[37] indicate that a limited restriction of party self-determination with respect to entry to the process and participation is not regarded as a denial of mediation's nature and identity and thus should not be considered as part of the core definitive features of mediation.

The above analysis establishes a *core descriptive definition* of mediation and of the role of mediators in Anglo-American countries. Mediation is a *process in which a third person assists parties to an actual or potential conflict in maintaining a dialogue in order to enable them to make decisions regarding the conflict and reach an agreement when they wish to do so.* The different styles or models of mediation are in effect *additional layers* to the core definition of mediation; variations on mediation's objectives and mediators' techniques that are not in consensus. For example, for the problem-solving mediator, the process should enable the parties to define issues, identify interests, explore options, and reach an agreement. The facilitative problem-solving mediator would stress the importance of party communication on the basis of needs, while the evaluative mediator would assign more weight to the legal rights of the parties and the likely court outcome.[38] On the other hand, the transformative mediator would use the mediation to take the parties through a process of empowerment and recognition to enhance their ability to make decisions,[39] while the narrative mediator would concentrate "on developing a relationship that is incompatible with conflict and that is built on stories of understanding, respect, and collaboration,"[40] and invite the parties "to view the plot of the dispute from a different vantage point [and] . . . lay the groundwork for the construction of an alternative story."[41] Each of these styles satisfies the core descriptive definition of

36 Compare Boulle and Nesic, *Mediation*, pp. 14–16 (discussing the difficulties in regarding voluntariness as a definitional element of mediation).

37 See, e.g., Dorcas Quek, "Mandatory Mediation: An Oxymoron? Examining the Feasibility of Implementing a Court-Mandated Mediation Program" (2010) 11 *Cardozo Journal of Conflict Resolution* 479.

38 See Note 4.

39 Joseph P. Folger, Robert A. Bauch Bush, and Dorothy J. Della Noce (eds.), *Transformative Mediation: A Sourcebook* (The Association for Conflict Resolution and the Institute for the Study of Conflict Resolution, 2010), pp. 24–25.

40 Winslade and Monk, *Narrative Mediation*, p. xi.

41 Id., p. 72.

mediation, and the lack of consensus in both academia and practice on a "true" process of mediation makes all of them legitimate.

3.3 Shared professional ideals

The core descriptive definition of mediation and of mediators' fundamental role is supplemented by some shared professional ideals of mediation practice. Every profession has ideals.[42] The professional ideals of mediation reflect the aims of mediation and mediators, what mediators aspire to and consider "good" in a professional sense. The core definition of mediation reveals two professional ideals shared by all mediators. The first ideal is an aspiration to *set conditions for constructive dialogue* between parties in conflict, i.e., to assist in communication; the second is an aspiration to *ensure party self-determination with respect to outcome*, whether or not that outcome ends the conflict.

The historical development of mediation as documented in mediation literature indicates two further shared professional ideals. One is an aspiration to *professionalization and to distinguishing mediation from other professions.* Mediators wish to develop a professional consciousness separate from other professionals, and to perform a unique role different from the one performed by judges, arbitrators, lawyers, therapists and other professionals.[43] For this reason mediators establish professional organizations, draft standards of conduct, and develop programs for learning, researching, and teaching mediation.

[42] See Chapter 1, Section 1.2.2.2.

[43] See, e.g., Folberg and Taylor, *Mediation*, pp. 13–14 (suggesting a philosophy of mediation that "will allow mediation to grow into a separate and distinct profession"). See also Model Standards, Standard VI.A.5 (noting that "[t]he role of a mediator differs substantially from other professional roles. Mixing the role of a mediator and the role of another profession is problematic and thus, a mediator should distinguish between the roles"); North Carolina Standards, Rule VI ("A mediator shall limit himself or herself solely to the role of mediator"); Australian Practice Standards, s. 2(2) ("Mediation processes are not a substitute for individual or organisational legal and/or other expert advice, or individual counselling or therapy. Mediation processes may not be appropriate for all disputants or all types of disputes"); id. s. 3(4)(g)(ii) ("if the mediator is a psychologist, counsellor or therapist, he or she shall inform the participants that he or she cannot counsel or practise therapy with either or any of the participants"); California Rules, Rule 3.857(d) ("A mediator must inform all participants, at or before the outset of the first mediation session, that during the mediation he or she will not represent any participant as a lawyer or perform professional services in any capacity other than as an impartial mediator").

Another shared ideal is an aspiration to contribute to the creation of *a better society* based largely on *consensual cooperation between individuals*. It focuses on society as a whole, rather than on particular individuals, and seeks to use mediation for the benefit of society. Although this *social* ideal does not follow from the core definition of mediation, it may still be considered a shared ideal of mediators because it is embedded in the stories that the different theories of mediation tell us to illustrate why mediation is valuable, the reasons for its rapid development, and its aims. For example, *problem-solving mediation* has developed, inter alia, in response to some of the illnesses of an adjudication-based justice system, such as the high costs of litigation both to disputants and the state, the case overload in the courts and the delays, injustice, and deteriorating trust in the justice system that follow, and the inability of the court system to offer tailor-made solutions to disputants.[44] The social ideal of problem-solving mediation is based on the assumption that if individuals solved conflicts consensually outside the courts, this would contribute to a better, more efficient, and more just society. The *transformative model* of mediation has an even more ambitious objective than the problem-solving model; it assumes that consensual cooperation between individuals in conflict can not only improve the justice system (for the benefit of both individuals and society at large), but also make people better in a moral sense,[45] and make society a better place to live in.[46] And *narrative mediation* seeks to promote social justice, and to assist individuals whose voice is not heard or is marginalized because of violence, racism, or sexism in making their voice heard.[47] Figure 3.1 illustrates the core descriptive definition of mediation and the shared professional ideals of mediation practice.

[44] See, e.g., Menkel-Meadow, Love and Schneider, *Mediation*, pp. 93–96 (discussing the advantages of mediation).

[45] See Robert A. Baruch Bush and Joseph P. Folger, *The Promise of Mediation: The Transformative Approach to Conflict*, Rev. edn. (San Francisco: Jossey-Bass, 2005), pp. 78–80 (discussing the private value of conflict transformation).

[46] See, e.g., Robert A. Baruch Bush and Joseph P. Folger, "Mediation and Social Justice: Risks and Opportunities" (2012) 27 *Ohio State Journal on Dispute Resolution* 1, 19–21 (discussing the potential of mediation to produce "macro-level social justice"). See also Bush and Folger, *The Promise of Mediation* (2005), pp. 81–82 (discussing the public value of conflict transformation).

[47] See, e.g., Winslade and Monk, *Narrative Mediation*, pp. 100–101.

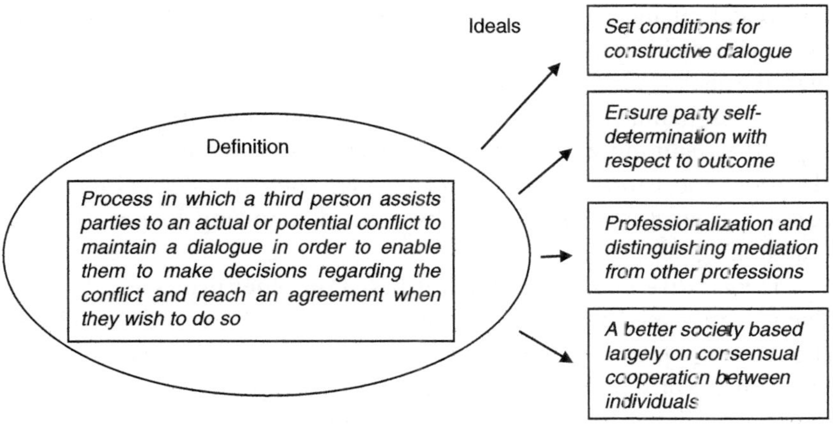

Figure 3.1: Core descriptive definition and shared professional ideals

3.4 Separate professionals ideals

Beyond the four professional ideals shared by all mediators, each mediation style has another set of professional ideals that follow from its assumptions about the nature of conflicts and its objectives.

For example, *problem-solving, court-connected* mediators aspire to *reach an agreement* resolving the dispute,[48] and to *efficiency* in terms of saving time and money both for the disputants and the court.[49] They strive, for example, to reach a quality agreement, that is, a sustainable agreement that will last and that the disputants will honor, making future resort to the court regarding the dispute unnecessary. Problem-solving mediators with a *facilitative orientation* will aspire, in addition, to allow the disputants to take *an active part* in the resolution of the conflict,[50] to assist the disputants in identifying their *needs and interests* and reaching an agreement that reflects them,[51] and to find a *creative, pie-enlarging, win-win solution* as opposed to a mere compromise that is based on rights.[52]

Transformative mediation differs from the problem-solving style in that it focuses on the process that the disputants undergo in the course of

[48] See, e.g., Wayne D. Brazil, "Should Court-Sponsored ADR Survive?" (2006) 21 *Ohio State Journal on Dispute Resolution* 241, 265–266 (referring to a "settlement obsession" of court ADR programs).

[49] Id., p. 247.

[50] See, e.g., Nancy A. Welsh, "The Thinning Vision of Self-Determination in Court-Connected Mediation: The Inevitable Price of Institutionalization?" (2001) 6 *Harvard Negotiation Law Review* 1, 16.

[51] See, e.g., Boulle and Nesic, *Mediation*, p. 28.

[52] Id., p. 29.

the mediation and does not consider a mediated agreement that resolves the dispute a vital goal of mediation. Some of its professional ideals (other than the shared ideals) include aspirations to *empower* the disputants,[53] so they can handle the conflict effectively from a position of strength; to support *recognition* shifts that help the parties to be more responsive and able to connect to the other;[54] and to "help the parties transform their conflict interaction from destructive and demonizing to positive and humanizing."[55]

The *narrative mediation* model is based on other professional ideals. The narrative mediator aspires in addition to the shared values to bring about an *engagement* of the parties[56] and "establish a relationship of trust and respect with the parties";[57] to demonstrate *reflexivity* in the practice of mediation, that is, an awareness of the implications of his actions for the parties, transparency of conduct, and take into consideration the parties' wishes;[58] to conduct the mediation with *curiosity*, for example by asking questions that are truly designed to learn what the parties think and what significance they attach to different elements in their story (as opposed to "technical" questioning designed to gather information or confirm the mediator's speculations);[59] to *deconstruct* the conflict stories of the parties[60] and point to other possible perspectives that emphasize respect and cooperation between them;[61] and to build *an alternative story* that will allow the parties to cooperate with each other.[62]

3.5 Flexible and diverse practice

Over the years common practices of mediation have been formed, documented in mediation literature, and taught in mediators' training courses. The literature on the practice of mediation provides readers with information on the practical methods that mediators use in order to achieve the process objectives, such as the stages of the process, common techniques, and tools for overcoming difficulties. It is a vast body of knowledge that has grown out of practice and remains largely

[53] See, e.g., Bush and Folger, *The Promise of Mediation* (1994), p. 85; Folger, Bush, and Della Noce, *Transformative Mediation*, p. 25.
[54] See, e.g., Bush and Folger, *The Promise of Mediation* (1994), p. 89; Folger, Bush, and Della Noce, *Transformative Mediation*, p. 25.
[55] See, e.g., Folger, Bush, and Della Noce, *Transformative Mediation*, p. 26.
[56] See Winslade and Monk, *Narrative Mediation*, p. 62. [57] See id., p. 116.
[58] See id., pp. 120–123. [59] See id., pp. 125–126. [60] See id., p. 38. [61] See id., p. 72.
[62] See id., p. 82.

unregulated by mediation associations and legislatures. Furthermore, mediation is a relatively young practice that continues to mature, develop, and change. As a result, mediators are left with extensive discretion as to choice of style, process design, and use of techniques. The variety in the methods and techniques that mediators employ to achieve the ideals of mediation is also possible because often there is no consensus within the mediation community on the right interventions or mediator moves. Yet, as some authors have suggested, despite the varieties of practice, mediators of each of the main mediation styles share some common practices.[63] For example, a typical *problem-solving mediation*[64] often begins with a joint meeting. The mediator introduces himself, gets to know the parties, and provides them with information about the process, the mediator's role and duties, and the rights of the parties participating in the process. Next, each party presents the conflict from his point of view. The mediator listens to both sides, makes sure he understands their stories, and asks questions for clarification and to elicit more information if necessary. Then, with the assistance of the mediator, the parties identify the issues in dispute and their interests. In doing so, the mediator reframes and restates the issues and some of the parties' statements in order to show them in a different, less offensive light. Next, the parties negotiate with the help of the mediator the various alternatives that are on the table, and examine various options and ideas that can move them forward. Sometimes the mediator will meet with the parties separately in order to allow them to express themselves more freely, air their feelings, and raise options for resolving the dispute. After

[63] See, e.g., Kovach, *Mediation*, p. 35 (commenting that "Authors and trainers have outlined the stages or segments of mediation. They may range from a four or five stage model to one with ten or more stages. The majority of models set forth similar basic concepts and recognize the inherent fluidity of the process"). See also Folger, Bush, and Della Noce, *Transformative Mediation*, pp. 31–50 (discussing the core practices of transformative mediation); John Winslade and Gerald Monk, *Practicing Narrative Mediation: Loosening the Grip of Conflict* (San Francisco: Jossey-Bass, 2008), pp. 1–39 (discussing the hallmarks of narrative mediation).

[64] For variations of this "basic model," see, e.g., Kovach, *Mediation*, pp. 35–37 (describing a twelve-stage model including preliminary arrangements, mediator's introduction, opening statements by parties, ventilation, information gathering, issue and interest identification, agenda setting, caucus, option generation, reality testing, bargaining and negotiation, agreement, closure). Compare Folberg and Taylor, *Mediation*, p. 32 (describing a seven-stage process including introduction, fact finding and isolation of issues, creation of options and alternatives, negotiation and decision making, clarification and writing a plan, legal review and processing, implementation, review, and revision); Moore, *The Mediation Process*, pp. 66–70 (describing twelve stages of mediation).

completing the negotiation stage, the parties may reach an agreement ending the conflict. The agreement can then be submitted to a court and be given the force of a judgment.

A *transformative mediation* is less structured.[65] The mediator invites the parties to have a conversation about their problem. He or she follows the conversation rather than directing it and responds to the ongoing interaction between the parties. He or she intervenes in order to help the parties get a better understanding of their and the other's views and options, and to support empowerment and recognition shifts. He or she does so by employing several techniques or skills: "listening; reflecting; summarizing; questioning to open doors, to invite further discussion on a subject raised by the parties; 'checking in' on what the parties want to do at a choice point in the discussion; backing out or staying out to allow for party exchange or silent party deliberation – and avoiding directive impulses."[66] The mediator's support of parties' empowerment and recognition can lead to an agreement on specific solutions, if the parties choose to have such an agreement.[67]

A *narrative mediation* will usually start with separate meetings with the parties that are aimed at enabling the parties to discuss the issues openly with the mediator, building trust, and clarifying the parties' expectations and hopes for the mediation.[68] At the first joint session the mediator explains his or her role as a facilitator of conversation, and the parties' place in making decisions on how to realize their hopes. He or she then works to create a respectful and safe relational climate that will enable the parties to engage in a constructive dialogue and decide how to go on. He or she does so using techniques such as engaging in double listening, externalizing and mapping the effects of the conflict, identifying openings to an alternative story, building stories of cooperation, and generating understanding on how to go on from the conflict situation.[69]

65 See, e.g., Bush and Folger, *The Promise of Mediation* (2005), pp. 109–112 (discussing the key elements of transformative practice).

66 Folger, Bush, and Della Noce, *Transformative Mediation*, p. 48. For a detailed discussion of the core practices of transformative mediation see id., pp. 31–49.

67 Id., p. 26.

68 See Gerald Monk and John Winslade, *When Stories Clash: Addressing Conflict with Narrative Mediation* (Taos Institute, 2013), pp. 19–22; Winslade and Monk, *Narrative Mediation*, pp. 137–140.

69 For a detailed discussion, see Winslade and Monk, *Practicing Narrative Mediation*, pp. 1–35 (discussing the hallmarks of narrative mediation); Monk and Winslade, *When Stories Clash*, pp. 25, 44–95 (discussing the techniques of narrative mediation).

One such understanding could take the form of an agreement that resolves the conflict between the parties.[70]

It seems, therefore, that mediation practice is diversified, although practitioners of each of the main styles of mediation have much in common in terms of the way they conduct mediations. However, this begs the question of the possibility of subjecting the varied styles to a single theory of ethics for mediators.

3.6 The shared normative features of mediators' conduct

A review of codes of conduct for mediators reveals *a set of mediation norms* that almost all codes of conduct for mediators in Anglo-American societies adopt in one combination or another. Most of these norms are also recognized and supported as norms of mediation by the mediation literature.[71] Without discussing the content of these norms at the moment, a list of these shared mediation norms would collectively include the following: mediator *competence*,[72] *impartiality*,[73] *conflict of*

[70] See Winslade and Monk, *Narrative Mediation*, p. 82; Winslade and Monk, *Practicing Narrative Mediation*, pp. 31–32.

[71] Compare Carrie Menkel-Meadow, "The Lawyer as Consensus Builder: Ethics for a New Practice" (2002) 70 *Tennessee Law Review* 63, 105 (suggesting core values for consensus-building facilitators that "inform the work of many who serve as professional facilitators of public participation and deliberative processes and may serve as a basis for an ethics code for this portion of the field"). See also Carrie Menkel-Meadow, "Are Cross-Cultural Ethics Standards Possible or Desirable in International Arbitration?", in Peter Gauch, Franz Werro and Pascal Pichonnaz (eds.) *Melanges en l'honneur de Pierre Tercier* (Zurich, Switzerland: Schulthess Verlag, 2008), p. 901 (arguing that despite legal cultural differences "it is still possible and desirable to formulate rules of practice, conduct and ethics for transnational legal proceedings, such as (or especially in) international commercial arbitration").

[72] See, e.g., Australian Ethical Guidelines, s. 4; Australian Practice Standards, s. 7; Family Mediation Canada Code, Article 5; Alabama Code, Standard 1(a); California Rules, Rule 3.856; Florida Rules, Rule 10.630; Illinois Standards, Standard I; Model Standards, Standard IV; North Carolina Standards, Rule I; Standards of Conduct for New York State Community Dispute Resolution Center Mediators available at www.nycourts.gov/ip/adr/Publications/Info_for_Programs/Standards_of_Conduct.pdf (NY-CDRC Standards), Standard IV; Oregon Standards, Standard V; Texas Guidelines, s. 5. See also Kovach, *Mediation*, pp. 429–435 (discussing the assurance of quality control for mediators); Ellen A. Waldman, "The Challenge of Certification: How to Ensure Mediator Competence While Preserving Diversity" (1996) 30 *University of San Francisco Law Review* 723; Bobby Marzine Harges, "Mediator Qualifications: The Trend Toward Professionalism" (1997) 1997 *Brigham Young University Law Review* 687.

[73] See, e.g., Australian Ethical Guidelines, s. 2; Australian Practice Standards, s. 5; ADR Canada Code, s. 4; Family Mediation Canada Code, Article 8; Alabama Code, Standard 5;

interest,[74] *confidentiality*,[75] party *self-determination*,[76] *integrity* of the mediator[77] and the process,[78] *fairness*,[79] and norms relating to *advertising*

California Rules, Rule 3.855; Florida Rules, Rules 10.330 and 10.620; Georgia Standards, Standard III; Illinois Standards, Standard IV; Model Standards, Standard II; North Carolina Standards, Rule II; NY-CDRC Standards, Standard II; Oregon Standards, Standard III; Texas Guidelines, s. 9; Wisconsin Association of Mediators Ethical Guidelines for the Practice of Mediation (1997) available at www.wamediators.org/publication/ethical-guidelines-practice-mediation (Wisconsin Association Guidelines), s. 4. See also Folberg and Taylor, *Mediation*, p. 247; Kovach, *Mediation*, pp. 211–213; Spencer and Brogan, *Mediation Law*, p. 156; Boulle and Nesic, *Mediation*, pp. 450–454.

74 See, e.g., Australian Ethical Guidelines, s. 3; Alabama Code, Standard 5; California Rules, Rule 3.855; Florida Rules, Rule 10.340; Model Standards, Standard III; North Carolina Standards, Rule VII; NY-CDRC Standards, Standard III; Texas Guidelines, s. 4. See also Kovach, *Mediation*, p. 212.

75 See, e.g., Australian Ethical Guidelines, s. 5; Australian Practice Standards, s. 6; ADR Canada Code, s. 6; Family Mediation Canada Code, Article 7; Alabama Code, Standard 6; California Rules, Rule 3.854; Florida Rules, Rule 10.360; Georgia Standards, Standard II; Illinois Standards, Standard II; Model Standards, Standard V; North Carolina Standards, Rule III; NY-CDRC Standards, Standard V; Oregon Standards, Standard IV; Texas Guidelines, s. 8; Wisconsin Association Guidelines, s. 5. See also Lawrence R. Freedman and Michael L. Prigoff, "Confidentiality in Mediation: The Need for Protection" (1986) 2 *Ohio State Journal on Dispute Resolution* 37; Edward F. Sherman, "Confidentiality in ADR Proceedings: Policy Issues Arising from the Texas Experience" (1997) 38 *South Texas Law Review* 541; Folberg and Taylor, *Mediation*, p. 264; Kovach, *Mediation*, pp. 262–266; Spencer and Brogan, *Mediation Law*, pp. 85–86; Boulle and Nesic, *Mediation*, p. 458.

76 See, e.g., ADR Canada Code, s. 3; Alabama Code, Standard 4; California Rules, Rule 3.853; Florida Rules, Rule 10.310; Georgia Standards, Standard I; Model Standards, Standard I; North Carolina Standards, Rule V; NY-CDRC Standards, Standard I; Oregon Standards, Standard I. See also Folberg and Taylor, *Mediation*, p. 245; Spencer and Brogan, *Mediation Law*, pp. 87–88 (discussed under voluntariness); Ellen Waldman (ed.), *Mediation Ethics: Cases and Commentaries* (San Francisco: Jossey-Bass, 2011), p. 3 (discussing disputant autonomy); Welsh, "The Thinning Vision"; Shapira, "Sharing Decision-Making."

77 Alabama Code, Standard 1(a); Florida Rules, Rule 10.620; Family Mediation Canada Code, Article 4. See also Richard M. Calkins, "Caucus Mediation-Putting Conciliation Back into the Process: The Peacemaking Approach to Resolution, Peace, and Healing" (2006) 54 *Drake Law Review* 259, 311.

78 See, e.g., North Carolina Standards, Rule VIII. See also Maureen E. Laflin, "Preserving the Integrity of Mediation Through the Adoption of Ethical Rules for Lawyer- Mediators" (2000) 14 *Notre Dame Journal of Law, Ethics and Public Policy* 479, 498; Nolan-Haley, "Informed Consent", 826.

79 See, e.g., Australian Practice Standards, s. 9; Family Mediation Canada Code, Article 9; Georgia Standards, Standard IV. See also Folberg and Taylor, *Mediation*, pp. 245–249; Boulle and Nesic, *Mediation*, pp. 455–456; Waldman, *Mediation Ethics*, pp. 4–6; Joseph B. Stulberg, "Fairness and Mediation" (1998) 13 *Ohio State Journal on Dispute Resolution* 909; Joseph B. Stulberg, "Mediation and Justice: What Standards Govern?" (2005) 6 *Cardozo Journal of Conflict Resolution* 213; Omer Shapira, "Conceptions and Perceptions of Fairness in Mediation" (2012) 54 *South Texas Law Review* 281.

and public statements,[80] *fees* and charges,[81] and the *advancement of mediation.*[82]

The codes consistently refer to a few other norms though less frequently: (a) *respect toward colleagues*, discussed in standards such as professional relationships,[83] relationships with other mediators,[84] and inter-professional relations[85]; (b) *diligence*, found in standards such as quality of the process,[86] mediation process,[87] and rules of fair practice[88]; (c) a demand for maintaining the *reputation* (sometimes referred to as the integrity) of mediators, of the mediation process, and of mediators' affiliated organizations (a court or mediation association), discussed in standards such as quality of the process,[89] impartiality,[90] and conflicts of interest standard[91]; (d) *honesty* and *compliance with authority* in mediators' relationship with the courts that nominate them;[92] and (e) *treating parties with respect*, referred to in a demeanor standard[93] and more fully developed in mediation literature.[94]

The norms that belong to this set of shared mediation norms are sometimes confusingly given other labels by the drafters of codes, when in reality the different terminology makes mediators accountable to a similar normative framework. For example, codes might include a

[80] See, e.g., Australian Ethical Guidelines, s. 8; Australian Practice Standards, s. 13; ADR Canada Code, s. 8; Family Mediation Canada Code, Article 14; Alabama Code, Standard 10; California Rules, Rule 3.858; Florida Rules, Rule 10.610; Illinois Standards, Standard VII; Model Standards, Standard VII; NY-CDRC Standards, Standard VI; Oregon Standards, Standard VIII; Wisconsin Association Guidelines, s. 7. See also Boulle and Nesic, *Mediation*, p. 459.

[81] See, e.g., Australian Ethical Guidelines, s. 9; Australian Practice Standards, s. 12; ADR Canada Code, s. 9; Family Mediation Canada Code, Article 15; Alabama Code, Standard 8; California Rules, Rule 3.859; Florida Rules, Rule 10.380; Model Standards, Standard VIII; Oregon Standards, Standard VII; Texas Guidelines, s. 3; Wisconsin Association Guidelines, s. 6. See also Boulle and Nesic, *Mediation*, p. 459.

[82] See, e.g., Alabama Code, Standard 12; Florida Rules, Rule 10.690; Model Standards, Standard IX.

[83] Illinois Standards, Standard V. [84] Florida Rules, Rule 10.660.

[85] Family Mediation Canada Code, Article 6; Australian Practice Standards, s. 4.

[86] California Rules, Rule 3.857(a); Model Standards, Standard VI.A.

[87] Alabama Code, Standard 3(c). [88] Georgia Standards, Standard V.

[89] ADR Canada Code, s. 7.4. [90] California Rules, Rule 3.855(f)(2).

[91] Model Standards, Standard III.E.

[92] For *responsibilities to courts* standards, see, e.g., Alabama Code, Standard 2; Florida Rules, Rule 10.500; Texas Guidelines, s. 15.

[93] Florida Rules, Rule 10.350.

[94] See, e.g., Stulberg, "Fairness and Mediation", 912–913; Nancy A. Welsh, "Making Deals in Court-Connected Mediation: What's Justice Got to Do with It?" (2001) 79 *Washington University Law Quarterly* 787, 820.

termination of mediation standard that in fact addresses concerns about integrity[95] and party self-determination[96] mentioned earlier; a *power issues* standard in effect addresses concerns about mediator competence, party self-determination, and integrity;[97] a *potential disqualification* standard actually addresses concerns about impartiality and conflicts of interest;[98] and a *quality of the process* standard in reality addresses a variety of concerns relating to party self-determination,[99] fairness,[100] promotion of respect among participants,[101] mediator competence,[102] integrity of the mediator and the process,[103] diligence,[104] and termination and withdrawal.[105]

The purpose of the preceding review of the codes and literature is to support a claim that there is a list of mediation norms that are repeatedly referred to as norms of conduct expected of mediators. The list of norms is consistent to a large degree, and constitutes a relatively clear public representation made by professional organizations of mediators, mediation programs, practitioners, and academics as to a set of core norms that mediators can be expected to follow. Thus, from this perspective-from-below that is based on the practice of mediation, mediators ought to be competent and impartial, disclose conflicts of interest, keep mediation communications confidential, and so on. Yet this perspective faces difficult challenges: (a) why should mediators who have *not* submitted to any code of conduct be subject to this set of norms? (b) Why should mediators who *have* submitted to a *particular* code of conduct be subject to

[95] See, e.g., Australian Ethical Guidelines, s. 6; Australian Practice Standards, s. 11; ADR Canada Code, s. 11; Family Mediation Canada Code, Article 13.

[96] Texas Guidelines, s. 13. [97] See, e.g., Australian Practice Standards, s. 4.

[98] See, e.g., ADR Canada Code, s. 5.

[99] See, e.g., ADR Canada Code, s. 7.1 and s. 7.2; California Rules, Rule 3.857(c); Model Standards, Standard VI.A.

[100] See, e.g., California Rules, Rule 3.857(b); Model Standards, Standard VI.A.

[101] See, e.g., ADR Canada Code, s. 7.2; Model Standards, Standard VI.A.

[102] See, e.g., ADR Canada Code, s. 7.3.

[103] See, e.g., ADR Canada Code, s. 7.4; California Rules, Rule 3.857(d); Model Standards, Standard VI.B and C.

[104] California Rules, Rule 3.857(a); Model Standards, Standard VI.A.

[105] California Rules, Rule 3.857(i). This list can go on and on. For example, the codes might include a *goal of process and roles* standard that addresses concerns about fairness (Family Mediation Canada Code, Article 3(1) and party self-determination (Family Mediation Canada Code, Article 3(2) and 3(3)); a *mediation process* standard that in fact addresses concerns about party self-determination (Alabama Code, Standard 3(a); Texas Guidelines, s. 6), integrity (Alabama Code, Standards 3(a) and (b)), and diligence (Alabama Code, Standard 3(c)); a *mediation practice* standard that addresses concerns relating to advancement of mediation (Oregon Standards, Standard X); etc.

norms that are not present in the particular code that applies to them? And (c) can a *shared meaning* of each of these norms be established in view of the variations in the content of these norms among the codes and literature, the vagueness of some of the terms used in connection with these norms, and the differences in mediators' styles of practice? Furthermore, the list of shared norms is based on publicly available codes of conduct that primarily address problem-solving mediators. To the best of my knowledge, there is no code that specifically addresses transformative or narrative mediators. Does the list of shared norms reflect the norms that apply to transformative and narrative mediators as well?

These challenges cannot be properly addressed by a perspective-from-below because there is no coherent theory that explains the grounds of mediator accountability and clarifies the rationale implicit in the norms that comprise the core norms of mediation practice. Such a theory, it is argued, requires a perspective-from-above and can be constructed on the basis of a role-morality theory of professional ethics.

3.7 From general ethics of roles to the ethics of mediators: the ethical relationships of mediators

Chapter 2 identified, on the basis of a theory of professional ethics, the *moral norms* that apply to professional role-holders and determine how professionals ought to behave. It argued that professionals have ethical relationships with their clients, their profession, the public, and their employers or principals. It then went on to list the norms that oblige professionals. This perspective-from-above of professional ethics can now be applied to mediators.

This chapter has established, on the basis of mediation literature and codes of conduct for mediators, a core descriptive definition of mediation and mediators' role, and a statement of their shared professional ideals. The core definition and shared ideals together comprise the *practice norms* of mediation that determine what ought to be considered the role of mediators and the practice of mediation. The integration of the moral norms of role-holding and the practice norms that determine the role of mediators produces a general theory of mediators' ethics. It requires us to explore the obligations of mediators in their relationships with mediation parties, the mediation profession, the public, and their employers or principals (when they have any). The resulting theory consists of the *ethical norms* of mediation practice that determine how mediators ought to

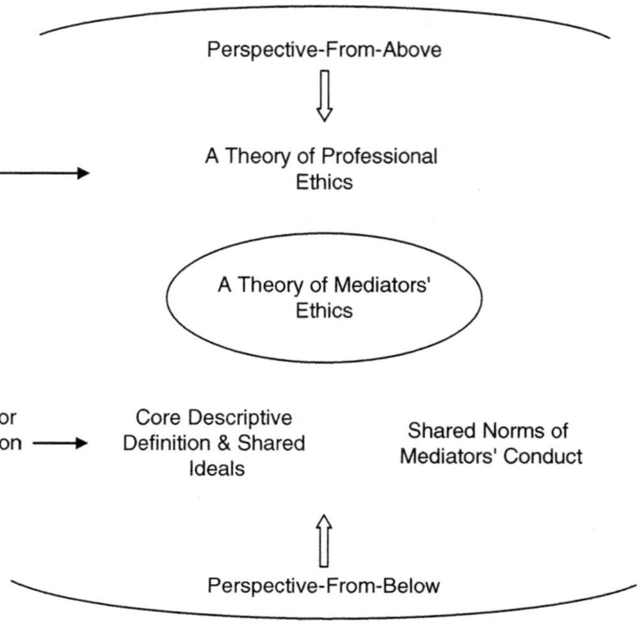

Figure 3.2: Perspectives from below and above of mediators' ethics

behave. According to this theory, *all* mediators must comply with these ethical role-holding norms in the practice of *any* style of mediation.

As we shall see, this perspective-from-above of professional ethics and the perspective-from-below that is based on the codes for mediators and mediation literature are interconnected and affect each other (see Figure 3.2). On the one hand, provisions from the codes are cited in this section in order to illustrate and support the general theory and its set of norms. On the other hand, the perspective of professional ethics is used to justify the shared norms of mediators according to the codes and literature, simplify existing codes, expose inconsistencies, externalize rationale, and fill in gaps in the codes. Later, after the *set* of mediation norms has been justified, we will turn to discussing how the *content* of these norms is to be determined and how variations in the codes, mediation literature, and mediators' style can be accounted for and addressed.

The mediator–parties relationship

Any person who calls him or herself "mediator" and the process he or she conducts "mediation," or who takes on a mediation case as a mediator, chooses by his or her conduct to limit his or her freedom of action, because the words "mediator" and "mediation" have meanings that have been determined by mediation practitioners, mediation scholars, mediation legislation, and codes of conduct for mediators. Therefore, for any person to explicitly or implicitly state "I am a mediator" constitutes a declaration or promise to the world at large that others are entitled to rely upon, be they mediation parties, colleagues, the general public, or employers or principals of the mediator. The meaning of that promise changes according to its recipients. *Mediation parties* expect mediators to honor this promise with respect to conduct that might affect *them*. They expect mediators to *act in accordance with the common standards of the field of mediation and those standards which follow from the nature and definition of the role of mediators* to the extent they are relevant to the provision of mediation services to parties. Here the perspective-from-below that is based on the codes for mediators and mediation literature becomes relevant for identifying the norms of mediation. For example, it can be established that all mediators are expected to act impartially, with competence, and to respect the parties' right to self-determination because, as we have seen, these standards are deeply grounded in mediation practice, literature, and legislation.

The obligations of mediators are also affected by the nature of their relationship with the parties. The relationship between mediators and mediation parties places mediators in a position of *power* and parties in a position of *dependence*.[106] The position of power is the result of, inter alia, the information and expertise that are in the mediator's possession, while the parties' dependency follows from, inter alia, the fact that the parties are asking the mediator to assist them in doing what they cannot do themselves. The parties need the mediator to help them communicate effectively, negotiate constructively, reach understandings, and otherwise assist them in doing what they have been unsuccessful in doing by themselves or with the help of their representatives prior to the mediation. The power that mediators have in their relationship with the parties and their influence on the parties' affairs establish ethical responsibility;[107] mediation parties rely on mediators to act in a manner that does not abuse the mediators' power or the parties' dependence and reliance. It is a relationship of *trust* that codes of conduct for mediators and mediation scholars expressly acknowledge. The

106 See generally Omer Shapira, "Exploring the Concept of Power in Mediation: Mediators' Sources of Power and Influence Tactics" (2009) 24 *Ohio State Journal on Dispute Resolution* 535.

107 On the connection between power and responsibility, see Chapter 2, Section 2.2.2.

Alabama Code of Ethics for Mediators (Alabama Code), for example, states that "[a] mediator occupies a position of trust with respect to the parties,"[108] and similarly the *Florida Rules for Certified and Court-Appointed Mediators* (Florida Rules) declare that "[a] mediator holds a position of trust."[109] Some scholars agree with these statements. Jacqueline M. Nolan-Haley, for example, argued that "[m]ediators . . . are fiduciaries. They occupy a position of trust with disputing parties."[110] Professors Arthur Chaykin and Rebekah Ryan Clark also thought that mediators owe fiduciary duties to the parties and considered the possible effect of these duties on mediators' legal liability.[111] Professor Chaykin argued that "[t]rust is such an essential element of the mediator's work, it could be argued, that mediators generally should be held to the virtually per se rule applied to trustees and attorneys. Like attorneys, mediators agree to act for the benefit of others; like trustees, they provide advice, guidance, and expertise on affairs of grave importance to the parties."[112] Professor Michael Moffitt on the other hand thought it less probable that courts would view the mediator–parties relationship as a fiduciary one for the purpose of legal sanctioning.[113] If we embark on an ethical analysis of the mediator–parties relationship as opposed to a legal one, then ethically speaking the relationship of trust establishes a legitimate expectation of mediators to be *trustworthy*, that is, to conduct themselves in a way that does not violate the parties' trust. A relationship of trust, as we saw in Chapter 2, requires professionals, and for that purpose mediators as well, to be *competent*, disclose *conflicts of interest*, respect the parties' autonomy or *self-determination*, exhibit professional *integrity*, act *impartially* and *diligently*, treat the parties with *respect, dignity*, and *honesty*, maintain *confidentiality*, and act *fairly*.

The mediator–profession relationship

Mediation is a profession, or at least a field of professional activity on its way to becoming a profession.[114] The term "mediation profession" is an

108 Alabama Code, Standard 8. 109 Florida Rules, Rule 10.380(a).

110 Nolan-Haley, "Informed Consent", 825. See also id., 826 ("the mediator has a special fiduciary relationship with both parties to a dispute").

111 See, e.g., Chaykin, "Mediator Liability", 732; Rebekah Ryan Clark, "Writing on the Wall: The Potential Liability of Mediators as Fiduciaries" (2006) 4 *Brigham Young University Law Review* 1033, 1059–1060.

112 Chaykin, "Mediator Liability", 745.

113 See, e.g., Michael Moffitt, "Suing Mediators" (2003) 83 *Boston University Law Review* 147, 168.

114 See Chapter 1, Section 1.1.3.

abstract one that includes (a) mediation practitioners, (b) mediation institutions and organizations working in the field, representing mediators, and providing mediation services, and (c) the mediation process as a social institution. Mediators' codes of conduct acknowledge the obligations of mediators to their profession. For example, the *Florida Rules* impose on mediators responsibility to the mediation profession[115] and to the process;[116] the *Professional Standards of Practice for Mediators* adopted by the Mediation Council of Illinois (Illinois Standards) state that "[t]he mediator's commitment shall be to the participants and the process."[117] The *Code of Professional Conduct for Labor Mediators* (Code of Labor Mediators) provides that "[mediators] must be aware that their duties and obligations relate to ... every other mediator,"[118] and the *Australian National Mediator Accreditation Standards: Practice Standards* (Australian Practice Standards) provide that "the Practice Standards are intended to govern the relationship of mediators with ... their professional colleagues."[119] These codes are correct in assigning to mediators a responsibility to the profession. From the perspective of professional ethics, when a person represents him or herself as a mediator and conducts mediations he or she voluntarily associates him or herself with the professional community of mediators and identifies him or herself with the mediation profession. As a result, that person enjoys benefits that accrue due to the linkage with the mediation community such as status, reputation, and potential earnings. The group of mediators follows certain standards, and if that person does not follow them he or she enjoys an unfair advantage. Therefore, on the basis of *fairness* considerations, the mediation profession legitimately expects any person who chooses to engage in mediation to act "as mediator" and *follow all the standards applicable to mediators.*[120]

In addition, a person who identifies him or herself with the mediation profession is perceived by the public as a representative of the profession and his or her actions potentially affect the attitude of the public to the mediation profession. That person must realize that his or her behavior could have both positive and negative impact on the social status and

[115] Florida Rules, Rule 10.600. [116] Florida Rules, Rule 10.400.

[117] Illinois Standards, Definition s. E.

[118] Code of Professional Conduct for Labor Mediators, the Federal Mediation and Conciliation Service of the United States and the Association of Labor Mediation Agencies available at ethics.iit.edu/ecodes/node/3410 (Code of Labor Mediators), Preamble.

[119] Australian Practice Standards, s. 1(1). [120] See generally Chapter 2, Section 2.3.2.

reputation of the mediation profession and the community of mediators. Therefore, the decision of a person to associate him or herself with the mediation profession establishes a legitimate expectation that he or she will *refrain from conduct that could harm the legitimate interests of the mediation profession and maintain the profession's standing and public trust in the profession.* For example, The *Standards of Practice for California Mediators* adopted by the California Dispute Resolution Council (CDRC) (California-CDRC Standards) provide that "[e]very mediator bears the responsibility of conducting mediations in a manner that instills confidence in the process."[121] The North Carolina *Revised Standards of Professional Conduct for Mediators* adopted by the Supreme Court of North Carolina (North Carolina Standards) provide that "mediation must be built upon public understanding and confidence. Persons serving as mediators are responsible ... to conduct themselves in a manner that will merit that confidence."[122] And *Georgia Ethical Standards for Mediators* (Georgia Standards) provide that "[m]ediators have an obligation to the integrity of the mediation process."[123]

The duties of mediators to avoid harming the profession, preserve its standing, and maintain public trust in the profession are supported by considerations of promise keeping, reciprocity, and fairness: joining the community of mediators could be considered as an implied promise not to injure the group of professionals (and undermining the profession's standing and the public's trust in it is an injury to the group); the benefits that mediators derive from the existence of the professional group require them to reciprocate by refraining from harming the group; and mediators should avoid the unfair advantage embedded in a situation in which they allow themselves to act in ways that undermine public trust in the profession, while their colleagues restrict their freedom of action for the benefit of the group in order to instill public confidence in the profession.[124] From the perspective of professional ethics, discussed in Chapter 2, mediators are expected to avoid professional conduct that harms the profession and undermines public trust, *treat colleagues, professional organizations, and other people or bodies with honesty and respect*, and they are encouraged to *help the profession to fulfill its social role.*

121 The California Dispute Resolution Council (CDRC) Standards of Practice for California Mediators available at www.cdrc.net/adr-practice/mediator-standards/ (California-CDRC Standards), Preamble.

122 North Carolina Standards, Preamble. See also California Rules, Rule 3.850.

123 Georgia Standards, Standard V.

124 See generally Chapter 2, Section 2.3.2.

The mediator–public relationship

Codes of conduct for mediators acknowledge that mediators have obligations toward the public, as well as duties to the parties and the mediation profession. For example, The *Code of Labor Mediators* provides that "[mediators] must be aware that their duties and obligations relate to . . . the general public."[125] The *Australian Practice Standards* provide that "[t]he Practice Standards are intended to govern the relationship of mediators with . . . the general public."[126] The *California Rules of Conduct for Mediators in Court-Connected Mediation Programs for Civil Cases* (California Rules) provide that "[m]ediators in court-connected programs are responsible to . . . the public,"[127] and the *North Carolina Standards* provide that "[p]ersons serving as mediators are responsible to . . . the public."[128] What justifies these statements?

From the perspective of professional ethics, when a person performs the role of mediator he enjoys benefits that are associated with the role, such as social status resulting from the professional status, income, opportunities, and special legal protections (for example, confidentiality privilege). The mediator is expected in return to *reciprocate* and conduct himself in a manner that benefits society, or at least *does not harm its interests.*[129]

Although it is easier to support this argument with respect to court-connected mediators who are paid for their services and sometimes enjoy a certain degree of legal immunity from litigation,[130] I think that mediators who are not court-mediators and are unpaid still share some benefits, either directly or indirectly, as an outcome of their membership in the community of mediators. For example, the good reputation of court-connected mediators improves the reputation and attractiveness of mediation practice in general, thus contributing to the social status and earning potential of non-court mediators as well.

Furthermore, mediators, like other professionals, are in a position of *power and social influence*, resulting from their knowledge, expertise, and the social acquiescence to the provision of professional services by them. Their decisions have an impact on the lives of people other than those

125 Code of Labor Mediators, Preamble. 126 Australian Practice Standards, s. 1(1).
127 California Rules, Rule 3.850(a). 128 North Carolina Standards, Preamble.
129 See Chapter 2, Section 2.4.2.
130 See, e.g., Arthur A. Chaykin, "The Liabilities and Immunities of Mediators: A Hostile Environment for Model Legislation" (1986) 2 *Ohio State Journal on Dispute Resolution* 47, 53 note 28.

participating in mediations. Here, too, it is easier to establish this claim with respect to court-connected mediators who are considered sometimes as the long arm of the court, thus performing a public role,[131] but in my view it applies to other mediators as well. For example, mediated agreements in family disputes affect the children of mediation parties; the outcome of a mediation between two homeowners can affect other homeowners in a condominium; and a mediation between a manufacturer and consumer over an alleged defective product, or between a polluting factory and an alleged victim, affects broad social interests such as the rule of law, and public health and safety. As we have seen, those who are in a position of power and influence are expected to act out of responsibility for those who may be affected by their conduct.[132] Mediators, therefore, must conduct mediations in a manner that is *worthy of the public's trust, promotes the public good, and avoids harming important social interests.*

Maintaining and preserving the rule of law and the rules of critical morality are important social interests,[133] and therefore mediators must avoid harming them while conducting mediations. In addition, there is a public interest in the maintenance and preservation of the institution of mediation, so that disputes are resolved by agreement, social harmony is promoted, and public funds are saved. Thus mediators must conduct mediations in a manner that will earn the public's trust and attract people to using mediation to resolve conflicts; and they must refrain from conducting mediations in ways that might harm this social interest, that is, they must maintain the profession's standing in order to realize its social objective. Harming the profession, therefore, is not only a breach of duty to the profession: when the breach is serious enough to undermine public confidence in the profession it is also a breach of duty toward the public.

From the perspective of professional ethics discussed in Chapter 2, mediators have three general ethical duties toward the public: a duty to *maintain the standing of the mediation profession*, a duty to *follow the*

131 See, e.g., Elad Finkelstein and Shahar Lifshitz, "Bargaining in the Shadow of the Mediator: A Communitarian Theory of Post-Mediation Contracts" (2010) 25 *Ohio State Journal on Dispute Resolution* 667, 682–684; Judith L Maute, "Mediator Accountability: Responding to Fairness Concerns" (1990) 1990 *Journal of Dispute Resolution* 347, 348, 358.

132 See Chapter 2, Section 2.4.2.

133 See, e.g., Hart, *Concept of Law*, pp. 86–87, 169–170 (arguing that moral rules and legal rules reflect fundamental ground rules that apply to all members of society).

rules of law and critical morality in the course of practice, and a duty *to prevent process abuse or substantive defects in the process.*

The mediator–employer/principal relationship

Mediators sometimes provide mediation services as employees of another mediator, a private sector mediation company, a court, or a public body. Others are not employed but act on behalf of another with whom they have a close relationship that could be described (for lack of an exact term) as a type of agency relationship in an ethical sense. For example, community mediation centers, where mediators volunteer and provide mediation services to members of the community on behalf of the center, or court programs that mediators are affiliated with and provide mediation services in court-referred cases could be considered as mediators' principals. In these cases the mediation centers or courts have put the mediators in the position of mediation services suppliers, and the services they supply are closely connected with the centers or the courts as well as with the mediators. As a result, the mediators' conduct affects their status, reputation, economic interests (for example, the willingness of potential clients to seek mediation for fee), and legal interests (for example, liability for damages allegedly caused by the mediators in the course of practice). This type of relationship establishes a legitimate expectation that mediators act in a manner that is *worthy of the trust* of their employers or principals and that they *comply with their instructions.*[134]

Indeed, some codes of conduct for mediators expressly refer to the obligations of mediators to bodies with which they have connections regarding the provision of mediation services. For example, the *Code of Labor Mediators* provides that "[mediators] must be aware that their duties and obligations relate ... to the agencies which administer the practice of mediation"[135] and that "[t]he mediator should constantly bear in mind that he and his work are not judged solely on an individual basis but that he is also judged as a representative of his agency. Any improper conduct or professional shortcoming, therefore, reflects not only on the individual mediator but upon his employer."[136] Moreover, codes of conduct for mediators in court-connected programs tend to refer explicitly to mediators' responsibility to the court. For example, The *Australian Practice*

134 See Chapter 2, Section 2.5.2.

135 See, e.g., Code of Labor Mediators, Preamble.

136 Id., s. 3.

Standards provide that "[t]he Practice Standards are intended to govern the relationship of mediators with the … courts."[137] The *Florida Rules* provides in a rule entitled "Mediator's Responsibility to the Courts" that "[a] mediator is accountable to the referring court."[138] The *California Rules* provide that "[m]ediators in court-connected programs are responsible … to the courts."[139] And so do the *North Carolina Standards*.[140] These obligations are quite similar to the obligations mediators owe mediation parties, and their content will be discussed in Chapter 14.

3.8 The norms of mediators' ethics

At this point a set of mediation norms that apply to mediators has been established. The set of norms is compatible with both a perspective-from-below that reflects the collective approach of codes of conduct for mediators and mediation literature on the duties of mediators, and a perspective-from-above that reflects a professional ethics approach to the duties of professionals in general. The set of norms includes the following: Competence, Conflicts of Interest, Party Self-determination, Professional Integrity, Impartiality, Diligence, Respect and Dignity, Honesty, Confidentiality, Fairness, Maintaining the Profession's Standing and Public Trust in the Profession, Advancement of the Profession, Advertising and Solicitation, Fees, and Obligations to Employers and Principals. All the norms have a basis in codes of conduct for mediators and mediation literature. Three of the norms – Advertising and Solicitation, Fees, and Obligations to Employers and Principals – are not genuine or primary norms from the perspective of professional ethics, but secondary or contingent. They are not *necessarily* associated with holding a role – one can hold a role without advertising, soliciting, charging fees, or being employed – and their content is to a large extent simply an application of the primary norms to the relevant factual situations, for example exhibiting Honesty in advertising, soliciting, charging fees, or in the relationship with an employer or principal; maintaining Impartiality in advertising, soliciting, charging fees, or in the relationship with an employer or principal; and so on. These norms have been included in the set of mediation norms because they appear in codes of conduct for mediators and because they are not incompatible with a theory of professional ethics.

[137] Australian Practice Standards, s. 1(1). [138] Florida Rules, Rule 10.500.
[139] California Rules, Rule 3.850(a). [140] North Carolina Standards, Preamble.

The resulting theory of mediators' ethics applies to all mediators in Anglo-American societies regardless of style or type of case, even in the absence of an applicable code of conduct, because (a) its norms are attached to the *role* of mediators, and the norms are based on the legitimate expectations of mediation parties, the profession, the public, and employers and principals that mediators act in certain ways, and (b) the norms are supported by codes of conduct for mediators and mediation literature in Anglo-American societies. Though the codes and literature have a dominant problem-solving orientation, in the absence of any codes of conduct that focus exclusively on mediators of other styles and of any literature that offers an alternative set of norms applicable to mediators of other styles, it is argued that the proposed set of norms applies to transformative and narrative mediators as well as to problem-solving mediators.[141] When a mediator *is* subject to a code of conduct, the theory provides an *additional* source for norms that would have to be considered in the process of establishing the extent of that mediator's responsibility.[142]

3.9 The meaning of the norms: understanding the meaning of mediators' ethical duties and resolving tensions between duties

After the *set* of norms that apply to mediators has been established, the *content and meaning* of these norms has to be addressed and ascertained. What does mediator competence mean? When can it be said that a mediator has satisfied the norm of impartiality? What does a mediation process respecting party self-determination look like? Does a shared meaning of the norms for all styles of mediation exist? Part II explores the meaning of mediators' duties with the assistance of several sources of meaning.

(a) Definition considerations

The core descriptive definition of mediation and mediators' role and the shared professional values of mediators shape the meaning of the norms

[141] Compare Australian Practice Standards, s. 1(4) ("These Practice Standards set out minimum practice requirements and recognise that some mediators who practise in particular areas or with particular models may choose to develop or comply with additional standards or requirements").

[142] On the ethical status of the code's provisions, see Chapter 1, Section 1.2.3.2 (noting that a provision in a code might fail to establish an ethical duty if it is inconsistent with (a) the definition and nature of the role, or (b) morality).

of mediation. For example, mediators by definition have more than one client per case, which means that they have to be worthy of the trust of several clients with conflicting interests at the same time. This affects the extent of legitimate interactions between mediators and their clients, reflected in the content of mediation norms such as mediator impartiality (for example, a duty not to favor one client's case over another's), confidentiality (for example, a duty to keep information disclosed by one client confidential vis-à-vis other clients in the same case), and conflicts of interest (for example, a duty to disclose prior relationships with any of the clients in the case). Another example of the implications of the core definition on the meaning of mediation norms is the definition's component stating that the outcome of the process is determined by the parties. This obviously shapes the meaning of the norm of party self-determination (for example, distinguishing the process from arbitration and adjudication), but also the norm of integrity (for example, affecting mediators' discretion and decision-making) and the norm of advertising and public statements (for example, prohibiting the mediator from promising a certain result).

The core definition shapes the *minimum* requirements for mediation practice. For example, all mediators must be competent to conduct an effective mediation. Yet these requirements may be expanded with the expansion of mediators' role. For example, the content of the norm of mediator competency may change with the style of mediation: while a problem-solving mediator needs to know how to work with interests, a transformative mediator must be able to support empowerment and recognition shifts, and a narrative mediator must be able to identify and elaborate unique outcomes. However, the effect of mediation style or type of case on the content of mediation norms should not be exaggerated. Clearly, norms such as conflicts of interest, confidentiality, respect and dignity, and honesty are hardly affected by these factors, and, as the next chapters show, so are more hotly debated concepts in mediation discourse such as impartiality and party self-determination.

(b) Role considerations

Role-morality is another source of meaning that affects the content of mediation norms. Role-morality suggests that mediators have ethical relationships with the parties, the profession, the public, or an employer or principal. The process of ascertaining the content and meaning of the ethical norms of mediation practice is therefore one of *negotiation and balancing* between the *different* legitimate expectations of the *various groups* that have an ethical relationship with the mediator with respect to each norm, with the aim of allowing these expectations to exist harmoniously side by side. For example, the content and meaning of the duty relating to conflicts of interest requires an articulation of the accumulative expectations of the parties, the profession, the public, and employers or principals. This is why ethical obligations are relative, not absolute: they must satisfy at the same time the legitimate expectations of different groups.

It is helpful to consider ethical duties as consisting of *layers* that reflect the legitimate expectations of the various groups (see Figure 3.3). The most basic layer of mediators' duties is their duties to the parties, who are the main recipients of the professional service that mediators provide. However, this is only the starting point for understanding the obligations of mediators. The content of mediators' duties is affected by their duties to the other groups, and the guiding principle for mediators is to find that interpretation or understanding of their obligations toward the parties that enables them to comply with their obligations toward the other groups.

For example, the ethical duty of mediators to be competent to provide mediation services to mediation parties reflects the legitimate expectation of parties that mediators be worthy of their trust. But in addition, this duty must also reflect the expectations of the profession, the public, and employers or principals that mediators be competent. It follows that even where parties are satisfied with the qualifications and skills of the mediator in their case, this might not suffice, because the level of competence of that mediator in that particular case could be unsatisfactory from the point of view of the profession, the public, or the mediator's employer or principal. If such a mediator were to conduct the mediation he or she could jeopardize the profession's standing, the reputation of a court with which the mediator has been closely working, and the public's trust in it.[143]

It is argued that in the vast majority of cases the legitimate expectations of the various groups *can be reconciled*, that is, a way can be found that allows for acting in a way that does not violate a duty toward any of the groups. For example, an incompetent mediator from the profession's or public's perspective can overcome his incompetence by collaborating with an experienced, competent mediator who will mediate the case

[143] See Chapter 5, Section 5.3.

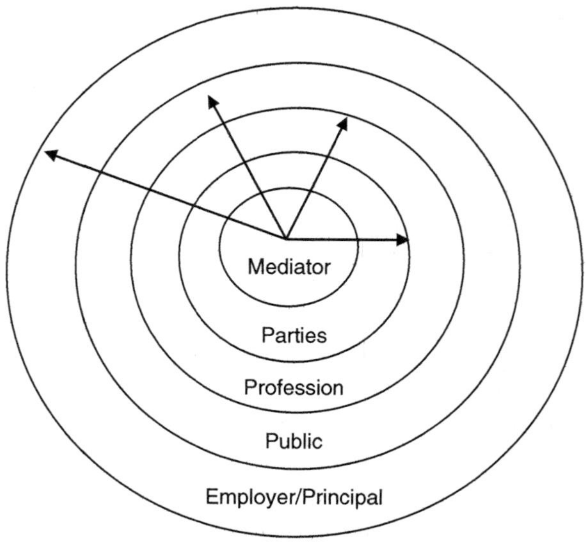

Figure 3.3: The layers of meaning of mediator duties

with him. In the rare events in which a mediator is unable to fulfill his or her obligations toward all the groups, I would argue that he or she must *refrain from conducting the mediation*, that is, refuse to take the case or withdraw or terminate the mediation if the mediation has already started. This follows from the premise that there is no hierarchy among the ethical duties of mediators,[144] that is, no duty has a prima facie priority over another. Having said that, it should be noted that in exceptional cases the discontinuation of mediation will not be sufficient to relieve the mediator of his ethical duties, for example in circumstances in which the mediator finds that one party intends to cause serious bodily injury to a person who is not a participant in the mediation. The mediator is legally and morally obligated to warn that person, although doing so would be a violation of his or her duty of confidentiality vis-à-vis the parties to the mediation.[145]

[144] See, e.g., Model Standards, Note on Construction ("These Standards are to be read and construed in their entirety. There is no priority significance attached to the sequence in which the Standards appear"). See also Model Standards Reporter's Notes, available at moritzlaw.osu.edu/programs/adr/msoc/pdf/reportersnotes-092005final.pdf, p. 7 ("The Standards are to be read and construed in their entirety. The interpretative principle that mandates that each Standard be read and interpreted in such a manner as to promote consistency with all other Standards is the presumed operative principle guiding the drafting of the Model Standards").

[145] See Chapter 10, Section 10.4.4.1.

In these rare cases, despite the absence of a hierarchy among ethical obligations, *assigning more weight* to one duty over another could be justified. The typical characteristics of such cases are the following: (a) the mediator is under a moral or legal obligation to take a certain action, (b) he or she cannot morally justify failure to take that action, (c) as a result of that action he or she violates a duty towards one of the groups of reference with whom he or she has an ethical relationship, and (d) terminating the mediation would not prevent the violation. The mediator in these cases must carry out the violating action in a way that will *minimize* as far as possible the harm resulting from the violation.[146]

The possibility of mediating between the conflicting obligations should not be neglected even in these situations. For example, if the mediator discusses the threat with the party who had made it and becomes convinced that the threat is not real, the duty to warn will not stand; and if he or she considers the threat to be credible but succeeds in obtaining the consent of the threatening party to waive confidentiality and talk with the threatened person or invite him or her to participate in the mediation, the violation of duty could be prevented altogether.

(c) The content and meaning mediation norms are given in codes of conduct for mediators and mediation literature

The core descriptive definition of mediation and of the role of mediators and the expectations that can be attached to that role on the basis of role-morality are too thin to support a comprehensive summary of the content of the norms of mediation. The expectations of parties and the public at large that mediators behave in certain ways have been shaped by institutional acts – mediation legislation and codes of conduct for mediators – and by mediation literature. These sources can provide *additional* meaning beyond the content of the norms that can be ascertained using the core definition and its interaction with the moral norms of role-holding. As I have observed, the codes and literature on mediation ethics are predominantly problem-solving-oriented, with esoteric discussion of its application to other styles of mediation. As a result, the contribution of these sources to a transformative or narrative mediators' ethics is very limited. Current codes of conduct and mediation literature do provide

146 See, e.g., Gert, *Common Morality*, p. 69 (suggesting that actions that cause less harm or would not involve a violation of a moral rule are morally preferable to actions that cause harm or violate moral rules).

valuable (though sometimes inconsistent) information on the possible meaning of party self-determination (for example, its components and extent), impartiality (for example, its manifestations), conflicts of interest (for example, types of conflicts and on the circumstances for disclosure), fees (for example, what are considered legitimate fee arrangements), and on the meaning of advancing mediation and the profession of mediation. From the perspective of professional ethics, the information in these resources is valuable so long as it is not inconsistent with the moral norms of the role of mediators, in line with the core definition of mediation. In other words, it is valuable as long as the codes and literature expand and elaborate on rather than diminish the ethical responsibility of mediators.

(d) Literature on moral philosophy and ethics in other professional fields

Mediators' ethics is part of moral philosophy in general and professional ethics or morality of roles in particular. Therefore, turning to philosophy literature on concepts such as autonomy, self-determination, impartiality, respect and dignity, and integrity could be helpful. Insight can also be gained from the experience of other professional fields that grapple with the definition of concepts that are relevant to professionals other than mediators such as informed consent, conflicts of interest, and confidentiality. This enquiry must be carried out with caution, because the unique features of particular roles inform the content of the norms that apply to each role. However, it can be helpful in pointing out and exploring essential elements in the definition of concepts, for example, the components of capacity and voluntariness in autonomy or self-determination, and possible definitions of conflicts of interest.

(e) Fairness considerations: applying a substantive, realist perspective of fairness to the interpretation of mediation norms

Mediation norms could have more than one meaning, and a choice has to be made between competing interpretations. In such cases I favor a substantive-realist-purposive approach to finding meaning over a formal approach. This approach has been described in Chapter 2 as a substantive fairness perspective that is committed to searching for a true, reality-based meaning of norms that is compatible with the spirit and purpose of the norm and of mediation as social practice. Thus, for example, where the core definition of mediation and mediators' role and codes of conduct for mediators support both a wide and narrow interpretation of party self-determination, the substantive-realist approach would favor the wider interpretation,[147] and where impartiality can be interpreted both as formal equality and as substantive equality the latter would prevail.[148]

3.10 A *proposed model code of conduct for mediators*

The search for meaning for the set of mediation norms produces a *Proposed Model Code of Conduct for Mediators* at the end of the book. The *Proposed Code* represents my reasoned understanding of the ethical norms that apply to all mediators in Anglo-American societies based on a comprehensive theory of mediators' ethics. It may be useful first and foremost to mediators who are not subject to a formal code of conduct and need guidance. But what about mediators, mediator organizations, legislators, and scholars who think otherwise and adopt or advocate norms that differ from the *Proposed Code*? I consider the *Proposed Code* as laying down minimum requirements applicable to all mediators. However, as a practical matter I realize that the content and meaning of the duties of a *particular* mediator may depart from the *Proposed Code* in several ways.

(a) One possibility is that an individual mediator has made promises and statements regarding his or her role in a particular mediation process that *enhance* his or her ethical responsibility relative to the *Proposed Code*. This is a matter of personal choice that raises no difficulty. For example, if a mediator practices evaluative mediation or narrative mediation he or she must be competent to provide these types of services that go beyond the core definition of mediation.
(b) Another possibility is that an enhanced responsibility – for example, a sweeping confidentiality duty with no exceptions – is imposed by mediation legislation or a binding code of conduct. This scenario differs from the first in that the enhanced responsibility is not a matter of personal choice.
(c) Yet another possibility is that either the individual mediator or the binding code make statements or include provisions that *diminish* the ethical responsibility of mediators relative to the *Proposed Code*,

147 See Chapter 4, Section 4.2.2. 148 See Chapter 7, Section 7.3.4.

for example by authorizing mediators to make extensive disclosures from the mediation room or restrict the parties' right to self-determination to a large extent.

In the event of scenarios (b) and (c) I would suggest the following. First, that the mediator, or the code or legislation drafters, should be able to *justify* their decision on the basis of a competing theory of mediators' ethics. The *Proposed Code* would provide them with resources for *thinking critically* about their decision, and they should be able to give *good reasons* for departing from it. And second, as codes of conduct for mediators are often vague, abstract, and have gaps, the *Proposed Code* may be useful for complementing existing codes by offering tools for interpreting such codes in a manner consistent as far as possible with the *Proposed Code* and for filling in lacunae in codes in light of the *Proposed Code.*

3.11 A road map for the next chapters

The rest of Part II examines in detail the standards of ethics that apply to mediators. Chapters 4–11 explore the duties of mediators in the order they have been presented when discussing the duties of professionals toward clients in Chapter 2, with two exceptions: party self-determination and impartiality. The duty to respect party self-determination has a special place in the context of mediation and its wide influence on the interpretation of other mediator duties warrants its discussion first in Chapter 4. Chapter 5 follows with a focus on mediator Competence and Chapter 6 on Conflict of Interest. Chapter 7 then discusses Mediator Impartiality because of the special connection between conflicts of interest and mediator impartiality in the context of mediation. Chapter 8 focuses on Professional Integrity, Chapter 9 on Diligence, Respect and Dignity, and Honesty, Chapter 10 on Confidentiality, and Chapter 11 on Fairness. As explained, these duties should not be solely understood or classified as "duties toward parties" because their content is shaped by the duties of mediators toward the profession of mediation, the public, and possibly employers and principals. The most notable duties toward the profession and the public are discussed in Chapter 12, which focuses on Maintaining the Profession's Standing and Public Trust in the Profession, and on the ideal of Advancement of the Profession. Duties toward the profession and the public are also discussed in the earlier chapters. Chapter 8 on Professional Integrity discusses mediators' duty to

Table 3.1 *The duties of mediators and corresponding standards*

Ch.	Standard	Duties to Parties	Duties to the Profession	Duties to the Public	Duties to Employers and Principals	Other Duties
4	Party Self-determination	Respect Party Self-determination				
5	Competence	Competence				
6	Conflict of Interest	Disclosure of Conflicts of Interest				
7	Impartiality	Act Impartially				
8	Professional Integrity	Exhibit Professional Integrity		Prevent Process Abuse or Substantial Defects in the Process		
	Diligence	Act Diligently				
9	Respect and Dignity	Treat Parties with Respect and Dignity	Treat Colleagues, Professional Organizations, and			

Table 3.1 (*cont.*)

Ch.	Standard	Duties to Parties	Duties to the Profession	Duties to the Public	Duties to Employers and Principals	Other Duties
			other People or Bodies with Respect			
	Honesty	Act Honestly	Treat Colleagues, Professional Organizations, and other People or Bodies with Honesty			
10	Confidentiality	Maintain Confidentiality				
11	Fairness	Act Fairly (toward Parties)	Act Fairly (toward Colleagues)	Act Fairly (toward the public) (Follow the Rules of Law and Critical Morality in the Course of Practice)		
12	Maintaining the Profession's Standing		Maintain the Profession's Standing and Public Trust in the Profession	Maintain the Profession's Standing and Public Trust in the Profession		

	Advancement of the Profession	Help the Profession in Fulfilling its Social Role (Ideal)		
13	Advertising and Solicitation			Advertising and Solicitation
	Fees			Fees
14	Obligations to Employers and Principals		Obligations to Employers and Principals	

the public to Prevent Process Abuse or Substantial Defects in the Process; Chapter 9 on Diligence, Respect and Dignity, and Honesty discusses mediators' duties to Treat Colleagues, Professional Organizations, and other People or Bodies with Respect and Honesty; and Chapter 11 on Fairness discusses mediators' duty of fairness toward their colleagues, and their duty to the public to Follow the Rules of Law and Critical Morality in the Course of Practice. These duties toward the profession and the public are not discussed in separate chapters because they are intertwined with the duties mediators have toward the parties. Chapter 13 discusses Advertising and Solicitation, and Fees. These duties are separate from the other duties because they do not derive directly from the ethical relationships of mediators and the core definition of their role. Instead they express the application of other standards such as Honesty, Impartiality, and Maintaining the Profession's Standing to common professional practices in which mediators engage, that is, advertising, solicitation, and charging fees. Similarly, the Obligations to Employers and Principals are left to Chapter 14 because they are not general ethical duties that apply to all mediators, but contingent on an employment relationship or a type of agency that some but not all mediators are in. Table 3.1 highlights the content of the chapters and the overlap between the duties.

4

Party self-determination

4.1 Introduction

It has been shown in the first part of this book that anyone who occupies a professional role must respect, as part of their duty to be worthy of their clients' trust, a number of ethical standards that reflect the legitimate expectations of their clients, including their right to self-determination. Our current goal is to examine what the meaning of self-determination is in the context of *mediation*. The underlying assumption is that the meaning of self-determination is not fixed, but changes with the type of professional activity in question because the role definition and nature of the provided services vary, and therefore clients' legitimate expectations of professionals vary as well. Self-determination in the context of mediation is not the same, then, as it is in the context of other professional–client relationships such as lawyer–client or doctor–patient.

The self-determination of mediation parties is presented as a fundamental principle of mediation both in codes of conduct for mediators and in the mediation literature. One Advisory Committee Comment to the *California Rules*, for example, states that "[v]oluntary participation and self-determination are fundamental principles of mediation";[1] the *Georgia Standards* consider the self-determination of the parties to be "a hallmark of mediation";[2] and the Oregon Mediation Association *Core Standards of Mediation Practice* (Oregon Standards) provide that "[s]elf-determination is a fundamental principle of mediation."[3] Mediation scholars express similar views. Rene L. Rimelspach, for example, argued that "[i]t is understood that a basic tenet of mediation is that the parties are autonomous and should have the ability to devise their own agreement";[4] and Laura E. Weidner, in her discussion of the *Model Standards*

[1] California Rules, Advisory Committee Comment to Rule 3.853.

[2] Georgia Standards, Standard I. [3] Oregon Standards, Standard I.

[4] See Rene L. Rimelspach, "Mediating Family Disputes in a World with Domestic Violence: How to Devise a Safe and Effective Court-Connected Mediation Program" (2001) 17 *Ohio State Journal on Dispute Resolution* 95, 109.

of Conduct for Mediators (2005) (Model Standards), noted "the overarching importance of party self-determination" in mediation.[5]

Notwithstanding the consensus on the importance and wide application of the principle of self-determination in mediation, it has been variously phrased and interpreted. As a result, there is no agreement with respect to the *extent of the principle's application* (which decisions and issues it applies to), its *meaning* (when a party's decision can be said to have been made in accordance with the principle of self-determination), and the *duties of mediators* stemming from it (how mediators should conduct mediations on the basis of party self-determination).

For example, a mediator who conducts a mediation in accordance with the *Model Standards* is directed to respect party self-determination on all mediation issues, at every stage of the mediation, and as regards decisions on both process and outcome.[6] In other words, the parties have a right to extensive self-determination, though the Standards qualify that right under certain circumstances.[7] Similarly, the *Florida Rules* recognize an extensive right of parties to self-determination, stating that "[a] mediator shall not make substantive decisions for any party."[8] However, they do not define "substantive decisions" or non-substantive decisions, leaving some uncertainty with respect to the extent of the application of parties' self-determination.[9] The *California Rules* specify several issues regarding which the parties have self-determination: process outcome, participation in the process, and withdrawal.[10] This approach leaves uncertainty as to the extent of self-determination regarding other

5 See Laura E. Weidner, "Model Standards of Conduct for Mediators (2005)" (2006) 21 *Ohio State Journal on Dispute Resolution* 547, 554–555. See also Welsh, "The Thinning Vision", 7–8, 15–20; Kimberlee K. Kovach, "Good Faith in Mediation – Requested, Recommended, or Required? A New Ethic" (1997) 38 *South Texas Law Review* 575, 584; John D. Feerick, "Toward Uniform Standards of Conduct For Mediators" (1997) 38 *South Texas Law Review* 455, 460; Donald T. Weckstein, "In Praise of Party Empowerment – and of Mediator Activism" (1997) 33 *Willamette Law Review* 501, 531; Omer Shapira, *Use of Power and Influence in Mediation: Practice and Applied Ethics* (Ono Academic College Press, 2007), pp. 169–87 [Hebrew]; Gabriel Hallevy, "The Defense Attorney as Mediator in Plea Bargains" (2009) 9 *Pepperdine Dispute Resolution Law Journal* 495, 502.

6 Model Standards, Standard I.A.

7 For example, the Model Standards provide in Standard I.A.1 that "a mediator may need to balance . . . party self-determination with a mediator's duty to conduct a quality process." However, the Model Standards do not explain what balancing means and whether the mediator's power of balancing applies to decisions on issues other than process design. For further discussion see Shapira, "Sharing Decision-Making", 927–928.

8 Florida Rules, Rule 10.310(a). See also Alabama Code, Standard 4(a).

9 See Shapira, "Sharing Decision-Making", 929–930.

10 California Rules, Rule 3.853.

decisions, e.g., whether to hold separate meetings with the parties, what to place on the agenda, and the order of speakers.[11]

There are different approaches to the meaning of the principle as well. Codes of conduct for mediators describe the principle using terms such as voluntariness, lack of coercion, informed consent, and avoidance of undue pressures.[12] The meaning of these terms is not adequately discussed in the codes, and the mediation literature suggests various interpretations of them.[13]

The purpose of this chapter is to define and justify an ethical standard of self-determination for mediation parties, which applies to all mediators. The definition of the standard and its justification rely on the core definitions of the process of mediation and the role of mediators;[14] on the ethical relationships between mediators, who exercise a professional role, and the mediation parties who are their clients, the mediation profession, and the public; and on the legitimate expectation that mediators be worthy of the mediation parties' trust and meet their obligations toward the profession and the public. This analysis will enable us to present a comprehensive standard of party self-determination at the end of the chapter.

4.2 The extent of party self-determination and the allocation of decision-making authority between mediators and parties

4.2.1 The normative sources of party self-determination

Self-determination is recognized as a fundamental principle of mediation. Codes of conduct for mediators refer to this principle, usually in an

11 See Shapira, "Sharing Decision-Making", 930–931 (discussing the vagueness of the California Rules).

12 See, e.g., Alabama Code, Standard 4 (using terms such as informed and voluntary agreement, prohibition of coercion, unfair influence, and misrepresentation, and balanced process to describe the standard of self-determination). See also California Rules, Rule 3.853 (using terms such as voluntary agreement and refraining from coercion in describing the rule on voluntary participation and self-determination); Oregon Standards, Standard I and II (describing in standard I self-determination with concepts such as freedom of choice, autonomy, and informed and voluntary decisions, and informed consent in standard II which is described as "a critical part of a participant's ability to exercise Self-Determination"); Florida Rules, Rule 10.310 (using terms such as informed and voluntary decisions, prohibition on coercion, improper influence, and misrepresentation).

13 See, e.g., Welsh, "The Thinning Vision." See also Nolan-Haley, "Informed Consent".

14 See Chapter 3, Section 3.2.

independent standard, separate from other standards. However, it is argued that even in the absence of an express right to self-determination in a formal code of conduct, mediation parties have such a right. Party self-determination derives from two *general* normative sources. The first is *ordinary morality* that applies to all persons, protects their personal autonomy, and grants them a moral right to determine how to conduct their lives.[15] The second source is the *ethical relationship* between mediators as role-holders and the parties as their clients. This relationship protects the legitimate expectation of mediation parties that mediators be worthy of their trust and respect their decisions regarding the provided mediation services.[16]

As we have seen in Chapter 3, the nuclear definition of the mediation process includes a component of party self-determination that applies, in the minimalist scenario, to the determination of the process *outcome*. In other words, it is impossible to consider a process as "mediation" where the outcome is determined by the professional who conducts the process instead of by the parties. The definition and nature of mediation construct the parties' legitimate expectation that mediators respect their self-determination regarding the *outcome*, establishing a right of mediation parties to determine the mediation outcome and a duty of mediators to conduct a process that respects that right. However, the parties' legitimate expectation of self-determination is not limited to control of the process outcome. The history of mediation, academic writing in the field, practitioner literature, and numerous codes of conduct for mediators all inform us that party self-determination covers more ground and applies to many other issues beyond the mediation outcome. Thus, despite the nuclear definition of mediation, which supposedly establishes a legitimate expectation of self-determination with respect to outcome alone, the message to mediation parties is that they are entitled to more than that. The question is: what are they entitled to? What are the issues and decisions that are subject to party determination?

Codes of conduct for mediators offer limited and inconsistent guidance on the extent of party self-determination. Self-determination is often defined with abstract and vague terms such as process, outcome, procedural issues, and substantive decisions.[17] In addition, depending on the particular code, concrete instances are often defined in which the parties have a right to self-determination, for example with respect to

[15] See Chapter 2, Section 2.2.3.3. [16] Ibid. [17] See Section 4.1.

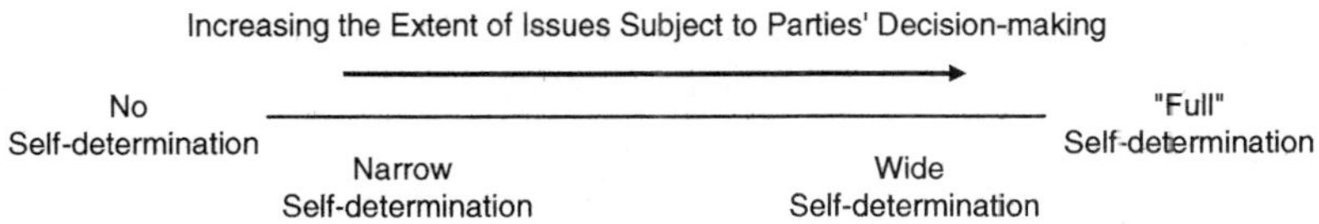

Figure 4.1: Wide and narrow self-determination

mediator selection,[18] participation and withdrawal,[19] and consultation with a lawyer.[20] It follows that had we to rely on codes of conduct for mediators as a sole source of party self-determination, the extent of self-determination would change in accordance with the provisions of each code, and theoretically fluctuate on a continuum ranging from *narrow* self-determination, which is limited to decisions on outcome, to *wide* self-determination that applies to all mediation issues (see Figure 4.1). In practice, however, codes of conduct for mediators guarantee a right to self-determination that is never restricted to the determination of outcome alone, and some refer to wide self-determination that applies to all mediation issues.[21]

The difficulty in establishing the extent of mediation parties' legitimate expectations of self-determination is reflected in the variety of opinions in the professional literature as well. For example, Jacqueline M. Nolan-Haley argued that "mediation autonomy . . . gives the mediator power to control only the process in which parties' decisionmaking occurs, while the parties retain the power to decide and control the outcome,"[22] while other scholars argue that parties have a right to make substantive decisions and mediators are responsible for making non-substantive decisions.[23] In other words, these writers suggest that the distinction between process

[18] See Model Standards, Standard I.A. See also NY-CDRC Standards, Standard I Comment 1.

[19] See Model Standards, Standard I.A. See also California Rules, Rule 3.853(2); Georgia Standards, Standard I.A.6; Family Mediation Model Standards, Standard I.D.

[20] See Alabama Code, Standard 3(a). See also Georgia Standards, Standard I.A.8.

[21] See NY-CDRC Standards, Standard I.

[22] See Nolan-Haley, "Informed Consent", 790–791. See also Kovach, *Mediation*, p. 46; Leonard L. Riskin, "Decisionmaking in Mediation: The New Old Grid and the New New Grid System" (2003) 79 *Notre Dame Law Review* 1, 43 note 145 and Boulle and Nesic, *Mediation*, p. 19 (recognizing this approach in the literature and practice).

[23] See, e.g., John Lande and Gregg Herman, "Fitting the Forum to the Family Fuss: Choosing Mediation, Collaborative Law, or Cooperative Law for Negotiating Divorce Cases" (2004) 42 *Family Court Review* 280, 282. See also Nancy Ver Steegh, "Yes, No, and Maybe: Informed Decision Making About Divorce Mediation in the Presence of Domestic Violence" (2003) 9 *William and Mary Journal of Women and the Law* 145, 173–174.

and outcome or between substantive and non-substantive issues determines the extent of party self-determination. Conversely, some authors and practitioners profess a deep commitment to party self-determination that is allegedly reflected in the subordination of all mediation issues to party consent, including decisions on process design.[24]

The following section justifies an extensive understanding of party self-determination. However, as we shall see, (a) it is *practically impossible* to submit all mediation decisions to the parties; and (b) since all norms are relative, party self-determination might have to give way to other ethical norms in appropriate circumstances.[25]

4.2.2 *Justifying wide self-determination for mediation parties*

Despite the fact that party self-determination is not absolute, there are good reasons to support a claim that mediation parties have a right to extensive self-determination. Such a right ought not to be restricted, in the absence of convincing justifications, to the determination of the mediation outcome or to a few other decisions that are rightly perceived as being of special importance, such as mediator selection and withdrawal from the process. The following arguments support a wide interpretation of party self-determination.

First, mediation parties have a general moral right (that every person has) to make decisions in matters that affect them, unless intervention in their affairs can be justified.[26] Our starting point is, therefore, that mediation parties' right to self-determination applies to all mediation issues, and it is for mediators to justify interventions that restrict parties' freedom of choice.

Second, as we have seen, mediation parties have a fundamental, indisputable right to determine the mediation outcome. However, in practice the outcome of mediation is affected by numerous decisions that are made in the course of mediation, such as decisions on agenda, order of speakers, and choice to focus on particular issues at the expense of others.[27] Although from a formal point of view these are not decisions on outcome, from a realist, substantive perspective they affect and design

[24] See Menkel-Meadow, Love, and Schneider, *Mediation*, p. 94 (suggesting that mediation parties are entitled to control both process and outcome). See also Welsh, "The Thinning Vision", 80 (advocating a wide meaning for party self-determination).

[25] See Section 4.2.3. [26] See Note 15.

[27] See Omer Shapira, "Joining Forces in Search for Answers: The Use of Therapeutic Jurisprudence in the Realm of Mediation Ethics" (2008) 8 *Pepperdine Dispute Resolution Law Journal* 243, 256. See also Riskin, "Decisionmaking in Mediation", 31 note 123.

the outcome. Michael Watkins, for example, observed in discussing principles of persuasion that "[d]ecision-making processes are like rivers: big decisions draw on preliminary tributary processes that define the problem, identify alternatives, and establish criteria for evaluating costs and benefits. By the time the problem and the options have been defined, the actual choice may be a foregone conclusion. This is why it is so important to shape the decision-making agenda early on."[28] It is practically impossible to fully distinguish between process and outcome decisions or between procedural decisions and decisions on substance.[29] Thus, if one agrees that decisions on outcome are in the jurisdiction of mediation parties alone, one must acknowledge that other decisions made in the course of mediation must be made by the parties in accordance with a wide concept of self-determination. The legitimate expectations of parties to determine the outcome include a legitimate expectation to make all other mediation decisions unless mediators can justify their intervention in the parties' right.

Third, the prominent feature of mediation in comparison to adjudication and arbitration is party decision-making. The essence of mediators' role is to assist parties in making decisions, not make decisions for them. This feature of the process of mediation and of the role of mediators must be preserved as far as possible for reasons of integrity. Mediator decision-making undermines the uniqueness and identity of the mediation process. Thus, intervention in party self-determination must be limited and for appropriate reasons.[30]

Fourth, an acknowledgment of wide self-determination for mediation parties is consistent with the modern perspective of the professional–client relationship, which has been transferring more and more decision-making authority and responsibility from professionals to their clients. This perspective is evident, for example, in doctor–patient and lawyer–client relationships. It reflects the rising significance that is being ascribed to the value of personal autonomy in society, and should apply to the mediator–parties relationship as well.[31]

[28] Michael Watkins, "Principles of Persuasion" (2001) 17 *Negotiation Journal* 115, 129. See also Riskin, "Decisionmaking in Mediation", 28; Boulle and Nesic, *Mediation*, pp. 20, 26; Macfarlane, "Mediating Ethically", 59; Forrest S. Mosten, "Collaborative Law Practice: An Unbundled Approach to Informed Client Decision Making" (2008) 2008 *Journal of Dispute Resolution* 163, note 4.

[29] See Shapira, "Sharing Decision-Making", 933–934. [30] See id., 937.

[31] See Omer Shapira, "On Human Dignity in Mediation: The Effect of The Basic Law: Human Dignity and Liberty on Mediation" (2008) 8 *Kiryat Hamishpat* 373, 385–388 [Hebrew].

Fifth, research shows that the exercise of self-determination improves the psychological welfare of individuals.[32] Therapeutic jurisprudence is a relatively new body of knowledge that argues for the modification of social arrangements in order to increase individuals' psychological well-being.[33] Thus, in accordance with this approach a wide concept of party self-determination should be preferred to a narrow one.[34] And sixth, participation in mediation can educate parties on constructive methods of coping with future conflicts outside mediation, without the assistance of a third party. The more mediators enable parties, as part of a wide concept of self-determination, to take an active part in making decisions relating to their conflict, the greater their contribution toward meeting that end.[35]

4.2.3 Exercising wide self-determination through shared decision-making; limitations on self-determination

As we have seen, there is no consensus among mediation experts and code draftsmen on the appropriate allocation of decision-making authority between mediators and mediation parties. Sometimes mediators are presented as responsible for the process and the parties for the outcome; sometimes it is said that mediators may make procedural decisions while the parties are responsible for making substantive decisions; and sometimes mediators are instructed to respect party self-determination with regard to all mediation issues, unless the decision jeopardizes the quality of the process. This state of affairs creates uncertainty with regard to the extent of party self-determination. What is needed is a *different model* for sharing decision-making authority in mediation, one that can guide both mediators and parties on the decisions that are within the authority of the mediator and decisions that are to be made by the parties.

A wide conception of self-determination assumes that each party has a *preemption right* to make decisions in relation to the mediation. This

[32] See Bruce J. Winick, "On Autonomy: Legal and Psychological Perspectives" (1992) 37 *Villanova Law Review* 1705, 1707. See also Amy D. Ronner and Bruce J. Winick, "Silencing the Appellant's Voice: The Antitherapeutic Per Curiam Affirmance" (2000) 24 *Seattle University Law Review* 499, 502.

[33] See Christopher Slobogin, "Therapeutic Jurisprudence: Five Dilemmas to Ponder" (1995) 1 *Psychology, Public Policy and Law* 193, 196 (noting that "[TJ is] [t]he use of social science to study the extent to which a legal rule or practice promotes the psychological and physical well-being of the people it affects").

[34] See Shapira, "Joining Forces", 257–259.

[35] See Shapira, "Sharing Decision-Making", 937.

right overrides the mediator's right to make a decision unless the transfer of decision-making authority to the mediator can be justified. Thus, mediators must realize that parties have a right to make decisions on all issues, procedural or substantive, at any stage of the mediation, including on mediator selection, participation in or withdrawal from the process, and outcome.

However, the parties' authority cannot be unlimited. Mediation parties cannot legitimately expect mediators to avoid making decisions that are necessary for the process to be carried out in accordance with its nature and principles. Parties must realize that mediators exercise a professional role, and that role entrusts them with the *authority to make those decisions which are necessary for conducting the mediation in accordance with the standards that apply to the process*. Mediators, on the other hand, must realize that in view of the general application of the parties' right to self-determination they must, whenever possible, share the decision-making with the parties and *seek the parties' consent* to the decision that is made.

For example, the decision on the order of speakers should be made by the parties, irrespective of whether it is a procedural decision or substantive. If the parties cannot agree on this issue the mediator should assist them in making the decision, and may suggest the order of speakers and put it to their approval. In no case has the mediator the authority to impose his or her will on the parties on this issue, though he or she might have to inform them that if they do not reach an agreement on that point it will be impossible to continue with the mediation.

Mediators may make decisions *without sharing* the decision-making with the parties in two cases. First, when it is *impossible* as a practical matter to share the decision-making with the parties. For example, decisions on the questions to be asked, or on whether and when to use reflection,[36] cannot be shared with the parties. And second, mediators may be under an *ethical duty* not to share particular decisions with the parties. For example, mediators might be prohibited by the standards of impartiality or confidentiality from sharing information with parties.

In all other cases, mediators must share the decision-making with the parties. However, sharing decision-making and securing the parties' consent to a decision are not always the same. Sometimes the mediator will be under an obligation to make a decision *against the*

[36] See Folberg and Taylor, *Mediation*, pp. 109–115 (discussing questions, reflection, summary, and clarification as mediator tools for enhancing communication between parties).

wishes of the parties.[37] Some codes of conduct for mediators express this idea by reference to a mediator's duty to uphold the quality of the mediation process. The *Standards of Conduct* for New York State Community Dispute Resolution Center Mediators (NY-CDRC Standards), for example, provide that "[a]lthough party self-determination is a fundamental principle of mediation practice, a mediator may need to balance party self-determination with a duty to conduct a quality mediation process."[38] The *NY-CDRC Standards* do not discuss the occasions on which balancing is required or the meaning of balancing. I argue that mediators must not follow the parties' wishes in two situations. First, where following the parties' wishes could jeopardize the mediator's *professional integrity*, because to do as the parties wish would be inconsistent with the nature and definition of the professional role and the standards that apply to the mediation.[39] And second, where following the parties' wishes could undermine the *standing of the mediation profession* and public faith in it.[40] For example, mediators must decline a mediation, notwithstanding the parties' wishes that they take on the case, when they do not have the necessary competence, i.e., the necessary skills and knowledge, to conduct an effective mediation process.[41] A mediator acting with professional integrity must be objectively convinced that he is capable of conducting mediation in accordance with the process's definition and nature. He must also be convinced that the level of his competence does not endanger the profession's standing and public confidence in the profession. This rationale also explains why mediators would have to terminate a mediation or withdraw against the wishes of the parties when they are in a serious conflict of interest;[42] why they must refuse parties' request for the mediator's professional opinion of their case;[43] or why they would have to disclose to a non-participant, in accordance with a legal order, confidential information that a mediation party insists should remain secret.[44] Figure 4.2 illustrates the allocation of decision-making authority between mediators and mediation parties.

[37] See Shapira, "Sharing Decision-Making", 938–944. See also Spiegel, "Lawyering and Client Decisionmaking", 113–123 (discussing limitations on client decision-making in lawyer-client relationships).

[38] NY-CDRC Standards, Standard I Comment 2. See also Model Standards, Standard I.A.1.

[39] See Chapter 8. [40] See Chapter 12. [41] See Chapter 5. [42] See Chapter 6.

[43] See Chapter 8. [44] See Chapter 10.

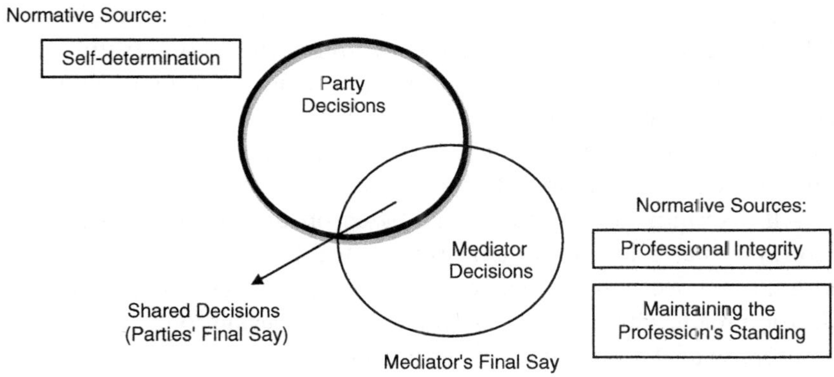

Figure 4.2: The extent of party self-determination and the allocation of decision-making authority between mediators and parties

4.3 The meaning of party self-determination: the elements and quality of self-determination

4.3.1 Distinguishing between the extent of self-determination and its elements

Thus far the discussion has focused on the *extent* of party self-determination, that is, on the type of decisions that are subject to party self-determination, and examined the allocation of decision-making authority between mediation parties and mediators. The following discussion focuses on the *conditions* that must be met for parties to exercise self-determination. This is a crucial step in the understanding of self-determination because making a decision and exercising self-determination are not necessarily the same.

Codes of conduct for mediators and mediation literature use terms such as voluntariness, lack of coercion, free choice, consent, and informed decisions to describe decisions that are the product of self-determination.[45] These are vague terms that are often left undefined. Moreover, the relationship between these terms is not explained. My purpose is to clarify the meaning of self-determination by deconstructing this concept into its constituent elements. As we shall see, the exercise of self-determination requires the convergence of three accumulative elements: competency to make decisions, voluntariness and lack of coercion at the time of decision-making, and the availability and understanding of

[45] See Section 4.1.

the information relevant to the decision-making. It will be helpful in the following discussion to distinguish between the factual observation that an *autonomous* decision has been made, and its *value* or *quality*. An autonomous decision must satisfy the first two conditions of self-determination: it must be made with competence, and be voluntary and uncoerced. An autonomous decision need not satisfy the third condition of self-determination, and could be based on inadequate information. However, such a decision would be of low quality. To put it differently, an uninformed decision is an exercise of *formal* self-determination, while a decision made with awareness of information relevant to the decision is an exercise of *substantive* self-determination.

Another point to bear in mind in discussing the meaning of self-determination is that the autonomy of decisions and their quality are relative values on a *scale*. Each of the elements of self-determination can be present or absent to a certain *degree*. The more the elements of self-determination are present and realized, the more likely it is that the decision is the product of substantive rather than formal self-determination. The exact point that separates substantive self-determination from formal self-determination might sometimes be blurred. However, it seems to me that the legitimate expectation of mediation parties is for "true," i.e., substantive, self-determination, not formal self-determination. This expectation of a real, substantive exercise of rights is sometimes described as an expectation of fairness or justice.[46] The remainder of this chapter will consider the meaning of each of the elements of self-determination and the responsibility of mediators for the realization of these elements in the mediation process. Figure 4.3 illustrates the relationship between the elements of self-determination and the value or worth of self-determination.

4.3.2 Competency to make decisions

Competence does not have a single acceptable definition,[47] and the meaning ascribed to it in this book is the *capacity* to perceive information, process it, and understand the information and its implications in order to make and communicate a decision.[48] Incompetence could

[46] See Chapter 11.

[47] See, e.g., Beauchamp and Childress, *Biomedical Ethics*, pp. 112–117 (discussing various definitions, standards, and tests of competence). See also Gert, Culver and Clouser, *Bioethics*, p. 219.

[48] Compare Beauchamp and Childress, *Biomedical Ethics*, p. 113 (arguing that in the context of medicine "[p]atients or prospective subjects are competent to make a decision if they

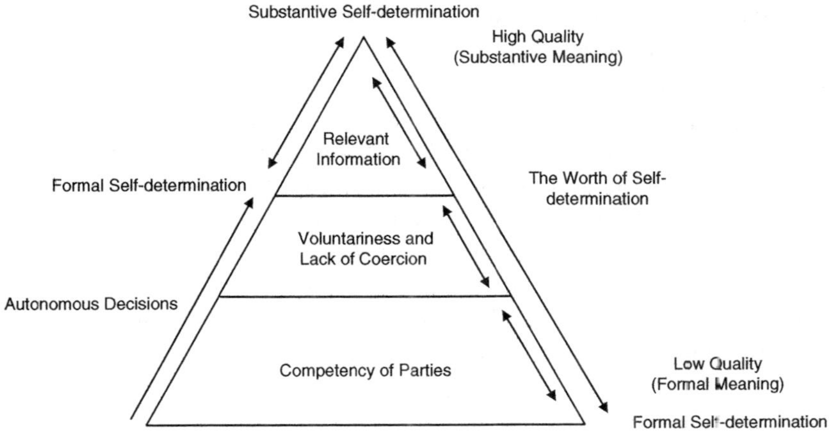

Figure 4.3: The elements of self-determination: between formality and substance

follow from reasons such as mental retardation, mental illness, or hallucinations that impair one's capacity to process information and make judgment. Incompetence could depend on the *type* of the decision that is made. For example, a mentally retarded person may have the capacity to decide what to eat but lack the capacity to manage his or her finances because he or she does not appreciate the value of money and does not understand the meaning of saving and interest. Incompetency can be *temporary*, due to drugs, alcohol, anxiety, or language illiteracy. In sum, one may be competent to make decisions in general, but incompetent to make decisions on a particular issue at a certain time.

A person with the *capacity* to understand the information required for making a decision is competent to make that decision even though he or she does not understand the information *in fact*. The difficulty in such a situation is not the person's incompetence to make the decision, but rather concerns the *low quality* of the decision-making process, which has been based on inadequate or erroneous information.[49] That some professionals such as lawyers and doctors are tempted to make decisions for their clients or patients may rest on a notion that their client or patient is "incompetent" to make a decision. However, if the latter is capable of understanding the reasons for a decision he or she should be deemed competent to make it.

have the capacity to understand the material information, to make a judgment about this information in light of their values, to intend a certain outcome, and to communicate freely their wishes to caregivers or investigators").

[49] See Section 4.3.4.

In some circumstances, one may have the competency to make a decision but the *level* of one's competence is *low* in comparison to one's usual capacity or the capacity of a reasonable person. For example, one may be under a mild influence of drugs or alcohol that lightly affects one's judgment (as opposed to a controlling influence that severely impairs one's judgment and temporarily renders one incompetent). In such case the decision could be autonomous, but the quality of the decision-making will be compromised. Alternatively, *high* competency, that is, a good and efficient processing of information that is free of interruption, contributes to the quality of the decision-making, i.e., to an exercise of substantive self-determination.

4.3.3 Voluntariness and lack of coercion

An autonomous decision is the product of free will or choice.[50] Coercive behavior, such as making threats, could result in a coerced decision that is not autonomous. *Coercive behavior* is the application of pressure intended to reduce one's options for choice.[51] A *coerced decision* is the result of coercive behavior that one could not resist, and is made out of feelings of distress, helplessness, and lack of choice.[52] Coerced decisions are easily identified in dramatic circumstances where a decision has been made following a threat of severe physical violence or an abuse of serious mental distress. Other cases, however, may not be so clear-cut. Voluntariness and coercion are at opposite ends of a continuum. The degrees of voluntariness and coercion can vary between cases, ranging on a scale from "full" voluntariness to "complete" coercion. An involuntary decision is considered coerced, but up to the point of coercion there are intermediate cases in which voluntariness may suffer yet the decision falls short of being coerced. However, coercive behavior is inappropriate in

[50] See, e.g., Beauchamp and Childress, *Biomedical Ethics*, p. 132 (arguing that "a person acts voluntarily if he or she wills the action without being under the control of another's influence"); Merriam-Webster Online Dictionary available at www.merriam-webster.com/dictionary/voluntary ("Voluntary – proceeding from the will or from one's own choice or consent; unconstrained by interference: self-determining; done by design or intention: intentional . . .; of, relating to, subject to, or regulated by the will . . .; having power of free choice . . . ").

[51] See Stanley I. Benn, *A Theory of Freedom* (Cambridge University Press, 1988), pp. 134–135.

[52] Compare Beauchamp and Childress, *Biomedical Ethics*, p. 133 (noting that "[c]oercion occurs only if a credible and intended threat displaces a person's self-directed course of action"). See also Gert, Culver and Clouser, *Bioethics*, p. 232.

itself, even when it does not succeed in bringing about a coerced decision, because it *undermines* self-determination. One's decision may still be autonomous, but the process of decision-making will have been defective, the quality of the decision-making wanting, and the exercise of self-determination not substantive.

4.3.4 *Knowledge of relevant information*

Decisions are always based on information that is perceived and processed by the decision-maker. Decisions that are based on inadequate or erroneous information are autonomous if made with the capacity to understand the information and if they are voluntary and uncoerced. However, such a decision is based on a defective decision-making process that represents formal, low-quality self-determination. In the words of Isabelle R. Gunning: "If self-determination is divorced from informed decision-making or voluntary consent, it cannot claim to constitute authentic self-determination."[53] Substantive self-determination reflects a high-quality decision-making process that relies on information that is *relevant* to the decision and on an understanding of the information and its implications. Relevant information is information the knowledge or ignorance of which could influence the decision or the choice made.[54] When a decision is made on the basis of relevant information, and the decision-maker understands its meaning and implications, the decision may be regarded as an *informed decision*, or, in the case of a decision to give consent, as *informed consent.*

4.3.5 *Summarizing the conditions for exercise of substantive self-determination*

In summary, for a decision to be autonomous the decision-maker must be competent and act voluntarily, thereby making an uncoerced decision. When one of these elements is missing, one cannot exercise self-determination. As Figure 4.4 shows, for a decision to be the product of "real," *substantive* self-determination, as opposed to illusory, formal

[53] Isabelle R. Gunning, "Know Justice, Know Peace: Further Reflections on Justice, Equality and Impartiality in Settlement Oriented and Transformative Mediations" (2004) 5 *Cardozo Journal of Conflict Resolution* 87, 93.

[54] Compare Davis, *Thinking Like an Engineer*, p. 168 (arguing that "[a] fact is 'relevant' to choice of an act if, and only if, exposure to it would, all else equal, strengthen or weaken the agent's resolve to do the act").

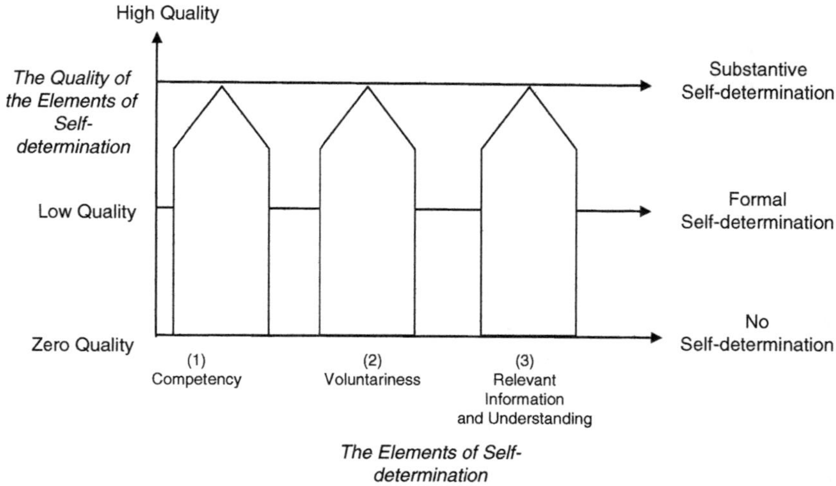

Figure 4.4: Substantive and formal self-determination

self-determination, each of the elements of self-determination must be of high quality: a high degree of *competence* in the sense of a high capacity to perceive and process information, as opposed to a low degree of competence following, for example, mental stress, confusion, or exhaustion; a high degree of *voluntariness* in the sense of a decision-making process free of coercive attempts, as opposed to a low degree of voluntariness following coercive acts and pressures that leave the decision-maker with feelings of helplessness and lack of choice; and decisions that are based on information *relevant* to the decision and understood by the decision-maker, as opposed to decisions that are based on inadequate information or on a misunderstanding of the information and its implications. When one or more of the elements of self-determination are of low quality, we will consider the decision-making process as reflecting the exercise of *formal* self-determination, and tend to treat it as unfair or unjust.[55]

The writing of Nancy A. Welsh on self-determination in mediation might give the impression that there is an additional condition for substantive self-determination of mediation parties. Welsh discusses the importance of *active participation* of mediation parties in the process, whereby the parties present their stories, take part in a dialogue, and

55 See Chapter 11.

design both the mediation process and the outcome.[56] In the terminology she suggests, active participation is part of the original concept of self-determination in mediation, as compared to the thin concept of self-determination that has developed in court-connected mediations that are dominated by lawyers, which restricts party participation and thereby reduces the quality of party self-determination.[57] I agree with Welsh that party participation is desirable, for research indicates that it promotes a perception of procedural fairness among participants and thus contributes to greater satisfaction on the part of mediation participants.[58] However, it should be noted that the degree of party participation in mediation is in itself a decision that is subject to party self-determination. Thus, active participation is not another element of the concept of self-determination, but another issue that parties should decide with competence, voluntarily, and on the basis of information that is relevant to that decision.

4.4 Waiver of self-determination

Self-determination refers to every decision parties make, including the decision not to exercise self-determination with regard to a particular issue. Mediation parties may decide to leave an issue to the mediator to decide. However, such a waiver should meet the three conditions of self-determination previously discussed: the parties must act with competency, voluntarily, and with an understanding of the implications of the waiver. For example, parties may decide not to consult a lawyer on their legal rights but must be aware of the consequences of their decision. Moreover, just as party self-determination is not unlimited, so too is their right to waive self-determination. For example, mediation parties cannot authorize a mediator, *as a mediator*, to make a decision on the mediation outcome. Mediators cannot make decisions on outcome because such conduct is inconsistent with the definition and nature of their role.[59] Authorizing a mediator to make a decision on the outcome of the mediation transforms the mediator into an arbitrator and the mediation into arbitration. The limitations on the parties' right to waive self-determination are determined by the standards that apply to mediation. For example, if parties ask the mediator to make a decision on

[56] See Welsh, "The Thinning Vision", 4. See also Mordehai Mironi, "Mediation v. Case Settlement: The Unsettling Relations between Courts and Mediation – A Case Study" (2014) 19 *Harvard Negotiation Law Review* 173, 179.

[57] Ibid. [58] See Welsh, "Making Deals", 792. [59] See Chapter 3, Section 3.2

the mediation agenda, he or she should (a) try to assist the parties to make the decision *themselves*, in accordance with the norm of party self-determination; (b) examine with the parties their understanding that it is an issue that they can determine themselves, and that decisions on agenda could affect the content of the mediation and its outcome; and (c) suggest an agenda, subject to the parties' approval, in a manner consistent with the other standards of mediation, for example in an impartial manner.

4.5 Mediators' duties regarding party self-determination

The correlative to the parties' right to self-determination is a duty of mediators to conduct mediation in a way that enables the parties to exercise self-determination, and to refrain from conducting mediation where a party is unable to do so. Mediators' duties regarding party self-determination can be sorted into two types of duties. First, mediators have a duty to refrain from conduct that could undermine party self-determination. This duty clearly follows from the legitimate expectation of parties that mediators avoid conduct that violates their rights or causes them harm. Second, mediators have a duty to take steps to prevent parties from making decisions in circumstances that do not meet the conditions of self-determination. This duty applies even where party self-determination is undermined not by the mediator but *by others*. The duty to intervene and prevent the undermining of party self-determination by others follows from the position of the mediator as a professional role-holder and the responsibility that comes with that role. For those who do not fulfill a role, preventing harm done by others is an ideal or aspiration, not a duty. However, preventing harm could become a duty for the role-holding professional.[60] The role of mediators is to assist parties to engage in a dialogue and make decisions on the basis of party self-determination. Thus, like lifeguards who are under a duty to save the life of drowning persons whom they did not put at risk, mediators must respond to the undermining of party self-determination by others. The remainder of this chapter addresses the specifications of mediators' duties with respect to each of the elements of self-determination.

[60] See Gert, Culver and Clouser, *Bioethics*, p. 82.

4.5.1 *Duties regarding party competency*

Mediators might meet parties who are incompetent due to their mental state (for example, due to major depression, high anxiety, or confusion), use of drugs or alcohol, or other reasons. In such circumstances, when a party does not have the capacity to perceive information, process it, and make a decision based on the information, mediators are expected to take necessary measures to prevent decision-making in a state of incompetency.

Mediation parties legitimately expect mediators to protect them from making decisions in a state of incompetency that makes them unaware of their incapacity to make a decision. It is also the duty of mediators toward the mediation profession and the public to do so, following from their obligation to maintain public confidence in mediation, which might be undermined if it appeared that mediations are conducted despite party incompetency. The *Georgia Standards*, for example, provide that "[t]he mediator has an obligation to assure that every party has the capacity to participate in the mediation conference";[61] and the *Family Mediation Model Standards* provide that "[a] family mediator shall ... assess [the participants'] capacity to mediate"[62] and "should not agree to conduct the mediation if the mediator reasonably believes one or more of the participants is unable ... to participate."[63]

It follows that mediators must be alert to parties' competence. If listening to a party makes the mediator suspect that the party does not understand what is going on or cannot process the information and appreciate its implications, he or she should take steps to help the party understand the information, such as slowing down the conversation or involving a representative of the party in the conversation. The *Model Standards*, for example, provide that "[a] mediator shall conduct a mediation ... in a manner that promotes ... party competency"[64] and "[i]f a party appears to have difficulty comprehending the process, issues, or settlement options, or difficulty participating in a mediation, the mediator should explore the circumstances and potential accommodations, modifications or adjustments that would make possible the party's capacity to comprehend, participate and exercise self-determination."[65] When the mediator's intervention is not successful, he or she must postpone the mediation (where the incompetence is temporary) or

[61] Georgia Standards, Standard I.B. [62] Family Mediation Model Standards, Standard III.
[63] Id., Standard III.C. [64] Model Standards, Standard VI.A.
[65] Model Standards, Standard VI.A.10.

bring it to an end. The Montana Mediation Association *Code of Ethics and Standards of Practice* (Montana Association Code), for example, provide that "[i]f, in the opinion of a mediator, the process is impeded by a party's use of a drug, alcohol or by other physical or mental incapacity, the mediator shall postpone a mediation session and/or withdraw from the mediation process and/or refer the parties to appropriate resources."[66] The obligation of the mediator is such that can be expected of a reasonable mediator. Clearly, mediators cannot be expected to diagnose mediation parties' capacity in the manner health specialists do. They are expected, however, to act as a reasonable mediator would have acted in the particular circumstances.

4.5.2 *Duties regarding voluntariness*

For mediation parties to make voluntary, uncoerced decisions, mediators must first refrain from conduct that undermines the voluntariness of party decision-making; and second, prevent coerced decisions that are the result of pressures by *other mediation participants* (such as another mediation party or a lawyer representing a party), or by *non-participants* (such as a referring court). We will not evaluate here the ethicacy of mandatory mediation that compels parties to participate in a mediation session by legal means.[67] Instead, our focus will be on the obligations of *mediators* regarding the voluntariness of decisions parties make.

4.5.2.1 A duty to refrain from undermining voluntariness

When an issue is subject to party decision-making, mediators must not impose their will on the parties,[68] and must refrain from acting in any manner that robs the parties of the opportunity to make their own decisions, despite their being inconsistent with the mediators' desires.[69] The *California Rules*, for example, direct mediators to "refrain from

[66] Montana Mediation Association Code of Ethics and Standards of Practice (2014) available at mtmediation.org/wp-content/uploads/2015/04/mtma-code-of-ethics-standards-of-practice-rev-2-13-14-reviewed-by-committee.pdf (Montana Association Code), s. IX.

[67] See, e.g., Holly A. Streeter-Schaefer, "A Look at Court Mandated Civil Mediation" (2000) 49 *Drake Law Review* 367.

[68] See, e.g., Weckstein, "Party Empowerment", 502 (noting that "[a] coerced settlement is inconsistent with a legitimate mediation process, as is any resolution that lacks voluntary and informed consent of the disputants").

[69] However, mediators may sometimes make decisions against the parties' will (see Section 4.2.3).

coercing any party to make a decision";[70] and the *Florida Rules* provide that "[a] mediator shall not coerce . . . any party to make a decision or unwillingly participate in a mediation."[71]

Mediator coercion, which makes parties feel helpless and with no control of the situation, could follow from mediator threats to deliver harmful information to the court,[72] mediator refusal to let parties leave the mediation room,[73] or aggressive evaluation by mediators.[74] Coercive behavior is inappropriate even where parties successfully resist it because it undermines the quality of voluntariness and thus the quality of the exercise of self-determination by the parties. True, "full" voluntariness is an ideal that can hardly be achieved, because everyone is subject to some pressures. However, in view of mediators' role assisting parties to make decisions, they are expected to refrain from undermining the degree of voluntariness of party decision-making. Thus, mediators have a duty not only to refrain from *coercing* parties to make decisions, but also to refrain from *exerting pressures* that fall short of coercion. The *North Carolina Standards*, for example, provide that "[a] mediator shall not exert undue pressure on a participant, whether to participate in mediation or to accept a settlement";[75] and the *Florida Rules* provide that "[a] mediator shall not . . . improperly influence any party to make a decision or unwillingly participate in a mediation."[76]

Codes of conduct for mediators recognize the temptation that mediators face to put pressure on parties, and warn them to avoid such conduct. The *Model Standards*, for example, provide that "[a] mediator shall not undermine party self-determination by any party for reasons such as higher settlement rates, egos, increased fees, or outside pressures from court personnel, program administrators, provider organizations, the media or others."[77]

It should be noted that exerting pressure on parties is not always ethically inappropriate. Mediator pressure is inappropriate when it is designed to *reduce party choice*, for example, by pushing parties to agree to a particular option or outcome,[78] or do without expert advice. Mediator pressure is

[70] California Rules, Rule 3.853(3). [71] Florida Rules, Rule 10.310(b).

[72] See, e.g., Omer Shapira, "Exploring the Concept of Power", 543.

[73] See, e.g., Kovach, "Good Faith", 584. [74] See, e.g., Shapira, "Joining Forces", 261.

[75] North Carolina Standards, Rule IV.B. [76] Florida Rules, Rule 10.310(b).

[77] Model Standards, Standard I.B. See also Illinois Standards, Definitions E.

[78] See, e.g., Andrew Schepard and James W. Bozzomo, "Efficiency, Therapeutic Justice, Mediation, and Evaluation: Reflections on a Survey of Unified Family Courts" (2003) 37 *Family Law Quarterly* 333, 352 (discussing pressure tactics of mediators).

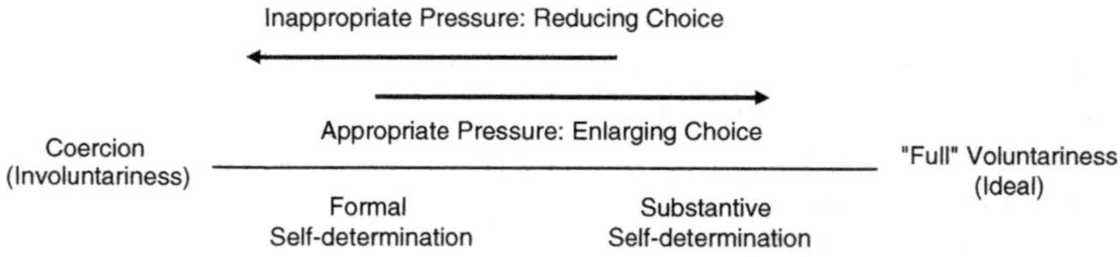

Figure 4.5: Voluntariness and lack of coercion

legitimate when it is designed to *enlarge the range of options for choice*, for example by urging parties to look for information, and to raise and consider options.[79] The *North Carolina Standards*, for example, provide that "a mediator shall encourage parties to consider both the benefits of participation and settlement and the costs of withdrawal and impasse";[80] and the Advisory Committee to the *California Rules* notes that mediators may legitimately try to persuade mediation parties not to withdraw from mediation so long as they do not do so in a coercive manner.[81] This positive type of pressure advances both party self-determination and the purposes of mediation, while pressures that reduce party choice harm them. Thus mediators have a duty to refrain from exerting pressures that reduce party choice, and as we will see in the next section, must intervene and take measures to reduce or disarm inappropriate pressures exerted by others. Figure 4.5 illustrates the relationship between types of pressures and self-determination.

4.5.2.2 A duty to prevent coerced decisions

Coercion may be attempted and successfully achieved by mediation parties, lawyers representing parties, and referring courts. Mediation parties expect mediators, who are responsible for conducting mediation according to its rules, to conduct mediations in a manner that enables them to make voluntary, uncoerced decisions. This means that mediators are expected to make sure that the *conditions* necessary for the exercise of party self-determination are present. Mediators must not remain passive if they are to shoulder this responsibility. They must *respond* to the exertion of inappropriate pressures and take necessary measures to prevent situations in which mediation parties make

[79] See, e.g., Robert Baruch Bush, "Efficiency and Protection, or Empowerment and Recognition? The Mediator's Role and Ethical Standards in Mediation" (1989) 41 *Florida Law Review* 253, 278.

[80] North Carolina Standards, Rule IV.B.

[81] California Rules, Advisory Committee Comment to Rule 3.853.

coerced decisions. This duty does not require a balancing of power in cases of imbalance of power between mediation parties; it instructs mediators to provide a *safety net*, designed to ensure that parties do not make decisions out of coercion.[82]

Codes of conduct for mediators recognize a mediator obligation to ensure conditions for the exercise of self-determination, and often instruct mediators to discontinue the process when a party cannot exercise self-determination. The *Model Standards*, for example, provide that "[a] mediator shall conduct a mediation based on the principle of party self-determination"[83] and "[i]f a mediator believes that participant conduct ... jeopardizes conducting a mediation consistent with these Standards, a mediator shall take appropriate steps-including, if necessary, postponing, withdrawing from or terminating the mediation."[84] The *California Rules* instruct the mediator to "conduct the mediation in a manner that supports the principles of voluntary participation and self-determination by the parties"[85] and in a procedurally fair manner where "each party is given an opportunity to participate and make uncoerced decisions."[86] The *Florida Rules* provide that "[i]f, for any reason, a party is unable to freely exercise self-determination, a mediator shall cancel or postpone a mediation."[87]

The termination of mediation should be a last resort,[88] and mediators should consider several measures before making that decision. First, mediators should remind parties of the rules of behavior in mediation. When a participant attempts to coerce a mediation party the most elementary duty of mediators is to remind all participants that mediation is a voluntary process. And second, mediators should call a recess in order to check with the decision-maker his or her state of mind. If mediators have the impression that a party has made or is about to make a coerced decision, that is, make a decision out of feelings of helplessness and lack

82 For the implication for mediators' duty of impartiality see Chapter 7.

83 Model Standards, Standard I.A. 84 Model Standards, Standard VI.C.

85 California Rules, Rule 3.853. 86 California Rules, Rule 3.857(b).

87 Florida Rules, Rule 10.310(d). See also Florida Mediator Ethics Advisory Committee (MEAC), Opinion 2006–002 available at www.flcourts.org/core/fileparse.php/283/urlt/MEAC-Opinion-2006-002.pdf, p. 2 (noting that "the mediator must carefully monitor the parties' participation in the mediation to ascertain the parties' ability to exercise self-determination and must be prepared to terminate the mediation if any party is unable or unwilling to participate meaningfully in the process").

88 See, e.g., Family Mediation Canada Code, Article 13.3 ("Mediators have a duty not to withdraw their services except for good cause and upon reasonable notice to the participants").

of choice,[89] they must postpone the decision-making in order to enable that party to recompose himself, reflect on his or her reasons for making the decision, evaluate the justifiability of his or her feelings, and reconsider his or her decision. As a part of this timeout, mediators should remind the party of his or her ethical rights in mediation, in particular his or her rights to make his or her own decisions, to reject offers that are unacceptable to him or her, and to withdraw from mediation at any time. Such a reminder may possibly ease some of the pressure felt by the party and allow him or her to exercise self-determination.

At the end of this break, if the party wishes to proceed with the decision, mediators must respect that party's choice (i.e. the party's right to self-determination) even if they would have made a different choice themselves. However, mediators will be justified in terminating the mediation at that point, and indeed are under a duty to do so, in two situations. First, mediators must terminate mediation in the rare situation where the party is in a state of incompetency and does not have the capacity to make the decision. A mediator's decision in such case is justified by the standard of self-determination itself and the obligations of the mediator toward the decision-maker. Second, the termination of mediation could follow from the obligations mediators owe to the profession of mediation and to the public. Mediators must not allow an abuse of the process of mediation or loss of public trust in mediation. For example, mediators must intervene to prevent a fundamentally unfair or unconscientious mediation outcome despite party agreement.[90]

4.5.3 *Duties regarding the availability of relevant information*

For parties to exercise self-determination, their decisions must be based on information that is relevant to making the decision that they understand (see Figure 4.6). The *Illinois Standards*, for example, declare that "[t]he mediation process relies upon the ability of participants to make their own ... informed decisions."[91] We will discuss mediators' duties

[89] For such a case, see Florida MEAC, Opinion 2006–004 available at www.flcourts.org/core/fileparse.php/283/urlt/MEAC-Opinion-2006–004.pdf. The advisory opinion focused on other issues, but the facts described in the Opinion illustrate in my view undue influence by one of the parties that gravely undermined the other party's ability to exercise self-determination and called for a mediator intervention.

[90] See Chapter 8 and Chapter 12.

[91] Illinois Standards, Definition s. A. See also Gabriel Hallevy, "Therapeutic Victim-Offender Mediation within the Criminal Justice Process – Sharpening the Evaluation of

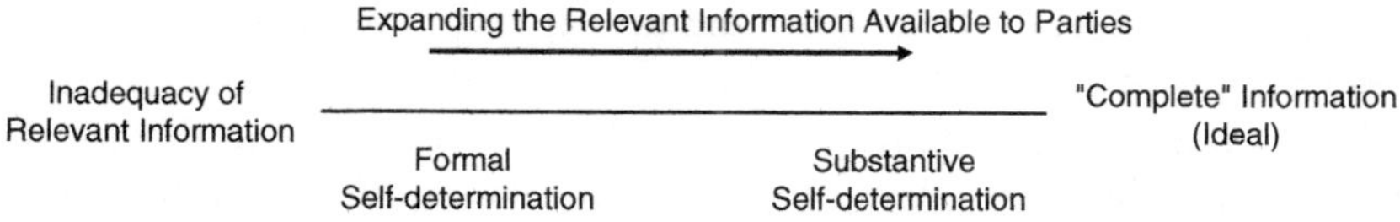

Figure 4.6: The element of information in the exercise of self-determination

regarding relevant information under two headings: (1) a duty to refrain from providing inaccurate information; and (2) a duty to take measures to generate the conditions for making informed decisions, which includes (a) a mediator duty to disclose or supply information to the parties (direct provision of information); (b) a duty to make information accessible to parties (indirect provision of information); and (c) a duty to terminate mediation as a last resort.

4.5.3.1 A duty to refrain from provision of inaccurate information

Mediators have a duty not to undermine party self-determination. Thus, they must refrain from providing parties with inaccurate information that is relevant to the decision and would distort the decision-making process. The *Alabama Code*, for example, provides that "[a] mediator shall not intentionally misrepresent material facts or circumstances in the course of a mediation."[92] In effect, misrepresentations that do not relate to "material" facts or to information relevant to a particular decision could very well be ethically inappropriate when they are inconsistent with standards of honesty and maintenance of the profession's standing.[93]

4.5.3.2 A duty to take measures to generate conditions for making informed decisions

Mediators must take measures to *generate the conditions* that enable parties to make informed decisions. The *Illinois Standards*, for example, provide that "[t]he mediator has a duty to ensure that clients make informed decisions"[94] and that "the understanding of each of the parties with respect to the relevant information is adequate to allow balanced negotiation."[95] This means that when mediators believe that parties are unknowingly about to make decisions on the basis of inadequate

Personal Potential for Rehabilitation while Righting Wrongs under the ADR Philosophy" (2011) 16 *Harvard Negotiation Law Review* 65, 85.

92 Alabama Code, Standard 4(c). See also Model Standards, Standard VI.A.4.

93 See Chapter 9 and Chapter 12. 94 Illinois Standards, s. VI. 95 Ibid.

information, they must intervene and take appropriate steps to bring the relevant information to the attention of the parties, subject to their other ethical obligations, in particular their duty to conduct the mediation impartially. This duty follows from the expectation of parties that mediators, who are considered responsible for conducting an intact process, take measures to ensure as far as possible that innocent parties are unharmed by the process. The Florida Committee to the *Florida Rules* noted, for example, that "[a] mediator must not ... knowingly allow a participant to make a decision based on misrepresented facts or circumstances."[96] Furthermore, the mediation profession expects mediators to maintain the profession's standing.[97] Uninformed decision-making by mediation parties could jeopardize public faith in mediation and deter potential disputants from using mediation to solve their differences.

Some codes of conduct for mediators are cautious in drafting this obligation, and stress that mediators cannot ensure that parties *in fact* make informed decisions. The *Oregon Standards*, for example, provide that "[w]hile a mediator cannot ensure that participants are making informed and voluntary decisions, mediators should help participants understand the process, issues, and options before them and encourage participants to make informed and voluntary decisions";[98] Family Mediation Canada *Members Code of Professional Conduct* (Family Mediation Canada Code) provides that "[a] mediator must endeavor to ensure that the participants reach agreement ... on the basis of informed consent"[99] and that the mediator has a duty "to actively encourage the participants to make decisions based upon sufficient information, knowledge and advice";[100] and the *Alabama Code* provides that "[a] mediator shall assist the parties in reaching an informed ... agreement."[101] These wordings do not relieve mediators of their responsibility to take all available measures that are necessary for parties to make informed decisions. Such measures may include (a) provision of information to the parties directly by mediators; (b) making information accessible to parties by indirect means; and (c) discontinuing the process as a last resort.

[96] Florida Rules, Committee Notes to Rule 10.310. [97] See Chapter 12.

[98] Oregon Standards, Standard I Comment 4. See also A Guide for Federal Employee Mediators (2006) available at www.adr.gov/pdf/final_manual.pdf (Federal Employee Mediators Guide), Standard I.A.2.

[99] Family Mediation Canada Code, Article 9.1. [100] Id., Article 10.1.

[101] Alabama Code, Standard 4(a).

(a) A duty to provide information directly to parties Mediators are in a position of trust with respect to mediation parties, and duties of disclosure are affected by relations of trust.[102] Mediators must provide parties with information that is in their possession and is relevant to making a decision, unless they are ethically justified in withholding the information, for example in order to meet their duties of confidentiality or impartiality. The duty to disclose information supports party self-determination, because decision-making that is not based on relevant information results in decisions of low quality that fail the test of substantive self-determination. The content of the information that must be disclosed to the parties varies with the type of decision that the parties are about to make. Three categories of information are discussed below.

(1) Information regarding the mediator

Information about the mediator includes information that is relevant for the parties to be able to make an informed decision on the *selection* of the mediator. Clearly, parties should be made aware of potential and actual conflicts of interest of the mediator.[103] In addition, parties should know the style of mediation that the mediator practices,[104] information that is closely connected to the mediator's duty to provide the parties with information about the *process* of mediation that will take place (discussed in this section).

Some codes of conduct for mediators suggest that mediators *must disclose* to the parties information about their *education, mediation training, and experience.*[105] However, the majority of the codes are content with the mediator having the information *available* for the parties and disclosing it upon request.[106] This is a tough issue to grapple with. Information on the mediator's qualifications and experience seems clearly relevant to the parties' decision to select a particular mediator, thus making the mediator, who is under a duty to be worthy of the parties' trust, responsible for disclosing the information to the parties.

[102] See, e.g., Nolan-Haley, "Informed Consent", 825–826 (discussing the fiduciary relationship between mediators and mediation parties and its implications for the disclosure requirements of mediators).

[103] See, e.g., California Rules, Rule 3.855(b). See also Model Standards, Standard III.C.

[104] See, e.g., Oregon Standards, Standard II Comment 2. See also Michael Moffitt, "Casting Light on the Black Box of Mediation: Should Mediators Make Their Conduct More Transparent?" (1997) 13 *Ohio State Journal on Dispute Resolution* 1.

[105] ADR Canada Code, s. 8.1(b).

[106] See, e.g., Federal Employee Mediators Guide, Standard IV.A.3; Oregon Standards, Standard V Comment 4.

The *Texas Ethical Guidelines for Mediators* (Texas Guidelines), for example, state that "[a] mediator's qualifications and experience constitute the foundation upon which the mediation process depends."[107] If this is indeed so, then the information is relevant to making an informed decision about mediator choice and "[a] mediator should inform the participants of the mediator's qualifications and experience,"[108] and not wait for the parties to request that information. On the other hand, practitioners might argue that such a demand is divorced from reality and cannot be met in practice. Should mediators begin their first meeting with the parties by saying that they recently underwent mediator training and this is their first, second, or fifth mediation? Obviously they must provide parties with accurate information if they are asked by them about their training and experience, but must they *volunteer* the information?

The practical difficulty is evident, as the sincerity of mediators may come at the cost of lost clients, who prefer more experienced mediators, and loss of confidence in the mediator, who may be viewed as less effective and as a result begin the process with one hand tied behind his back. Do we require lawyers to tell their clients that their case is their first? Do we ask surgeons to tell their patients that their operation is their fifth? However, these down-to-earth reasons do not provide an *ethical* justification for such practice. A possible justification could lie in the standard of party self-determination itself.

Mediators are under a duty to generate conditions that make informed decisions by parties possible. Mediation parties have a personal responsibility to seek information that is relevant to making decisions. They can ask questions, consult others, and collect information. The more the information is readily available to the parties, the more it is within their capabilities to seek it by themselves, and the more they are aware of the existence of that information and its relevancy to the decision they are about to make, the greater the personal responsibility of the parties to seek the information and the lower the onus of disclosure on the mediator. Thus, for example, the mediator must disclose conflicts of interest, because parties cannot be expected to be aware of them and might not suspect that the mediator as a trusted professional has such conflicts.[109] Similarly, mediators must disclose information about their mediation *style* because most parties are probably unaware that there are different mediation styles and that these differences have an impact on the conduct

[107] Texas Guidelines, Comment to s. 5. [108] Id., s. 5.
[109] This duty rests on reasons beyond the mediator–parties relationship. See Chapter 6.

of the mediation. However, all parties realize that mediators' training and experience are relevant to the selection of a mediator. They do not need the mediator to tell them that. Furthermore, this information may be available to them in various forms through the internet, advertising, court register, or simply by asking the mediator to supply them with the information. It therefore seems that mediators are not under a duty to disclose this information to the parties on their own initiative, although they must do so truthfully and accurately upon a party request.

(2) Information regarding the process

Parties reasonably expect mediators to provide them with information that is relevant to making an informed decision on whether to *participate* in the mediation. Information regarding the process can refer to the following:

- Information about the process,[110] the differences between mediation and other dispute resolution processes,[111] the possible use of separate meetings,[112] the role of the mediator,[113] and the importance of consulting outside experts when necessary.[114]

Mediators have a responsibility to provide this information or verify that parties are aware of it because an understanding of the nature of mediation is essential to exercising self-determination regarding participation in the process, yet it cannot be ruled out that parties either have received inaccurate information about the process from various sources or have not fully appreciated its meaning.

- Information about the risks of the process.

Mediators must not suffice with providing information about the advantages of mediation. An informed decision must be based on the hazards of mediation as well if it is to be a true exercise of self-determination.[115] Most notably, mediators must discuss with the parties the limitations of mediation confidentiality, limitations that could

[110] See, e.g., Montana Association Code, s. I.E.

[111] See, e.g., Family Mediation Canada Code, Article 11.1(a).

[112] See, e.g., id., Article 11.1(g). See also Alabama Code, Standard 3(a).

[113] See, e.g., ADR Canada Code, s. 3.2. See also Alabama Code, Standard 3(a); California Rules, Rule 3.857(d).

[114] See, e.g., Alabama Code, Standard 3(a).

[115] See, e.g., Nolan-Haley, "Informed Consent", 782–783 (discussing disclosure of risks in medical treatment). See also id., 791–792 and note 73 (discussing disclosure of risks in mediation).

result in disclosure of mediation information.[116] The *Oregon Standards*, for example, provide that "[i]n advance of receiving confidential communications, mediators should educate themselves and inform all participants about their reporting obligations (e.g., mandatory Child Abuse or Elder Abuse reporting) and how those obligations influence the way the mediators conduct mediation."[117] It is critical that innocent or unsophisticated parties do not participate in mediation under the mistaken assumption that mediation confidentiality grants full protection to their words and actions. When parties are legally represented the responsibility of the mediator is lighter because we assume that the lawyers will provide that information to their clients and protect their interests.

- Information about parties' rights and mediators' duties.

If parties are to make an informed decision on participation in mediation they need to know the extent of their control over the process and the standards that govern the mediator's conduct. For example, mediators are expected to provide parties with information regarding the decisions that are within their exclusive decision-making power, such as the decision to withdraw from mediation at any time,[118] the decision to accept or reject mediated agreements, and the decision to consult a lawyer or other outside experts.[119]

(b) A duty to make information accessible to parties by indirect means Supplementing the duty of mediators to directly provide information to the parties is a duty to take steps that will make information accessible to the parties. This duty is triggered in circumstances in which mediators are ethically *prevented* from providing the information directly to the parties, yet the information is relevant to the decision-making for otherwise the decision will be made on the basis of inadequate information. For example, mediators may be prevented from providing information that has been communicated to them in confidence by one of the parties, or where provision of the information might give an

[116] See Chapter 10.

[117] Oregon Standards, Standard IV Comment 2. See also California Rules, Rule 3.854(b); Federal Employee Mediators Guide, Standard V.C.

[118] See, e.g., Family Mediation Canada Code, Article 11.1(d). See also Alabama Code, Standard 3(a).

[119] Family Mediation Canada Code, Article 11.1(d).

impression of mediator partiality, or where the mediators do not have the competence (i.e. the qualifications and experience) to supply the information, for example where the mediator is not a lawyer but realizes that legal information is relevant to party decision-making. In such cases, mediators ought to try to bring the information to the attention of parties indirectly, by asking questions that stimulate parties to look for the information, or by referring parties to consult outside experts. The *North Carolina Standards*, for example, state that "[i]n appropriate circumstances, a mediator shall inform the parties of the importance of seeking legal, financial, tax or other professional advice before, during or after the mediation process";[120] And the *Family Mediation Canada Code* provides that "[i]n the event that a party needs either additional information or assistance in order for the negotiations to proceed in a fair and orderly manner or for an agreement to be reached, the mediator must refer the individual to appropriate resources."[121]

(c) A duty to terminate mediation When mediators believe that a party is about to make an uninformed decision, in circumstances in which their attempts to bring that information to the attention of the party have not been successful, they must terminate the mediation in order to prevent the making of an uninformed decision. This duty follows from the legitimate expectation of parties that the mediators in their case be worthy of their trust, that is, protect them from faulty decision-making that they are not aware of. The *Oregon Standards*, for example, provide that "[m]ediators should suspend, end, or withdraw from the mediation if they believe a participant is unable to give Informed Consent."[122]

However, the termination of mediation is a drastic intervention in party self-determination, and therefore should be a measure of last resort that is used sparingly only in *extraordinary* circumstances in which substantive self-determination is *severely undermined* because of the missing information. This requires us to adopt a strict definition of relevant information for the purpose of justifying a termination of mediation. In such case, the definition of inadequate relevant

120 North Carolina Standards, Rule IV.D.

121 Family Mediation Canada Code, Article 9. See also Model Standards, Standard I.A.2; New York MEAC, Opinion 2009–01 available at www.nycourts.gov/ip/adr/Publications/MEAC_Opinions/FormalPublishedOpinion2009-01.pdf, p. 5 (Mediator instructed to refer parties to seek expert advice).

122 Oregon Standards, Standard II Comment 5.

information that justifies termination must be *narrower* than the definition of relevant information that triggers a mediator duty to provide information to parties or to take steps that make such information accessible. In other words, mediators who are aware of the inadequacy of relevant information must take steps to address the situation, and failure to do so would be unethical. However, such failure does not mean that the mediation should have been terminated. After all, information about the differences between mediation and other conflict resolution processes and information regarding the duties of mediators is information that is relevant to party decision-making as well, yet it would be too extreme to view such mediator failure and such inadequacy of information as a reason for terminating a mediation.

In my view, a mediator's duty to terminate a mediation for lack of information relevant to a decision to be made is established where a reasonable party, being aware of that information, *would not have agreed to continue to participate in the process* or *would not have consented to the proposed mediated outcome*. Such occasions will probably be quite rare, where the inadequate information has an impact on *the content of the mediated agreement* or is about *an abuse of the process* of mediation. Think, for example, of a party who is not aware of the fact that the other party's action is barred by a statute of limitation, or of assets that are in the other party's possession in connection to which the other party lies, or of the other party's intention to collect information in the course of mediation for the purpose of litigation, which he or she intends to pursue later irrespective of the mediation. These are cases of bad faith, fraud, or unconscionability that had a reasonable party been aware of, he or she would not have agreed to participate in the mediation or accept its outcome. This kind of information might significantly affect the *mediation outcome* and thus the mediator in such cases has a duty to terminate the mediation.[123]

This analysis would not be complete without reference to the duties of mediators toward their profession. The duty to terminate mediation follows from mediators' duty toward their *profession* to conduct mediations with professional integrity and to preserve the profession's standing and public trust in it, as well as from their relationship with the parties. The mediator–profession perspective supports the *stricter* requirement for significant inadequacy of information as a condition for an obligation

[123] See, e.g., Family Mediation Canada Code, Article 13.1(b) and (c). See also Florida Rules, Rule 10.420(b)(4) (termination upon fraud or unconscionability).

to terminate the mediation. Not every decision that is made on the basis of inadequate information will endanger public confidence in the institution of mediation. However, sometimes the type of missing information and the consequences of the decision will be of such magnitude as to undermine the profession's standing and compel termination of the process.[124] Again, mediators should remember that the decision to terminate should be a decision of *last resort*, in circumstances in which other, less drastic interventions have failed.

4.6 Conclusion

Party self-determination is a fundamental standard of mediation. This chapter has presented, from a professional ethics perspective, the type of decisions this standard applies to, the division of decision-making authority between mediation parties and mediators, the conditions that must be met for self-determination to be exercised by parties, and the responsibility of mediators for the presence of these conditions in the course of mediation. The following proposed standard summarizes these insights.

4.7 A proposed standard of self-determination

A mediator shall conduct the mediation on the basis of party self-determination. Self-determination means that the parties are free to make voluntary, uncoerced, and informed decisions.

A. Parties have a right to exercise self-determination with respect to any issue that has to be decided in the course of mediation, procedural or substantive, at any stage of the mediation, including mediator selection, process design, participation in or withdrawal from the process, and outcome.
B. A mediator may make those decisions that are necessary to conduct the mediation in accordance with the Standards.[125] However, due to the general applicability of the parties' right to self-determination,

[124] See in this context Sarah Childs Grebe, Karen Irvin, Michael Lang, "A Model for Ethical Decision Making in Mediation" (1989) 7 *Mediation Quarterly* 133, 144 (arguing that while client self-determination is paramount, a mediator should consider "potential damage to his or her professional reputation" if the outcome of the mediation "may give an uninformed outsider a bad impression about how mediation is conducted and/or what mediation is").

[125] The Standards are the ethical norms identified in this book as applying to mediators.

when a mediator makes a decision he or she must involve the parties in the decision-making process, and either obtain their consent to the decision or follow the parties' determination on the issue.

C. Nevertheless:
   1. A mediator may make decisions without involving the parties in the decision-making process where doing so is practically impossible (for example, with regard to the type of questions to be asked) or is inconsistent with the Standards (for example, where sharing decision-making might give an appearance of partiality or violate confidentiality).
   2. After sharing decision-making with the parties when possible, the mediator shall decide, despite an express desire of the parties to the contrary:
      (a) To terminate, postpone, or withdraw from the mediation if he or she cannot conduct the mediation consistent with the Standards (for example, for reasons of incompetence[126] or serious conflict of interest[127]);
      (b) To refuse to perform an act requested by the parties, which would be inconsistent with the Standards (for example, refuse to give professional advice[128]);
      (c) To perform a specific act that he is under a duty to perform by an express provision in the Standards or by a compelling external standard (for example, disclose confidential information to non-participants in accordance with a legal order[129]).

D. Party Competency –
   A mediator shall not conduct a mediation in circumstances in which it is reasonable to believe that a party is incompetent to participate in the process. Party competency is the capacity of a party to perceive information, process it, and understand the information and its implications, in order to make and communicate the decision.
   1. Incompetence to participate in mediation may be temporary or permanent and result from reasons such as abuse of drugs or alcohol; lack of language proficiency; mental retardation, dementia, mental illness, or depression; or age.
   2. A mediator who suspects that a party's capacity to participate in the mediation and understand information is limited, shall take appropriate steps to assist the party to understand the information, participate in the process, and exercise self-determination,

[126] See Chapter 5. [127] See Chapter 6. [128] See Chapter 8. [129] See Chapter 10.

including postponing the mediation or involving a representative of the party in the process. When the mediator's intervention is neither possible nor successful the mediator shall terminate the mediation.

E. Voluntariness –
A mediator shall conduct the mediation under conditions that enable parties to make voluntary, uncoerced decisions.

1. A mediator shall not exert pressure designed to reduce party choice in decision-making.
   (a) A mediator shall not undermine party self-determination for reasons such as higher settlement rates, egos, increased fees, or outside pressures from court personnel, program administrators, provider organizations, the media, or others.
2. A mediator shall take appropriate steps to prevent the exertion of pressure designed to reduce party choice in decision-making by other mediation participants.
   (a) A mediator shall be aware of power imbalances between parties. If the mediator suspects that a party has made or is about to make a decision out of feelings of helplessness and lack of choice, as a result of pressures of mediation participants or non-participants, he or she shall examine with that party the basis for those feelings and whether they are justified in the prevailing circumstances.
   (b) If subsequent to this clarification the party wishes to proceed with the decision the mediator shall respect his or her choice, provided that he or she is competent to participate in the mediation.

F. Informed decisions –
A mediator shall conduct the mediation under conditions that enable parties to make informed decisions. An informed decision is a decision that has been made on the basis of the information that is relevant to the decision-making.

1. A mediator cannot ensure that parties make decisions that are based on complete information. However, the mediator shall take steps, consistent with the Standards, so that party decision-making is based on the information relevant to the decision-making. Relevant information is information the knowledge or ignorance of which could influence the decision or the choice made.

2. The information that a mediator shall provide the parties with includes the following:
   (a) The process of mediation, the differences between mediation and other dispute resolution processes, the role of the mediator, the style of mediation practiced by the mediator, the possible use of separate meetings, and the risks of the process;
   (b) The duties of the mediator according to the Standards;
   (c) The parties' right to withdraw from the mediation at any time;
   (d) The parties' right to consult other professionals and the importance of such consultation when it is required for decision-making.
3. A mediator shall terminate the mediation for lack of information where all the following conditions are met:
   (a) A party does not possess relevant information and is unaware of its existence; and
   (b) The information is such that a reasonable party, being aware of the information, would not have agreed to continue to participate in the process or would not have consented to the proposed mediated outcome; and
   (c) The mediator has taken all possible steps consistent with the Standards to make the information accessible to the party, including asking questions and referring the party to outside experts.

5

Mediator competence

5.1 Introduction

Mediator competence is hotly debated in the mediation discourse. What qualifications and skills are required of mediators? What kind of training should mediators undergo? Should mediators be licensed like lawyers, doctors, and other professionals? In the United States, Canada, Australia, and many other states there are no legal requirements for the practice of mediation in private settings. Any person can practice mediation if he or she is acceptable to the parties. However, there is a requirement for qualifications in many mediation programs established by states, courts, and professional mediator organizations. Persons who wish to conduct mediations in connection with these programs and be on their list of mediators must meet minimum requirements that vary from program to program. Some programs set requirements according to the *type* of mediated cases, requiring *general* qualifications for civil cases and *special* qualifications for categories of cases such as family or divorce,[1] child custody,[2] or domestic violence.[3] Court programs sometimes set requirements that vary in accordance with the *court* with which mediators are listed, be it a civil court, family court, superior court, or other.[4] The qualifications required of mediators may include requirements for good character; X hours of approved mediation training (for example, 20 hours in Alabama,[5] 30 hours in

[1] See, e.g., Indiana Rules of Court, Rules for Alternative Dispute Resolution (Indiana Rules) available at www.in.gov/judiciary/rules/adr/, Rule 2.5.

[2] See, e.g., California Rules of Court available at www.courts.ca.gov/cms/rules/index.cfm?title=five, Rule 5.210.

[3] See, e.g., Georgia Alternative Dispute Resolution Rules, Appendix B available at www.godr.org/files/CURRENT%20ADR%20RULES%20COMPLETE%209-4-2013(1).pdf.

[4] See, e.g., Florida Rules, Rule 10.100.

[5] See Alabama Center for Dispute Resolution, Mediator Standards and Registration Procedures, available at www.alabamaadr.org/web/roster-documents/med_Stds_Reg_Procedures.php (Alabama Mediator Standards and Registration Procedures), Appendix I.

Minnesota,[6] 38 hours according to the Australia National Mediator Accreditation System,[7] 40 hours in Indiana,[8] or 180 hours according to the ADR Canada Chartered Mediators Accreditation Program[9]); being a licensed attorney with X years of practice of law (for example, 4 years in Alabama,[10] or 5 years in North Carolina[11]) or having a degree in certain fields (for example, psychology, accountancy, social work) with X years of practice; completing X hours of continuing education every X years;[12] or an undertaking to provide X hours of pro bono mediation services to the public every X years.[13]

Developing requirements for mediator qualification, training courses, and continuing education programs is an important step in the process of professionalization. This chapter applies the lens of professional ethics to this issue. It begins with an explanation of the *normative basis* for a duty of mediator competence, and then explores the *meaning* of competence in view of the core definition of mediation and mediators' role. It establishes two levels of competence that mediators are required to have: a minimum requirement of basic competence that all mediators must satisfy, and a contingent requirement of specific competence that mediators sometimes need to satisfy, depending on the circumstances. The chapter concludes with a *proposed standard* of mediator competence that applies, from the perspective of a theory of mediators' ethics, to all mediators.

5.2 A duty of competence to mediation parties

Mediators perform a role in the service of mediation parties. As a matter of role-morality, and like other role-holders, mediators must be

[6] See Minnesota General Rules of Practice available at www.revisor.mn.gov/court_rules/rule.php?type=gp&id=114, Rule 114.13(a) (Civil Facilitative/Hybrid Neutral Roster).

[7] See Australia National Mediator Accreditation System Approval Standards available at www.msb.org.au/sites/default/files/documents/Approval%20Standards.pdf, s. 5.

[8] See Indiana Rules, Rule 2.5.

[9] See ADR Canada Chartered Mediators Accreditation Program available at www.adrcanada.ca/resources/documents/CMedCriteriaSept2011.pdf.

[10] See Alabama Mediator Standards and Registration Procedures, Appendix I.

[11] See North Carolina Mediated Settlement Conference Rules available at www.nccourts.org/Courts/CRS/Councils/DRC/MSC/Certification/Apply/Default.asp, Rule 8.B(1).

[12] See, e.g., CME Requirements for Certified Mediators, How to Become A Florida Supreme Court Certified Mediator Step By Step Guide, Attachment D available at www.floridamediation.com/about/HowToBecomeAMediatorCurrent.pdf.

[13] See, e.g., Alabama Mediator Standards and Registration Procedures, Appendix I (10 hours annually).

competent if they are to be worthy of the trust of their clients.[14] Parties who come to mediation expect the mediator to be competent to mediate their case. These parties rely on the competence of their mediator and assume that he or she has special qualifications and skills beyond those of the parties themselves that enable him or her to fulfill his or her role and provide the requested service. Persons who accept the role of mediator implicitly promise the parties by doing so that they have the competence to fulfill the role of a mediator.

Not surprisingly, a mediator duty of competence can be found in virtually every code of conduct for mediators.[15] The *Model Standards*, for example, state that "[a] person who offers to serve as a mediator creates the expectation that the person is competent to mediate effectively";[16] the *Florida Rules* state that "[a] mediator shall acquire and maintain professional competence in mediation";[17] and the *Australian Practice Standards* provide that "[m]ediators must be competent and have relevant skills and knowledge."[18]

If mediators have a duty toward parties to *be competent* to mediate, then surely they must *decline* a case when they are not competent, and *withdraw* if they lose competence at some stage of the mediation. Indeed, the *Georgia Standards*, for example, provide that "[m]ediators are obligated not to undertake cases for which their training or expertise is inadequate";[19] the *North Carolina Standards* provide that "[a] mediator shall maintain professional competency in mediation skills and, where the mediator lacks the skills necessary for a particular case, shall decline to serve or withdraw from serving";[20] and the *Model Standards* provide that "[i]f a mediator's ability to conduct a mediation is impaired by drugs, alcohol, medication or otherwise, the mediator shall not conduct the mediation."[21]

5.3 The profession's and public expectations of mediator competence: the professional and social interests in mediator competence

Mediators' duty of competence is shaped not only by the expectations of mediation parties, but also by the expectations of the mediation

14 See Chapter 2, Section 2.3.1. 15 For examples, see Chapter 3, Section 3.6.
16 Model Standards, Standard IV.A.1. 17 Florida Rules, Rule 10.630.
18 Australian Practice Standards, s. 7. 19 Georgia Standards, Standard V.
20 North Carolina Standards, Rule I. See also Alabama Code, Standard 1(a); California Rules, Rule 3.856(d).
21 Model Standards, Standard IV.C.

profession and the general public. Incompetent mediators compromise the interests of both the profession and the public that mediation should flourish, provide work for practitioners, and contribute to peaceful and efficient handling of disagreements. From a professional ethics perspective, the mediation profession and the public expect mediators to have a degree of competence that does not jeopardize the standing of the profession or the public trust in it. Some codes of conduct for mediators express this rationale in their standards of competence. *The Australian Ethical Guidelines*, for example, state that "[a] person who agrees to act as a mediator holds out to the parties *and the public* that she or he has the competence to mediate effectively";[22] the *Florida Rules* state, under a Mediator's Responsibility to the Mediation Profession Rule, that "a mediator is responsible for maintaining professional competence";[23] and the *Wisconsin Association Guidelines* also regard professional competency as mediators' responsibility to the *profession*.[24] The responsibilities to the profession and the public affect, as we will see, the meaning of mediator competence.

5.4 The meaning of mediator competence

5.4.1 Distinguishing between the expectations of particular parties and the expectations of reasonable parties

People come to mediation with various expectations regarding the mediator's competence. One approach to defining the requirement of competence could be to treat competence as a *variable* to be determined by the reasonable expectations of the *parties* in any *particular* case. For example, the *Model Standards* provide that "[a] mediator shall mediate only when the mediator has the necessary competence to satisfy the reasonable expectations of the parties."[25] A better approach would link the concept of competence to the expectations of *reasonable parties*. The expectations of reasonable parties represent a *minimum threshold* of *basic competence* that all mediators must meet irrespective of the expectations of the parties in the particular cases they mediate. Such a concept is needed because the parties' actual expectations might be *lower* than the expectations of reasonable parties with regard to basic competence.

There are two reasons why an approach of basic competence, which in effect commits the mediator to requirements of competence that might

[22] Australian Ethical Guidelines, s. 4. [23] Florida Rules, Rule 10.600.
[24] See Wisconsin Association Guidelines, s. 2.1. [25] Model Standards, Standard IV.A.

surpass the parties' actual expectations, is warranted. First, from a role-morality perspective, mediators are in a relationship of trust with the parties and must refrain from causing them injury. Since lack of basic competence could reasonably harm the parties, mediators who do not have basic competence must not accept cases despite the parties' desire that they do so. One could respond to this argument by bringing up the principle of party self-determination, and arguing that mediators who disclose their qualifications to the parties who in turn decide to select them as mediators should be exempt from an ethical duty to possess basic competence. It seems to me that this is the *Model Standards* approach, according to which "[a]ny person may be selected as a mediator, provided that the parties are satisfied with the mediator's competence and qualifications."[26] However, this approach should be rejected due to a second reason that supports a requirement for basic competence: mediators have a duty toward the profession and the public to protect the standing of mediation even where the parties in a particular case have limited expectations of their mediator. The public's trust in the profession of mediation and in the process of mediation could be undermined if unqualified mediators conduct mediations. Thus, parties' choice of mediators cannot relieve the latter of their duty to have basic competence, and where mediators do not possess this level of competence they must withdraw notwithstanding the parties' wishes.

It should be noted that parties' actual expectations of competence could be *similar* to or *higher* than the expectations of reasonable parties. Similar expectations raise no ethical difficulty because they reflect an expectation of basic competence. Higher expectations of parties represent a requirement for special or *specific competence*, beyond basic competence. Having specific competence, as we shall see, is not a general duty of mediators; it emerges in circumstances that establish an expectation of a competence over and above the basic competence required of mediators. But first we must understand what basic competence stands for.

5.4.2 *Basic competence*

5.4.2.1 Knowledge and skills

A concept of basic competence deals with the general requirement of qualifications that all mediators must satisfy if they are to have the capacity to perform the role of mediator and conduct a process of

[26] Model Standards, Standard IV.A.1.

mediation. A concept of mediator competence must have at least three components: (a) a basic, taken-for-granted ability to grasp information and understand communications (for example, not being intoxicated); (b) *knowledge* and *understanding* of the role, process, and responsibilities attached to the role; and (c) the *skills* necessary for the execution of the role.

As the core definition of mediators' role is to *assist parties to an actual or potential conflict to maintain a dialogue in order to enable them to make decisions regarding the conflict,*[27] mediators must have the knowledge and skills necessary for assisting parties in conflict to communicate, negotiate, and make decisions effectively.[28] Most codes of conduct for mediators rarely discuss the competence required of mediators and simply declare that mediators must be competent. Still, one can learn from the mediation literature and codes of conduct for mediators that do elaborate on mediator competence[29] that it should include:

Knowledge and understanding of:

- The nature of conflicts and their effect on people;
- Theories of communication, negotiation, and persuasion, including issues of power and abuse of power in negotiation; ways of assisting people to communicate, and overcoming obstacles to communication;
- The nature of mediation (what it is) and its stages (how it is done);
- The role of mediators (what mediators do) and the ethical and legal responsibilities attached to it, such as a commitment to party self-determination, impartiality, and confidentiality;
- The possibility that the law may affect the rights of mediation parties and the importance of the parties being aware of these legal implications.

Skills to:

- Assess suitability of case and parties to mediation;
- Communicate, negotiate, and assist the parties to communicate and negotiate. Such skills include listening, asking questions, reframing, summarizing, addressing power-imbalances and obstacles to communication and negotiation.

[27] See Chapter 3, Section 3.2.

[28] For a requirement that mediators have competence to mediate *effectively*, see, e.g., Australian Ethical Guidelines, s. 4; Model Standards, Standard IV.A.1; California Rules, Rule 3.856(d).

[29] See, e.g., Australian Practice Standards, s. 7.

Though all mediators must have basic competence, the *meaning* of basic competence is affected by the *style* of mediation with which the mediator associates himself. For example, the *knowledge* required of problem-solving mediators with respect to the nature of conflict, the nature of mediation, and the role of the mediator differs from that required of transformative or narrative mediators. Similarly, the basic *skills* that are deemed necessary for effective communication and negotiation receive a different interpretation.

The mediation literature and codes of conduct for mediators suggest that *problem-solving* mediators have an understanding of conflict as a clash between conflicting positions in a state of insufficient information. Mediators must therefore be familiar with both principled collaborative win-win negotiation and its rival, win-lose competitive negotiation; understand the difference between interests and positions; appreciate the importance of objective criteria for developing options; and be aware of rational and irrational barriers to negotiation. When the mediator engages in evaluation of the parties' cases he or she must have a knowledge of, or expertise in, the subject-matter of the content of the mediation as well. The skills of the problem-solving mediator require,[30] inter alia, good communicating, active listening, defining and clarifying issues, identifying and uncovering parties' needs and interests, reframing, exploring and assessing possible options and solutions, and use of separate meetings and reality testing when appropriate.

In terms of the knowledge required of *transformative mediators*, the mediation literature tells us that it involves an understanding of conflict as a destructive and demonizing experience that disempowers parties and harms their capacity to interact and "recognize" the other. It follows that mediators must be aware of the ways that empowerment and recognition shifts can occur in circumstances of dispute and transform the

[30] See, e.g., Boulle and Nesic, *Mediation*, pp. 158–174; Moore, *The Mediation Process*, pp. 211–268. See also, the definition of mediation in the Model Standards, Preamble ("Mediation serves various purposes, including providing the opportunity for parties to define and clarify issues, understand different perspectives, identify interests, explore and assess possible solutions, and reach mutually satisfactory agreements, when desired"); Advisory Committee Comment to California Rules, Rule 3.856(d) (noting that "Core mediation skills include communicating clearly, listening effectively, facilitating communication among all participants, promoting exploration of mutually acceptable settlement options, and conducting oneself in a neutral manner"); Nebraska Office of Dispute Resolution Manual of Standards and Ethics for Center Mediators, Directors and Staff, available at supremecourt.nebraska.gov/5530/professional-ethics-mediators (Nebraska Standards), s. I.C (listing "skills necessary for competency as a mediator").

relationship between the parties.[31] The skills transformative mediators are required to possess are listening, reflecting, summarizing, questioning that invites further discussion, "checking in" on what parties want to do, and avoiding directiveness and backing or staying out to allow for party participation.[32]

The type of knowledge required of *narrative mediators* differs from that of both problem-solving and transformative mediators. Narrative mediators need have an understanding of social constructionism – for example, that stories construct meaning and that social and cultural narratives affect personal narratives – and of postmodern ideas such as the denial of a single truth or the existence of objective descriptions (for example, denial of the existence of a single correct point of view of an event). They need to understand how the stories parties tell create reality and meaning for the parties. For the narrative mediator, conflicts are not about interests and needs but concern conflicting notions of entitlements. He or she must therefore be aware of the way notions of entitlements develop in order to challenge them, deconstruct the parties' stories, and help the parties build alternative stories.[33] The skills that narrative mediators rely on are double listening,[34] asking curious questions,[35] externalizing,[36] mapping the effects of the conflict, identifying openings to an alternative story,[37] building stories of cooperation,[38] and generating understanding on how to go on from the conflict situation.[39]

Thus the basic competence of mediators – the requirement for knowledge and skills – takes on a different *meaning* according to the style of the mediator. To illustrate again the point of difference, take listening as an example. Listening is a core skill of all mediators, irrespective of style. It contributes to the development of trust in the mediator and to a positive experience of parties, who feel that they are heard, and provides the mediator with valuable information to work with. But the meaning of

[31] See, e.g., Folger, Bush, and Della Noce, *Transformative Mediation*, pp. 36–37.

[32] See, e.g., id., p. 48. For a detailed discussion of the core practices of transformative mediation see id., pp. 31–49.

[33] See, e.g., Winslade and Monk, *Narrative Mediation*, p. 72.

[34] See, e.g., Winslade and Monk, *Practicing Narrative Mediation*, pp. 7-12.

[35] See Winslade and Monk, *Narrative Mediation*, pp. 78, 123–129.

[36] See id., pp. 79, 143–147.

[37] See Winslade and Monk, *Practicing Narrative Mediation*, pp. 26–31.

[38] See id., pp. 31–35.

[39] For a detailed discussion, see id., pp. 1–35 (discussing the hallmarks of narrative mediation); Monk and Winslade, *When Stories Clash*, pp. 25, 44–95 (discussing the techniques of narrative mediation).

listening varies among the mediation styles, because mediators have different goals in practicing listening. While the problem-solving mediator listens carefully in order to identify underlying needs and interests that can later establish common ground for a resolution, the transformative mediator listens for expressions of weaknesses that could be transformed by empowerment and for expressions of self-centeredness that could be transformed into recognition, yet the narrative mediator listens to the narratives of the parties in order to reveal the "positioning" or role that each party assumes for himself and assigns to the other, and later intervenes to destabilize these descriptions so that alternative descriptions or stories can develop.[40] Thus, all mediators must have listening skills as part of their basic competence to mediate, but the meaning of this skill depends on the style of mediation they associate themselves with.

5.4.2.2 A requirement for training and experience

The previous discussion of the knowledge and skills required of mediators to be able to perform their role has a bearing on the question whether basic competence to mediate involves (a) mediator training and (b) mediation experience. Mediator training involves a structured course designed to supply candidates with the knowledge and skills that mediators need, while a requirement for mediation experience is designed to complement mediator training with real-case mediation experience in practice and supervision. Most people have some of the knowledge required of mediators: they have some idea regarding conflicts, communication, and negotiation, and they may have, to some degree, the skills of mediators: they may be good listeners, communicators, or negotiators. This is one reason for favoring an approach to mediator competence that resists a requirement for training and experience as a prerequisite for mediation practice. This view is often raised in the debate over the need for mediator certification and licensing.[41] Those who oppose such a move raise various concerns, for example the difficulty in deciding on the criteria for certification; that people who have natural qualifications to be mediators would be prevented from conducting mediations; that the costs of mediation to parties would increase; and that parties should be free to choose and nominate mediators in their cases. For example, the

[40] See Winslade and Monk, *Practicing Narrative Mediation*, pp. 7–12.

[41] See, e.g., Donald T. Weckstein, "Mediator Certification: Why and How" (1996) 30 *University of San Francisco Law Review* 757; Ellen A. Waldman, "The Challenge of Certification"; Sarah Rudolph Cole, "Mediator Certification: Has the Time Come?" (2005) 11 *Dispute Resolution Magazine* 7.

California-CDRC Standards state that "[u]se of any degree or license as a criterion for determining competence could restrict competent persons from serving as a Mediator. The freedom of disputants to select their own Mediator should not be denied by restricting that choice, as any restriction would be inconsistent with mediation's voluntary nature and would deprive disputants of access to Mediators with a rich diversity of occupational backgrounds and mediation styles."[42]

From a professional ethics perspective, it is necessary to look at the issue of training and experience in view of the *practice* that mediators are expected to perform (the descriptive definition of the role and its ideals) and the *responsibilities* associated with that role (role-morality). The previous section discussed the kinds of knowledge and skills required of mediators. Persons with no training and experience are unlikely to have the *level* of knowledge and skills that would make them competent to mediate. What it requires is *a deep, high-level* understanding of the theories and processes involved in mediation (of conflict, communication, negotiation, responsibility, etc.) and the use of skills and techniques of mediators in practice, together with an *awareness* of that knowledge and understanding. This combination of high-level understanding of what is going on in the process of the mediation with a reflective use of skills that is informed by theory is the reason why mediator competence almost certainly requires training and experience. People who are "natural mediators" because they are great listeners or have excellent communication and negotiation skills are not competent mediators, in the same way that an extremely wise and supportive friend would not be considered a competent therapist, nor a persuasive person representing another's case a competent lawyer. Putting aside for the moment the legal question of regulation and licensing, from an ethical perspective these persons do not satisfy the ethical requirement of basic competence: they do not have sufficient knowledge about the relevant practice (what it is, the theories behind it, and the responsibilities of the role) and sufficient awareness of the proper use of the skills that are used to achieve the purpose of that practice (how the skills are to be used in light of the theories and responsibilities). Thus, as a matter of both role-definition and role-morality, formal mediator training and experience are important ingredients of basic competence. They follow from the expectations of reasonable mediation parties, and they certainly reflect the expectations of the mediation profession and of employers and principals of

[42] California-CDRC Standards, s. 5. See also Boulle and Nesic, *Mediation*, p. 424.

mediators. They also reflect mediators' shared ideal of professionalization and distinguishing themselves from other professionals.

This also is the approach taken by the majority of codes of conduct for mediators and mediation legislation that support a requirement for training, and to a lesser extent for mediation experience. For example, the *Alabama Code* states that "[a] mediator is obligated to acquire knowledge and training in the mediation process";[43] and the *Model Standards* provide that "[t]raining, experience in mediation, skills, cultural understandings and other qualities are often necessary for mediator competence."[44] As we have seen, mediation programs, especially court-connected programs that seek to protect the reputation of court-connected mediators, require training and experience as a condition for inclusion on their lists of mediators. Though a professional ethics perspective cannot tell us exactly *how many* hours of training and experience are required, it points to the need for this condition to be met and to the substantive goals that such training and experience should achieve. The actual numbers and specifics may legitimately vary from program to program as long as they meet this ethical end. Furthermore, the question of training and experience should not be understood as an issue between mediators and parties alone. As we have already observed, mediation parties cannot release mediators from the requirement for basic competence by their consent, because of the expectations of such competence of the profession, the public, and employers or principals. However, mediators may sometimes be able to overcome certain types of incompetence, such as lack of experience, by mediating cases together with a competent experienced mediator,[45] and by appropriate disclosure when disclosure is required by the norm of party self-determination.[46]

5.4.2.3 The question of mediator qualities

The mediation literature sometimes discusses various qualities or traits that are considered important for the practice of mediation, such as empathy, creativity, patience, listening ability, being non-judgmental, persuasiveness, optimism, flexibility, and commonsense.[47] These qualities should not be seen as forming part of a *duty* of mediator competence, but as professional *ideals* that mediators aspire to and are encouraged to develop and nurture. For example, a model mediator might always be non-judgmental and patient, but most mediators will experience

[43] Alabama Code, Standard 9(a). [44] Model Standards, Standard IV.A.1.
[45] See Section 5.5. [46] See Section 5.6. [47] See Boulle and Nesic, *Mediation*, pp. 111–112.

moments of criticism and impatience and can only strive to achieve these worthy ideals. Indeed, competence standards in codes of conduct for mediators do not include these qualities. Clearly, however, persons whose dominant qualities are the opposite will likely find it difficult to comply with the ethical norms of mediation. For example, a judgmental person will find it hard to conduct mediations in consistence with a norm of impartiality, an impatient person might have a problem with a norm of respect, and a person who has difficulty listening to people might not be able to adequately exercise the skill of listening and thus lack competence and undermine the parties' opportunity to participate in the process in accordance with a norm of party self-determination.

5.4.3 *Specific competence*

Specific competence represents special kinds of knowledge and skills beyond basic competence, namely knowledge and skills that differ from the knowledge and skills that are needed in order for mediators to be able to exercise their core role. Specific competence could refer, for example, to expertise in the subject-matter of the dispute or to knowledge of the parties' culture and language. Mediators may be required to have specific competence for several reasons.

5.4.3.1 An expectation of subject matter expertise due to role definition

The core definition of mediation and of the role of mediators requires mediators to have *process* expertise, that is, to have the knowledge and skills necessary for conducting a process of assisted communication and negotiation between parties in conflict. According to this approach, basic competence is not dependent on the *type* of case and does not require special knowledge of the subject-matter of the dispute. For example, mediators need not have prior knowledge of the law of negligence and the technicalities of medical practice in order to mediate a case of a malpractice claim against a doctor. It is assumed that basic competence suffices for them to conduct an efficient mediation process, because their function as facilitators of communication and negotiation between the parties does not require subject-matter expertise for that purpose. Echoing this approach, the *North Carolina Standards* state that "[a] mediator's most important qualification is the mediator's competence in procedural aspects of facilitating the resolution of disputes rather than the mediator's familiarity with technical knowledge relating to the subject of the dispute."[48] Similarly, the Georgia Supreme Court *ADR Rules* provide that "[a]lthough mediators do not necessarily need subject matter expertise, they must have process expertise."[49] The situation changes when the mediator assumes a different role that takes him farther from the core role of mediators. For example, if the mediator assumes an *evaluative* role in response to the parties' request or on his or her own initiative, he or she must have sufficient knowledge of the area of evaluation in order to form a precise evaluation, and sufficient skills to collect the information for the evaluation and to deliver it in accordance with the norms of mediation, in particular the norms of impartiality and self-determination.[50] Thus, mediators should have subject matter expertise if they (1) make a representation that they have such expertise; or (2) if they undertake a role that requires such expertise.

5.4.3.2 An expectation of subject matter expertise due to case complexity and related factors

It cannot be ruled out that in certain circumstances procedural expertise or basic competence will be insufficient even where the mediator exercises his or her core role as facilitator of communication and negotiation. Take, for example, a complex dispute regarding intellectual property rights that most people know little about. Can a mediator help the parties negotiate their differences without an understanding of issues such as what intellectual property rights are? What can and cannot be subject to such rights? How does one protect such rights? What are the limitations on using such rights? This is a complicated matter and I can only point to some factors that could be relevant in considering a requirement for specific competence in the area of dispute.

(1) The more the subject-matter of the dispute is *technical and remote* from the everyday experience of most people in general, of the particular mediator in particular, the stronger the requirement for specific knowledge of that area. This factor may be affected by *mediators' personal attributes*. The more experienced the mediator is, the quicker he or she learns, and the more confident he or she is in his or her abilities – the easier he or she will find the challenge of

[48] North Carolina Standards, Rule I.A.

[49] Georgia Supreme Court ADR Rules, Requirements for Qualification and Training of Neutrals available at www.godr.org/index.php?option=com_content&view=article&id=58&Itemid=57, Appendix B s. I(A).

[50] See, e.g., Boulle and Nesic, *Mediation*, pp. 114–115 (discussing the issue of expertise in the subject matter of the dispute).

navigating the process, the parties, and their representatives without detailed knowledge of the area of dispute.

(2) The more critical an understanding of key concepts and details of the subject-matter is to *the ability to assess the parties' capacity to participate* in the process, to *assist party communications*, and to *prevent harm* to participants and non-participants – the stronger the requirement for specific knowledge of that area. For example, many mediation programs require specific competence of mediators in family, divorce, and child custody disputes. It is thought that without adequate understanding of the legal and psychological aspects of family disputes and their implications for all those involved, mediators will not be able to facilitate an effective and safe dialogue. This rationale could apply to non-family disputes as well.

(3) The more *dependent* the parties are on the mediator's knowledge of the subject-matter of the dispute, the stronger the requirement for specific knowledge of that area. If the parties have a good grasp of the area of conflict, or if they are assisted by experts (for example, a lawyer or other professional experts), there is less need for specific mediator knowledge because he or she can focus on helping them communicate on the basis of the parties' knowledge. When one or more of the parties do not have that knowledge, or when one or more of them do not have access to an expert, the need for mediator input in terms of guiding the parties, referring them to relevant information, understanding the information himself and helping the parties understand it is greater, and so too is the requirement for specific competence.

5.4.3.3 An expectation of subject matter expertise due to institutional rules

Mediators who practice in connection with mediation programs or as employees must satisfy the qualification requirements set by them. Most programs are satisfied with basic competence and do not require substantive knowledge of the content of the dispute. One notable exception is *family mediation*. Mediation programs that provide mediation services in family disputes and family mediator organizations require specific qualifications that include, for example, knowledge of family law relating to divorce, psychological issues in divorce, the recognition of domestic violence, and an understanding of children's needs in divorce.[51] Specific

[51] See, e.g., Academy of Professional Family Mediators (APFM) Training Program Guidelines at www.apfmnet.org/pg38.cfm; Vermont Superior Court Family Mediation Program

qualifications are sometimes required by court programs that certify mediators according to the *court* with which they are affiliated (for example, county court, circuit court, appellate court). These programs might require special knowledge relating to the law and procedures that govern the type of cases that are dealt with in these courts.[52]

5.4.3.4 An expectation of cultural knowledge or language skills

Basic competence may be insufficient when the mediator and one or more of the parties come from different cultures. Our cultural background affects the way we understand, communicate, and interact with other people, and thus awareness of cultural differences may be important for conducting mediation.[53] When the mediator and one or more of the parties do not speak the same language or have a low command of the shared language, the mediator might not be able to fulfill his or her role effectively and may need the assistance of someone who has this specific competence.

Figure 5.1 describes the types and build-up of mediator competence.

5.5 Bridging competence gaps

From a professional ethics perspective, a mediator who does not have sufficient competence to mediate a case does not have to decline the case or withdraw if he or she can overcome his or her deficiency by bringing the missing competence into the process with the assistance of other persons. For example, a person who has just completed a mediator training course and never mediated a real case probably lacks basic competence to mediate because he or she has no mediation experience. Such a person should co-mediate first with experienced mediators in order to reach the required level of basic competence. Similarly, when a mediator does not have specific competence where such competence is required, for example,

(VSCFMP) available at www.vermontjudiciary.org/GTC/Family/Shared Documents/Mediator%20Application%20Packet%209%2029%202013%20FINAL.pdf; Lake County 19th Judicial Circuit Family Mediation Program available at 19thcircuitcourt.state.il.us/services/Pages/fmp.aspx#how%20to%20become%20a%20family%20mediator.

52 See, e.g., Florida Mediation Training Standards and Procedures available at www.floridasupremecourt.org/clerk/adminorders/2013/AOSC13-41.pdf; Virginia Guidelines for the Training and Certification of Court-Referred Mediators available at www.courts.state.va.us/courtadmin/aoc/djs/programs/drs/mediation/training/tom.pdf.

53 See, e.g., Harold Abramson, "Crossing Boarders into New Ethical Territory: Ethical Challenges When Mediating Cross-Culturally" (2008) 49 *South Texas Law Review* 921.

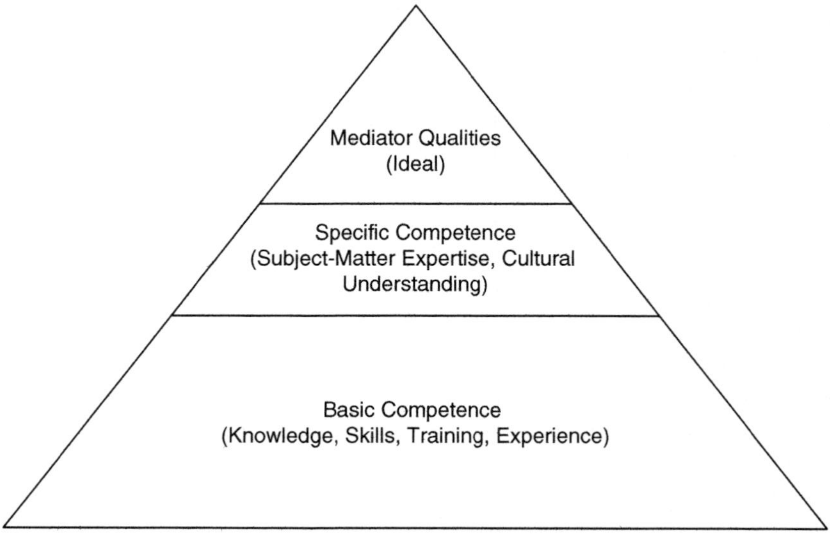

Figure 5.1: Mediator competence

because legal or psychological issues that need to be addressed have arisen in the mediation and the mediator has no subject-matter expertise, the mediator should close this competence gap through the use of persons who have the desired expertise. For example, mediators in such case may involve the parties' lawyers in the discussion, refer the parties to outside experts or invite experts to take part in the mediation, or collaborate with a co-mediator who has the necessary specific competence.[54]

5.6 Providing information regarding mediator competence

Mediators may be required to provide information to the parties regarding their competence at the outset of the mediation. The information regarding the mediator's competence might be needed to enable the parties to make an informed decision whether the particular mediator is suitable for their needs. The provision of such information could be considered to be a *duty* of the mediator, stemming from his or her duty to respect the parties'

[54] See, e.g., Alabama Code, Standard 1(a)(3) (noting that the mediator shall request technical assistance); Michigan Standards of Conduct for Mediators (2013) available at courts.mi.gov/Administration/SCAO/Resources/Documents/standards/odr/Mediator%20Standards%20of%20Conduct%202.1.13.pdf (Michigan Standards), Standard IV(b) (requesting appropriate assistance).

right to self-determination, because knowledge of the mediator's qualifications seems necessary for making an informed decision about mediator selection. This approach may have prompted the drafters of the *Texas Guidelines* to comment that "[a] mediator's qualifications and experience constitute the foundation upon which the mediation process depend," and to hold that "[a] mediator should inform the participants of the mediator's qualifications and experience."[55] However, an automatic duty to provide such information at the beginning of any mediation seems harsh to mediators, especially those who are making their first steps in the field. Such mediators might fear that the provision of such information, even when unsolicited by the parties, could undermine their professional authority in the eyes of the parties and jeopardize the effectiveness of the process. They might question whether lawyers, doctors, therapists, and other professionals are required to disclose their qualifications at the first meeting with their clients. It is no wonder, then, that many codes of conduct for mediators do not mandate unsolicited disclosure of mediator qualifications. The *Model Standards*, for example, require that mediators "should have available for the parties information relevant to the mediator's training, education, experience and approach to conducting a mediation";[56] and the *California Rules* provide that "[u]pon a request by any party, a mediator must provide truthful information regarding his or her experience, training, and education."[57] This approach can be reconciled with party self-determination because parties know that training and experience are relevant to mediator selection, and this information is often available to them or can simply be asked for from the mediator. It therefore seems that mediators are not under a duty to disclose information about their training and experience to the parties on their own initiative.[58] In contrast, however, mediators must disclose information about their mediation *style*, because most parties are probably unaware that there are different mediation styles and that these differences have an impact on the conduct of the mediation.[59]

5.7 Maintaining competence

To be competent, mediators must *maintain* their competence. They can do that in various ways: reading professional literature, participating in

[55] Texas Guidelines, s. 5.
[56] Model Standards, Standard IV.A.3. See also Georgia Standards, Standard V.
[57] California Rules, Rule 3.856(b). [58] See Chapter 4, Section 4.5.3.2(a)(1). [59] Ibid.

workshops, discussing practice issues with colleagues, and mediating cases. From a substantive-realist professional ethics perspective, the exact details of *how* mediators maintain the competence they already have is a matter of personal choice and responsibility. The *California-CDRC Standards* reflect this point when they provide that "[e]very mediator is personally responsible for his or her professional growth. A Mediator should endeavor to continually improve and increase his or her knowledge about the practice of mediation."[60] The *Model Standards* are somewhat more direct and provide that "[a] mediator should attend educational programs and related activities to maintain and enhance the mediator's knowledge and skills related to mediation."[61] Yet, some mediation programs and professional organizations go further and adopt institutional rules that make formal continuing education *mandatory*. The *Alabama Code*, for example, provides that "[a] mediator shall maintain professional competence in mediation skills. This includes ... [r]egularly engaging in educational activities promoting professional growth";[62] and the *Florida Rules* provide that "[a] mediator shall regularly participate in educational activities promoting professional growth."[63] A requirement for continuing education requires the mediation program or organization to develop a continuing mediator education program, decide on its content, and adopt criteria for courses, certified trainers, and reporting.[64] A mediator enlisted in these mediation programs must attend specified educational activities in order to be certified. For other mediators, participation in such educational activities is encouraged as an ideal.

5.8 Conclusion

Mediators must be competent to carry out their role. The normative requirement for mediator competence stems from (a) mediators' duty to the *parties* to be worthy of their trust, that is, to meet the parties' expectation that they have the ability to conduct the mediation effectively; (b) their duty to the *profession* to maintain the standing and reputation of the profession so it can function and support its members, a duty that can only be met when mediators have competence to mediate;

60 California-CDRC Standards, s. 5. 61 Model Standards, Standard IV.A.2.

62 Alabama Code, Standard 1(a). 63 Florida Rules, Rule 10.630.

64 See, e.g., Florida Continuing Mediator Education available at www.flcourts.org/resources-and-services/alternative-dispute-resolution/information-trainers-legal-professionals/continuing-mediation-education/; Indiana Rules, Rule 2.5(c).

and (c) their duty to the *public* to maintain public confidence in mediation and the profession so that the public interest in the use of mediation to resolve disputes is furthered.

Any person conducting mediation must have *basic competence*, that is, the qualifications necessary for carrying out the role of mediator in an effective manner in accordance with the core, shared definition of mediation. Basic competence generally requires *knowledge and understanding* of conflicts, communication, and negotiation theories, as well as an understanding of the process of mediation, the role of mediators, and their responsibilities. In addition, mediators must have the *skills* to facilitate communication, negotiation, and decision-making among disputants. The meaning of basic competence varies between the styles of mediation because they offer different accounts of conflicts, communication, and negotiation, and because they set different goals for mediation that go beyond the core, shared definition of the process.

Sometimes mediators are expected to have *specific competence* beyond the qualifications required for basic competence. Specific competence includes, for example, subject-matter expertise, cultural understanding, and language skills. An expectation of specific competence in a particular case can follow from representations of the mediator, requests of mediation parties, or circumstances such as the complexity of the case or cultural differences between the mediator and the parties.

A professional ethics perspective has little to say on the *exact criteria* or minimum requirements of mediator competence. Institutional decisions that require mediators to have 40 versus 60 or 80 hours of training, a BA or LLB versus MA degree, or X number of years of experience as a precondition for licensing, can all comply with the ethical requirement of competence notwithstanding the variation between them, as long as they actually equip mediators with the knowledge and skills they need for conducting effective mediations.

Mediators who do not possess basic competence or lack specific competence when such is required must decline to mediate unless they can "remedy" the state of incompetence. This can be accomplished by disclosure of their qualifications to the parties, provided that the level of competence of the mediator is not wanting to a degree that might jeopardize the standing of the profession and public trust in it, and by seeking the assistance of persons that can provide the missing competence, for example by inviting a co-mediator to join the process, involving the parties' representatives, or consulting outside experts. Mediators who are unable to overcome their incompetence must withdraw.

5.9 A proposed standard of mediator competence

A mediator shall mediate only when he or she has the competence to conduct the mediation.

A. Competence to mediate –
   1. Basic competence – A mediator shall mediate only when he or she has the knowledge and skills necessary for carrying out his or her role in an effective way. An effectively conducted mediation assists the parties to communicate, negotiate, and make decisions.
      (a) Basic competence will normally require mediation training and experience.
      (b) A mediator enlisted with a mediation program or organization shall comply with the qualification requirements set by it.
   2. Specific competence – A mediator shall have special knowledge and skills beyond basic competence when he or she is reasonably expected to have them on the basis of his or her own representations, institutional (mediation program or organization) rules, or circumstances. Specific competence may include subject-matter expertise, cultural knowledge, or language skills.
   3. Maintaining competence – A mediator must maintain his or her competence to mediate and is encouraged to improve his or her knowledge and skills relating to mediation through continuing education and related activities.

B. A mediator shall provide the parties upon request with information regarding his or her training, education, and experience.

C. Incompetence –
   1. A mediator lacking basic competence, or specific competence when such is required, shall notify the parties and decline to mediate notwithstanding the parties' wishes that he or she mediate the case, unless his or her incompetence can be adequately addressed and compensated for through the involvement of other persons in the mediation.
   2. A mediator shall decline to mediate when his or her ability to mediate is impaired by drugs, alcohol, medication, or other reasons.

6

Conflicts of interest

6.1 Introduction

Mediators are expected to further the interests of mediation parties and avoid harming them. This expectation clearly follows from mediators' position of trust regarding the parties. But mediators have interests of their own that are not necessarily consistent with the parties'. They are not unique in that respect, as all professionals might find themselves in a conflict of interest vis-à-vis their clients. For these reasons, issues of conflicts of interest are discussed in the literature on professional ethics[1] and addressed in various professional codes of conduct.[2] Mediators and mediation parties need to be aware of circumstances that give rise to conflicts of interest and of the actions that mediators should take in response. This chapter explores the meaning of a conflict of interest in the context of mediation and its implications for mediators' conduct.

6.2 The inevitability of mediator conflicts of interest

A realistic approach to professional ethics accepts that conflicts of interest between professionals and their clients in general and between mediators and mediation parties in particular are unavoidable and cannot be completely eliminated.[3] Consider the following examples in the context of mediation practice:

[1] See, e.g., Michael Davis and Andrew Stark (eds.), *Conflict of Interest in the Professions* (New York: Oxford University Press, 2001).

[2] See, e.g., APA Ethical Principles and Code, Standard 3.06; ABA Model Rules, Rules 1.7 and 1.8; Model Standards, Standard III; ASCE Code of Ethics for Engineers, Canon 4; Code of Ethics for Arbitrators in Commercial Disputes, Canon II.

[3] See, e.g., Boulle and Nesic, *Mediation*, pp. 18–19.

6.2.1 *Mediator fees*

Mediators who charge fees for their services have an interest in increasing their fees while reducing the amount of work done for these fees. This potential conflict of interest is inherent in any professional relationship: therapists might have to resist the temptation to prolong treatment when remunerated on an hourly basis, and lawyers might be torn between a desire to take on a case for a high fee and their professional evaluation that the case has no legal merits. Codes of conduct for mediators recognize these difficulties. The *Model Standards*, for example, provide that "a mediator shall not undermine party self-determination . . . for reasons such as . . . increased fees";[4] and the *North Carolina Standards* state that "[a] mediator shall not prolong a mediation for the purpose of charging a higher fee."[5]

6.2.2 *Agreement as a goal*

Problem-solving mediation often considers a mediated agreement to be the purpose of mediation. On such an approach, the attainment of an agreement, possibly *any* agreement, irrespective of the parties' needs, is in the mediator's interest.[6] Furthermore, mediators are motivated to push for an agreement because they want to attract more work, build up their reputation, and satisfy case-referring institutions that equate mediation success with mediated agreements.[7] Some codes of conduct for mediators explicitly address such concerns. The *Model Standards*, for example, provide that "[a] mediator shall not undermine party self-determination . . . for reasons such as higher settlement rates . . ., or outside pressures from court personnel, program administrators, provider organizations, the media or others";[8] and the *Florida Rules* state that "[w]hether the parties

[4] Model Standards, Standard I.B. [5] North Carolina Standards, Rule VII.G.

[6] See, e.g., Bush and Folger, *The Promise of Mediation* (1994), pp. 76, 104–106.

[7] See, e.g., Debra Shapiro, Rita Drieghe, and Jeanne Brett, "Mediator Behavior and the Outcome of Mediation" (1985) 41 *Journal of Social Issues* 101, 113 (" . . . mediators' successes or failures are never private. Indeed, mediators know that a 'second invitation' rests on their effective first performance and that subsequent invitations rest similarly on continuing successes"). See also Scott R. Peppet, "Contractarian Economics and Mediation Ethics: The Case for Customizing Neutrality through Contingent Fee Mediation" (2003) 82 *Texas Law Review* 227, 256–257 (" . . . a mediator might be self-interested vis-à-vis the outcome of the mediation because she wants the dispute to settle to increase her settlement rate and thereby bolster her reputation. She is not neutral in the sense of being purely self-disinterested"); Deborah Kolb & Associates, *When Talk Works: Profiles of Mediators* (San Francisco: Jossey-Bass, 1994), p. 480.

[8] Model Standards, Standard I.B.

involved in a mediation choose to resolve their dispute is secondary in importance to whether the mediator conducts the mediation in accordance with these ethical standards."[9]

6.2.3 *Psychological needs, prejudice, and bias*

Mediators, like anyone else, strive to satisfy *personal basic needs* such as having a sense of power, self-esteem, and confidence. These psychological needs do not necessarily work for the benefit of mediation parties. Recognizing this, the *Model Standards* provide that "[a] mediator shall not undermine party self-determination ... for reasons such as ... egos."[10] Moreover, mediators may have a personal interest in the content and outcome of mediation due to *personal prejudice and preferences*. Susan Oberman observed that "[m]ediators cannot avoid bringing their experience, education and personal perspectives into the process."[11] Every mediator has a personal worldview and values that affect his notion of the "right" outcome for a dispute.[12] Thus mediators have an interest in steering mediation parties in certain directions, and when the views and values of one party are close to the mediator's the potential for favoritism increases.

6.2.4 *A duty to take action*

In some circumstances a mediator may be, or feel that he is, under a legal, moral, ethical, religious, conscientious, or other *duty to act* in a way that is inconsistent with the interests of one or more of the parties. For example, divorce mediation often involves decisions that have an effect on the parties' children, and mediators might be under a duty to ensure that the interests of the children are considered by the parties even where the parties do not wish to do so.[13] Furthermore, some codes of conduct for mediators impose on mediators a duty to prevent certain types of

[9] Florida Rules, Rule 10.200. [10] Model Standards, Standard I.B.

[11] Susan Oberman, "Mediation Theory vs. Practice: What Are We Really Doing? Re-Solving a Professional Conundrum" (2000) 20 *Ohio State Journal on Dispute Resolution* 775, 819.

[12] Bush and Folger, *The Promise of Mediation* (1994), p. 70.

[13] See, e.g., Boulle and Nesic, *Mediation*, p. 459. See also Orna Cohen, Naomi Dattner, and Ahron Luxenburg, "The Limits of the Mediator's Neutrality" (1999) 16 *Mediation Quarterly* 341, 343–344; Florida Rules, Rule 10.320 ("A mediator shall promote awareness by the parties of the interests of persons affected by actual or potential agreements who are not represented at mediation"); Family Mediation Model Standards, Standards VIII and IX; California-CDRC Standards, s. 3; Illinois Standards, s. IV.C.

mediated agreements, such as illegal and unconscionable agreements.[14] As a result, the mediator becomes an interested person in the outcome and might have to take action against the wishes of the parties.[15]

From a professional ethics perspective, the unavoidable nature of conflicts of interest points to the need to distinguish between an *ideal* of complete freedom from conflicts of interest and a workable *duty* regarding conflicts of interest that seeks to (a) make such conflicts transparent through a requirement of disclosure, and (b) limit their potential harm by identifying types of conflicts of interest that cannot be tolerated and requiring mediators in such circumstances to decline cases or withdraw.[16]

6.3 Defining mediator conflicts of interest

Any duty relating to a conflict of interest situation must first define what a mediator conflict of interest is. The meaning of a conflict of interest in a mediation setting is shaped by the definition of mediation and the role of mediators. The core definition of mediation stipulates that two or more disputing parties are assisted in communication, negotiation, and decision-making by a mediator.[17] If we consider the simple case of two-party mediation, it follows that the interests of mediators might be in conflict with (a) the interests of *one* of the parties, or (b) the interests of *both* parties. It is important to distinguish between these two cases because each of them reveals a different ethical concern that provides for a different rationale for limiting the freedom of action of mediators.

(a) In the first scenario, an interest of the mediator is inconsistent with an interest of *one party* and matches the interest of the other. For example, mediators might be tempted to favor the interest of a party

[14] See Chapter 8, Section 8.2.4.3(a) and (c).

[15] See, e.g., Gunning, "Know Justice", 93 (noting that "a mediator's concern for a just outcome does affect mediator 'neutrality' as defined as having an interest in the outcome of the conflict"). See also Bush, "Efficiency and Protection", 265.

[16] Note that conflicts of interest are not necessarily harmful and sometimes might be welcomed by disputing parties. A close relationship of a party with the mediator might benefit the other party in two respects. First, the mediator might feel obliged to pacify the other party; and second, a prior relationship puts the mediator in a better position of influence and a party in a close relationship might find it more difficult to resist the mediator's interventions. See generally Dean G. Pruitt, "Kissinger As A Traditional Mediator With Power", in Jeffrey Z. Rubin (ed.), *Dynamics of Third Party Intervention: Kissinger in the Middle East* (New York: Praeger, 1981), pp. 141, 144.

[17] See Chapter 3, Section 3.2.

with whom they have a personal or business relationship. From a professional ethics perspective, such favoritism illustrates conduct in violation of the norm of *mediator impartiality*.[18] This approach to conflicts of interest is taken by many codes of conduct for mediators. The *Florida Rules*, for example, provide that "a conflict of interest arises when any relationship between the mediator and the mediation participants or the subject matter of the dispute compromises or appears to compromise the mediator's impartiality,"[19] and the *Model Standards* warn the mediator of involvement or relationships that "reasonably raises a question of a mediator's impartiality."[20]

(b) In the second scenario, an interest of the mediator is inconsistent with an *interest shared by all of the parties*. For example, the mediator might have a stake in a business that could be affected by the mediation, and the mediator might be exposed to trade secrets that could be useful to that business. From a professional ethics perspective, the possibility of an abuse of process illustrates a concern that the mediator might act on an *irrelevant consideration* in violation of the norm of *professional integrity*.[21] This concern may have led the drafters of the *North Carolina Standards* to provide in a Conflicts of Interest Rule that "[a] mediator shall not use information obtained or relationships formed during a mediation for personal gain or advantage,"[22] and the *Australian Practice Standards* to state that "[a] mediator will not use information about participants obtained in mediation for personal gain or advantage."[23] Other codes of conduct refer to a concern that a conflict of interest might impair mediators' professional judgment or increase the risk of exploiting the parties[24] or raise "a question about the . . . self-interest on the part of the mediator."[25]

The two scenarios reveal a dual rationale for regulating mediator conflicts of interest: the concern that mediators might unjustifiably favor one party over another in violation of the norm of impartiality, and the concern that mediators might make decisions on the basis of irrelevant considerations in violation of professional integrity (see Figure 6.1). Some codes of conduct for mediators exclusively define a conflict of

18 See Chapter 7. 19 Florida Rules, Rule 10.340(a).

20 Model Standards, Standard III.A. For other codes that link conflict of interest with impartiality see, e.g., Alabama Code, Standard 5, California Rules, Rule 3.855.

21 See Chapter 8, Section 8.2.1. 22 North Carolina Standards, Rule VII.D.

23 Australian Practice Standards, s. 5(4).

24 See, e.g., Family Mediation Canada Code, Article 4.1.

25 Michigan Standards, Standard III.A.

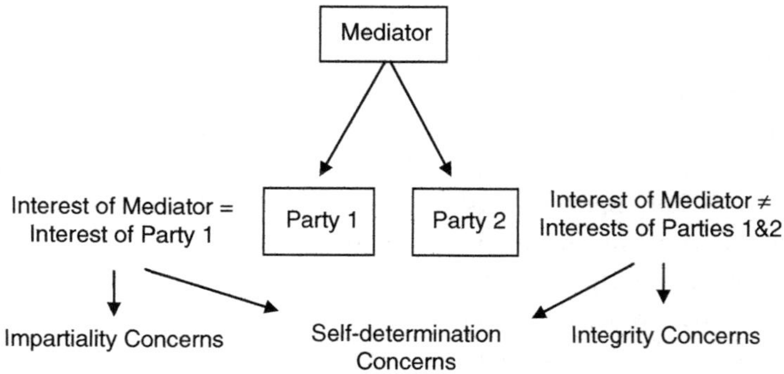

Figure 6.1: Why mediators' conflicts of interest matter to mediation parties?

interest by its likely effect on mediator impartiality. For example, the Florida Rule mentioned above provides that "a conflict of interest arises when any relationship between the mediator and the mediation participants or the subject matter of the dispute *compromises or appears to compromise the mediator's impartiality.*"[26] However, as we have seen, as a matter of definition the relationship or subject matter need not only affect the mediator's impartiality in order to qualify as a conflict of interest; it can impair his professional judgment without necessarily violating impartiality.

Furthermore, mediator conflicts of interest raise another concern that parties should be aware of: mediators might *feel* or *be* obliged to act in a way that is inconsistent with the wishes (or "interests") of one or all of the parties, contrary to the norm of *party self-determination.* For example, the mediator might be under a legal obligation to disclose mediation communication to the authorities despite the wishes of one or all of the parties for confidentiality.

A workable definition of a mediator conflict of interest cannot simply repeat the phrase "conflict of interest" if it is to effectively guide mediators and parties. The nature of the interests that might conflict in a mediation setting can be learnt from common sense, real cases arising out of mediation practice, and the language of conflicts of interest provisions in codes of conduct for mediators. Such an inquiry would suggest that mediators are likely to find themselves in a conflict of interest situation in the following circumstances, where:

[26] Florida Rules, Rule 10.340(a) (emphasis added).

(a) The mediator has or had in the past a personal, professional, or business *relationship with a mediation participant* (party or his representative) or a person related to a mediation participant. For example, the mediator might have studied with a party at the same class in university, or been employed by the law firm now representing a party,[27] or is a partner in a law firm that provides legal services to a law firm now representing a party.[28] Many codes of conduct for mediators include a provision of such content. For example, the *Model Standards* provide that "[a] conflict of interest can arise ... from any relationship between a mediator and any mediation participant, whether past or present, personal or professional ... ";[29] and the *Alabama Code* provides that "[a] mediator must disclose to the disputing parties ... [a]ny current or past representation of or consulting relationship with any party or the attorney of any party involved in the mediation."[30]

(b) The mediator has an emotional or financial *involvement* in the *content or outcome* of the dispute. Imagine, for example, a mediator who strongly objects to abortions mediating a case between a man and a woman who are debating whether to have an abortion, as the man wants, or keep the baby, as the woman wants. Again, codes of conduct for mediators often have provisions to that effect. The *Model Standards*, for example, provide that "[a] conflict of interest can arise from involvement by a mediator with the subject matter of the dispute ... ";[31] and the *Oregon Standards* provide that "[m]ediators avoid actual, potential, or perceived conflicts of interest that can arise from a mediator's involvement with the subject matter of the controversy ... "[32]

(c) The mediator has or believes he has a legal, moral, ethical, religious, conscientious, or other *duty* to act in a way that is inconsistent with the interests of one of the parties or all of them. For example, the mediator might feel obliged to follow a particular religious norm that supports one of the parties, or might have an ethical duty to

27 See, e.g., Florida MEAC, Opinion 2001–009 available at www.flcourts.org/core/fileparse.php/283/urlt/MEAC-Opinion-2001–009.pdf.

28 See, e.g., Florida MEAC, Opinion 2009–009 available at www.flcourts.org/core/fileparse.php/283/urlt/MEACOpinion2009-009.pdf (concluding that "It is a conflict of interest for a mediator to mediate a case when one of the mediator's law partners is currently performing transactional legal services for the law firm representing the party to the mediation").

29 Model Standards, Standard III.A.

30 Alabama Code, Standard 5(b)(A).

31 Model Standards, Standard III.A.

32 Oregon Standards, Standard III.

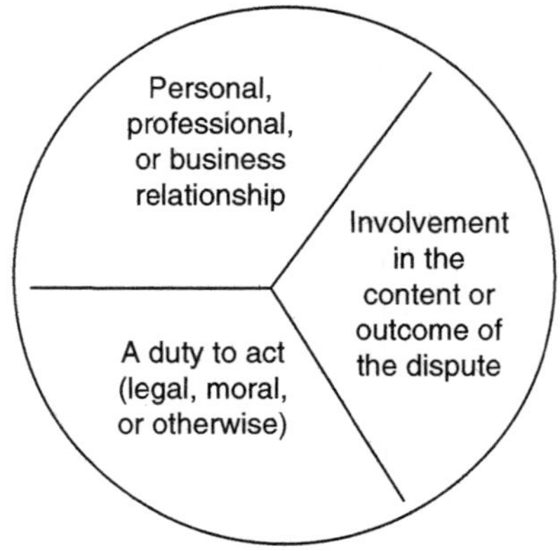

Figure 6.2: Circumstances of mediators' conflicts of interest

terminate the mediation notwithstanding the wishes of the parties to proceed. This type of potential conflict of interest is largely ignored by codes of conduct for mediators in the definition they provide for a mediator conflict of interest.

Figure 6.2 illustrates the circumstances of mediators' conflicts of interest.

6.4 The normative implications of mediator conflicts of interest

6.4.1 The legitimate expectations of parties in a conflict of interest situation

If mediators, as a matter of fact, cannot possibly avoid conflicts of interest altogether, then parties cannot legitimately expect mediators to be completely free of such conflicts. Furthermore, the expectation of parties is that mediators do not *harm* them, and being in a state of conflict does not *in itself* cause any harm to the parties; harm might be caused where mediators *act* on a conflict of interest for their benefit and to the parties' disadvantage. Thus, from a professional ethics perspective, focusing on the parties–mediator relationship, the first thing mediators are expected to do is to *inquire* whether they are in a conflict of interest situation, reflect on their position, and be satisfied that they are capable of conducting the mediation without allowing their conflicting interest to affect their judgment. If a mediator feels he might not be able to resist the temptation to act on his interest, thereby favoring one of the parties in violation of impartiality, or acting on irrelevant considerations thereby violating integrity, he must *withdraw*. Such a duty of withdrawal can be found, for example, in the *Alabama Code*, which states that "[i]f the mediator believes that the relationship or interest would affect the mediator's impartiality, he or she should withdraw."[33]

Once a mediator is satisfied that the conflict of interest will not affect his or her behavior, he or she must go on to consider whether he or she should *disclose* the conflict of interest to the parties. A trustworthy mediator is expected to disclose to the parties information in his or her knowledge and control that is necessary for the parties to make a decision on whether to accept or reject him or her as mediator. Parties cannot make an informed decision on the selection of the mediator and on participation in the mediation when they are not aware of actual or potential conflicts of interest of the mediator that might harm them in the course of mediation. The disclosure requirement is a condition for party self-determination,[34] and the extent of the information that must be disclosed with respect to a conflict of interest depends on whether the information could reasonably affect the parties' decision whether to accept or reject the mediator. Indeed, many codes of conduct for mediators make disclosure requirements in support of party self-determination. The *Model Standards*, for example, provide that "[a] mediator shall disclose, as soon as practicable, all actual and potential conflicts of interest that are reasonably known to the mediator and could reasonably be seen as raising a question about the mediator's impartiality. After disclosure, if all parties agree, the mediator may proceed with the mediation."[35] Again, the correct linkage between a conflict of interest and mediator impartiality should not be taken to mean that questions of impartiality are the *only* ground for disclosure. As conflicts of interest may result from other reasons as well, the disclosure requirement will be triggered by any conflict of interest that might reasonably be seen as raising a question about the appropriateness of the mediator's considerations for decisions, the possibility that the mediator might be required to make an intervention against parties' wishes, as well as the question of mediator favoritism. Thus, if an actual or potential conflict of interest raises a reasonable concern regarding mediator impartiality or the preference of an interest of the mediator over the parties' interest, the

[33] Alabama Code, Standard 5. [34] See Chapter 4, Section 4.5.3.2(a).

[35] Model Standards, Standard III.C. See also Alabama Code, Standard 5; Florida Rules, Rule 10.340(b); California Rules, Rule 3.855(c); Texas Guidelines, s. 4.

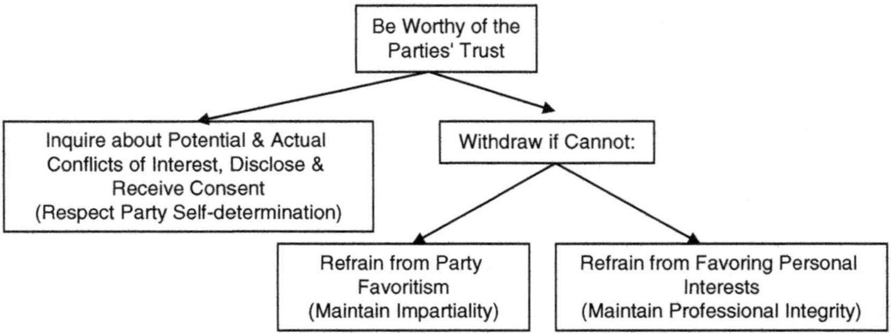

Figure 6.3: The expectations of parties regarding a conflict of interest

mediator must disclose the conflict of interest to the parties. If there is no such concern, then from a professional ethics perspective the mediator has no duty of disclosure. Figure 6.3 illustrates the expectations of parties regarding a conflict of interest.

This analysis leaves us at the moment with two types of conflicts of interest in terms of severity: conflicts of interest that raise a reasonable concern that the mediator might favor a party or might conduct the mediation on the basis of irrelevant considerations; and *trivial* conflicts of interest that do not raise any such reasonable concern. For example, if *one of the parties* to the mediation had participated in a previous mediation that the mediator had conducted, the mediator must disclose to the other party this past professional relationship. The information is relevant to party decision-making on mediator selection because of the possibility that the mediator and that party developed a close relationship that might affect the mediator's attitude toward him or her in the present mediation. But what about a previous professional relationship with a party's *representative*, who represented another party in another mediation conducted by the same mediator? Such a conflict of interest might at first be considered trivial, as the concern that the mediator will favor the lawyer's new client is probably smaller than in the first scenario. However, it seems to me that reasonable parties would need to know about the relationship in order to make a decision whether to accept the mediator and stay alert for expressions of favoritism during the mediation, or reject him or her altogether. Most of the codes of conduct do not refer to such a circumstance, and the few that do are not in agreement. The *Alabama Code*, for example, provides that "mediators are strongly encouraged to disclose . . . prior relationships" such as "[p] rior service as a mediator in a mediation involving a party or an attorney for a party."[36] Conversely, the Advisory Committee Comment to the *California Rules*, for example, requires disclosure with respect to prior service and provides that "[t]he interests, relationships, and affiliations that a mediator may need to disclose ... include: (1) prior, current, or currently expected service as a mediator in another mediation involving any of the participants in the present mediation."[37] It seems to me that the better approach would require disclosure. A cautious approach in favor of disclosure is taken by some codes such as the *Family Mediation Model Standards* and the *Michigan Standards*, for example, providing that a "mediator should resolve all doubts in favor of disclosure."[38]

To summarize, mediation parties expect mediators to disclose conflicts of interest, receive their consent to proceed with the mediation despite a conflict of interest, and withdraw when a mediator cannot avoid acting on the basis of a conflict of interest.

6.4.2 The legitimate expectations of the profession and the public in a conflict of interest situation

From a professional ethics perspective, the meaning of a mediator conflict of interest is also shaped by mediators' responsibility toward the mediation profession and toward the public to *maintain the standing of the profession and the public trust in it.* The key difference between the parties' expectations regarding mediator conflicts of interest and the expectations of the profession and the public is the former's focus on *factual*, actual or potential conflicts of interest and the latter's focus on the *appearance* of conflicts of interest. While the parties are concerned that the mediator not act against their interest in their particular case, the profession and the public are concerned that mediators not be in a conflict of interest that conveys an *impression* that the process has been *faulty*, because such an impression could undermine public faith in mediators and in the process of mediation and result in fewer people being willing to resort to mediation.[39] The ethical responsibility of mediators to maintain public

36 Alabama Code, Standard 5(b)(D).

37 Advisory Committee Comment to California Rules, Rule 3.855(b).

38 See Family Mediation Model Standards, Standard IV.E; Michigan Standards, Standard III.C. See also James Coben and Peter N. Thompson, "Disputing Irony: A Systematic Look at Litigation About Mediation" (2006) 11 *Harvard Negotiation Law Review* 43, 140 (recommending such an approach as a means of reducing the likelihood of legal actions against mediators).

39 Compare Kipnis, "Conflict of Interest", 274 (quoting the court decision in *State* v. *Horan*, 21 Wis. 2d 66, 123 N.W.2d 488 (1963) that "[A]n attorney must avoid not only the fact,

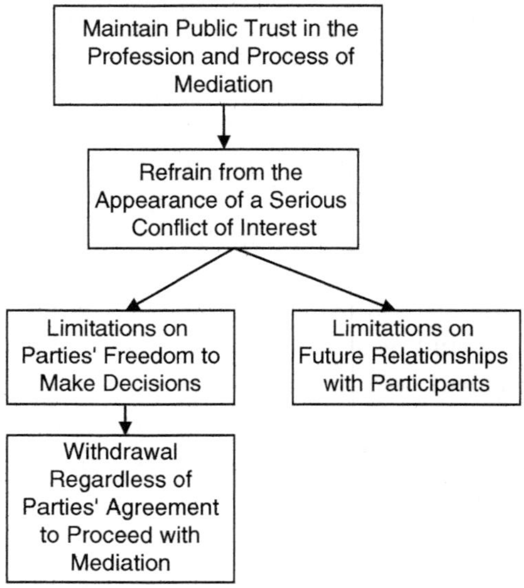

Figure 6.4: The expectations of the mediation profession and the public regarding mediators' conflicts of interest

confidence in the profession and process of mediation has several implications in the context of mediators' conflicts of interest (see Figure 6.4). First, it limits the freedom of *mediators* to take on new mediation cases, requires their withdrawal from mediation, and limits their freedom to establish relationships with mediation participants subsequent to a mediation when the conflict of interest is *serious* to a degree that might reasonably jeopardize public trust in the profession and process; and second, it limits the freedom of mediation *parties* to give effective consent on such occasions.

6.4.2.1 Serious conflicts of interest

A serious conflict of interest is one that would cause a reasonable person observing the mediation from the outside to suspect that the mediator is unable to avoid partiality or conduct on the basis of irrelevant considerations. As serious conflicts of interest could undermine public trust in the profession and process of mediation, they cannot be left to the determination of the parties in a particular mediation, because the parties might

but even the appearance, of representing conflicting interests" and arguing that "[I]f the system of adjudication is to work, if it is to succeed in generating judicial decisions that are likely to be just and that the community *can accept* as just, it must preserve appearances" [italics in the original]).

subjectively believe that the mediator is able to fulfill his or her role to their satisfaction, while a reasonable outsider would have a different impression. Codes of conduct for mediators recognize that serious conflicts of interest charge mediators with the responsibility to decline a mediation or withdraw notwithstanding the parties' wishes. The *NY-CDRC Standards*, for example, provide that "if a conflict of interest casts serious doubt on the integrity of the process, the mediator shall withdraw or decline to proceed regardless of the express agreement of the parties";[40] the *Florida Rules* provide that "if a conflict of interest clearly impairs a mediator's impartiality, the mediator shall withdraw regardless of the express agreement of the parties";[41] the *California Rules* provide that "[r]egardless of the consent of the parties, a mediator either must decline to serve as mediator or, if already serving, must withdraw from the mediation if . . . Proceeding with the mediation would jeopardize the integrity of the court or of the mediation process";[42] and the *Model Standards* state that "[i]f a mediator's conflict of interest might reasonably be viewed as undermining the integrity of the mediation, a mediator shall withdraw from or decline to proceed with the mediation regardless of the expressed desire or agreement of the parties to the contrary."[43]

This analysis of a serious conflict of interest from the perspective of the profession and the public adds a third type of conflict of interest to the two already identified from the perspective of mediation parties. The three types of conflicts of interest in terms of severity thus include *minor* conflicts of interest that raise a reasonable concern that the mediator might favor a party or might conduct the mediation on the basis of irrelevant considerations; *trivial* conflicts of interest that do not raise any such reasonable concern; and *serious* conflicts of interest that raise a reasonable concern that the mediation might appear faulty, thereby undermining the standing of the profession and jeopardizing public trust in the profession and process of mediation. While *minor* conflicts of interest require mediators to disclose the conflict of interest to the parties and obtain their consent, *trivial* conflicts of interest do not necessitate disclosure, although it is recommended, and *serious* conflicts of interest require mediators to decline the case or withdraw regardless of the parties' wishes. Figure 6.5 illustrates the implications of the type of conflict of interest for the conduct expected of the mediator.

[40] NY-CDRC Standards, Standard III.B. [41] Florida Rules, Rule 10.340(c).
[42] California Rules, Rule 3.855(f).
[43] Model Standards, Standard III.E. See also Georgia Standards, Standard III.C; Family Mediation Model Standards, Standard IV.

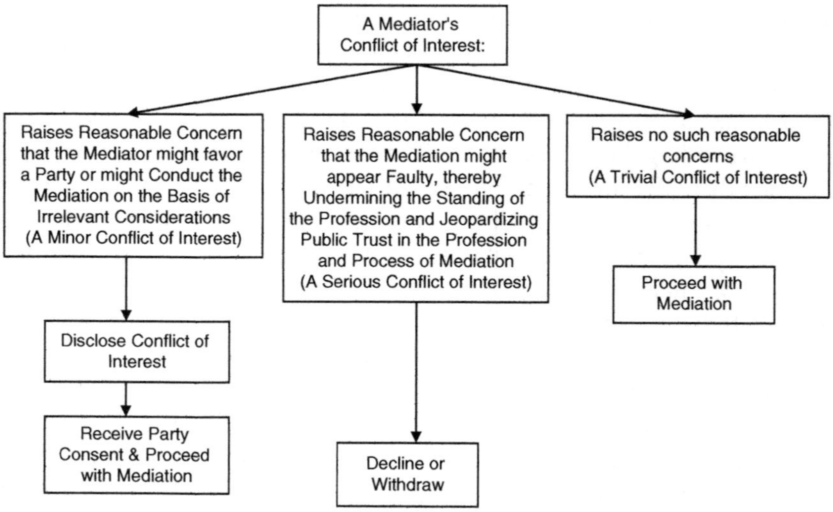

Figure 6.5: The severity of a conflict of interest and its implications

The lines between trivial and minor conflicts of interest on the one hand, and minor and serious conflicts of interest on the other hand are bound to be blurred sometimes, as they rest on a judgment of what raises a *reasonable* concern. Some guidance may be found in codes of conduct for mediators and in the opinions of mediator ethics advisory boards.

Mediator *fees*, for example, could raise a concern that mediators prefer their own interest in securing and maximizing their fees over the parties' interest in obtaining high-quality service for a pre-estimated fee.[44] Accordingly, most codes of conduct for mediators instruct mediators to provide parties with information regarding their fees and obtain the parties' agreement. The *Model Standards*, for example, provide that "[a] mediator shall provide each party or each party's representative true and complete information about mediation fees, expenses and any other actual or potential charges that may be incurred in connection with a mediation";[45] and the *California Rules* provide that "[b]efore commencing the mediation, the mediator must disclose to the parties in writing

[44] See, e.g., North Carolina Dispute Resolution Commission, Advisory Opinion 13-27 available at www.nccourts.org/Courts/CRS/Councils/DRC/Documents/13-27_2014.pdf (holding, after learning that one of the parties had no funds to pay for his services, that "the mediator mixed his own financial business with the business of the parties in settling their dispute").

[45] Model Standards, Standard VIII.A.

any fees, costs, or charges to be paid to the mediator by the parties."[46] Charging fees is a *minor* conflict of interest because it is inherent to the provision of professional services. Fees are common in the case of all professionals, and therefore do not jeopardize public faith in professionals and in the process they conduct. On the other hand, in the context of mediation, allowing a mediator to charge a fee that is *contingent* on securing an agreement or a particular outcome would raise a reasonable concern that the mediator is unable to conduct a fair mediation according to its rules, without harming the parties. Thus, a contingent mediation fee is considered by codes of conduct for mediators as a *serious* conflict of interest that must be avoided notwithstanding the parties' consent. The *Model Standards*, for example, provide that "[a] mediator should not enter into a fee agreement which is contingent upon the result of the mediation or amount of the settlement";[47] the *California Rules* provide that "[t]he amount or nature of a mediator's fee must not be made contingent on the outcome of the mediation";[48] and the *Alabama Code* provides that "[a] mediator shall not charge or accept a contingent fee or base a fee in any manner on the outcome of the mediation process."[49] From a mediators' ethics perspective, these principles relating to fees equally apply where no formal code regulates a mediator's conduct or where a code does not refer to mediators' fees.

A *personal, professional, or business relationship* between a mediator and a mediation participant creates a potential conflict of interest that could tempt a mediator to conduct the mediation with partiality. The severity of such a conflict of interest might vary considerably. A *continuing, long, close, and intensive* relationship would reasonably raise a question about the ability of the mediator to conduct the mediation impartially, thereby endangering public faith in the profession and process of mediation and necessitating mediator withdrawal. An example of a *serious* conflict of interest would be a family relationship between a mediator and a participant. The Florida Mediator Ethics Advisory Committee, for example, held that "[a]n example of a clear conflict would exist if you were asked to mediate a case your daughter is personally handling as opposed to a case from her firm with which she has no involvement. A case your daughter is personally handling would be nonwaivable, clear conflict, while her firm's case with which she had no involvement, may be waivable after disclosure, depending on the

[46] California Rules, Rule 3.859(b).
[47] Model Standards, Standard VIII.E.1.
[48] California Rules, Rule 3.859(c).
[49] Alabama Code, Standard 8(d).

circumstances."[50] The Florida committee similarly considered a situation in which the party's lawyer is the mediator's ex-husband or ex-wife as non-waivable.[51] An intimate or close professional or business relationship should arguably be considered to give rise to a serious conflict of interest as well, for example where a party is a close friend of a mediator, or a party's lawyer is employed by a law firm in which a mediator is a partner. The Florida Committee considered it to be "a clear (non-waivable) conflict of interest for a mediator to mediate a case in which his/her former law partners represented any of the parties while the dissolved partnership was in effect, regardless of whether the parties would like to waive the conflict."[52] In the committee's view, if the mediator's former law partner is representing a party as an advocate subsequent to the mediator leaving the law firm, the conflict of interest might be non-waivable, depending on the elapsed time since the partnership dissolved and the appearance of partiality. In the Committee's words, "[a] mediator may want to consider whether an outsider, hearing about the conflict for the first time and being unaware of a waiver, could believe the mediator should have declined service or removed him/herself from the mediation process."[53] The *Australian Practice Standards* provide in this context that "[e]xcept where culturally required, practitioners will not facilitate disputes involving close friends, relatives, colleagues/supervisors or students."[54]

The more the relationship is *remote, sporadic, superficial or a matter of the past*, the greater the tendency to regard it as trivial, not necessitating disclosure, as opposed to a *present, ongoing* professional relationship that requires disclosure. If, for example, the mediator was in law-school with the party's attorney 20 years ago, this might seem a trivial conflict, not requiring disclosure. Yet, as we have seen before, disclosure should probably be the rule rather than the exception to the rule. The better approach is to consider the fact of prior service as relevant information that the parties are entitled to be aware of in exercising self-determination with respect to mediator selection.

50 Florida MEAC, Opinion 2004–008 available at www.flcourts.org/core/fileparse.php/283/urlt/MEAC-Opinion-2004–008.pdf.

51 Florida MEAC, Opinion 2013–010 available at www.flcourts.org/core/fileparse.php/283/urlt/MEACOOpinionO2013-010OFINALOSIGNED.pdf.

52 Florida MEAC, Opinion 2012–004 available at www.flcourts.org/core/fileparse.php/283/urlt/MEACOpinion2012-004.pdf.

53 Ibid. 54 Australian Practice Standards, s. 5(6).

Worldview and personal values are also hard to categorize. Mediators naturally have their own views, values, and prejudices, and these in turn create a potential conflict of interest that could lead them to favor a party or a particular outcome. Think, for example, of an ultraorthodox Jewish mediator who strongly believes that living together without marrying first is a sin. The mediator is asked to mediate a case between a man and a woman who are deliberating whether to move together to a joint accommodation as the man wishes, or postpone the move until they are married as the woman prefers. The easy case is where the mediator feels that he or she would not be able to remain impartial in the course of the mediation. In this scenario, it follows from his or her duty to be worthy of the trust of the parties that he or she must decline to take the case. But assume that the mediator has reflected on his position and does not see a problem in proceeding with the mediation. Could his decision be justified? The mediator in this case has a *strict, uncompromising worldview and personal values* as opposed to a pluralistic approach that is tolerant of competing views and values. The mediator's worldview and personal values raise a reasonable concern that he might not act impartially. Therefore, it is clear that he must disclose his view of the matter to the parties and obtain their agreement to go on with the mediation. However, assume that both parties agree to waive the conflict of interest and ask the mediator to proceed. The question is whether the conflict of interest is waivable in the first place. Arguably it is not. A reasonable person looking at the process would doubt that the mediator, so strongly committed to one view of the situation, is capable of impartially conducting the mediation. Carrying on with the mediation would raise serious doubt whether the mediation was conducted fairly, in accordance with the principles of party self-determination and mediator impartiality. It follows from the mediator's responsibility to maintain the standing of the profession and public faith in the profession and the process that he or she must decline the case.

Table 6.1 summarizes the examples discussed above.

6.4.2.2 Conflicts of interest subsequent to mediation

Mediators and mediation participants might wish to form relationships with each other *subsequent* to the mediation. For example, a party might contact a mediator for romantic reasons and ask her for a date, or ask a mediator to provide other professional services that he or she is qualified for as a therapist or lawyer, or a party's lawyer may refer a new case to a mediator. Although the mediation has already ended, such incidents could raise concerns about the way a mediator had conducted the

Table 6.1 *Illustrating the severity of a conflict of interest*

Degree of Severity	Trivial	Minor	Serious
Required Action	None (Disclosure Recommended)	Disclosure + Parties' Consent	Decline/Withdraw
Mediator Fees	–	Fixed or hourly fee	Contingent Fee
Personal, Professional, or Business Relationship	Brief, Superficial, Insignificant Interaction long Ago	Short, Formal, Past or Present Relationship (e.g., distant family tie; same school)	Continuing, Long, Close, Intensive Relationship (e.g., father/son/brother; business partners)
Worldview and Personal Values	Pluralistic Worldview	–	Strict, Uncompromising Worldview and Personal values

mediation. Was he or she *really* impartial? Did he or she have the future relationship in mind at the time of the mediation and let it influence his or her actions during the mediation? From a professional ethics perspective, as far as the parties are concerned the mediator should be free to enter any new relationship he or she chooses as long as the new relationship does not compromise any current or future interest of the parties, or should obtain their consent in the event that an interest of the parties might be compromised, in accordance with the principle of party self-determination.

However, besides their obligations to the parties, mediators have a continuing responsibility to maintain the profession's standing and public trust in the profession before, during, and after mediation. Any public *appearance* of impropriety that might be harmful needs to be controlled, therefore mediators must not establish relationships subsequent to the mediation that could raise a reasonable concern that the mediator had been in a conflict of interest and conducted a faulty mediation that might undermine the profession's standing and public trust in the profession and process of mediation. Many codes of conduct for mediators reflect this concern. The *Model Standards*, for example, provide that "subsequent to a mediation, a mediator shall not establish another relationship with any of the participants in any matter that would raise questions about the integrity of the mediation."[55] Sometimes this concern is addressed by a prohibition on solicitation during mediation. The *Nebraska Standards*, for example, provide that "a mediator shall not use the mediation process to solicit, encourage or otherwise incur future services with either party."[56]

This understanding from a professional ethics perspective of the rationale for the limitation on future mediator relationships explains why the consent of the parties cannot be a sole requirement for future relationships with a mediator. First, the parties' consent is not sufficient to ensure public confidence in mediators and in mediation because the parties may agree to a relationship but a reasonable concern of improper conduct would still arise from a public perspective. Second, a party may refuse to consent to contact with the other party for unjustified reasons, that is, in circumstances where the future relationship does not compromise his interests or does not raise a concern of improper conduct at the time the mediation was conducted. The better approach, then, is one that instead of insisting on receiving the parties' consent to future relationships,[57] conditions future relationships on circumstances that do not raise a concern of partiality or impropriety during the mediation and maintain public confidence in the process.

It is difficult to provide in advance clear-cut guidelines on the appropriateness of future relationships. The decision would probably depend on factors such as the time elapsed since the mediation ended, the nature of the new relationship, and the type of the proposed services to be provided.[58] The Georgia Commission on Dispute Resolution's Committee on Ethics, for example, discussing a *personal relationship of a romantic nature* between a mediator and a party, noted that "[a] reasonable person could easily conclude that having two dinners with a party three months after a contentious 12-hour divorce mediation, and prior to the final divorce decree, would create a perceived or actual conflict of interest for the mediator. Perceived or actual conflicts of

[55] Model Standards, Standard III.F. See also Georgia Standards, Standard III.C(f); NY-CDRC Standards, Standard III.D.

[56] Nebraska Standards, s. III.B.4. See also NY-CDRC Standards, Standard III.C; Alabama Code, Standard 5.

[57] Such an approach was taken by the 1994 version of the Model Standards that did include a requirement for the parties' consent, providing that "[w]ithout the consent of all parties a mediator shall not subsequently establish a professional relationship with one of the parties in a related matter, or in an unrelated matter under circumstances which would raise legitimate questions about the integrity of the mediation process."

[58] See, e.g., Model Standards, Standard III.F.

interest that raise questions about a mediator's impartiality, especially in the case of a dual relationship with a participant, should be avoided during and after the mediation."[59]

The Florida MEAC, discussing the possibility that a mediator might become a *party's lawyer* in a matter related to a mediation he had mediated, held that "[t]here is a clear conflict of interest when a mediator, having mediated a dispute, subsequently represents or otherwise takes a position for or against a former party in a related matter."[60] In another Opinion, the Florida MEAC asserted that "[i]f the mediator were permitted to accept an appointment to serve as cocounsel for the plaintiff in a personal injury suit he or she had mediated, regardless of the passage of time, both the integrity of the mediator and the integrity of the mediation process itself would be severely compromised."[61] The position could be different where a party contacted a mediator subsequent to a mediation in order to engage him or her as a *lawyer in an unrelated matter*. In such case, depending on the time elapsed since the end of the mediation, the concern that the mediator might appear not to have acted impartially in order to secure future work might subside, as well as the concern that he or she might use information from the mediation to the detriment of the other party. The Florida MEAC reached such a decision where one of the parties to a divorce mediation contacted the mediator *one and a half years* after the mediation had ended and asked her to represent him as a lawyer in his second, unrelated, dissolution of marriage.[62]

The North Carolina Dispute Resolution Commission, discussing the appropriateness of an agreement by a mediator in a dispute between heirs to serve as the *estate's administrator/fiduciary*, noted that the mediator "failed to give due regard to the conflict between the parties' interests and the fact that he stood to gain personally and financially

[59] See Georgia Commission on Dispute Resolution's Committee on Ethics, Opinion 5-2012 available at www.godr.org/files/Ethics%20Opinion%205.pdf.

[60] See Florida MEAC, Opinion 2008-008 available at www.flcourts.org/core/fileparse.php/283/urlt/MEACOpinion2008-008.pdf. See also North Carolina Dispute Resolution Commission, Advisory Opinion 04-06 available at www.nccourts.org/Courts/CRS/Councils/DRC/Documents/04-06_final.pdf (A mediator who conducts a mediation for a couple that is separating may not thereafter represent either the husband or wife in divorce proceedings).

[61] Florida MEAC, Opinion 94-002 available at www.flcourts.org/core/fileparse.php/283/urlt/1994-Opinion-002.pdf.

[62] Florida MEAC, Opinion 97-002 available at www.flcourts.org/core/fileparse.php/283/urlt/1997-Opinion-002.pdf.

from his appointment as administrator."[63] The Commission, which seems to have been influenced by the fact that one of the heirs/parties objected to the appointment and the mediator ignored that objection, concluded that "[a] mediator should remain focused exclusively on his or her role as mediator and should not solicit or accept an appointment as a fiduciary that flows from the mediation process. A mediator who accepts such an appointment creates the perception that he or she manipulated the mediation process and the parties to his or her own advantage in obtaining the appointment and, thus, compromised his/her neutrality in the process."[64] The Commission was concerned that "[s]uch perceptions serve to discredit the mediator, the mediation process, the Clerk Mediation Program and, ultimately, the Commission and courts."[65]

In another Opinion, the North Carolina Dispute Resolution Commission held that a mediator is not prohibited in principle from serving as an *arbitrator* in the same dispute, provided that he or she obtains the parties' informed consent to the change in role, and that the relationship he or she formed with the parties during the mediation and the information he or she learned in caucuses does not cloud his judgment or compromise his neutrality.[66] The Commission was influenced in its decision by the shared dispute-resolution goal of both mediators and arbitrators, and by the accepted method of "med-arb" in the professional practice of dispute resolution.[67] Indeed, many codes of conduct for mediators expressly allow mediators to switch to another *dispute resolution role* with the parties' consent. The *Model Standards*, for example, provide that "[a] mediator shall not undertake an additional dispute resolution role in the same matter without the consent of the parties. Before providing such service, a mediator shall inform the parties of the implications of the change in process and obtain their consent to the change."[68]

63 North Carolina Dispute Resolution Commission, Advisory Opinion 08-15 available at www.nccourts.org/Courts/CRS/Councils/DRC/Documents/15-08_final120408.pdf.

64 Ibid. 65 Ibid.

66 North Carolina Dispute Resolution Commission, Advisory Opinion 10-17 available at www.nccourts.org/Courts/CRS/Councils/DRC/Documents/10-17_2010.pdf.

67 Ibid.

68 Model Standards, Standard VI.A.8. See also NY-CDRC Standards, Standard VI Comment 7; Committee Notes to Florida Rules, Rule 10.310; Michigan Standards, Standard VII.B.6.

6.5 Conclusion

Conflicts of interest might tempt mediators to prefer their interest over the parties' interests, thereby frustrating the parties' legitimate expectation that they ignore considerations that are irrelevant to the nature of the professional service mediators provide and conduct the mediation in a manner worthy of the parties' trust. A notable feature of mediation practice and an important interest of mediation parties is that mediators avoid favoritism and bias in the conduct of mediation. Thus, a paramount concern of a theory of mediators' ethics is the control of actual and potential conflicts of interest that could reasonably raise a question about mediators' impartiality. However, as conflicts of interest cannot be completely avoided, a realistic theory of mediators' ethics instructs mediators to disclose them to the parties and enable the parties to exercise self-determination with regard to whether to accept or reject the mediator in their case. Furthermore, as mediators have a responsibility to the profession of mediation and to the public to conduct mediations in a manner that does not harm the profession and the process of mediation, mediators are required to avoid any conduct that jeopardizes public faith in them. Accordingly, mediators must avoid the appearance of conflicts of interest at all stages of mediation as well as subsequent to mediation, decline to accept a mediation, and withdraw from mediation when the conflict of interest is severe to a degree that might undermine public trust in the profession or process of mediation.

6.6 A proposed standard of conflicts of interest

A mediator shall avoid a conflict of interest or the appearance of a conflict of interest at all stages of mediation or act to neutralize it in accordance with this standard. A conflict of interest is a situation in which an interest of a mediator conflicts with an interest of one party or more, and can arise, inter alia (1) from involvement of a mediator with the subject matter of the dispute or its outcome; (b) from a personal or professional relationship, whether past or present, between a mediator and any mediation participant or a person related to a mediation participant; or (c) from a legal, moral, ethical, religious, conscientious, or other duty to act in a particular way.

A. The existence of an actual or potential conflict of interest is relevant information for the parties because it raises a concern regarding mediator partiality or possible preference of the mediator's interest over the interests of the parties. A mediator shall disclose a conflict of interest to the parties so as to enable them to exercise self-determination with regard to selection of the mediator and participation in the mediation.

1. Prior to accepting a mediation –
   (a) A mediator shall make a reasonable inquiry to determine whether there are any facts that a reasonable person would consider likely to create a potential or actual conflict of interest for the mediator.
   (b) If following the inquiry a conflict of interest has been found the mediator shall disclose it to the parties as soon as practicable.
   (c) After disclosure, if all parties agree, the mediator may proceed with the mediation.
2. During a mediation –
   (a) If a mediator learns any fact after accepting a mediation that raises a question of a potential or actual conflict of interest, the mediator shall disclose it to the parties as soon as practicable.
   (b) After disclosure, if all parties agree, the mediator may proceed with the mediation.
   (c) A mediator shall not solicit or otherwise incur any future professional services, including future mediations, beyond the sessions necessary for the mediation.

B. A serious conflict of interest –

Notwithstanding the aforesaid, if a conflict of interest raises a reasonable concern that the mediator will not be able to refrain from harming a party's interest, and as a result the process might be publicly perceived as faulty, thereby jeopardizing the standing of the mediation profession and public trust in the profession and the process, the mediator shall withdraw or decline to proceed regardless of the express agreement of the parties.

C. Subsequent to a mediation –

A mediator shall not establish a personal or professional relationship with parties, other individuals or organizations, following a mediation in which they were involved, that would raise a reasonable concern that the mediator had a conflict of interest and conducted a faulty process that could undermine the profession's standing and public trust in the profession and process of mediation. In making the decision, the mediator should consider factors such as the time elapsed since the mediation, the nature of the relationship established, and the type of services offered.

7

Mediator impartiality

7.1 Introduction

The obligation of mediators to conduct mediations impartially can be found in virtually every code of conduct for mediators. Most mediation scholars agree on the importance and centrality of impartiality to the theory and practice of mediation,[1] although some – especially transformative and narrative mediation experts – are skeptical of the possibility of ever achieving impartiality in real practice.[2] Some practitioners use the term "neutrality" interchangeably with impartiality,[3] but neutrality is hardly used these days as a standard in codes of conduct for mediators. The problem with the neutrality discourse is that it is not refined enough and leaves uncertainty as to the intentions of those who make statements on the neutrality of mediators.[4] In fact, the meaning of neutrality in the context of mediation encompasses both mediator *impartiality* and the obligations of mediators in connection with *conflicts of interest*. When a mediator's neutrality is questioned, it could mean that the mediator acted with partiality, i.e., that he or she favored one party over another, or that he was not acting disinterestedly, i.e., that he or she had an interest in the process or outcome in conflict with an interest of one or more parties. Each of these statements has a different meaning that should be appreciated and fully understood by mediators. Thus, impartiality and conflict of interests are dealt with separately in this book, and these terms are preferred to neutrality.

1 See, e.g., Moore, *The Mediation Process*, p. 53; Kovach, *Mediation*, p. 211; Boulle and Nesic, *Mediation*, p. 18.

2 See Section 7.5. 3 See Kovach, *Mediation*, p. 212.

4 See, e.g., Boulle and Nesic, *Mediation*, p. 448 (distinguishing between different aspects of neutrality that includes, in their view, impartiality, and arguing that "neutrality is not an indispensable feature of mediation, whereas impartiality is"). See also id., p. 18 (noting that "[w]hile impartiality must be a constant feature of mediation, the existence of neutrality will always be a question of degree").

Understanding the meaning of impartiality is a key to the ethical practice of mediation. Impartiality has become so intertwined with the public image of mediation that mediators acting impartially in the exercise of their role can be considered a professional undertaking. The exact limits of this norm, however, are uncertain, not only because of different suggested definitions of impartiality, but also because of the tension between impartiality and other recognized norms of conduct applicable to mediators, in particular the obligation to conduct a process that respects party self-determination. This chapter explores the normative sources of mediators' ethical duty of impartiality, ascertains its meaning, and suggests how it can be reconciled with other norms that are binding on mediators.

7.2 The sources of mediators' duty of impartiality

7.2.1 The reasonable expectations of mediation parties

The reasonable expectations of mediation parties are constructed upon (a) the common standards of mediation practice, and (b) the relationship of trust between parties and mediators. Any person taking on a case of mediation represents by virtue of his conduct an undertaking to carry on the mediation in accordance with the common standards of the field of mediation and those standards that follow from the nature and definition of the role of mediators.[5] Parties may legitimately expect any mediator to keep that promise, and as impartiality is presented in all codes of conduct for mediators as a mediation norm, and since it is depicted by most mediation experts as a fundamental principle of mediation, they may legitimately expect any mediator to act impartially. Second, since mediators are in a position of power while parties are in a position of dependence, parties are entitled to expect mediators to exercise their role in a manner worthy of the parties' trust.[6] Acting impartially is one such manifestation, while favoritism by mediators will be reasonably considered unworthy of the parties' trust.

7.2.2 The reasonable expectations of the profession and public

Mediators have an ethical obligation toward the profession of mediation and the public to maintain the standing of the profession in order

[5] See Chapter 3, Section 3.7. [6] Ibid.

to protect legitimate interests of the profession (that mediation be used by the public for the benefit of the profession so that the profession is preserved) and the interests of the public (that mediation be used by the public for the benefit of the public in order to promote consensual dispute resolution within a harmonious society).[7] The profession and public reasonably expect mediators to conduct mediations impartially because partiality on the part of mediators is likely to jeopardize public trust in the profession and process of mediation.[8] Moreover, the expectation that mediators act impartially is shared by principals (e.g., mediation programs with which mediators are associated) and mediators' employers, as partiality might adversely affect their standing.

7.2.3 A practical source

The normative reasons that establish a mediator obligation of impartiality are supported by practical considerations. The mediation literature tends to explain the duty of impartiality by pragmatic reasons.[9] Mediator impartiality is viewed as essential to mediation success because parties would hesitate to cooperate with a partial mediator and decline to reveal sensitive information or offer concessions. Moreover, a partial mediator would be less effective in offering parties a detached, "objective" point of view of their problem that could be productive in moving on the dialogue between them.

7.3 The meaning of the duty of impartiality

7.3.1 A legitimate expectation of parties of freedom from favoritism and bias

Impartiality is a commonly used word that indicates equality of treatment and nondiscrimination. The Merriam-Webster Online Dictionary, for example, defines the word impartial as "not partial or biased: treating

[7] See Chapter 3, Section 3.7 (The mediator–profession and mediator–public relationships).

[8] See, e.g., *N.L.R.B.* v. *Joseph Macaluso* 618 F.2d 51, 52–54 (9th Cir. 1980) (noting "the public interest in maintaining the perceived and actual impartiality of federal mediators" (p. 54) and pointing out that "the purpose of excluding mediator testimony . . . is to avoid a breach of impartiality, not a breach of confidentiality" (at note 3).

[9] See, e.g., Peppet, "Contractarian Economics", 255–256. See also Boulle and Nesic, *Mediation*, p. 451 (noting that "[i]mpartiality of the mediator aims to ensure that the parties can trust the process and the mediator").

or affecting all equally";[10] and the Oxford Dictionaries define it as "[t]reating all rivals or disputants equally."[11] One source that can shed light on the meaning of impartiality in the context of mediation is the nature and definition of mediation. The core definition of mediation is "a *process in which a third person assists parties to an actual or potential conflict to maintain a dialogue in order to enable them to make decisions regarding the conflict and reach an agreement when they wish to do so.*"[12] Mediators, therefore, provide services to parties with (at least some) conflicting interests. As a result, each party expects the mediator to refrain from conduct that *favors* other parties and *discriminates* against him or her. This expectation is justified by the relationship of trust between parties and mediators. No party would agree to receive mediation services from a person who favors the other party; a mediator who favors one party would not be worthy of the trust of the other party; thus, from a professional ethics perspective, persons who exercise the role of mediators should be viewed as if they have promised to avoid favoritism between the parties. Note that the criterion for mediator discrimination is his or her behavior toward *other* parties. A mediator attempting to coerce one party is *not* acting impartially vis-à-vis the other party, while a mediator attempting to coerce *all* parties *is*; he or she is treating the parties in the same manner, and his or her wrongdoing is due to the violation of the norm of party self-determination, not the norm of impartiality.

The reasonable expectations of parties are shaped by the practice of mediation. Thus, a second source of meaning for mediator impartiality can be found in standards of mediation practice that are common in the field of mediation. Virtually all codes of conduct for mediators call for mediator impartiality. While some codes decline to define what impartiality is,[13] most codes do so with reference to the terms favoritism and bias,[14] and a few refer to the term evenhandedness.[15] The *Florida Rules*,

10 See Merriam-Webster Online Dictionary available at www.merriam-webster.com/dictionary/impartial.

11 See Oxford Dictionaries available at www.oxforddictionaries.com/definition/english/impartial.

12 See Chapter 3, Section 3.2.

13 See, e.g., California Rules, Rule 3.855(a). See also ADR Canada Code, s. 4; Maryland Standards of Conduct for Mediators, Arbitrators and Other ADR Practitioners available at www.courts.state.md.us/macro/pdfs/standardsfinal.pdf (Maryland Standards), Standard II.

14 See, e.g., Australian Practice Standards, s. 5. See also Model Standards, Standard II.A; Family Mediation Model Standards, Standard IV.A; Alabama Code, Standard 5(A); Family Mediation Canada Code, Article 8.

15 See, e.g., Oregon Standards, Standard III. See also Australian Ethical Guidelines, s. 2.

for example, provide that "[i]mpartiality means freedom from favoritism or bias . . . and includes a commitment to assist all parties, as opposed to any one individual";[16] and the *Model Standards* state that "[i]mpartiality means freedom from favoritism, bias or prejudice."[17]

Most codes, then, prefer to define impartiality in a negative way, that is, to focus on what mediators are *not* expected to do (exhibit favoritism, bias, or prejudice). A few codes *positively* instruct mediators on what they should do (act evenhandedly; assist all parties as opposed to one party). What becomes clear is that the codes refrain from using the term "equality." They do not express the meaning of impartiality through the use of the term equality, and do not state, for example, that mediators should treat parties equally or give them equal treatment. There are good reasons for that, which are discussed in Section 7.3.4. Still, it should be appreciated that ordinarily, mediators are expected to treat parties *in the same way.* Questions of partiality are likely to arise when mediators (a) treat parties differently, for example, allocate them different time, address them differently, or make an intervention such as holding a caucus or providing advice with respect to one party but not to another; or (b) take an action that seems to be the same treatment but in fact has a *different impact* on the parties. For example, a decision by the mediator to provide information, refer parties to an expert, or terminate the mediation, may work to the benefit of one party and to the disadvantage of another. As an illustration, consider the facts of one Florida mediation grievance case. It "was a county court contract case involving two corporations, which were both represented by counsel at mediation. The corporation which was being sued allegedly was bankrupt and thus judgment proof. During mediation, in joint session, the mediator pointed out to both parties that the individual who had appeared at mediation on behalf of the defendant corporation had signed the contract in his individual capacity, not on behalf of the corporation, and thus could be sued individually. This was not a fact that had previously been raised by either party."[18] The complaint committee found probable cause that the mediator failed to maintain impartiality. It is apparent that the mediator's suggestion aligned him with one of the parties.

This may seem a clear case of mediator intervention that gives an advantage to one party at the expense of another. It is also clear that

[16] See Florida Rules, Rule 10.330(a).

[17] See Model Standards, Standard II.A. See also Georgia Standards, Standard III.

[18] FL-1992–95-GV available at www.americanbar.org/directories/mediator_ethics_opinion/11.html.

favoritism on the basis of reasons such as the parties' race, sex, values, or opinions would be wrong, and some codes in fact warn mediators to avoid such conduct. The *Model Standards*, for example, provide that "[a] mediator should not act with partiality or prejudice based on any participant's personal characteristics, background, values and beliefs, or performance at a mediation ... "[19] However, from a professional ethics perspective, impartiality is more than "same treatment." Mediator interventions that treat parties differently or have a different impact on them may be justified under a proper interpretation of the norm of impartiality where parties are unable to participate meaningfully in a mediation according to the process's norms. This point will be explored in Section 7.3.4, after the distinctions between external and internal impartiality and factual and perceived impartiality have been made.

7.3.2 *Internal and external impartiality: between ideal and duty*

A professional ethics perspective distinguishes between ideals that inspire professionals and duties that bind them.[20] If professional ethics is to be treated with respect, it must not be divorced from reality. Ethical duties, therefore, must be limited to behavior that professionals can reasonably be expected to exhibit. When this is applied to mediators' impartiality, it becomes clear that a realistic ethical duty of impartiality cannot relate to the *internal* feelings, views, and beliefs of mediators. Mediators are human beings, and as such are bound sometimes to experience feelings of sympathy for one party or resentment toward another.[21] This inevitable truth leads some mediation scholars and practitioners to the conclusion that mediation impartiality is a myth or an unrealistic ideal.[22] The better view from a professional ethics perspective is to focus on the *behavior* that mediators can be reasonably expected to control. It is an *external* aspect of impartiality that refers to freedom from favoritism or bias *in word or action*, to an extent that mediators can

[19] Model Standards, Standard II.B.1. See also NY-CDRC Standards, Standard II Comment 1.

[20] See Chapter 1, Section 1.2.1.2. See also Gert, Culver and Clouser, *Bioethics*, p. 43.

[21] See, e.g., Cohen, Dattner, and Luxenburg, "The Limits of the Mediator's Neutrality", 342. See also Trina Grillo, "The Mediation Alternative – Process Dangers for Women" (1991) 100 *Yale Law Journal* 1545, 1592–1593; Jonathan G. Shailor, *Empowerment in Dispute Mediation: A Critical Analysis of Communication* (Westport, CT: Praeger, 1994), pp. 78–79 (describing such events on the basis of observations of mediations).

[22] See, e.g., Grillo, "The Mediation Alternative", 1587. See also Weckstein, "In Praise of Party Empowerment", 510.

reasonably be expected to maintain. The norm of impartiality, thus, serves to warn mediators to separate their feelings and views from their conduct,[23] and to keep an open mind to enable them to assist parties who have values and views different from theirs.[24]

Indeed, many codes of conduct for mediators refer to an external aspect of impartiality in their definition of impartiality. The *Florida Rules*, for example, provide that "impartiality means freedom from favoritism or bias in word, action, or appearance,"[25] and the *Georgia Standards* state that "a mediator must demonstrate impartiality in word and deed."[26] The Committee Notes to the impartiality standard of the *NY-CDRC Standards* stress this idea in providing that "the *Committee's* emphasis is on the mediator's **action** with regard to any bias he or she may hold. A mediator who may have a particular bias towards a party for any reason must not act with partiality due to her or his views" (emphasis in the original).[27]

7.3.3 Avoiding perceived partiality or the appearance of it

As a practical issue, there is much logic in requiring mediators to avoid the *appearance* of partiality, as well as partiality *in fact*. Assume, for example, that a mediator makes an aggressive evaluation of each of the parties' cases in separate meetings in order to convince them to make concessions. This mediator does not in fact favor one party over another, but each party may wrongly suspect the mediator of favoring the other. A

[23] See, e.g., Moore, *The Mediation Process*, pp. 53–54.

[24] Compare Judge Scalia's definition of judicial impartiality in *White v. Minnesota Republican Party*, 536 U.S. 765 (2002) as cited in Gunning, "Know Justice", 92: "Justice Antonin Scalia, who wrote the majority decision, defined three meanings for impartiality: (1) having no bias against or favor towards any party; (2) the impossible – having no preconception in favor of or against any particular legal view; and (3) open-mindedness – a willingness to be open to being persuaded in spite of your preconceived notions".

[25] See Florida Rules, Rule 10.330(a). See also Family Mediation Model Standards, Standard IV.A; Family Mediation Canada Code, Article 8(1); Alabama Code, Standard 5(a); North Carolina Standards, Rule II; NY-CDRC Standards, Standard II.A; Texas Guidelines, s. 9 Comment; Virginia Standards, s. G.1. Compare to the California Rules, Rule 3.855(a) stating that the mediator "must *maintain* impartiality" and to the Model Standards, Standard II.A stating that "impartiality means *freedom from* favoritism, bias or prejudice" and instructing the mediator in Standard II.B to "conduct a mediation in an impartial manner" (emphasis added). These formulations leave uncertainty as to whether the mediator's duty is to avoid *expressions* of impartiality in conducting mediation, or alternatively to refrain from conducting mediation in *a state of mind* of impartiality.

[26] See Georgia Standards, Standard III.A.

[27] See NY-CDRC Standards, Committee Notes Comment 1 to Standard II.

mediator that *appears* partial might lose the parties' trust and the ability to carry on his or her role. The *Illinois Standards*, for example, state that "mediators can serve effectively only when all parties to the dispute are confident of the mediator's impartiality."[28] In addition, the behavior of a mediator could have implications that go beyond the particular case which is mediated by him or her. Parties might share their experience with relatives, friends, and the community at large. Thus, the damaging repercussions of behavior that is perceived as partial can extend far beyond the immediate parties involved.[29]

From a professional ethics perspective, the ethical obligation of mediators to exercise their role impartially includes a commitment to avoiding *an appearance* of partiality as well. Avoiding the appearance of partiality is not a duty owed to the *parties*, because the appearance of partiality, in contrast to actual partiality, does not cause harm to the parties. In fact, this obligation is owed to the *mediation profession* and to *the public*, and it stems from the legitimate expectations of the profession and the public that mediators conduct themselves in a manner that does not undermine public trust in the profession so that the process of mediation continues to serve the legitimate needs (and interests) of the profession and the public. If mediators appeared to be partial, the standing of the profession of mediation would be undermined, to the detriment of both the profession and the public. Capturing this idea, the *NY-CDRC Standards* state that "[g]iven the central role that a mediator's impartiality assumes to promote the integrity and effectiveness of the mediation process, a mediator should avoid conduct that undermines the public's or party's perception of her or his impartiality";[30] and Gaines observes that "an appearance of impartiality promotes public confidence in the fairness of [mediation]."[31] As an illustration, consider the facts of a complaint filed with the Committee on Ethics of the Georgia Commission on Dispute Resolution. In a mediated divorce case, the drafting of the mediation agreement was done in a room in the presence

[28] Illinois Standards, s. IV. See also Family Mediation Model Standards, Overview and Definitions ("Effective mediation requires ... that the mediator be impartial"); Laflin, "Preserving the Integrity of Mediation", 498.

[29] This point had been raised in an ethics opinion discussing a mediator's vulgar, offensive and demeaning remarks made in the course of a mediation. See the Committee on Ethics of the Georgia Commission on Dispute Resolution, Opinion 2002–1, available at www.godr.org/files/Formal%20opinion%202002–1%203–23–04TP.pdf.

[30] See NY-CDRC Standards, Standard III Comment 1.

[31] See Michelle D. Gaines, "A Proposed Conflict of Interest Rule for Attorney-Mediators" (1998) 73 *Washington Law Review* 699, 703.

of one of the parties. The other party's perception was that "the conversation was more flirtatious than professional. The mediator admitted that the mediation agreement was drafted in a relatively small area and if someone saw them together in the room without hearing their discussion, one could assume that the mediator's conversation with the opposing party was social rather than professional."[32] The Ethics Committee held that the mediator failed to maintain impartiality and his actions caused the party to question the integrity of the mediation.[33]

Indeed, many codes of conduct for mediators require mediators to avoid the appearance of partiality. The *Model Standards*, for example, provide that "a mediator shall conduct a mediation in an impartial manner and avoid conduct that gives the appearance of partiality";[34] the *Georgia Standards* provide that "[a] mediator must scrupulously avoid any appearance of partiality";[35] and the *Australian Practice Standards* provide that "[i]mpartiality means freedom from favouritism or bias either in word or action, or the omission of word or action, that might give the appearance of such favouritism or bias."[36] Some codes explicitly refer to the receipt of gifts and benefits from parties and to the giving of gifts and benefits to parties as a type of conduct that might raise concerns of partiality. The *California Rules*, for example, provide that "[a] mediator must not at any time solicit or accept from or give to any participant or affiliate of a participant any gift, bequest, or favor that might reasonably raise a question concerning the mediator's impartiality."[37]

As a practical matter, however, it is very hard and sometimes even impossible to completely avoid conduct that raises a suspicion of partiality in the eyes of the parties. When mediators make decisions within mediation, ask questions, reflect parties' stories, provide information, and refer parties to outside experts, their actions could sometimes be construed as partiality.[38] In this respect, mediators *cannot* completely

32 See the Committee on Ethics of the Georgia Commission on Dispute Resolution, Opinion 5-2012 available at www.godr.org/files/Ethics%20Opinion%205.pdf.

33 Id., p. 2. 34 See Model Standards, Standard II.B.

35 See Georgia Standards, Standard III.A.

36 Australian Practice Standards, s. 5(1). See also Alabama Code, Standard 5(a); Florida Rules, Rule 10.330(a); Family Mediation Canada Code, Article 8(1); Australian Ethical Guidelines, s. 2(ii); Texas Guidelines, s. 9.

37 California Rules, Rule 3.859(d). See also Model Standards, Standard II.B.2 and B.3; Florida Rules, Rule 10.310(c); Georgia Standards, Standard III.B.

38 See, e.g., John Forester and David Stitzel, "Beyond Neutrality: The Possibilities of Activist Mediation in Public Sector Conflicts" (1989) 5 *Negotiation Journal* 251, 260.

avoid conduct that might be interpreted as partiality, even though they have tried hard to avoid such an impression. It is clear, therefore, that the demand addressed at mediators must be "reasonable," not absolute, and that the test for reviewing mediators' conduct cannot be the impressions of the parties alone. In other words, not every subjective feeling of a party that a mediator has been partial will be followed by ethical responsibility.[39]

It is not surprising, therefore, that the test adopted by many codes for identifying an appearance of partiality is one of *reasonableness*: would a reasonable person consider (even mistakenly) that the mediator had acted with partiality? The *NY-CDRC Standards* provide that "[i]n the event circumstances arise during a mediation that would reasonably be construed to impair or compromise a mediator's impartiality, the mediator is obligated to withdraw";[40] and the California Advisory Committee Comment to the Rule on impartiality state that "[a] mediator's overarching duty under [the Impartiality Rule] is to make a 'reasonable effort' to identify matters that, in the eyes of a reasonable person, could raise a question about the mediator's ability to conduct the mediation impartially."[41] This approach is also evident in the *Model Standards'* rule on gifts. While the Standards hold that "[a] mediator should neither give nor accept a gift, favor, loan or other item of value that raises a question as to the mediator's actual or perceived impartiality,"[42] they provide at the same time that "[a] mediator may accept or give *de minimis gifts* or incidental items or services that are provided to facilitate a mediation or respect cultural norms so long as such practices do not raise questions as to a mediator's actual or perceived impartiality" (emphasis added).[43]

Adopting a test of reasonableness for recognizing the appearance of partiality should not be taken as a license to ignore the subjective feelings of parties. If parties lose faith in the mediator because they suspect his or her impartiality, the mediator will be unable to conduct the mediation in that particular case, and if the parties circulate their feelings it could harm the profession and the process as well. Thus, mediators should aspire to conduct mediations free of an appearance of partiality in its subjective

[39] Compare Family Mediation Canada Code, Article 8(3) ("The perception by one or both of the participants that the mediator is partial does not in itself require the mediator to withdraw, but in such circumstances, the mediator must remind both parties of their right to terminate the mediation"). See also Australian Practice Standards, s.5(5).

[40] NY-CDRC Standards, Standard II Comment 2.

[41] See Advisory Committee Comment to California Rules, Rule 3.855(b).

[42] See Model Standards, Standard II.B.2. [43] Id., Standard II.B.3

sense, i.e., in the eyes of the parties, insofar as is possible. The implications for practice are that mediators should choose that course of action that *minimizes* (though does not necessarily eliminate) the risk of an appearance of partiality. The main method for overcoming perceived impartiality is the use of separate meetings with parties.[44] Separate meetings (or caucuses) are frequently used by mediators, though some scholars oppose them.[45] They enable mediators and parties to raise issues that cannot be freely discussed in the presence of all the parties, gain a better understanding of the parties' interests, assist parties to air strong emotions and frustrations, examine with the parties options for settlement, overcome impasses, and reinforce the parties' trust in the mediator.[46] With impartiality concerns in mind, separate meetings can give mediators more room for action, although not unlimited as we have seen with the aggressive evaluation example earlier.[47]

To summarize the obligations of mediators regarding the appearance of partiality, mediators *should* take measures to avoid the appearance of partiality, as viewed by the parties;[48] and *must not* conduct a mediation in a manner that could impair or compromise a mediator's impartiality in the eyes of a reasonable person.

7.3.4 Between impartiality and equality: substantive interpretation of impartiality

As noted previously, all codes of conduct for mediators require mediators to act impartially, often defined negatively as freedom from favoritism and bias, rather than positively as treating the parties equally. There is a good reason for this limited approach to defining impartiality in the

[44] On the use of separate meetings in order to maintain the appearance of impartiality, see e.g., Boulle and Nesic, *Mediation*, p. 136. See also Susan Nauss Exon, "The Effects that Mediator Styles Impose on Neutrality and Impartiality Requirements of Mediation" (2008) 42 *University of San Francisco Law Review* 577, 609; Bush, "Efficiency and Protection", 282; Jean Poitras, "The Strategic Use of Caucus to Facilitate Parties' Trust in Mediators", IACM 23rd Annual Conference Paper, available at ssrn.com/abstract=1612880.

[45] See, e.g., Gary Friedman and Jack Himmelstein, "The Understanding-Based Model of Mediation", in Carrie Menkel-Meadow, Lela Porter Love, and Andrea Kupfer Schneider, *Mediation: Practice, Policy and Ethics* (New York: Aspen, 2006), p. 120.

[46] See, e.g., Boulle and Nesic, *Mediation*, p. 136.

[47] Wrong use of separate meetings can result in partiality or the appearance of partiality. See, e.g., Boulle and Nesic, *Mediation*, p. 458 (noting that a perception of partiality can arise "when a mediator spends more time with one party than another in a private session").

[48] See, e.g., Virginia Standards, s. G.2.

context of mediation: mediation parties are often *unequal* in terms of their intellectual capabilities, education, negotiation skills, financial resources, social status, and emotional state. If impartiality were defined as equal treatment, the mediator would presumably be required to ignore parties' inequalities, and as a result the process would harm weak parties and favor stronger ones.[49] Still, defining impartiality as freedom from favoritism and bias is inadequate as a practical guideline for mediators who face unequal parties, because mediators need to know what conduct would and would not count as favoritism or bias and what distinguishes freedom from favoritism or bias from a concept of formal equality. Codes of conduct for mediators do not provide such guidance, and while some scholars suggest that in appropriate circumstances mediators should assist weak parties, the ethical rationale for such mediator intervention and its limitations remain vague.

The following discussion analyses the meaning of "freedom from favoritism and bias in word or action" as a relative obligation of mediators that must accommodate other ethical obligations that are binding on mediators. A professional ethics perspective supports a substantive, realist interpretation of impartiality that prefers a substantive concept of equality over a formal one. It justifies, within limits, legitimate interventions by mediators that are instances of different treatment of unequal parties. It does so, on the basis of (a) the legitimate expectations of parties for a fair process, and (b) the legitimate expectations of the profession and the public that mediators protect the process of mediation and the profession's standing. Such conduct might be *formally* seen as an act of partiality, but from a professional ethics perspective that adopts a more complex, relative, and substantive approach to the interpretation of the ethical norms that bind mediators, such conduct would be treated as substantively impartial.

7.3.4.1 Legitimate expectations of parties for a fair process

The relationship of trust between parties and mediators supports a fundamental expectation of every party that the mediator in his or her case conduct a *fair* process[50] that is *not harmful* or *abusive* to the parties.[51] These expectations are sometimes given explicit expression in codes of conduct for mediators. The *Georgia Standards*, for example, state that "a

[49] See, e.g., Gunning, "Know Justice", 93; Penelope Eileen Bryan, "The Coercion of Women in Divorce Settlement Negotiations" (1997) 74 *Denver University Law Review* 931.

[50] See generally Chapter 11. [51] See Chapter 8, Section 8.2.4.

mediator acts as guardian of the overall fairness of the process,"[52] and the *Ontario Family Mediation Code* imposes on the mediator a "Duty to Minimize Harm or Prejudice to Participants" and provides that "it is the obligation of the mediator to suspend or terminate mediation whenever continuation of the process would harm or prejudice one or more of the participants."[53] Such expectations are legitimate even in the absence of similar code provisions, because reasonable parties would regard the mediator in their case as responsible for the conduct of a due process that is not used (with the mediator's awareness) to harm them, and would consider a mediator who allowed such abuse unworthy of their trust. These expectations have a bearing on the meaning of the obligation of impartiality: mediators cannot justify nonintervention in such circumstances in the name of impartiality, and the obligation is mitigated by considerations of fairness and professional integrity to the effect that certain conduct cannot be properly considered favoritism or bias.

The best example of this idea is the interplay between the obligation of mediator impartiality and the norm of respecting party self-determination. The latter directs mediators to support a true exercise of party decision-making as opposed to a formal, low-value decision-making, by conducting a process in which to the extent the mediator can reasonably be satisfied, the parties are competent and the decisions they make are voluntary, uncoerced, and informed.[54] Mediators would not be living up to the standard of party self-determination if they adhered to a formal, restricted interpretation of impartiality. Such mediators would face a dilemma when a party is unable to exercise self-determination because he or she suffers from incompetency or is ignorant of important relevant information, for example about his or her legal rights: if the mediator does nothing he or she in fact favors the strong party, and if he or she assists the weak party he or she favors him or her over the other. Both action and inaction have an effect on the parties and formally favor one over the other. However, if we accept, in accordance with the nature and definition of mediation, that a central part of the role of mediators is to assist parties to make decisions, it follows that in circumstances in which mediators become aware that a party is unable to exercise self-determination, they may not remain passive. If they were to do so, they

[52] See Georgia Standards, Introduction and Standard IV.

[53] See Ontario Association for Family Mediation Code of Professional Conduct (2013), available at www.oafm.on.ca/membership/policies/standards-of-practice (Ontario Family Mediation Code), s. 9.

[54] See Chapter 4.

would be lending a hand to the conduct of a defective process of mediation and decision-making that seriously undermines the fundamental right of every mediation party to make decisions concerning his affairs. Thus, when a party in unable to exercise self-determination the primary duty of mediators is to assist that party to realize his or her right to self-determination; for example, to refer parties to an expert when a party is ignorant of relevant information and cannot make an informed decision,[55] or to postpone the mediation when a party temporarily suffers from incompetence due to emotional stress.[56]

Still, the obligation to assist parties in the exercise of self-determination, strong and fundamental as it is, is not an overriding duty that trumps all other mediation norms. It does elasticize the meaning of impartiality to allow, from a formalistic point of view, a form of "soft favoritism,"[57] but within limits. One such limitation stems from the fact that the mediator serves several masters. The mediator is committed to *all* parties. The legitimate expectation of Party A that the mediator assist him or her in the exercise of self-determination must be balanced with the legitimate expectation of Party B that the mediator limit his or her intervention to the *minimum required* for enabling Party A to realize his or her self-determination or other ethical rights, so that the harm to Party B's interests is minimal. Therefore, the mediator must choose that intervention that is *necessary yet the least harmful* to the other party's right to impartiality. For example, if the mediator believes that a party is in need of relevant information for making an informed decision (i.e. that making a decision absent that information would render the decision-making defective), referring the parties to consultation would be "justified favoritism" consistent with the norm of impartiality, while the mediator's providing the information directly to that party would be unjustified favoritism in breach of impartiality. The difference between the two scenarios is that referring the parties to obtain advice might reach the same goal as the provision of the information by the mediator, but with only a minor intervention on the part of the mediator that involves a lesser harm to his or her impartiality.[58] This course of action meets the

[55] See, e.g., Florida Rules, Rule 10.370. See also Illinois Standards, s. IV.

[56] See, e.g., Alabama Code, Standard 7(c).

[57] Compare Ronit Zamir, "The Disempowering Relationship between Mediator Neutrality and Judicial Impartiality: Toward a New Mediation Ethic" (2011) 11 *Pepperdine Dispute Resolution Law Journal* 467 (discussing the concept of "equal partiality").

[58] Compare Florida MEAC, Opinion 2006-006, available at www.flcourts.org/core/fileparse.php/283/urlt/MEAC-Opinion-2006-006.pdf.

legitimate expectations of both parties: the one in need of relevant information expects the mediator to prevent a faulty decision-making process in the absence of the information, and the one who is aware of the information expects the mediator to limit his or her intervention to the minimum necessary for ensuring an exercise of self-determination by the ignorant party.

This construction of the meaning of mediator impartiality can be further illustrated by contrasting legitimate *empowerment* with illegitimate *balancing of power*. Boulle and Nesic write that "empowerment refers to all those ways in which the strengths of the mediation process increase the parties' ability to perform well and to feel good about their performance. It includes interventions which assist the parties to understand their situations, to communicate effectively, to negotiate assertively, to make decisions confidently, and to feel satisfied with the mediation process and its outcome."[59] Mediators empower parties through various interventions, for example, by meeting with the parties separately, allocating more time to parties who experience difficulties in relating their stories, and by preventing interruptions.[60] The *Georgia Standards* refer to another method of empowerment, providing that "[i]f there is a serious imbalance of power between parties, the mediator should consider whether the presence of an attorney, family member, or friend would give the needed support."[61]

In contrast, a balancing of powers would be an intervention seeking to equalize the power positions of the parties. Parties cannot legitimately expect mediators to balance the powers of the participants. First, it will often be unrealistic to expect mediators to do so. Mediators cannot turn a poor party into a wealthy one, an unintelligent party into a sophisticated one, or a party with wanton legal representation into a well-represented one. Second, such intervention would be *beyond* what is required for enabling the weak party to realize his or her ethical right to self-determination. While empowerment assists the weaker party more than it assists the other party, thereby affecting the balance of power between the

(holding that "[a] mediator is obligated to advise a party of the *right* to seek counsel, if the mediator believes that the party does not understand or appreciate how an agreement may adversely affect the party's legal rights or obligations, but is prohibited from giving 'a personal or professional opinion intended to coerce the parties, unduly influence the parties, decide the dispute, or direct a resolution of any issues,'" i.e., from delivering the information by himself).

59 See Boulle and Nesic, *Mediation*, pp. 167–168.

60 Id., pp. 167–169 (discussing ways of empowering parties).

61 See Georgia Standards, Standard I.B, Recommendation.

parties, it does not seek nor effect an equality of powers; it seeks to provide a *minimum safety-net* ensuring that all parties have the basic conditions for exercising self-determination within the mediation. The empowering mediator, unlike the balancing mediator, does not take a stand on the parties' cause or on the content of a proposed solution. He or she simply strengthens the decision-making capacity of parties, realizing that different parties need different kinds of support in order to make decisions. The *Georgia Standards*, for example, express this idea by noting that "[h]elping a party to present his or her needs and interests in a way that can be heard by the other side is not a breach of neutrality but is, rather, an important part of the mediator's role. When the mediator helps each side to communicate effectively, the mediator is assisting the parties in establishing the common ground upon which a solid agreement can be based."[62] To take another illustration, a Florida mediator asked MEAC whether he may inform a mediation party of a right, which he seemed ignorant of, to make a legal claim.[63] The Committee thought that he may not do so, irrespective of the fact that the party was or was not legally represented, because this would constitute prohibited "professional advice" that would necessarily compromise his impartiality. In the words of the Committee, "advice inevitably will favor one party over another and thus, by its very nature, advice can not be provided while maintaining impartiality." Instead, the Committee suggested that the proper intervention would be to check with the party whether he had consulted a lawyer and considered his legal rights, and advise him to seek legal counsel. This more limited intervention was aimed at assisting the party in exercising his right to self-determination. If he were already represented or had made an informed decision not to seek legal advice, the mediator could legitimately assume that the party had exercised self-determination.

So one limitation on what might be termed from a formalistic point of view "justified favoritism" (although under a substantive approach, the intervention does not really favor a party but rather ensures that the ground rules of the game of mediation are maintained), is that the intervention is necessary in order to protect an ethical right of one of the parties and there is no other possible intervention with lesser impact on the mediator's impartiality. A second limitation is derived from the

[62] See Georgia Standards, Standard III.A, Recommendation.

[63] See Florida MEAC, Opinion 1996–003, available at www.flcourts.org/core/fileparse.php/283/urlt/1996-Opinion-003.pdf.

ongoing commitment of mediators to abide by other norms of ethics applicable to them. Mediators are expected to abide by all the ethical norms applicable to them, and find that course of action that mediates between their various obligations.[64] Accordingly, a mediator might be prevented from assisting Party A or empowering him or her with particular information because, for example, he or she is not *competent* to provide such information, because providing such information would be considered prohibited *professional advice*, or because he or she learnt the information in a separate meeting with Party B and must keep it in *confidence*. In addition, as mediators are bound to avoid conduct that might undermine the standing of the profession and public faith in the profession and process of mediation, mediators must be satisfied that the intervention is not likely to have such an impact. This takes us back to the discussion of the *appearance* of partiality and the limitations that it places on mediators' conduct.

7.3.4.2 Legitimate expectations of the profession and the public that mediators protect the process of mediation and the profession's standing

A substantive understanding of the meaning of impartiality also follows from the expectations of the profession and the public. The profession and the public expect mediators to conduct mediations in a manner that does not harm the profession and the process. This expectation affects the meaning that should be given to the obligation of mediator impartiality, that is, the meaning of what should be considered favoritism and bias in the conduct of mediators, because if mediators rigidly committed themselves to equal treatment of parties irrespective of context (i.e. to formal impartiality or equality, irrespective of the particular circumstances of the parties and the case) their conduct would seriously endanger public trust in the profession and the process of mediation. Thus, the duty of mediators to maintain public trust in the profession and process provides an additional source for a substantive interpretation of the obligation of mediator impartiality. For example, a mediator terminating a mediation notwithstanding the wishes of the parties, where the parties are about to reach a fundamentally unfair or unconscionable agreement that is extremely harmful to one of them,[65] might be considered, from a formalistic point of view, as partial for taking a stand and protecting one of the parties. However, from a professional ethics perspective, such an act

[64] See Chapter 3, Section 3.9(b). [65] See Chapter 8 Section 8.2.4.3(c).

should not be considered as an exercise of partiality because (a) it is a limited intervention that (b) would not be perceived as an act of partiality in the eyes of a reasonable person and thus would not result in a loss of public trust in the profession and process of mediation, and (c) it is in fact *necessary* for the preservation of public trust in the profession and process of mediation. Note that the duty to maintain public trust serves at the same time both as a *justification* for a mediator intervention and a *limitation* on the *extent* of such intervention.

In summary, the meaning of mediator impartiality is indeed freedom from favoritism or bias in word, action, or appearance. Ordinarily this would simply mean treating the parties in the same way in order to avoid favoring the interests of one party over another's (impartiality as formal equality). Sometimes, however, treating the parties in the same way might promote the interests of one party to the disadvantage of another. In such case, different treatment by a mediator would be justified if certain conditions are met (impartiality as substantive equality) (see Figure 7.1). The mediator should first ask him or herself whether his or her intervention is (a) required in order to give effect to an ethical right of the parties, for example their right to self-determination, or (b) necessary for the preservation of public trust in the profession and process of mediation. If the answer is affirmative, the mediator should limit his or her intervention to one that is (a) the minimum necessary for the realization of the parties' right, for example, an intervention that ensures minimum conditions for the exercise of party self-determination, (b) can be reconciled with other mediator obligations, and (c) would not be perceived as an act of partiality in the eyes of a reasonable person and thus would not result in a loss of public trust in the profession and process of mediation.

7.4 Refusal of cases and withdrawal

If a mediator cannot meet the legitimate expectations for impartiality, he or she must not accept a case for mediation, or withdraw if he or she has already taken on the case. A mediator who *believes* that he or she is not or will not be able to conduct the mediation impartially (*factual* partiality) must not accept the case or withdraw. This expectation is reflected in many of the codes. The *Family Mediation Model Standards*, for example, state that "[a] family mediator should not accept a dispute for mediation if the family mediator cannot be impartial";[66] and the

[66] See Family Mediation Model Standards, Standard IV.C.

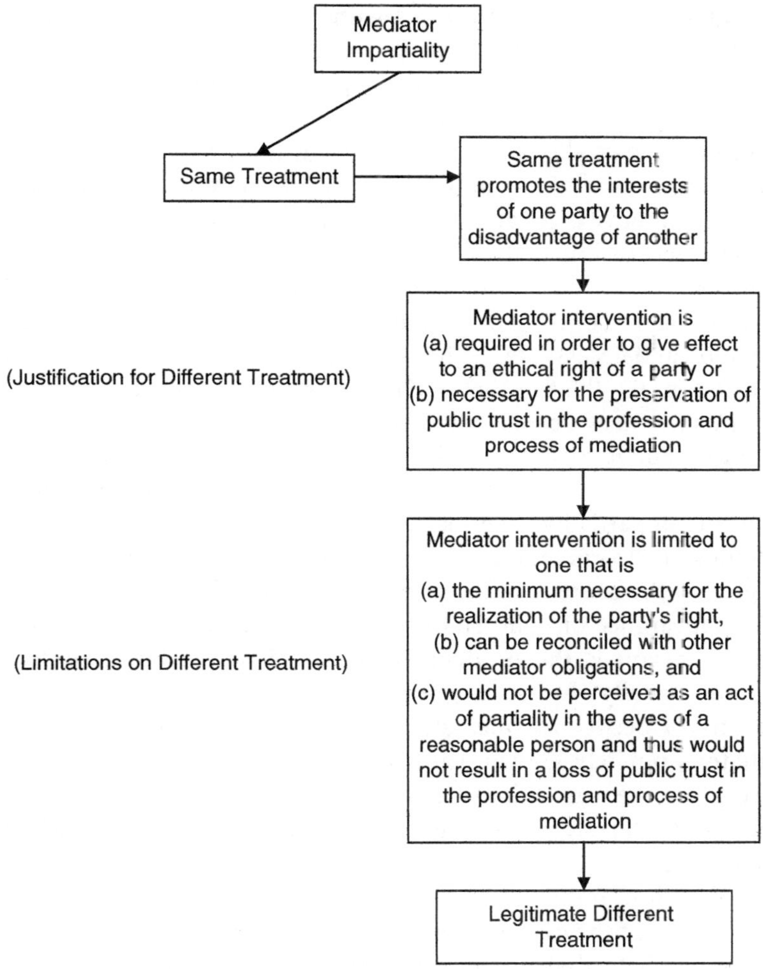

Figure 7.1: The meaning of mediator impartiality

California Rules provide that "[r]egardless of the consent of the parties, a mediator either must decline to serve as mediator or, if already serving, must withdraw from the mediation if: (1) The mediator cannot maintain impartiality toward all participants in the mediation process."[67]

[67] See California Rules, Rule 3.855 (f)(1). See also Michigan Standards, Standard II.B.

In addition, refusal of a case or withdrawal is obligatory where the mediator is *reasonably perceived or likely to be perceived* as partial in circumstances that could undermine public trust in the process (the *appearance* of partiality). Some codes simply refer to the reasonable suspicion of partiality as a ground for withdrawal. The Committee Notes to the *Florida Rules* on impartiality, for example, provide that "in the event circumstances arise during a mediation that would reasonably be construed to impair or compromise a mediator's impartiality, the mediator is obligated to withdraw."[68] It seems that in the drafters' view any reasonable concern of partiality might endanger public faith in mediation and necessitates withdrawal. However, in view of the rationale for withdrawal – the fear that public faith in mediation would suffer – if the circumstances are such that the concern for partiality does not jeopardize public trust, the mediator should not be obliged to withdraw. The phrasing of the *California Rules* on that point is illustrative, providing in the impartiality Rule that the mediator must decline to serve or withdraw if "[p]roceeding with the mediation would jeopardize the integrity of the court or of the mediation process."[69]

An appearance or concern of mediator partiality before the mediation has begun is the product of an actual or perceived *conflict of interests*, usually due to a prior *personal, professional, or business relationship* between a mediator and a mediation participant, or a mediator's publicly known *worldview and personal values* that have a bearing on the case. The mediator will have to identify potential conflicts of interest, assess their severity, and reach a decision whether they are trivial conflicts that allow him or her to accept the case or proceed with it; minor conflicts that require disclosure and allow him or her to accept the case or proceed with it with the parties' consent; or serious conflicts that are non-waivable and compel him or her to decline the case or withdraw.[70] These considerations are discussed in detail in Chapter 6 on "Conflict of Interests." For example, a mediator

[68] See Committee Notes to Florida Rules, Rule 10.330. See also, Florida Rules, Rule 10.330(a); Family Mediation Model Standards, Standard IV.A; Alabama Code, Standard 5; Georgia Standards, Standard III.A; NY-CDRC Standards, Standard II.A. The Model Standards require mediators to conduct mediations impartially and without an appearance of partiality (Standard II.B), but impose a duty to decline a case or withdraw when a mediator is unable to conduct the mediation impartially, not mentioning the appearance of partiality as a trigger of such a duty (Standard II.A and II.C). The other codes mentioned above avoid such an outcome by defining impartiality as including an appearance of partiality.

[69] See California Rules, Rule 3.855 (f)(2).

[70] See Chapter 6, Section 6.4.2.

must decline a case where the party's lawyer is the mediator's daughter[71] or ex-husband or ex-wife.[72]

7.5 Criticism of impartiality

Scholars, especially those belonging to the transformative and narrative mediation schools, criticize the central role assigned to impartiality by the problem-solving style of mediation. This criticism, I argue, can be challenged by the professional ethics perspective. One criticism is that impartiality is an internal, psychological condition beyond mediators' control that mediators cannot meet while conducting mediations.[73] Rifkin, Millen, and Cobb, for example, refer to impartiality as "the ability to interact in the absence of feelings, values, or agendas in themselves"[74] and as "the ability to suspend judgment."[75] A professional ethics perspective considers this view of impartiality as an *ideal* of impartiality that encourages mediators to *aspire* to impartiality in mind, as opposed to a *duty* of external impartiality that prohibits manifestations of partiality in word or deed. While the ideal aspect of impartiality cannot be achieved, its duty aspect can.

According to another criticism of impartiality, while mediators are encouraged by codes and writers to ensure that the interests of the parties are represented in the mediation process,[76] mediators who in fact engage in such practice are bound to favor one side or another at a given moment,[77] and lose their impartiality as a result. Cobb and Rifkin term this practice "equidistance," and argue that "if mediators are equidistant, they cannot be impartial, and if they are impartial, they cannot be equidistant."[78] Winslade and Monk embrace that critique in their

[71] See Florida MEAC, Opinion 2004–008 available at www.flcourts.org/core/fileparse.php/283/urlt/MEAC-Opinion-2004–008.pdf.

[72] See Florida MEAC, Opinion 2013–010 available at www.flcourts.org/core/fileparse.php/283/urlt/MEACOOpinionO2013-010OFINALOSIGNED.pdf.

[73] See Sara Cobb and Janet Rifkin, "Practice and Paradox: Deconstructing Neutrality in Mediation" (1991) 16 *Law and Social Inquiry* 35, 42–43.

[74] See Janet Rifkin, Jonathan Millen, and Sara Cobb, "Toward a New Discourse for Mediation: A Critique of Neutrality" (1991) 9 *Mediation Quarterly* 151, 152.

[75] See id., 153.

[76] See Cobb and Rifkin, "Practice and Paradox", 45. See also Alison Taylor, "Concepts of Neutrality in Family Mediation: Contexts, Ethics, Influence, and Transformative Process" (1997) 14 *Conflict Resolution Quarterly* 215, 226–227, 233 (discussing a concept of expanded neutrality that accepts empowering and power balancing by mediators).

[77] See Cobb and Rifkin, "Practice and Paradox", 44.

[78] See id., 45. See also Rifkin, Millen, and Cobb, "Toward a New Discourse for Mediation", 153–154.

narrative approach to mediation. They argue that mediators "can either promote social justice and attend equity and fairness, or reinforce unjust dominant cultural practices."[79] They suggest that mediators may "make efforts to assist those whose voices are often silenced or marginalized . . . in a manner that does not alienate the party who appears to be the most advantaged as the mediation begins."[80] A professional ethics perspective addresses this critique by rejecting a formal interpretation of impartiality that ignores context and differences between parties, and adopts a substantive, realist interpretation of impartiality that accommodates, within limits, different treatment of parties.

A third line of criticism focuses on the goal of problem-solving mediation and argues that mediators with such an orientation are bound to lose their *neutrality*. Bush and Folger state this difficulty as follows: "Mediators, as interveners in conflict, necessarily carry their own interest with them. In problem-solving mediation, given the underlying view of conflict and resolution, the mediator's interest is in finding a good solution to a problem that is blocking the parties' satisfaction. This interest leads mediators to be directive in shaping both problems and solutions, and they wind up influencing the outcome of mediations in favor of settlement generally and in favor of terms of settlement that comport with their views of fairness, optimality, and so forth."[81] Bush and Folger go on to suggest "a new conception of neutrality that makes sense given the reality of mediator influence."[82] "The meaning of mediator neutrality, in the context of inevitable influence, is a *commitment to use influence only for the sake of keeping the ultimate decision on outcome in the parties' hands*" (emphasis in the original).[83] It seems to me that the main concern of this critique is with what is arguably a lack of respect for parties' right to *self-determination* among mediators with a problem-solving orientation. From a professional ethics perspective, these legitimate concerns should be addressed by a proper construction of the norm of party self-determination to the effect that parties are adequately involved in the decisions that are made by mediators during mediations. The "new conception of neutrality" is one illustration of the limitations that the norm of party self-determination imposes on mediator influence,

[79] See Winslade and Monk, *Narrative Mediation*, p. 100. [80] Id., p. 101.

[81] See Bush and Folger, *The Promise of Mediation* (1994), p. 104. See also Weckstein, "In Praise of Party Empowerment", 510 (" . . . inherent in the nature of the mediator's calling is a 'bias' in favour of settlement. In fact, many mediators push hard to achieve that end . . ."); Winslade and Monk, *Narrative Mediation*, pp. 36, 47.

[82] Bush and Folger, *The Promise of Mediation* (1994), p. 105. [83] Ibid.

and it cannot replace a norm of impartiality that prohibits mediators from favoring one party over another.

7.6 Conclusion

Impartiality is an ethical norm that binds all mediators. In essence, it instructs mediators to avoid favoritism and bias between parties in word or action. It does not and cannot control the internal feelings and views of the mediator, but only their external manifestations. Transformative and narrative mediation scholars have not yet offered a comprehensive concept of impartiality in replacement of the "defective" problem-solving concept. Thus, from a professional ethics perspective, any mediator, regardless of style, must conduct a mediation impartially in the sense discussed in this chapter:[84] a problem-solving mediator must implement impartiality while assisting parties to reach an agreement; a transformative mediator while facilitating empowerment and recognition shifts; and a narrative mediator while deconstructing the story of conflict and assisting the parties to construct an alternative story.

Mediators are expected to avoid the appearance of partiality, as well as partiality in fact. *Practically* they should strive to avoid perceptions of partiality in the eyes of the *parties*, in order to secure their cooperation; *ethically*, they must avoid the appearance of partiality in the eyes of a *reasonable person*, where such could undermine the standing of the profession and process of mediation and public faith in it.

Important as it is, impartiality is a relative norm like all other ethical norms. It therefore should be interpreted in conjunction with other ethical norms that are binding on mediators. A substantive, realist interpretation of impartiality allows for different treatment under certain circumstances.

7.7 A proposed standard of impartiality

A mediator shall exercise his role impartially. Impartiality means freedom from external manifestations of favoritism or bias between parties in word or action.

[84] Compare Gaines, "A Proposed Conflict of Interest Rule", 702 (noting that "[r]egardless of mediator style and context, the mediator's impartiality is critical to the success of the mediation and the protection of the parties' rights. Mediator impartiality instills trust, enables the parties to collaborate and share information with the mediator and other parties").

A. Accepting Cases and Withdrawal
   A mediator shall not accept a case for mediation or withdraw if:
   1. He or she cannot conduct the mediation impartially; or
   2. There is a reasonable concern that he or she is not or will not be able to conduct the mediation impartially or without an appearance of partiality, in circumstances that could jeopardize the standing of the profession and process of mediation and public trust in it.

B. In Conducting a Mediation and Exercising his or her Role –
   1. A mediator shall avoid partiality in fact, and any conduct that might reasonably appear as an act of partiality.
      (a) A mediator shall not act with partiality on the basis of reasons such as participants' race, sex, religion, personal characteristics, background, values and beliefs, or conduct at a mediation.
      (b) A mediator shall neither give nor accept a gift, favor, loan or other item of value that raises a question as to the mediator's impartiality. A mediator may accept or give de minimis gifts or services that are provided to facilitate a mediation or respect cultural norms so long as such practices do not raise questions as to a mediator's impartiality.
   2. A mediator shall treat parties differently where –
      (a) Same treatment would favor the interests of one party and disadvantage another; and
      (b) The mediator's intervention is (1) required in order to give effect to an ethical right of a party (in particular self-determination), or (2) necessary for the preservation of public trust in the profession and process of mediation.

      Any such intervention shall be limited to one that is –
      (a) The minimum necessary for the realization of the party's right; and
      (b) Can be reconciled with other mediator obligations; and
      (c) Would not be perceived as an act of partiality in the eyes of a reasonable person and thus would not result in a loss of public trust in the profession and process of mediation.

8

Professional integrity

8.1 Introduction

From a professional ethics perspective, professional integrity is a fundamental ethical norm that describes the state of *being committed to the nature and definition of the professional role and to the wholeness of the professional service provided.*[1] Mediation literature and codes of conduct for mediators, however, have not dedicated much space to it. They tend to focus on the integrity of the *process* of mediation and on mediators' duty to maintain *process* integrity, rather than on the more general norm of professional integrity of *mediators* and their duty to maintain *professional* integrity in their conduct of mediations, a norm that encompasses a duty to maintain process integrity but is not limited to it.

Jacqueline M. Nolan-Haley, for example, has noted that "the mediator is said to represent the *integrity of the mediation process*"[2] and argued that "[t]he mediator … owes an obligation to both parties to maintain *the integrity of the mediation process*";[3] the *Georgia Standards* provide in a Fairness standard that "[a] mediator is the guardian of the *integrity of the mediation process*"[4] and that he or she "must protect the *integrity of the process.*"[5] The *Model Standards* use the term integrity in the context of two standards: the Conflicts of Interest standard provides that "a mediator shall withdraw from or decline to proceed with the mediation" if "a mediator's conflict of interest might reasonably be viewed as undermining the *integrity of the mediation*";[6] and the Advertising and Solicitation standard provides that "[a] mediator shall not solicit in a manner that

1 See Chapter 2, Section 2.2.3.4.
2 See Nolan-Haley, "Informed Consent", 826 (emphasis added).
3 See id., p. 825 note 236 (emphasis added). See also Nolan-Haley, "Lawyers, Non-Lawyers and Mediation", 295 (noting that "the mediator's primary concern should be to uphold the integrity of the process").
4 See Georgia Standards, Standard IV.B (emphasis added).
5 See id., Standard IV (emphasis added).
6 Model Standards, Standard III.E (emphasis added).

gives an appearance of partiality for or against a party or otherwise undermines the *integrity of the process*."[7] The *California Rules* provide that mediators in court-connected programs are responsible for conducting themselves in a manner that merits "broad public confidence in the *integrity and fairness of the process*,"[8] and hold in the context of an Impartiality and Conflicts of Interest rule that a mediator must withdraw from the mediation if "[p]roceeding with the mediation would jeopardize the *integrity ... of the mediation process*";[9] lastly, the *Virginia Standards* provide in a Quality of the Process standard that "[t]he mediator shall terminate the mediation when, in the mediator's judgment, the *integrity of the process* has been compromised."[10]

Only a few codes and scholars refer explicitly to the integrity of *mediators*. The *Florida Rules*, for example, provide in an Integrity and Impartiality standard that "[a] mediator shall not accept any engagement, provide any service, or perform any act that would compromise the *mediator's integrity* or impartiality";[11] the *California-CDRC Standards* provide that "[e]very mediator bears the responsibility of conducting mediations in a manner that instills confidence in the process, [and] promotes trust in the *integrity* and competence *of mediators*";[12] and Richard M. Calkins argued that "[m] ediators must operate under the highest ethical standards in the profession because of the very nature of their work. They must be principled, trustworthy, dependable, and *act with integrity*."[13]

I would argue that when the drafters of codes of conduct for mediators use the terminology of integrity, they are referring to what is in fact a general duty of mediators to protect *the institution of mediation* (i.e. the profession and process of mediation) and *the public's trust in it*. The duty to maintain the integrity of the mediation process reflects a concern of the drafters that a damaged process, a process that is seen as lacking the quality of wholeness or completeness, or a process that is viewed as being abused, will not earn the public's confidence, which is essential to the survival and

7 Id., Standard VII.B (emphasis added).
8 California Rules, Rule 3.850 (emphasis added).
9 Id., Rule 3.855(f)(2) (emphasis added).
10 Virginia Standards, s. K.4 (emphasis added). See also ibid., (noting that the integrity of the process might be compromised " ... For example, by inability or unwillingness of a party to participate effectively; gross inequality of bargaining power or ability; and unfairness resulting from nondisclosure, where there is a legal duty to disclose, or fraud, by a participant.").
11 Florida Rules, Rule 10.620 (emphasis added).
12 California-CDRC Standards, Preamble (emphasis added).
13 Calkins, "Caucus Mediation", 311 (emphasis added).

development of mediation.[14] But preserving process integrity and protecting the public's trust in the process are not necessarily the same. A process may lack completeness or wholeness in varying degree; it might sometimes lead to loss of public trust, at other times not. What current codes lack is a clear expression of *two* independent mediator standards: one that relates to a duty to conduct mediation in a manner that does not jeopardize the public's trust in the institution of mediation;[15] and another that relates to a duty of mediators to conduct mediation with professional integrity, that is, in a state of true commitment to the role of a mediator and to the wholeness of the mediation process. A duty to act with professional integrity includes a duty to maintain the integrity of the mediation process because a mediator who is truly committed to his or her role must conduct a "whole" or "complete" process; and the integrity of the mediation process is dependent on the mediator's integrity because the mediator is a key participant in the process.[16] This chapter seeks to establish professional integrity as an independent standard of mediators' ethics. Professional integrity is discussed in the context of mediators' duties under four headings:[17] Decision-Making and the Exercise of Professional Discretion; Separation of Professional Roles; Appropriateness of Case to Process; and Prevention of Process Abuse or Substantial Defects in the Process (see Figure 8.1).

14 See, e.g., Nancy D. Erbe, "Appreciating Mediation's Global Role in Promoting Good Governance" (2006) 11 *Harvard Negotiation Law Review* 355, 357 (noting that "If mediators and parties to mediation fail to safeguard the integrity of their process, mediation's growing popularity may erode"). I do not define mediation integrity "as an adherence to mediation practice norms" (see, e.g., John Lande, "Using Dispute System Design Methods to Promote Good-Faith Participation in Court-Connected Mediation Programs" (2002) 50 *University of California Los Angeles Law Review* 69, 75), a definition which is reserved in this book for fairness: see Chapter 11, Section 11.2; Chapter 2, Sections 2.2.3.4 and 2.2.3.10.

15 See Chapter 12.

16 See, e.g., Luis Miguel Diaz, "Mediation Furthers the Principles of Transparency and Cooperation to Solve Disputes in the NAFTA Free Trade Area" (2001) 30 *Denver Journal of International Law and Policy* 73, 80 (noting that "the integrity and quality of a mediation is very dependent on the mediator"). See also Gaines, "A Proposed Conflict of Interest Rule", 699 (noting that "the integrity of mediation as an alternative form of dispute resolution depends largely on the ethics of mediators"). Compare Fuller and Randall, "Professional Responsibility", 200 (noting that "the integrity of the adjudicative process itself depends upon the participation of the advocate").

17 See Chapter 2, Section 2.2.3.4.

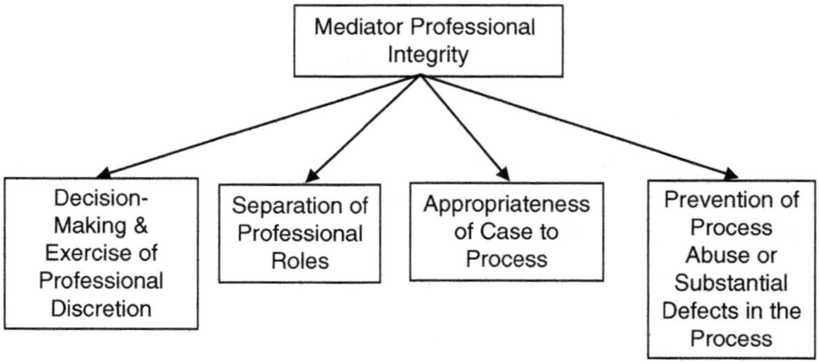

Figure 8.1: Mediator professional integrity

8.2 Mediators' duty to conduct mediation with integrity

8.2.1 Decision-making and the exercise of professional discretion

Mediation parties that seek mediation services expect the mediator to act "as a professional" as opposed to an ordinary person, that is, they expect him or her to examine and analyze their case on the basis of his or her *professional knowledge* and assist them in conducting a constructive dialogue on the basis of his or her *professional skills*. In order to examine and analyze a case and provide assistance to the parties, a mediator must engage in *decision-making* in the execution of his role. A mediator cannot perform his or her role without making decisions; and in order to make decisions he or she must exercise *professional discretion*, that is, he or she must make decisions on the basis of *professional considerations* that are *relevant* to the provision of mediation services, as opposed to extraneous, irrelevant considerations. It follows that professional integrity is in fact the *ethical source* of the *general authority* of mediators to make decisions in the conduct of mediation.

Codes of conduct for mediators do not usually include an explicit standard dealing with the authority of mediators to make decisions or with the exercise of discretion, but such authority is often implied by various standards. The *Model Standards*, for example, authorize the mediator in a Quality of the Process standard to make decisions necessary in order to "conduct a mediation in accordance with [the] Standards and in a manner that promotes diligence, timeliness, safety, presence of the appropriate participants, party participation, procedural fairness, party competency and mutual respect among all participants."[18] Conflicts of interest

[18] See Model Standards, Standard VI.A.

standards often authorize mediators to terminate a mediation in certain circumstances,[19] and confidentiality standards authorize the mediator to withhold confidential information from interested persons.[20] Still, the general source of both the authority and responsibility of mediators for making decisions and for exercising discretion in the course of mediation, so that the process is conducted consistent with the applicable standards, remains the norm of professional integrity. Numerous mediator interventions stem from the norm of professional integrity. Asking questions, reflecting, reframing, engaging in reality testing, caucusing, and withdrawal are all professional interventions aimed at moving the process forward. Any such intervention must rely on professional considerations and respect party self-determination.[21]

An example of the exercise of professional integrity in decision-making is a mediator's duty to *take steps so that appropriate participants are part of the process*. Sometimes the presence of individuals other than the disputing parties is important for a mediation process to be effective. For example, in public issues that involve environmental or planning policy, identifying possible stakeholders could be vital to a successful mediation.[22] Recognizing the need to invite other individuals into the process is a product of professional competence. The exercise of this competence, that is, the analysis and evaluation of the conflict and the use of professional insight in the course of providing a professional service, is an expression of professional integrity on the part of the mediator, who in doing so demonstrates a commitment to his or her role. In view of the parties' right to self-determination, the mediator should bring the need to involve other persons in the process to the attention of the disputing parties. Still, many codes of conduct for mediators do not address this issue at all. The *Model Standards*, which do deal with this issue, do so unsatisfactorily. They provide that "[t]he presence or absence of persons at a mediation depends on the agreement of the parties and the mediator. The parties and mediator may agree that others may be excluded from particular sessions or from all sessions."[23] The Standards are correct in raising this issue and instructing the mediator to involve the parties in the decision regarding who should attend the mediation; but they fail to impose on the mediator the responsibility for *bringing up* this issue in the first place.

19 See Chapter 6, Section 6.4.2.1. 20 See generally Chapter 10.
21 See generally Chapter 4. 22 See, e.g., Boulle and Nesic, *Mediation*, pp. 122–123.
23 Model Standards, Standard VI.A.3.

Another example concerns *participants' authority to bind parties.* Some mediations are conducted in the absence of one or all of the disputing parties, who are represented by other participants, for example by lawyers or by corporate officers in the case of a party-corporation. A mediator must be aware of possible limitations on the authority of representatives to bind their principals.[24] A party participating in a mediation legitimately expects the other party's representative to have the authority to make binding offers unless the opposite is explicitly stated. A mediator's awareness of that is an expression of his or her professionalism, of his or her obligation to execute his or her role as a professional rather than as an ordinary person, that is, of his or her obligation to conduct mediation with professional integrity. It is the mediator's responsibility to make sure that the other party or his or her representative is aware of a limitation of authority if such limitation exists. That information is relevant to their making an informed decision to participate in the mediation, consistent with a norm of party self-determination. The responsibility of the mediator is distinctly elevated where only one of the parties is unrepresented, but even where both parties are represented the mediator has a responsibility to ensure that the mediation is not abused by one of the representatives and he or she should raise the issue of authority with them.

8.2.2 Separation of professional roles

Mediators come from various backgrounds. Some mediators may belong to another profession and engage in another professional practice such as law, healthcare, education, or engineering. These mediators must be able to distinguish between their role as a mediator and their other professional roles. The first reason for that is because this is a matter of the *ideal.* Mediation is a new, developing profession that is still struggling for recognition. One of the shared professional ideals of mediators as a collective is an aspiration to *professionalization and to distinguishing mediation from other professions.*[25] If mediators fail to separate their professional roles, mediation will not succeed in maintaining its own character and be absorbed by other professions. However, the limitations of this consideration should be clear: an ideal sets goals to be aspired to rather than a duty to be complied with.

[24] See, e.g., Boulle and Nesic, *Mediation*, pp. 120–121. [25] See Chapter 3, Section 3.3.

A second reason for the separation of professional roles is the professional–client relationship. When a person contacts a professional he or she expects to be provided with a service *compatible with the definition and nature of the role* the professional is identified with;[26] likewise, a mediation party legitimately expects a mediator to provide him or her with mediation services, rather than other professional services such as arbitration, legal advice, or therapy. To provide other services without making it clear to the parties would be a misrepresentation on the part of the mediator. Still, *a party* may ask the mediator to supply him or her with an *additional service during* the mediation, that is, to perform a *dual role* at the same time. For example, a party might ask the mediator to make a binding decision in the course of a mediation on a mediation issue such as who should talk first (i.e. act as an arbitrator), give him legal advice (i.e. act as a lawyer), or provide psychological treatment (i.e. act as a therapist). In view of the mediation norm of party self-determination, the wishes of parties carry much weight, and such a request could be construed as an authorization by the parties of the mediator to perform another professional role (dual role) that eliminates any concern of misrepresentation about the mediator's role. Reflecting this idea, the *Model Standards*, for example, provide that "[a] mediator shall not undertake an additional dispute resolution role in the same matter without the consent of the parties. Before providing such service, a mediator shall inform the parties of the implications of the change in process and obtain their consent to the change."[27]

However, the consent of parties must be subject to limitations if mediators are to comply with applicable ethical norms *other than* self-determination. Mediators are expected by parties, by the mediation profession, and by the public to conduct the mediation *in accordance with the standards of practice that apply to mediators*, which include, inter alia, impartiality, confidentiality, and preserving the profession's standing and public trust in the process and profession of mediation. Once a mediator departs from his role in the course of mediation, he or she risks violating norms that apply to him or her in his or her capacity as a mediator, a situation that the parties' agreement is incapable of

[26] See Chapter 2, Section 2.2.3.4.

[27] Model Standards, Standard VIA.8. See also Federal Employee Mediators Guide, Standard VIA.8. The language of these standards is somewhat ambiguous as it is unclear whether the additional role is undertaken as a dual role *in the course of a mediation* or as a new and separate role *subsequent* to a mediation. The first possibility is considered here, and the latter in the last two paragraphs of this section.

remedying. For example, parties cannot legitimize mediator partiality. It is beyond their competence, because the duty to maintain impartiality is owed to the profession and to the public as well as to the parties, in order to preserve the profession's standing and public faith in the process and profession of mediation. Some codes of conduct for mediators reflect these concerns. The *Model Standards*, for example, provide that "[t]he role of a mediator differs substantially from other professional roles. Mixing the role of a mediator and the role of another profession is problematic and thus, a mediator should distinguish between the roles";[28] and the *NY-CDRC Standards* note that "to ensure a quality mediation process, the mediator should not mix the role of mediator with that of any other professional role."[29] The problematic nature of mixing roles and the concern about reduced quality are not alleviated by the parties' consent. Thus, a third reason for separating professional roles is a concern that the dual role might make it impossible for a mediator to observe mediation norms by which he or she is bound irrespective of the parties' wishes.

This is a major consideration for holding that mediators must not provide *legal or other professional advice* to parties, because doing so would almost certainly result in their violating impartiality. Indeed, many codes of conduct for mediators explicitly forbid mediators from giving professional advice[30] or offering a professional opinion.[31] The *North Carolina Standards*, for example, hold that "[a] mediator shall limit himself or herself solely to the role of mediator, and shall not give legal or other professional advice during the mediation";[32] and the *Federal Employee Mediators Guide* provides that "[a] federal employee mediator must limit his/her role to that of mediator and must never assume the role of advocate or advisor of any sort for any party's interests during the mediation process."[33]

In an effort to support informed decision-making by parties, and in order to accommodate a practice of "soft" evaluation or reality-testing by mediators, some codes seek to distinguish between the legitimate *provision*

[28] See Model Standards, Standard VI.A.5. See also Federal Employee Mediators Guide, Standard VI.A.5.; Virginia Standards, Comment to s. F.

[29] NY-CDRC Standards, Standards Committee Meeting August 2009, General Notes at 14.

[30] See, e.g., Georgia Standards, Standard I.E; North Carolina Standards, Rule VI; Texas Guidelines, s. 11; ADR Canada Code, s. 3.3.

[31] Florida Rules, Rule 10.370(c); Alabama Code, Standard 7(d).

[32] North Carolina Standards, Rule VI.

[33] Federal Employee Mediators Guide, Guidance Note to Standard III.

of information by mediators that is consistent with mediator impartiality and party self-determination, and illegitimate professional advice or opinion. The *Model Standards*, for example, state that "[a] mediator may provide information that the mediator is qualified by training or experience to provide, only if the mediator can do so consistent with these Standards,"[34] and the Reporter's Notes comment that this language "supports the mediator sharing information that he or she is qualified by training or experience to provide only if it is done in a manner consistent with other Standards, most notably promoting party self-determination and sustaining mediator impartiality."[35] The *Florida Rules* elaborate on this point, holding that "[a] mediator shall not offer a personal or professional opinion intended to coerce the parties, unduly influence the parties, decide the dispute, or direct a resolution of any issue. Consistent with standards of impartiality and preserving party self-determination however, a mediator may point out possible outcomes of the case and discuss the merits of a claim or defense. A mediator shall not offer a personal or professional opinion as to how the court in which the case has been filed will resolve the dispute."[36] In practice, the distinction between offering advice and providing information might be blurred. In general, advice or opinion involves the *application* of professional principles to the facts of the case, thus risking partiality and narrowing the spectrum of options rather than enlarging it, as is consistent with party self-determination, while providing information tends to be more general, avoids application to the facts of the case, and leaves more room for party choice. Thus, the provision of information approach could be justified from a professional ethics perspective, as it strikes a delicate balance between the competing norms. Still, where a mediator has reason to believe that providing the information might interfere with the parties' self-determination or with his own impartiality, he should refer the parties to *consult an outside expert* rather than provide the information himself. Many codes of conduct for mediators draw mediators' attention to this option. The *NY-CDRC Standards*, for example, provide that "[w]here appropriate, a mediator should recommend that parties seek outside professional advice or services";[37] The *Texas Guidelines* provide that "[i]n appropriate circumstances, a mediator should encourage the parties to seek legal, financial, tax or other professional advice before, during or after the mediation

34 Model Standards, Standard VI.A.5. See also Family Mediation Model Standards, Standard VI.B.

35 Model Standards, Reporter's Notes, p. 18. 36 Florida Rules, Rule 10.370(c).

37 NY-CDRC Standards, Standard VI Comment 5.

process";[38] and the *Virginia Standards* hold that "[t]he mediator shall encourage the parties to obtain independent expert information and/or advice when such information and/or advice is needed to reach an informed agreement or to protect the rights of a party."[39]

A different ethical issue arises where a mediator is asked to fulfill a different professional role *after* the mediation has been terminated. This time the mediator is not undertaking a dual role in the course of the mediation; he or she abandons his role as mediator and switches to another professional role in another professional process. For example, the parties might ask the mediator to act as an arbitrator or as a neutral evaluator in their case *subsequent* to the mediation. Again, the first step mediators must take in such cases is to secure the parties' informed consent to the change of role, as is consistent with the norm of party self-determination. Still, mediators should be aware that some mediation norms have a *continuing application* that lasts after mediation and impose on mediators an enduring responsibility despite the change of role. This means that the duty to maintain professional integrity *as a mediator*, that is, the commitment to the role of a mediator, could remain in effect after the mediation has ended. For example, a mediator might be precluded from taking the role of an arbitrator or neutral evaluator because he or she had been exposed to confidential information during caucuses that he or she must not use in the execution of his or her new role. Furthermore, the limitation on taking the new role could derive from the ethical norms of the new role. For example, a mediator who had been exposed to confidential information during caucuses might find it impossible to remain objective *as an arbitrator* or *neutral evaluator*.[40]

Another way of looking at the ongoing responsibility of mediators subsequent to a mediation is by considering the potential *conflict of interest* in taking another professional role after mediation. A mediator must decline to serve the parties in another professional capacity where accepting a different role after the mediation would reasonably raise a question about the propriety of the mediator's actions at the time of the mediation, to the effect that a reasonable concern might arise that the process had been faulty and that public trust in the process and profession of mediation could be undermined.[41]

38 Texas Guidelines, s. 11 Comment (a). 39 Virginia Standards, s. F.1.

40 See, e.g., North Carolina Dispute Resolution Commission, Advisory Opinion 10–17 available at www.nccourts.org/Courts/CRS/Councils/DRC/Documents/10–17_2010.pdf (discussing the ability of a mediator to serve as an arbitrator in the same dispute).

41 See Chapter 6, Section 6.4.2.2.

8.2.3 *Appropriateness of case to process*

From a professional ethics perspective, a person seeking professional service legitimately expects a professional to accept a case only when he or she considers the case appropriate for the process he or she is conducting, and to decline a case or withdraw when it is inappropriate for professional intervention of the type he or she is conducting.[42] Similarly, mediation parties expect mediators to conduct mediation in cases that are appropriate for mediation and decline a mediation or terminate it when the case is inappropriate for mediation. In this spirit, the *Florida Rules*, for example, provide that "[a] mediator is responsible for confirming that mediation is an appropriate dispute resolution process under the circumstances of each case";[43] and the *Texas Guidelines* note that "[a] mediator should postpone, recess, or terminate the mediation process if it is apparent to the mediator that the case is inappropriate for mediation."[44]

A mediator mediating a case which is inappropriate for mediation lacks professional integrity because he or she is not truly committed to his or her role and to the nature of the professional process for which he or she is responsible. In doing so he or she is unworthy of the parties' trust, his or her actions mislead the parties, and he or she jeopardizes public faith in mediation irrespective of the parties' agreement to his or her taking on their case.

Identifying the content of this duty is not easy, and codes of conduct for mediators do not elaborate on it. I suggest that mediation cases should meet two tests of appropriateness: *factual* and *normative*. A practical-factual appropriateness test asks whether a process of mediation, in view of its definition and intervention techniques, *could* as a practical matter achieve its goal; a normative appropriateness test asks whether a case *should*, in light of mediators' ethical norms, be dealt with in a mediation. For example, from a practical-factual perspective, mediation could assist two criminals in distributing the proceeds of a robbery committed by them, thus making that case appropriate for mediation. However, from a normative perspective, the case is inappropriate for mediation because any connection of mediation to the prohibited illegality raises a concern that the standing of the profession of mediation might suffer.

The duty to consider the appropriateness of the case to mediation is an ongoing duty that continues during the mediation. For example, a

[42] See Chapter 2, Section 2.2.3.4. [43] Florida Rules, Rule 10.400.

[44] Texas Guidelines, s. 13. See also Florida Rules, Rule 10.420(b)(3).

mediator may realize in the course of mediation that there is *no reasonable likelihood that the parties will reach a mediated agreement*. In court-connected mediation or other mediation in which a mediated settlement is the stated goal of the process, proceeding with the mediation might be inconsistent with professional integrity, because if the process is incapable of solving the dispute the case is inappropriate for the process. Assuming that the normative test of inappropriateness does not apply in the circumstances (i.e. the content of the case raises no difficulties), the practical-factual test would require the mediator to consider whether the possibilities of moving the parties toward a solution have been exhausted. If the answer is yes, the mediator must consider the termination of the mediation consistent with professional integrity. However, termination may not necessarily be mandatory. According to the principle of party self-determination, the mediator should share his or her thoughts with the parties and solicit their views on the matter. The parties may disagree with his or her view and wish to proceed with the mediation. They might think that an agreement is possible, or value the continuation of a dialogue even where an agreement is unlikely. The mediator in such circumstances would have no duty to end the mediation, as long as proceeding with the mediation does not jeopardize the standing of the profession and process of mediation.

Another situation that requires a mediator's attention is where *a party acts in a way that makes the conduct of mediation impossible*. For example, a party might continuously disrupt the other party's story, use demeaning and abusive language, or refuse to participate in a dialogue with the mediator or the other party. That party need not act in this way for malicious reasons.[45] It may truly be his or her personality, style of expression, or degree of self-restraint. But according to a test of appropriateness for mediation in a practical-factual sense, as a matter of practice his or her type and level of participation are not appropriate for a mediation process that is based on a dialogue and cooperation between parties. A mediator in such case cannot conduct the mediation, and he or she should reflect that state of affairs to that party and, in the event that the party is unwilling or unable to change his or her conduct, terminate the mediation. From a professional ethics perspective, the duties of a mediator toward the profession and the public support a discontinuation of the mediation, because proceeding with the mediation in these conditions might harm the standing of the mediation profession

[45] See Section 8.4.3.

and deter members of the public from going to mediation. For this reason, I believe, the *Florida Rules* correctly state that a mediator shall "adjourn or terminate the mediation if . . . any party is . . . unwilling to participate meaningfully in the process."[46]

Where a mediator has reason to believe that other dispute resolution processes are more appropriate for the parties, he should recommend that the parties consider resolving their conflict through other processes.[47]

8.2.4 Prevention of process abuse or substantial defects in the process

8.2.4.1 Process abuse by mediators

From a professional ethics perspective, clients expect professionals to conduct themselves and the process in a way consistent with the definition of the process and its goals. Any use of the process for some *other purpose* would not be worthy of the client's trust.[48] Furthermore, an abuse of a professional process would be inconsistent with the legitimate expectations of the profession and the public, who expect professionals to refrain from harming legitimate interests of the profession and the public, in particular the standing of the profession and the process, and public faith in them.[49]

Similarly, mediation parties expect mediators to refrain from using mediation for purposes for which it was not designed. For example, mediation parties legitimately expect mediators *not to use information revealed to them during mediation for any purpose not connected to the mediation.* From a professional ethics perspective, parties are entitled to assume that information which a mediator has been exposed to during mediation *because of* his role, which he would not have been likely to be exposed to otherwise, will be used for the purpose of advancing the process, and not for the personal interests of the mediator. A mediator

[46] See Florida Rules, Rule 10.420(b)(3). See also Texas Guidelines, s. 13; Virginia Standards, s. K.4.

[47] See, e.g., Georgia Standards, Standard IV.B and Commentary (providing in Standard IV.B that "A mediator is the guardian of the integrity of the mediation process" and commenting that "While there is room for variation in mediation style from the more directive to the more therapeutic, the mediator should recognize the line between mediation and a more evaluative process and be prepared to refer the party to another process if that would be more appropriate"). See also Michigan Standards, Standard VII.B.5; Model Standards, Standard VI.A.7.

[48] See Chapter 2, Section 2.2.3.4. [49] See Chapter 2, Section 2.4.3.

who uses such information for a purpose unrelated to the mediation is abusing the process in breach of the parties' trust. Some codes of conduct for mediators adopt provisions to that effect. The *Texas Guidelines*, for example, provide that "[a] mediator should not use information obtained during the mediation for personal gain or advantage."[50]

8.2.4.2 Process abuse by other participants – the parties' expectations

Mediation parties legitimately perceive mediators as responsible for the conduct of mediation in accordance with its rules and goals. Thus, they expect mediators not only to refrain from abusing the process themselves, but also to take necessary measures to prevent an abuse of the process (i.e. use of mediation for a purpose other than the purpose of mediation) by *other participants*, or prevent a defect in the process that is inconsistent with its nature. This general expectation is reflected in some of the codes of conduct for mediators. The *Florida Rules*, for example, provide that as part of his responsibility to the process "[a] mediator is responsible for safeguarding the mediation process";[51] The *Family Mediation Canada Code* provides that "[i]t is the duty of the mediator to suspend or terminate mediation whenever continuation of the process is likely to harm or prejudice one or more of the participants";[52] and the *NY-CDRC Standards* provide that "[a] mediator shall terminate the mediation, withdraw from service, or take other appropriate steps if she or he believes that participant conduct, including that of the mediator, jeopardizes sustaining a quality mediation process."[53]

The following scenario can illustrate this aspect of professional integrity. If a mediator has reason to believe that one party is concealing vital information from the other party – for example, a party is participating in the process with the sole intention of fishing for information for an upcoming trial, or a party is concealing information regarding hidden assets that are relevant to the dispute – he or she has a duty to take some action to prevent the process from being abused. The North Carolina Dispute Resolution Commission dealt with such a case where "a mediator learned, in a confidential private session with the wife and her attorney, that they intentionally had not disclosed to her husband and

[50] Texas Guidelines, s. 2 Comment (a). See also North Carolina Standards, Rule VII.E; Family Mediation Model Standards, Standard IV.H.

[51] Florida Rules, Rule 10.400. [52] Family Mediation Canada Code, Article 13.1.

[53] NY-CDRC Standards, Standard VI.B. See also Family Mediation Model Standards, Standard XI.A.6; Model Standards, Standard VI.C; North Carolina Standards, Rule VIII.

his attorney the existence of a valuable marital asset . . . the wife and her attorney told the mediator that they would not reveal the asset to the other side and they reminded the mediator of her duty [of confidentiality]."[54] The Commission held that "[w]hen a mediator learns of the intentional non-disclosure, it is best practice for the mediator to engage the offending participant in private conversation about the consequences of that party's decision. If the party persists in non-disclosure, the mediator must terminate the session and, if the party's decision remains the same, withdraw from the mediation altogether."[55] In another mediation case, the complainant party silently took notes for almost an hour while the other party spoke, and the mediators "reasonably believed that the complainant was abusing the process by attending for the sole purpose of obtaining discovery."[56] The NY-CDRC Mediator Ethics Advisory Committee held that based on these facts the mediators had a duty to intervene to ensure that the mediation was conducted in a manner consistent with the standards that applied to the mediation.[57]

8.2.4.3 Process abuse and prevention of substantial defects in the process – the professional and public aspects

The expectation that mediators take action in cases of an abuse of process or of a defective process is not only the parties' expectation, but also the legitimate expectation of the profession and the public. This follows from a reasonable concern that if mediation were to be abused by participants or suffer from a substantial defect, and the mediator could have prevented that state of affairs but did not intervene, the standing of the profession and the process and public faith in them would be undermined.[58] Thus, from a professional ethics perspective, the consent of participants to an abuse of the process by some participants or by a mediator, or to conduct that makes the process defective, cannot justify such conduct and cannot absolve a mediator of his or her responsibility

[54] See North Carolina Dispute Resolution Commission, Advisory Opinion 10–16 available at www.nccourts.org/Courts/CRS/Councils/DRC/Documents/10-16r_2010.pdf.

[55] Ibid.

[56] See New York MEAC, Opinion 2013–01 available at www.nycourts.gov/ip/adr/MEAC_Opinion_2013-01.pdf.

[57] Ibid. In fact the mediation turned out to be a success after the complainant responded to a question and started participating in the dialogue, but the mediators sought the committee's opinion assuming the complainant had remained quiet and not said anything.

[58] See, e.g., Scott H. Hughes, "The Uniform Mediation Act: To the Spoiled Go the Privileges" (2001) 85 *Marquette Law Review* 9, 75 (noting that "Any agreement completed where the mediator is aware of contractual misconduct would impugn the integrity of mediation").

(owed to the profession and the public) to prevent such conduct. This idea is widely reflected in codes of conduct for mediators. A large number of codes provide that a mediator should not allow the mediation to be used to *further criminal conduct,*[59] even where, I would add, the parties wish to do so; and the *Model Standards* provide that "[a] mediator shall not conduct a dispute resolution procedure other than mediation but label it mediation in an effort to gain the protection of rules, statutes, or other governing authorities pertaining to mediation,"[60] again, I would add, even where the parties consent to such conduct; more generally, the *Kansas Ethical Standards for Mediators* state in an "Obligations to the Mediation Process" standard that "[m]ediators have an obligation . . . to correct abuses."[61]

Furthermore, even though the determination of *the outcome* of mediation is in the hands of the parties, as is consistent with the definition of mediation and the norm of party self-determination, there will be times, from a professional ethics perspective, where a mediator's duty to respect parties' self-determination regarding the outcome gives way to the legitimate expectations of the profession and the public that the mediator prevent an abuse of process or a substantial defect in the process. The *public* expects mediators, on the basis of considerations of reciprocity and trust,[62] to prevent harm to vital social interests such as the rule of law, critical morality, public policy, and the survival of the institution of mediation; and the *profession* of mediation expects mediators to conduct mediations in a manner that maintains the standing of the profession and process of mediation. It follows that from a professional ethics perspective, a mediator has a duty to *terminate* a mediation if, after taking all possible steps consistent with mediation standards to induce a change in the parties' position, he believes that a mediated agreement *might harm a vital social interest.* The following cases, in which the parties are about to reach a mediated agreement, might be considered as harming a vital social interest.

[59] See, e.g., California Rules, Rule 3.857(i)(1); Family Mediation Model Standards, Standard XI.A.5; Model Standards, Standard VI.A.9.

[60] See Model Standards, Standard VI.A.6.

[61] Kansas Ethical Standards for Mediators Prefatory Comment, Rule 903 adopted by the Supreme Court of Kansas available at www.kscourts.org/rules/Rule-Info.asp?r1=Court+Rules+Relating+to+Mediation&r2=316 (Kansas Ethical Standards for Mediators), Comment to Standard (i).

[62] See Chapter 3, Section 3.7.

(a) The agreement is illegal The duty of mediators to prevent illegal mediated agreements is widely acknowledged by codes of conduct for mediators and scholars. The *Georgia Standards*, for example, state that "[a] mediator should not be a party to an agreement which is illegal";[63] the *Nebraska Standards* provide that "[a] mediator shall not knowingly allow the parties to sign an illegal agreement";[64] and the *Federal Employee Mediators Guide* notes that "[i]f, in a federal employee mediator's informed judgment, an agreement desired by the parties will contravene federal law or regulation, the mediator should raise the issue for the parties to consider. If the parties cannot satisfy the mediator's concerns and nevertheless insist on executing such an agreement, the mediator should withdraw from the mediation immediately."[65] John W. Cooley argued that a mediator must "as a last resort, withdraw as mediator and terminate the mediation" where the agreement is illegal;[66] and Robert A. Baruch Bush correctly revealed the rationale for these statements by commenting that "if [the mediator] does nothing, he may bring mediation into disrepute if the illegal agreements are later discovered."[67]

(b) The agreement is immoral according to critical morality, that is, in the eyes of a rational, impartial person Mediators' duty to prevent the signing of an immoral agreement is recognized by at least one code of conduct for mediators,[68] and I would argue that it is a well justified duty on two grounds.[69] First, the rules of morality are binding on everyone and no one should be a party to an immoral agreement or facilitate such an agreement. The rules of morality, like legal rules, are the ground rules of society and the public legitimately expects mediators not to facilitate immoral agreements. This expectation is part of the expectation that mediators be worthy of the public's trust. In addition, immoral agreements might jeopardize the standing of the institution of mediation and the public's trust in it, and therefore mediators should prevent immoral agreements as part of their duty to protect the institution of mediation. A

63 Georgia Standards, Standard IV.A. 64 Nebraska Standards, s. III.E.3.

65 Federal Employee Mediators Guide, Standard I, Guidance Notes 1.

66 John W. Cooley, "A Classical Approach to Mediation – Part I: Classical Rhetoric and the Art of Persuasion in Mediation" (1993) 19 *University of Dayton Law Review* 83, 130. See also Maute, "Mediator Accountability", 361.

67 Robert A. Baruch Bush, "A Study of Ethical Dilemmas and Policy Implications" (1994) 1 *Journal of Dispute Resolution* 1, 24. See also Shapira, "Conceptions and Perceptions of Fairness", 339–340.

68 Takanot Batei-Mishpat (Gishur) [Hebrew], s. 8(b)(4a).

69 See Chapter 2, Section 2.4.3.

potential objection to a duty of mediators to prevent immoral agreements might contend that morality is indeterminate and subjective and that such a duty might result in uncontrolled mediator intervention in parties' self-determination. The answer to this objection is that critical morality differs from positive morality;[70] and that the immorality that triggers the mediator's duty to intervene is such that every reasonable and impartial person would recognize to be immoral. Vagueness of circumstances should work in favor of nonintervention by the mediator. Where reasonable persons would disagree, the mediator is expected to exercise professional discretion and should not be criticized for any decision reached as a result of such due process.

(c) The agreement is unconscionable or grossly unfair, that is, its terms deviate from common social norms to a degree that jeopardizes the standing of the profession and public trust in the profession A mediator's duty to prevent a grossly unfair or unconscionable agreement receives support from both scholars and codes of conduct for mediators. Cooley, for example, argued that "where the mediator or nonparties perceive, or could perceive, the resulting agreement to be ... grossly inequitable ... the mediator must apprise the parties of the problem, redirect their efforts toward generating new, acceptable options, and, as a last resort, withdraw as mediator and terminate the mediation";[71] Judith Maute argued for mediator intervention when the mediated agreement is grossly unfair;[72] and the *Florida Rules* provide that "[a] mediator shall... terminate a mediation entailing... unconscionability."[73] Some codes use more permissive language that seems to leave discretion to the mediator in such circumstances. The *Georgia Standards*, for example, provide that "[a] mediator may refuse to draft or sign an agreement which seems fundamentally unfair to one party";[74] and the *Illinois Standards* state that "should parties come to an understanding that the mediator finds unconscionable or grossly unfair, the mediator is not obligated to write up a mediation agreement."[75] It is argued, however, that the duty of mediators to terminate the mediation in such circumstances should be understood strictly, because the goal of these provisions is to preserve the public's

70 See Hart, *Law, Liberty, and Morality*, p. 20. See also Chapter 1, Section 1.2.1.1 (last paragraph).
71 Cooley, "A Classical Approach to Mediation", 130.
72 Maute, "Mediator Accountability", 361. 73 Florida Rules, Rule 10.420(b)(4).
74 Georgia Standards, Standard IV.A.
75 Illinois Standards, s. IV.A. See also Family Mediation Model Standards, Standard XI.A.4.

faith and confidence in the institution of mediation.[76] This goal is also the key to understanding the meaning of this abstract term, unconscionability, in the context of mediation. Unconscionability comes to fill in a possible lacuna concerning outcomes that are perhaps not illegal, according to the local laws applicable to the mediation, and not immoral, according to the demanding tests of critical morality, yet cannot be tolerated by society.[77] It reflects a serious deviation from the common social norms that are accepted by the society in which mediation is practiced, and its meaning could change between communities. Unconscionability, therefore, is connected to positive morality and guides the mediator to be alert to the values of the general public that he or she serves, so that mediation outcomes are not perceived as an attack on public norms and do not depreciate public trust in the profession and process of mediation.

(d) The agreement might cause serious harm to nonparticipants
Causing harm to others is morally wrong. The philosopher Peter Singer once argued that "if it is in our power to prevent something bad from happening, without thereby sacrificing anything of comparable moral importance, we ought, morally, to do it."[78] A mediator might find himself in a position where a nonparticipant could suffer harm caused by the decisions of mediation parties. The *Florida Rules*, for example, provide that "a mediator shall … terminate any mediation if the physical safety of any person is endangered by the continuation of mediation."[79] Laurence Boulle and Miryana Nesic discussed a wider basis for termination of mediation where "there is evidence of danger to life or property";[80] and the *California Rules* provide that "[a] mediator may suspend or terminate the mediation or withdraw as mediator when … Continuation of the process would cause significant harm to any participant or a third party."[81] These, it is argued, are mere illustrations of a wider ethical duty of the mediator to prevent mediation outcomes that harm others to an extent that would

76 See Shapira, "Conceptions and Perceptions of Fairness", 322–324, 327.

77 See id., 338. See also, Kevin Gibson, "Mediator Attitudes toward Outcomes: A Philosophical View" (1999) 17 *Mediation Quarterly* 197, 209 (noting that "mediation should not endorse [unconscionable] agreements that would not be sanctioned by society").

78 Peter Singer, "Famine, Affluence, and Morality" (1973) 1 *Philosophy and Public Affairs* 229 quoted in Beauchamp and Childress, *Biomedical Ethics*, p. 200.

79 Florida Rules, Rule 10.420(b)(5).

80 Boulle and Nesic, *Mediation*, p. 173.

81 California Rules, Rule 3.857(i)(3).

jeopardize the institution of mediation.[82] The mediator is in a position to prevent that outcome by terminating the mediation (though he or she cannot prevent the parties from signing the agreement outside the mediation if they so insist); and by doing so he or she is doing right both morally as a person (attempting to prevent harm to others) and ethically as a professional (preventing harm to the institution of mediation).[83]

(e) The agreement might cause harm to minors or incapacitated persons related to the dispute As a variation of the rule on preventing harm to nonparticipant third parties, codes of conduct for family mediators discuss the duties of family mediators to children and incapacitated persons related to the parties and to the dispute. The justification of a separate duty toward minors and incapacitated persons is that they are weak, helpless, and dependent on the parties. Ordinarily we would expect the parties to take care of the interests of those who depend on them, but if they do not act on this expectation it becomes an issue of public policy that their interests be safeguarded and the mediator is expected to perform that task.

The *Illinois Standards*, for example, provide that "the mediator . . . has a responsibility to assist participants in considering the best interests of children and other persons who are unable to give voluntary, informed consent ... If the mediator believes that any proposed agreement between the parties puts the children at risk, the mediator has a duty to attempt to facilitate further discussion of the proposed agreement."[84] The *Illinois Standards* further state that the mediator may suspend or terminate the mediation if "a serious risk of harm may result to the minor children because their needs and interest(s) are not being considered by the parties."[85] Other codes and scholars focus on the safety and wellbeing of the children. Boulle and Nesic, for example, discussed the termination of mediation where "a child is suffering or is likely to suffer harm";[86] the *Family Mediation Model Standards* provide that "a mediator should consider suspending or terminating the mediation . . . [where] the safety of a participant or well-being of a child is threatened";[87] and the

[82] Of course, where the harm to a nonparticipant is illegal, immoral in a critical sense, or unconscionable, the discussion above would apply as well.

[83] Sometimes the termination of mediation will not suffice to discharge the mediator of his duties. See, e.g., the discussion of the duty to warn nonparticipants in Chapter 10, Section 10.4.4.1.

[84] Illinois Standards, s. IV.C. [85] Id., s. III.D.5.e.

[86] Boulle and Nesic, *Mediation*, p. 173.

[87] Family Mediation Model Standards, Standard XI.A.1.

California-CDRC Standards provide that "[i]f a Mediator believes that the continuation of the process would harm any participant or a third party (such as children in a marital dissolution matter) . . . the Mediator shall inform the parties and shall discontinue the mediation."[88] The message to mediators should be clear-cut: a mediator who is worthy of the public's trust and who is committed to the process must prevent the conclusion of a mediated agreement that harms the helpless.

(f) The agreement jeopardizes the institution of mediation and the public's trust in it There is a social interest in the flourishing of mediation as a form of consensual method for resolving conflicts among members of society and in the maintenance of public trust in mediators and in the mediation profession.[89] Mediators owe a duty to the public and to the mediation profession to conduct the mediation in a manner that does not jeopardize the institution of mediation;[90] thus they should prevent mediation outcomes that might jeopardize the public's trust in mediation, or, as some codes of conduct for mediators term it, they should terminate the mediation when the integrity of the process is threatened.[91]

To sum up, the rationale that justifies mediator intervention in each of the abovementioned cases is that the mediated outcome, despite being agreed upon by the parties, is incompatible with the goals of mediation and could cause the process to be perceived as defective or abused. It is assumed that every professional process, including mediation, is aimed at promoting a social good. Thus, where the process outcome harms vital social interests, the process is likely to be perceived as defective, that is, as lacking integrity. The duty of mediators is to conduct mediation with professional integrity; they must conduct a "whole" process that is not defective, is not abused for purposes it was not designed to serve, and does not undermine the standing of the profession to a degree that could jeopardize public faith in the profession and process of mediation; and they must take action to prevent such outcomes.

88 California-CDRC Standards, s. 3.

89 See Chapter 3, Sections 3.3 and 3.7 (The mediator–public relationship).

90 See Chapter 3, Section 3.7 (The mediator–profession relationship; The mediator–public relationship).

91 See Section 8.1.

8.3 Conclusion

The norm of professional integrity reflects a commitment of mediators to their role as mediators and the process of mediation they conduct. Professional integrity is a source of the general authority of mediators to make those decisions that are necessary for exercising their role, and it legitimizes the exercise of professional discretion. The professional integrity of mediators is closely connected to what is sometimes called "the integrity of (the process of) mediation," that is, the wholeness of the process, or its freedom from substantial defects. A mediator acting with professional integrity is committed to maintaining the integrity of the process in that he must prevent an abuse of the process or substantive defects in the process. Professional integrity is connected to preservation of the profession's standing and of the public's trust in the process, in the sense that the integrity of a mediator, and the maintenance of process integrity that follows, promote the standing of the profession and public trust in the profession and process of mediation.

8.4 A proposed standard of professional integrity

A mediator shall conduct mediation with professional integrity. A mediator's conduct reflects professional integrity when he or she is committed to the nature and definition of both his or her role as a mediator and mediation.

A. Decision-Making and Exercise of Professional Discretion –
   A mediator shall make those decisions that are necessary for the execution of his role.
   1. A mediator shall make decisions consistent with the standard of self-determination on the basis of relevant professional considerations and good reasons that could be reasonably justified.
   2. A mediator shall take steps to the effect that appropriate participants take part in the process.

B. Separation of Professional Roles –
   A mediator shall distinguish between his or her role as a mediator and other professional roles.
   1. A mediator shall not undertake in the course of a mediation an additional professional role simultaneously in the same matter, unless (a) he or she has informed the parties of the implications of undertaking such an additional role and obtained their consent; and (b) he or she can proceed with the conduct of the mediation

consistent with his or her obligations as a mediator in accordance with the Standards.

2. A mediator shall not give parties professional advice or a professional opinion that applies professional (e.g., legal) principles to the facts of the mediation case.
   (a) A mediator may provide parties with general information that he or she is qualified by training or experience to provide, without mixing his or her role as a mediator and another professional role, as is consistent with the standard of self-determination and the standard of impartiality.
   (b) A mediator may recommend parties, when appropriate, to seek outside professional advice, a professional opinion, or other professional services.

C. Appropriateness of Case to Process –
A mediator shall only conduct a mediation in cases that are appropriate and suitable for mediation in light of the nature of mediation and its principles and methods.

1. A mediator shall recommend that parties consider resolving their dispute through other processes such as arbitration, counseling, or neutral evaluation, when they are more appropriate than mediation.
2. A mediator shall take appropriate steps, including terminating the mediation, if he or she believes that the case is inappropriate for mediation, or that there is no reasonable likelihood that the parties will reach a mediated agreement, or where a party acts in a way that makes the conduct of mediation impossible.

D. Prevention of Process Abuse or Substantial Defects in the Process –
A mediator shall prevent an abuse of process (i.e. use of mediation for purposes which it has not been designed to serve), or a substantial defect in the process. In doing so a mediator shall:

1. Prevent a use of mediation to further illegal conduct.
2. Not use information revealed to him or her during a mediation for any purpose not connected to the mediation, unless authorized to do so in accordance with the Standards.
3. Not present a dispute resolution procedure other than mediation as a mediation in an effort to gain the protection of rules, statutes, or other governing authorities pertaining to mediation.
4. Take appropriate steps, including terminating the mediation, when a participant is abusing the process.

5. Terminate the mediation if, after taking all possible steps consistent with the Standards to induce a change in the parties' position, he or she believes that a mediated agreement might harm a vital social interest. In this context, any of the following agreements are to be considered as harming a vital social interest:
   (a) An illegal agreement;
   (b) An immoral agreement according to critical morality, that is, in the eyes of a rational, impartial person;
   (c) An unconscionable or grossly unfair agreement, that is, its terms deviate from common social norms to a degree that jeopardizes the standing of the profession and public trust in the profession;
   (d) An agreement that might cause serious harm to nonparticipants;
   (e) An agreement that might cause harm to minors or incapacitated persons related to the dispute;
   (f) An agreement that jeopardizes the institution of mediation and the public's trust in it.

9

Diligence, respect and dignity, and honesty

9.1 Diligence

9.1.1 A duty to conduct mediation with diligence

From a professional ethics perspective, a mediator, like any role-holder worthy of his or her client's trust,[1] must fulfill his role diligently in order to be worthy of the trust of parties to whom he or she is providing mediation services. The expectation of diligence complements the expectation of competence: it is not enough that a mediator is competent to exercise the role of a mediator; he or she must utilize his or her competence for the benefit of the parties at the right time and place, without undue delay. No reasonable mediation party would be satisfied with sloppy, long-delayed service, and any reasonable mediator can be taken to have made an implied representation or promise to supply careful service on time. This is a legitimate expectation of the mediation profession and the public, as well as the parties, because such conduct is necessary if mediators are to maintain the standing of the profession and process of mediation, and instill public trust in them. It is not surprising, then, that codes of conduct of various professions provide for a standard of diligence, whose content varies according to the nature and definition of the professional role they perform.[2] Codes of conduct for mediators, however, do not usually include an independent standard of diligence, but provide for such a duty in other standards such as a Quality of the Process standard,[3] Competence,[4] Scheduling Mediation,[5] and Rules of Fair Practice.[6] These codes can shed some light on the meaning of diligent practice of mediators.

[1] See Chapter 2, Section 2.2.3.6. [2] For examples, see ibid.

[3] See, e.g., Model Standards, Standard VI.A. See also Federal Employee Mediators Guide, Standard VI.A; Virginia Standards, s. K.1; California Rules, Rule 3.857 (a) (Quality of mediation process – Diligence); Alabama Code, Standard 3(c) (The Mediation Process).

[4] See, e.g., Family Mediation Canada Code, Article 5.

[5] See, e.g., Florida Rules, Rule 10.430. [6] See, e.g., Georgia Standards, Standard V.

9.1.2 The meaning of diligence in mediation

9.1.2.1 Attention to the parties and their case

A mediator is expected to dedicate the time, resources, and attention required for the provision of high-quality service to the parties. The *Georgia Standards*, for example, provide under a heading of Diligence that "[m]ediators will exercise diligence in scheduling the mediation, drafting the agreement if requested to do so, and returning completed necessary paperwork to the court or referring agency."[7] Diligence here seems to refer to the duty of mediators to attend to their tasks – be it scheduling a session, drafting a mediated agreement, or returning paperwork – *without delay*.[8] This duty applies to other routine tasks such as making telephone calls to parties and their representatives, reviewing documents, and writing down understandings. The *Florida Rules* convey this meaning without using the word diligence, stating that "[a] mediator shall perform mediation services in a timely fashion, avoiding delays whenever possible."[9]

Another element of diligence that comes up in the codes is a mediator's *ability to commit the necessary time and attention to the process*. The *Model Standards*, for example, provide that "[a] mediator should agree to mediate only when the mediator is prepared to commit the attention essential to an effective mediation,"[10] and "[a] mediator should only accept cases when the mediator can satisfy the reasonable expectation of the parties concerning the timing of a mediation."[11] Similarly, the *California Rules* provide that "[m]ediators are required to advance the mediation in a timely manner and keep the time period scheduled for mediation free from other commitments."[12]

9.1.2.2 Preparation for mediation?

Mediators who prepare for mediation demonstrate diligence on their part because they invest time and effort to assist them (so they believe) in better accomplishing the goals of the mediation. Preparation may include collecting and analyzing information about the parties and the

[7] Ibid. [8] Ibid. [9] Florida Rules, Rule 10.430. See also Alabama Code, Standard 3(c).

[10] Model Standards, Standard VI.A.1. See also Michigan Standards, Standard VII.A.1.a; Federal Employee Mediators Guide, Standard VI.A.1; NY-CDRC Standards, Standard VI Comment 1.

[11] Model Standards, Standard VI.A.2. See also Michigan Standards, Standard VII.A.1.b; Federal Employee Mediators Guide, Standard VI.A.2; NY-CDRC Standards, Standard VI Comment 2.

[12] California Rules, Rule 3.857 (a).

dispute,[13] designing a plan for the mediation,[14] and mental preparation.[15] The degree of preparation depends on the complexity and nature of the dispute.[16] From a professional ethics perspective, preparation might be required if a professional cannot exercise his role without it. While some mediation scholars are of the view that preparation for mediation can contribute to an effective mediation,[17] no one suggests that the mediator is under a duty to prepare for mediation. In practice, some mediators, especially in community mediation programs, receive information about the case and the parties very close to the mediation session,[18] and in court-connected mediations the mediator may only receive a short summary of the disputants' claims.[19] Moreover, while some mediation models refer to preparation for mediation as one of the stages of the mediation process,[20] others do not.[21] Thus, it cannot be said that mediators who do not prepare for mediation are acting unethically. However, if parties sent the mediator information on their initiative or on his or her request, this may create an expectation that the mediator will have reviewed that information prior to meeting with the parties or will inform the parties that his or her approach to mediation is to refrain from such preparation, if that is the case.

9.1.3 Care

A mediator must conduct the mediation with *care* in order to avoid, as far as possible, any harm to the parties. The standard of diligence instructs mediators on the *state of mind* they must maintain at the time of conducting mediations: they must act with caution when they exercise their role. For example, while the standard of professional integrity instructs mediators to *refrain from actions* that inflict harm on mediation parties, and to take steps necessary in order to prevent their suffering harm due to their participation in the mediation process,[22] the standard of diligence instructs mediators to take care in carrying out any of their interventions. While the standard of professional integrity focuses on an *action* that

[13] See, e.g., Moore, *The Mediation Process*, pp. 118–144. [14] Id., pp. 145–165.
[15] See, e.g., Kovach, *Mediation*, p. 143.
[16] Id., pp. 142–143. See also Moore, *The Mediation Process*, p. 119.
[17] Boulle and Nesic, *Mediation*, p. 118. [18] See, e.g., Kovach, *Mediation*, p. 143.
[19] See, e.g., Boulle and Nesic, *Mediation*, p. 119.
[20] See, e.g., Spencer and Brogan, *Mediation Law*, p. 49. See also Moore, *The Mediation Process*, pp. 68–69.
[21] See, e.g., Folberg and Taylor, *Mediation*, pp. 38–70. [22] See Chapter 8, Section 8.2.4.

should or should not be taken, the standard of diligence focuses on the *attitude* of the mediator in taking an action. Similarly, where the standard of impartiality, for example, warns against *actions* of partiality, the standard of diligence demands that the mediator *be cautious* in his or her actions so as not to violate the standard of impartiality. It is a duty of care in an ethical, not legal, sense and it reflects the degree of care that can be expected of a reasonable mediator in the circumstances.

9.1.4 A proposed standard of diligence

A mediator shall conduct a mediation with diligence.

A. A mediator shall only accept cases –
   1. When he or she is prepared and able to commit to the parties and the process the attention necessary for an effective mediation.
   2. When he or she can be available to the parties, respond to their need without undue delays, and satisfy the reasonable expectation of the parties concerning the timing of the mediation.

B. A mediator shall exercise his or her role –
   1. Dedicating the time and resources required for the provision of high-quality service that responds to the parties' needs.
   2. With due care to avoid harm to the parties.

9.2 Respect and dignity

9.2.1 Treating mediation parties with respect and dignity

Mediators, like other professionals who perform a role in a relationship of trust, are expected to treat their clients with respect and dignity.[23] Morally every person is expected to respect others; yet from a professional ethics perspective, professionals, including mediators, have an enhanced duty of respect and dignity for two reasons. First, one has higher expectations of persons with whom one has a professional relationship, in comparison to persons with whom one does not have any special relationship. Second, showing disrespect and acting in a manner that does not acknowledge the dignity of another could undermine the standing of the profession and have an adverse effect on the public's faith in the profession, in violation of the legitimate expectations of the

[23] See Chapter 2, Section 2.2.3.7.

profession and the public that the standing of the profession be maintained.

Morally, the expectation of being treated with respect and dignity sets a minimum standard of behavior that is necessary for preserving human dignity. Morality demands that one avoid the use of others as a means rather than an end and refrain from humiliating and discriminating against others.[24] Professional ethics, on the other hand, sets a higher threshold for the conduct of professionals. A professional is expected not only to avoid such immoral expressions of behavior, but to exhibit patience, dignity, and courtesy in their professional conduct. This attitude is reflected in many professional codes of conduct,[25] and should apply in the case of mediators as well.

Indeed, some codes of conduct for mediators recognize the importance of respect for the parties and refer to such a duty in their Preamble[26] or within standards such as Demeanor,[27] Balanced Process,[28] Research,[29] and Responsibility to Parties.[30] The codes, however, do not often dwell on the meaning of respect and dignity, although some do. The *Florida Rules*, for example, provide that "a mediator shall be patient, dignified, and courteous during the mediation process."[31] Of course, a realistic approach to professional ethics must distinguish ideals from duties,[32] and no mediator can be reasonably expected in circumstances of stress and high feelings always to remain patient and courteous; yet still a mediator must avoid conduct and use of language that are humiliating, degrading, and harmful to either the parties or the process.

As an illustration, in one mediation case a mediator used offensive and humiliating language in the course of mediation. He said to a party "that he didn't understand what she ever saw in her former husband, and that ' . . . he must've had a really big ****.' He further told Complainant that she needed to 'start thinking with what's between your shoulders'."[33] The Committee on Ethics of the Georgia Commission on Dispute Resolution, discussing the mediator's behavior, observed that "[t]he mediator's

24 Ibid. 25 Ibid.

26 North Carolina Standards, Preamble ("Mediation ethics derive from the mediator's respect for each party's . . . dignity").

27 See Florida Rules, Rule 10.350. 28 Id., Rule 10.410. 29 Illinois Standards, s. VIII.

30 Wisconsin Association Guidelines, s. 1.1 ("As WAM members, we treat all persons with respect and seek to prevent discriminatory incidents in the practice of mediation").

31 Florida Rules, Rule 10.350. 32 See Chapter 1, Section 1.2.1.2.

33 The Committee on Ethics of the Georgia Commission on Dispute Resolution, Opinion 2002–1, available at www.godr.org/files/Formal%20opinion%202002–1%203-23-04TP.pdf.

conduct in this matter violated the dignity of the parties and the integrity of the process." The Committee noted that "the conduct at issue in this case is never acceptable in any mediation process," adding that "it is particularly harmful in a court-mandated mediation. The parties are required to participate by the court, and the mediator serves as a representative of the court system. Vulgar, offensive and demeaning remarks are a reflection on the referring court, the local ADR program and the process of mediation in general. As was clear from the evidence in this case, parties will likely share their experience in mediation with relatives, friends and the community at large. Thus, the damaging repercussions of such behavior can extend far beyond the immediate parties involved." The Committee thought that "[t]he scrupulous demeanor of respect for all participants in mediation is essential."

In another mediation case a mediator used foul language is addressing a party whom he thought had lied to him. The North Carolina Dispute Resolution Commission found the mediator's behavior to be inappropriate and opined that "[m]ediators have a duty to protect the integrity of the mediation process and to conduct the mediation with decorum. The Commission strongly cautions all mediators against using profanity, even in instances where the parties and their attorneys are using it."[34]

9.2.2 Treating participants and nonparticipants with respect and dignity

In the course of exercising their role, mediators have contact with participants other than the parties, such as the parties' lawyers and co-mediators. They may also have interactions with *nonparticipants* such as colleagues (mediators), courts or other case-referring organizations, and the media. Treating others with respect and dignity is a precondition for maintaining public confidence in the profession.[35] As mediators are bound to act in a manner that preserves the standing of the profession and process of mediation, and the standing of the agencies with which they are connected, they must treat non-parties with respect and dignity as well. Aspects of this duty appear in some codes of conduct for

[34] North Carolina Dispute Resolution Commission, Advisory Opinion 07–13, available at www.nccourts.org/Courts/CRS/Councils/DRC/Documents/13-07_final.pdf.

[35] Compare ABA Model Rules, Preamble and Scope, s. 5 ("A lawyer should demonstrate respect for the legal system and for those who serve it, including judges, other lawyers and public officials. While it is a lawyer's duty, when necessary, to challenge the rectitude of official action, it is also a lawyer's duty to uphold legal process").

mediators. The *Code of Labor Mediators*, for example, provides that "where more than one mediator is participating in a particular case, each mediator ... should extend every possible courtesy to his fellow mediator. The mediator should carefully avoid any appearance of disagreement with or criticism of his fellow mediator";[36] and the *Model Standards* provide that "[a] mediator should demonstrate respect for differing points of view within the field."[37]

9.2.3 *Promoting respect among participants*

Mediation sessions can get tense and hostile. While mediators cannot always ensure a warm and friendly environment in the midst of a conflicted dispute, they must not remain passive when participants act with disrespect toward each other. A mediator is in charge of the process and must take appropriate steps to ensure that participants are not harmed and the process is not abused.[38] Participants reasonably expect the mediator in their case to intervene and prevent an attack on their dignity; furthermore, the profession and the public expect mediators not to allow in the course of mediation any kind of behavior that could bring the profession and process of mediation into disrepute. Codes of conduct for mediators do not spell out this rationale but encourage mediators to promote respect among participants. The *Nebraska Standards*, for example, state that "a mediator shall seek to establish a tone of reasonableness, respect, and honesty during mediation";[39] the *Florida Rules* state that "[a] mediator shall promote mutual respect among the mediation participants throughout the mediation process";[40] and the *Michigan Standards* provide that "[a] mediator shall conduct mediation ... in a manner that promotes ... mutual respect among all participants."[41]

Of course, a mediator cannot be expected to control every uttering by the participants, and he or she must simultaneously honor the parties' right to self-determination and his or her duty of impartiality. Still, a mediator cannot remain inactive where a participant is continuously

[36] Code of Labor Mediators, Standard 2.

[37] Model Standards, Standard IX.B. See also Federal Employee Mediators Guide, Standard IX.B; Oregon Standards, Standard X Comment 7.

[38] See Chapter 8, Section 8.2.4. [39] Nebraska Standards, s. III.D.2.a.

[40] Florida Rules, Rule 10.410.

[41] Michigan Standards, Standard VII.A. See also ADR Canada Code, s. 7.2; Federal Employee Mediators Guide, Standard VI.A; Model Standards, Standard VI.A; North Carolina Standards, Rule VIII.

treating another participant with disrespect and derision. He or she should remind all the participants (in an impartial manner) that respect is one of the ground rules of behavior in mediation, and that a dialogue of mutual respect could contribute to an effective process. In the rare event of consistently injurious behavior of a party, the mediator will have to consider termination of the mediation in order to protect the integrity of the process and the standing of the profession and mediation.

9.2.4 *The relationship between respect and other standards*

A norm of respect and dignity can be construed widely as overlapping with other recognized ethical and moral norms. For example, respect and dignity is closely connected with *autonomy* or *self-determination*, for to respect somebody is to honor his or her right to make those decisions that have an effect on his or her life. Thus, a mediator treating parties with respect and dignity will honor their right to self-determination. Still, an independent standard of respect and dignity is justified because its content could cover other ground. The Committee on Ethics of the Georgia Commission on Dispute Resolution, for example, correctly noted that "it is important to be aware that any conduct by a mediator that is insulting to a party risks also being intimidating, and any conduct that is intimidating may be coercive and thus undermine the parties' self-determination."[42] But a party expects the mediator in his or her case to treat him or her with respect and dignity irrespective of his or her ability to make decisions. He or she expects the mediator not to belittle or insult him or her, and not suffice with respecting his or her right to make decisions. Thus the duty of a mediator to treat parties with respect and dignity should be considered separately and independently of the other ethical duties of the mediator.

A norm of respect and dignity is also connected to a norm of *equality*, for to respect a person is to treat them as an equal.[43] The moral norm of equality is implemented in mediation through an ethical standard of *impartiality* that prohibits partiality on the part of the mediator. Disrespectful mediator conduct might violate the standard of impartiality. The Committee on Ethics of the Georgia Commission on Dispute Resolution, for example, noted in one of its opinions that "[derogatory] inappropriate remarks made in caucus gave a strong appearance that

[42] Opinion 2002-1 at Note 33.

[43] See, e.g., Dworkin, *Taking Rights Seriously*, pp. 272–273.

impartiality had been compromised as to both parties."[44] Yet here again a separate and independent standard of respect and dignity is justified; a mediator might treat *all* parties with disrespect and derision, that is, without violating the norms of equality or impartiality vis-à-vis the parties, but he or she would be in breach of the norm of respect and dignity.

9.2.5 *Conclusion*

A mediator has an ethical duty to treat mediation participants with respect and dignity. He or she has a similar duty when communicating with nonparticipants such as colleagues, courts, other referring bodies, and the media. Furthermore, mediators are expected to promote mutual respect among participants and to intervene in cases in which participants behave in a disrespectful manner that is harmful to other participants or the process. Ideally we would have liked mediators to always be patient, dignified, and courteous. More realistically, we expect them to refrain from use of abusive, discriminatory, humiliating, and profane language. This minimum standard of conduct is necessary, from a professional ethics point of view, to meet the expectations of mediation parties, the profession of mediation, the public, and employers and referring agencies.

9.2.6 *A proposed standard of respect and dignity*

A mediator shall conduct a mediation in a manner that respects and acknowledges the dignity of others.

A. A mediator shall treat the parties, their representatives, co-mediators, and other participants with dignity and respect, and shall endeavor to conduct the mediation with patience and courtesy.
B. A mediator shall refrain in the exercise of his or her role from the use of abusive, discriminatory, humiliating, and profane language.
C. A mediator shall promote mutual respect among the participants.
D. A mediator shall treat with respect and dignity colleagues, other professionals, courts and other referring agencies, and the media.

[44] Opinion 2002–1 at Note 33.

9.3 Honesty

9.3.1 Honesty toward mediation parties

A professional must be honest in order to be worthy of his or her clients' trust.[45] Mediation parties, therefore, legitimately expect mediators to be truthful in their communications with them and refrain from deception and lying. As Professor Arthur A. Chaykin noted, "a mediator actively seeks to gain the trust of the mediatrants in order to maximize effectiveness ... The parties rely on the mediator to be truthful and honest."[46] Codes of conduct for mediators reflect this obligation of honesty in standards such as Informed Consent,[47] Quality of the Process,[48] Skills Necessary for Competency as a Mediator,[49] and Standards for Conducting Mediation.[50] The *Virginia Standards*, for example, provide that a mediator shall not "engage in conduct involving dishonesty, fraud, deceit or misrepresentation which reflects adversely on the mediator's fitness to provide mediation services."[51]

The duty of honesty is closely related to the parties' right to self-determination. If mediators were allowed to withhold information relevant to decision-making or to provide wrong information, the parties' ability to exercise meaningful informed decision-making would suffer. For this reason, codes of conduct for mediators often provide, some of them in a Self-determination standard,[52] that mediators "shall not knowingly misrepresent any material fact or circumstance in the course of a mediation."[53] It is important, however, to realize that the requirement of honesty is *wider* than the requirement to respect party self-determination. A mediator is expected to refrain from providing deceiving or false information even where the parties will not rely on the information in making a decision, because deception and lying to the parties are inappropriate and unworthy of their trust *per se*. Furthermore, from a professional ethics perspective, the requirement of honesty is aimed at protecting public confidence in the profession and the process of mediation, as well as protecting the parties' legitimate

45 See Chapter 2, Section 2.2.3.8. 46 See Chaykin, "Mediator Liability", 744.
47 Oregon Standards, Standard II Comment 4. 48 Virginia Standards, s. K.5.
49 Nebraska Standards, s. I.C.6. 50 California-CDRC Standards, s. 3.
51 Virginia Standards, s. K.5.b.
52 See, e.g., Alabama Code, Standard 4(c). See also Florida Rules, Rule 10.310(c).
53 Model Standards, Standard VI.A.4. See also Alabama Code, Standard 4(c); Federal Employee Mediators Guide, Standard VI.A.4; Texas Guidelines, s. 10.

expectations. Thus, a mediator must avoid dishonesty wherever the dishonesty is of a nature that could jeopardize public trust in mediation.

9.3.2 *Honesty toward participants and nonparticipants*

The legitimate expectations of the profession and the public that mediators be honest in the performance of their professional role, in order for the profession and the process to maintain their standing, result in an obligation of honesty with regard to participants other than the parties (for example, representatives and co-mediators), and nonparticipants (for example, other mediators, courts, and the media). Thus, from a professional ethics perspective, mediators must be truthful in communicating information to participants and nonparticipants alike. The *Alabama Code*, for example, reflects this rationale, inter alia, in providing that mediators shall be truthful with regard to "advertising or any other communication with the public concerning mediation services offered by the mediator,"[54] and the *California Rules* provide that a mediator must be truthful in representing "his or her background to the court and participants"[55] and "in marketing his or her mediation services."[56]

9.3.3 *Honesty among participants*

Mediation parties expect the mediation process to be different than direct negotiations. The presence of a third-party mediator and the title "mediation process" indicate different rules of behavior. The ethos of mediation is collaboration between participants, exchange of information, and goodwill. In practice, mediation parties and their representatives often bring into the process competitive negotiating tactics that involve withholding of information and deception.[57] Parties sometimes conceal information from mediators and deceive them in order to bring about a better outcome.[58] Yet some codes of conduct correctly instruct the

54 Alabama Code, Standard 10. See also Federal Employee Mediators Guide, Standard VII. A; Florida Rules, Rule 10.610; Oregon Standards, Standard VIII.

55 California Rules, Rule 3.856(b).

56 Id., Rule 3.858(a). See also California-CDRC Standards, s. 6.

57 See, e.g., Charles B. Craver, "Negotiation Ethics: How to Be Deceptive Without Being Dishonest/How to Be Assertive Without Being Offensive" (1997) 38 *South Texas Law Review* 713, 714–718 (noting that parties often make inaccurate opening statements that do not reflect their true positions).

58 See, e.g., John W. Cooley, "Mediation Magic: Its Use and Abuse" (1997) 29 *Loyola University Chicago Law Journal* 1, 6.

mediator to "promote honesty and candor between and among all participants."[59] The mediator cannot ensure participants' honesty or good faith, but he or she should encourage it in order to preserve the unique nature of mediation. Moreover, when mediators are made aware of participants' dishonesty that undermines party self-determination or otherwise jeopardizes the integrity of the process, thereby jeopardizing public faith in the institution of mediation, they must take steps to prevent such an outcome, including termination of the mediation.[60] For example, if the mediator knows that one party is concealing assets that are unknown to the other party and are important to the decision making of that party, he or she must discuss this matter with the party that has concealed the information, consider terminating the mediation, and must not allow the mediation to conclude with an agreement to which the ignorant party cannot give informed consent. The Ethical Board of Oregon State Bar, for example, discussed the obligations of a lawyer-mediator when "[d]uring the mediation, Party *A* discloses to the mediator the existence of assets that are unknown to Party *B*. Lawyer-Mediator knows that the assets are important to decision-making by Party *B*. Party *A* instructs Lawyer-Mediator to withhold these facts from Party *B*."[61] The Board decided that "a lawyer who is also a mediator cannot engage in a knowing misrepresentation or concealment of a material fact ... It follows that Lawyer-Mediator cannot complete a mediation based in whole or in part on the fraud of a mediating party."[62]

9.3.4 Legitimate exceptions to the norm of honesty

Ethical standards are not absolute. In principle, therefore, in some circumstances a mediator could be justified in providing incorrect or inaccurate information. This possibility is discussed in the literature of some professions. For example, health professionals sometimes find themselves in a dilemma whether to communicate bad news to a patient who has been diagnosed as suffering from a terminal disease. The principle of patient autonomy seems to support full disclosure, but disclosure could have

59 Model Standards, Standard VI.A.4. See also Federal Employee Mediators Guide, Standard VI.A.4; Oregon Standards, Standard VI Comment 1; Virginia Standards, s. K.3; Nebraska Standards, s. III.D.2.a.

60 See Chapter 4 and Chapter 8.

61 Ethical Board of Oregon State Bar, Formal Opinion OR-2005-167 available at www.osbar.org/_docs/ethics/2005-167.pdf.

62 Ibid.

serious implications, such as making the patient experience depression, stress, and loss of hope, and possibly reduce his or her chances of recovery. In such case, it could be argued that withholding or manipulating the information is justified because of the greater harm that is likely to follow a full disclosure.[63] Another example comes from legal practice. While Model Rule 8.4 prohibits lawyers from "engag[ing] in conduct involving dishonesty, fraud, deceit or misrepresentation,"[64] Model Rule 4.1 "legitimizes some deceitful negotiation techniques and only prohibits fraudulent misrepresentations about material matters."[65] But Rule 4.1, which is termed "Truthfulness In Statements To Others," concerns transactions with persons *other than clients*; it does not legitimize misrepresentations to clients. Similarly, it is hard to imagine a case where a mediator would be justified in deceiving *his or her clients*, the mediation parties. Mediators might be tempted to misrepresent facts in order to help the parties communicate effectively and solve their conflict, but it seems to me that the harm to the parties' right to make their own decisions (and mistakes) and the risk of a depreciation of trust in mediators and in the mediation process outweighs any possible benefit of such conduct.

There are, however, a few "soft" forms of deception that mediators may justify. First, mediators cannot tell parties all that they think or feel about the case because statements to that effect might be inconsistent with their duty of *impartiality*. It is natural for a mediator to sympathize with a party or disagree with another, but his or her duty to refrain from expressions of favoritism requires him or her to carefully choose his or her words and actions and make them seem neutral even where they do not reflect his or her views and feelings accurately. Second, as a result of their duty of confidentiality, mediators cannot disclose information received in confidence from another party or even indicate that such information is in their possession. Thus, mediators might lead parties to falsely believe that they are unaware of certain information. The *California-CDRC Standards* reflect that idea in stating that "[s]ubject to duties of nondisclosure of confidential information, a Mediator is obligated to be truthful."[66] Third, mediators restate and reframe parties'

[63] See, e.g., Beauchamp and Childress, *Biomedical Ethics*, pp. 289–293. See also Gert, Culver and Clouser, *Bioethics*, pp. 270–273.

[64] See ABA Model Rules, Rule 8.4 (c).

[65] See Art Hinshaw and Jess K. Alberts, "Attorney Negotiation Ethics: An Empirical Assessment" available at www.law.yale.edu/documents/pdf/Intellectual_Life/Hinshaw_AttorneyNegEethics.pdf, note 13.

[66] California-CDRC Standards, s. 3.

statements in order to ease the reception of information by opponent parties. In doing so they are not wholly loyal to the messages of the parties. However, restating and reframing are common mediation tactics, openly discussed in mediation literature, transparently performed by mediators, and identified with the process. Thus, notwithstanding the tension between the duty of honesty and restating and reframing, these tactics exhibit only a minor degree of deception and should be considered legitimate. And fourth, mediators sometimes present offers as their own in order to overcome the phenomenon of devaluation, that is, the negative attitude one adopts in a conflict situation toward the proposal of an adversary.[67] Although the mediator misrepresents the *true author* of the offer, this mild deception may be considered acceptable because the deception relates to the identity of the initiator, not to its content, and it is clear to the offeree that if accepted the agreement would be with the other party. I presume that such a deception would not be viewed as an act of dishonesty on the part of the mediator and would not jeopardize the public image of mediators.

Separate meetings with parties provide mediators with ample opportunities to manipulate information and deceive parties, because parties who receive information that originated from a separate meeting from the mediator are often unable to verify its truth.[68] Mediators should act cautiously when they make a choice as to the type and scope of information they pass on to the other party. John W. Cooley brings an example of a landlord–tenant mediation concerning an eviction lawsuit.[69] The landlord tells the mediator in a caucus that he would agree to dismiss the action if the tenant complied with several conditions, one of which, termed by the landlord as "non-negotiable," is that the tenant stop working on his car in front of the house. The mediator then meets separately with the tenant to discuss the landlord's concerns, and when the tenant asks directly about the car issue the mediator answers "I wouldn't worry about it" and moves on to discuss other matters. At a later stage, the mediator tells the tenant that an agreement is about to be achieved if a "minor" obstacle can be tackled – the working on the car. Eventually the mediator succeeds in persuading the parties to make mutual concessions on the issue of the car and agree on a solution that allows the tenant to work on his car in an empty garage behind the house.

67 See, e.g., Kenneth J. Arrow et al. (ed.), *Barriers to Conflict Resolution* (New York: W.W. Norton, 1995), p. 15.

68 Moore, *The Mediation Process*, pp. 375–376.

69 See, e.g., Cooley, "Mediation Magic", 72.

Deborah Kolb described another case, in which a mediator met with party A, presented him with party B's offer, and received a counter-offer. He then told party A that he would pass on his offer to party B but in fact waited for some time without approaching party B, and came back to party A with another portion of the original offer that party B had made. In other words, in order to make the original offer more attractive the mediator made party A believe that he had met party B again and that party B had made additional concessions.[70]

These are borderline cases of mediator deception, which, I would argue, should be avoided. On the positive side, the mediator assisted the parties to successfully negotiate an agreement that they desired and accepted. On the negative side, the mediator acted paternalistically, withholding relevant information from the parties and undermining their right to self-determination. In the first scenario the mediator took a risk that the landlord would not be willing to modify his position regarding the car, and knowingly provided false information to the tenant. The tenant relied on this information and agreed on its basis to participate in the mediation. What would the mediator have done had the landlord stubbornly stuck to his original position? How could he have explained that to the tenant without being seen as a liar, unworthy of the tenant's trust? How can he justify having tricked the tenant into participating in a mediation that was conducted under a secret precondition unknown to him? The second scenario is even more troubling. The mediator deceived one of the parties, causing him to believe that an inferior offer had been made. What if that party had accepted the offer? The mediator would have had to confess that he had lied and that the offer was in fact more generous, otherwise he would have betrayed that party's trust, undermined his right to self-determination, given preference to the interests of the other party, and possibly lost the trust of the other party as well. Moreover, this tactic, however effective, jeopardizes trust in mediators. Could one trust offers made by mediators if mediators were allowed to manipulate offers?

9.3.5 *Conclusion*

A mediator must be truthful and avoid lies and deceit, because otherwise he or she would not be worthy of the parties' trust. He or she must be truthful in contacts with nonparticipants as well in order to preserve

[70] Deborah M. Kolb, *The Mediators* (MIT Press, 1983), p. 50.

public faith in the profession and process of mediation. The nature of the role of mediators justifies to a certain extent inaccurate statements that embellish the facts rather than reflect to the letter the information received by the mediator or the mediator's personal views. Such statements might be justified if they are (a) necessary in order for the mediator to be able to perform his or her role, that is, to assist the parties to communicate effectively about their conflict; and (b) if they are consistent with his or her other ethical duties, in particular his or her duty to conduct a process that is based on party self-determination (i.e. there is no concern that a mediator's statement might cause a party to make a decision on the basis of wrong information), and his or her duty to maintain the standing of the profession (that is, there is no concern that making a statement gives an impression that the process has been defective and leads to depreciation in public confidence in the profession and process).

9.3.6 A proposed standard of honesty

A mediator shall conduct a mediation with honesty.

A. A mediator shall treat the parties, the parties' representatives, and other participants with honesty. A mediator shall be truthful, avoid lying, and refrain from misrepresentations that could undermine party self-determination.

B. A mediator shall encourage the participants to be honest with each other.

C. A mediator shall be honest in contacts with colleagues, referring bodies such as courts, the media, and the general public.

10

Confidentiality

10.1 Introduction

The confidentiality aspects of mediation are extensively discussed in the mediation literature. Mediation confidentiality has been the subject of dozens of articles, and many textbooks on mediation devote a chapter to confidentiality matters that arise in mediation practice. The discussion, however, primarily focuses on the *legal* aspects of confidentiality.[1] Scholars describe, interpret, and criticize the scope of mediation confidentiality in statutes, case-law, and codes of conduct for mediators. In contrast, this chapter concentrates on the *ethical* duty of mediators to maintain the confidentiality of the mediation process, addressing some of the legal aspects of the duty when they affect its ethical scope. The chapter employs the perspective of professional ethics to determine the extent of mediators' obligation of confidentiality, and the grounds for justified disclosure of information obtained in the exercise of their role.

10.2 Expectations of confidentiality

10.2.1 The parties' expectations of mediator confidentiality

Mediation parties contact mediators for their services. They are clients receiving a professional service, and as such they are entitled to expect that information about them or their case, to which the mediator is exposed in the provision of mediation services, is kept in confidence by the mediator and not disclosed to anyone without their permission.[2] The parties' expectations are based on several grounds: first, on the *relationship of trust* that exists between the parties and the mediator. Professor Kovach, for example, correctly commented that "[t]rust is an

[1] For an exception, see Kevin Gibson, "Confidentiality in Mediation: A Moral Reassessment" (1992) 1992 *Journal of Dispute Resolution* 25 (discussing the policies and considerations that underlie the law on mediation confidentiality).

[2] On the legitimate expectation of clients to confidentiality, see Chapter 2, Section 2.2.3.9.

element of mediation closely related to confidentiality";[3] and the New York State Community Dispute Resolution Center Mediator Ethics Advisory Committee (MEAC) observed that "[c]onfidentiality is integral to the mediation process. It fosters trust among the parties and between each party and the mediator, and it also promotes trust among parties in the mediation process itself."[4] My argument is that mediators must maintain confidentiality in the exercise of their role in order to be worthy of the parties' trust; second, the parties' expectations of confidentiality rest on *a promise* of the mediator to keep in confidence the information to which he is exposed in the course of exercising his role. This promise may be an *explicit* one, as is the case with many mediators who begin a mediation with a promise of confidentiality in order to elicit the parties' cooperation and the sharing of information that is vital to the success of the process;[5] or it may be *implied* from the public representations of the profession of mediation, its members, mediation scholars, and drafters of mediation legislation and codes. These recurring public representations have shaped an image of mediation as a private process, designed to offer an alternative to a public and open adjudicative process; a process conducted under a widely accepted norm of confidentiality, which is extensively discussed in mediation literature,[6] and found in virtually every code of conduct for mediators.[7] To give a few examples, the *Tennessee Standards of Professional Conduct for Rule 31 Neutrals* (Tennessee Standards), for example, provide that "[a] Neutral shall preserve and maintain the confidentiality of all dispute resolution proceedings except where required by law to disclose information";[8] the *NY-CDRC Standards* provide that "[a] mediator shall maintain the confidentiality of all information obtained by the

[3] See, e.g. Kovach, *Mediation*, p. 263. See also Ellen E. Deason, "The Need for Trust as a Justification for Confidentiality in Mediation: A Cross-Disciplinary Approach" (2006) 54 *University of Kansas Law Review* 1387 (discussing the importance of trust to the functioning of mediation and the value of confidentiality in developing trust).

[4] New York MEAC, Opinion 2006-01 available at www.nycourts.gov/ip/adr/Publications/MEAC_Opinions/FormalPublishedOpinion2006-01.pdf, p. 2.

[5] See, e.g., Moore, *The Mediation Process*, pp. 218–219.

[6] See, e.g., Kovach, *Mediation*, pp. 262–338. See also Folberg and Taylor, *Mediation*, pp. 263–280; Spencer and Brogan, *Mediation Law*, pp. 312–345; Boulle and Nesic, *Mediation*, pp. 488–506.

[7] See, e.g., Family Mediation Canada Code, Article 7. See also Texas Guidelines, s. 8; Family Mediation Model Standards, Standard VII; Model Standards, Standard V.A; Florida Rules, Rule 10.360(a); Illinois Standards, s. II; North Carolina Standards, Rule III.

[8] Tennessee Standards of Professional Conduct for Rule 31 Neutrals, Rule 31 Appendix A available at www.tsc.state.tn.us/rules/supreme-court/31 (Tennessee Standards), s.7(a).

mediator during a mediation";[9] and the *Nebraska Standards* provide that "[t]o encourage a frank and full exploration of issues between parties, the mediator has a duty to maintain confidentiality for all verbal or written information relating to the subject matter of a dispute between the parties in mediation to the extent permitted by the law."[10] Lastly, the parties' expectations of confidentiality are supported by their right to *self-determination*, that is, their right to make decisions regarding information that concerns them.

As each of the mediation parties has a separate relationship of trust with the mediator, a party may expect the mediator to maintain confidentiality vis-à-vis *other participants* in the process. If, for example, party A discloses personal or sensitive information to the mediator in the absence of party B, it should be assumed that party A expects the mediator to refrain from disclosing the information to party B as well as to anyone else. Accordingly, codes of conduct for mediators often include a provision to such effect. The *California Rules*, for example, provide that "[e]xcept as required by law, a mediator must not disclose information revealed in confidence during . . . separate communications unless authorized to do so by the participant or participants who revealed the information";[11] and the *North Carolina Standards* provide that "[a] mediator shall not disclose, directly or indirectly, to any non-participant, information communicated to the mediator in confidence by any other participant in the mediation process, unless that participant gives permission to do so."[12]

10.2.2 The profession's and public expectations of mediator confidentiality

The protection of mediation confidentiality is often presented in the literature as a key aspect of the ability of mediators to perform their role successfully, and as a condition for obtaining parties' cooperation.[13] The *Oregon Standards* state that "[c]onfidentiality is a fundamental attribute of

[9] NY-CDRC Standards, Standard V.A. [10] Nebraska Standards, s. III.C.1.

[11] California Rules, Rule 3.854(c).

[12] North Carolina Standards, Rule III.B. See also Federal Employee Mediators Guide, Standard V.B; Florida Rules, Rule 10.360(b).

[13] See, e.g., Kovach, *Mediation*, pp. 263–264. See also Folberg and Taylor, *Mediation*, p. 264; Spencer and Brogan, *Mediation Law*, p. 312; Ellen E. Deason, "The Quest for Uniformity in Mediation Confidentiality: Foolish Consistency or Crucial Predictability?" (2001) 85 *Marquette Law Review* 79, 80–84; Georgia Standards, Standard II.

mediation";[14] the *Georgia Standards* provide that "[w]ithout the protection of confidentiality, parties would be unwilling to communicate freely, and the discussion necessary to resolve disputes would be seriously curtailed";[15] and the North Carolina Dispute Resolution Commission observes that "[i]f confidentiality is not preserved, the integrity of the mediation process is compromised. Participants will no longer feel free to speak frankly with their mediators and the public will no longer view mediated settlement as a confidential alternative to a public trial."[16] From a professional ethics perspective, maintaining the confidentiality of mediation information is a professional and public interest as well as an interest of the parties. If mediators were to disclose mediation information with no good cause, they would jeopardize the standing of the profession and public faith in the profession and process. Thus, the expectation that mediators maintain confidentiality is not only the parties', but the expectation of the profession and the public as well, in view of their legitimate concern that the profession's standing be preserved. Where the mediator is employed or carries out his or her role in connection with a mediation program, the preservation of confidentiality becomes an interest of the employer or principal as well, because a breach of confidentiality on the part of the mediator might adversely affect the standing of the employer or principal.

10.2.3 Participants' obligation of confidentiality

The scope of confidentiality that mediation can offer parties depends to a large extent on the commitment of the *participants* to confidentiality. As we have seen, from a professional ethics perspective, the ethical obligation of mediators to maintain the confidentiality of mediation information stems from the fact that they perform a *professional role* in the service of the parties. The parties, however, are not in such a position and thus are not subject to an ethical duty of confidentiality. Therefore, unless the parties and other participants are placed under a legal obligation to refrain from disclosing mediation information, one participant or more may possibly feel free to disclose information that has come up in the mediation to nonparticipants.[17] The North Carolina Dispute

14 Oregon Standards, Standard IV. 15 Georgia Standards, Standard II.

16 North Carolina Dispute Resolution Commission, Opinion 09-06 available at www.nccourts.org/Courts/CRS/Councils/DRC/Documents/09-06_final.pdf.

17 A limited legal duty not to disclose personal and sensitive information might derive from other legal sources such as laws of privacy. See, e.g., Restatement (Second) of Torts s. 652(a) (1977).

Resolution Commission, for example, noted that while "Standard III [the confidentiality standard] of the Standards of Professional Conduct for Mediators places a duty of confidentiality on mediators . . . the parties and their counsel are not bound by Standard III and are free to talk to the public or press about statements or conduct occurring in the mediation. If the parties want to negotiate their own confidentiality agreement, the mediator should assist them."[18] Conversely, other mediation programs have elected to impose on participants a requirement of confidentiality. The *ADR Canada Code*, for example, provides that "[t]he Mediator, the parties, their experts and advisors, and any other persons who accompany a party to a Mediation session shall keep confidential and shall not disclose to any non-party all information, documents, and communications that are created, disclosed, received, or made available in connection with the Mediation except . . . ";[19] and the *Florida Rules* succinctly state that "communications made during the process are confidential, except where disclosure is required or permitted by law,"[20] leading the Florida MEAC to hold that all mediation participants are obligated by the confidentiality provision.[21]

10.2.4 Knowledge about the scope of confidentiality

It is clear, then, that knowledge of the scope of confidentiality that applies to mediation is important to both mediators and parties. *Mediators* must be aware of the extent to which they are bound to keep mediation information in confidence and of exceptions to confidentiality, because otherwise (a) they will not be able to distinguish between legitimate and prohibited disclosures, thereby risking a violation of their ethical and possibly legal duties; and (b) they will not be able to accurately represent to the parties the extent of confidentiality that they can expect from the mediator and other participants. *Parties* must be aware of the scope of confidentiality that applies to the mediator as well as to themselves and to other participants if they are to exercise self-determination regarding participation in a mediation, because this information is relevant to making the decision whether to participate in the mediation and on the terms of participation.

[18] North Carolina Dispute Resolution Commission, Opinion 12–22 available at www.nccourts.org/Courts/CRS/Councils/DRC/Documents/12–22_2012.pdf.

[19] ADR Canada Code, s. 6.2. [20] Florida Rules, Rule 10.420(a)(3).

[21] See Florida MEAC, Opinion 2005–003 available at www.flcourts.org/core/fileparse.php/283/urlt/MEAC-Opinion-2005–003.pdf.

Thus, from a professional ethics perspective, mediators must first educate themselves about the scope of confidentiality that applies to them and to the parties in ethics and in law; and second, ensure that parties understand the extent and limitations of confidentiality that apply to the process. The Georgia Commission on Dispute Resolution correctly observed, in my view, that "[i]t is the mediator's responsibility to ensure that all mediation attendees understand the concept and benefit of, and the obligation embedded in, mediation confidentiality."[22] The *California Rules* provide that "[a]t or before the outset of the first mediation session, a mediator must provide the participants with a general explanation of the confidentiality of mediation proceedings";[23] the *Virginia Standards* provide that "[i]n order to inform the participants about confidentiality in mediation, the mediator shall use an Agreement to Mediate that contains the statutory language relating to confidentiality and any requirements for mandatory reporting that are applicable to the mediation";[24] and the *Family Mediation Canada Code* provides that "[t]he mediator shall inform the participants at the outset of mediation of the limitations to confidentiality and the fact that confidentiality cannot be guaranteed."[25]

The mediator's responsibility should not be understood as a duty to provide a detailed explanation of the law that applies to confidentiality, because the mediator is not the parties' legal advisor, and should not indulge in such practice.[26] The *Florida Rules*, for example, provide that a mediator "shall inform the mediation participants that: . . . communications made during the process are confidential, except where disclosure is required or permitted by law."[27] The Florida MEAC was of the opinion that "there is no requirement that [the mediator] go into detail as to any specific statutory provisions."[28] The *Model Standards*, to take another example, do not refer to a specific duty of the mediator to discuss with the parties the extent of the *mediator's* obligation of confidentiality, but do state that "[a] mediator shall promote understanding among the parties

22 Georgia Commission on Dispute Resolution, Opinion 8 available at www.godr.org/files/Advisory%20Opinion%208.pdf, p. 1.

23 California Rules, Rule 3.854(b). See also Family Mediation Model Standards, Standard VII B; Oregon Standards, Standard IV.

24 Virginia Standards, s. H.1.

25 Family Mediation Canada Code, Article 7.3. See also id., Article 11.1(c).

26 See Chapter 8, Section 8.2.2.

27 Florida Rules, Rule 10.420(a)(3).

28 Florida MEAC, Opinion 2000–010 available at www.flcourts.org/core/fileparse.php/283/urlt/2000-Opinion-010.pdf, p. 2. See also Florida MEAC, Opinion 2003–003 available at www.flcourts.org/core/fileparse.php/283/urlt/MEAC-Opinion-2003–003.pdf.

of the extent to which *the parties* will maintain confidentiality of information they obtain in a mediation."[29]

At the end of the day, it is argued, in order to ensure the exercise of party self-determination with regard to participation in the mediation, the mediator must, as a minimum, make sure that (a) the parties understand that his duty of confidentiality is not absolute and that disclosures could be required or permitted in rare circumstances by law or morality, and (b) that the parties are aware of the scope of confidentiality that applies to themselves and to participants other than the mediator. The mediator must then be prepared to answer further questions that the parties might have with respect to confidentiality. As mediation confidentiality in general and mediation privilege in particular are to a large extent *legal* issues, the mediator might legitimately elect to involve the parties' legal representatives (when they have such) in clarifying confidentiality and privilege issues to the parties; he or she may provide additional information that he or she is qualified by training or experience to provide; or refer the parties to outside experts for advice.

10.3 Defining the type of information that is subject to expectations of confidentiality

The type of information that mediators are ethically bound to keep in confidence from a professional ethics perspective is shaped by the legitimate expectations of the parties, the profession, the public, and the employer or principal. The protected information that mediators should keep in confidence is (a) information that parties can reasonably expect a mediator not to disclose if he or she is to be worthy of their trust, and (b) information that the profession, public, and possibly an employer or principal (when there is one) can reasonably expect a mediator not to disclose, that is, information the disclosure of which might harm the standing of the profession or the employer/principal and public trust in it. How is the content of these expectations to be ascertained?

The expectations of the parties are context-related. Mediators are exposed to mediation information because of the professional role they exercise. The relationship of trust between mediators and parties entitles parties to expect that (a) any information about the parties and their case obtained by the mediator in the course of exercising his or her role that

[29] Model Standards, Standard V.C (emphasis added). See also Federal Employee Mediators Guide, Standard V.C; Virginia Standards, s. H.6.

could adversely affect their interests, show them in a bad light, or embarrass them, is not disclosed without a compelling reason. The parties are also entitled to expect that (b) the mediator will respect any rules of critical morality and law that possibly protect the confidentiality of information, because morality and law are ground rules of society that everyone is legitimately expected to follow. For example, when the mediator promises to keep information confidential or where he or she is subject to a legal duty of confidentiality, either in mediation legislation or in a code of conduct that has the force of law, the parties are entitled to expect that he or she keep his or her promise and abide by his or her legal duties.

These expectations of parties of extensive confidentiality are backed by the expectations of the profession, the public, and employers or principals. They wish the process of mediation to flourish, and realize that disclosure of information by mediators could harm the standing of the profession (and possibly the standing of employers or principals) and public trust in it. Thus, they legitimately expect that (c) any information that could undermine public trust in the profession, or in an employer or principal when there is one, be kept in confidence, unless there is a compelling reason to disclose it. In addition, they too expect mediators to keep their promises regarding confidentiality, and to obey any law that protects the confidentiality of mediation.

It seems, therefore, that almost everything said or done by the parties or on their behalf in connection with the mediation that is communicated to the mediator before, during, and after the mediation, is mediation information that has been revealed to the mediator in the exercise of his or her role and should not be disclosed (see Figure 10.1). If a mediator wishes or is required to disclose such information, he or she has to make sure that the information is not covered by the expectations of confidentiality discussed above and that there is a justified cause for disclosure.

Of course, the reasonable expectations of confidentiality may vary between *specific* mediation parties. Still, it is suggested that the working assumption of mediators, at least before clarifying the position of the *particular* parties in a mediation, and before ascertaining the *legal* definition of the protected information in law or the confidentiality rules of an employer/principal that apply to the particular mediation, should be that all communications made in connection with the mediation that could harm parties are to be kept in confidence; that parties do not wish anyone beside the participants to know how they have acted during the mediation; and that they want their anonymity to be protected in the event that

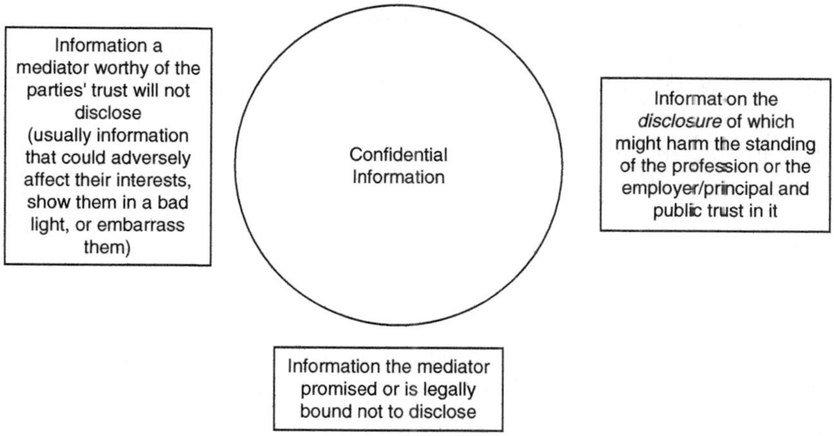

Figure 10.1: Confidential information

the mediator discusses the mediation with others for legitimate purposes such as peer consultation, training, or research.

Perhaps some parties might be satisfied with a more *limited* scope of confidentiality, but it is the duty of the mediator to verify it with the parties rather than assume that is the case. Conversely, some parties might have *higher* expectations of confidentiality, for example, they might not want nonparticipants to know that they have participated in a mediation *at all*. This would probably not be the expectation of parties who have been referred to mediation by a court, for their dispute is already in the public arena, but it might be the expectation of, for example, divorcing couples who have not yet told their children, friends, and colleagues of their plans and wish to keep the fact of their participation in mediation a secret for some time. These expectations of confidentiality would probably be openly expressed by the parties, but they can also be implied from the circumstances, and mediators should be alert to such reasonable expectations and clarify them with the parties.

As previously noted, mediators must be knowledgeable regarding the extent of their *legal* duty of confidentiality, which varies according to the jurisdiction and mediation program within which they operate.[30] Legislation, court rules, and codes of conduct for mediators vary considerably in the language used to define the information that must be kept

[30] See Section 10.2.4.

confidential. The Uniform Mediation Act, for example, takes an extensive approach and defines a confidential mediation communication as "a statement, whether oral or in a record or verbal or nonverbal, that occurs during a mediation or is made for purposes of considering, conducting, participating in, initiating, continuing, or reconvening a mediation or retaining a mediator."[31] Note, however, that the Act does not address communications made *after* the mediation has been concluded, although such communications might be connected to events that occurred during the mediation. In addition, The Act does not refer to the need to protect the *anonymity* of the parties in certain circumstances.

The drafters of the *North Carolina Standards* phrase the confidentiality provision differently, providing that "[a] mediator shall not disclose, directly or indirectly, to any non-participant, any information communicated to the mediator by a participant within the mediation process, whether the information is obtained before, during, or after the mediated settlement conference."[32] The Revised Standards address the issue of protecting the anonymity of parties in connection with the use of mediation information for instruction, evaluation, and monitoring, allowing such use "so long as the parties or the specific circumstances of the parties' controversy are not identified or identifiable."[33] The *Model Standards*, which do not have the force of law,[34] provide more succinctly that "[a] mediator shall maintain the confidentiality of all information obtained by the mediator in mediation,"[35] leaving some uncertainty as to the meaning of an "in mediation" communication. The Standards supplement this obligation with a couple of statements to the effect that "[a] mediator should not communicate to any non-participant

[31] Uniform Mediation Act, available at www.uniformlaws.org/shared/docs/mediation/uma_final_03.pdf (Uniform Mediation Act), s. 2(2).

[32] North Carolina Standards, Rule III.A. See also Georgia Commission on Dispute Resolution, Advisory Opinion 8 available at www.godr.org/files/Advisory%20Opinion%208.pdf ("Confidentiality covers anything said or done in the mediation, and the process, procedures and conduct of all of those present. Confidential communications include the mediator's and the attendees' words, actions, documents, information, and conduct in mediation, including the mediator's notes and records" (p. 3), "any statements made as part of intake by ADR court program staff in preparation for a mediation are confidential" (p. 4), and "[e]xcept in cases where an exception applies, confidentiality applies forever. Confidentiality does not end by virtue of a resolution, whether arrived at during the mediation, after the mediation, or as a result of trial. Confidentiality continues after the conclusion of the mediation session" [p. 6]).

[33] North Carolina Standards, Rule III.E. [34] See Model Standards, Note on Construction.

[35] Model Standards, Standard V.A. See also Family Mediation Model Standards, Standard VII; Florida Rules, Rule 10.360(a); Illinois Standards, s. II.

information about how the parties acted in the mediation"[36] and that "the mediator should protect the anonymity of the parties and abide by their reasonable expectations regarding confidentiality" when he participates in "teaching, research or evaluation of mediation."[37]

From a professional ethics perspective, these formulations of confidentiality should be complemented as suggested in this section. Bearing in mind the ethical rationale of the requirement of mediator confidentiality, and taking into account the wide scope of confidentiality associated with mediation according to mediation legislation, codes, and literature, it is suggested that an *ethical* duty of mediators to keep mediation information in confidence relates to information that could adversely affect the parties' interests, show them in a bad light, or embarrass them, including (a) communications made in connection with the mediation, whether before, during, and after the mediation, including communications made in separate meetings; (b) information regarding how the parties acted in the mediation; and (c) information connecting the parties with the mediation, where the anonymity of the parties is reasonably expected. The underlying assumption should be that parties wish all such information to be kept in confidence, unless they indicate otherwise, and that in case of doubt, in line with the norm of party self-determination, the mediator should check with the parties what their wishes are.

In view of the general application of the theory of professional ethics, all mediators must abide by this ethical duty, whether or not they are subject to a code of conduct or to confidentiality legislation, subject to the exceptions of justified disclosures discussed in the next section. Where the duty of confidentiality under a code or under the law is more limited, mediators must abide by the wider ethical duty if they are to conduct themselves ethically. If the legal or institutional rules of confidentiality are wider than the ethical duty of confidentiality, mediators should respect the wider formulation of confidentiality because of the general expectation that they follow the law or the rules of their institutions.

10.4 Justified grounds for disclosure

A theory of professional ethics assumes that no ethical norm is absolute. Therefore, there will be times at which disclosure of confidential

36 Model Standards, Standard V.A.2. See also Oregon Standards, Standard IV, Comment 4; Virginia Standards, s. H.4.

37 Model Standards, Standard V.A.3. See also below s. 4.5.

information by mediators will be justified. The grounds for justified disclosure derive from an exploration of the interaction between the expectations of confidentiality of the parties, the profession, the public, and employers/principals. From a professional ethics perspective, disclosure may be ethically justified when (1) it is not harmful to the parties; or (2) when the disclosure is harmful to the parties yet justified, either because the parties (a) waived or agreed to limit the scope of confidentiality and in fact authorized the disclosure, or (b) despite the parties' objection to the disclosure, the harm of nondisclosure to important public and professional interests is considered higher than the harm of disclosure to the parties, that is, the reasonable expectations of disclosure of the profession (and sometimes of the mediator as a professional), the public, and the employer/principal (when there is one) exceed the expectations of confidentiality of the parties.

Ethically *permitted* disclosures have, from a professional ethics perspective, limitations. One limitation derives from the expectations of confidentiality of the profession and the public. Since maintaining confidentiality is aimed at preserving public trust in the profession and process of mediation, disclosure in the mentioned instances would only be acceptable where (1) it would not jeopardize the standing of the profession and public trust in it. A second limitation derives from the overall commitment of mediators to abide by all the norms of ethics, without sacrificing one norm at the expense of another. Thus, such disclosure must (2) be consistent with other norms of ethics applicable to the mediator, such as impartiality, because the other norms continue to be binding upon the mediator.

Nonetheless, in exceptionally rare cases the ethical permission to disclose can turn into an *ethical duty*. A mediator will have a *duty* to disclose confidential information where the disclosure is required in order to protect highly important public interests. This limited category of interests may be identified by the demand that a *non-disclosure* of the information, if the information and the mediator's decision not to disclose it were to become public, could jeopardize the standing of the profession and public trust in it. In such rare cases, the possible harm to the protected interests would be considered so severe that the disclosure would not jeopardize the standing of the profession and public trust in it. Such circumstances could even justify legitimate exceptions to other norms of ethics applicable to the mediator, such as impartiality, because a flexible approach to the meaning of the norm is essential in order to preserve public trust in the profession and process. A detailed discussion of the grounds for justified disclosure follows. Figure 10.2 summarizes these grounds.

10.4.1 Disclosure with the parties' consent

If the main purpose of the confidentiality obligation of mediators, insofar as reasonable mediation parties are concerned, is that mediators keep to themselves information that parties reasonably expect them not to disclose so that they be worthy of the parties' trust, it follows that parties are entitled to *relieve* mediators of that obligation toward them to the extent that the disclosure does not violate the obligations mediators owe others, that is the profession, the public, or an employer or principal. Parties may do so by virtue of their right to make decisions concerning the mediation (according to the norm of self-determination), authorizing the mediator to disclose mediation information to nonparticipants. This exception to confidentiality is common in mediation legislation and codes of conduct for mediators. The *Model Standards*, for example, provide that "[i]f the parties to a mediation agree that the mediator may disclose information obtained during the mediation, the mediator may do so";[38] The *Family Mediation Canada Code* provides that "[a] mediator shall not voluntarily disclose to anyone who is not a party to the mediation any information obtained through the mediation process except . . . (b) with the written consent of the participants to the mediation contract";[39] and the *Australian Ethical Guidelines* provide that "[a] mediator should not disclose any matter that a party requires to be kept confidential . . . unless: (i) the mediator is given permission to do so by all persons attending at the mediation with an interest in the preservation of the confidence."[40]

Of course, when the mediator owes the duty of confidentiality to *one* party, as is the case with communications in separate meetings, for the disclosure to be justified the mediator must first obtain the consent of the party that communicated the information to him.[41]

[38] Model Standards, Standard V.A.1. [39] Family Mediation Canada Code, Article 7.1(b).

[40] Australian Ethical Guidelines, s. 5 Comment (c)(i). See also Family Mediation Model Standards, Standard VII.

[41] See, e.g., Model Standards, Standard V.B. See also California Rules, Rule 3.854(c); Federal Employee Mediators Guide, Standard V.B.

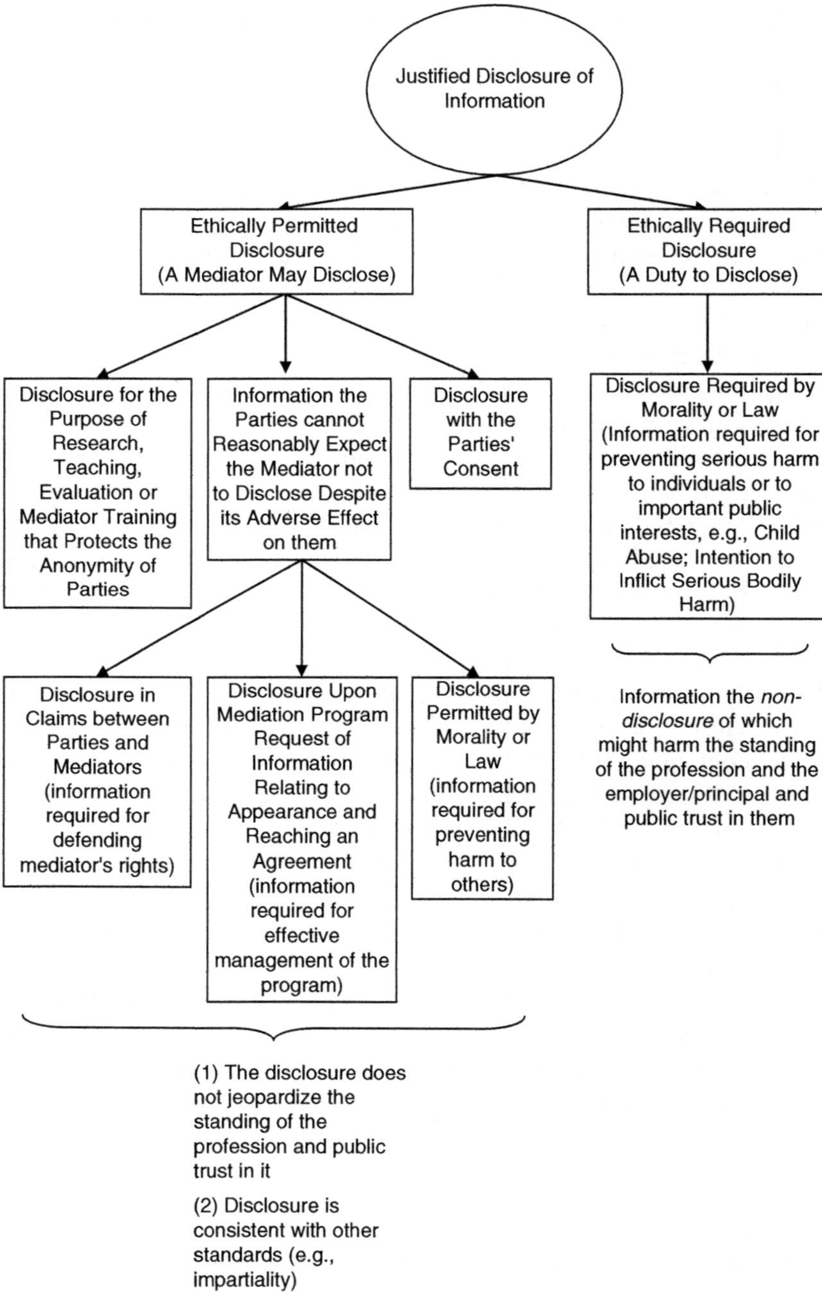

Figure 10.2: Justified disclosure of information

10.4.2 *Disclosure in claims between parties and mediators*

10.4.2.1 Claims or complaints against mediators

Malpractice claims in court against mediators are quite rare but do occur from time to time.[42] More often, disappointed parties file complaints with ethical or disciplinary boards that have been set up by mediation programs or mediator associations.[43] Inevitably, legal or disciplinary actions of such nature often make reference to mediation information, and it seems only logical that by the commencement of these proceedings the parties have waived the mediator's ethical and legal obligation of confidentiality to the extent needed for him or her to be able to present his or her case before the court or the disciplinary body and explain his or her actions. On an ethical analysis, the parties in such case cannot reasonably expect the mediator to refrain from disclosing the information required to defend his or her rights. Such an exception to confidentiality is sometimes incorporated into mediators' codes of conduct, providing that the confidentiality requirement does not apply in actions alleging misconduct of the mediator.[44] Note, however, that the mediator's ethical duty of confidentiality remains in force toward *anyone else* except the court or the body that makes an enquiry into the complaint, because the mediator is still expected to conduct him or herself in a manner that is worthy of the parties' trust and avoid harming the standing of the profession and process of mediation.

In *law*, a legal action against the mediator will also usually override a mediation evidentiary *privilege*, if such privilege applies to the mediation. The Uniform Mediation Act, for example, which many states have adopted, provides that "[t]here is no privilege . . . for a mediation communication that is: . . . sought or offered to prove or disprove a claim or complaint of professional misconduct or malpractice filed against a mediator."[45]

10.4.2.2 A mediator claim for fees

Ethically, a mediator who has not received his or her fees as agreed upon in the initial contract for the supply of mediation services may

42 See, e.g., Coben and Thompson, "Disputing Irony." See also Moffitt, "Suing Mediators."

43 See, e.g., Florida Rules, Rule 10.700. See also California Rules of Court (Revised June 8, 2015), Division 8 (Alternative Dispute Resolution), Chapter 3 (General Rules Relating to Mediation of Civil Cases), Article 3 (Requirements for Addressing Complaints About Court-Program Mediators) available at www.courts.ca.gov/cms/rules/index.cfm?title=three.

44 See, e.g., Virginia Standards, s. H.1(ii); North Carolina Standards, Rule III.F.

45 Uniform Mediation Act, s. 6(a)(5).

legitimately bring a suit against the defaulting party to recover his or her fees. The claim might require limited disclosure of mediation information regarding the fees that each party has agreed to pay, and possibly regarding other mediation expenses that have been incurred with the parties' consent, such as an outside expert opinion that has been arranged for by the mediator on behalf of the parties. In these circumstances, the mediator will be partially relieved of his or her ethical duty of confidentiality to the extent needed to establish his or her claim for the unpaid fees, because the parties' reasonable expectations of confidentiality should not bar the mediator from realizing his or her pre-agreed right to be remunerated for his or her services. The Alabama Supreme Court Commission for Dispute Resolution, for example, held that the *Alabama Code* does not prohibit the mediator from reporting to the court that his or her mediator's fee has not been paid.[46]

10.4.3 Disclosure upon mediation program request of information relating to the appearance of parties and as to whether an agreement has been reached

Mediators receive cases in various ways. Some parties approach a mediator and hire his or her services directly, while others are referred to a mediator through a mediation program operated by a court, public agency, or private body. The mediator in these cases will normally be subject to rules of conduct adopted by the program that referred the case to him or her, either by agreement between the program and him or herself, as in the case of a mediator who is conducting mediations under the auspices of a community or a private mediation center, or by virtue of legislation or court rules, as is the case with many court-connected mediation programs. From a professional ethics perspective, conducting mediations in accordance with the rules of a specific mediation program is part of the mediator's obligations toward his or her employer or principal, and these obligations do not relieve the mediator of the ethical duties established by the theory of professional ethics toward the parties, the profession, and the public. The mediator is still under a duty, for example, to respect the parties' right to self-determination, remain impartial, act with professional integrity, and maintain the standing of the profession and public trust in it. Similarly, the mediator's obligation

[46] Alabama Supreme Court Commission for Dispute Resolution, Opinion 001–2010 available at www.alabamaadr.org/web/roster-documents/med_Ethical_Opinions.php.

to confidentiality remains intact, thus requiring the mediator to be able to justify any disclosure to the program's staff not only by the program's rules, but also by the norms of professional ethics that apply to all mediators.

Mediation programs can justify a request from a mediator to disclose mediation information on relatively *narrow* grounds, when the disclosure is needed for proper administrative management of the program. Generally speaking, an informed choice of parties to mediate their case with a program can be seen as an agreement to limitations on confidentiality contained in the rules of the program. However, it would be wrong for a program or for its mediators to rely on the parties' choice to mediate their case with the program as a sweeping consent to *any* disclosure requirement that might be contained in the program's rules. The Reporter's Notes to the *Model Standards*, for example, state in this context that "the Joint Committee explicitly supports the position widely adopted in practice and program rules that a mediator can override confidentiality, if required, for only two purposes: to report whether parties appeared at a scheduled mediation or to report whether the parties reached a resolution; the Joint Committee rejected overriding the confidentiality requirement for any other purpose."[47] In addition, the Reporter's Notes refer with approval to mediator disclosures that are required for the purpose of monitoring and evaluation, provided that the anonymity of the parties is preserved. Similarly, the *Federal Employee Mediators Guide* provides that "[a] mediator should not communicate to any non-participant information about how the parties acted in the mediation. A mediator may report, if required, whether parties appeared at a scheduled mediation and whether or not the parties reached a resolution,"[48] and "[i]f a mediator participates in . . . evaluation of mediation, the mediator should protect the anonymity of the parties and abide by their reasonable expectations regarding confidentiality."[49]

This approach is consistent with a professional ethics perspective because it limits the extent of information disclosed to (a) information whose disclosure is needed for the effective management of the program, along with the legitimate interests of the program, and (b) information whose disclosure by the mediator does not involve a breach of the trust the parties are entitled to expect of the mediator, or a violation of the duty

[47] Model Standards Reporter's Notes, p. 10. See also NY-CDRC Standards, Standard V, Comment 4.

[48] Federal Employee Mediators Guide, Standard V.A.2. [49] Id., Standard V.A.3.

the mediator owes the profession of mediation to refrain from conduct that might harm the standing of the profession and public trust in it. For example, from a professional ethics perspective it would be wrong in principle for the mediator to disclose to the program's staff information about the content of sessions, statements of the parties, their interests, or concessions they made. Such disclosure is not ordinarily required for the management of the program. This is not to say that such disclosure would *never* be permitted. The program could require, for example, that the mediator report to the staff a credible intention of a participant to assault another participant or an actual assault that occurred in the course of the mediation, in order to ensure that the offending participant is not allowed to participate in a mediation in the future without proper precautions. The offending participant cannot reasonably expect the mediator to withhold such information, which is completely divorced from the nature and purpose of mediation as a forum for the conduct of voluntary dialogue about differences; the disclosure of the information is unlikely to harm the standing of the profession and public trust in it; and it could probably be reconciled with the norm of impartiality as well, as it is required for maintaining public trust in the profession.[50] Other possible justified disclosures to program staff could occur, for example, for training purposes, provided that the *anonymity* of the parties is protected. When the parties cannot be identified or connected with the facts of the case, their expectations of confidentiality are not frustrated and the mediator may disclose the information for a legitimate purpose.

10.4.4 *Disclosure required or permitted by morality or law*

10.4.4.1 Ethically required disclosure (a mediator duty to disclose)

The obligation to follow the norms of critical morality and law is a fundamental obligation owed by mediators to the public (as a matter of trust and reciprocity),[51] to the profession (in order to preserve the standing of the profession and public trust in it),[52] and possibly to themselves (as a matter of personal morality and conscience). Mediation parties cannot legitimately expect mediators to maintain confidentiality when this, in effect, would result in the mediator acting in violation of norms of critical morality or law. For example, parties cannot reasonably expect mediators to refrain from disclosing mediation

[50] See Chapter 7, Section 7.3.4.2. [51] See Chapter 3, Section 3.7. [52] Ibid.

information that is necessary to save the lives of innocent, unaware nonparticipants who might be seriously harmed by a participant's conduct. Warning an intended victim is morally, and probably legally, required, and the mediator would be violating his or her obligations toward the public and the profession if he or she failed to take such action. From a professional ethics perspective, then, an ethical duty to disclose mediation information arises when the information is required to prevent serious harm to individuals or to important public interests. A mediator will be able to recognize such an instance when non-disclosure of the information, if later learnt by the public, could harm the standing of the profession (and of an employer/principal when there is one) and public trust in it.

A mediator is expected to follow the law. Therefore, he or she might not be able to justify a disclosure where he or she is under a strict legal duty of confidentiality. But legal exceptions to confidentiality do exist. Indeed, there are common exceptions to confidentiality that are often recognized by law, depending on the jurisdiction in which the mediator conducts the mediation, and by codes of conduct for mediators, imposing on mediators a duty to disclose information to the authorities in relation to child abuse,[53] or a duty to warn an intended victim of an intention to inflict on him serious bodily harm.[54] The *Family Mediation Model Standards*, for example, provide that "[t]he mediator shall disclose a participant's threat of suicide or violence against any person to the threatened person and the appropriate authorities if the mediator believes such threat is likely to be acted upon as permitted by law";[55] the *Illinois Standards* provide that "[t]he mediator shall inform the participants in writing that confidentiality will not apply when there is a threat to inflict bodily harm and suspected child abuse or neglect";[56] and the *Family Mediation Canada Code* provides that "[a] mediator shall not voluntarily disclose ... any information obtained through the

[53] See, e.g., Florida Statutes, s. 44.405(4)(a)3 and s. 39.201.

[54] See, e.g., *Tarasoff* v. *Regents of the University of California* 17 Cal.3d 425, 131 Cal.Rptr. 14, 551 P.2d 334 (1976) (a duty of a professional to warn a person who is threatened by his client with serious bodily harm). See also John R. Murphy III, "In the Wake of Tarasoff: Mediation and the Duty to Disclose" (1985) 5 *Catholic University Law Review* 209, 210–211 (suggesting that a duty to disclose may apply to a mediator).

[55] Family Mediation Model Standards, Standard VII.C.

[56] Illinois Standards, s. II. See also Kovach, *Mediation*, p. 275 and Uniform Mediation Act, Comment 8 to s. 6(a)(7), pp. 30–31 (listing mediation confidentiality statutes that recognize an exception for child abuse and neglect).

mediation process except: ... (d) when the information discloses an actual or potential threat to human life or safety."[57]

The underlying rationale of these common exceptions to confidentiality, as revealed by the theory of professional ethics, is that declining to disclose information in the unique circumstances referred to above will probably jeopardize the standing of the profession and the process, and violate the rules of law and morality because the mediator, being in a professional capacity that triggers duties toward the profession and the public, has failed to assist innocent and vulnerable people. Some codes of conduct for mediators explicitly acknowledge such considerations. The 1999 version of the *Illinois Standards* provided that "[w]here there is clear and imminent danger to an individual or to society, the obligation of the mediator to maintain confidentiality will not apply";[58] and the *North Carolina Standards* provide that " ... a mediator has discretion to report otherwise confidential conduct or statements ... Where public safety is an issue."[59]

However, even in these rare cases mediators should take great care before making a decision to disclose information from mediation, as it runs contrary to their initial obligation of confidentiality. As a first step, mediators should verify as far as possible the basis for their suspicion that a situation of abuse, threatened violence, or future crime is at stake. Next, they should share if possible their suspicions with the parties and examine together with them the possibility that *they* disclose the information, or that *they* consent to disclosure by the mediators, thereby minimizing the harm to the parties' rights to confidentiality and self-determination. In the event that the mediators cannot avoid disclosure, they should make every effort to limit the extent of the information revealed. The *Family Mediation Canada code* reflects this idea correctly by stating that "[a]ny information so divulged shall be limited to what is absolutely necessary to accomplish such purposes."[60]

10.4.4.2 Ethically permitted disclosure (information mediators may disclose)

The incidents discussed in the previous section are extreme cases in which morality and law would probably be united in the requirement for disclosure. They pose little difficulty for the mediator because the

57 Family Mediation Canada Code, Article 7.1(d).

58 Illinois Standards (1999) available at www.mediate.com/mobile/article.cfm?id=293, s. II.

59 North Carolina Standards, Rule III.C(2).

60 Family Mediation Canada Code, Article 7.2.

ethical and legal duties of disclosure are likely to overlap, and in the event they do not, there is a strong moral reason to disclose the information in breach of legal confidentiality.[61] More difficult are cases where the disclosure is (a) required by law (through legislation, court rules, program rules, or other institutional or mediator rules agreed by the parties) but does not seem to be required by ethics, because the potential harm to the public or to an innocent bystander is not severe; or (b) legally *permitted* by a particular provision or through a narrow definition of the confidential information, thereby leaving the decision to the mediator's discretion.[62]

Although mediators are expected to follow the law, they should realize that the mere existence of a *legal* permission for, or even a requirement of, disclosure does not automatically absolve them of their *ethical* duty of confidentiality; mediators should be able to justify the disclosure on ethical grounds, the legal permission or duty of disclosure being only one consideration, though one of considerable weight in favor of disclosure, in the decision. From a professional ethics perspective, the mediator has to ask him or herself whether (a) there is a moral reason that supports disclosure (i.e. the disclosure is aimed at preventing some harm); (b) the disclosure would not jeopardize the standing of the profession and public trust in it; and (c) the disclosure would be consistent with other binding standards, such as impartiality. Since following the law is an important factor in the shaping of public trust, it is assumed that in most cases a mediator who discloses information according to a legal requirement or permission would not be jeopardizing the standing of the profession, and if he or she can make the disclosure without violating other applicable ethical standards the disclosure is ethically permissible.

Consider the following case as an illustration. Party A physically assaults Party B or the mediator in the course of mediation. May the mediator disclose information regarding the assault in a police investigation or in legal proceedings against Party A? On such facts, the Tennessee Alternative Dispute Resolution Commission held that "the mediator may provide a statement to law enforcement or be called as a witness if an assault is committed against someone other than the mediator . . . or when the mediator is the victim of an assault during the mediation,"

[61] Compare Gibson, "Confidentiality in Mediation", 32 (noting that "situations remain where it might be appropriate for mediators to go against the letter of the law and break confidentiality").

[62] See, e.g., Florida Rules, Rule 10.360(a) (referring to disclosure permitted by law).

provided that he or she be "careful and moderate his statement and testimony to avoid disclosing information pertaining to the underlying dispute and may only testify as to the assault."[63] The Committee based its decision on an interpretation of the scope of confidential information according to the relevant Tennessee Rule, holding that by such disclosure "[t]he mediator is not divulging information regarding the underlying dispute but only collateral issues."[64]

Now let us distinguish between the legal and ethical questions. The Committee, I believe, answered the legal question, holding that the law permits such disclosure, but is the disclosure consistent with the theory of professional ethics? I tend to agree that an act of violence during mediation is not an act that parties can reasonably expect mediators to keep in confidence. Acts of violence in the midst of mediation are both immoral and illegal, and are too remote from the purpose and spirit of mediation, a process committed to voluntary dialogue and decision-making that respects party self-determination. Therefore, it seems that in principle the mediator is ethically permitted to disclose that information if the disclosure can be made consistent with norms of ethics other than confidentiality that apply to mediators. It would be helpful to further distinguish between a case in which the mediator is the victim of violence and a case in which another participant has been assaulted.

If the mediator is assaulted, a disclosure to the police could be justified in order to protect his or her rights, and such ground for disclosure has been discussed previously.[65] Moreover, such disclosure is not likely to undermine public faith in the profession and is consistent with the norm of impartiality because it cannot be considered as an act of favoritism between the parties.

When another participant is assaulted the matter becomes more complex. First, what is the moral reason for the disclosure? What is the harm that the disclosure comes to address? Violent behavior is unacceptable in a mediation setting and should not be tolerated. The mediator must not allow the process to continue in such circumstances and should probably put an end to the process and in this way intervene to protect the injured party and the process. Any further action on the part of the mediator should be further justified. The injured party is the initiating force of disclosure and the mediator's intervention could be morally justified if he

[63] Tennessee Alternative Dispute Resolution Commission, Opinion 2010–0002 available at www.tncourts.gov/sites/default/files/adrc_advisory_opinion_2010–0002.pdf.
[64] Ibid. [65] See above s. 4.2.

or she is asked to assist in the investigation where the investigation cannot proceed without his or her help. If the investigation can proceed without him or her, he or she should stay out of it for the reasons discussed below.

Second, the disclosure must not harm public trust in the profession and process. The public expects mediators to keep confidences for utility purposes, that is, to enable them to solicit the cooperation and trust of the participants that is needed for the success of mediations. Violent conduct of participants during mediation is not the type of information that is expected to be kept in confidence and therefore its limited disclosure in an official investigation is not likely to lead to a loss of faith in the profession or process. However, as the next point illustrates, public faith could be undermined for reasons other than confidentiality.

The third condition for justified disclosure that must be considered is whether the disclosure would be consistent with other binding ethical norms, in particular impartiality. If the mediator assists in the investigation, he or she takes a position that aligns him or her with the injured party and could give an appearance of partiality. This is not partiality with regard to the subject matter of the original dispute between the parties, but an appearance of partiality in the stance of the mediator that could possibly affect the public image of mediators and consequently also public trust in the profession and the process of mediation (this concern would not have arisen to such a degree if, for example, Party A assaulted *his or her* lawyer, and the mediator were asked to assist in the lawyer's complaint, because then the mediator's disclosure would not give an appearance of partiality between the parties).[66] Here *the severity of the assault* seems to be a relevant factor. If the assault and its consequences are minor, the mediator might be seen as a tool in the ongoing struggle

[66] Compare Florida MEAC, Opinion 2012–007 available at www.flcourts.org/core/fileparse.php/283/urlt/MEACOpinion2012-007.pdf (holding that under Florida Rules there is no *mandatory* obligation for a mediator to report that a sworn indigent form is false or that the crime of perjury is being committed. The mediator *may* disclose to an appropriate authority a "mediation communication that is willfully used to plan a crime, commit or attempt to commit a crime, conceal ongoing criminal activity, or threaten violence," but if he or she makes the disclosure he or she will inevitably exhibit the appearance of partiality and must withdraw from the mediation. I agree that if the mediator reports the incident he or she *must withdraw* because of the appearance of partiality in continuing the mediation, but in my view if the mediator *withdrew* from the mediation and reported the perjury he or she *would have probably not appeared to be impartial* to a degree that could undermine public trust in the profession and process because the reported act had nothing to do with the other party or with the subject-matter of the case, and it related to an illegal attempt to abuse the process).

between the parties, thereby unnecessarily risking his or her and the process's image of impartiality. In such case, the mediator should make an effort to refrain as far as possible from taking part in the investigation or testimony. The greater the gravity of the assault and its consequences, the less likely it is that the mediator's cooperation will be considered inappropriate in the public eye, thus making such conduct ethically permissible.

This condition for justified disclosure can raise concerns other than impartiality. For example, mediators are bound to act with professional integrity that requires them, among other things, to exercise professional discretion in making decisions with regard to the process and to refrain from abusing the process – for example, avoid using information revealed to them during a mediation for any purpose not connected to the mediation, unless authorized to do so in accordance with the norms of ethics.[67] While in the circumstances described above cooperating with an official police inquiry or giving testimony in a court of law may be considered legitimate use of information learnt in mediation, sharing that information with the media without preserving the anonymity of the parties would be an inappropriate violation of the norm of professional integrity.

10.4.4.3 A note on mediation privilege and court ordered disclosure

Sometimes the mediation does not put a stop to legal proceedings between mediation parties, or its content might be of relevance in other proceedings in which one of the parties is involved. In such cases, as we have already seen, the mediator could become a valuable witness in the ensuing legal proceedings, and attempts made to solicit mediation information from him or her, deposit him or her, or summon him or her as a witness in court to give evidence. The mediator might find himself facing a court order requiring him or her to testify in conflict with his ethical duty of confidentiality. Again, as discussed in the previous section, the mediator should strive to find ethical justifications for the disclosure; look for ways that make the disclosure unnecessary; and limit the extent of disclosure as far as possible where disclosure is inevitable. However, a new factor that the mediator should take into consideration where the disclosure is aimed at bringing mediation information before a court is the issue of mediation *privilege* that might provide a legal reason in

[67] See Chapter 8, Section 8.2.1 and 8.2.4.1.

support of the mediator's ethical duty of confidentiality. An evidentiary privilege means an exemption from the duty to reveal information to court in legal proceedings.[68] When a mediator is able to point to a recognized mediation privilege, he or she can maintain the confidentiality of the mediation by invoking the privilege before the court. According to the ADR Rules of Georgia, for example, "neither the neutral nor any observer present with permission of the parties in a court-annexed or court-referred ADR process may be subpoenaed or otherwise required to testify concerning any type of ADR proceedings in any subsequent administrative or judicial proceeding. If mediators or observers receive a subpoena to testify about a mediation, they should file a Motion to Quash the subpoena."[69]

The question whether a mediation privilege exists depends on the jurisdiction in which the mediator practices. It may have a statutory basis or derive from case-law, and vary in scope.[70] The privilege could be *absolute*, denying the court's authority to force the mediator to disclose information in legal proceedings, or *relative*, authorizing the court to order disclosure if it believes that disclosure is justified in the circumstances; the privilege may belong to the parties, thus allowing them to waive it and compel the mediator to testify, belong to the mediator, allowing him or her to refuse disclosure despite the parties' wishes that he or she testify, or have an independent status, incapable of being waived even with the parties' and the mediator's agreement. The rationale of a mediation privilege that cannot be waived with the parties' consent is that disclosure of mediation information by mediators, even with the parties' consent, could be perceived as if the mediator is taking sides and the appearance of partiality could jeopardize public trust in the profession and process of mediation.

[68] See, e.g., Welsh S. White, "Evidentiary Privileges and the Defendant's Constitutional Right to Introduce Evidence" (1989) 80 *Journal of Criminal Law and Criminology* 377, 377 note 1 (noting, while referring to C. McCormick, *Evidence*, 3rd edn. (1984), pp. 170–277, that "Evidentiary privileges may be defined as rules that bar the admission of evidence in order to promote a social policy such as safeguarding an individual's privacy or protecting a confidential relationship").

[69] Georgia Commission on Dispute Resolution, Opinion 8 available at www.godr.org/files/Advisory%20Opinion%208.pdf, pp. 3–4. See also North Carolina Dispute Resolution Commission, Opinion 03-01 available at www.nccourts.org/Courts/CRS/Councils/DRC/Documents/03-01_final.pdf (holding that a mediator should not give an affidavit nor should he provide information at a deposition regarding mediation communications).

[70] See, e.g., Kovach, *Mediation*, p. 272.

This rationale led the court in *N.L.R.B.* v. *Joseph Macaluso* to support a mediation privilege and conclude that "the public interest in maintaining the perceived and actual impartiality of federal mediators does outweigh the benefits derivable from [the mediator's] testimony";[71] and it led the court in *Olam* v. *Cong. Mortgage* to observe that "[t]o force [mediators] to give evidence that hurts someone from whom they actively solicited trust ... rips the fabric of their work and can threaten their sense of the center of their professional integrity."[72] However, if this rationale is correct, then it cannot be said that mediator testimony will *always* undermine public faith in mediation, because there could be circumstances in which the harm to the profession and process of mediation would be greater, in terms of loss of public trust, in the event of *non-disclosure* than in the event of disclosure, thus justifying the disclosure of mediation information to the court by the mediator. This view has been endorsed in *Re Anonymous* by the United States Court of Appeals, which, after quoting the *Olam* judgment, continued to hold that "we will consent for the Circuit Mediator to disclose confidential information only where such disclosure is mandated by manifest injustice, is indispensable to resolution of an important subsequent dispute, and is not going to damage our mediation program."[73]

The Uniform Mediation Act is a notable example, followed by many states, of instances that are regarded by many as legitimate exceptions to confidentiality that justify discovery and admission of information to court. The Act provides that "[t]here is no privilege ... for a mediation communication that is: ... (3) a threat or statement of a plan to inflict bodily injury or commit a crime of violence; [or] (4) intentionally used to plan a crime, attempt to commit a crime, or to conceal an ongoing crime or ongoing criminal activity."[74]

Mediators should therefore educate themselves about the legal rules of confidentiality and be ready to invoke them in defense of their ethical duty of confidentiality. If mediators are summoned to testify or requested to submit mediation information to a court, they should bring up the issues of mediation confidentiality and privilege and ask the court to rule

[71] See *N.L.R.B.* v. *Joseph Macaluso* 618 F.2d 51 (9th Cir. 1980). See also Kovach, id., p. 265.

[72] *Olam* v. *Cong. Mortgage Co.*, 68 F. Supp. 2d 1110, 1134 (N.D. Cal. 1999).

[73] See *In Re Anonymous* 283 F.3d 627 (United States Court of Appeals, 4th Cir. 2002), in Kovach, *Mediation*, p. 325.

[74] Uniform Mediation Act, s. 6(a)(3) and (4). See also Comment 4 to s. 6(a)(3), p. 28 and Comment 5 to s. 6(a)(4), pp. 28–29 (listing mediation confidentiality statutes that recognize similar exceptions).

on their application to the particular facts of the case. If following the mediator's request the court goes on to make a ruling to the effect that the mediator is under a duty to disclose the information, it constitutes a good reason for the mediator to do so and defend his or her conduct as ethically permissible. In this context, the ABA Section of Dispute Resolution Committee on Mediator Ethical Guidance held that "[t]he Model Standards themselves do not impose an affirmative duty on the mediator to resist compelled disclosure of confidential communications," but observed that "[a]t a minimum, good practice would suggest that the mediator inform the court, or the party seeking the confidential information, of the mediator's ethical requirements under the Model Standards, as well as any applicable statutes, rules, or contracts of the parties that protect the confidentiality of mediation communications."[75]

10.4.5 Disclosure for the purpose of research, teaching, evaluation or mediator training that protects the anonymity of parties

Advancement of the profession of mediation is an ideal for all mediators. Experienced mediators can contribute to the professionalization of others for the benefit of the public at large. Disclosure of inside information about the conduct of mediations that is used for research, training, monitoring, and evaluation serves a good cause and advances the profession and the quality of services provided to the public. These legitimate goals can be achieved without harming the parties' interests where the disclosure of the information is done with the parties' consent, or in a manner that protects the anonymity of the parties. In fact it could be argued that information that protects the anonymity of the parties is not confidential at all, as long as it cannot adversely affect the parties' interests, show them in a bad light, or embarrass them. Such disclosures are therefore justified from a professional ethics perspective, and indeed provisions to such effect are often found in codes of conduct for mediators. The *NY-CDRC Standards*, for example, provide that "[n]othing in [the Confidentiality] Standard should be construed to prohibit monitoring, research, and evaluation of mediation activities or the continuing education of mediators";[76] the *Australian Ethical Guidelines* provide that "[a] mediator should render anonymous all identifying information.

[75] ABA Section of Dispute Resolution, Committee on Mediator Ethical Guidance, Opinion 2008-3 available at apps.americanbar.org/dch/committee.cfm?com=DR018600.

[76] NY-CDRC Standards, Standard V, Comment 5. See also North Carolina Standards, Rule III.E.

When materials emanating from a mediation are used for research, supervision, or training purposes, the mediator should remove all identifying information from them";[77] the *Florida Rules* provide that "[a] mediator . . . shall not disclose any identifying information when materials are used for research, training, or statistical compilations";[78] and the *Illinois Standards* provide that "[m]ediators who present personal information obtained during the course of professional work in writings, lectures, or other public forums need either to obtain adequate prior written informed consent or to disguise identifying information of the persons involved."[79]

10.5 Conclusion

From a professional ethics perspective, mediators must maintain the confidentiality of information relating to the parties, which they have been exposed to in connection with the mediation they are conducting. Mediators must do so if they are to meet the legitimate expectation of parties that they be worthy of the parties' trust, and if they are to meet the legitimate expectations of the profession and the public that they maintain public trust in the profession and process of mediation. These expectations of confidentiality are intertwined with mediation practice to a degree that unjustified deviation from them might seriously jeopardize the standing of the mediation profession and public trust in it. The ethical duty of confidentiality is often recognized by law, depending on the jurisdiction within which mediators operate, thus frequently making the duty of mediators to refrain from disclosing mediation information a legal duty as well.

The ethical duty of confidentiality is not absolute, and is subject to legitimate exceptions. According to the theory of professional ethics, disclosure by mediators could be ethically justified (a) by the norm of party self-determination, where the parties consent to the disclosure; (b) by the rights of mediators to protect their good name and livelihood, in proceedings between parties and mediators; (c) by the reasonable expectations of mediation programs that mediators are associated with and whose rules they are bound to follow, that limited information necessary for the proper management of the program be disclosed; (d) by the reasonable expectations of the public and the profession that mediators

[77] Australian Ethical Guidelines, s. 5 Comment (i). [78] Florida Rules, Rule 10.360(c).
[79] Illinois Standards, s. II.B.

follow the rules of critical morality and law, and disclose information required to prevent harm to others; and (e) by the ideal of advancement of the profession, where the disclosure is for the legitimate purposes of research, teaching, evaluation, or training, when the anonymity of the parties is protected. Any such disclosure, in order to be ethically permissible, must not (1) undermine the standing of the profession and public trust in it, and (2) be consistent with other standards of ethical mediation practice, such as impartiality.

A disclosure is ethically *required*, i.e., becomes an ethical *duty* of the mediator, where the disclosure is necessary in order to prevent a serious harm to an individual (for example, an innocent nonparticipant) or to important public interests (for example, public safety), i.e., in circumstances where *non-disclosure*, were it to come to public attention, would harm the standing of the profession and public trust in it.

Since mediation confidentiality is often regulated by law, mediators must be aware of the scope of confidentiality according to the law applicable to them and to the process they conduct. They must recognize the type of information that they are not allowed to disclose according to the law, and be familiar with an applicable evidentiary mediation privilege, where one exists. Moreover, mediators must be ready to reconcile possible tensions between their ethical and legal duties of confidentiality. Where disclosure is legally permissible, mediators should avoid disclosure unless it can be shown to be ethically permissible as well. Where disclosure is legally required, mediators are not absolved of their ethical responsibilities, but mandatory disclosure is most likely to be ethically permissible because mediators are reasonably expected to follow the law and mandatory disclosures are usually reserved to exceptional cases of severe harm to individuals or to the public, which are recognized as exceptions to confidentiality by both ethics and law. Similarly, where disclosure is legally prohibited, it would probably be prohibited ethically as well, because mediators are reasonably expected to abide by the law and it is very likely that the ethical protection of confidentiality covers the information protected by the law.

The centrality of confidentiality to mediation practice on the one hand, and the variety of formulations attached to it in mediation legislation, codes, and literature on the other, illuminate the importance of parties being knowledgeable about the extent of the duty of confidentiality that applies to the mediator in their case, the circumstances in which mediator disclosure would be justified, and the extent of confidentiality that they themselves are bound to follow. Mediators should take the necessary steps so that parties participate in the mediation with that knowledge.

10.6 A proposed standard of confidentiality

A mediator shall maintain the confidentiality of information that came to his or her knowledge in the exercise of his or her role. Maintaining confidentiality means refraining from disclosure of information without a justified cause as provided in this Standard. The extent of confidentiality applying to a mediation will depend on applicable law, on rules agreed upon by the parties, or on other rules determined by the mediator or a mediation program that the parties agreed to abide by.

A. Discussion of the extent of confidentiality with the parties
   1. A mediator shall promote understanding among the parties of the extent of confidentiality that applies to the process and to the mediator, and the existence or nonexistence of a mediation privilege and its scope. At a minimum, a mediator shall explain that confidentiality is not absolute and has exceptions. Where appropriate, the mediator may refer the parties to obtain legal advice on the extent of mediation confidentiality and privilege.
   2. A mediator shall promote understanding among the parties of the extent to which the parties will maintain confidentiality of information they obtain in a mediation.

B. Confidential information

   A mediator shall not disclose information that could adversely affect the parties' interests, show them in a bad light, or embarrass them, including:
   1. Communications made in connection with the mediation, whether before, during, or after the mediation, including communications made in separate meetings.
   2. Information regarding the conduct of the parties in the mediation.
   3. Information connecting the parties with the mediation, where the anonymity of the parties is reasonably expected.

C. Disclosure of information
   1. A mediator may disclose mediation information where the disclosure (1) does not undermine the standing of the profession and public trust in it, and (2) is consistent with the other Standards, in the following circumstances:
      (a) The parties agreed to the disclosure.

(b) The information was obtained in a private session and the disclosing party agreed to the disclosure.
(c) The disclosure is required or permitted by morality in order to prevent harm to others, or by law, either by legislation, case-law, or court order.
(d) The disclosure is required by a mediation program that referred the case to the mediator for its efficient management with regard to whether parties appeared at a mediation and whether or not the parties reached an agreement.
(e) The disclosure is made for the purpose of research, teaching, evaluation, or training, provided that the anonymity of the parties is protected as well as their reasonable expectations regarding confidentiality.
(f) The disclosure is required in connection with resolving claims between a mediator and parties.

2. A mediator shall disclose mediation information where the disclosure is morally or legally required in order to prevent a serious harm to an individual or to important public interests, and where non-disclosure, were it to come to public attention, would harm the standing of the profession and public trust in it.

11

Fairness

11.1 Introduction

Fairness is considered an important value of mediation. Jacqueline M. Nolan-Haley, for example, noted that "[t]here is little dispute that fairness is the fundamental goal of any dispute resolution process including mediation,"[1] and Ellen Waldman described fairness in her casebook on mediation ethics as an underlying value of mediation practice that influences mediators' ethical decision making.[2] However, the terms "fairness" and "unfairness" are used in numerous contexts in codes of conduct for mediators and in mediation literature without being adequately defined.[3] As a result, the meaning of statements such as "the mediator must act fairly," "the mediator should conduct a fair process," and "mediation should produce fair outcomes" remains vague. Moreover, without a clear definition of fairness these statements cannot be fully evaluated, agreed with, or rejected. This chapter briefly explains the meaning of fairness in the context of mediation for the purpose of ascertaining its implications for the ethical conduct of mediators. After distinguishing between a *norm* of fairness and a *perception* of fairness, it argues that statements about the fairness of mediation often simply mean that the mediator, the mediation process, or the mediation outcome comply with the standards of mediation practice. It then goes on to suggest several ways in which an understanding of fairness from a professional ethics perspective can contribute to the ethics of mediators: it offers guidance on the proper approach to the *interpretation* of the norms that regulate the conduct of mediators, that is, the adoption of a substantive interpretation that is grounded in reality and committed to the spirit and purpose of the norms of mediation; it provides a normative basis for an obligation of mediators (toward the profession) to follow all

1 See Nolan-Haley, "Informed Consent", 787 note 57.
2 See Ellen Waldman, *Mediation Ethics*, p. 3.
3 See Omer Shapira, "Conceptions and Perceptions of Fairness", 283–290.

the standards of mediation; and it explains the obligation of mediators (toward the public) to follow the rules of law and critical morality in the exercise of their professional role.

11.2 Understanding the meaning of fairness in mediation

For our purposes, fairness should be looked at from two perspectives: fairness as a normative term and fairness as a perception.[4] *Normative* fairness represents a norm of behavior that should be followed. Its *formal* sense is playing by the rules;[5] thus, adherence to the rules would be considered fair while breaking the rules would be considered unfair. For example, one of the rules of mediation requires mediators to act impartially. Thus, a mediator exhibiting partiality would be considered to have acted unfairly. Laurence Boulle and Miryana Nesic seem to adopt such a view in describing impartiality as "fairness towards the parties during the mediation process."[6]

Mediation is a social practice or "game." As members of society, we participate in many social games, each with its own rules. To look at mediation and its rules in isolation from other games would be to adopt a *narrow* approach to the question of fairness. Alternatively, we can adopt a *wide* perspective of fairness that takes account of the obligatory social rules that all members of society must adhere to. All members of society participate in the grand game of living in society and must respect the ground rules of law and morality in its critical sense.[7] Members of society who participate in mediation are thus subject both to the obligatory rules of society and to the rules of mediation. It follows that a mediator who conducts a mediation in an illegal or immoral manner is acting unfairly, at least from a wide perspective of fairness. Such a conception of fairness, I would argue, can explain Kevin Gibson's claim that "[w]here issues of harm to self or others are involved, the mediator cannot be neutral in the sense of disinterested; he or she has an affirmative obligation to make sure that some kinds of

4 See id., 290–304.

5 See, e.g., Brad Hooker, "Fairness" (2005) 8 *Ethical Theory and Moral Practice* 329, 329 (noting that "It is often thought that there is a kind of minimal fairness that involves interpreting and applying rules consistently-i.e., applying the same rules impartially and equally to each agent. Call this formal fairness.").

6 Boulle and Nesic, *Mediation*, p. 17.

7 See Hart, *Concept of Law*, pp. 86–87, 169–170 (discussing the special nature of legal and moral rules in comparison with other social rules). See also Hart, *Law, Liberty, and Morality*, p. 20 (discussing the difference between critical and positive morality).

settlement are questioned";[8] it is also reflected in Judith Maute's suggestion that court-connected mediators are accountable for the effect of mediation on public interests.[9]

Normative fairness has another important aspect. Sometimes mere commitment to the letter of the rules would produce a result that is divorced from their purpose. In the words of philosopher Craig L. Carr, "[i]t seems. . . that sometimes insisting upon a strict adherence to rule can actually constitute a form of unfair play."[10] A mediation party, for example, might agree to an outcome which he or she does not fully understand. Formally speaking, he or she consented to the mediated agreement and exercised his or her right to self-determination, but from a *substantive*, realist perspective his consent was illusionary; he did not exercise real self-determination and thus the process should not be considered fair from a substantive perspective of fairness.[11] Carr explains this idea of fairness by using the word fidelity: "fidelity to the game means making sure things go as they should even when the rules might work in the other direction."[12]

A different perspective of fairness concentrates on the *experience* of conduct, process, or outcome as fair or unfair. *Perceptions* of fairness concern how people perceive a social game, not how the game should (normatively) be played. For example, mediation parties may subjectively feel that the mediation was unfair (a personal sense of fairness); empirical research on the psychology of fairness may suggest the conditions under which mediation parties are more likely to perceive the process as fair (a psychological sense of fairness); and it is also possible to view the fairness of mediation from a public perspective and focus on the experience of the general public.

The variety of perspectives on fairness calls for caution in the use of the term "fairness" in the context of mediation. In fact, when one makes an assertion of fairness or unfairness with regard to the mediator's conduct, the mediation process, or the mediation outcome, it could mean any of the following statements:[13]

- The mediator's conduct, the mediation process, or the mediation outcome is in accordance with or in violation of *the rules of mediation* (a narrow-formal normative fairness claim). For example, a mediator who discloses information in breach of his or her duty of

[8] See Gibson, "Mediator Attitudes", 209. [9] See Maute, "Mediator Accountability", 358.
[10] See Carr, "Fairness", 44. [11] See Chapter 4, Section 4.3.5. [12] Carr, "Fairness", 44.
[13] For elaboration see Shapira, "Conceptions and Perceptions of Fairness", 290–304.

confidentiality can be said to have acted unfairly and conducted an unfair process because he or she departed from the confidentiality rule (standard) of mediation.

- The mediator's conduct, the mediation process, or the mediation outcome is in accordance with or in violation of *obligatory social rules of critical morality or law* (a wide-formal normative fairness claim). For example, a mediator using (illegal) violence in the course of mediation would be acting unfairly; and the use of mediation for illegal purposes would make the process unfair. The *Georgia Standards* exhibit such an approach to fairness in providing in a Fairness Standard that "[a] mediator should not be a party to an agreement which is illegal or impossible to execute,"[14] because they consider the defective outcome to be unfair.
- The mediator's conduct, the mediation process, or the mediation outcome is in accordance with or in violation of the *spirit and purpose of the rules of mediation* (a substantive normative fairness claim). For example, a mediator who ignores power imbalances between parties and allows the abuse of a weaker party does not truly respect that party's right to self-determination and thus acts unfairly and makes the process unfair; and a mediated outcome to which a party consented without understanding its meaning and implications is not a product of a true exercise of self-determination and is thus unfair. Using this sense of fairness, Jacqueline M. Nolan-Haley commented in discussing the connection between self-determination and justice in court-connected mediation that "[e]ven mediation's most favored virtue, self-determination, may be of limited value as an indicator of the justice of court mediation. Without knowledge of their legal rights, the exercise of self-determination is simply a feel-good process."[15] More generally, the Florida MEAC observed that "[w]hen forming opinions on standards of conduct, it is essential to look not only at the letter of the rules, but also at their intent."[16]
- The mediator's conduct, the mediation process, or the mediation outcome has been *subjectively perceived by the parties* as fair or unfair (a personal perceived fairness claim). For example, parties might

[14] Georgia Standards, Standard IV.A.

[15] See Jacqueline M. Nolan-Haley, "Court Mediation and the Search for Justice Through Law" (1996) 74 *Washington University Law Quarterly* 47, 87.

[16] See Florida MEAC, Opinion 2012-008 available at www.flcourts.org/core/fileparse.php/283/urlt/MEACOpinion2012-008.pdf.

perceive the mediator to have acted with partiality and thus unfairly, or feel that the process was unfair because it did not meet their needs, or that the outcome is unfair because it does not meet their expectations.[17] Kevin Gibson, Leigh Thompson, and Max H. Bazerman make that point while discussing the shortcomings of neutrality in mediation, arguing that "[w]hat is considered fair by one party may differ dramatically from what is considered fair by another, with both points of view equally convincing, yet conflicting."[18]

- The mediator's conduct, the mediation process, or the mediation outcome is *likely to be perceived* as fair or unfair on the basis of *empirical research* on the psychology of fairness (a psychological perceived fairness claim). Nancy A. Welsh, for example, argues on the basis of procedural justice research that a neutral mediator, as also a mediation process, would probably be perceived as fair if it enables the parties to have a voice;[19] and a mediated outcome is likely to be perceived as fair if it follows a fair process.[20]
- The mediator's conduct, the mediation process, or the mediation outcome is perceived or might be perceived *by the general public* as fair or unfair (a public perceived fairness claim). For example, a mediator who charges excessive fees and expenses for mediation services is acting dishonestly and would be perceived by the public as having acted unfairly;[21] a mediation process conducted by a mediator who is in a serious conflict of interest that "might reasonably be viewed as undermining the integrity of the mediation"[22] would be perceived by the public as a faulty, unfair process; and unconscionable mediated outcomes "that would not be sanctioned by society"[23] would be perceived by the public as unfair.

[17] See, e.g., Jonathan M. Hyman and Lela P. Love, "If Portia Were a Mediator: An Inquiry into Justice in Mediation" (2002) 9 *Clinical Law Review* 157, 164.

[18] See Kevin Gibson, Leigh Thompson, and Max H. Bazerman, "Shortcomings of Neutrality in Mediation: Solutions Based on Rationality" (1996) 12 *Negotiation Journal* 69, 75.

[19] See Nancy A. Welsh, "Making Deals", 792. See also Paula M. Young, "Take It or Leave It. Lump It or Grieve It: Designing Mediator Complaint Systems that Protect Mediators, Unhappy Parties, Attorneys, Courts, the Process, and the Field" (2006) 21 *Ohio State Journal on Dispute Resolution* 721, 782–783.

[20] See Nancy A. Welsh, "Perceptions of Fairness in Negotiation" (2004) 87 *Marquette Law Review* 753, 761.

[21] See Alabama Code, Standard 8(a). [22] See Model Standards, Standard III.E.

[23] See Gibson, "Mediator Attitudes", 209.

11.3 Mediators' duty of fairness

11.3.1 Fairness toward mediation parties: an expectation that mediation be conducted in accordance with its standards

The discussion on the meaning of fairness in mediation can now be implemented in regard to the conduct of mediators. A mediator's duty to conduct a fair process means first and foremost *an obligation to conduct mediation in accordance with the standards that apply to mediation*. This duty follows from the legitimate expectation of mediation parties that mediators abide by those standards of practice that are commonly acceptable in mediation practice and follow from the definition and nature of mediation.[24] It is a legitimate expectation of *normative* fairness, i.e., the parties are entitled to expect that the process is conducted according to its rules.

In addition, it is argued that mediation parties expect mediators to *interpret and apply the standards of mediation in accordance with their substantive, realist meaning*, that is, they expect substantive rather than formal fairness. It is reasonable to assume that mediation parties expect mediators to truly respect their rights and that they would not be satisfied with a formal exercise of rights that does not fulfill the spirit and purpose of the standards. For example, parties legitimately expect mediators to obtain their *informed* consent to decisions they make,[25] and they reject a formal conception of impartiality and legitimately expect mediators to intervene in the process in certain circumstances, for example, to prevent a grossly unfair or unconscionable agreement.[26]

The mediator's duty to conduct the mediation fairly (i.e. to follow the standards of mediation in accordance with the parties' expectations) falls into three subcategories that may overlap. First is a duty of the mediator to conduct *him or herself* according to the standards of mediation. For example, a fair mediator respects the parties' right to self-determination, conducts the mediation with impartiality and honesty, and avoids disclosure of confidential information. Second is a duty to maintain *process fairness*, that is, taking steps to ensure that the standards of mediation are followed in the course of mediation. For example, the mediator must take

24 See Chapter 3, Section 3.7 (The mediator-parties relationship).

25 See Shapira, "Conceptions and Perceptions of Fairness", 298–299 (discussing the substantive meaning of self-determination in the writings of Joseph Stulberg and Jacqueline M. Nolan-Haley).

26 See id., 304–310 (suggesting a substantive interpretation and application of the principle of mediator impartiality).

appropriate steps to enable the parties to exercise their right to self-determination, and refrain from conducting a mediation where the case is unsuitable for mediation or where one of the parties does not cooperate with the mediator. And third is a duty to prevent an unfair mediation *outcome*, that is, an outcome that is inconsistent with the standards of mediation. For example, the mediator must not allow the mediation to conclude with an agreement that the parties have not consented to in accordance with the standard of self-determination.

11.3.2 Fairness toward the profession, the public, and an employer or principal: an expectation that mediation be conducted without causing harm to the institution of mediation, to important social interests, and to the standing of the employer or principal

The duty to act with fairness, which is primarily a duty to follow the standards of mediation, is a duty owed to nonparties as well as to the mediation parties. Chapter 3 discussed the expectations of the mediation profession, the public, and mediators' employers and principals that mediators conduct mediations in accordance with the rules of mediation. The *profession* expects mediators to follow mediation rules because the failure of some mediators to do so would give them an advantage over rule-abiding mediators, and because departure from the rules might undermine the standing of the profession and public trust in it; the *public* has that expectation because one's choice to conduct mediations establishes a public commitment on his part to follow the rules of mediation; and *employers and principals* have that expectation because a breach of mediation rules might jeopardize their standing. Thus, from a professional ethics perspective, a mediator should ask him or herself whether his or her conduct is fair toward the profession, the public, and his or her employer or principal, as well as to the parties. In practice, this would require him to ensure that his or her conduct complies with his or her various obligations toward the profession, the public, and his or her employer or principal, for example with the standards of Maintaining the Standing of the Profession (protecting the institution of mediation for the benefit of the profession and the public),[27] Professional Integrity (seeking the prevention of process abuse or substantial defects in the process for the benefit of the profession and the public, as well as the parties),[28] and Obligations toward Employers or Principals (making compliance with employers' or principals' rules and

[27] See Chapter 12. [28] See Chapter 8.

maintaining the employers' or principals' standing an issue of fairness).[29] As these standards are part of the rules of mediation that all mediators are expected to follow, complying with them is therefore another expression of mediators' duty to fairly conduct mediations.

It follows that mediators' duty of fairness toward mediation parties is affected and shaped by the expectations of the mediation profession, the public, and mediators' employers or principals. Their expectations, that mediators conduct mediations without harming their legitimate interests, go beyond the parties' expectations and inject additional meaning into mediators' duty of fairness. They require mediators to respect *social norms* that mediation parties do not necessarily expect mediators to follow. They commit mediators to a wide perspective of fairness (an adherence to rules of law and critical morality) and to maintaining a public *perception* of fairness, which are vital for the protection of the interests of the profession, the public, and employers or principals. For example, the parties might agree on an illegal solution to the conflict, which in their view promotes their interests. However, an illegal mediation outcome jeopardizes the standing of the profession and process of mediation (in breach of the standard of Maintaining the Standing of the Profession), undermines the rule of law (in breach of the standards of Fairness and Professional Integrity), and devaluates the standing of the mediator's employer or principal (in breach of the standard of Obligations toward Employers or Principals). Thus, an illegal outcome is inconsistent with the standards of mediation; it is therefore unfair and the mediator must take steps to prevent such a mediation outcome.[30]

It is worth noting that the expectations of mediation parties that mediators interpret and apply the rules of mediation in a substantive-realist manner receive support from the expectations of the mediation profession, the public, and mediators' employers or principals. A formal interpretation and application of rules by mediators that is divorced from reality could harm the standing of the profession and process of mediation (i.e. the institution of mediation) and the standing of employers and principals, as well as the parties.

11.4 Conclusion

Mediators' duty of fairness reflects a normative sense of fairness that instructs mediators on how mediations should be conducted. Fairness

[29] See Chapter 14. [30] See Chapter 8, Section 8.2.4.3(a).

can also be understood as a perception, which describes, for example, mediation parties' experience of mediation processes in which they participated, the findings of empirical research on what constitutes fair mediation in the eyes of mediation participants, and the public's view of mediation.

Mediation fairness as a normative concept means an adherence to the standards of mediation. Thus, conducting mediations fairly requires mediators to be familiar with the standards of mediation and follow them. Since the standards of mediation include the legitimate expectations of mediation parties, the profession, the public, and employers or principals, a duty of fairness refers to compliance with all these expectations and is not limited to the expectations of the parties alone.

Mediators discharge their duty to conduct a fair *process* when they conduct mediations in accordance with the standards of mediation. For example, they conduct a fair process when they act with competence and impartially and maintain confidentiality. Mediators discharge their duty of fairness with regard to mediation *outcomes* when they conduct mediation processes whose outcomes do not violate the standards of mediation and terminate mediations whose outcomes are inconsistent with mediation standards. For example, mediators protect the fairness of outcomes by taking steps to prevent mediated outcomes that are coerced, uninformed, illegal, or unconscionable.

A further meaning of mediation fairness is that mediators employ a substantive-realist rather than a formal-technical approach to the interpretation and application of mediation standards, in accordance with the spirit and purpose of the standards. For example, they intervene to address circumstances in which parties seem to be ignorant of relevant information in order to ensure a true as opposed to formal exercise of party self-determination.

11.5 A proposed standard of fairness

A mediator shall perform his or her role fairly. Fairness means following the standards of mediation in accordance with their spirit and purpose.

12

Maintaining the profession's standing and advancement of the profession

12.1 Maintaining the profession's standing

12.1.1 Introduction

From a professional ethics perspective, every professional has an ethical duty toward his or her profession and the public to maintain his or her profession's standing and avoid conduct that could undermine it.[1] That duty applies to mediators as well, and they are expected to avoid conduct that might harm the profession and undermine public trust.[2] I consider mediation to be a profession, or a practice that is undergoing a professionalization process that justifies its treatment as a profession.[3] The profession of mediation consists of the collective of individuals who practice mediation and present themselves as mediators, organizations that represent mediators, and the mediation process as a social institution.

This view from role-morality is supported by the practice of mediation. Mediators' codes of conduct acknowledge that mediators owe obligations to their profession in provisions that refer either directly to the profession, or indirectly to the elements that make up a profession, i. e., the process that the profession is associated with and the individuals and bodies that are involved in the practice of mediation. The *Florida Rules*, for example, explicitly refer to mediators' obligation to the profession in a Rule titled "Mediator's Responsibility to the Mediation Profession," which states that "[a] mediator shall preserve the quality of the profession."[4] In addition, as the process of mediation "belongs" to the profession as well as to the parties in the sense that both have legitimate interests in the way it is conducted, codes that recognize mediators' responsibility to the *process* of mediation indirectly acknowledge a

[1] See Chapter 2, Section 2.3.3.2 and 2.4.3.
[2] See Chapter 3, Section 3.7 (The mediator–profession relationship).
[3] See Chapter 1, Section 1.1.3. [4] Florida Rules, Rule 10.600.

responsibility to the profession as well. The *Illinois Standards*, for example, state that "[t]he mediator's commitment shall be to . . . the *process*";[5] The *Florida Rules* have a Rule titled "Mediator's Responsibility to the Mediation *Process*";[6] the *California-CDRC Standards* provide that "[e]very mediator bears the responsibility of conducting mediations in a manner that instills confidence in the *process*";[7] and the *Georgia Standards* provide that "[m]ediators have an obligation to the integrity of the mediation *process*."[8] Other codes refer to the responsibility of mediators to their *colleagues*, which is another aspect of an obligation toward the profession. The *Code of Labor Mediators*, for example, provides that "[mediators] must be aware that their duties and obligations relate to . . . every *other mediator*";[9] and the *Australian Practice Standards* provide that "the Practice Standards are intended to govern the relationship of mediators with . . . their *professional colleagues*."[10]

12.1.2 The meaning of maintaining the standing of the profession

Maintaining the profession's standing means refraining from conduct that could undermine the standing of the profession in the public eye, that is, avoiding conduct that might jeopardize public faith in the profession.[11] It also means protecting the quality and integrity of the process and treating colleagues in a manner that instills public trust in the profession. The linkage between the duty to maintain the profession's standing and *public trust* in the profession brings some uncertainty to the exact meaning of the duty, because the term "public trust" is not a precise one and is sometimes difficult to assess. The use of the term is intended to reflect a *reasonable assessment* of the likely public *perception* of a mediator's conduct or of the process, and the *willingness* of the public to use mediation processes. Accordingly, the main manifestations of public trust in the profession are twofold: first, a *positive public image* of mediation – the more positive the image of the profession, the higher the degree of public faith in the profession and process; and second, the *extent of public use* of mediation services – the more use made of

5 Illinois Standards, Definition s. E (emphasis added).
6 Florida Rules, Rule 10.400 (emphasis added).
7 California-CDRC Standards, Preamble (emphasis added).
8 Georgia Standards, Standard 5 (emphasis added).
9 Code of Labor Mediators, Preamble (emphasis added).
10 Australian Practice Standards, s. 1(1) (emphasis added).
11 See Chapter 2, Section 2.3.3.2.

mediation by the public, the higher the indicated level of public trust in the profession and process. Note that the degree of use of a professional service is a suitable factor in evaluating public trust only where the public has a real choice whether to use these services or decline them. Thus, for example, public trust in most medical, legal, and governmental services cannot be evaluated by a degree-of-use test because the clients of doctors, lawyers, and governmental agencies are to a large extent captive clients who cannot manage without the professional's assistance. There is, of course, a connection between the two aspects of public trust. A positive image of the profession and process of mediation will probably contribute to greater public willingness to use mediation.

With the benefit of the above discussion, it is possible to hone the meaning of the duty of mediators to maintain the profession's standing and public trust in it. It means that mediators must *refrain from conduct that might devaluate the public perception of the mediation profession, harm the profession's image or reputation, or diminish the willingness of the public to use mediation.* This duty clearly applies to the actions of mediators in the course of conducting mediations, but in view of its rationale, there is good reason to expect mediators to similarly conduct themselves *outside* the course of practice.[12]

12.1.3 Implications of the duty to maintain the standing of the profession for the conduct of mediators

The duty to maintain the profession's standing applies to *all* of mediators' actions. This has two major consequences. First, mediators must *consider* their conduct and the decisions they make in light of their potential impact on the standing of the profession and public trust in it. For example, decisions they make on how to advertise their services, whether to accept cases, how to make interventions in the course of mediation, whether to withdraw, and whether to form a relationship with a party subsequent to a mediation are all decisions that should be taken with consideration of their possible impact on the profession of mediation.

To put it slightly differently, mediators must *interpret* the meaning of their various duties – toward the parties, the profession, the public, and their employers or principals – in a manner that enables them to command public trust. We saw, for example, that a mediator's duty to act without partiality between the parties extends to an *appearance* of

[12] Ibid.

partiality in order to protect public faith in the profession and process of mediation,[13] and that his or her duty to treat parties with respect, dignity, and honesty extends to his or her *colleagues* in order to maintain the standing of the profession.[14] I believe that this is the rationale that lies behind many provisions in codes of conduct for mediators that do not refer explicitly to the mediator's obligation to the profession, yet require the mediator to act in a manner that will protect it. For example, the *Illinois Standards* provide in a Professional Relationships Standard that "[m]ediators, whether functioning independently or as part of an organization, shall act professionally and with proper decorum at all times";[15] the *Model Standards* provide in a Conflicts of Interest Standard that "[i]f a mediator's conflict of interest might reasonably be viewed as undermining the integrity of the mediation, a mediator shall withdraw from or decline to proceed with the mediation regardless of the expressed desire or agreement of the parties to the contrary";[16] and the *Georgia Standards* provide in a Competence Standard that "[m]ediators are obligated not to undertake cases for which their training or expertise is inadequate."[17] In other words, the duty toward the profession to maintain its standing and public trust in it serves as a *limit* on the extent to which a mediator may act in his or her own personal interest, or on the requests of the parties, his or her employer, or an interested member of the public. If, for example, the parties or the employer insist that the mediator take on a case for which he or she lacks the necessary qualifications and skills, he or she must decline to do that, regardless of his or her duty to respect the parties' right to self-determination or the employer's right to issue instructions. As the professional ethics perspective shows, the coexistence of the duties toward the parties, the profession, the public, and employers shapes their content in order to enable mediators to concurrently meet all of their obligations.

The second consequence of the application of the duty to maintain the profession's standing to all mediators' actions and decisions is that potentially *any* breach of duty by the mediator (for example, acting with partiality) can turn into a breach of his or her responsibility to the profession if it is *serious* to a degree that raises a concern of loss of public faith in the profession. When a breach is not perceived by the public as serious, the public is able to distinguish between the conduct of the

13 See Chapter 7, Section 7.3.3. 14 See Chapter 9, Section 9.2.2 and 9.3.2.

15 Illinois Standards, s. V.B. 16 Model Standards, Standard III.E.

17 Georgia Standards, Standard V.

particular wanton mediator and the practice of mediators in general, and between the particular mediation in question and mediation processes in general. If this is the case, a loss of faith in the particular mediator and mediation process might occur without undermining public trust in the mediation profession and process. For example, not every potential or actual conflict of interests of a mediator and failure to disclose it to the parties will necessarily result in a loss of public trust in the profession and process of mediation. If a mediator fails to disclose that he or she once mediated a case that one of the parties was a party to, his or her conduct will probably be in violation of his or her ethical duty of disclosure. However, even though the mediator might lose the parties' trust, it is quite likely that his or her actions will not have an impact on the image and reputation of the profession of mediation in general.

On the other hand, when a mediator's conduct is perceived as a *serious* breach of duty, and as a consequence the process is perceived to be *substantively defective*, the ethical violation of the mediator could trigger a linkage between the conduct of the individual mediator and the practice of other mediators, and between the particular mediation and mediation processes in general, thereby jeopardizing public trust in the profession and process, and undermining the reputation of mediation and the public inclination to participate in mediation. For example, if a mediator were to conduct a mediation between a family relative of his or her and a stranger, this would probably be treated as a serious violation of his or herduty to avoid this type of conflict of interests and partiality that might harm the standing of the profession and put it into disrepute.[18] In such cases, the breach is serious enough to be considered a breach of the duty toward the profession, as well as a breach of duty toward the parties.

12.1.4 The duty to maintain the standing of the profession as a duty to the public

Maintaining the standing of the profession is a *public* interest as well as an interest of the profession.[19] It is in the public interest that the institution of mediation be preserved for the benefit of society. Mediators have a responsibility to the public to conduct mediations in a manner that is worthy of

[18] See Chapter 6, Section 6.4.2.1 and Chapter 7, Section 7.4.
[19] See Chapter 2, Section 2.4.3.

the public's trust and will attract people to use mediation, and in order to meet that responsibility must maintain the profession's standing.[20] If mediators conduct themselves and mediation processes in a manner that devaluates the institution of mediation, they are violating not only their obligation to the profession but to the public as well. Consider, for example, a mediator mediating a defective product case between an injured party and a large manufacturer. The parties are about to reach a confidential settlement that will enable the manufacturer to continue marketing the product in the future. What should the mediator do? A mediator who is fixed on his or her duties to the parties might think that the parties' right to self-determination can justify such a mediated outcome. However, if the mediator has reason to believe that the mediated settlement poses a threat to the wellbeing of innocent nonparticipants, he or she cannot remain passive and allow the parties to reach such an agreement. The parties might want such an agreement, which satisfies their right to self-determination, but to allow that would be to violate the mediator's duties toward the profession and the public. The duty to the profession is breached because such an agreement, if it were ever to become public, would undermine public trust in the profession and process of mediation. The duty to the public is not met because undermining public trust in the profession threatens the realization of the social interest in resolving conflicts through mediation and because the agreement is clearly immoral and threatens to harm innocent people.[21]

12.1.5 Conclusion

Mediators have an ongoing obligation toward the mediation profession to conduct themselves in a way that maintains the profession's standing and instills public trust in the profession and process of mediation. Mediators should be constantly aware of that obligation in making decisions in the exercise of their role, and make sense of their other obligations, for example their duties toward the parties, in light of that responsibility.

12.1.6 A proposed standard of maintaining the profession's standing

A mediator shall exercise his or her role in a manner that maintains the profession's standing and public trust in the mediation profession and

[20] See Chapter 3, Section 3.7 (The mediator–public relationship).
[21] See Chapter 8, Section 8.2.4.3.

process. Maintaining the profession's standing means refraining from conduct that might devaluate the public perception of the mediation profession, harm the profession's image or reputation, or diminish the willingness of the public to use mediation.

A. A mediator shall exercise his or her role and discharge his or her duties in a manner that maintains the profession's standing and is worthy of the public's trust.
B. A mediator shall refrain from conducting a mediation in a manner or in circumstances that raise a reasonable concern that the process is substantially defective.

12.2 Advancement of the profession

12.2.1 The ideal of advancing the profession

While a *duty* to maintain the profession's standing is supported by both morality of role and provisions of codes of conduct for mediators, a norm of advancing the profession does not enjoy such normative status. From a professional ethics perspective, it is easier to establish a duty to *refrain* from harmful conduct or to prevent such an outcome than to impose a duty to *act* in a beneficent manner. Advancement of the profession seems to belong to the ethics of *aspirations* that indicates values that guide professionals, rather than to the ethics of duties that sets a minimum threshold of behavior.[22] Distinguishing between duties and aspirations can be a complex task,[23] but in the case of the advancement of mediation a review of codes of conduct for mediators reveals wide agreement that positive actions that are aimed at advancing the process and profession of mediation are treated by the mediation community as aspirational rather than compulsory. Provisions on the advancement of the profession and process of mediation are often found in codes of conduct for mediators.[24] The codes commonly refer to activities that can potentially promote the profession and process of mediation and suggest that mediators *should* (as opposed to *shall*) engage in them.[25] They describe these activities using terminology

[22] See Chapter 1, Section 1.2.1.2(a). [23] See Chapter 1, Section 1.2.1.2(c).

[24] See, e.g., Model Standards, Standard IX; Alabama Code, Standard 12; Federal Employee Mediators Guide, Standard IX; Florida Rules, Rule 10.690; NY-CDRC Standards, Standard VIII.

[25] See, e.g., Model Standards, Standard IX; NY-CDRC Standards, Standard VIII.

that discloses an intention to set aspirational goals rather than impose strict obligations. Mediators, for example, are encouraged to foster diversity, strive to make mediation accessible, participate in research when given the opportunity, assist newer mediators, respect different points of view, and seek to learn from others.

12.2.2 *The meaning of advancement of the profession*

The process of mediation addresses public needs and therefore constitutes a social good. The profession of mediation represents a collective effort of those involved in the field of mediation to address these public needs and promote this social good. Advancement of the profession includes the numerous actions that can help the profession realize its goals. The theory of mediators' ethics, however, focuses on the activities in which *individual mediators* are encouraged to participate in order to advance the profession and process of mediation. Clearly, there are many other stakeholders who can and do advance mediation. For example, legislatures introduce programs of mediation into various areas; schools train staff and students in mediation; academics engage in research and teaching of mediation; mediation centers make mediation services accessible to the public and draw new mediators to the field; and mediators' organizations develop criteria for certification and professional practice. A professional ethics perspective that is focused on mediators guides mediators regarding the type of activities that *they* can initiate or be party to in order to make the process and profession of mediation successful. Generally, this would include actions that enhance the qualifications and skills of mediators, improve the quality of mediation processes, and increase public awareness of the process, the inclination to use it, and its accessibility to potential users. Code drafters suggest that mediators can help to achieve these goals by fostering diversity in the field, learning from each other,[26] making mediation accessible, by, for example, providing pro bono services or services at a reduced rate,[27] assisting research in

[26] See, e.g., Model Standards, Standard IX.B; NY-CDRC Standards, Standard VIII Comment 6.

[27] See, e.g., Model Standards, Standard IX.A.2; Florida Rules, Rule 10.690(a); NY-CDRC Standards, Standard VIII Comment 2; Oregon Standards, Standard X Comment 5; Virginia Standards, s. N.

the field,[28] promoting public awareness and appreciation of mediation,[29] and assisting newer mediators at the beginning of their career.[30]

12.2.3 A proposed standard of advancement of the profession

Advancement of the mediation profession is an ideal in the realization of which every mediator should assist. A mediator can do so in some or all of the following:[31]

A. Demonstrate respect for differing points of view within the field, seek to learn from other mediators, and work together with other mediators to improve the profession and better serve people in conflict.
B. Strive to make mediation accessible to the public, including providing services at a reduced rate or on a pro bono basis as appropriate.
C. Participate in research in the field when given the opportunity, including obtaining participant feedback when appropriate.
D. Participate in outreach and education efforts to assist the public in developing an improved understanding of, and appreciation for, mediation.
E. Assist newer mediators through training, mentoring and networking.

[28] See, e.g., Model Standards, Standard IX.A.3; Alabama Code, Standard 12; Florida Rules, Rule 10.690(c); NY-CDRC Standards, Standard VIII Comment 3; Oregon Standards, Standard X Comment 3.

[29] See, e.g., Model Standards, Standard IX.A.4; Alabama Code, Standard 12; Florida Rules, Rule 10.690(c); NY-CDRC Standards, Standard VIII Comment 4; Oregon Standards, Standard X Comment 1.

[30] See, e.g., Model Standards, Standard IX.A.5; Florida Rules, Rule 10.690(b); NY-CDRC Standards, Standard VIII Comment 5; Oregon Standards, Standard X Comment 2.

[31] This Standard largely reproduces Model Standards, Standard IX and NY-CDRC Standards, Standard VIII.

13

Advertising, solicitation, and mediator fees

13.1 Introduction

As a practical matter, it is not uncommon for mediators to advertise their services, solicit work, and charge fees. These activities will naturally increase in scope as mediation becomes more professionalized and is practiced by people who consider it their main occupation. Engaging in these marketing and business activities can raise ethical concerns that need to be addressed by a theory of mediators' ethics. Indeed, codes of conduct for mediators usually include provisions on advertising and solicitation,[1] and on mediator fees.[2] It should be noted, however, that these are not genuine or primary norms of ethical conduct, in the same sense as party self-determination, mediator competence, impartiality, and the other ethical norms discussed in the previous chapters. While the latter norms derive directly from role-morality or what I have called a perspective-from-above of mediators' ethics, advertising, solicitation, and fees are norms that derive from the actual practice of mediation as reflected in many codes of conduct for mediators, to which I have referred as a perspective-from-below of mediators' ethics.[3] While every mediator *must* respect the parties' ethical right to self-determination, must be competent to conduct the mediation, and must maintain confidentiality, advertising, solicitation of cases, and charging fees are not compulsory and mediators may decide not to engage in these activities. However, once a mediator does engage in these activities, his or her conduct need be

[1] See, e.g., Virginia Standards, s. M; Oregon Standards, Standard VIII; NY-CDRC Standards, Standard VII; Model Standards, Standard VII; Family Mediation Model Standards, Standard XII; Georgia Standards, Standard V; Florida Rules, Rule 10.610; California Rules, Rule 3.858; Alabama Code, Standard 10; ADR Canada Code, s. 8.

[2] See, e.g., Australian Ethical Guidelines, s. 9; Australian Practice Standards, s. 12; ADR Canada Code, s. 9; Family Mediation Canada Code, Article 15; Alabama Code, Standard 8; Federal Employee Mediators Guide, Standard VIII; Florida Rules, Rule 10.380; Illinois Standards, s. III.C; Family Mediation Model Standards, Standard V; Model Standards, Standard VIII.

[3] See Chapter 3, Section 3.7.

regulated by the norms of role-morality – i.e., his or her activity must conform to the norms of party self-determination, mediator impartiality, etc. – and by any particular norms regulating these activities that are contained in a particular code of conduct applicable to him or her, if any. The consistency with which many codes of conduct for mediators handle advertising, solicitation and mediator fees, together with the guidance of the norms of role-morality, makes it possible to suggest a minimum content for ethical advertising, solicitation and fees provisions that are applicable to all mediators. This chapter discusses briefly the rationale for such norms from a mediators' ethics perspective and the content of these norms.

13.2 Advertising and solicitation

13.2.1 The purpose of regulating mediator advertising and solicitation

Rules on advertising mediation services and solicitation have two main objectives: the first is to prevent deceptive and misleading practices of advertising and solicitation in order to protect potential clients of mediators from being misled and to enable them to make informed decisions on whether to appoint a mediator or hire his or her services. The *Australian Practice Standards*, for example, provide that "[t]he purpose of public statements concerning mediation processes should be to: (a) educate the public about the process in order to help the public make informed judgments and choices ... "[4] A second goal of these provisions is to prevent advertising and solicitation practices that might depreciate the image and reputation of mediation and discourage people from using mediation. In other words, they are intended to maintain the standing of the profession of mediation and public trust in it. The *Georgia Standards*, for example, provide that "[m]ediators have an obligation to the integrity of the mediation process ... It is important to the public perception of mediation that advertisements by mediators are not only accurate, clear, and truthful, but that they are in no way misleading";[5] and the Florida MEAC held that a mediator cannot use "Litigation Terminators" as his or her business name for advertising his or her mediation services because "[i]t would be misleading and untruthful to advertise the role of a mediator as a 'terminator' of the

[4] Australian Practice Standards, s. 13.1. [5] Georgia Standards, Standard V.

litigation process when that role is different from and beyond the scope of the mediator's permitted duties and responsibilities" and because it "demeans the dignity of the mediation process and the judicial system."[6]

13.2.2 The content of advertising and solicitation provisions in codes of conduct for mediators

Codes of conduct for mediators attempt to protect potential mediation parties and the profession of mediation by provisions that guide mediators to *be truthful and refrain from deception* in advertising, solicitation, or provision of information about their qualifications, experience, the type of services offered, and fees. The *Virginia Standards'* provision is typical, providing that "[a] mediator shall be truthful in advertising, solicitation, information distributed electronically through a website, or other communication about the mediator's qualifications, experience, services and fees."[7] These provisions are simply an application of the general norm of honesty[8] to the specific activities of advertising and solicitation.

Some codes elaborate on this theme of truthfulness or honesty by including a provision that prohibits mediators from making *promises as to the outcome of the mediation.* The *Oregon Standards*, for example, state that "[m]ediators do not make promises or guarantees of specific results."[9] Such a demand of mediators is justified because as a matter of definition their role does not allow them to guarantee any outcome, so any such promise would be conduct inconsistent with their duty of professional integrity, which requires them to be committed to the role of mediator.[10] Moreover, keeping that promise would most probably result in the mediator putting pressure on the parties to settle, thereby

[6] See Florida MEAC, Opinion 2011–009 available at www.flcourts.org/core/fileparse.php/283/urlt/MEACOpinion2011-009.pdf.

[7] Virginia Standards, s. M. See also NY-CDRC Standards, Standard VII; Model Standards, Standard VII.A; Family Mediation Model Standards, Standard XII; Florida Rules, Rule 10.610; California Rules, Rule 3.858(a); Alabama Code, Standard 10; ADR Canada Code, s. 8.1(b).

[8] See Chapter 9, Section 9.3.

[9] Oregon Standards, Standard VIII. See also NY-CDRC Standards, Standard VII Comment 1; Model Standards, Standard VII.A.1; Family Mediation Model Standards, Standard XII.A; California Rules, Rule 3.858(c); Alabama Code, Standard 10; ADR Canada Code, s. 8.1(a).

[10] See Chapter 8, Section 8.2.2.

losing his or her impartiality and violating his or her duty to respect party self-determination. One Florida MEAC Opinion illustrates this point in a different context. The Committee held that a mediator may not advertise the mediation services he or she provides as "a dispassionate evaluation by a neutral party" because "[m]ediation and early neutral evaluation (ENE) are two separate and distinct alternative dispute resolution processes. It is misleading for mediators to advertise that they are providing evaluation services under the guise of mediation services."[11]

Some codes apply the honesty/truthfulness norm to the issue of *mediator certification*, prohibiting mediators who have not been certified by a recognized, publicly scrutinized entity from presenting themselves as certified mediators. The *Model Standards*, for example, provide that "[a] mediator should only claim to meet the mediator qualifications of a governmental entity or private organization if that entity or organization has a recognized procedure for qualifying mediators and it grants such status to the mediator."[12] The Florida MEAC held in this context that "[i]t is misleading and inappropriate for a mediator who has completed a Florida Supreme Court mediation training but is not yet certified to advertise him/herself as Florida Supreme Court County Court 'Trained' Mediator."[13] The Missouri Bar issued an Informal Advisory Opinion holding that an attorney who has completed the training course for mediators that satisfies the requirements of the Missouri Supreme Court Rules cannot state that he or she is a "court-certified" mediator because the relevant Supreme Court Rule "does not indicate, in any way, that people who attend the required training are certified by the court."[14]

Other common code provisions on advertising and solicitation apply to these activities the norm of *impartiality*, providing, for example, that "[a] mediator should not solicit in a manner that could give an appearance of partiality for or against a party,"[15] and the norm of party

[11] See Florida MEAC, Opinion 1995–007 available at www.flcourts.org/core/fileparse.php/283/urlt/1995-Opinion-007.pdf.

[12] Model Standards, Standard VII.A.2. See also Oregon Standards, Standard VIII Comment 2; NY-CDRC Standards, Standard VII Comment 2; Family Mediation Model Standards, Standard XII.B.

[13] See Florida MEAC, Opinion 2011–010 available at www.flcourts.org/core/fileparse.php/283/urlt/MEACOpinion2011-010.pdf.

[14] See Missouri Bar, Informal Advisory Opinion 990099 available at www.mobar.org/ethics/InformalOpinionsSearch.aspx.

[15] See NY-CDRC Standards, Standard VII Comment 3. See also Oregon Standards, Standard VIII Comment 3; Model Standards, Standard VII.B.

self-determination, providing, for example, that "[a] mediator shall not communicate to others, in promotional materials or through other forms of communication, the names of persons served without their permission."[16] The rationale for maintaining public faith in the mediation profession and process is often inexplicit in the language of the codes, but is in some cases made explicit, as in the *Oregon Standards*, for example, which refer to solicitation that might "undermine the integrity of mediation as a viable process to resolve disputes,"[17] and the *Model Standards* that refer to solicitation that "undermines the integrity of the process."[18]

13.2.3 A proposed standard of advertising and solicitation

The discussion in the previous section makes it possible to suggest a standard of advertising and solicitation that may be considered ethically obligatory on mediators generally, as it is representative of the content of such provisions in major codes of conduct for mediators and is at the same time compatible with the norms of role-morality. The standard reads as follows:

A mediator may advertise his or her mediation services and solicit mediation work in accordance with these Standards.

A. A mediator shall be truthful and refrain from misleading in advertising, solicitation, or provision of information about his or her qualifications, experience, the type of services offered, and fees.
   1. A mediator shall not make any promises as to outcome.
   2. A mediator may indicate that he or she has state, national or private organization qualifications only if the entity referred to has a procedure for qualifying mediators, and the mediator has been duly granted the requisite status.

B. A mediator shall not solicit in a manner that could give an appearance of partiality for or against a party.

C. A mediator shall not list names of mediation parties served without their prior permission.

[16] See Model Standards, Standard VII.C. See also Oregon Standards, Standard VIII Comment 4; NY-CDRC Standards, Standard VII Comment 4.

[17] Oregon Standards, Standard VIII Comment 3. [18] Model Standards, Standard VII.B.

13.3 Mediator fees

13.3.1 The purpose of regulating mediator fees and other mediation charges

Mediators, like many other role-holders who provide services, may charge fees for the services rendered. Still, some mediators choose to provide mediation services for free, or are required to do so in accordance with the rules of the mediation program with which they are associated. For example, mediators who volunteer in community mediation centers are usually not remunerated for mediations they conduct, and some court-connected programs require that some cases be mediated on a pro-bono basis. Mediators do not have an ethical duty to charge fees for their work, but once they have decided to do so, their decision on the fees arrangement, its communication to the parties, and the parties' consent to that arrangement become subject to the general ethical norms applicable to all mediators and to any particular norms established by the mediation program or organization with which the mediators are affiliated. As with the standard on advertising and solicitation, the purpose of the standard on mediator fees is twofold: first, to enable mediation parties to make an informed decision on participation in the process with an understanding of the costs of the process and transparency with regard to the financial interests of the mediator in terms of remuneration. The *Kansas Ethical Standards for Mediators*, for example, typically provide that "[p]arties should be provided sufficient information about fees at the outset of a mediation to determine if they wish to retain the services of a mediator."[19] The second objective of fee standards is to guide mediators on the type of fee arrangements that are compatible with the nature of mediation and with the ethical norms that are expected of mediators, in order to prevent fee arrangements that might jeopardize the standing of the profession and public trust in the mediation profession and process. The *Alabama Code*, for example, illustrates this concern by stating that "[a] mediator occupies a position of trust with respect to the parties and the court system. In charging for services and expenses, the mediator must be governed by the same high standards of honor and integrity that apply to all other phases of the mediator's work. A mediator shall be scrupulous and honest in billing and must avoid charging excessive fees and expenses for mediation services."[20]

[19] Kansas Ethical Standards for Mediators, Standard (h).

[20] Alabama Code, Standard 8(a).

13.3.2 The content of mediator fees standards in codes of conduct for mediators

Codes of conduct for mediators correctly require mediators to provide mediation parties with information regarding their fees and other charges that the parties might incur in the course of the mediation, because that information is necessary if parties are to exercise self-determination with regard to the fees of the mediator in their case. The *Model Standards*, for example, typically provide that "[a] mediator shall provide each party or each party's representative true and complete information about mediation fees, expenses and any other actual or potential charges that may be incurred in connection with a mediation."[21] Clearly, every party has a right to know the cost of using the mediator's services.

Mediators are free to determine their fees, unless their fees are predetermined by the program of mediation with which they are affiliated. They may charge by the hour or set a fee for the entire mediation.[22] There is a consensus in the codes, however, that mediators are not permitted to charge *fees contingent upon the outcome or amount of the mediation.*[23] This type of fee arrangement is inappropriate for mediation because it places the mediator in a serious conflict of interests that could tempt mediators to pressure parties to settle, in breach of their duty to respect party self-determination. In addition, such arrangements are likely to fuel public mistrust of the profession and process of mediation, raising questions as to mediators' integrity. These concerns are recognized by some codes of conduct for mediators and mediation scholars. The *Georgia Standards*, for example, explain that rule by stating that "[i]t is imperative that the mediator have no 'stake' in the outcome";[24] Robert P. Schuwerk refers to such fee arrangements as "an agreement to allow the mediator to receive a form of compensation that compromises his neutrality and calls the process by which any

[21] Model Standards, Standard VIII.A. See also Australian Ethical Guidelines, s. 9; Australian Practice Standards, s. 12.1; ADR Canada Code, s. 9.1; Alabama Code, Standard 8(f); California Rules, Rule 3.859(b); Federal Employee Mediators Guide, Standard VIII.A; Family Mediation Model Standards, Standard V.A.

[22] See, e.g., Georgia Standards, Standard V.

[23] See, e.g., Australian Ethical Guidelines, s. 9 Comment (c); Australian Practice Standards, s. 12.3; ADR Canada Code, s. 9.2; Family Mediation Canada Code, Article 15.3; Alabama Code, Standard 8(d); California Rules, Rule 3.859(c); Federal Employee Mediators Guide, Standard VIII.B.1; Florida Rules, Rule 10.380(f); Family Mediation Model Standards, Standard V.C; Model Standards, Standard VIII.B.1.

[24] Georgia Standards, Standard V.

mediated settlement was arrived at into question," which, "if allowed, could affect the overall integrity of the mediation process";[25] and Carrie Menkel-Meadow considers such fee agreements a public injury, calling mediation as a process into question.[26]

Most codes of conduct for mediators do not refer to a right of mediators to end the mediation if the parties do not pay their fees.[27] I speculate that this is so because that right seems to the code-drafters too obvious to mention. However, an explicit acknowledgment of such a right is required because termination of mediation after the process has begun should only take place where the mediator can adequately justify his or her decision. A justification is required because a withdrawal of the mediator services could harm the parties: they may have invested time, money, and effort in the process, the mediator's termination of the mediation could take its toll emotionally and financially, and the parties will possibly have to find a new mediator and start all over again or go to court. Therefore, any termination of mediation requires a good justification, and nonpayment of mediator fees on the part of the parties can provide such justification.

Some of the rules on fee agreements that can be found in the codes are not *necessarily* derived from a professional ethics perspective. For example, the *ADR Canada Code* requires a *written fee agreement*, providing in a Fees Standard that "[t]he Mediator shall give the parties as soon as practicable after his or her appointment a *written* statement of a fee structure, likely expenses, and any payment retainer requirements."[28] Similarly, the *California Rules* provide that "[b]efore commencing the mediation, the mediator must disclose to the parties in *writing* any fees, costs, or charges to be paid to the mediator by the parties."[29] Yet other codes leave mediators' discretion as to that matter, although they tend to encourage mediators to reduce fee agreements into writing. The *Australian Ethical Guidelines*, for example, state that "[t]he better practice is to record in writing the arrangements in respect of fees and

[25] See Robert P. Schuwerk, "Reflections on Ethics and Mediation" (1997) 38 *South Texas Law Review* 757, 762–763, note 31.

[26] See Carrie Menkel-Meadow, "Ethics in Alternative Dispute Resolution: New Issues, No Answers from the Adversary Conception of Lawyers' Responsibilities" (1997) 38 *South Texas Law Review* 407, 448–451, referred to by Schuwerk, ibid.

[27] For exceptions, see, e.g., Takanot Hagishur [Hebrew], s. 8(b)(8); The Ethical Rules of the Mediation Association [Hebrew], s. 1.8.1.e.

[28] ADR Canada Code, s. 9.1(emphasis added).

[29] California Rules, Rule 3.859(b) (emphasis added). See also Florida Rules, Rule 10.380(c).

costs."[30] There is nothing in role-morality to demand written mediator fee agreements and there is no consensus in the field on that matter. On the other hand, such rules are not incompatible with the professional ethics perspective. Thus, rules that require written agreements on fees may legitimately be considered as binding upon mediators who have voluntarily *agreed* to be bound by a code that adopted such rules, but they do not form a part of the general theory of mediators' ethics that binds all mediators.

Another rule that can sometimes be found in the codes permits mediators to charge parties *unequal fees*.[31] This is a problematic rule because, as the *Model Standards* Reporters' Notes acknowledge, "unequal payments of fees almost always creates a perception of partiality,"[32] and the reason for including it in the codes is the "reality of contemporary practice in some sectors."[33] The drafters of these codes believe that disclosure of the arrangement to the parties and the exercise of caution by the mediator not to act partially are sufficient to legitimize this practice. The *Model Standards* typically provide that "[w]hile a mediator may accept unequal fee payments from the parties, a mediator should not allow such a fee arrangement to adversely impact the mediator's ability to conduct a mediation in an impartial manner."[34] This practice was discussed and reaffirmed in 2008 by the ABA Section of Dispute Resolution Committee on Mediator Ethical Guidance.[35] It is questionable, however, whether this rule and opinion satisfy the Reporters' Notes' own condition that "the Standard should require the mediator to be attentive to how that practice, even when acceptable to all parties, *impacts the integrity of the process*."[36] To rephrase the question, the question from a professional ethics perspective is whether such practice raises concerns as to the equal commitment of mediators to all the parties to a degree that is capable of undermining public trust in the profession, irrespective of the subjective belief of the individual mediator of his or her ability to conduct the

[30] Australian Ethical Guidelines, s. 9 Comment (b). See also Model Standards, Standard VIII.A.2; Australian Practice Standards, s. 12.2; Federal Employee Mediators Guide, Standard VIII.A.2; Family Mediation Model Standards, Standard V.B.

[31] See, e.g., Model Standards, Standard VIII.B.2; Oregon Standards, Standard VII Comment 1; Federal Employee Mediators Guide, Standard VIII.B.2.

[32] See Model Standards Reporter's Notes, p. 21. [33] Id., p. 20.

[34] Model Standards, Standard VIII.B.2.

[35] See ABA Section of Dispute Resolution, Committee on Mediator Ethical Guidance, Opinion 2008–4 available at apps.americanbar.org/dch/committee.cfm?com=DR018600.

[36] See Model Standards Reporter's Notes, p. 21 (emphasis added).

process impartially. It is far from clear that unequal fees practice can satisfy this test.

13.3.3 A proposed standard of mediator fees

On the basis of the discussion in the previous sections, a minimum ethical requirement of mediators with regard to fees would be as follows:

A mediator may charge fees for mediation services provided in accordance with these Standards and with any applicable institution or program rules.

A. A mediator shall discuss with the parties, before the mediation begins, the mediation fees and any charges that may be incurred in connection with the mediation.
B. Mediation fees shall not be contingent upon the outcome or amount of the mediation.
C. A mediator may terminate the mediation if the parties do not pay due fees.

14

Obligations to employers and principals

14.1 Introduction

Mediators may be self-employed, mediating cases for parties who contact them directly. These mediators are not acting on behalf of an employer or principal, and therefore have no obligations toward any such entity. Their duties are to the parties, the mediation profession, and the public, and the content of these duties has been considered in the chapters hitherto. Alternatively, a mediator might supply mediation services on behalf of an employer, for example a mediation firm, or on behalf of another entity that is not his or her employer but may be considered his or her principal (in an *ethical* rather than legal sense) because of the nature of their close relationship, for example, a community mediation center in which the mediator volunteers or a court that runs a mediation program with which the mediator is affiliated. These employers or principals legitimately expect the mediators who are connected to them to exercise their role and conduct mediations in a manner that is *worthy of their trust*, in *compliance with their instructions* (to the extent that the employer or principal issued such instructions or adopted rules with regard to the provision of mediation services), and in accordance with the *general standards applicable to mediators.*[1] To be worthy of the trust of his or her employer or principal, it has been suggested that a mediator must be competent, disclose conflicts of interests between his or her affairs and the affairs of his or her employer or principal, respect the authority (autonomy) of his or her employer or principal and obey his or her instructions, conduct him or herself with professional integrity, diligence, and impartiality between different employers or principals, treat his or her employer or principal with respect and honesty, maintain confidentiality with regard to his or her employer's or principal's matters, protect the standing of his or her employer or principal, and act fairly.[2] This chapter briefly addresses the obligations that mediators owe their

[1] See Chapter 2, Section 2.5 and Chapter 3, Section 3.7. [2] Ibid.

employers and principals on top of their duties to the parties, the profession, and the public. They are illustrated by reference to the relationship between court-connected mediators and the court, and between community mediators and the community mediation center with which they are connected.

14.2 The obligations of court-connected mediators to the court

Court-connected mediation programs are designed to reduce court caseload and delays, enable judges to devote more time to disputants, and improve the quality of justice delivered to disputants both directly through adjudication and indirectly through mediation.[3]

Mediators operate in connection with court mediation programs with varying degrees of court involvement. A court's involvement may be quite limited – merely an offer to parties to try mediation, the services themselves being offered by private mediators.[4] The court's involvement may be greater – referring parties to mediators who are employed by the court or to mediators who are on the court's list of approved mediators; or even more intensive – making the referral to approved mediators compulsory, a process sometimes termed mandatory mediation.[5]

Judges and scholars have suggested that mediators who conduct mediations in court-referred cases function to some degree as agents of the court. They perform a public role and are perceived by the public as a long arm of the court.[6] The court in *Vitakis-Valchine* v. *Valchine*, for example, considered a court-appointed mediator to be an agent of the court, holding that "[d]uring a court-ordered mediation, the mediator is no ordinary third party, but is, for all intent and purposes an agent of the court carrying out an official court-ordered function."[7] Similarly, mediation expert Wayne D. Brazil argued that "[a] mediator who works in a court-sponsored program will be viewed by the parties and their lawyers, at least in some measure, as an agent of the court,"[8] and stated more generally that "[n]eutrals in court-sponsored programs are perceived by

[3] See, e.g., Brazil, "Should Court-Sponsored ADR Survive", 246–249. [4] See id., 271–272.

[5] On mandatory mediation see, e.g., Campbell C. Hutchinson, "The Case for Mandatory Mediation" (1996) 42 *Loyola Law Review* 85.

[6] See, e.g., Finkelstein and Lifshitz, "Bargaining in the Shadow of the Mediator", 682–684; Maute, "Mediator Accountability", 348, 358.

[7] *Vitakis-Valchine* v. *Valchine*, 793 So. 2d 1094, 1099 (Fla. 4th D.C.A. 2001).

[8] Wayne D. Brazil, "Comparing Structures for the Delivery of ADR Services by Courts: Critical Values and Concerns" (1998) 14 *Ohio State Journal on Dispute Resolution* 715, 728.

litigants, lawyers, and the public generally as agents of the court—representatives of the court."[9] While these observations may not suffice to establish an agency relationship in *law*, they indicate the close relationship between mediators and referring courts that supports a view of the mediator as an agent or representative of the court from an *ethical* standpoint.

Courts with mediation programs usually adopt rules of conduct for mediators, and a few go even further and set up a procedure for reviewing complaints against mediators.[10] Still, courts have limited ability to supervise the ongoing conduct of mediators participating in their programs and must rely to a large extent on the commitment of the mediators to their role and duties. The *Alabama Code*, for example, states that "[a] mediator occupies a position of trust with respect to . . . the court system,"[11] and goes on to require in a Responsibilities to Courts Standard that "[a] mediator shall be candid, accurate, and fully responsive to a court concerning the mediator's qualifications, availability, and other matters pertinent to his or her being selected to mediate. A mediator shall observe all administrative policies, procedural rules, and statutes that apply to mediation. A mediator shall refrain from any activity that has the appearance of improperly influencing a court to secure placement on a roster of mediators or appointment to a case."[12]

Similarly, the *Florida Rules* hold that "[a] mediator shall be candid, accurate, and fully responsive to the court concerning the mediator's qualifications, availability, and other administrative matters,"[13] and "[a] mediator shall comply with all statutes, court rules, local court rules, and administrative orders relevant to the practice of mediation."[14]

Code-drafters, courts, and scholars agree that the conduct of court-connected mediators can have an impact on the public image of the court system and that this calls for certain responsibilities toward the courts. The *California Rules*, for example, declare that "[m]ediators in court-connected programs are responsible to . . . the courts for conducting themselves in a manner that merits [broad public confidence in the integrity and fairness of the process]."[15] The Rules state that one purpose of the standards of conduct for mediators adopted by the court is "to

[9] Wayne D. Brazil, "Continuing the Conversation About the Current Status and the Future of ADR: A View from the Courts" (2000) 2000 *Journal of Dispute Resolution* 11, 24.

[10] See, e.g., California Rules, Rule 3.865. See also Florida Rules, Part III.

[11] Alabama Code, Standard 8. [12] Id., Standard 2. [13] Florida Rules, Rule 10.510.

[14] Id., Rule 10.520.

[15] California Rules, Rule 3.850(a). See also North Carolina Standards, Preamble.

promote public confidence in the mediation process and the *courts*,"[16] and they instruct the mediator to withdraw "if proceeding with the mediation would jeopardize the *integrity of the court*."[17] In one ethics opinion, the Committee on Ethics of the Georgia Commission on Dispute Resolution highlighted this point while discussing the behavior expected of court-connected mediators and its rationale, holding that "[w]hile the conduct at issue in this case is never acceptable in any mediation process, it is particularly harmful in a court-mandated mediation. The parties are required to participate by the court, and the mediator serves as a representative of the court system. Vulgar, offensive and demeaning remarks are a reflection on the referring court, the local ADR program and the process of mediation in general. As was clear from the evidence in this case, parties will likely share their experience in mediation with relatives, friends and the community at large. Thus, the damaging repercussions of such behavior can extend far beyond the immediate parties involved."[18] Mediation scholar Brazil stressed the same point, commenting that "[w]hen the parties see their court-sanctioned mediator sliding out of process character just to move them closer to a deal, or when they feel their mediator pressuring them to abandon objections to proposed terms, their respect for the court fades and their cynicism about their public institutions grows."[19] He also argued that "[a] mediator who is ... viewed [as an agent of the court] must act in ways that conform to the most fundamental norms by which our judicial institutions are guided,"[20] and that "[i]f [neutrals in court-sponsored programs] perform badly, if they make process mistakes or ethical mistakes or substantive mistakes, or if their conduct is insufficiently constrained and dignified, or if they fail to follow the process protocols that the court's rules and literature lead parties to expect, they will erode public trust in the court."[21]

From a professional ethics perspective, then, the relationship that is established between a court that refers a case to a mediator for mediation,

[16] California Rules, Rule 3.850(a) (emphasis added).

[17] Id., Rule 3.855(f)(2) (emphasis added).

[18] Georgia Commission on Dispute Resolution Committee on Ethics, Opinion 2002-1, available at www.godr.org/files/Formal%20opinion%202002-1%203-23-04TP.pdf.

[19] Brazil, "Should Court-Sponsored ADR Survive", 266.

[20] Brazil, "Comparing Structures", 728. See also ibid. ("Because she is likely to be perceived as a representative of the court, a mediator must behave in ways that will foster respect for judicial institutions").

[21] Brazil, "Continuing the Conversation", 24–25. See also Wayne D. Brazil, "Hosting Mediations as a Representative of the System of Civil Justice" (2007) 22 *Ohio State Journal on Dispute Resolution* 227, 233–234.

and the mediator who conducts the mediation, justifies an expectation that the mediator act in a manner that is worthy of the court's trust. This ethical responsibility adds up to the mediator's responsibilities to the parties, the profession, and the public. The mediator is publicly perceived as connected to the court, and even as a representative of the court. The closer the relationship between the court and the mediator, the greater the likely impact of the mediator's conduct on the standing and reputation of the court and on the level of public trust in the court, and the higher the expectation of the court that the mediator conduct him or herself in a manner that will not undermine public trust in the court. Every mediator of a court-referred case must bear that responsibility in mind in the course of conducting the mediation.

14.3 The obligations of volunteering mediators to the community mediation center

The ethical analysis of the relationship between court-connected mediators and the court can be applied to other institutions in connection with which mediators supply mediation services as well. The *Code of Labor Mediators*, for example, refers to the relationship between governmental agencies that provide mediation services and mediators employed by them. It provides that "[a]gencies responsible for providing mediation assistance to parties engaged in collective bargaining are a part of government. The mediator must recognize that, as such, he is part of government. The mediator should constantly bear in mind that he and his work are not judged solely on an individual basis but that he is also judged as a representative of his agency. Any improper conduct or professional shortcoming, therefore, reflects not only on the individual mediator but upon his employer and, as such, jeopardizes the effectiveness of his agency, other government agencies and the acceptability of the mediation process."[22] In this section I focus on community mediation centers that are very widespread in the United States and in other countries, providing a great variety of mediation services to their communities through thousands of volunteering mediators who are not

22 Code of Labor Mediators, Standard 3. See also Orna Rabinovich-Einy, "Technology's Impact: The Quest for a New Paradigm for Accountability in Mediation" (2006) 11 *Harvard Negotiation Law Review* 253, 262 (arguing that "professional mediators must be held accountable to parties, providers that rely on their services, relevant regulatory authorities, and the general public for the delivery of procedurally fair mediation services that meet accepted standards of mediator performance").

paid for their work.[23] These mediators are subject to the duties discussed in the previous chapters, namely duties to the mediation parties, the mediation profession, and the public, and in addition have responsibilities toward the mediation center with which they are connected.

Mediators who choose to volunteer in community mediation centers should be praised for dedicating time and personal effort for the good of others. They should, however, realize that their involvement with the mediation program of these centers comes with responsibilities and limits their freedom of action in comparison to ordinary members of the public. Mediators who join these centers enjoy benefits and opportunities beyond those enjoyed by the general public. For example, they receive professional training, participate in continuing professional education activities arranged by the centers, accumulate mediation experience and skills that can later be utilized for attracting paying mediation clients, and enjoy the social recognition awarded to volunteers. In return, mediation centers expect the mediators to observe the center's rules and refrain from conduct that could harm the center. A center's rules are likely to be similar to the common standards that can be found in major codes of conduct for mediators, with certain variations that address local preferences as to, for example, the type of qualifications required of the mediators, the type of information that the mediators are expected to report to the center's management, mediation charges, and the (in)eligibility of mediators for mediation fees. The *NY-CDRC Standards*, for example, provide in a Competence Standard that "[a] mediator shall mediate only when the mediator has the necessary competence to satisfy the reasonable expectations of the parties and the *sponsoring organization* for which she or he mediates."[24] The mediator "should obtain the training, skills, experience in mediation, cultural understanding, and other qualities that are necessary for effective mediation,"[25] and "attend educational programs and related activities to enhance and strengthen his or her personal knowledge of and skills in the mediation process, consistent with the *sponsoring organization* for which she or he mediates."[26] The *NY-CDRC Standards* state in a Confidentiality Standard that "[a] mediator may report, pursuant to the policies of the *local center*, whether

[23] On community mediation, see generally the National Association for Community Mediation site available at www.nafcm.org/.

[24] NY-CDRC Standards, Standard IV.A (emphasis added).

[25] Id., Standard IV Comments 1 (emphasis added).

[26] Id., Standard IV Comments 3 (emphasis added).

parties appeared at a scheduled mediation and whether or not the parties reached a resolution."[27]

From a professional ethics perspective, mediators who take part in the activities of mediation centers are *representatives* of the centers. The centers have placed the mediators in a position of power vis-à-vis the users of the center's mediation services, a position that enables them, in exercising their role as mediators, to influence the affairs of the users of the center's services. The center relies on the mediators that are affiliated with its activities to exercise their power and influence in a manner that is *worthy of the center's trust*. Moreover, in the public eye, mediation centers and the mediators that conduct mediations on their behalf are connected, so that the centers are judged, inter alia, by the conduct of the mediators. Thus, mediation centers legitimately expect those mediators to act in a manner that will not undermine their *public image*. If the standing of the centers were undermined, the public would hesitate to use the centers' services, thereby jeopardizing the attainment of one of the centers' most important public missions: contributing to consensual conflict resolution and social harmony in the communities they serve.

Codes of conduct for community mediators are not as common as codes for court-connected mediators, making it more difficult to illustrate this perspective in the case of community mediation centers. One code that makes an explicit reference to the organizational setting of the provision of mediation services and its impact on the relationship between the organization and the mediators connected to it is the *Illinois Standards*. The code provides in a Professional Relationships Standard that "[m]ediators, whether functioning independently or as part of an organization, shall act professionally and with proper decorum at all times. When mediators function as employees of organizations providing mediation services or as independent mediators serving clients in an organizational context, mediators seek to support the integrity, reputation, and proprietary rights of the host organization."[28] This approach, it is submitted, is correct with respect to community mediation centers and their mediators.

From a professional ethics perspective, then, a community mediation center legitimately expects the mediators of the center to conduct themselves in a manner that *will not harm the center*. The mediation center, like mediation parties, expects the mediators to act in a manner that is worthy of trust. The question of what constitutes an unjustified infliction of harm

[27] Id., Standard V Comment 4 (emphasis added). [28] Illinois Standards, s. V.B.

on the center may sometimes be difficult to answer. In general, the mediators should not harm the economic interests of the center, its image and reputation, or public faith in the center. For example, a community mediation center might deliberate over whether to forbid volunteering mediators from handing out their personal business cards at the end of a mediation.[29] On the one hand, it is understandable that volunteering mediators would want to promote their private practice, for example their law or mediation practice, by using the exposure that their volunteering work gives them. On the other hand, the mediation center must protect the public perception of the center as a public body that operates for the public benefit on the basis of social rather than profit considerations. Volunteers who use the center's activities (such as mediations) for solicitation of work for personal gain jeopardize the center's public image and reputation as a nonprofit organization operating for the benefit of the community, and send a confusing message to the center's "clients" and the public that the center has business interests as well. The mediation center, therefore, might choose to adopt a rule that prohibits self-solicitation by, for example, handing out business cards to the mediation parties.

14.4 Conflicting duties

A mediator's duties toward his or her employer or principal should be considered as complementing his or her duties toward the parties, the profession, and the public rather than replacing or superseding them. A mediator's employer or principal cannot legitimately expect the mediator to act in breach of his or her obligations toward the parties, the profession, and the public, because by allowing the mediator to provide mediation services in connection with the employer or principal, the latter impliedly accepts that the mediator shall act "as a mediator" in accordance with the standards that apply to mediators, that is, consistent with his or her ethical duties toward the parties, the profession, and the public.

Some court-connected codes of conduct for mediators explicitly endorse this idea. The *North Carolina Standards*, for example, provide that "[t]he mediator shall place the interests of the parties above the interests of any court or agency which has referred the case, if such interests are in conflict."[30] Similarly, the *Florida Rules* state that

[29] This issue was discussed in Kiryat-Ono Community Mediation Center Ethics Forum, Opinion 1-2012 (on file with the author).

[30] North Carolina Standards, Rule VII.A.

"[a] mediator is accountable to the referring court with ultimate authority over the case. Any interaction discharging this responsibility, however, shall be conducted in a manner consistent with these ethical standards."[31] The *Florida Rules* also remind the mediator that "[w]hether the parties involved in a mediation choose to resolve their dispute is secondary in importance to whether the mediator conducts the mediation in accordance with these ethical standards."[32]

The Florida MEAC Opinions on cases involving a possible clash between the mediator's duty to abide by the court's instructions and his or her other duties are instructive. In one opinion, for example, the MEAC stated that "[w]hen a mediator receives a court order in advance of a mediation, which contains provisions which are contrary to the mediator's role and requires the mediator to act in a manner that is inconsistent with the mediator's ethical rules, the mediator should decline participation in the mediation."[33] In another opinion, the committee held that "if a mediator believes a court is asking the mediator to violate the mediator's Standards of Professional Conduct, the mediator shall decline to do so."[34] From a professional ethics perspective, the mediator's duties toward his or her employer or principal add another layer of responsibility to the responsibilities he or she already has toward the parties, the profession, and the public. Ordinarily, these responsibilities will overlap and complement each other because they often serve common interests. It is the employer's or principal's interest that the mediator comply with his or her duties to the parties, the profession, and the public, because such compliance is essential for maintaining the standing of the employer or principal, that is, for maintaining his or her reputation, attracting potential clients to use his or her services, and instilling public trust in him or her. Thus, an employer or principal cannot relieve the mediator of any of his or her responsibilities. However, he or she may choose to *intensify* them. For example, an employer or principal might adopt rules prohibiting the acceptance of any gifts or any solicitation of work that are *stricter* than the rules sanctioned by the relationship of trust between the mediator and the parties and the need to maintain the standing of the profession.

31 Florida Rules, Rule 10.500. 32 Id., Rule 10.200.

33 Florida MEAC, Opinion 2004–006 available at www.flcourts.org/core/fileparse.php/283/urlt/MEAC-Opinion-2004–006.pdf.

34 Florida MEAC, Opinion 2010–012 available at www.flcourts.org/core/fileparse.php/283/urlt/MEACOpinion2010-012.pdf.

14.5 Conclusion

A mediator exercising a mediator's role as an employee, an agent, or a representative must meet all his or her ethical responsibilities to the mediation parties, the mediation profession, and the public. A mediator in such a capacity has additional obligations toward his employer or principal, requiring him to ensure that his conduct is consistent with the rules of his employer or principal and does not undermine the employer's or principal's standing. These obligations do not justify a breach of duty toward the parties, the profession, or the public, but can supplement them with additional obligations (in the form of rules or instructions issued by the employer or principal) or support an interpretation of the duties that enables the mediator to maintain the standing of the employer or principal.

14.6 A proposed standard of obligations to employers and principals

A mediator exercising the role of a mediator as an employee, agent, or representative of another, such as a mediation center, mediation program, court, or organization, shall exercise his or her role consistent with the rules of his or her employer or principal, in a manner that will not undermine the employer's or principal's standing and public trust in it, and in accordance with these Standards. Maintaining the employer's or principal's standing means refraining from conduct that might devaluate the public perception of the employer or principal, harm the employer's or principal's image or reputation, or diminish the willingness of the public to receive mediation services from the employer or principal.

A. A mediator shall exercise his or her role and discharge his or her duties in a manner that is worthy of his or her employer's or principal's trust.

   To be worthy of the trust of his or her employer or principal, a mediator must be competent, disclose conflicts of interests between his or her affairs and the affairs of his or her employer or principal, respect the authority (autonomy) of his or her employer or principal and obey his or her instructions, conduct him or herself with professional integrity, diligence, and impartiality between different employers or principals, treat his or her employer or principal with respect and honesty, maintain confidentiality with regard to his or her employer's or principal's matters, protect the standing of his or her employer or principal, and act fairly.

B. A mediator shall observe and interpret his or her employer's or principal's rules and instructions in a manner consistent with the Standards.

PART III

Dealing with ethical problems

15

Ethical decision-making

15.1 Introduction

Parts I and II laid down a theory of professional ethics, applied it to the role of mediators, and extrapolated a reasoned list of ethical standards to regulate the conduct of mediators. Chapter 3 posited the foundations for analyzing ethical problems in mediation, providing a prism for understanding the content and meaning of the ethical standards that apply to mediators, drawing attention to the coexisting relationships that mediators have with the mediation parties, the mediation profession, the public, and sometimes an employer or principal, and pointing to the mutual influence that the standards exert on one another following these relationships. Chapters 4–14 elaborated on the meaning and content of mediators' ethical standards, demonstrating the process for ascertaining the standards' meaning and content, and yielding a *Proposed Model Code of Conduct for Mediators.*[1]

Part III takes this project a step further. It seeks to demonstrate how these standards can be utilized by mediators in the practice of mediation. The exercise of the mediator's role necessitates decision-making by mediators. Decisions have to be made with respect to various aspects of the process, such as the time and place of the mediation, types of interventions, postponement, withdrawal and termination, information disclosed to parties and nonparties, and so on. These decisions can be evaluated through the lens of professional ethics, so that the ethical norms provide behavioral guidelines for mediators.

The present chapter describes, in general terms, what ethical decision-making is, in order to provide mediators with tools for making ethical decisions. It stresses the importance of ethical sensitivity, elaborates on the features of easy and hard cases or questions in mediation, and provides mediators with an ethical decision-making procedure for making decisions in both "easy" and hard cases. The next chapter then takes a

[1] See Appendix I.

more concrete and contextualized approach and demonstrates how the theory of mediators' ethics and ethical decision-making can be applied to various scenarios that raise ethical questions for mediators.

15.2 On ethical decision-making

Ethical decision-making is a process by which decisions or choices are made on the basis of ethical norms. It should be a rational and informed process, based on reflection, careful consideration of facts and norms, and logical application of the relevant norms to factual situations. Intuitions are important for the purpose of making ethical decisions, but must not be allowed to replace reasoned judgment and consistency. Ethical determinations must never be arbitrary; they require justifications based on general considerations that go beyond the circumstances of a particular case.

James Rachels and Stuart Rachels, for example, explain that "moral judgments must be backed by good reasons; and [that] . . . morality requires the impartial considerations of each individual's interests."[2] They note that "[t]he morally right thing to do is always the thing best supported by the arguments."[3] Michael S. Pritchard develops the idea of justification as part of ethical thinking. He says that justification requires good reasons, and "[g]ood reasons are reasons one is willing to commend to others."[4] In addition, he says that "one's reasons must be generalizable to similar situations," which is a kind of impartiality requirement.[5] Frederic G. Reamer, writing on social work ethics, suggests that codes of ethics, ethical theories, and ethical principles can help practitioners make ethical decisions.[6] However, he observes that "[n]o precise formula for resolving ethical dilemmas exists. Reasonable, thoughtful social workers can disagree about the ethical principles and criteria that ought to guide ethical decisions in any given case. But ethicists generally agree that it is important to approach ethical decisions systematically, to follow a series of steps to ensure that all aspects of the ethical dilemma are addressed."[7]

In the context of mediation practice, Ellen Waldman in her book on mediation ethics argued that "[a]dopting a practical approach to mediation ethics requires recognizing that value compromises and trade-offs are an

[2] Rachels and Rachels, *Moral Philosophy*, p. 10. [3] Id., p. 11.
[4] Pritchard, *Professional Integrity*, pp. 26–27. [5] Id., p. 27.
[6] Reamer, *Social Work Values*, pp. 43–72. [7] Id., p. 73.

integral part of doing ethics in this field."[8] Waldman followed philosopher W. D. Ross's approach, which maintains that there are no absolute duties, therefore conflicting duties need to be weighed and balanced upon consideration of all the circumstances. She observed that this approach is intuitive and fluid, saying that "Ross didn't think there was any magic to the process of weighing and balancing the competing values at stake. No one rule could be laid down as to how to do it – other than to think hard and carefully about what is at stake and which duties seem most pressing under the circumstances."[9] Julie Macfarlane suggested that mediators should adopt a reflective-practice approach to ethical decision making, arguing that "[t]he outcomes of ethical judgments by mediators must be supported by the reasoned and contextual perspective of that mediator and that mediation."[10] The reflective-practice approach, according to Macfarlane, "focuses on teasing out the values and assumptions behind the choices often made intuitively by mediation practitioners when they face ethical dilemmas in the course of their practice and the values they imply. These values can then be debated, critiqued, and diversified across different frames of action."[11]

I agree with Waldman, Macfarlane, and other mediation scholars[12] who argue that mediation ethics cannot rely on abstract principles alone, and must be contextualized, grounded in the particularities of mediation cases. I do believe, however, that more structure must be brought into mediation ethical analysis if we want to give mediators practical tools for engaging in ethical decision-making. I would argue that ethical decision-making can sometimes be straightforward, although at other times quite difficult. Frequently, the norms of ethics provide sufficient guidance for mediators. There are "easy" cases that raise no difficulty because the outcome of applying the norms to the facts of the case is clear. Other cases may prove more difficult because the application of the norms does not yield a clear-cut result. This

[8] Waldman, *Mediation Ethics*, p. 6. [9] Id., p. 9.

[10] Macfarlane, "Mediating Ethically", 71. [11] Id., 74.

[12] See, e.g., Menkel-Meadow, "Ethics in Alternative Dispute Resolution"; Brad Honoroff and Susan Opotow, "Mediation Ethics: A Grounded Approach" (2007) 23 *Negotiation Journal* 155; Rachael Field, "Rethinking Mediation Ethics: A Contextual Method to Support Party Self-Determination" (2011) 22 *Australasian Dispute Resolution Journal* 8; Samantha Hardy and Olivia Rundle, "Applying the Inclusive Model of Ethical Decision Making to Mediation" (2012) 19 *James Cook University Law Review* 70.

may be so for various reasons: the facts of the case may be unclear, which ethical norms are relevant may be uncertain, the content of the relevant ethical norms may be vague and open to several interpretations, the norms may allow a number of possible ethical courses of action to choose from, or the norms may mandate conflicting courses of action that cannot be reconciled. Mediators, like other role-holders, sometimes find themselves involved in such hard cases. They then have to make a choice among different possible courses of action. The alternative courses of action will follow from a process of fact-determination, identification of the relevant ethical norms, interpretation of the norms, and balancing and weighing of the norms or of the alternative courses of action (thereby giving more weight to one ethical norm or one course of action over another).

Figure 15.1 and the accompanying discussion are aimed at providing mediators with milestones for making ethical decisions in the course of exercising their role.

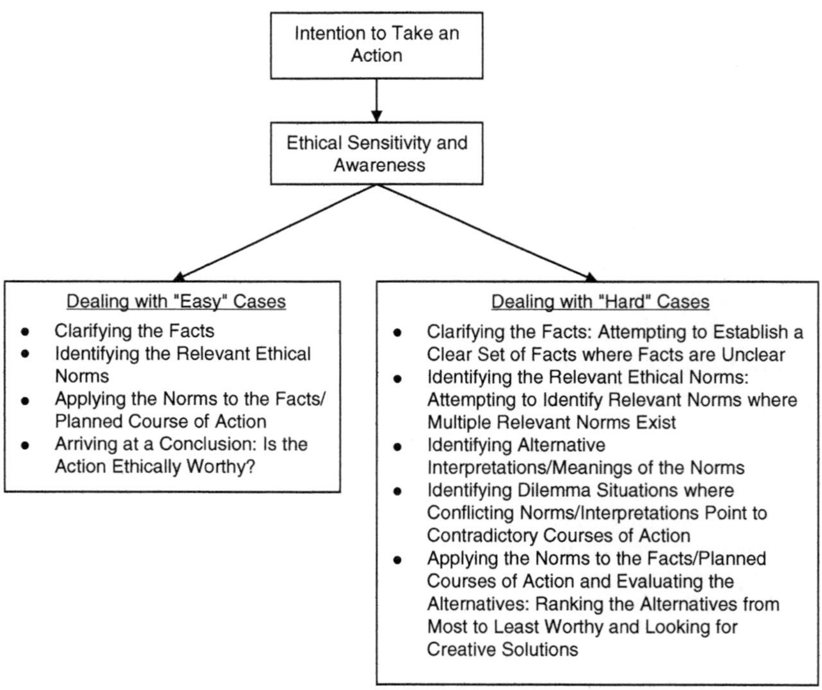

Figure 15.1: Ethical decision-making

15.3 Ethical questions and ethical sensitivity

15.3.1 Ethical questions

Generally, ethical questions are questions about the right thing that role-holders should do from a professional ethics perspective. Such questions typically arise when a role-holder intends to take an action in the course of exercising his or her role, or in response to actions taken by others, for example clients. Mediators, for example, might ponder over the right intervention, in an ethical sense, in circumstances when one party is intimidating another party in order to make him or her agree to his terms of settlement.

One might think that it is possible to distinguish between ethical questions and technical, practical, or professional questions. In fact, such distinctions are very hard to maintain. Macfarlane, for example, observed that "[m]ediators must constantly choose which types of intervention techniques and strategies they will use" and went on to consider whether "all such choices raise questions of ethics."[13] In discussing that topic, she illustrated the problem in the following way: "[s]ome choices appear to be functional; for example, whether to use a round table or a rectangular one. Other choices are apparently dictated by practical circumstances; for example, can the first meeting between the parties be scheduled in the evening, as the plaintiffs prefer? Yet others are simply expedient; for example, what should a mediator do to silence Party A in order to prevent Party B from leaving?"; she then observed that "this distinction may not be very helpful in the context of mediation. Even the most mundane and mechanical decisions have a habit of turning into issues of principle in the volatile climate of conflict . . . Even the design of the meeting table may convey an important message about the values of the mediation process . . . The mediator makes innumerable choices while managing the process and interaction between the parties, and these choices go to the root of the values that the mediation process espouses. Accordingly, each time an intervention is made, there is at least the potential for a principled choice that seeks either consciously or unconsciously to promote those values."[14] Macfarlane, then, seems to believe that ethical decision-making by mediators relates to decisions which may initially be perceived as merely functional or technical.

Experts on professional ethics, writing on the ethics of engineers, have made similar claims. Michael Davis, for example, argued that "insofar as

[13] Macfarlane, "Mediating Ethically", 57–58. [14] Ibid.

the distinction between 'ethical standard' and 'technical standard' suggests that technical standards have nothing to do with ethics, the distinction is misleading. For any profession, part of acting ethically is satisfying technical standards";[15] and Robert J. Baum commented that "ethical judgments can be made about *every* decision; thus, it is misleading to describe any decision as 'ethical' (or 'moral') if this is intended to distinguish it from decisions that are (mistakenly) considered to be *purely engineering* – legal, economic, or scientific."[16]

In my view, mediators engaging in ethical analysis of decisions they intend to make in the course of mediation are likely to find the theory of mediators' ethics a valuable source of guidance. The distinction between an ethical decision and a technical, practical, or professional decision is of not much importance, because almost any decision mediators make may be subjected to an ethical evaluation. Of course, such an evaluation need not result in the imposition of an ethical duty on the mediator to take a certain action; it could point to an ideal or aspiration that the mediator is merely encouraged to pursue.[17] But either way, mediators can benefit from an ethical reflection on their choices.

15.3.2 Intention to take an action

An ethical decision-making process begins when a mediator is deliberating over whether an action he or she is about to take is "right" in an ethical sense, or when he or she is already in the course of taking an action and is deliberating whether it would be right to continue with it. For example, a mediator might reflect on whether it would be ethical for him or her to take on a mediation case in the first place, or consider the appropriateness of continuing with the mediation after it has begun.

15.3.3 Ethical sensitivity and awareness

Ethical decision-making rests on ethical sensitivity to and awareness of circumstances that give rise to ethical questions and dilemmas.[18]

15 See Davis, *Thinking Like an Engineer*, p. 115.

16 See Robert J. Baum, "Engineers and the Public: Sharing Responsibilities", in Wueste, *Professional Ethics*, p. 122 (emphasis in the original).

17 See Chapter 1, Section 1.2.1.2.

18 See, e.g., Alice Woolley and Sara L. Bagg, "Ethics Teaching in Law School" (2007) 1 *Canadian Legal Education Annual Review* 85, 94–95 (discussing moral sensitivity and arguing that "[m]oral sensitivity can be understood as a basic awareness of how our

Mediators should be alert to the fact that by exercising their role they affect others and that ethics might have something to say about the appropriateness of their actions. It is important, therefore, that mediators be familiar with the standards of ethics that apply to them. Davis, for example, stated the obvious by commenting that "[a] code of ethics cannot actually guide conduct unless those to be guided know the code . . . Education is probably the primary means by which a profession puts its code into practice."[19] This could be a weakness of the field of mediation. Kimberlee Kovach argued that "[t]he subject of ethics has generally been part of the basic mediation training, but is often considered as filler or merely an afterthought."[20] As a result, the ability of mediation practitioners to recognize an ethical problem and respond to it suffers. Kovach claimed that "[t]he need for mediators to immediately recognize ethical dilemmas is imperative. [However] [i]n discussions with colleagues about ethical cases, many report that the mediators were unaware that an ethical dilemma or situation had arisen."[21] She went on to suggest that mediators should receive training and education focusing solely on mediator ethics.[22] Another mediation expert, Charles Pou, supports this message, writing about the "need to find better ways of sensitizing mediators . . . to their ethical obligations to the field and to parties. Moreover, efforts should focus on preparing neutrals to recognize dilemmas and to avoid or deal with them in 'real time'."[23]

15.4 Easy cases/questions

Sometimes the relevant norms of ethics that guide a mediator in the exercise of his or her role are easily recognized, their content and meaning are clear, and their application to the circumstances yields a single course of action. In such cases it can be said that the mediator is facing an

actions may affect others' welfare"). See also Donald Buckingham, "Rules and Roles: Casting Off Legal Education's Moral Blinders for an Approach that Encourages Moral Development" (1996) 9 *Canadian Journal of Law and Jurisprudence* 111, 121–122 (applying the concept of moral sensitivity to legal education).

19 Davis, *Thinking Like an Engineer*, p. 112.

20 Kimberlee K. Kovach, "Musings on Idea(l)s in the Ethical Regulation of Mediators: Honesty, Enforcement and Education" (2005) 21 *Ohio State Journal on Dispute Resolution* 123, 161. See also Charles Pou, "'Embracing Limbo': Thinking About Rethinking Dispute Resolution Ethics" (2003) 108 *Penn State Law Review* 199, 204.

21 Kovach, "Musings on Idea(l)s", 153.

22 Id., 161. See also id., 155–160 (discussing teaching methods of mediator ethics).

23 Pou, "'Embracing Limbo'", 204.

easy case that raises no real difficulty in an ethical sense. For example, when a mediator is asked by one mediation party about statements made by the other party in caucus he or she must decline to answer unless the other party consents to the disclosure. The guidance of the norm of confidentiality on the right choice by the mediator is very clear. It is suggested that in making an ethical decision the mediator should go through the following stages:

15.4.1 Clarifying the facts

Ethical decision-making requires a clear understanding of the facts on which the decision is based. When the facts are not clear the case becomes hard to decide, or even worse, it may lead to wrong conclusions. For example, if the mediator in a divorce case suspects family violence, the clarification of this fact is crucial to making appropriate decisions on the design and conduct of the mediation. It is difficult to guide mediators in advance on the criteria for identifying the relevant facts of a case, as these will vary in accordance with the ethical issue in question. The relevant facts of a case may include, for example, the capacity of the parties to understand the process, legal representation of the parties, and the existence of an applicable code of conduct for mediators or a legal privilege provided by state laws.

15.4.2 Identifying the relevant ethical norms

The conduct of mediators is regulated by a large number of norms. Mediators therefore have to identify those ethical norms that are relevant in the circumstances of any particular case. In some cases, recognizing the relevant norms may be straightforward. For example, non-mandatory mediations are conducted on the premise that the parties voluntarily participate in the mediation. The mediator is therefore expected, as is consistent with the ethical norm of party self-determination, to tell the parties that they are free to leave the mediation at any time. The ethical norms that apply to mediators have been discussed in Part II and are summarized in the *Proposed Model Code of Conduct for mediators*. In addition, a mediator who is subject to a code of conduct by virtue of his affiliation with a mediation court program or a mediators' professional organization, should consult that code as well.

15.4.3 *Applying the norms to the facts and arriving at a conclusion*

When the meaning of the relevant norms is clear the norms can be immediately applied to the facts or to any planned course of action, and lead to a conclusion according to which the considered action is either ethically permissible or prohibited. If the planned action is unethical, the mediator must refrain from taking that action and modify it. For example, if an acquaintance of a mediator inquires as to the behavior of a mediation party in the course of the mediation, the mediator must refuse to disclose the information because such disclosure would clearly be in breach of his or her ethical duty of confidentiality. It is an easy case or question because we can see no legitimate good reason for the disclosure that could challenge the norm of confidentiality in mediation.

15.5 Hard cases/questions and dilemmas

Difficult cases or questions are bound to come up in any professional setting. Pritchard, for example, writes that "[n]o doubt many cases will be straight-forwardly analyzable as morally acceptable or unacceptable. However, more challenging cases require the exercise of interpretative and critical skills."[24] What makes a case or question "hard," and how mediators should approach it and make right ethical choices are discussed below.

15.5.1 *Indeterminacy of* facts: *attempting to establish a clear set of facts where facts are unclear*

As noted, ethical decision-making is a logical process based on facts. The determination of the facts is highly important because different sets of facts will produce different outcomes. For example, if the mediator has been appointed by a court (factual scenario A), the standards applicable to the mediator's conduct might vary in comparison with a mediator who has been hired by the parties directly, with no involvement of a court (factual scenario B). When there is disagreement about the facts of a case it is difficult to arrive at a clear decision on the ethical course of action, because each set of facts might point to a different course of action. Again, consider the following scenarios: a mediator who knows that one mediation party is lying to the other party with regard to a material

[24] Pritchard, *Professional Integrity*, p. 25.

fact (scenario A) will have an ethical responsibility to take an action to prevent a mediated agreement based on the misrepresentation,[25] while a mediator who has no reason to suspect such misrepresentation will not have to make such a decision (scenario B).

15.5.2 Uncertainty as to the identity *of the relevant ethical norms: attempting to identify relevant norms where multiple norms exist*

Ethical decision-making requires the mediator to apply ethical norms to the facts of a given case. However, identifying the relevant norms out of the many available and having to *choose* those that are relevant to the case in question may prove difficult. What are, for example, the relevant ethical norms that should be applied to circumstances in which a mediation party exhibits difficulty in presenting his or her case? Is it the standard of Party self-determination that is relevant? Is Impartiality a relevant norm here? Is it a matter of Fairness? Are all these norms of relevance? Are there any available Ethical Opinions on similar issues?[26] The range of norms and the need to choose between them (and later balance or reconcile them) creates complexity, and the choice of norms could sometimes justify different courses of action. Again, there are no easy guidelines for recognizing the relevant ethical norms. The exercise of common sense is inevitable and the benefit of ethical training and experience cannot be overstated. A solid familiarity with the ethical norms of mediation practice could be helpful in that regard, and the *Proposed Model Code of Conduct for Mediators* supplies mediators with a list of the norms and their meanings that they can consult.

15.5.3 Ambiguity of the norms' content: *identifying alternative interpretations or meanings of the norms*

Ethical norms that are easily identifiable may still be ambiguous in content. Moreover, normative ambiguity can give rise to alternative, sometimes even contradictory, interpretations of the relevant norm or norms, requiring the mediator to identify the possible interpretations and choose between them and between corresponding alternative

25 See Chapter 8, Section 8.2.4.2; Chapter 9 Section 9.3.3.

26 See, e.g., National Clearinghouse for Mediator Ethics Opinions available at www.americanbar.org/directories/mediator_ethics_opinion.html for a potential source for ethical opinions in mediation.

courses of action. For example, how should a decision on the mediation agenda be made? Should the mediator make that decision alone, as the manager of the process, or should it be left to the parties to make with the assistance of the mediator? The mediator may correctly recognize the standard of party self-determination as a relevant norm to be applied in that case, but face difficulty in ascertaining the meaning of that norm and finding an answer to the question that troubles him. The mediator at this stage of ethical analysis has to clarify for him or herself the meaning of the relevant norms. The discussion of the norm of self-determination in codes of conduct for mediators and in mediation literature is likely to leave the mediator with unclear guidance on that issue. Should the mediator, for example, adopt a "thin" or "thick" meaning of self-determination?[27]

There are many theories of interpretation and there is no agreement on the best method for establishing meaning.[28] A reference to a *better* interpretation or course of action requires criteria for the evaluation of alternative interpretations or courses of action, and a method for identifying the alternatives and choosing between them. This book adopts a *purposive* approach to interpretation. The meaning of ethical norms is examined in light of the norms' objectives, and their objectives are deduced from the position of holding a role, the definition and nature of the particular role (in our case: the role of a mediator), the professional ideals attached to that role, and the interaction of these role-norms with the norms of morality.[29] Part II has demonstrated the application of this type of interpretation to the ethical norms that regulate mediators' conduct such as party self-determination, in order to assist mediators engaging in ethical decision-making and reduce the ambiguity that surrounds mediation norms. It is suggested, therefore, that mediators who are unsure about the meaning of a relevant ethical norm consult the relevant chapter dedicated to that norm and apply to the norm the purposive interpretation approach described.[30]

[27] See, e.g., Welsh, "The Thinning Vision."

[28] In the legal context, for example, there is a vast literature on the methods of interpreting legal texts. See, e.g., Andrei Marmor (ed.), *Law and Interpretation: Essays in Legal Philosophy* (Oxford University Press, 2006).

[29] See Chapter 3.

[30] For an answer to the question posed above (on the determination of the process agenda), see Chapter 4, Section 4.2.2. See also Shapira, "Joining Forces", 257–258 (arguing that it is a decision which should be made by mediation parties).

15.5.4 Conflicting *ethical norms or meanings: identifying ethical dilemmas*

There is a tendency among mediation practitioners and scholars to refer to hard cases or questions as dilemmas, but for the sake of clarity it is noted that not every case of uncertainty and indecisiveness constitutes a dilemma. The term ethical dilemma suits a case where the norms of ethics mandate *conflicting* courses of action, placing the professional in the difficult position of having to choose between ethical norms or to balance them and consequently having to choose one course of action over another. However, often the possible courses of action between which a choice must be made are not conflicting but stand *side by side*. The difficulty and hesitancy inherent in such cases, belonging to Section 15.5.3, stem from the need to choose the *better* interpretation of the ethical norm or the better course of action in ethical terms, rather than from having to choose between conflicting and *irreconcilable* interpretations or courses of action. The following discussion addresses the issue of ethical dilemmas in the context of mediation.

15.5.4.1 Ethical dilemmas

Ethical decision-making is extremely hard in dilemma situations. A typical dictionary definition of a dilemma describes it as "[a] situation in which a difficult choice has to be made between two or more alternatives, especially ones that are equally undesirable."[31] A closer look at the literature on moral dilemmas reveals two situations that can give rise to ethical dilemmas:

(1) The first is a situation in which the decision-maker is guided by *conflicting ethical norms*. According to one norm, a certain conduct is ethically correct, while at the same time such action is ethically prohibited by another ethical norm, and as a result the decision-maker must make a hard and bewildering choice between alternative courses of action that cannot be taken simultaneously.[32] For

[31] See, e.g., Oxford Dictionaries available at www.oxforddictionaries.com/definition/english/dilemma. See also Dictionary.Com ("a situation requiring a choice between equally undesirable alternative") available at dictionary.reference.com/browse/dilemma.

[32] Beauchamp and Childress make this point, commenting that in a dilemma " . . . one or more moral norms obligate the agent to do x and one or more moral norms obligate the agent to do y, but the agent cannot do both in the circumstance" (Beauchamp and Childress, *Biomedical Ethics*, p. 11). Daniel Statman suggests that moral dilemmas have three features: "the agent ought to do both of two incompatible actions; . . . the agent is forced to do evil; [and] . . . the options at stake are incommensurable" (Daniel Statman,

example, when mediation parties reach an agreement in the course of mediation the mediator is normally expected to defer to the parties' wishes even where the content of the agreement does not meet his or her sense of justice. This expectation follows directly from the norm of party self-determination and possibly from the norm of impartiality as well. Suppose, however, that the parties reach a grossly unfair agreement. In such case, the mediator may rightly feel torn between the norm of professional integrity that guides him or her to terminate the mediation and the norm of party self-determination that directs him or her to respect the parties' wishes.[33]

(2) A second situation entailing an ethical dilemma is where an ethical norm is *ambiguous* and can be *construed* at the same time as both permitting and prohibiting a certain conduct. In such case, the decision-maker must make a choice between the conflicting *interpretations* of an ethical norm and the conflicting alternative courses of action that follow. Tom Beauchamp and James Childress put it this way: "[s]ome evidence or argument indicates that an act is morally permissible and some evidence or argument indicates that it is morally wrong, but the evidence or strength of argument on both sides is inconclusive."[34] For example, some mediation practitioners and commentators believe that the norm of party self-determination applies to the "substantive" decisions that parties need to make in the course of mediation, leaving "procedural," "process," and "non-substantive" decisions to the mediator. Other practitioners and commentators, myself included, argue that this approach misinterprets the norm of party self-determination, which in fact applies to procedural, process, and non-substantive decisions as well.[35] If both approaches are correct, we have here a dilemma situation that may be resolved either way, that is, actions justified by either approach

Moral Dilemmas [Amsterdam: Rodopi, 1995], p. 27). In addition, Statman, id., p. 7, stresses the distressing or painful state of the decision-maker in a state of a dilemma, distinguishing between "moral conflicts, situations where good reasons exist for two incompatible actions, and moral dilemmas, where the nature of the conflict is more serious and the agent consequently feels anguish and is at a loss as to what he or she ought to do." Another scholar, David E. Cooper, looks at dilemmas from a reasonable man point of view, defining a moral dilemma "as a value conflict that is so complex that reasonable members of a community can disagree with each other about the proper solution" (See Cooper, *Ethics for Professionals*, pp. 42–43).

[33] See Chapter 8, Section 8.2.4.3.

[34] See Beauchamp and Childress, *Biomedical Ethics*, p. 11.

[35] See Chapter 4, Section 4.2.2.

may be treated as ethically correct. If, however, the latter approach is the correct one, as I argue, then there is no real dilemma in these cases and the expansive interpretation of party self-determination is the one to be preferred. Note that the normative ambiguity in a dilemma situation referred to here differs from the ambiguity of a hard case that does not constitute a dilemma in a strict sense, referred to in Section 15.5.3. In the latter case, the norm can be interpreted in several ways and yield alternative courses of action, all of which are ethically *permissible*. In such case, the decision-maker might deliberate over the *best* course of action, but as the choice is not between ethically prohibited alternatives, it is more accurate not to refer to such a case as a dilemma.

15.5.4.2 Non-ethical dilemmas

Decision-makers may feel torn between conflicting values, and constrained to make tough choices between alternative courses of action, yet their choices would not be appropriately considered ethical dilemmas. For a dilemma to be ethical, it must be based on *ethical* reasons or norms, while a non-ethical dilemma is based on *non-ethical* reasons or norms. For example, a mediator concluding that the mediation parties have no chance of reaching a mediated agreement (in a mediation in which the parties set the signing of a mediated agreement as the mediation's goal) may feel torn between the ethical norms of professional integrity and honesty that guide him or her to terminate the mediation,[36] and his or her personal self-interest that tempts him or her to continue with the process in order to increase his or her fees that are charged on an hourly basis. While the mediator might find that decision very vexing, it does not constitute an ethical dilemma.[37]

Moreover, as noted earlier, dilemmas strictly understood involve a conflict between courses of action both of which are ethically undesirable at the same time. Mediators sometimes find themselves in a *professional or practical* "dilemma" that is not strictly speaking also an ethical dilemma because all the alternative courses of action meet the demands of ethics. Again, such cases may be hard on the decision-maker but they do not constitute ethical dilemmas, although ethical analysis of the possible courses of action could yield some guidance on the better ethical

[36] See Chapter 8, Section 8.2.3.

[37] See, e.g., Beauchamp and Childress, *Biomedical Ethics*, pp. 11–12 (discussing practical dilemmas).

practice. For example, if a mediator has a difficult time making a choice between two interventions that are both correct from a practical point of view, and one of the interventions empowers the parties more than the other, the ethical norm of party self-determination would support the more empowering intervention.

15.5.4.3 Dilemmas resulting from conflicting ethical and legal duties

When law and ethics appear to be in conflict, mediators could find themselves in a dilemma whether to abide by their legal duty or follow their ethical obligation. For example, mediators have an ethical obligation of confidentiality to the mediation parties; what should a mediator do if summoned to court and ordered by the judge to testify about events that took place during the mediation? The ethical duty of confidentiality conflicts with the legal duty of disclosure and puts the mediator in a dilemma situation: should he or she disclose mediation information in breach of his or her ethical duty of confidentiality or maintain the confidentiality of the mediation in breach of the legal duty of disclosure?[38]

Since norms can be both legal and ethical at the same time, conflicting legal and ethical norms can raise an ethical dilemma situation where the legal norm has ethical force as well. For example, Bernard Gert, like other scholars, considers the obedience to law as a (non-absolute) moral rule and the violation of law as requiring adequate justification.[39] On such analysis, the legal versus ethical conflict could turn into a conflict between ethical norms, constituting an ethical dilemma for the mediator. However, as law and ethics do not *necessarily* overlap, it cannot be said that obedience to law will *always* be morally right and therefore the mediator will have to engage in ethical thinking in order to reach a reasoned conclusion on that issue.[40]

15.5.5 Resolving hard cases: evaluating, ranking, and choosing between alternative courses of action

Once the facts and the relevant ethical norms are sorted out and determined, the mediator will have to choose between competing

[38] For discussion, see Chapter 10, Section 10.4.4. See also Chapter 16, 16.2.3.
[39] See, e.g., Gert, *Common Morality*, p. 47.
[40] See Chapter 1, Section 1.2.3.2. See also Chapter 10, Section 10.4.4.1.

interpretations of the relevant ethical norm or between competing ethical norms. This choice of norms will be translated into a choice between different courses of action. For example, choosing Meaning A for the norm of party self-determination will likely lead to Action 1 while Meaning B will direct Action 2. Alternatively, choosing Norm A over Norm B, for example party self-determination over impartiality, will likely produce a different choice among the available courses of action. Thus, the choice of norms (and their meanings) and the choice of courses of action are intertwined and hard to separate.

At the level of reconciling *competing norms*, it is helpful to remember that no ethical norm is absolute, that is, no ethical norm overrides all other norms all the time. Philosopher Bernard Gert illustrated this idea by commenting that "[m]oral agents agree that some violations of the moral rules are justified. Even killing may be justified if it is done in self-defense."[41] The idea is that *context and circumstances matter* in ethical analysis and can provide justifications for departure from a norm, that is, for its non-application or partial application in certain circumstances and for giving more weight to another norm. James Wallace argued in this context that "there are no algorithms for harmonizing moral norms in the abstract,"[42] and Pritchard commented that "for Wallace, individual moral norms are not 'absolutes' – that is none can be stated in terms of 'always' or 'never'."[43] Pritchard explains that "moral norms must be understood in relation to each other as well as in relation to the practices and activities that give them their life."[44] He then concludes: "So, an 'absolute' maxim such as 'Always tell the truth' is unworkable, as it does not take into account the variety of contexts in which truthfulness is only one practical consideration among many that matter to us."[45] This approach has been utilized in the context of mediation throughout Part II in exploring and reconciling the tension between, for example, party self-determination and impartiality, or self-determination and professional integrity. For example, it has been shown that the clash between self-determination and professional integrity where the parties wish to conclude the mediation with a grossly unfair agreement is resolved by limiting the scope of the norm of party self-determination to choices that would not jeopardize public trust in the profession and process of mediation.[46]

[41] See Gert, *Common Morality*, p. 56.

[42] Pritchard, *Professional Integrity*, p. 42 quoting from James Wallace, *Ethical Norms, Particular Cases* (Cornell University Press, 1996), p. 101.

[43] Id., p. 43. [44] Ibid. [45] Id., p. 44. [46] See Chapter 8, Section 8.2.4.3.

When the case or question is perceived to be hard because of *competing interpretations of the same norm* that in turn produce different courses of action, it is helpful to address the choice between the competing interpretations and courses of action through a purposive approach to interpretation.[47] Here the idea is to find interpretations and courses of action that *better* suit the purpose of mediation, the role of mediators, their definition, nature, and ideals.[48] The idea of *ranking interpretations* or courses of action is not new. Gert argued that "[a]lthough there is not always only one morally acceptable way of acting, in every moral situation there are always morally better and morally worse ways of acting."[49] Many practical decisions in the course of mediation fall into this category: a decision whether to hold separate or joint sessions, to have party A or party B relate his or her story first, to involve the parties' legal representatives in the discussion or ask them to leave the stage to the parties. In general, all these alternatives are ethically permissible and mediators have discretion to choose between them. However, the *criteria* for ranking the alternative courses of action are not fixed or easily recognizable.

One way of ranking ethically permissible alternatives is by reference to ethical *ideals*.[50] Actions that do not violate any ethical duty may nevertheless be more or less in line with the ethical ideals that particular role-holders are encouraged to aspire to, and these ideals may provide some guidance to a deliberating role-holder. For example, court-connected mediators share ideals of effectiveness (time and cost saving) and outcome (considering a mediated agreement a good, aspired outcome of mediation). They are likely to rank the alternatives of using caucuses, letting the plaintiff talk first, and permitting extensive involvement of lawyers higher than the other alternatives. In contrast, for transformative mediators the ideals of party empowerment and recognition will probably lead mediators to rank higher the use of joint sessions, the personal choice of the parties with regard to who will talk first, and the active involvement of parties at the expense of lawyers' involvement.

Another method for ranking alternatives is by exposing them to a test of *substantive fairness*, that is, by looking for courses of action that correspond to a realist (as opposed to formalist) understanding of the norms. Mediators, for example, should rank actions that support informed consent higher than actions that support formal consent.[51]

[47] See Section 15.5.3. [48] See Chapter 3. [49] Gert, *Common Morality*, p. 137.
[50] See Chapter 1, Section 1.2.1.2. [51] See Chapter 11.

Other commentators have suggested a resort to common moral theories that could offer guidance as to the ranking of alternatives such as utilitarianism (preferring actions that cause less harm)[52] and rights-based theories (preferring actions that respect the rights of affected persons and minimize injury to those rights),[53] although that guidance might be partial and sometimes inconsistent.

15.5.6 *Dead-ends and creative solutions*

In hard cases and dilemma situations, one should be ready to admit that sometimes there is simply no ultimate right answer, and that the best one can do is to make an honest, rational, and reasoned attempt to find a defendable solution to the problem in question.

Beauchamp and Childress argued that "[n]either morality nor ethical theory has the resources to provide a single solution to every moral problem."[54] They noted that "various moral principles ... conflict in the moral life. These conflicts sometimes produce irresolvable moral dilemmas. When forced to a choice, we may 'resolve' the situation by choosing one option over another, but we still may believe that neither option is morally preferable to the competing option ... In some cases, the dilemma may only become more difficult and remain unresolved even after most careful reflection."[55] Philosopher Bernard Gert similarly argued that many moral issues are not resolvable.[56] He also observed that

[52] See, e.g., Beauchamp and Childress, *Biomedical Ethics*, p. 23 (discussing factors that should affect the balancing (infringement) of moral norms – and thus relevant for the ranking of alternative actions – such as "[t]he lowest level of infringement, commensurate with achieving the primary goal of the action, has been selected" and "[a]ny negative effects of the infringement have been minimized"). See also Gert, *Common Morality*, p. 69 (suggesting that actions which cause less harm are to be preferred), id., pp. 60–61, 66–67, 79 (treating the evils or harms that an action causes and the benefits or goods that it promotes as relevant to ethical decision-making and ranking of alternatives). But see id., pp. 146–147 (noting that often there will be differences in the estimates of the ranking of consequences by different people); Marian Mattison, "Ethical Decision Making: The Person in the Process" (2000) 45 *Social Work* 201, 204 (suggesting that social workers should consider when they engage in ethical decision-making the possible consequences that might result from any given intervention).

[53] See, e.g., Reamer, *Social Work Values*, pp. 69–70 (discussing "rights-based theories about the most appropriate way to rank conflicting duties," which basically argue that "when choosing among duties that may result in harm, one should do that which results in the least harm." These approaches are sometimes called minimization of suffering or negative utilitarianism).

[54] Beauchamp and Childress, *Biomedical Ethics*, p. 24. [55] Id., p. 12.

[56] Gert, *Morality*, p. 383.

"[s]ome persons have such strong views about how people ought to behave in . . . morally controversial situations that they do not recognize that it is morally acceptable to have a different view."[57]

Mediation experts express similar views. Macfarlane argued that "[m] ediators confronting ethical dilemmas, as they are defined in this article, are more likely to be looking for the 'best' course rather than a universal 'right' one. While they may certainly wish to avoid a 'wrong' decision which might harm the parties or the process, they are unlikely to find an uncontentious and universally applicable solution to any of the dilemmas they encounter in practice."[58] Mediation expert Charles Pou commented that "context matters and many ethical dilemmas will not have a single, 'right' response. There may be some distinct 'no-no's,' but often the mediator will have to think through several potential approaches to arrive at an evenhanded, defensible response for the specific situation. And, as with the evolution of any situation, there will often be a broad range of possible mediator behavior that allows one to respond with a surprising degree of nuance."[59]

One way of confronting hard cases or questions, including dilemmas, is by looking for *creative solutions* that avoid the need to choose between the conflicting norms and alternative courses of action. Daniel Statman, for example, noted that *integration* is a preferred strategy for resolving dilemmas.[60] Integration and exploration of creative solutions are familiar concepts to mediators. They are trained to look for interests that lie behind positions and for interest-based solutions that satisfy the parties' needs rather than settle for a compromise. In a hard case, one should treat the conflicting alternatives as positions and the goals they are set to achieve as interests, thereby looking for other alternatives that can meet those interests. For example, mediators are not allowed to provide parties with legal advice. However, they may, with some limitations, provide parties with *information* that they have the competence and experience to provide. The line between these two actions is often blurred, and mediators regularly deliberate whether the provision of information by them would be ethically permitted or prohibited. One way of getting around this difficult choice is by avoiding the provision of information *directly* to the parties by the mediator while taking steps to the effect that the parties will be informed through other channels. For example, the mediator might ask the parties questions that will prompt them to look for the

[57] Gert, *Common Morality*, p. 140.
[58] See, e.g., Macfarlane, "Mediating Ethically", 65.
[59] Pou, "'Embracing Limbo'", 210.
[60] See Statman, *Moral Dilemmas*, p. 8.

information themselves; involve the parties' lawyers, if they have ones, in the process; or refer the parties to outside experts.[61]

Creativity, in my view, cannot be replaced by readily available solutions. Macfarlane, for example, suggested that " . . . a dilemma that can be readily anticipated and easily identified, because a clear and uniform best practice has been set out, is no longer a true dilemma but rather a formalized professional response."[62] Such professional responses could indeed be helpful, but a critical approach to these responses may still be in place. For example, a code of conduct for mediators might attempt to solve the ethical dilemma of confidentiality versus disclosure in advance, by providing, as the *Model Standards* do, that "[a] mediator shall maintain the confidentiality of all information obtained by the mediator in mediation, unless otherwise agreed to by the parties or required by applicable law."[63] However, this general exception or readymade professional response does not really solve the ethical dilemma of a mediator who faces, for example, a subpoena to appear in court. First, as noted before, there could be cases, however rare, in which ethics would trump a legal obligation. Second, acceptance of the supremacy of the law should not be translated into mechanical obedience. The mediator should be open to considering creative ways to solve the dilemma. For example, is it possible to convince the court that the mediator's testimony is not necessary in the circumstances because the information sought could be discovered through other channels or witnesses? Could the court be persuaded that the testimony should not be compelled for policy reasons, in order to support the impartiality of mediators and the standing of the profession?[64]

15.6 Conclusion

Ethical decision-making is a process based on ethical sensitivity and principled logical analysis of the facts of a given scenario and of the relevant ethical norms applicable to those facts. It is a process that cannot be justified solely by intuition or subjective feelings. On the contrary, it must be justified on the basis of rational reasons capable of generalization. Thus, mediators' ethical decision-making cannot be satisfied with a personal statement such as "I think/believe that this is the right

[61] See Chapter 4, Section 4.5.3.2. See also Chapter 16, Sections 16.2.1 and 16.2.2.

[62] Macfarlane, "Mediating Ethically", 61 note 32.

[63] See, e.g., Model Standards, Standard V.A. [64] See Chapter 16, Section 16.2.3.

thing to do," because ethical decision-making rests on external (ethical) standards that must be met and support the personal convictions of mediators.

Professional ethics comes to assist mediators in exercising their role in a worthy, ethical manner. In order to accomplish that goal, mediators must be familiar with the ethical standards applicable to them, and assimilate and internalize these norms so they are readily available for application. The process of making decisions should be a reflective one: mediators should continuously ask themselves what they must do to discharge their ethical duties and what guidance they can receive from the ideals of mediation.

As ethical duties are relative and no duty overrides all other duties in all circumstances, mediators must be ready to examine any given ethical norm in light of other ethical norms that govern their conduct. The meaning of these duties, therefore, is not fixed, but changes as a result of the negotiation between the meanings of the relevant ethical norms and the circumstantial context. The answer to a given ethical question will not necessarily be straightforward or even unitary. Mediators should strive to construct several courses of action and attempt to choose the one most worthy. In the end of the day, however, we should appreciate that mediators have discretion (although not unlimited) to choose the alternative that may be justified on a rational and impartial basis. The next chapter illustrates how this can be done.

16

Case illustrations

16.1 Introduction

The purpose of this chapter is to demonstrate the usefulness of the theory of mediators' ethics in the analysis of ethical questions, and to illustrate the ethical guidance it can offer in difficult cases. The discussion will be of particular interest to mediation practitioners, members of mediator ethics committees, and mediation scholars. Five case scenarios have been drawn from a variety of sources, including questions that were referred to a community mediation center's ethics forum (committee), which I head,[1] opinions published by mediator ethics committees in court-connected mediation programs, ethical dilemmas on the American Bar Association Dispute Resolution Section site,[2] and cases and commentaries from Ellen Waldman's casebook on mediation ethics.[3] The *number* of cases selected for discussion is not larger for reasons of space, but the theory may be similarly applied to other cases raising ethical questions for mediators. The ethical *issues* that were chosen for discussion are only a sample of the many ethical questions that come up in mediation practice. They seemed to me, however, questions that many readers will relate to, and their discussion will hopefully enable readers to apply the theory to other cases as well.

[1] The Kiryat-Ono Community Mediation Center was founded in 2006. The center has 45 volunteer mediators who mediate cases referred to it by the municipality, the police, the courts, and the community. The Ethical Forum was established in 2012. It consists of 10–12 mediators who meet regularly once a month, discuss ethical questions that are referred to the Forum and publish opinions on these questions. The objectives of the Forum are to receive ethical questions from mediators and mediation centers and respond to these questions; develop tools for dealing with ethical questions in mediation; and collect, preserve and disseminate knowledge among mediators. The Forum is not a disciplinary body. It aims to draw conclusions for the future, and contribute to the professionalization of mediators.

[2] See www.americanbar.org/groups/dispute_resolution/resources/Ethics.html.

[3] See Waldman, Mediation Ethics.

Applying theory to practice as illustrated by this chapter serves to highlight the potential contribution of the theory of mediators' ethics to ethical discourse in the field of mediation. As the following discussion of the cases shows, the theory provides a reasoned normative basis for the examination of ethical questions in mediation that may be useful when no code of conduct for mediators applies to the mediator, or when an applicable code exists but needs to be interpreted. The theory organizes the norms of mediators' ethics in an accessible way, enabling mediators/members of ethics committees/commentators to orient themselves and focus on the relevant ethical standards; it provides a detailed explanation of the meaning of the ethical norms that apply to mediators, enabling the reader to apply them to factual scenarios; it exposes the rationale behind the norms of mediators' ethics, and therefore behind the provisions of many codes of conduct for mediators that are silent on that point, enabling the reader to better understand the obligations of mediators and reconcile tensions between these obligations; and it provides a common ethical basis for evaluating, justifying, and criticizing mediator interventions or advocated courses of action of advisory ethics committees and commentators.

The analysis of the cases is based on the theory of mediators' ethics articulated in Part II, and uses the *Proposed Model Code of Conduct for Mediators*[4] that summed up the detailed discussion, explanation, and justification of the theory. Therefore, in order to appreciate the full force of the arguments presented in this chapter, the reader is advised to consult the relevant chapters that comprehensively discuss and justify those arguments.

16.2 Case illustrations

16.2.1 *The uninformed wife:* party self-determination (informed decision-making) and mediator impartiality

The Uninformed Wife case was referred to the Ethics Forum of the Kiryat-Ono Community Mediation Center, Israel, by one of its volunteer mediators.[5] The Forum, which I head, analyzed the ethical issues arising from the reference using the professional ethics perspective advocated by this book. The mediator who sent the question to the Forum was not acting at the time under any applicable formal code of conduct for

[4] See Appendix I.

[5] Kiryat-Ono Community Mediation Center Ethics Forum, Opinion 2–2012 (on file with the author).

mediators, so the Forum had to point to alternative sources of mediators' ethical norms that regulated the mediator's conduct. The following is a summary of the facts of the case, and an elaborated discussion of the main issues referred to in the Forum's Opinion.

The facts

The mediator, a lawyer and accountant volunteering at the mediation center, was contacted privately by a couple and hired to mediate their divorce. One of the issues at the mediation was the division of the couple's property, and the husband and wife disclosed their assets for that purpose. The husband, who was the owner of a company, argued that the company was in debt and therefore its value for the purpose of property division was low. The wife, who was not involved in the business, had limited financial understanding and expected the mediator to protect her rights. On examining the company's financial reports, the mediator realized that although the company owed a large amount of money to the banks, it was a thriving business and in fact was owed money by some of its clients. The mediator became suspicious that the husband had misrepresented the true value of the company, but the wife was impressed by the company's debts and tended to accept her husband's offer for settlement. The mediator asked for the Forum's opinion on the appropriate way to proceed with the case. She raised several concerns, including (a) the imbalance of power between the husband and wife; (b) the difficulty to maintain impartiality in the circumstances; (c) her fear that the wife would accept an inferior offer (in the mediator's view) based on inadequate or even wrong information; and (d) her concern that if she referred the wife to an outside expert the wife would end the mediation, and if the mediator withdrew the parties would simply find another mediator willing to mediate the case despite all those concerns.

Discussion

(a) Party self-determination and its sources The Uninformed Wife case is primarily about party self-determination, which is a fundamental principle of mediation. The core meaning of self-determination in mediation is that the decision on the outcome of mediation rests with the parties who must agree to it. Three conditions must be met for the exercise of party self-determination: (1) the parties must have mental capacity to make the decision; (2) the decision must be voluntary, free, and uncoerced; and (3) the decision must be informed, made on the basis of the relevant information necessary for making the decision.[6] When one of these features is missing the right to self-determination is not realized. For example, if a party suffers from major depression (incapacity), or is under strong pressure to settle (compromised voluntariness), or unknowingly makes a decision on the basis of wrong or inadequate information (uninformed decision) his or her self-determination is called into question.

Mediators are responsible toward the parties of a case they mediate to conduct the mediation on the basis of party self-determination. This responsibility has several sources.[7] First, when mediators present themselves as mediators they can be taken to have promised to act like mediators in accordance with the definition and nature of the role of a mediator. There is a consensus among mediators and scholars about the right of mediation parties to make decisions for themselves during mediation. Any mediator operating under an applicable formal code of conduct (for example, the *Model Standards* or any code of a court-connected mediation program) will be subject to a right of mediation parties to self-determination that is widely recognized in virtually every code of conduct for mediators. Parties who participate in mediations are entitled to rely on this right as a promise made by their mediator. Second, the role of mediators places them in a position of power and influence with regard to the parties. The parties, who rely on their mediator's knowledge and skills, are entitled to expect him or her to conduct the mediation in a manner worthy of their trust. A mediator knowingly allowing parties to make decisions in a state of incapacity, lacking free will, or on the basis of wrong or inadequate information will not be worthy of the parties' trust.

Thus, every mediator has an ethical duty toward the parties of a case he or she is mediating to conduct the mediation under conditions that enable the parties to exercise their right to self-determination, and to refrain from conducting the mediation in circumstances in which the parties are incapable of realizing that right. This duty applies to the mediator in the present case despite the fact that she is not subject to a formal code of conduct for mediators.

(b) Party self-determination, informed decisions, and the tension with impartiality The mediator in this case suspects that the information provided by the husband is inadequate or misleading. If her suspicion is right it is likely that the wife will make an uninformed decision on the

6 See Chapter 4, Section 4.3.1. 7 See Chapter 4, Section 4.2.1.

terms of settlement. The mediator has a duty toward the wife to conduct the mediation on the basis of self-determination, namely under conditions that enable her to make informed decisions.[8] This duty is even more apparent in view of the imbalance of power between the husband and wife that has placed the wife in an inferior bargaining position: the wife does not have the husband's knowledge of business and finances or the husband's access to information about the company's performance. The difficulty, however, is that if the mediator takes action in support of the wife's right to self-determination she might appear partial in violation of the obligation of *impartiality*. Like party self-determination, mediator impartiality is an ethical obligation of all mediators. It is recognized by virtually every code of conduct for mediators and derives from the duty of mediators to be worthy of the parties' trust.[9] Thus, every party is entitled to expect the mediator in his case to conduct the mediation impartially. Impartiality requires mediators to avoid favoritism toward one party over another or conduct that gives an appearance of favoritism. This set of facts creates for the mediator a conflict between the wife's right to self-determination and the mediator's duty to conduct the mediation impartially. How can she support the wife's right to self-determination without violating the norm of impartiality?

(c) Self-determination and impartiality are not absolute norms and must be reconciled The ethical rights of parties and the ethical obligations of mediators are not absolute. The wife's right to make an informed decision cannot be interpreted as a right to base her decision on complete information, because realistically no one can have access to all the information regarding any decision one makes. Moreover, every person bears personal responsibility for their decisions, and that responsibility extends to the decision on the amount of information one collects for the purpose of making a decision. The duty of mediators, therefore, cannot be interpreted as an obligation to ensure that parties make decisions based on complete information. Still, the mediator is the person in charge of the mediation, and he or she is perceived by the parties, the profession, and the public as responsible for the process. He or she is expected to "conduct the mediation under conditions that enable parties to make informed decisions,"[10] where informed decision-making is defined more

[8] See Chapter 4, Section 4.5.3. See also Appendix I: Proposed Model Code of Conduct for Mediators (Proposed Code), Standard IV.

[9] See Chapter 7, Sections 7.1 and 7.2.

[10] See Chapter 4, Section 4.5.3.2; Proposed Code, Standard IV.F.

narrowly as decision-making based on *relevant* information, namely "information the knowledge or ignorance of which could influence the decision or the choice made."[11] It is clear that the wife cannot make an informed decision about the husband's proposal unless she recognizes that her understanding of the company's financial position is wanting and until she understands the consequences of accepting the husband's proposal without more information.

Impartiality, like party self-determination, should not be understood in absolute terms. In practice, taking action that somewhat benefits one party more than another cannot be completely avoided, and passivity cannot be a prescription for impartiality because it favors powerful and sophisticated parties.[12] Thus the real question is whether a mediator's intervention can be (a) justified and (b) carried out in a manner that maintains the mediator's appearance of impartiality.[13] Practically, if a mediator is perceived as partial he or she is likely to lose the parties' cooperation; ethically such a mediator would undermine the standing of the profession and public faith in the profession and process of mediation, compromising his or her responsibilities toward the profession and the public. From a professional ethics perspective, the mediator's intervention can be justified if it is necessary for securing the ethical rights of the parties. In the current case, the wife cannot exercise her right to self-determination and the mediator will be justified in empowering her, provided that her intervention is limited to (a) the minimum required for the wife to exercise self-determination, and (b) to measures that do not give an appearance of partiality.[14] For these reasons, the mediator may not tell the wife *directly* that she suspects that the company's financial state is better than as represented. Doing so will be taking a side and she will lose impartiality. However, she equally cannot remain passive and let the wife make an uninformed decision. Instead, she should take steps that *indirectly* enable the wife to make an informed decision.

In the *Proposed Code*, the balance between impartiality and self-determination is described as follows:

> 2. A mediator shall treat parties differently where –
>
> (a) Same treatment would favor the interests of one party and disadvantage another; and

[11] See Chapter 4, Section 4.3.4; Proposed Code, Standard IV.F.1.
[12] See Chapter 7, Section 7.3.1. [13] See Chapter 7, Section 7.3.4. [14] Ibid.

(b) The mediator's intervention is (1) required in order to give effect to an ethical right of a party (in particular self-determination), or (2) necessary for the preservation of public trust in the profession and process of mediation.

Any such intervention shall be limited to one that is -

(a) The minimum necessary for the realization of the party's' right; and
(b) Can be reconciled with other mediator obligations; and
(c) Would not be perceived as an act of partiality in the eyes of a reasonable person and thus would not result with a loss of public trust in the profession and process of mediation.

(d) Professional integrity (separation of professional roles) It is very tempting to the mediator in this case to use her qualifications and knowledge as a lawyer and accountant to empower the wife. However, her role in this case is that of a *mediator*, a role that differs in nature and definition from the role of a lawyer or an accountant. Professional integrity considerations require that she distinguish between her professional roles and commit herself to that of a mediator.[15] As a mediator, it is not her role to give the wife legal advice on her rights in law, act as her legal representative, or provide her with a financial assessment of the company's assets.

(e) Reconciling self-determination, impartiality, and professional integrity: possible interventions to consider Here are some of the steps the mediator may consider taking, allowing her to meet her ethical obligations:

- Point out to the parties in *joint session* (1) the importance that decisions on property division be made on a wide and verified basis of information; (2) the advantages of seeking together a neutral evaluation of the value of the company and of the other assets belonging to the parties; (3) the importance that each of them seek independent legal advice; and (4) that despite the fact that the mediator is a lawyer and accountant as well as a mediator, her dual duty of trust toward both parties and concerns of professional integrity and impartiality prevent her from giving a professional opinion or advice on the value of their assets and rights, because such opinion or advice is beyond the definition of her role as a mediator and would make her appear partial.

[15] See Chapter 8, Section 8.2.2.

- Point out to the *husband* in a *separate* session (1) that the information regarding the company's financial state may be incomplete and encourage him to provide more information; (2) that this state of affairs might be to his disadvantage if in the future the wife decides to challenge the validity of the agreement; (3) that if the mediation does not produce an agreement and the parties go to court the information regarding the company will likely be discovered; and (4) that if the wife remains in her current state of knowledge the mediator will have to consider the termination of the mediation because she has an ethical obligation toward both parties and the profession to prevent the signing of a mediated agreement that is based on the wife's ignorance of relevant information.
- Point out to the *wife* in a *separate* session (1) the importance that she receive professional advice from an accountant and a lawyer to extend her understanding of her financial state and legal rights; (2) the possibility that the information regarding the company is incomplete and the desirability of receiving more information about it; (3) the fact that her role as mediator in the case does not allow her to act as the wife's representative and prevents her from providing her with the type of information that an outside expert can; (4) the consequences of refusing to consult outside experts, while verifying that the wife understands the implications of a decision to accept the husband's proposal on the basis of the available information.

(f) Proceeding with or withdrawing from mediation and party waiver of self-determination Following the interventions by the mediator, the mediation could develop in several directions. First, the wife might receive the relevant information through outside sources. In such case, the mediation can proceed as usual because the wife will be able to make informed decisions on the outcome, and the mediator will be able to maintain impartiality and professional integrity. In another scenario, the wife might become aware of the importance of obtaining the relevant information and the possible consequences that could follow from proceeding with the mediation without access to that information, yet still decide to proceed with the mediation without the information. In such case, the mediator may continue with the mediation because the wife has exercised her right to self-determination in her informed decision to make an uninformed decision.[16] Possible exceptions could

[16] See Chapter 4, Section 4.4.

arise in (a) circumstances that do not satisfy one of the other conditions of self-determination, for example the wife is temporarily incompetent to make the decision due to emotional distress that necessitates a postponement of the mediation; or (b) circumstances that do not meet the mediator's responsibility toward the profession and the public, for example, the mediated agreement that the wife is willing to sign is unconscionable or grossly unfair, that is, "its terms deviate from common social norms to a degree that jeopardizes the standing of the profession and public trust in the profession."[17] The mediator has to bear in mind that other than in exceptional circumstances (such as illegality or unconscionability of the agreement), the decision on the outcome belongs to the parties and a decision of the wife, albeit unsatisfactory in the mediator's judgment, should not be disturbed.

(g) Professional integrity (decision-making by professionals) and the concern for loss of business The mediator raised concerns that if she were to refer the wife to an outside expert the wife might choose to end the mediation, or if she were to withdraw the parties might simply find another mediator willing to mediate the case. These concerns cannot justify an omission to act on her part for reasons of professional integrity. From a professional ethics perspective, the mediator is expected to make decisions on the basis of professional considerations that are relevant for the provision of mediation services, as opposed to extraneous, irrelevant considerations. The *Proposed Code* makes this point by stating that the duty of a mediator is to make "those decisions which are necessary for the execution of his role . . . on the basis of relevant professional considerations and good reasons that could be reasonably justified."[18]

The mediator's concerns in the current case are speculative because no one can tell what will happen if the mediator makes those decisions. If, for example, the wife opts for consultation she will probably receive additional relevant information. Following that the wife might indeed decide to withdraw, but otherwise she might decide to proceed with the husband raising his initial offer, or the mediation might come to an impasse. It is also true that if the mediator decides to terminate the mediation the parties might go to another mediator, but this would simply leave the other mediator with the responsibility to conduct the mediation in an ethical manner.

[17] See Proposed Code, Standard V.D.5(c); Chapter 4, Section 4.5.3.2(c)
[18] Proposed Code, ibid.

16.2.2 *Ziba and Ahmed's Iranian-American divorce:* party self-determination and professional integrity (unacceptable mediation outcomes and separation of professional roles)

This hypothetical is taken from Ellen Waldman's casebook on mediation ethics.[19] In the book, the hypothetical is followed by the comments of Professor Carrie Menkel-Meadow and Harold Abramson. Below you will find a summary of the facts and commentaries, followed by an analysis from a professional ethics perspective. Employing this perspective enables me to evaluate the commentators' ethical analysis of the case and compare it to the approach taken by the theory of mediators' ethics.

The facts

Ziba (17) and Ahmed (41) are married for four years and have two sons aged three and two. Ziba is miserable in the marriage because of Ahmed's behavior: he has been very controlling, limited her freedom, taken a second wife, and devoted less and less time to her and the children. Ziba wants a divorce, but also wants to remain part of the local Muslim community that expects Ziba and Ahmed to follow the principles of Islamic law. Ziba and Ahmed were advised that according to Islamic law (a) Ziba cannot receive a divorce without Ahmed's consent; (b) if Ziba initiates the divorce she will lose her right to the marriage contract payment (40,000 dollars) and any other financial support for herself; and (c) the children will stay with Ziba until they are seven years old and at that point the custody will revert to Ahmed. Ziba and Ahmed come to mediation where Ahmed agrees to the divorce on the following terms: (a) Ziba will forfeit any right to marriage dissolution payment and any other financial support for herself; and (b) Ziba will give up custody of the children at the age of five. Ziba "capitulates and tearfully" agrees to Ahmed's terms. Ahmed believes that the agreement is "within the norms of the Iranian community in which they live."

The commentaries

Menkel-Meadow explains that she will not take the case (p. 320) but will hold pre-mediation joint and caucus sessions in which she, as a lawyer mediator, will "give legal advice and counsel to both of them at the same time and tell them what American law provides" (p. 321). Her

[19] See Waldman, *Mediation Ethics*, pp. 318–337.

understanding of the law, which she intends to share with the parties, is that (a) the marriage is not legal under American law because Ziba was thirteen when she married; thus (b) the marriage could be legally annulled; (c) Ahmed might be guilty of statutory rape; and (d) Ziba would likely be entitled to financial support, as well as custody of the children (p. 321).

Menkel-Meadow then gives several reasons for declining the case, referring to the relevant provisions in the *Model Standards of Conduct for Mediators* (2005) (pp. 321–322): (1) she is not impartial because she is judging the validity of the marriage and giving legal advice; (2) she is not competent to mediate the case because it involves Islamic law, which she does not know much about; (3) the process is not a "quality process" because it lacks in safety, participation of parties, party competency, and mutual respect among the participants; and (4) she has a conflict of interest because she is a publicly known feminist and secular who is committed to equality in marriage and rights of women to no-fault divorce thus could not possibly be seen as impartial by Ahmed.

Moreover, Menkel-Meadow states that "in my view, no mediator (and certainly not this mediator) should participate in a mediation that she thinks will lead to a morally, legally, or ethically 'unconscionable' result" (p. 323). Still, for Menkel-Meadow "[w]hat is unconscionable is, of course, subjective, personal, and nonuniversal" (p. 323). She stresses that her decision is based on *her* sense of ethics, culture, and justice (p. 326) and suggests that Ziba and Ahmed find another mediator (p. 327).

Indeed, the other commentator and mediator, Harold Abramson, is willing to take the case. And he is willing to do so for two reasons: (a) working with Ziba and Ahmed would not violate universally accepted international principles of human rights; and (b) the mediation can get them "'the least bad' outcome – an outcome that involves the least amount of moral violence and coercion for all involved" (p. 328). For Abramson, mediators should be careful to avoid cultural imperialism and respect cultural pluralism. The difficulty in Ziba and Ahmed's case in Abramson's view is that "[b]oth parties agree broadly to a rule that, when they apply it, results in a mediated agreement that is unfair according to the mediator's Westernized values and may even violate Western domestic law" (p. 328). In his opinion, the agreement that the parties reached "is likely to be invalid and unenforceable" under American law (p. 328), but assuming that the parties have legal counsel, are supported by family members or friends, and are aware of the applicable law, he would not withdraw (pp. 331–333), although he later qualifies this by saying that he will "try to mediate the best agreement the parties are willing to enter into, so long as the agreement is not illegal" (p. 335). He supports his decision with two main reasons. First, he argues, the *Model Standards* focus on party self-determination and process fairness but "steer clear of discussions of fairness, equity, and substantive justice" (p. 329). Thus Abramson interprets the Standards as exempting mediators from the burden of judging the fairness of the parties' desired outcomes (p. 330). A second reason for accepting the case and outcome is the lack of a universally recognized norm of gender equality in international treaties. In his words, "[m]y forays into international law revealed no principled source of internationally recognized standards that could be the basis for withdrawing from the mediation" (p. 334).

Menkel-Meadow's and Abramson's commentaries illustrate the complexity of ethical analysis and the type of reasoning mediators can adopt when facing difficult questions. However, as Menkel-Meadow's analysis seems very personal, based on *her* sense of ethics, culture, and justice, its guidance for mediators in general might be limited. The danger is that mediators might perceive her account as communicating a message that mediators' ethics is subjective, a matter of personal taste. Mediators might think to themselves that it is all about personal choice: Menkel-Meadow felt she lacked competence – they do not see it as a problem; Menkel-Meadow decided to give legal advice – they would have avoided that; Menkel-Meadow could not personally live with the process and outcome, but they, like Abramson, could. It is also hard to generalize from Abramson's commentary to the practice of mediators in general. We are not told the normative basis for his using international law and the "least bad outcome" tests for accepting or rejecting a case for mediation. Menkel-Meadow, for example, did not refer to such considerations in her decision-making. Abramson does refer to the *Model Standards* to justify mediators' responsibility to process rather than to outcome, thus legitimizing the decision to proceed with the mediation, but then mentions other codes that expect mediator accountability to outcome (in note 21) and would have pointed at withdrawal. What should mediators make of seemingly conflicting codes? Can the codes be reconciled? Moreover, Abramson gives much weight to norms of international law. Why does the lack of a legal norm of gender equality in international treaties justify a mediation agreement that is almost certainly, according to his legal analysis, in breach of American law? What is the role of law in mediators' ethics?

Analysis from a professional ethics perspective

I now turn to the theory of mediators' ethics. I base the analysis on the facts of the case as summarized above plus the legal evaluation of both Menkel-Meadow and Abramson that the agreement that the parties have reached is most likely in violation of American law. Instead of relying on the *Model Standards*, I refer to the *Proposed Code* whose provisions have been explained, reasoned, and justified in Part II. As ethical decision-making begins with ethical awareness and knowledge of the relevant ethical standards that apply to mediators, I assume such familiarity with the *Proposed Code* and refer the reader to Appendix I and to the relevant chapters for a more detailed account.

(a) Preliminary issues: the decision on whether to take the case

1) Competence If the mediator of this hypothetical is of a different culture than the parties and is not familiar with Muslim culture and Islamic law, then *competence* becomes a relevant ethical issue. Mediators are expected to have the competence to conduct the mediation.[20] If the mediator is an experienced one he or she probably has the knowledge and skills for assisting parties in general to communicate, negotiate, and make decisions (*basic* competence), but the circumstances in our case raise a reasonable expectation that he or she have *specific* competence that includes cultural knowledge of the norms of the Muslim community and subject-matter expertise of Islamic law.[21] This means that (a) the mediator must notify the parties that he or she does not have that knowledge, if this is the case, and (b) decline to mediate unless he or she can fill in this competence gap. This could be done, for example, by bringing in a co-mediator with knowledge of the culture and principles of Islam[22] or by acquiring that knowledge, as Abramson did.

2) Impartiality and conflict of interest Impartiality may be a relevant ethical issue for many Western mediators because of the sharp contrast between Western norms and Muslim community norms as described in the hypothetical. Mediators have a duty to exercise their role impartially. "Impartiality means freedom from external manifestations of favoritism or bias in word or action between parties,"[23] and it guides the mediator

[20] See Chapter 5, Section 5.2; Proposed Code, Standard I.

[21] On basic and specific competence see Chapter 5, Sections 5.4.2 and 5.4.3.

[22] See id., Section 5.5. [23] Proposed Code, Standard II.

on the acceptance of cases. The *Proposed Code* offers the following guidance:

> A mediator shall not accept a case for mediation or withdraw if:
>
> 1. He or she cannot conduct the mediation impartially; or
> 2. There is a reasonable concern that he or she will not be able or is not able to conduct the mediation impartially or without an appearance of partiality, in circumstances that could jeopardize the standing of the profession and process of mediation and public trust in them.[24]

The test is therefore twofold. First, the mediator should ask him or herself if *he or she*, personally, would be able to avoid partiality; and second, if he or she believes he or she can maintain impartiality, whether he or she would also be able to conduct the mediation with an *appearance* of impartiality that maintains the standing of the profession and process of mediation. If, for example, the mediator is strongly and publicly committed to gender equality and no-fault divorce, as Menkel-Meadow is, this raises reasonable concern about his or her ability to conduct the mediation impartially without favoring Ziba. Such a personally held belief or commitment of the mediator places him or her in a conflict of interest due to his or her involvement with the subject matter of the dispute or due to his or her belief that he or she is under a moral or conscientious duty to act in favor of the wife.[25] It is a *serious* conflict of interest that cannot be waived by the parties because "the process might be publicly perceived as faulty, thereby jeopardizing the standing of the mediation profession and public trust in the profession and the process."[26] The mediator has a duty to avoid such an outcome due to his or her responsibilities toward the profession of mediation and the public.[27] Therefore, if these are the circumstances the mediator will have a duty to decline the case.

(b) Issues relating to process and outcome

1) Party self-determination Mediators have a duty to conduct the mediation on the basis of party self-determination.[28] "Self-determination means that the parties are free to make voluntary, uncoerced, and informed decisions."[29] The hypothetical describes Ziba as the weaker party. Ahmed had controlled her actions and movements for years

[24] Id., Standard II.A. [25] Chapter 6, Section 6.3; Proposed Code, Standard III.
[26] Proposed Code, Standard III.B; Chapter 6, Section 6.4.2.1.
[27] See Chapter 6, Section 6.4.2. [28] See Chapter 4, Section 4.2.1.
[29] Proposed Code, Standard IV; Chapter 4, Section 4.3.1.

during their marriage in accordance with their community and religious norms. These norms place her at a disadvantage in negotiating the divorce and financial and custody issues. This raises a question about Ziba's ability to make a *voluntary* decision. Another issue relates to the knowledge or ignorance of both parties of their rights and obligations under American law. The concern is that without such knowledge the decisions made by the parties in the mediation will not be *informed.*

a. Voluntariness Ziba is acting under enormous pressures. She wants a divorce but she also wants to stay part of the Iranian-American community. To do that she has to abide by the community norms that would deny her right to divorce without Ahmed's consent, deny her financial assistance following the divorce, and limit her custody rights. Ahmed is using these community norms to exert even more pressure and insists on getting the custody of the children at an earlier age. Ziba "capitulates and tearfully" agrees, but is this a voluntary decision?

In an ideal world, mediation parties would have been able to make decisions without any pressures. Realistically, however, this is not often the case. From a professional ethics perspective, the task of the mediator is to support the voluntariness of the parties' decision-making in the face of existing pressures. He or she can do so by calling a kind of "time out," giving each party an opportunity to reflect on his or her reasons for making a particular decision and carefully consider whether he or she wishes to go on with the decision. If after this pause for reflection and consideration the party wishes to proceed with the decision, mediators should consider that choice as an exercise of self-determination.[30] The *Proposed Code* describes that position in the following way:

> (a) A mediator shall be aware of power imbalances between parties. If the mediator suspects that a party has made or is about to make a decision out of feelings of helplessness and no choice, as a result of pressures of mediation participants or nonparticipants, he or she shall examine with that party the basis for those feelings and whether they are justified in the prevailing circumstances.
> (b) If subsequent to this clarification the party wishes to proceed with the decision the mediator shall respect his or her choice, provided that he or she is competent to participate in the mediation.[31]

[30] See Chapter 4, Section 4.5.2.2. [31] Proposed Code, Standard IV.E.2.

The pressures on Ziba are real, but Ziba is a competent person that has the capacity "to perceive information, process it, and understand the information and its implications, in order to make and communicate the decision."[32] The mediator cannot shield Ziba from these pressures, only discuss them with her, help her evaluate them, and give her time and space to consider alternative courses of action. The mediator might postpone the mediation for some time, encourage her to consult close friends or family, and even use professional help. But in the end of the day, however constrained by the circumstances and by Ahmed's insistence, Ziba's choice is her choice and the mediator cannot justify an intervention in her choice for the paternalistic reason that he or she knows better what is right for *her.*[33]

b. Informed decision Decisions that are made on the basis of inadequate information do not represent a true exercise of self-determination.[34] Thus, the *Proposed Code* provides that "[a] mediator shall conduct the mediation under conditions that enable parties to make informed decisions. An informed decision is a decision that has been made on the basis of the information that is relevant for the decision-making."[35] Relevant information is defined as "information the knowledge or ignorance of which could influence the decision or the choice made."[36]

In the case of Ziba and Ahmed, it is fairly obvious that American law on the right of Ziba to divorce despite Ahmed's disagreement, her rights to a portion of the family assets and to financial assistance, her rights with respect to the children, and the possible voidability of the mediated agreement should undoubtedly be in the parties' mind while making a decision on the divorce. Of course, a mediator cannot ensure that parties make decisions that are based on complete information. However, the mediator must take steps, consistent with his other ethical obligations, so that party decision-making is based on the information relevant for the decision-making.[37] In our hypothetical the mediator will have to make sure that the parties are legally represented or are aware of that information through other means, or otherwise refer them to outside legal experts.

32 Id., Standard IV.D. See also Chapter 4, Section 4.3.2; Section 16.2.4.
33 But see Section b(4) in this chapter (Professional integrity (prevention of substantial defects in the process)).
34 See Chapter 4, Section 4.3.4. 35 Proposed Code, Standard IV.F.
36 Id., Standard IV.F.1; Chapter 4, Section 4.3.4.
37 Id., Standard IV.F.1; Chapter 4, Section 4.5.3.

3) Professional integrity (separating professional roles) and impartiality

Providing the information directly to the parties would seem to be wrong for reasons of *professional integrity*. "A mediator's conduct reflects professional integrity when he is committed to the nature and definition of both his role as a mediator and mediation."[38] Providing legal information or advice on Ziba's rights is the task of a lawyer. When mediators, including lawyer-mediators, conduct mediations they must distinguish between their role as mediators and other professional roles, otherwise they are not truly committed to their role as mediators.[39] Therefore, the *Proposed Code*, like many other codes of conduct for mediators, guides mediators to refrain from giving legal advice, providing that "[a] mediator shall not give parties professional advice or professional opinion that applies professional (e.g., legal) principles to the facts of the mediation case."[40] A common exception to that rule seeks to distinguish between the provision of information as opposed to giving advice, and accordingly the *Proposed Code* like other codes states that "[a] mediator may provide parties with general information that he is qualified by training or experience to provide, without mixing his role as a mediator and another professional role, consistent with the standard of self-determination and the standard of impartiality."[41] However, in Ziba and Ahmed's case it is impossible to provide general information without losing impartiality, because the information clearly favors Ziba. Thus, although the mediator in Ziba and Ahmed's case must take steps to ensure that they are aware of their legal rights and obligations, the mediator must not provide that information by him or herself.

4) Professional integrity (prevention of substantial defects in the process)

Mediators' responsibilities are not only to the parties but also to the profession and the public.[42] Mediators are responsible that the process of mediation not be abused and that its outcomes not harm important social interests such as the rule of law, the rules of critical morality, and the institution of mediation.[43] Although the parties have a right to self-determination, they cannot legitimately expect mediators to assist them in concluding agreements that are illegal, immoral, or unconscionable. Self-determination as an ethical norm does not extend to such conduct. Moreover, the profession and the public expect mediators to prevent

[38] Id., Standard V. [39] See Chapter 8, Section 8.2.2. [40] Proposed Code, Standard V.B.2.
[41] Id., Standard V.B.2(a). [42] See Chapter 3, Section 3.7.
[43] See Chapter 8, Section 8.2.4.3.

such mediation outcomes because mediators are perceived, at least partly, as responsible for outcomes that were reached in a process that they conducted, outcomes that they could have frustrated by terminating the process.[44]

The two commentators argue that if the agreement that Ziba and Ahmed agree on is in violation of American law the mediator should not proceed with the mediation, and this argument is supported by the theory of mediators' ethics. Menkel-Meadow believes that "no mediator (and certainly not this mediator) should participate in a mediation that she thinks will lead to a morally, legally, or ethically 'unconscionable' result" (p. 323), but then goes on to state that "[w]hat is unconscionable is, of course, subjective, personal, and nonuniversal" (Ibid.). This personal account of morality, ethics, and unconscionability is probably shared by Abramson, who chooses to put his personal values aside and look for "universally accepted international [legal] principles of human rights" (p. 328) on which to base his decision to proceed with the mediation. Following philosophers of morality such as Bernard Gert and H.L.A. Hart, the theory of mediators' ethics offers a different account of morality and ethics that has a non-subjective dimension, and distinguishes between personal senses and values of morality, ethics, and judgments of unconscionability on the one hand, and standards that are *external* to the mediator and to a local community located within a larger one on the other.[45]

There is a sound moral basis for criticizing norms that systematically give men power over women (for example, to control their movements and decisions), subjugate women's rights to men's will (for example, condition divorce on the consent of men), or automatically place children with their father without reference to their actual needs (for example, reverting custody at a certain age). It is not a matter of personal values alone, and a charge of cultural imperialism should not deter one who is willing to expose his judgment to impartial and rational moral testing. Cultural sensitivity and humility are not the same as mechanical acceptance of all the norms of another culture. Patriarchic and discriminating norms are morally wrong even when and where they are widely accepted. The fact that Iran or other Middle Eastern states have not *legally* endorsed certain conventions or treaties (as suggested by Abramson) does not mean that they are not *morally* bound by fundamental norms of equality. The immorality of Ziba and Ahmed's

[44] Ibid. [45] See Chapter 1, Section 1.2.1.1.

agreement is indeed based on a concept of morality and ethics developed in the West, but this fact does not indicate that this concept is wrong and that it cannot serve as a legitimate guide for human action so long as a more convincing concept has not emerged. Thus, the concept of critical morality guides the mediator to decline to proceed with the agreement.

Moreover, like morality, the concept of unconscionability is not wholly subjective as well. When used in the context of mediation and from a professional ethics perspective, it comes to indicate conduct that grossly deviates from acceptable social norms to a degree that could jeopardize public faith in the profession and process of mediation.[46] Such conduct need not be illegal, or immoral in a critical sense, because it is connected to the actual norms that dominate a given society in which mediation is practiced, sometimes referred to as positive morality.[47] From a role-morality perspective, the responsibilities of a mediator who is a member of a Western community, conducts the mediation in a Western country, and is perceived by the Western public as a representative of the profession of mediation are *to the general Western public and to the Western community of mediators with whom he or she is associated.* The "constituency" of the mediator in Ziba and Ahmed's case is not the Iranian-American community (or Iran or other Muslim states, for that matter) but the American public at large, which is likely to view the agreement as grossly unfair due to its departure from acceptable American social norms. Abramson captured this notion by remarking: "I would not want the *mediation process* (or me) to be associated with . . . an unfair mediated result" (p. 335, emphasis added), yet preferred to follow the parties' wishes. However, if the likely outcome of the mediated agreement is so detrimental to the profession and process of mediation, then this is a strong argument for the mediator not to facilitate such agreement notwithstanding the parties' wishes.

Conclusion

The challenging case of Ziba and Ahmed and the comments of Professor Menkel-Meadow and Abramson provide an opportunity to illustrate the contribution of the theory of mediators' ethics to the analysis of difficult cases and to the practice of mediation.

Both Menkel-Meadow (p. 321) and Abramson (p. 329) used the *Model Standards* as an authoritative statement of "our profession's norms," but in fact found little help in it. The theory offers a complementary source of

[46] See Chapter 8, Section 8.2.4.3(c). [47] See Chapter 1, Section 1.2.1.1.

guidance. Moreover, other mediators who do not take the *Model Standards* as an authoritative guide, or find it wanting, need an alternative source of guidance. For example, some mediators might find the *Model Standards*' choice to "steer clear of discussions of fairness, equity and substantive justice" (p. 329) unsatisfactory.

Both Menkel-Meadow and Abramson believe that self-determination concerns require that Ziba should be aware of her rights under American law. The question for the mediator is how that information should be made available to her. Menkel-Meadow decides to provide the information herself, while Abramson conveniently assumes that Ziba is legally represented. The theory helps mediators who find themselves in such circumstances by reminding them of their duty of professional integrity to *distinguish between the role of mediator and other professional roles such as the role of lawyer*. This duty applies to all mediators, including lawyer-mediators, in order to construct and preserve mediation as a separate and independent profession. Thus, reasons of professional integrity, together with impartiality, would support the view that such information should be made available through open questions, use of the parties' lawyers (if they have ones), or through referral to outside experts.

Both commentators deal with the case by asking themselves what the parties want, what the *Model Standards* state, what the law prohibits, and what their personal values mandate. I assume that many mediators would follow that line of thinking, and in the likely event that the law and the *Model Standards* are indeterminate will feel justified in following their personal values. The theory helps mediators by suggesting a different set of questions: (1) what are your obligations as a mediator to the parties? (2) What are your obligations to the profession? And (3) what are your obligations to the public? The last two questions are only rarely explicitly raised and considered by mediators. The theory's *Proposed Code* is more elaborated on these points in comparison to existing codes and thus more suitable in offering guidance to mediators. Thus the theory provides *justifications beyond the mediator's personal convictions*, and points not only to the mediator's responsibilities toward the parties but to his or her obligations toward the profession and the public as well.

Bringing into the discussion the responsibilities of mediators toward the profession and the public is helpful in the evaluation of alternative courses of action and their justifications. Thus, the theory is able to reinforce Menkel-Meadow's decision to withdraw, while criticizing her decision to provide legal advice to the parties (decisions that she has based on her personal values); and to support Abramson's decision to gain competence by familiarizing himself with the parties' culture, while criticizing his decision to proceed with the process and outcome.

16.2.3 *The probing judge and the ordering court:* confidentiality and disclosure of mediation information to court

The Probing Judge and the Ordering Court case is based on two sources: a hypothetical on the American Bar Association Section of Dispute Resolution site titled "The Judge Beckons," presented by Professor Tim Hedeen,[48] and a mediator question referred to the Ethics Forum of the Kiryat-Ono Community Mediation Center about court-ordered mediator testimony.[49]

The facts

The Probing Judge hypothetical describes a mediation between two legally represented parties that concluded in a signed agreement. A week after the mediation, Party A asked the court to set aside the agreement because, she argued, she was incompetent to contract. With the consent of both parties, the judge decided to contact the mediator and ask for her assessment of Party A's condition during the mediation.

The Ordering Court case takes this scenario further. A husband and wife used mediation for their divorce. They were not legally represented at the mediation, but the mediated agreement was approved by the court. Sometime later, Party A asked the court to set the agreement aside for various reasons, including alleged incompetence to contract, undue influence and pressures to settle exerted by both Party B and the mediator, and failure to understand the terms of the agreement and its consequences. Both parties agreed that the mediator should testify on these issues, and the court summoned the mediator to testify.

Commentary

The commentary to the hypothetical summarizes the various responses of mediators to the hypothetical: (a) mediators noted that according to common provisions of confidentiality laws mediators must not disclose information about the *content* of a mediation; (b) confidentiality, they

48 See The Judge Beckons available at www.americanbar.org/groups/dispute_resolution/resources/Ethics.html.

49 Kiryat-Ono Community Mediation Center Ethics Forum, Opinion 6–2014 (on file with the author).

thought, arguably did not apply to the mediator's judgment of a party's demeanor and ability to participate, though some mediators were concerned that by explaining his assessment the mediator would probably have to refer to communications with the parties, thus breaking confidentiality; the commentator raised concerns that (c) mediators are not sufficiently trained to assess the psychological fitness of parties to mediation; and (d) that their testimony on that issue is predictable and of limited utility because a mediator is not likely to say that he thought a party is incompetent yet decided to proceed with the mediation; still (e) some mediators thought the mediator should respect the parties' decision to waive confidentiality in accordance with their right to self-determination; though in the end of the day (f) the dominant response was that the mediator should decline to offer any information regarding the mediation other than that a mediation was held between the parties.

The theory of mediators' ethics perspective

(a) The probing judge hypothetical What is the theory's contribution to the analysis of this hypothetical? The first point to note is the difference between legal and ethical protection of mediation confidentiality. The responding mediators were right in their concern to establish the extent of the *legal* protection of mediation confidentiality according to local laws, because this could help them clarify the type of information mediators are *legally prohibited* from disclosing. However, this exercise should not replace an examination of the extent of the information they are *ethically prohibited* from disclosing, which might be wider. The theory of mediators' ethics draws mediators' attention to the law/ethics distinction in order to make them realize that permission to disclose information in *law* (because disclosure is not legally prohibited) does not constitute a permission to do so in *ethics*.[50]

Second, mediators responding to the hypothetical gave much weight to the right of parties to *self-determination*, which they understood as allowing the parties to waive confidentiality protection. However, the respondents arrived at the conclusion that the mediator should *not* disclose the information, despite the parties' wishes. What is missing in the responses and the commentary is the *normative basis* for this conclusion. Indeed, the commentary explicitly referred to the lack of ethical guidance on the tension between party self-determination and confidentiality, noting that "[h]ow the standards of self-determination and

[50] See Chapter 10, Section 10.3.

confidentiality function in relation to one another is not prescribed in the Model Standards of Conduct for Mediators." The theory of mediators' ethics, however, does provide guidance on that issue.[51] The conclusion of the commentary, that the mediator should not disclose the information to the judge despite the parties' waiver of confidentiality, is supported by the theory's account of mediators' responsibilities toward *the profession and the public*. On this account, the parties' right to self-determination is not without limitations, as the parties cannot legitimately expect the mediator to act in breach of his other ethical responsibilities. From this perspective, one realizes that the gist of the hypothetical is not the effect of the disclosure on the *parties* and their interests in maintaining confidentiality, but its effect on the *process* of mediation and the interests of the profession and the public in maintaining the standing of the profession and public trust in the profession and the process. More pointedly, the question that the mediator in the hypothetical should ask himself is whether the disclosure of legally permitted information might compromise his *appearance of impartiality*, thereby undermining public confidence in the process of mediation. The Standard of Confidentiality in the *Proposed Code* thus provides that "[a] mediator may disclose mediation information where the disclosure (1) does not undermine the standing of the profession and public trust in it, and (2) is consistent with the other Standards."[52] Note that if the mediator were to provide the judge with his assessment of Party A's competence to contract he would necessarily be taking a side in the legal dispute between the parties, because his input would be advantageous to one party and detrimental to the other. This is the ethical reason why the mediator should decline to provide the information to the judge, not the protection of confidentiality per se.

(b) The ordering court case The facts of the Ordering Court case add complexity to the hypothetical. The parties were not legally represented, so we might be more concerned about how well their rights had been protected during the mediation; the court *ordered* the mediator to appear before the court, so he might be *legally required* to provide the information to the court; and Party A claimed that both Party B *and the mediator* were responsible for his defective consent to the mediated agreement. The basic ethical analysis, however, does not change, though it is more complicated because the mediator has to convince the court that he should not be compelled to provide the information sought.

[51] See Chapter 10, Sections 10.2.2 and 10.4.4.2. [52] See Proposed Code, Standard IX.C.1.

First, the mediator should find out whether an applicable mediation privilege exists in the jurisdiction in which he or she operates that covers the information sought and that is independent of the parties' will. An affirmative answer could solve the ethical problem, because the mediator would then be able to rely on the privilege and have a *legal reason* for maintaining the confidentiality of mediation information. Alternatively, in a jurisdiction in which a mediation privilege has not been recognized yet, or when an existing privilege is relative or its limits unclear, the mediator should raise before the court the *possibility* that the information sought is privileged and seek the court's decision on that point before giving testimony.[53]

Second, in the event that the privilege does not apply for some reason, the mediator should make sure that he or she is not *ethically obligated* to decline to provide the information. Basically this means that he or she should consider whether the provision of the information could undermine the standing of the profession and public trust in the profession and process of mediation.[54] As a general statement, the use of a mediator's testimony for the purpose of deciding a legal suit between the parties would seem to be detrimental to the mediation process and profession because potential users of mediation would be (a) hesitant to cooperate with and trust mediators, knowing that their conduct and communications might be used against them in future litigation; and (b) less willing to try mediation because testifying mediators would lose their reputation and the public perception of them as impartial third parties.

This general statement has to be *specified* in the context of the particular facts of any given case, because the ethical obligations of mediators are not absolute and there may be cases in which a mediator's testimony would be ethically legitimate. For example, *a mediator sued* by a party would be ethically justified to disclose information from the mediation to the extent necessary for his legal defense.[55] Similarly, there may be exceptional cases where the mediator's testimony would be ethically permissible in *litigation in which both parties were involved*, for example, where the mediator witnessed an assault on one party by another resulting in serious bodily harm.[56] It is suggested that the mediator should reflect on the following considerations in making the decision whether

[53] See Chapter 10, Section 10.4.4.3. [54] See Proposed Code, Standard IX.C.1.

[55] See Chapter 10, Section 10.4.2.1.

[56] See id., Section 10.4.4.2. See also Tennessee Alternative Dispute Resolution Commission, Opinion 2010–0002 available at tncourts.gov/sites/default/files/adrc_advisory_opinion_2010–0002.pdf.

his or her testimony is ethically permissible:[57] (1) would the provision of information in the given circumstances be likely to give an outside observer the impression that the mediator is taking sides in the dispute between the parties or is being used by the parties to further their interests? (2) Would that impression jeopardize the mediator's impartial standing and the standing of the profession to an extent that might undermine public faith in the profession and process of mediation? And (3) is the information crucial to the litigation in view of the severity of the case, and can it be obtained by other means than the mediator's testimony? These considerations should also be communicated to the court in an attempt to convince the court to exempt the mediator from testifying or to limit the type of information he or she is required to provide. The court, of course, may nonetheless order disclosure in circumstances where the mediator believes he should not make a disclosure on ethical grounds, but in most cases I assume that obeying the court (and the rule of law for that matter) would serve as a good justification for the disclosure in ethics as well.

Informed by the theory's approach and applying these considerations to the particular facts of the Ordering Court case, the Ethics Forum thought that there were good reasons for the mediator to refrain from providing the information to the court. First, the mediated agreement had been approved by the court in the presence of the parties, after the parties answered questions relating to the content of the agreement directed at them by the court. Second, the mediator's testimony was not crucial to the litigation because the information could be obtained through the parties' testimonies, cross examinations, and other forms of evidence. Third, the party's claims that sought to invalidate the mediated agreement on the basis of party incompetence, undue influence, and lack of informed consent were not supported by any shred of evidence. The Forum thought that such claims must be backed by at least some evidence to justify the mediator's testimony, otherwise any such claim, which could be made by any party to a mediation, would automatically result in mediators being summoned to court on a regular and frequent basis (the mediator himself was not sued by any of the parties). And fourth, the circumstances of the case were not exceptional enough in their severity to justify having the mediator testify. The Ethics Forum suggested that the mediator bring up these considerations before the court so that the judge

[57] See id., Section 10.4.4.2.

be made aware of the professional ethics dimension of having the mediator testify and the stakes for the mediation process and profession.

Using the perspective of mediators' ethics theory, the Forum then went on to discuss the types of information that the mediator might be asked to provide, classified them as more or less detrimental to the perception of the mediator as being impartial, and suggested possible responses to such questions in the event that the court insisted on getting an answer. First, questions that could be viewed as *technical*, such as questions about the dates mediation sessions took place, were considered the least harmful, because answering them was less likely to give an appearance of partiality or portray the mediator as a means in the hands of one party. Second, questions that could be framed as *general* questions about *procedure*, for example whether an explanation of the process was given to the parties, whether the agreement was discussed with the parties, and whether the parties where pressured to settle, were considered "middle ground" questions in terms of their potential harm. On the one hand, it seemed that no harm could follow from answering these questions since the answers to them were predictable: it is clear that any mediator properly conducting a mediation would explain the process, discuss the agreement, and avoid undue influence. On the other hand, the only reason for eliciting these answers from the mediator seemed to be to support Party B's (the defendant's) claim that the mediated agreement was valid, with the harmful consequence of causing the mediator to be seen as collaborating with one party against the other. The Forum suggested that if answering such questions could not be avoided the mediator should attempt to answer them in a general manner, saying, for example, "I always explain about the process," or "I would not allow parties to make an agreement in circumstances that make me suspect coercion or misunderstanding of the agreement." And third, *concrete* questions about the state of mind or conduct of a party were considered the most problematic in terms of maintaining the standing of the profession and process of mediation, because by answering them the mediator would have clearly become a witness associated with one of the parties, in the present case Party B, that sought to support his claim that Party A had been competent to contract and that the agreement was voluntarily entered into. If compelled to answer, it was again suggested that the mediator should try to distance himself from the particular case and provide a more generalized answer, saying, for example, "I would not proceed with a mediation and allow parties to make an agreement in circumstances in which I suspect the parties do not understand the process or the agreement or make a coerced agreement."

Conclusion

The discussion of the Probing Judge hypothetical and the Ordering Court case from the theory of mediators' ethics perspective shows that court requests or even demands for disclosure of mediation information should be treated with great caution, because the ethical responsibility of mediators to refrain from such disclosure goes beyond their legal obligation of confidentiality or evidentiary privilege when one exists. Such disclosure can be ethically justified in exceptional circumstances only because it could jeopardize public trust in the process and profession of mediation and in the role of mediators. The primary reason for avoiding such conduct, despite parties' waiver of confidentiality, is not the protection of the confidentiality of the process, but the need to maintain the impartial standing of mediators and the standing of the profession, and to secure the readiness of the public to continue using mediation as a voluntary means of resolving disputes. Since judges are trained to do legal justice, and since mediation is a young profession, judges might not be sensitive enough to these professional concerns. Mediators who are contacted by judges, court personnel, and lawyers and asked to provide mediation information should raise these ethical concerns, along with legal reasons (if any) that support nondisclosure, such as statutory confidentiality protection or applicable evidentiary privilege. Where mediators are nevertheless legally compelled to make such disclosure, they should limit their answers as far as possible to technical and procedural aspects of the mediation (for example, the dates mediation sessions were held on or explanations given on the process), avoiding as far as possible concrete descriptions of the parties' conduct during the mediation and subjective assessments of their mental state.

16.2.4 *The emotional interrupting party:* party self-determination (party incompetency) and respect and dignity

The facts

A small-claims court case, co-mediated by community mediation center volunteers, gave rise to a mediator query that came before the Ethics Forum of the Kiryat-Ono Community Mediation Center.[58] The defendant renovated her flat, and in the course of the renovation water leaked to the plaintiff's flat on a lower floor, causing damage to the plaintiff's

[58] Kiryat-Ono Community Mediation Center Ethics Forum, Opinion 2–2013 (on file with the author).

belongings. The plaintiff brought an action for damages; the defendant argued that the water leak resulted from actions taken by another neighbor. During the mediation, the plaintiff, an old woman and a Holocaust survivor, became very emotional. She continuously shouted at the defendant, a younger woman, describing at length the troubles she went through in the process of immigrating to Israel from Russia, the loss of her husband, the hardships of raising her son as a single mother, and her medical problems. She repeatedly denounced the plaintiff as a liar, patronizing, and racist, complaining that the defendant, born in Israel, was condescending and humiliating in her behavior. The mediators addressed these high feelings by offering empathy and space for ventilation. The plaintiff's outbursts, however, continued. The mediators then met with both parties separately, allowing the plaintiff more time to air her feelings and discuss her story. During these sessions, the defendant agreed to pay some compensation and was willing to raise her offers, but the plaintiff kept on attacking the defendant, rejecting her proposals and expressing strong feelings of insult, anger, injustice, and deprivation. At that stage, the mediators decided to terminate the mediation, but were left with the thought that they should have done so at an earlier stage, possibly at the stage that the plaintiff related her story for the first time. One of the mediators told the Forum that she had concerns about the competency of the plaintiff to participate in the process and about the limits of acceptable behavior during mediation.

Discussion

The Forum, informed by the theory of mediators' ethics approach, thought that the facts did not indicate party incompetence, but considered the termination of the mediation to be correct because the plaintiff's behavior (a) substantially departed from the norm of respect and dignity, and (b) undermined the quality of the process to a degree that made proceeding with the mediation futile. The Forum considered various steps that the mediators might have taken consistent with the norms of professional integrity and maintaining the profession's standing. A summary of the Opinion follows, with references to the relevant provisions of the *Proposed Code.*

(a) The question of party competence A major concern raised by the mediators was the emotional capacity of the plaintiff to participate in the mediation. Party competence is an essential element for exercising self-determination, which is a fundamental feature of mediation.[59] "Party competency is the capacity of a party to perceive information, process it, and understand the information and its implications, in order to make and communicate the decision."[60] Emotional stress, depression, and anxiety can undermine a party's competence, sometimes temporarily, and require the mediator to take measures that address that problem.[61] The *Proposed Code* therefore provides that "[a] mediator who suspects that a party's capacity to participate in the mediation and understand information is limited, shall take appropriate steps to assist the party to understand the information, participate in the process, and exercise self-determination, including postponing the mediation or involving a representative of the party in the process. When the mediator's intervention is neither possible nor successful the mediator shall terminate the mediation."[62] The facts described by the mediators in the present case, however, did not indicate party incompetency. Although the plaintiff continuously "lost control," shouted at the other party, used inflammatory language, and did not respond to the mediators' attempts to engage her in a constructive dialogue, it seems that she understood what she was doing and chose to act the way she did. The mediators were therefore not under an ethical duty to terminate the mediation due to party incapacity.

(b) Respect and dignity Mediators are expected to conduct mediations "in a manner that respects and acknowledges the dignity of others" and to "promote mutual respect among the participants."[63] They cannot remain passive when one participant attacks the dignity of another participant because they are in charge of the process. Participants reasonably expect the mediator in their case to intervene and prevent an ongoing attack on their dignity, and the profession and the public expect mediators not to enable behavior that could bring the profession and process of mediation into disrepute.[64]

Insulting, shouting, and cursing are not expressions of respect. At the beginning of mediation, mediators commonly present the parties with the process rules, including a requirement for mutual respect, and the parties agree to abide by the rules of the process. Naturally, in the course

[59] See Chapter 4, Section 4.3.1.
[60] See Proposed Code, Standard IV.D; Chapter 4, Section 4.3.2.
[61] See Chapter 4, Section 4.5.1. [62] See Proposed Code, Standard IV.D.2.
[63] See Proposed Code, Standards VII and VII.C; Chapter 9, Section 9.2.
[64] See Chapter 9, Section 9.2.3.

of mediation tensions can rise and parties will express their anger and frustration in different ways, some of them abusive and unpleasant. Mediation need not be a calm, reserved process, because such an environment would not suit all participants in every type of dispute. Still, the role of mediators in such cases is to place limits on parties' conduct, reminding them of the process rules and norms. If parties *repeat* their abusive behavior *over and over again* in disregard of the mediator's intervention, the process should be brought to an end because it does not respect other parties, the mediator, the profession, and the mediation center in connection with which the process takes place.

(c) Professional integrity Mediators must conduct mediations with professional integrity.[65] "A mediator's conduct reflects professional integrity when he is committed to the nature and definition of both his role as a mediator and mediation."[66] The essence of mediation is a dialogue between disputing parties. Like any dialogue, mediation has its ups and downs, with barriers to communication, parties holding to their positions or narratives, and impasses. Still, when a party *continuously* acts in a way that makes the dialogue *impossible* and rejects all suggestions that he modify his behavior, a point may come at which the mediator has no choice but to terminate the process because he cannot conduct "a mediation process." In the circumstances described above, the plaintiff either did not want or was not able to participate in an effective dialogue. After making continuing efforts to reach the plaintiff, the mediators were justified in their decision to terminate the mediation as a last resort, believing that the plaintiff acted in a way that made the conduct of mediation impossible, and probably thinking that there was no reasonable likelihood that the parties would be able to reach a mediated agreement,[67] a stated goal of this court-connected mediation.

(d) The profession and the mediation center's standing Mediators must exercise their role in a manner that maintains the profession's standing and public trust in the mediation profession and process.[68] Moreover, when mediators conduct mediations on behalf of a mediation center, they must do so in a manner that will not undermine the employer's or principal's standing and public trust in it.[69] A mediation

[65] See Chapter 8, Section 8.1. [66] See Proposed Code, Standard V.
[67] See Chapter 8, Section 8.2.3; Proposed Code, Standard V.C.2.
[68] See Chapter 12, Section 12.1.1. [69] See Chapter 14, Section 14.1 and 14.3.

process that is dominated by party shouting, insults, racist statements and general disrespect to other participants might undermine the profession and center's standing, namely devaluate the public perception of them, harm their image or reputation, and diminish the willingness of the public to use mediation in general or receive mediation services from the center in particular. By terminating the mediation in the case described, the mediators sent a message to the parties and to others through them that the mediation profession and the mediation center are worthy of both respect and confidence.

Conclusion

What made this case difficult in an ethical sense for the mediators involved was that the mediators felt that they had a responsibility to bring the mediation to an end, but were unsure for what reasons, because both parties were willing to proceed with the process. The theory of mediators' ethics perspective indicated that the relevant concerns in the particular case beyond party self-determination were professional integrity (the quality of the process and its integrity) and the profession and center's standing (the process's potential adverse effect on the reputation of the profession and the mediation center). Terminating a mediation should always be the last resort after all other measures have been taken. The type of required interventions will vary in accordance with the mediators' skills and orientation. For example, other mediators might have been able to reach that party using various techniques. It is also possible that breaking up the process into separate meetings at an earlier stage in order for the plaintiff to ventilate her high emotions might have made a difference. Mediators, however, should appreciate that if their efforts are not well received by parties, their obligations to the parties themselves, the profession, and in this case to the mediation center could require their withdrawal.

16.2.5 *Post-mediation psychiatric treatment:* conflict of interest

The facts

The Tennessee Alternative Dispute Resolution Commission was asked to provide an opinion on the question whether a court-connected [Rule 31] mediator, who is a psychiatrist, is permitted to "provide post-mediation psychiatric treatment to a participant in the mediation."[70] The Commission treated the question as one depending solely on the issue of *confidentiality*, reminding mediators that they are not allowed to disclose information obtained by them during the course of mediation and noting that this obligation continues after the mediation ends. The Commission was concerned with the propriety of such practice, but thought that it raised a *medical* rather than a mediation ethics question. The Commission thus noted that "[i]t is difficult to imagine how a psychiatrist could undertake to subsequently treat a patient, who was a party to a prior mediation. One would think that the best treatment would need to proceed with the open mind of the provider. However, this would seem to be a medical ethics question, and not one for consideration by this Commission."

Theory of mediators' ethics perspective

The Commission's decision would have read differently had it applied the theory of mediators' ethics. The Commission would have appreciated that at the heart of the question was a genuine mediation ethics issue of *conflict of interest subsequent to mediation.*[71] With that in mind, the Commission would have likely interpreted Rule 31 as warning mediators against such practice as a matter of ethical *mediator* practice.

As noted in Chapter 6, entering into a professional relationship with a former mediation client after the mediation has ended raises concerns about the way the mediator conducted the mediation.[72] Was the mediator impartial? Was he or she thinking about the future engagement at the time the mediation took place? Did it affect his or her judgment? Did he or she solicit or incur the future professional service?

These concerns have the potential to undermine public trust in the profession and process of mediation, calling on mediators to exercise caution in establishing any professional relationship with mediation parties subsequent to mediation. Rule 31, like other codes of conduct for mediators, includes a conflict of interest provision that could be interpreted in that spirit. Section 6(b)(5) of Tennessee Rule 31 states that "[a] Neutral shall not use the dispute resolution process to solicit, encourage, or otherwise incur future professional services with either party." Section 1(a) refers to the purpose of the rules, providing that "[t]

[70] See Tennessee Alternative Dispute Resolution Commission, Opinion 2014-0002 available at www.tncourts.gov/sites/default/files/docs/adrc_ethics_advisory_opinion_2014-0002-04-22-14.pdf.

[71] See Chapter 6, Section 6.4.2.2. [72] Ibid.

hese rules are intended to instill and promote public confidence in the Alternative Dispute Resolution process," and reminds mediators that they "are responsible to the parties, the public, and the courts to conduct themselves in a manner which will merit that confidence." Section 2(a)(1) goes on to provide that "[a] Neutral shall not accept any engagement, perform any service, or undertake any act which would compromise the Neutral's integrity." Taking a *mediator* professional ethics perspective, the Commission would have realized that avoiding a conflict of interest and the maintenance of public confidence in the mediation process, as well as confidentiality, are obligations that continue after the mediation has ended.[73] It would and should have treated the question whether a mediator is permitted to provide post-mediation psychiatric services as a genuine ethical question of mediator practice, while observing (as it did) that it has a medical ethics dimension as well.

Taking this approach, the Commission would have been able to point to the *type of considerations* other than maintaining the confidentiality of information obtained in the mediation that mediators in general and the mediator who submitted the question in particular should consider before providing post-mediation psychiatric treatment to an individual involved in the mediation. For example, it would have looked at the *time elapsed* following the mediation, noting that the longer the time elapsed the lesser the risk that the mediator's conduct might be perceived as inappropriate; it would have considered the *nature of the relationship*, noting, for example, that the concern for a conflict of interest would have been lesser if the mediator had been a public servant treating the party for free as part of his public clinic; and it would have examined in more detail the *nature of the offered services*, noting, for example, the difference between a onetime meeting for the purpose of prescribing anti-depression pills as opposed to a long and expensive therapeutic process. The Commission's original message of cautious reserve regarding such practice would have remained the same. With the theory's perspective, however, the reasons for the Commission's stand would have been more substantiated, and the guidance to mediators more exact.

[73] See ibid. and the references there (e.g. to provisions in codes that limit future relationships in order to protect the "integrity of the mediation," and to Georgia Commission on Dispute Resolution's Committee on Ethics, Opinion 5-2012 arguing that perceived or actual conflicts of interest should be avoided after as well as during the mediation).

APPENDIX I A PROPOSED MODEL CODE OF CONDUCT FOR MEDIATORS

The *Proposed Model Code of Conduct for Mediators* (Proposed Code) is the end product of the theory of mediators' ethics. It builds upon codes of conduct for mediators adopted in Anglo-American countries, including the United States, Canada, and Australia.[1] The *Proposed Code* reflects in its Standards the minimum ethical norms of conduct that mediators in Anglo-American societies are expected to observe.[2]

Introduction

Mediation is a process in which a third person – a mediator – assists parties to an actual or potential conflict in maintaining a dialogue in order to enable them to make decisions regarding the conflict and reach an agreement when they wish to do so. The provision of mediation services is a social interest: mediation enables people to engage in dialogue and address disagreements on a consensual basis, absent state or individual coercion, and with savings of both private and public resources. Moreover, mediation promotes a better society based on dialogue, social harmony, and agreement.

The purpose of the *Proposed Code* is to –

(a) Inform mediators about the Standards of conduct for mediators and offer guidance for conducting mediation;
(b) Inform mediation parties about the mediation process, their rights and obligations while participating in mediation, and the obligations and rights of mediators in conducting mediation;
(c) Enhance public confidence in the mediation process and profession.

The *Proposed Code* is aimed at supplementing, not replacing, legislation, case-law, court rules or other professional rules of obligatory force applicable to mediators.

[1] A version of the Proposed Code was adopted by the Kiryat-Ono Community Mediation Center, Israel in 2014. I thank the members of the center's Ethics Forum for their valuable contribution and suggestions in discussing various provisions of the Proposed Code.
[2] See Chapter 3, Section 3.10.

The *Proposed Code* Standards include different levels of guidance:

(a) Obligations – the Standards state the duties of mediators, using the terms "shall" and "must" to indicate actions that mediators have to take or refrain from taking.
(b) Permissions – the Standards use the term "may" to indicate actions that mediators are permitted to take or refrain from taking. Professional discretion must be exercised on the basis of relevant considerations and good reasons that can be reasonably justified.
(c) Aspirations – all duty-imposing Standards indicate ideals (as well as obligations) that call for the realization of each Standard beyond its compulsory threshold. The ideal feature of the Standards corresponds to excellence in ethical conduct that exceeds the demands of duty; a goal accomplished by excellent mediators committed to the highest level of ethical conduct. Mediators are encouraged to reach that ethical bar but cannot be criticized for failing to do so.

The *Proposed Code* reflects the obligations of mediators toward mediation parties, the mediation profession and colleagues, the public, and employers or principals.

(a) Mediation Parties – a mediator has a duty to exercise his or her role in a manner worthy of the parties' trust.
(b) The Mediation Profession and Colleagues – a mediator has a duty to exercise his or her role in a manner that maintains the standing of the profession and public trust in the profession and process of mediation.
(c) The Public – a mediator has a duty to exercise his or her role in a manner that avoids harming important social interests such as the maintenance of the rule of law and the institution of mediation.
(d) Employers and Principals – a mediator conducting a mediation on behalf of or in connection with an organization (for example, a mediation center or a referring court) has a duty to exercise his or her role in a manner that is worthy of the institution's trust, maintains the standing of the institution and public confidence in it, and is consistent with the institution's rules.

The *Proposed Code* should be read, interpreted, and applied in its entirety. The obligations of mediators are relative, not absolute, and no obligation has a prima-facie priority over another. Therefore, when obligations seem to conflict, a mediator shall –

(a) Search for an alternative course of action that is consistent with all of his or her obligations; and

(b) Terminate or withdraw from the mediation when he or she cannot prevent the violation, minimizing as far as possible the harm resulting from the violation.

The standards

I. Competence

A mediator shall mediate only when he or she has the competence to conduct the mediation.

A. Competence to Mediate –

1. Basic Competence – A mediator shall mediate only when he or she has the knowledge and skills necessary for carrying out his or her role in an effective way. An effectively conducted mediation assists the parties to communicate, negotiate, and make decisions.
   (a) Basic competence will normally require mediation training and experience.
   (b) A mediator enlisted with a mediation program or organization shall comply with the qualification requirements set by it.
2. Specific Competence – A mediator shall have special knowledge and skills beyond basic competence when he or she is reasonably expected to have them on the basis of his or her own representations, institutional (mediation program or organization) rules, or circumstances. Specific competence may include subject-matter expertise, cultural knowledge, or language skills.
3. Maintaining Competence – A mediator must maintain his or her competence to mediate and is encouraged to improve his or her knowledge and skills relating to mediation through continuing education and related activities.

B. A mediator shall provide the parties upon request with information regarding his or her training, education, and experience.

C. Incompetence –

1. A mediator lacking basic competence, or specific competence when such is required, shall notify the parties and decline to mediate notwithstanding the parties' wishes that he or she mediate the case, unless his or her incompetence can be adequately addressed and compensated for through the involvement of other persons in the mediation.
2. A mediator shall decline to mediate when his or her ability to mediate is impaired by drugs, alcohol, medication, or other reasons.

II. Impartiality

A mediator shall exercise his or her role impartially. Impartiality means freedom from external manifestations of favoritism or bias between parties in word or action.

A. Accepting Cases and Withdrawal
   A mediator shall not accept a case for mediation or withdraw if:
   1. He or she cannot conduct the mediation impartially; or
   2. There is a reasonable concern that he or she is not or will not be able to conduct the mediation impartially or without an appearance of partiality, in circumstances that could jeopardize the standing of the profession and process of mediation and public trust in it.

B. In Conducting a Mediation and Exercising his or her Role –
   1. A mediator shall avoid partiality in fact, and any conduct that might reasonably appear as an act of partiality.
      (a) A mediator shall not act with partiality on the basis of reasons such as participants' race, sex, religion, personal characteristics, background, values and beliefs, or conduct at a mediation.
      (b) A mediator shall neither give nor accept a gift, favor, loan or other item of value that raises a question as to the mediator's impartiality. A mediator may accept or give de minimis gifts or services that are provided to facilitate a mediation or respect cultural norms so long as such practices do not raise questions as to a mediator's impartiality.
   2. A mediator shall treat parties differently where –
      (a) Same treatment would favor the interests of one party and disadvantage another; and
      (b) The mediator's intervention is (1) required in order to give effect to an ethical right of a party (in particular self-determination), or (2) necessary for the preservation of public trust in the profession and process of mediation.

      Any such intervention shall be limited to one that is –
      (a) The minimum necessary for the realization of the party's' right; and
      (b) Can be reconciled with other mediator obligations; and
      (c) Would not be perceived as an act of partiality in the eyes of a reasonable person and thus would not result in a loss of public trust in the profession and process of mediation.

III. Conflicts of interest

A mediator shall avoid a conflict of interest or the appearance of a conflict of interest at all stages of mediation or act to neutralize it in accordance with this standard. A conflict of interest is a situation in which an interest of a mediator conflicts with an interest of one party or more, and can arise, inter alia, (1) from involvement of a mediator with the subject matter of the dispute or its outcome; (b) from a personal or professional relationship, whether past or present, between a mediator and any mediation participant or a person related to a mediation participant; or (c) from a legal, moral, ethical, religious, conscientious, or other duty to act in a particular way.

A. The existence of an actual or potential conflict of interest is relevant information for the parties because it raises a concern regarding mediator partiality or possible preference of the mediator's interest over the interests of the parties. A mediator shall disclose a conflict of interest to the parties so as to enable them to exercise self-determination with regard to selection of the mediator and participation in the mediation.
   1. Prior to accepting a mediation –
      (a) A mediator shall make a reasonable inquiry to determine whether there are any facts that a reasonable person would consider likely to create a potential or actual conflict of interest for the mediator.
      (b) If following the inquiry a conflict of interest has been found the mediator shall disclose it to the parties as soon as practicable.
      (c) After disclosure, if all parties agree, the mediator may proceed with the mediation.
   2. During a mediation –
      (a) If a mediator learns any fact after accepting a mediation that raises a question of a potential or actual conflict of interest, the mediator shall disclose it to the parties as soon as practicable.
      (b) After disclosure, if all parties agree, the mediator may proceed with the mediation.
      (c) A mediator shall not solicit or otherwise incur any future professional services, including future mediations, beyond the sessions necessary for the mediation.

B. A serious conflict of interest –
   Notwithstanding the aforesaid, if a conflict of interest raises a reasonable concern that the mediator will not be able to refrain from harming a party's interest, and as a result the process might be publicly perceived as faulty, thereby jeopardizing the standing of the mediation profession and public trust in the profession and the process, the mediator shall withdraw or decline to proceed regardless of the express agreement of the parties.

C Subsequent to a mediation –

A mediator shall not establish a personal or professional relationship with parties, other individuals or organizations, following a mediation in which they were involved, that would raise a reasonable concern that the mediator had a conflict of interest and conducted a faulty process that could undermine the profession's standing and public trust in the profession and process of mediation. In making the decision, the mediator should consider factors such as the time elapsed since the mediation, the nature of the relationship established, and the type of services offered.

IV. Party self-determination

A mediator shall conduct the mediation on the basis of party self-determination. Self-determination means that the parties are free to make voluntary, uncoerced, and informed decisions.

A. Parties have a right to exercise self-determination with respect to any issue that has to be decided in the course of mediation, procedural or substantive, at any stage of the mediation, including mediator selection, process design, participation in or withdrawal from the process, and outcome.
B. A mediator may make those decisions that are necessary to conduct the mediation in accordance with the Standards. However, due to the general applicability of the parties' right to self-determination, when a mediator makes a decision he or she must involve the parties in the decision-making process, and either obtain their consent to the decision or follow the parties' determination on the issue.
C. Nevertheless:
    1. A mediator may make decisions without involving the parties in the decision-making process where doing so is practically impossible (for example, with regard to the type of questions to be asked) or is inconsistent with the Standards (for example, where sharing decision-making might give an appearance of partiality or violate confidentiality).
    2. After sharing decision-making with the parties when possible, the mediator shall decide, despite an express desire of the parties to the contrary:
        (a) To terminate, postpone, or withdraw from the mediation if he or she cannot conduct the mediation consistent with the Standards (for example, for reasons of incompetence or serious conflict of interest);
        (b) To refuse to perform an act requested by the parties, which would be inconsistent with the Standards (for example, refuse to give professional advice);

(c) To perform a specific act that he or she is under a duty to perform by an express provision in the Standards or by a compelling external standard (for example, disclose confidential information to non-participants in accordance with a legal order).

D. Party Competency –
A mediator shall not conduct a mediation in circumstances in which it is reasonable to believe that a party is incompetent to participate in the process. Party competency is the capacity of a party to perceive information, process it, and understand the information and its implications, in order to make and communicate the decision.

1. Incompetence to participate in mediation may be temporary or permanent and result from reasons such as abuse of drugs or alcohol; lack of language proficiency; mental retardation, dementia, mental illness, or depression; or age.
2. A mediator who suspects that a party's capacity to participate in the mediation and understand information is limited, shall take appropriate steps to assist the party to understand the information, participate in the process, and exercise self-determination, including postponing the mediation or involving a representative of the party in the process. When the mediator's intervention is neither possible nor successful the mediator shall terminate the mediation.

E. Voluntariness –
A mediator shall conduct the mediation under conditions that enable parties to make voluntary, uncoerced decisions.

1. A mediator shall not exert pressure designed to reduce party choice in decision-making.
   (a) A mediator shall not undermine party self-determination for reasons such as higher settlement rates, egos, increased fees, or outside pressures from court personnel, program administrators, provider organizations, the media or others.
2. A mediator shall take appropriate steps to prevent the exertion of pressure designed to reduce party choice in decision-making by other mediation participants.
   (a) A mediator shall be aware of power imbalances between parties. If the mediator suspects that a party has made or is about to make a decision out of feelings of helplessness and lack of choice, as a result of pressures of mediation participants or non-participants, he or she shall examine with that party the basis for those feelings and whether they are justified in the prevailing circumstances.
   (b) If subsequent to this clarification the party wishes to proceed with the decision the mediator shall respect his or her choice, provided that he or she is competent to participate in the mediation.

F. Informed decisions –

A mediator shall conduct the mediation under conditions that enable parties to make informed decisions. An informed decision is a decision that has been made on the basis of the information that is relevant to the decision-making.

1. A mediator cannot ensure that parties make decisions that are based on complete information. However, the mediator shall take steps, consistent with the Standards, so that party decision-making is based on the information relevant to the decision-making. Relevant information is information the knowledge or ignorance of which could influence the decision or the choice made.
2. The information that a mediator shall provide the parties with includes the following:
   (a) The process of mediation, the differences between mediation and other dispute resolution processes, the role of the mediator, the style of mediation practiced by the mediator, the possible use of separate meetings, and the risks of the process;
   (b) The duties of the mediator according to the Standards;
   (c) The parties' right to withdraw from the mediation at any time;
   (d) The parties' right to consult other professionals and the importance of such consultation when it is required for decision-making.
3. A mediator shall terminate the mediation for lack of information where all the following conditions are met:
   (a) A party does not possess relevant information and is unaware of its existence; and
   (b) The information is such that a reasonable party, being aware of the information, would not have agreed to continue to participate in the process or would not have consented to the proposed mediated outcome; and
   (c) The mediator has taken all possible steps consistent with the Standards to make the information accessible to the party, including asking questions and referring the party to outside experts.

V. Professional integrity

A mediator shall conduct mediation with professional integrity. A mediator's conduct reflects professional integrity when he or she is committed to the nature and definition of both his or her role as a mediator and mediation.

A. Decision-Making and Exercise of Professional Discretion –

A mediator shall make those decisions which are necessary for the execution of his or her role.

1. A mediator shall make decisions consistent with the standard of self-determination on the basis of relevant professional considerations and good reasons that could be reasonably justified.
2. A mediator shall take steps to the effect that appropriate participants take part in the process.

B. Separation of Professional Roles –
A mediator shall distinguish between his or her role as a mediator and other professional roles.
1. A mediator shall not undertake in the course of a mediation an additional professional role simultaneously in the same matter, unless (a) he or she has informed the parties of the implications of undertaking such an additional role and obtained their consent; and (b) he or she can proceed with the conduct of the mediation consistent with his or her obligations as a mediator in accordance with the Standards.
2. A mediator shall not give parties professional advice or a professional opinion that applies professional (e.g., legal) principles to the facts of the mediation case.
   (a) A mediator may provide parties with general information that he or she is qualified by training or experience to provide, without mixing his or her role as a mediator and another professional role, as is consistent with the standard of self-determination and the standard of impartiality.
   (b) A mediator may recommend parties, when appropriate, to seek outside professional advice, a professional opinion, or other professional services.

C. Appropriateness of Case to Process –
A mediator shall only conduct a mediation in cases that are appropriate and suitable for mediation in light of the nature of mediation and its principles and methods.
1. A mediator shall recommend that parties consider resolving their dispute through other processes such as arbitration, counseling, or neutral evaluation, when they are more appropriate than mediation.
2. A mediator shall take appropriate steps, including terminating the mediation, if he or she believes that the case is inappropriate for mediation, or that there is no reasonable likelihood that the parties will reach a mediated agreement, or where a party acts in a way that makes the conduct of mediation impossible.

D. Prevention of Process Abuse or Substantial Defects in the Process –
A mediator shall prevent an abuse of process (i.e. use of mediation for purposes which it has not been designed to serve), or a substantial defect in the process. In doing so a mediator shall:

1. Prevent a use of mediation to further illegal conduct.

2. Not use information revealed to him or her during a mediation for any purpose not connected to the mediation, unless authorized to do so in accordance with the Standards.
3. Not present a dispute resolution procedure other than mediation as a mediation in an effort to gain the protection of rules, statutes, or other governing authorities pertaining to mediation.
4. Take appropriate steps, including terminating the mediation, when a participant is abusing the process.
5. Terminate the mediation if, after taking all possible steps consistent with the Standards to induce a change in the parties' position, he or she believes that a mediated agreement might harm a vital social interest. In this context, any of the following agreements are to be considered as harming a vital social interest:
   (a) An illegal agreement;
   (b) An immoral agreement according to critical morality, that is, in the eyes of a rational, impartial person;
   (c) An unconscionable or grossly unfair agreement, that is, its terms deviate from common social norms to a degree that jeopardizes the standing of the profession and public trust in the profession;
   (d) An agreement that might cause serious harm to nonparticipants;
   (e) An agreement that might cause harm to minors or incapacitated persons related to the dispute;
   (f) An agreement that jeopardizes the institution of mediation and the public's trust in it.

VI. Diligence

A mediator shall conduct a mediation with diligence.

A. A mediator shall only accept cases –
   1. When he or she is prepared and able to commit to the parties and the process the attention necessary for an effective mediation
   2. When he or she can be available to the parties, respond to their need without undue delays, and satisfy the reasonable expectation of the parties concerning the timing of the mediation.

B. A mediator shall exercise his or her role –
   1. Dedicating the time and resources required for the provision of high-quality service that responds to the parties' needs.
   2. With due care to avoid harm to the parties.

VII. Respect and dignity

A mediator shall conduct a mediation in a manner that respects and acknowledges the dignity of others.

A. A mediator shall treat the parties, their representatives, co-mediators, and other participants with dignity and respect, and shall endeavor to conduct the mediation with patience and courtesy.
B. A mediator shall refrain in the exercise of his or her role from the use of abusive, discriminatory, humiliating, and profane language.
C. A mediator shall promote mutual respect among the participants.
D. A mediator shall treat with respect and dignity colleagues, other professionals, courts and other referring agencies, and the media.

VIII. Honesty

A mediator shall conduct a mediation with honesty.

A. A mediator shall treat the parties, the parties' representatives, and other participants with honesty. A mediator shall be truthful, avoid lying, and refrain from misrepresentations that could undermine party self-determination.
B. A mediator shall encourage the participants to be honest with each other.
C. A mediator shall be honest in contacts with colleagues, referring bodies such as courts, the media, and the general public.

IX. Confidentiality

A mediator shall maintain the confidentiality of information that came to his or her knowledge in the exercise of his or her role. Maintaining confidentiality means refraining from disclosure of information without a justified cause as provided in this Standard. The extent of confidentiality applying to a mediation will depend on applicable law, on rules agreed upon by the parties, or on other rules determined by the mediator or a mediation program that the parties agreed to abide by.

A. Discussion of the extent of confidentiality with the parties
    1. A mediator shall promote understanding among the parties of the extent of confidentiality that applies to the process and to the mediator, and the existence or nonexistence of a mediation privilege and its scope. At a minimum, a mediator shall explain that confidentiality is not absolute and has exceptions. Where appropriate, the mediator may

refer the parties to obtain legal advice on the extent of mediation confidentiality and privilege.

2. A mediator shall promote understanding among the parties of the extent to which the parties will maintain confidentiality of information they obtain in a mediation.

B. Confidential information

A mediator shall not disclose information that could adversely affect the parties' interests, show them in a bad light, or embarrass them, including:

1. Communications made in connection with the mediation, whether before, during, or after the mediation, including communications made in separate meetings.
2. Information regarding the conduct of the parties in the mediation.
3. Information connecting the parties with the mediation, where the anonymity of the parties is reasonably expected.

C. Disclosure of information

1. A mediator may disclose mediation information where the disclosure (1) does not undermine the standing of the profession and public trust in it, and (2) is consistent with the other Standards, in the following circumstances:
   (a) The parties agreed to the disclosure.
   (b) The information was obtained in a private session and the disclosing party agreed to the disclosure.
   (c) The disclosure is required or permitted by morality in order to prevent harm to others, or by law, either by legislation, case-law, or court order.
   (d) The disclosure is required by a mediation program that referred the case to the mediator for its efficient management with regard to whether parties appeared at a mediation and whether or not the parties reached an agreement.
   (e) The disclosure is made for the purpose of research, teaching, evaluation, or training, provided that the anonymity of the parties is protected as well as their reasonable expectations regarding confidentiality.
   (f) The disclosure is required in connection with resolving claims between a mediator and parties.
2. A mediator shall disclose mediation information where the disclosure is morally or legally required in order to prevent a serious harm to an individual or to important public interests, and where non-disclosure, were it to come to public attention, would harm the standing of the profession and public trust in it.

X. *Maintaining the profession's standing*

A mediator shall exercise his or her role in a manner that maintains the profession's standing and public trust in the mediation profession and process. Maintaining the profession's standing means refraining from conduct that might devaluate the public perception of the mediation profession, harm the profession's image or reputation, or diminish the willingness of the public to use mediation.

A. A mediator shall exercise his or her role and discharge his or her duties in a manner that maintains the profession's standing and is worthy of the public's trust.
B. A mediator shall refrain from conducting a mediation in a manner or in circumstances that raise a reasonable concern that the process is substantially defective.

XI. *Obligations to employers and principals*

A mediator exercising the role of a mediator as an employee, agent, or representative of another, such as a mediation center, mediation program, court, or organization, shall exercise his or her role consistent with the rules of his or her employer or principal, in a manner that will not undermine the employer's or principal's standing and public trust in it, and in accordance with these Standards. Maintaining the employer's or principal's standing means refraining from conduct that might devaluate the public perception of the employer or principal, harm the employer's or principal's image or reputation, or diminish the willingness of the public to receive mediation services from the employer or principal.

A. A mediator shall exercise his or her role and discharge his or her duties in a manner that is worthy of his or her employer's or principal's trust.
   To be worthy of the trust of his or her employer or principal, a mediator must be competent, disclose conflicts of interests between his or her affairs and the affairs of his or her employer or principal, respect the authority (autonomy) of his or her employer or principal and obey his or her instructions, conduct him or herself with professional integrity, diligence, and impartiality between different employers or principals, treat his or her employer or principal with respect and honesty, maintain confidentiality with regard to his or her employer's or principal's matters, protect the standing of his or her employer or principal, and act fairly.
B. A mediator shall observe and interpret his or her employer's or principal's rules and instructions in a manner consistent with the Standards.

XII. *Advertising and solicitation*

A mediator may advertise his or her mediation services and solicit mediation work in accordance with these Standards.

A. A mediator shall be truthful and refrain from misleading in advertising, solicitation, or provision of information about his or her qualifications, experience, the type of services offered, and fees.
   1. A mediator shall not make any promises as to outcome.
   2. A mediator may indicate that he or she has state, national or private organization qualifications only if the entity referred to has a procedure for qualifying mediators, and the mediator has been duly granted the requisite status.
B. A mediator shall not solicit in a manner that could give an appearance of partiality for or against a party.
C. A mediator shall not list names of mediation parties served without their prior permission.

XIII. *Mediator fees*

A mediator may charge fees for mediation services provided in accordance with these Standards and with any applicable institution or program rules.

A. A mediator shall discuss with the parties, before the mediation begins, the mediation fees and any charges that may be incurred in connection with the mediation.
B. Mediation fees shall not be contingent upon the outcome or amount of the mediation.
C. A mediator may terminate the mediation if the parties do not pay due fees.

XIV. *Advancement of the profession*

Advancement of the mediation profession is an ideal in the realization of which every mediator should assist. A mediator can do so in some or all of the following:[3]

A. Demonstrate respect for differing points of view within the field, seek to learn from other mediators, and work together with other mediators to improve the profession and better serve people in conflict.

[3] This Standard largely reproduces Model Standards, Standard IX and NY-CDRC Standards, Standard VIII.

B. Strive to make mediation accessible to the public, including providing services at a reduced rate or on a pro bono basis as appropriate.
C. Participate in research in the field when given the opportunity, including obtaining participant feedback when appropriate.
D. Participate in outreach and education efforts to assist the public in developing an improved understanding of, and appreciation for, mediation.
E. Assist newer mediators through training, mentoring and networking.

XV. Fairness

A mediator shall perform his or her role fairly. Fairness means following the standards of mediation in accordance with their spirit and purpose.

APPENDIX II MODEL STANDARDS OF CONDUCT FOR MEDIATORS (2005)

AMERICAN ARBITRATION ASSOCIATION
(ADOPTED SEPTEMBER 8, 2005)
AMERICAN BAR ASSOCIATION
(APPROVED BY THE ABA HOUSE OF DELEGATES AUGUST 9, 2005)
ASSOCIATION FOR CONFLICT RESOLUTION
(ADOPTED AUGUST 22, 2005)
SEPTEMBER 2005

The model standards of conduct for mediators 2005

The Model Standards of Conduct for Mediators was prepared in 1994 by the American Arbitration Association, the American Bar Association's Section of Dispute Resolution, and the Association for Conflict Resolution.[1] A joint committee consisting of representatives from the same successor organizations revised the Model Standards in 2005.[2] Both the original 1994 version and the 2005 revision have been approved by each participating organization.[3]

Preamble

Mediation is used to resolve a broad range of conflicts within a variety of settings. These Standards are designed to serve as fundamental ethical guidelines for persons mediating in all practice contexts. They serve three primary

[1] The Association for Conflict Resolution is a merged organization of the Academy of Family Mediators, the Conflict Resolution Education Network and the Society of Professionals in Dispute Resolution (SPIDR). SPIDR was the third participating organization in the development of the 1994 Standards.

[2] Reporter's Notes, which are not part of these Standards and therefore have not been specifically approved by any of the organizations, provide commentary regarding these revisions.

[3] The 2005 version to the Model Standards were approved by the American Bar Association's House of Delegates on August 9, 2005, the Board of the Association of Conflict Resolution on August 22, 2005 and the Executive Committee of the American Arbitration Association on September 8, 2005.

goals: to guide the conduct of mediators; to inform the mediating parties; and to promote public confidence in mediation as a process for resolving disputes.

Mediation is a process in which an impartial third party facilitates communication and negotiation and promotes voluntary decision making by the parties to the dispute.

Mediation serves various purposes, including providing the opportunity for parties to define and clarify issues, understand different perspectives, identify interests, explore and assess possible solutions, and reach mutually satisfactory agreements, when desired.

Note on construction

These Standards are to be read and construed in their entirety. There is no priority significance attached to the sequence in which the Standards appear.

The use of the term "shall" in a Standard indicates that the mediator must follow the practice described. The use of the term "should" indicates that the practice described in the standard is highly desirable, but not required, and is to be departed from only for very strong reasons and requires careful use of judgment and discretion.

The use of the term "mediator" is understood to be inclusive so that it applies to co-mediator models.

These Standards do not include specific temporal parameters when referencing a mediation, and therefore, do not define the exact beginning or ending of a mediation.

Various aspects of a mediation, including some matters covered by these Standards, may also be affected by applicable law, court rules, regulations, other applicable professional rules, mediation rules to which the parties have agreed and other agreements of the parties. These sources may create conflicts with, and may take precedence over, these Standards. However, a mediator should make every effort to comply with the spirit and intent of these Standards in resolving such conflicts. This effort should include honoring all remaining Standards not in conflict with these other sources.

These Standards, unless and until adopted by a court or other regulatory authority do not have the force of law. Nonetheless, the fact that these Standards have been adopted by the respective sponsoring entities, should alert mediators to the fact that the Standards might be viewed as establishing a standard of care for mediators.

Standard I. Self-determination

A. A mediator shall conduct a mediation based on the principle of party self-determination. Self-determination is the act of coming to a voluntary, uncoerced decision in which each party makes free and informed choices as to process and outcome. Parties may exercise self-determination at any stage of a mediation, including mediator selection, process design, participation in or withdrawal from the process, and outcomes.

1. Although party self-determination for process design is a fundamental principle of mediation practice, a mediator may need to balance such party self-determination with a mediator's duty to conduct a quality process in accordance with these Standards.
2. A mediator cannot personally ensure that each party has made free and informed choices to reach particular decisions, but, where appropriate, a mediator should make the parties aware of the importance of consulting other professionals to help them make informed choices.

B. A mediator shall not undermine party self-determination by any party for reasons such as higher settlement rates, egos, increased fees, or outside pressures from court personnel, program administrators, provider organizations, the media or others.

Standard II. Impartiality

A. A mediator shall decline a mediation if the mediator cannot conduct it in an impartial manner. Impartiality means freedom from favoritism, bias or prejudice.

B. A mediator shall conduct a mediation in an impartial manner and avoid conduct that gives the appearance of partiality.

1. A mediator should not act with partiality or prejudice based on any participant's personal characteristics, background, values and beliefs, or performance at a mediation, or any other reason.
2. A mediator should neither give nor accept a gift, favor, loan or other item of value that raises a question as to the mediator's actual or perceived impartiality.
3. A mediator may accept or give de minimis gifts or incidental items or services that are provided to facilitate a mediation or respect cultural norms so long as such practices do not raise questions as to a mediator's actual or perceived impartiality.

C. If at any time a mediator is unable to conduct a mediation in an impartial manner, the mediator shall withdraw.

Standard III. Conflicts of interest

A. A mediator shall avoid a conflict of interest or the appearance of a conflict of interest during and after a mediation. A conflict of interest can arise from involvement by a mediator with the subject matter of the dispute or from any relationship between a mediator and any mediation participant, whether past or present, personal or professional, that reasonably raises a question of a mediator's impartiality.

B. A mediator shall make a reasonable inquiry to determine whether there are any facts that a reasonable individual would consider likely to create a potential or actual conflict of interest for a mediator. A mediator's actions necessary to accomplish a reasonable inquiry into potential conflicts of interest may vary based on practice context.

C. A mediator shall disclose, as soon as practicable, all actual and potential conflicts of interest that are reasonably known to the mediator and could reasonably be seen as raising a question about the mediator's impartiality. After disclosure, if all parties agree, the mediator may proceed with the mediation.

D. If a mediator learns any fact after accepting a mediation that raises a question with respect to that mediator's service creating a potential or actual conflict of interest, the mediator shall disclose it as quickly as practicable. After disclosure, if all parties agree, the mediator may proceed with the mediation.

E. If a mediator's conflict of interest might reasonably be viewed as undermining the integrity of the mediation, a mediator shall withdraw from or decline to proceed with the mediation regardless of the expressed desire or agreement of the parties to the contrary.

F. Subsequent to a mediation, a mediator shall not establish another relationship with any of the participants in any matter that would raise questions about the integrity of the mediation. When a mediator develops personal or professional relationships with parties, other individuals or organizations following a mediation in which they were involved, the mediator should consider factors such as time elapsed following the mediation, the nature of the relationships established, and services offered when determining whether the relationships might create a perceived or actual conflict of interest.

Standard IV. Competence

A. A mediator shall mediate only when the mediator has the necessary competence to satisfy the reasonable expectations of the parties.

   1. Any person may be selected as a mediator, provided that the parties are satisfied with the mediator's competence and qualifications. Training, experience in mediation, skills, cultural understandings and other qualities are often necessary for mediator competence. A person who offers

to serve as a mediator creates the expectation that the person is competent to mediate effectively.

2. A mediator should attend educational programs and related activities to maintain and enhance the mediator's knowledge and skills related to mediation.
3. A mediator should have available for the parties' information relevant to the mediator's training, education, experience and approach to conducting a mediation.

B. If a mediator, during the course of a mediation determines that the mediator cannot conduct the mediation competently, the mediator shall discuss that determination with the parties as soon as is practicable and take appropriate steps to address the situation, including, but not limited to, withdrawing or requesting appropriate assistance.

C. If a mediator's ability to conduct a mediation is impaired by drugs, alcohol, medication or otherwise, the mediator shall not conduct the mediation.

Standard V. Confidentiality

A. A mediator shall maintain the confidentiality of all information obtained by the mediator in mediation, unless otherwise agreed to by the parties or required by applicable law.

1. If the parties to a mediation agree that the mediator may disclose information obtained during the mediation, the mediator may do so.
2. A mediator should not communicate to any non-participant information about how the parties acted in the mediation. A mediator may report, if required, whether parties appeared at a scheduled mediation and whether or not the parties reached a resolution.
3. If a mediator participates in teaching, research or evaluation of mediation, the mediator should protect the anonymity of the parties and abide by their reasonable expectations regarding confidentiality.

B. A mediator who meets with any persons in private session during a mediation shall not convey directly or indirectly to any other person, any information that was obtained during that private session without the consent of the disclosing person.

C. A mediator shall promote understanding among the parties of the extent to which the parties will maintain confidentiality of information they obtain in a mediation.

D. Depending on the circumstance of a mediation, the parties may have varying expectations regarding confidentiality that a mediator should address. The parties may make their own rules with respect to confidentiality, or the accepted practice of an individual mediator or institution may dictate a particular set of expectations.

Standard VI. Quality of the process

A. A mediator shall conduct a mediation in accordance with these Standards and in a manner that promotes diligence, timeliness, safety, presence of the appropriate participants, party participation, procedural fairness, party competency and mutual respect among all participants.

1. A mediator should agree to mediate only when the mediator is prepared to commit the attention essential to an effective mediation.
2. A mediator should only accept cases when the mediator can satisfy the reasonable expectation of the parties concerning the timing of a mediation.
3. The presence or absence of persons at a mediation depends on the agreement of the parties and the mediator. The parties and mediator may agree that others may be excluded from particular sessions or from all sessions.
4. A mediator should promote honesty and candor between and among all participants, and a mediator shall not knowingly misrepresent any material fact or circumstance in the course of a mediation.
5. The role of a mediator differs substantially from other professional roles. Mixing the role of a mediator and the role of another profession is problematic and thus, a mediator should distinguish between the roles. A mediator may provide information that the mediator is qualified by training or experience to provide, only if the mediator can do so consistent with these Standards.
6. A mediator shall not conduct a dispute resolution procedure other than mediation but label it mediation in an effort to gain the protection of rules, statutes, or other governing authorities pertaining to mediation.
7. A mediator may recommend, when appropriate, that parties consider resolving their dispute through arbitration, counseling, neutral evaluation or other processes.
8. A mediator shall not undertake an additional dispute resolution role in the same matter without the consent of the parties. Before providing such service, a mediator shall inform the parties of the implications of the change in process and obtain their consent to the change. A mediator who undertakes such role assumes different duties and responsibilities that may be governed by other standards.

9. If a mediation is being used to further criminal conduct, a mediator should take appropriate steps including, if necessary, postponing, withdrawing from or terminating the mediation.
10. If a party appears to have difficulty comprehending the process, issues, or settlement options, or difficulty participating in a mediation, the mediator should explore the circumstances and potential accommodations, modifications or adjustments that would make possible the party's capacity to comprehend, participate and exercise self-determination.

B. If a mediator is made aware of domestic abuse or violence among the parties, the mediator shall take appropriate steps including, if necessary, postponing, withdrawing from or terminating the mediation.
C. If a mediator believes that participant conduct, including that of the mediator, jeopardizes conducting a mediation consistent with these Standards, a mediator shall take appropriate steps including, if necessary, postponing, withdrawing from or terminating the mediation.

Standard VII. Advertising and solicitation

A. A mediator shall be truthful and not misleading when advertising, soliciting or otherwise communicating the mediator's qualifications, experience, services and fees.
   1. A mediator should not include any promises as to outcome in communications, including business cards, stationery, or computer-based communications.
   2. A mediator should only claim to meet the mediator qualifications of a governmental entity or private organization if that entity or organization has a recognized procedure for qualifying mediators and it grants such status to the mediator.

B. A mediator shall not solicit in a manner that gives an appearance of partiality for or against a party or otherwise undermines the integrity of the process.
C. A mediator shall not communicate to others, in promotional materials or through other forms of communication, the names of persons served without their permission.

Standard VIII. Fees and other charges

A. A mediator shall provide each party or each party's representative true and complete information about mediation fees, expenses and any other actual or potential charges that may be incurred in connection with a mediation.

1. If a mediator charges fees, the mediator should develop them in light of all relevant factors, including the type and complexity of the matter, the qualifications of the mediator, the time required and the rates customary for such mediation services.
2. A mediator's fee arrangement should be in writing unless the parties request otherwise.

B. A mediator shall not charge fees in a manner that impairs a mediator's impartiality.

1. A mediator should not enter into a fee agreement which is contingent upon the result of the mediation or amount of the settlement.
2. While a mediator may accept unequal fee payments from the parties, a mediator should not allow such a fee arrangement to adversely impact the mediator's ability to conduct a mediation in an impartial manner.

Standard IX. Advancement of mediation practice

A. A mediator should act in a manner that advances the practice of mediation. A mediator promotes this Standard by engaging in some or all of the following:

1. Fostering diversity within the field of mediation.
2. Striving to make mediation accessible to those who elect to use it, including providing services at a reduced rate or on a pro bono basis as appropriate.
3. Participating in research when given the opportunity, including obtaining participant feedback when appropriate.
4. Participating in outreach and education efforts to assist the public in developing an improved understanding of, and appreciation for, mediation.
5. Assisting newer mediators through training, mentoring and networking.

B. A mediator should demonstrate respect for differing points of view within the field, seek to learn from other mediators and work together with other mediators to improve the profession and better serve people in conflict.

BIBLIOGRAPHY

Abramson, Harold, "Crossing Borders into New Ethical Territory: Ethical Challenges When Mediating Cross-Culturally" (2008) 49 *South Texas Law Review* 921

Alberstein, Michal, "Forms of Mediation and Law: Cultures of Dispute Resolution" (2007) 22 *Ohio State Journal on Dispute Resolution* 321

Alberstein, Michal, *Jurisprudence of Mediation* (Jerusalem: The Hebrew University Magnes Press, 2007) [Hebrew]

Alberstein, Michal, "The Jurisprudence of Mediation: Between Formalism, Feminism and Identity Conversations" (2009) 11 *Cardozo Journal of Conflict Resolution* 1

Altman, William M., Parmelee, Patricia A., and Smyer, Michael A., "Autonomy, Competence, and Informed Consent in Long Term Care: Legal and Psychological Perspectives" (1992) 37 *Villanova Law Review* 1671

Appelbaum, David and Lawton, Sarah Verone (eds.), *Ethics and the Professions* (Englewood Cliffs, NJ: Prentice-Hall, 1990)

Arrow, Kenneth J. *et al.* (eds.), *Barriers to Conflict Resolution* (New York: W.W. Norton, 1995)

Baum, Robert J., "*Engineers and the Public: Sharing Responsibilities*", in Daniel E. Wueste (ed.), *Professional Ethics and Social Responsibility* (Lanham, MD: Rowman and Littlefield, 1994)

Bayles, Michael D., *Professional Ethics*, 2nd edn. (Belmont: Wadsworth, 1989)

Beauchamp, Tom L. and Childress, James F., *Principles of Biomedical Ethics*, 6th edn. (New York: Oxford University Press, 2009)

Benn, Stanley I., *A Theory of Freedom* (Cambridge University Press, 1988)

Boulle, Laurence and Nesic, Miryana, *Mediation: Principles, Process, Practice* (London: Tottel, 2001)

Brazil, Wayne D., "Comparing Structures for the Delivery of ADR Services by Courts: Critical Values and Concerns" (1998) 14 *Ohio State Journal on Dispute Resolution* 715

Brazil, Wayne D., "Continuing the Conversation About the Current Status and the Future of ADR: A View from the Courts" (2000) 2000 *Journal of Dispute Resolution* 11

Brazil, Wayne D., "Hosting Mediations as a Representative of the System of Civil Justice" (2007) 22 *Ohio State Journal on Dispute Resolution* 227

Brazil, Wayne D., "Should Court-Sponsored ADR Survive?" (2006) 21 *Ohio State Journal on Dispute Resolution* 241

Bryan, Penelope Eileen, "The Coercion of Women in Divorce Settlement Negotiations" (1997) 74 *Denver University Law Review* 931

Buckingham, Donald, "Rules and Roles: Casting Off Legal Education's Moral Blinders for an Approach that Encourages Moral Development" (1996) 9 *Canadian Journal of Law and Jurisprudence* 111

Bush, Robert A. Baruch, "A Study of Ethical Dilemmas and Policy Implications" (1994) 1 *Journal of Dispute Resolution* 1

Bush, Robert A. Baruch, "Efficiency and Protection, or Empowerment and Recognition? The Mediator's Role and Ethical Standards in Mediation" (1989) 41 *Florida Law Review* 253

Bush, Robert A. Baruch, and Folger, Joseph P., "Mediation and Social Justice: Risks and Opportunities" (2012) 27 *Ohio State Journal on Dispute Resolution* 1

Bush, Robert A. Baruch, and Folger, Joseph P., *The Promise of Mediation: Responding to Conflict through Empowerment and Recognition* (San Francisco: Jossey-Bass, 1994)

Bush, Robert A. Baruch, and Folger, Joseph P., *The Promise of Mediation: The Transformative Approach to Conflict*, Rev. edn. (San Francisco: Jossey-Bass, 2005)

Calkins, Richard M., "Caucus Mediation-Putting Conciliation Back into the Process: The Peacemaking Approach to Resolution, Peace, and Healing" (2006) 54 *Drake Law Review* 259

Carr, Craig L., "Fairness and Political Obligation-Again: A Reply to Lefkowitz" (2004) 30 *Social Theory and Practice* 33

Carter, Stephen, *Integrity* (New York: Basic Books, 1996)

Charles, Cathy, Gafnia, Amiram, and Whelan, Tim, "Decision-making in the Physician–patient Encounter: Revisiting the Shared Treatment Decision-making Model" (1999) 49 *Social Science and Medicine* 651

Chaykin, Arthur A., "The Liabilities and Immunities of Mediators: A Hostile Environment for Model Legislation" (1986) 2 *Ohio State Journal on Dispute Resolution* 47

Chaykin, Arthur A., "Mediator Liability: A New Role for Fiduciary Duties?" (1984) 53 *University of Cincinnati Law Review* 731

Clark, Rebekah Ryan, "Writing on the Wall: The Potential Liability of Mediators as Fiduciaries" (2006) 4 *Brigham Young University Law Review* 1033

Cobb, Sara and Rifkin, Janet, "Practice and Paradox: Deconstructing Neutrality in Mediation" (1991) 16 *Law and Social Inquiry* 35

Coben, James and Thompson, Peter N., "Disputing Irony: A Systematic Look at Litigation About Mediation" (2006) 11 *Harvard Negotiation Law Review* 43

Cochran, Robert F., "Legal Representation and the Next Steps Toward Client Control: Attorney Malpractice for the Failure to Allow the Client to Control Negotiation and Pursue Alternatives to Litigation" (1990) 47 *Washington and Lee Law Review* 819

Cohen, Elliot D. and Davis, Michael (eds.), *Ethics and the Legal Profession*, 2nd edn. (Amherst, NY: Prometheus Books, 2009)

Cohen, Orna, Dattner, Naomi, and Luxenburg, Ahron, "The Limits of the Mediator's Neutrality" (1999) 16 *Mediation Quarterly* 341

Cole, Sarah Rudolph, "Mediator Certification: Has the Time Come?" (2005) 11 *Dispute Resolution Magazine* 7

Cooley, John W., "A Classical Approach to Mediation - Part I: Classical Rhetoric and the Art of Persuasion in Mediation" (1993) 19 *University of Dayton Law Review* 83

Cooley, John W., "Mediation Magic: Its Use and Abuse" (1997) 29 *Loyola University Chicago Law Journal* 1

Cooper, David E., *Ethics for Professionals in a Multicultural World* (Upper Saddle River, NJ: Pearson Prentice Hall, 2004)

Cox, Damien, La Caze, Marguerite, and Levine, Michael P., *Integrity and the Fragile Self* (Aldershot, UK: Ashgate, 2003)

Coyle-Shapiro, Jacqueline A-M. and Kessler, Ian, "Exploring Reciprocity through the Lens of the Psychological Contract: Employee and Employer Perspectives" (2002) 11 *European journal of Work and Organizational Psychology* 69

Craver, Charles B., "Negotiation Ethics: How to Be Deceptive Without Being Dishonest/How to Be Assertive Without Being Offensive" (1997) 38 *South Texas Law Review* 713

Davis, Michael, "Introduction", in Michael Davis and Andrew Stark (eds.), *Conflict of Interest in the Professions* (New York: Oxford University Press, 2001)

Davis, Michael, *Thinking Like an Engineer: Studies in the Ethics of a Profession* (New York: Oxford University Press, 1998)

Davis, Michael and Elliston, Frederick A. (eds.), *Ethics and the Legal Profession* (Buffalo, NY, Prometheus Books, 1986)

Davis, Michael and Stark, Andrew (eds.), *Conflict of Interest in the Professions* (New York: Oxford University Press, 2001)

Deason, Ellen E., "The Quest for Uniformity in Mediation Confidentiality: Foolish Consistency or Crucial Predictability?" (2001) 85 *Marquette Law Review* 79

Deason, Ellen E., "The Need for Trust as a Justification for Confidentiality in Mediation: A Cross-Disciplinary Approach" (2006) 54 *University of Kansas Law Review* 1387

DeMartino, George F., *The Economist's Oath: On the Need for and Content of Professional Economic Ethics* (New York: Oxford University Press, 2011)

DeMott, Deborah A., "The Lawyer as Agent" (1998) 67 *Fordham Law Review* 301

Diaz, Luis Miguel, "Mediation Furthers the Principles of Transparency and Cooperation to Solve Disputes in the NAFTA Free Trade Area" (2001) 30 *Denver Journal of International Law and Policy* 73

Dinerstein, Robert D., "Client-Centered Counseling: Reappraisal and Refinement" (1990) 32 *Arizona Law Review* 501

Dworkin, Gerald, *The Theory and Practice of Autonomy* (New York: Cambridge University Press, 1988)

Dworkin, Roger B., "Getting What We should from Doctors: Rethinking Patient Autonomy and the Doctor-Patient Relationship" (2003) 13 *Health Matrix* 235

Dworkin, Ronald, *Taking Rights Seriously* (Cambridge, MA: Harvard University Press, 1978)

Emanuel, Linda L. and Emanuel, Ezekiel J., "Four Models of the Physician-Patient Relationship" (1992) 267 *Journal of the American Medical Association* 2221

Erbe, Nancy D., "Appreciating Mediation's Global Role in Promoting Good Governance" (2006) 11 *Harvard Negotiation Law Review* 355

Exon, Susan Nauss, "The Effects that Mediator Styles Impose on Neutrality and Impartiality Requirements of Mediation" (2008) 42 *University of San Francisco Law Review* 577

Faden, Ruth R. and Beauchamp, Tom L., *A History and Theory of Informed Consent* (New York: Oxford University Press, 1986)

Feerick, John D., "Toward Uniform Standards of Conduct For Mediators" (1997) 38 *South Texas Law Review* 455

Field, Rachael, "Rethinking Mediation Ethics: A Contextual Method to Support Party Self-Determination" (2011) 22 *Australasian Dispute Resolution Journal* 8

Finkelstein, Elad and Lifshitz, Shahar, "Bargaining in the Shadow of the Mediator: A Communitarian Theory of Post-Mediation Contracts" (2010) 25 *Ohio State Journal on Dispute Resolution* 667

Folberg, Jay and Taylor, Alison, *Mediation: A Comprehensive Guide To Resolving Conflicts Without Litigation* (San Francisco: Jossey-Bass, 1984)

Folger, Joseph P., Bush, Robert A. Bauch, and Della Noce, Dorothy J. (eds.), *Transformative Mediation: A Sourcebook* (The Association for Conflict Resolution and the Institute for the Study of Conflict Resolution, 2010)

Forester, John and Stitzel, David, "Beyond Neutrality: The Possibilities of Activist Mediation in Public Sector Conflicts" (1989) 5 *Negotiation Journal* 251

Freedman, Lawrence R. and Prigoff, Michael L., "Confidentiality in Mediation: The Need for Protection" (1986) 2 *Ohio State Journal on Dispute Resolution* 37

Freeman, M.D.A., *Lloyd's Introduction to Jurisprudence*, 8th edn. (London: Sweet & Maxwell, 2008)

Freidson, Eliot, *Professional Powers: A Study of the Institutionalization of Formal Knowledge* (Chicago: University of Chicago Press, 1986)

Freidson, Eliot, *Professionalism Reborn: Theory, Prophecy and Policy* (Chicago: University of Chicago Press, 1994)

Fried, Charles, "The Lawyer as Friend: The Moral Foundations of the Lawyer-Client Relationship" (1976) 85 *Yale Law Journal* 1060

Friedman, Gary and Himmelstein, Jack, "The Understanding-Based Model of Mediation", in Carrie Menkel-Meadow, Lela Porter Love, and Andrea Kupfer Schneider, *Mediation: Practice, Policy and Ethics* (New York: Aspen, 2006)

Frolik, Lawrence A., "Is a Guardian the Alter Ego of the Ward?" (2007) 37 *Stetson Law Review* 53

Fuller, Lon L., *The Morality of Law*, Revised edn. (New Haven: Yale University Press, 1969)

Fuller, Lon L. and Randall, John D., "Professional Responsibility: Report of the Joint Conference", in Elliot D. Cohen and Michael Davis (eds.), *Ethics and the Legal Profession*, 2nd edn. (Amherst, NY: Prometheus Books, 2009)

Gaines, Michelle D., "A Proposed Conflict of Interest Rule for Attorney-Mediators" (1998) 73 *Washington Law Review* 699

Gert, Bernard, *Common Morality: Deciding What to Do* (Oxford University Press, 2004)

Gert, Bernard, *Morality: Its Nature and Justification*, Revised edn. (Oxford University Press, 2005)

Gert, Bernard, Culver, Charles M. and Clouser, K. Danner, *Bioethics: A Systematic Approach*, 2nd edn. (Oxford University Press, 2006)

Gibson, Kevin, "Confidentiality in Mediation: A Moral Reassessment" (1992) 1992 *Journal of Dispute Resolution* 25

Gibson, Kevin, "Contrasting Role Morality and Professional Morality: Implications for Practice" (2003) 20 *Journal of Applied Philosophy* 17

Gibson, Kevin, "Mediator Attitudes toward Outcomes: A Philosophical View" (1999) 17 *Mediation Quarterly* 197

Gibson, Kevin, "The New Canon of Negotiation Ethics" (2004) 87 *Marquette Law Review* 747

Gibson, Kevin, Thompson, Leigh, and Bazerman, Max H., "Shortcomings of Neutrality in Mediation: Solutions Based on Rationality" (1996) 12 *Negotiation Journal* 69

Goldman, Alan H., *The Moral Foundations of Professional Ethics* (Totowa, NJ: Rowman and Littlefield, 1980)

Grebe, Sarah Childs, Irvin, Karen, Lang, Michael, "A Model for Ethical Decision Making in Mediation" (1989) 7 *Mediation Quarterly* 133

Grillo, Trina, "The Mediation Alternative – Process Dangers for Women" (1991) 100 *Yale Law Journal* 1545

Gunning, Isabelle R., "Know Justice, Know Peace: Further Reflections on Justice, Equality and Impartiality in Settlement Oriented and Transformative Mediations" (2004) 5 *Cardozo Journal of Conflict Resolution* 87

Hallevy, Gabriel, "The Defense Attorney as Mediator in Plea Bargains" (2009) 9 *Pepperdine Dispute Resolution Law Journal* 495

Hallevy, Gabriel, "Therapeutic Victim-Offender Mediation within the Criminal Justice Process - Sharpening the Evaluation of Personal Potential for Rehabilitation while Righting Wrongs under the ADR Philosophy" (2011) 16 *Harvard Negotiation Law Review* 65

Hardy, Samantha and Rundle, Olivia, "Applying the Inclusive Model of Ethical Decision Making to Mediation" (2012) 19 *James Cook University Law Review* 70

Harges, Bobby Marzine, "Mediator Qualifications: The Trend Toward Professionalism" (1997) 1997 *Brigham Young University Law Review* 687

Hart, H.L.A., *The Concept of Law*, 2nd edn. (Oxford University Press, 1994)

Hart, H.L.A., *Law, Liberty, and Morality* (Stanford: Stanford University Press, 1963)

Hofstein, David N., "Ethical Guidelines for Attorney-Mediators: Are Attorneys Bound by Ethical Codes for Lawyers When Acting as Mediators?" (1997) 14 *Journal of the American Academy of Matrimonial Lawyers* 267

Hohfeld, Wesley N., *Fundamental Legal Conceptions as Applied in Judicial Reasoning* (New Haven: Yale University Press, 1919)

Honoroff, Brad and Opotow, Susan, "Mediation Ethics: A Grounded Approach" (2007) 23 *Negotiation Journal* 155

Hooker, Brad, "Fairness" (2005) 8 *Ethical Theory and Moral Practice* 329

Hughes, Scott H., "The Uniform Mediation Act: To the Spoiled Go the Privileges" (2001) 85 *Marquette Law Review* 9

Hutchinson, Campbell C., "The Case for Mandatory Mediation" (1996) 42 *Loyola Law Review* 85

Hyman, Jonathan M. and Love, Lela P., "If Portia Were a Mediator: An Inquiry into Justice in Mediation" (2002) 9 *Clinical Law Review* 157

Kasher, Asa, "Ethics, Law, and Adjudication" in Aharon Barak (ed.), *Essays in Honour of President Meir Shamgar*, Vol. II (Tel Aviv: Israel Bar Publications, 2003) [Hebrew]

Kipnis, Ken, "Conflict of Interest and Conflict of Obligation", in Elliot D. Cohen and Michael Davis (eds.), *Ethics and the Legal Profession*, 2nd edn. (Amherst, NY: Prometheus Books, 2009)

Koehn, Daryl, *The Ground of Professional Ethics* (New York: Routledge, 1994)

Kolb, Deborah M., *The Mediators* (MIT Press, 1983)

Kolb, Deborah & Associates, *When Talk Works: Profiles of Mediators* (San Francisco: Jossey-Bass, 1994)

Kovach, Kimberlee K., "Good Faith in Mediation - Requested, Recommended, or Required? A New Ethic" (1997) 38 *South Texas Law Review* 575

Kovach, Kimberlee K., *Mediation: Principles and Practice*, 3rd edn., (St. Paul, MN: Thompson West, 2004)

Kovach, Kimberlee K., "Musings on Idea(l)s in the Ethical Regulation of Mediators: Honesty, Enforcement and Education" (2005) 21 *Ohio State Journal on Dispute Resolution* 123

Kovach, Kimberlee K., "New Wine Requires New Wineskins: Transforming Lawyer Ethics for Effective Representation in A Non-adversarial Approach to Problem Solving Mediation" (2001) 28 *Fordham Urban Law Journal* 935

Kovach, Kimberlee K., and Love, Lela P., "Evaluative Mediation Is An Oxymoron" (1996) 14 *Alternatives to High Cost Litigation* 31

Kovach, Kimberlee K., and Love, Lela P., "Mapping Mediation: The Risks of Riskin's Grid" (1998) 3 *Harvard Negotiation Law Review* 71

Kultgen, John, *Ethics and Professionalism* (Philadelphia: University of Pennsylvania Press, 1988)

Laflin, Maureen E., "Preserving the Integrity of Mediation Through the Adoption of Ethical Rules for Lawyer- Mediators" (2000) 14 *Notre Dame Journal of Law, Ethics and Public Policy* 479

Lande, John, "Using Dispute System Design Methods to Promote Good-Faith Participation in Court-Connected Mediation Programs" (2002) 50 *University of California Los Angeles Law Review* 69

Lande, John, "Toward More Sophisticated Mediation Theory" (2000) 2000 *Journal of Dispute Resolution* 321

Lande, John and Herman, Gregg, "Fitting the Forum to the Family Fuss: Choosing Mediation, Collaborative Law, or Cooperative Law for Negotiating Divorce Cases" (2004) 42 *Family Court Review* 280

Levin, Murray S., "The Propriety of Evaluative Mediation: Concerns About the Nature and Quality of an Evaluative Opinion" (2001) 16 *Ohio State Journal on Dispute Resolution* 267

Lo, Bernard, "Assessing Decision-Making Capacity" (1990) 18 *Law, Medicine and Health Care* 193

Luban, David, *Legal Ethics and Human Dignity* (New York: Cambridge University Press, 2007)

Lukes, Steven, *Power: A Radical View* (London: Macmillan, 1974)

Macfarlane, Julie, "Mediating Ethically: The Limits of Codes of Conduct and the Potential of a Reflective Practice Model" (2002) 40 *Osgoode Hall Law Journal* 49

Markovits, Daniel, *A Modern Legal Ethics: Adversary Advocacy in a Democratic Age* (Princeton University Press, 2008)

Marmor, Andrei (ed.), *Law and Interpretation: Essays in Legal Philosophy* (Oxford University Press, 2006)

Mattison, Marian, "Ethical Decision Making: The Person in the Process" (2000) 45 *Social Work* 201

Maute, Judith L., "Mediator Accountability: Responding to Fairness Concerns" (1990) 1990 *Journal of Dispute Resolution* 347

May, William F., *The Beleaguered Rulers: The Public Obligation of the Professional* (Louisville, KY: Westminster John Knox Press, 2001)

May, William F., "Professional Virtue and Self-Regulation", in Joan Callahan (ed.), *Ethical Issues in Professional Life* (New York: Oxford University Press, 1988)

McDermott, E. Patrick and Obar, Ruth, "'What's Going On' in Mediation: An Empirical Analysis of the Influence of a Mediator's Style on Party Satisfaction and Monetary Benefit" (2004) 9 *Harvard Negotiation Law Review* 75

McDermott, F. E. (ed.), *Self-determination in Social Work: A Collection of Essays on Self-determination and Related Concepts by Philosophers and Social Work Theorists* (London; Boston: Routledge and Kegan Paul, 1975)

McEwen, Craig, "Giving Meaning to Mediator Professionalism" (2005) 11 *Dispute Resolution Magazine* 3

McFall, Lynne, "Integrity" (1987) 98 *Ethics* 5

Menkel-Meadow, Carrie, "Are Cross-Cultural Ethics Standards Possible or Desirable in International Arbitration?", in Peter Gauch, Franz Werro and Pascal Pichonnaz (eds.) *Melanges en l'honneur de Pierre Tercier* (Zurich, Switzerland: Schulthess Verlag, 2008)

Menkel-Meadow, Carrie, "Are There Systemic Ethics Issues in Dispute System Design? And What We Should [Not] Do About it: Lessons from International and Domestic Fronts" (2009) 14 *Harvard Negotiation Law Review* 195

Menkel-Meadow, Carrie, "Ethics in Alternative Dispute Resolution: New Issues, No Answers from the Adversary Conception of Lawyers' Responsibilities" (1997) 38 *South Texas Law Review* 407

Menkel-Meadow, Carrie, "The Lawyer as Consensus Builder: Ethics for a New Practice" (2002) 70 *Tennessee Law Review* 63

Menkel-Meadow, Carrie, Love, Lela Porter, and Kupfer Schneider, Andrea, *Mediation: Practice, Policy and Ethics* (New York: Aspen, 2006)

Miller, John A., "Indeterminacy, Complexity, and Fairness: Justifying Rule Simplification in the Law of Taxation" (1993) 68 *Washington Law Review* 1

Minow, Martha, "On Being Religious Professional: The Religious Turn in Professional Ethics" (2001) 150 *University of Pennsylvania Law Review* 661

Mironi, Mordehai, "Mediation v. Case Settlement: The Unsettling Relations between Courts and Mediation - A Case Study" (2014) 19 *Harvard Negotiation Law Review* 173

Moffitt, Michael, "Casting Light on the Black Box of Mediation: Should Mediators Make Their Conduct More Transparent?" (1997) 13 *Ohio State Journal on Dispute Resolution* 1

Moffitt, Michael, "Schmediation and the Dimensions of Definition" (2005) 10 *Harvard Negotiation Law Review* 69

Moffitt, Michael, "Suing Mediators" (2003) 83 *Boston University Law Review* 147

Monk, Gerald and Winslade, John, *When Stories Clash: Addressing Conflict with Narrative Mediation* (Taos Institute, 2013)

Moore, Christopher W., *The Mediation Process: Practical Strategies for Resolving Conflict*, 3rd edn. (San Francisco: Jossey-Bass, 2003)

Moore, Wilbert E., *The Professions: Roles and Rules* (New York: Russell Sage Foundation, 1970)

Mosten, Forrest S., "Collaborative Law Practice: An Unbundled Approach to Informed Client Decision Making" (2008) 2008 *Journal of Dispute Resolution* 163

Murphy, John R. III, "In the Wake of Tarasoff: Mediation and the Duty to Disclose" (1985) 5 *Catholic University Law Review* 209

Nicolson, Donald and Webb, Julian, *Professional Legal Ethics: Critical Interrogations* (New York: Oxford University Press, 1999)

Nolan-Haley, Jacqueline M., "Court Mediation and the Search for Justice Through Law" (1996) 74 *Washington University Law Quarterly* 47

Nolan-Haley, Jacqueline M., "Informed Consent in Mediation: A Guiding Principle for Truly Educated Decisionmaking" (1999) 74 *Notre Dame Law Review* 775

Nolan-Haley, Jacqueline M., "Lawyers, Non-Lawyers and Mediation: Rethinking the Professional Monopoly from a Problem-Solving Perspective" (2002) 7 *Harvard Negotiation Law Review* 235

Norman, Richard, "Applied Ethics: What is Applied to What?" (2000) 12 *Utilitas* 119

Oberman, Susan, "Mediation Theory vs. Practice: What Are We Really Doing? Re-Solving a Professional Conundrum" (2000) 20 *Ohio State Journal on Dispute Resolution* 775

Padgett, Barry L., *Professional Morality and Guilty Bystanding: Merton's Conjectures and the Value of Work* (Newcastle upon Tyne, UK: Cambridge Scholars, 2009)

Peppet, Scott R., "Contractarian Economics and Mediation Ethics: The Case for Customizing Neutrality through Contingent Fee Mediation" (2003) 82 *Texas Law Review* 227

Pou, Charles, "'Embracing Limbo': Thinking About Rethinking Dispute Resolution Ethics" (2003) 108 *Penn State Law Review* 199

Pritchard, Michael S., *Professional Integrity: Thinking Ethically* (Lawrence: University Press of Kansas, 2006)

Pruitt, Dean G., "Kissinger As A Traditional Mediator With Power", in Jeffrey Z. Rubin (ed.), *Dynamics of Third Party Intervention: Kissinger in the Middle East* (New York: Praeger, 1981)

Quek, Dorcas, "Mandatory Mediation: An Oxymoron? Examining the Feasibility of Implementing a Court-Mandated Mediation Program" (2010) 11 *Cardozo Journal of Conflict Resolution* 479

Rabinovich-Einy, Orna, "Technology's Impact: The Quest for a New Paradigm for Accountability in Mediation" (2006) 11 *Harvard Negotiation Law Review* 253

Rachels, James and Rachels, Stuart, *The Elements of Moral Philosophy*, 6th edn. (Singapore: McGraw-Hill, International Edition, 2010)

Raz, Joseph, "Legal Principles and the Limits of Law" (1972) 81 *Yale Law Journal* 823

Raz, Joseph, *Practical Reasons and Norms* (Oxford University Press, 1999)

Rescher, Nicholas, *Introduction to Value Theory* (Englewood Cliffs, NJ: Prentice-Hall, 1969)

Rhode, Deborah L., "Ethical Perspectives on Legal Practice" (1985) 37 *Stanford Law Review* 589

Rifkin, Janet, Millen, Jonathan, and Cobb, Sara, "Toward a New Discourse for Mediation: A Critique of Neutrality" (1991) 9 *Mediation Quarterly* 151

Rimelspach, Rene L., "Mediating Family Disputes in a World with Domestic Violence: How to Devise a Safe and Effective Court-Connected Mediation Program" (2001) 17 *Ohio State Journal on Dispute Resolution* 95

Riskin, Leonard L., "Decisionmaking in Mediation: The New Old Grid and the New New Grid System" (2003) 79 *Notre Dame Law Review* 1

Riskin, Leonard L., "Understanding Mediators' Orientations, Strategies, and Techniques: A Grid for the Perplexed" (1996) 1 *Harvard Negotiation Law Review* 7

Ronner, Amy D. and Winick, Bruce J., "Silencing the Appellant's Voice: The Antitherapeutic Per Curiam Affirmance" (2000) 24 *Seattle University Law Review* 499

Rosenthal, Douglas E., *Lawyer and Client: Who's In Charge?* (New York: Russell Sage Foundation, 1974)

Schaap, Andrew, "Power and Responsibility: Should We Spare The King's Head?" (2000) 20 *Politics* 129

Schepard, Andrew and Bozzomo, James W., "Efficiency, Therapeutic Justice, Mediation, and Evaluation: Reflections on a Survey of Unified Family Courts" (2003) 37 *Family Law Quarterly* 333

Schuwerk, Robert P., "Reflections on Ethics and Mediation" (1997) 38 *South Texas Law Review* 757

Schwartz, Murray L., "The Professionalism and Accountability of Lawyers" (1978) 66 *California Law Review* 669

Shailor, Jonathan G., *Empowerment in Dispute Mediation: A Critical Analysis of Communication* (Westport, CT.: Praeger, 1994)

Shapira, Omer, "Conceptions and Perceptions of Fairness in Mediation" (2012) 54 *South Texas Law Review* 281

Shapira, Omer, "Exploring the Concept of Power in Mediation: Mediators' Sources of Power and Influence Tactics" (2009) 24 *Ohio State Journal on Dispute Resolution* 535

Shapira, Omer, "Joining Forces in Search for Answers: The Use of Therapeutic Jurisprudence in the Realm of Mediation Ethics" (2008) 8 *Pepperdine Dispute Resolution Law Journal* 243

Shapira, Omer, "On Human Dignity in Mediation: The Effect of The Basic Law: Human Dignity and Liberty on Mediation" (2008) 8 *Kiryat Hamishpat* 373 [Hebrew]

Shapira, Omer, "A Theory of Sharing Decision-Making in Mediation" (2013) 44 *McGeorge Law Review* 923

Shapira, Omer, *Use of Power and Influence in Mediation: Practice and Applied Ethics* (Ono Academic College Press, 2007) [Hebrew]

Shapiro, Debra, Drieghe, Rita, and Brett, Jeanne, "Mediator Behavior and the Outcome of Mediation" (1985) 41 *Journal of Social Issues* 101

Shaw, William H., *Business Ethics*, 6th edn. (Boston, MA: Wadsworth, 2008)

Sherman, Edward F., "Confidentiality in ADR Proceedings: Policy Issues Arising from the Texas Experience" (1997) 38 *South Texas Law Review* 541

Shultz, Marjorie Maguire, "From Informed Consent to Patient Choice: A New Protected Interest" (1985) 95 *Yale Law Journal* 219

Singer, Peter, "Famine, Affluence, and Morality" (1973) 1 *Philosophy and Public Affairs* 229

Slobogin, Christopher, "Therapeutic Jurisprudence: Five Dilemmas to Ponder" (1995) 1 *Psychology, Public Policy and Law* 193

Smith, M.B.E., "Is There a Prima Facie Obligation to Obey the Law" (1973) 82 *Yale Law Journal* 950

Spencer, David and Brogan, Michael, *Mediation Law and Practice* (Cambridge University Press, 2007)

Spiegel, Mark, "Lawyering and Client Decisionmaking: Informed Consent and the Legal Profession" (1979) 128 *University of Pennsylvania Law Review* 41

Statman, Daniel, *Moral Dilemmas* (Amsterdam: Rodopi, 1995)

Stempel, Jeffrey W., "Identifying Real Dichotomies Underlying the False Dichotomy: Twenty-First Century Mediation in an Eclectic Regime" (2000) 2000 *Journal of Dispute Resolution* 371

Stempel, Jeffrey W., "The Inevitability of the Eclectic: Liberating ADR from Ideology" (2000) *Journal of Dispute Resolution* 247

Strauss, Marcy, "Toward a Revised Model of Attorney-Client Relationship: The Argument for Autonomy" (1987) 65 *North Carolina Law Review* 315

Streeter-Schaefer, Holly A., "A Look at Court Mandated Civil Mediation" (2000) 49 *Drake Law Review* 367

Stulberg, Joseph B., "Fairness and Mediation" (1998) 13 *Ohio State Journal on Dispute Resolution* 909

Stulberg, Joseph B., "Mediation and Justice: What Standards Govern?" (2005) 6 *Cardozo Journal of Conflict Resolution* 213

Taylor, Alison, "Concepts of Neutrality in Family Mediation: Contexts, Ethics, Influence, and Transformative Process" (1997) 14 *Conflict Resolution Quarterly* 215

Van der Burg, W., "The Morality of Aspiration: A Neglected Dimension of Law and Morality", in W.J. Witteveen and W. van der Burg (eds.), *Rediscovering Fuller. Essays on Implicit Law and Institutional Design* (Amsterdam: Amsterdam University Press, 1999)

Velasquez, Manuel G., *Business Ethics: Concepts and Cases*, 5th edn. (Upper Saddle River, NJ: Prentice-Hall, 2002)

Ver Steegh, Nancy, "Yes, No, and Maybe: Informed Decision Making About Divorce Mediation in the Presence of Domestic Violence" (2003) 9 *William and Mary Journal of Women and the Law* 145

Waldman, Ellen A., "The Challenge of Certification: How to Ensure Mediator Competence While Preserving Diversity" (1996) 30 *University of San Francisco Law Review* 723

Waldman, Ellen (ed.), *Mediation Ethics: Cases and Commentaries* (San Francisco: Jossey-Bass, 2011)

Wallace, James, *Ethical Norms, Particular Cases* (Cornell University Press, 1996)

Watkins, Michael, "Principles of Persuasion" (2001) 17 *Negotiation Journal* 115

Weckstein, Donald T., "Mediator Certification: Why and How" (1996) 30 *University of San Francisco Law Review* 757

Weckstein, Donald T., "In Praise of Party Empowerment - and of Mediator Activism" (1997) 33 *Willamette Law Review* 501

Weidner, Laura E., "Model Standards of Conduct for Mediators (2005)" (2006) 21 *Ohio State Journal on Dispute Resolution* 547

Welsh, Nancy A., "All in the Family: Darwin and the Evolution of Mediation" (2001) 7 *Dispute Resolution Magazine* 20

Welsh, Nancy A., "Making Deals in Court Connected Mediation: What's Justice Got to Do with It?" (2001) 79 *Washington University Law Quarterly* 787

Welsh, Nancy A., "Perceptions of Fairness in Negotiation" (2004) 87 *Marquette Law Review* 753

Welsh, Nancy A., "The Thinning Vision of Self-Determination in Court-Connected Mediation: The Inevitable Price of Institutionalization?" (2001) 6 *Harvard Negotiation Law Review* 1

White, Welsh S., "Evidentiary Privileges and the Defendant's Constitutional Right to Introduce Evidence" (1989) 80 *Journal of Criminal Law and Criminology* 377

Whitney, Simon N., McGuire, Amy L. and McCullough, Laurence B., "A Typology of Shared Decision Making, Informed Consent, and Simple Consent" (2004) 140 *Annals of Internal Medicine* 54

Winick, Bruce J., "On Autonomy: Legal and Psychological Perspectives" (1992) 37 *Villanova Law Review* 1705

Winslade, John and Monk, Gerald, *Narrative Mediation: A New Approach to Conflict Resolution* (San Francisco: Jossey-Bass, 2000)

Winslade, John and Monk, Gerald, *Practicing Narrative Mediation: Loosening the Grip of Conflict* (San Francisco: Jossey-Bass, 2008)

Woolley, Alice and Bagg, Sara L., "Ethics Teaching in Law School" (2007) 1 *Canadian Legal Education Annual Review* 85

Wueste, Daniel E. (ed.), *Professional Ethics and Social Responsibility* (Lanham, MD: Rowman and Littlefield, 1994)

Young, Paula M., "Take It or Leave It. Lump It or Grieve It: Designing Mediator Complaint Systems that Protect Mediators, Unhappy Parties, Attorneys, Courts, the Process, and the Field" (2006) 21 *Ohio State Journal on Dispute Resolution* 721

Zamir, Ronit, "The Disempowering Relationship between Mediator Neutrality and Judicial Impartiality: Toward a New Mediation Ethic" (2011) 11 *Pepperdine Dispute Resolution Law Journal* 467

INDEX

Note: Boldface numbers indicate illustrations

ABA Model Rules, 51
Abbreviations list, xxviii–xxxi
Abramson, Harold, 373–384
Abuse of mediation process, 243–251, 253–254
  case illustration for, 380–382
  concealing vital information and, 244–245
  defects in process and, preventing, 245–251, 380–383
  disclosure of confidential information and, duty to disclose and, 288–290
  expectations of mediation parties and, 243–245
  expectations of the mediation profession and public and, 245–251
  grossly unfair agreements as, 248–249, 380–383, 406
  harm to nonparticipants as, 249–250, 254, 406
  harm to minors or incapacitated persons related to the dispute as, 250–251, 254, 406
  illegal agreements as, 247, 254, 380–383, 406
  immoral agreements as, 247–248, 254, 380–383, 406
  by mediators, 242–243
  mislabeling a process "mediation" as, 246, 253, 406, 417
  misuse of information as, 187, 243–244, 253, 406
  by participants, preventing, 158, 244–245
  preventing, 243–251, 253
  public trust and, 246–251
  reporting obligations and, 288–290
  respect among participants and, 261
  standing of the profession and, 243, 245–246
  termination of mediation and, 244–245, 248–249, 406
  unconscionable or unfair agreements as, 248–249, 254, 380–383, 406
  unruling parties and, 242, 253, 393, 405
  use of mediation to further illegal conduct as, 246, 253, 406
Accepting/refusing a case, 374–375, 376–382
  competence and, 165, 167, 376
  conflicts of interest and, 194–195, **194, 196**, 205, 376–377
  diligence and, 256, 258
  impartiality in, 224–227, 230
  integrity and, 241–243
  standing of the profession and, 313
ADR Canada, 91, 164. *See also* Canada standards
Advancement of the profession, 103, 114–115, 123, 317–319, 410–411
  codes of conduct and, 103, 317, 419
  ethics of aspiration and, 317
  ideal of, 317, 319, 410
  meaning of, 318–319
  Proposed Model Code of Conduct and, 410–411
  proposed standard of, 319

Advantage, unfair
  duties of professionals toward the profession and, 60
  mediator–profession relationship and, 109–110
  professional-profession relationship and, 59
Advertising and solicitation, 102–103, 114–115, 124, 320–324, 410, 418
  certification and, 323
  codes of conduct and, 102–103, 320, 322–324
  conflicts of interest and, 201, 203, 205, 395, 401
  honesty and, 321–324, 410, 418
  impartiality and, 323–324
  integrity and, 321–322, 324
  mediation outcome and, 322, 324, 410, 418
  Proposed Model Code of Conduct and, 410
  proposed standard of, 324
  public trust and, 321
  role-morality and, 321
  self-determination and, 324
  standing of the profession and, 321
  truthfulness in, 265, 321–324
Advice, professional. *See* Integrity
  case illustration for, 370–371, 380
  coercion and, 239
  impartiality and, 211, 220, 222, 237–239, 380
  integrity and, 237–240, 370, 380
  provision of information vs., 238–239
  self-determination and, 157, 160, 238–240, 253, 277, 361, 370–371, 380
Alabama and *Alabama Code of Ethics for Mediators*, 108, 151, 152, 163, 164, 173, 180, 189, 191–193, 197, 265, 286, 325, 332
Allocation of decision-making powers, 44–46, 134–136, **137**
Alternative courses of action, ranking and choosing between, 357–360
Ambiguities
  discretion and, 16
  ethical dilemmas and, 355–356
  norms' content and, 352–353
  rules and, 16
  values and, 16
American Bar Association, 364, 384
Analysis of ethical questions. *See* Ethical decision-making; Case illustrations
Anonymity of mediation parties
  confidentiality and, 278, 280–281, 300, 408
  disclosure of confidential information and, 287–288, 297–298, 301, 408
Appropriateness of case to process, 49, 62, 240–243, 253, 405
Aspiration, 12–19, **17, 24**, 26–27. *See also* Ideals
  Advancement of the profession and, 317
  competence and, 42
  duty vs, 17–19
  duties of professionals toward clients and, 41
  ethical, 17, **17**
  ethics of, 13
  moral, 12–13, 15, **17**, 17
  morality of, 12–13, 15, 17, 24–25, 27
Australian standards and *Australian National Mediator Accreditation Standards*, 91, 109, 113–114, 164, 165, 166, 187, 215, 283, 297, 321, 327–328
Authority
  decision-making, of mediators, 90, 129–136, **137**, 234–235, 252. *See also* Integrity; Self-determination (autonomy)
  decision-making, of professionals, 44–46, 48
  employers/principals and, 74, 330–339
  law vs. morality and, 27–28
Autonomy. *See* Self-determination (autonomy)
Awareness, in ethical decision-making, 348–349

Bad faith, 158
Bar, ethical, 30–31, **31**
Baserman, Max H., 306
Baum, Robert J., 348
Bayles, Michael D. xxv, 23, 39, 41, 42, 50, 51, 62, 64, 67, 68
Beauchamp, Tom, xxvi, 14, 17–18, 29, 60, 67, 360
Bias. *See* Conflicts of interest; Impartiality
Boulle, Laurence, 87–88, 221, 249, 250, 303
Brazil, Wayne D., 331–332, 333
Bush, Robert B. A., 228

California and *California Rules of Conduct for Mediators . . .*, 110, 111, 114, 127, 128, 146–149, 172, 179, 180, 193, 195–197, 215, 216, 225, 226, 231–232, 249, 250, 256, 265–268, 273, 276, 312, 327, 332–333
Calkins, Richard M., 232
Canadian standards, 91, 152, 164, 244, 275, 276, 283, 327
Care, diligence and, 51, 257–258
Carr, Craig L., 56, 304
Case illustrations, 364–396
Categorical imperative (Kant), 8–9
Certification, 171, 177, 318, 323
Chartered Mediators Accreditation Program (Canada), 164. *See also* Canadian standards
Chaykin, Arthur, 108, 264
Childress, James, xxvi, 14, 17–18, 29, 50, 67
Claims or complaints against mediators, 285, 301, 332, 408
Client autonomy or self-determination, 40, 43–46
Client-professional relationship. *See* Professional-client relationship
Clouse, Danner, 54
Cobb, Sara, 227
Code of Conduct for Mediators (Canada), 91. *See also* Canadian standards
Code of Conduct for United States Judges, The, 51, 53, 63
Code of Medical Ethics, 53
Code of Professional Conduct for Labor Mediators, 109, 111, 113, 261, 312, 334
Codes of Ethics and Standards of Practice (Montana), 146. *See also* Montana standards
Coercion,
- advice or opinion and, 239
- codes of conduct and, 91, 129, 137, 146–147, 239, 414
- duties regarding voluntariness and lack of, 146–148
- duty to prevent coerced decisions and, 148–150
- fairness and, 310
- impartiality and, 210
- Proposed Model Code of Conduct and, 402–403
- respect and, 252
- self-determination and, 129, 137, 140–142, 146–150, **148**, 161, 262, 366–367, 377–379
- termination of mediation and, 149–150
- voluntariness and lack of, 129, 137, 140–142, 146–150, **148**, 161, 262, 366–367, 377–379

Cohen, Elliot D, 50
Communication, *See also* Confidentiality; Dialogue in mediation; Disclosure of confidential information
- advertising, solicitation and, 322, 324
- competence and, 168–169, 171–172, 174–176, 181–182
- competency of mediation parties to make decisions and, 138, 160
- dependence of mediation parties and, 107
- honesty and, 264–267
- ideal of mediation and, professional, 95
- information subject to confidentiality, 277–281, **279**, 300, 408
- privileged communications, mediation privilege and, 294–297, 299, 384–390

Communication (cont.)
role of mediator and, 86–87, 94
truthfulness and, 264–267, 322, 324
Community mediation centers
case illustrations, 365–372, 384–394
duties of mediators toward, 113, 330, 334–337, 339
employers/principals and, 113, 330, 334–337
fees and, 325
mediator–employer/principal relationship and, 113
Proposed Model Code of Conduct and, 398, 409
volunteer mediators and, 7, 113, 325, 330, 334–337
Competence, 101, 104, 108, 114–115, 117, 122, 163–182, **178**, 399, 415–416
accepting/refusing a case based on, 165, 167, 376
basic, 166–173
basic, elements of, 168
basic vs. specific, 166, 182
bridging gaps in, 177–178
codes of conduct and, 101, 163–167, 415–416
complexity of case and, 175–176
consulting outside experts and, 178, 181
continuing education and, 179–180
court-connected mediation programs and, 163–164, 173, 177
cultural knowledge and, 177, 376
diligence and, 255
duty of, 164–166, 180–182
duty of, normative basis for, 164–165, 180–181
duty of, of professionals in professional-client relationship, 40, 41–42
education and training in, 163, 171–173, 179–180, 181
evaluative mediation and, 175
expectations of mediation parties for, 165, 166–167
expectations of the mediation profession and public for, 165–166
expectations of subject-matter expertise and, 174–177
experience in, 171–173
expertise and, process vs. subject-matter, 174–175
fairness and, 310
family mediation and, 176
ideal of professionalization and, professional, 173
impartiality and, 223
incompetence defined for, 182
integrity and, 235
knowledge in, 168–171, 181
language skills and, 177
licensing and, 163, 171–172
maintaining, 179–180, 182
meaning of mediator, **178**, 180–181
narrative mediation and, 170–171
"natural mediators" and, 172
problem-solving mediation and, 169, 171
professional and social interests of mediator in, 165–166
professionalization and, 164
Proposed Model Code of Conduct and, 399
proposed standard of, 182
providing information regarding, 178–179
public trust and, 165–167, 181
qualifications for, 181
qualifications for, in mediation laws, 163–164
qualities or traits of the mediator and, 173–174
relationship of trust and, 167
role-morality and, 164–165, 167, 172
self-determination and, 157, 178–179
self-determination and, limits to, 136, 167
skills in, 168–171, 181
specific, 167, 174–177
standing of the profession and, 166–167, 180–181, 314
styles of mediation and, 169–171
subject matter expertise and, 174–177

training and, 171–173
transformative mediation and, 169–171
volunteer mediators and, 335–336
withdrawal from mediation on the basis of, 165, 167, 177–178

Complaints against mediators, 285, 301, 332, 408

Complex cases,
competence and, 175–176
reasons for, in ethical decision-making, 346, 351–354

Compliance, in employer/principal relationship, 103, 113, 310, 330, 332, 338

Confidentiality, 54–55, 92, 93, 102, 108, 114–115, 123, 271–301, 407–408, 416–417. *See also* Disclosure of confidential information
anonymity and, 278, 280–281, 300, 408
awareness of, 275–277
case illustration, the probing judge and the ordering court, 384–390
codes of conduct and, 102, 272–273
competence and, 168
conflicts of interest and, 188
disclosure vs., justified grounds for, 281–298, **284**. *See also* Disclosure of confidential information
duty of, of professionals in professional-client relationship, 40, 54–55
employers/principals and, 78, 330
ethical duty of, 281, 300, 407
exceptions to. *See* Disclosure of confidential information
expectations of mediation parties for, 271–272, 277–279, 298
expectations of the mediation profession and public for, 273–274, 277–278, 298
fairness and, 305, 310
honesty and, 267
information about, providing to parties, 155–156, 275–277, 300
information subject to, defining, 277–281, **279**, 300, 408
institutional/program rules on, 275, 278–279, 281
legal rules of, knowledge of, 276, 289, 296, 299
obligation of participants to, 274–275
privileged communications, mediation privilege and, 294–297, 299, 384–390
promise of, 272
Proposed Model Code of Conduct and, 407–408
proposed standard of, 300–301
public trust and, 274, 278, **279**, 298–299
relationship of trust and, 271, 273, 277
scope of, knowledge of, 275–277
self-determination and, 155–156, 273, 275, 277, 281, 298
self-determination and, limits to, 136, 282, 290
standing of employer/principal and, 274, 278
standing of the profession and, 273–274, 277–278, **279**, 298–299
trust of parties and, 271–272, 273, 277–278, **279**, 298
warning others and, 118–119, 289–294

Conflict/dispute, 88–89, 168

Conflicts of interest, 16, 42–43, 101–103, 108, 114–115, 122, 183–206, 401–402, 414–415
abuse of process and, 187
accepting/refusing a case based on, 194–195, **194, 196**, 205, 376–377
actual, 191, **192**, 193, 204–205
appearance of, 193, **194**, 198, 204
bias in, 185, 204
case illustration for, post-mediation psychiatric treatment, 394–396
children's interests and, 185
circumstances of, 189–190, **190**
clear, 195, 197–198, 202. *See also* serious
codes of conduct and, 101–102, 184, 195–199, 200–203

Conflicts of interest (cont.)
  defining, 186–190, 204
  disclosure of, 191–192, **192, 196**, 198–199
  duty to act in, 185–186, 189–190
  duty to act in, of professionals in professional-client relationship, 40, 42–43
  duties outside of those of mediator (religious, etc.) and, 189–190, **190**, 199
  emotional involvement in outcome and, 189
  employers/principals and, 76, 337–338
  expectations of mediation parties and, 190–193, **192**
  expectations of the mediation profession and public and, 193–194, **194**
  factual, 193
  fairness and, 306
  fees and, 184, 196–197, 326
  financial involvement in outcome in, 189
  goals of mediation and, 184–185
  ideal vs. workable duty to act in, 186, 204
  impartiality and, 187–188, **188**, 191–192, **192**, 194, 197, 199, 200–203, 205, 207, 226–227
  importance of, 187–188, **188**
  inevitability of, 183–186
  informed decision-making and, 191, **192**
  integrity and, 187, 191, **192**, 195, 201–202, 231–232, 240
  irrelevant considerations and, 187, 194–195, **196**, 204
  lawyer-mediators and, 189, 198, 202–203
  minor, 195–197, **196**, 200, 226
  neutrality and, 207
  non-waivable, 197–198. *See also* serious
  outcomes and, 185–186, 189, **190**, 199, 204
  personal values in, 185, 189–190, **190**, 199, 200, 226
  post-mediation, 199–203, 205–206, 240, 394–396
  potential, 191, **192**, 193, 197, 199, 204–205
  prejudice in, 185, 199
  problem-solving mediation and, 184
  Proposed Model Code of Conduct and, 401–402
  proposed standard of, 204–206
  psychological needs and, 185
  public trust and, 193–194, **194**, 197, 200–203, 314–315
  rationale for regulating, 187, **188**
  relationship and, family, 197–198
  relationships (business, personal, professional) with participants and, prior relationship with participants and, 187, 189, **190**, 197–198
  relationships with participants and, future or subsequent to mediation, 199–203
  religion and, 189–190, 199
  self-determination and, 188, 191, **192**, 198, 204
  self-determination and, limits to, 136, 194–195, **194**, 197–198, 201
  serious, 194–200, **194, 196**, 205, 226, 306, 326, 377, 401
  severity of, 192, 194–199, **196, 200**, 205
  solicitation and, 201, 203, 205, 395, 401
  standing of the profession and, 193–194, **194**, 200–203, 314–315
  subsequent to mediation, 199–203, 205–206, 240, 394–396
  trivial, 192, 195–196, **196**, 198, 200, 226
  trust of parties and, 183, 191, **192**, 199, 204
  withdrawal of mediator in presence of, 191, **192**, 193, 194–195, **194, 196**, 197, 200, 204–205
  worldviews in, 185, 189–190, **190**, 199, 200, 226

Consent of mediation parties, 45, 76. *See also* Self-determination (autonomy)
abuse of mediation process and, 245–246
case illustrations and, 378, 388
codes of conduct and, 129, 264
conflicts of interest and, **192**, 193–197, **196**, 200–201
competence and, 173
disclosure of confidential information and, 283, **284**, 287, 295, 297–298, 300, 388
ethical decision-making and, 359
fairness and, 56, 304–305, 307–308, 359
fees and, 325
honesty and, 264, 266
impartiality and, 225–226
incapacitated persons, minors, and harm to, 250–251
informed, 56, 120, 129, 141, 152, 157–158, 203, 240, 250, 264, 266, 307, 359. *See also* informed decision-making, in Self-determination (autonomy)
integrity and, 237–238, 245–246, 252
mediation outcome and, 90, 305, 308. *See also* mediation outcome, in Self-determination (autonomy)
mediation privilege and, 295
participation in mediation, 93. *See also* participation in mediation, in Self-determination (autonomy)
Proposed Model Code of Conduct and, 402–405, 408
self-determination and, 129, 132, 135, 137, 141, 152, 157–158, 160, 162, 378
shared decision-making and, 134–135, 160.
termination of mediation and, 157–158, 162
Consulting outside experts
case illustrations, 366, 371–372, 379, 383
competence and, 178, 181
confidentiality and, 277
ethical decision-making and, 361–362
impartiality and, 215, 239
integrity and, 239, 253
self-determination and, 155–157, 162
Continuing education, competence and, 179–180. *See also* Education and training
Contracts and contract law, 28
Cooley, John W., 248, 263
Cooper, David E., 10
Core descriptive definition of mediation, 88–90, 94, 97. *See also* Mediation
Core Standards of Mediation (Oregon), 127. *See also* Oregon standards
Court-connected mediators, *See also* Courts and mediators
as agents of court, 331–332
claims or complaints against mediators and, 285
competence of, qualifications requirements for, 163–164, 173, 177
conflicting duties and, 337–338
duties of, toward the court, 113–114, 331–334, 339–340
duties of, toward the public, 111–112
ethical decision-making and, 350–351, 359
ideals of, professional, 97, 359
image of court and, 203, 260
integrity of court and, maintaining, 195, 226, 232, 333
Proposed Model Code of Conduct and, 397–398, 407–409
public trust in the courts and, maintaining, 232, 332–333
request of information by mediation programs and, 286–288
trust and, position of, 330, 332
Courts and mediators
case illustration, the probing judge and the ordering court, 384–390
claims or complaints against mediators, 285

Courts and mediators (cont.)
competence/qualifications requirements for mediators, 163–164, 173, 177
conflicting duties and, 337–338
court-ordered disclosure of confidential information, 294–297, 384–390
courts as employers/principals, 73, 113, 330
duties of mediators toward courts, 113–114, 330–334
honesty in contacts with courts, 265, 270
mandatory mediation, 93–94, 146, 331
problem-solving mediation and, 91, 97
Proposed Model Code of Conduct and, 397–398, 407–409
request of information by mediation program, 286–288
respect/dignity in contacts with courts, 260, 263
Cox, Damien, 47
Creative solutions, 360–362
Critical morality, 12, 70–71, 112–113, 246–249, 254, 278, 288, 299, 303, 305, 309, 380, 382, 406
Culture and ethical practice.
case illustration, 373–384
competence and, 173–174, 177, 181–182, 376, 400
impartiality and, 216, 228, 230, 376–377, 399
narrative mediation and, 170, 228
Cultural knowledge and competence, 177
Culver, Charles M., 54

Davis, Michael, xxv, 28–29, 50, 59, 63, 347–348
Deception, 54, 264–269, 322. *See also* Truthfulness
DeMartino, George, 67
Dependability, 15
Dependence issues in mediation, 107–108, 176, 208, 250
Dialogue in mediation,
basic features of mediation and, 89–90
competence related to, 168, 176
definition of mediation, core descriptive and, 94, **97**
ideal of, professional, 7, 95, **97**
integrity and, 242, 393
respect and, 261–262
role of mediator and, 89, 94, 100, 144
self-determination and, 144
Dignity. *See* Respect and dignity
Dilemmas in ethical decision-making, 354–362. *See also* Ethical decision-making
conflicting ethical norms and, 354–355
conflicting ethical vs. legal norms/duties and, 357
conflicting interpretations of ethical norms and, 355–356
creative solutions and, 360–362
dead-ends and, 360–362
ethical, 354–356
integration and, resolving dilemmas by, 361–362
non-ethical, 356–357
single "right" solution to, possibility of, 344–345, 360–361
Diligence, 108, 114, 255–258, 406
accepting/refusing a case based on, 256, 258
attention to parties and the case in, 256
care in, 257–258
codes of conduct and, 103–104, 255
competence and, 255
definitions of, 51
delay and, 255–256
duty of, 255
duty of, of professionals in professional-client relationship, 40, 51–52
employers/principals and, 77, 330
expectations of mediation parties for, 255
expectations of the mediation profession and public for, 255

impartiality and, 258
integrity and, 257
meaning of, 256
preparation for mediation and, 256–257
Proposed Model Code of Conduct and, 406
proposed standard of, 258
public trust and, 255
standing of the profession and, 255
timing and, 256
trust of parties and, 255
Dillon, Robin S., 52
Disclosing conflicts of interest, 191–192, **192, 196**, 198–199, 205, 401
Disclosure of confidential information, 281–298, **284**, 281
anonymity in, 287–288, 297–298, 301, 408
agreement and, information relating to parties reaching, 286–288, 301, 408
appearance of parties and, information relating to, 286–288, 301, 408
claims or complaints against mediators and, 285, 301, 408
consent of parties to, 283, **284**, 287, 295, 297–298, 300, 388, 408
court-ordered, 294–297, 384–390
ethical duty of mediators of, (ethically required disclosure), 282, **284,** 288–290, 301, 408
ethically permitted, 282–288, **284**, 290–298, 300–301, 408
fees and, claims for, 285–286, 301, 408
impartiality and, 293–294, 296
institutional/program rules on, 286–288, 291
integrity and, 294
legally permitted, vs. ethical duty of confidentiality, 291–292, 299
limits to ethically permitted, 282, 300, 408
mediation program's request for, 286–288, 301, 408
on status of negotiations/agreement, 286–288
privileged communication, mediation privilege and, 294–297, 299, 384–390
public trust and, 282, 288–291, 296, 299–301, 407–408
research, teaching, evaluation, training purposes and, 297–298, 301, 408
self-determination and, 283
self-determination and, limits to, 295
standing of the profession and, 282, **284**, 285, 288–291, 299–301, 407–408
trust of parties and, 287, 296
warning others of danger and, 118–119, 289–294
Discretion,
ethical decision-making and, 359, 363
inherent in professional practice, 44
integrity and, 48, 77, 233–235, **234**, 248, 252
mediation practice and, xxiii, 99, 234–236, 252,
uncertainty and ambiguity of norms necessitating exercise of, 16, 31, 359, 363
Dispute. *See* Conflict/dispute
Distinguishing features of mediation, 88–91
Diversity of practice in mediation, 98–101
Divorce mediation, 91, 163, 176, 185, 201–202, 214–215, 350, 365–384
Duties of mediators toward employers/principals, 113–114, 330–340. *See also* Duties of professionals toward employers/principals
agency relationship and, 331–332
autonomy of employer/principal in, 330
autonomy of employer/principal, limits to, 314, 338
codes of conduct and, 113–114, 332–333
conflicts of interest in, 330, 337–338

Duties of mediators (cont.)
competence in, 172–173, 330, 335
community mediation center and, 113, 330, 334–337
confidentiality in, 330
confidentiality in duties toward mediation parties and, 274, 277–278
conflicting duties, 337–338
court-connected mediators and, 331–334
courts and, 113–114, 330–334
courts and, standing of, 334
diligence in, 330
disclosure of confidential information and, 282–283, 286, 289
duties to mediation parties, the profession, and the public and, 337–339
duties of professionals toward employers/principals and, 75–79, **80**
fairness and, 308–309, 330
governmental agencies and, 334
honesty in, 330, 339
impartiality in, 330
impartiality in duties toward mediation parties and, 209
integrity in, 330
interpretation of norms and, 117, **118**, 313–314, 338–339
obedience to instructions of employer/principal in, 113, 330, 332, 335
principals in, 113, 330
Proposed Model Code of Conduct and, 398, 409
proposed standard of, 339–340
public image of employer/principal and, 332, 336–337, 339, 394
public trust in employers/principals and, 332–334, 393–394
public trust in the mediation profession and, 313–314
reputation of employer/principal and, 332, 336–339, 394
role-ethics and, 25
standing of the profession and, 313–314
standing of employer/principal in, maintaining, 330, 332–334, 336, 339, 393–394
respect in, 330
trust and, 113, 330, 334, 336
volunteer mediators and, 334–337
Duties of mediators toward mediation parties, 108, 122
Duties of mediators toward the mediation profession, 109–110, 122, 126
Duties of mediators toward the public, 112–113, 122, 126
Duties of professionals toward clients 38–57, **57**
appropriateness of case to process in, 49
aspiration aspect of, 41
client autonomy or self-determination in, 40, 43–46
competence in, 40, 41–42
confidentiality in, 40, 54–55
conflicts of interest in, 40, 42–43
decision-making and exercising discretion in, 48
dignity in, 40, 52–53
diligence in, 40, 51–52
discretion in, 48
ethical standards and, 40–41
fairness in, 40, 55–56
honesty in, 40, 54
impartiality in, 40, 49–51
integrity in, 40, 46–49
meaning of clients in, 38
mediators' duties toward mediation parties, 108
normative basis of, 38–40, **40**
process abuse or substantial defects in the process in, preventing, 49
professional-client relationship establishing, 38–40, **40**. *See also* Professional-client relationship
respect and dignity in, 40, 52–53
separation of professional roles in, 49
Duties of professionals toward employers/principals, 75–79, **80**

autonomy of employer/principal in, 76
conflicts of interest in, 76
competence in, 76
confidentiality in, 77
conflicting duties and, 76, 79
diligence in, 77
duties to clients and, 75, 79
duties of mediators toward employers/principals and, 113–114, 330–340
honesty in, 77
impartiality in, 77
integrity in, 77
normative basis of, 73–75, **75**
obedience to instructions of employer/principal in, 76
public trust in employers/principals and, 78
reputation of employer/principal and, 78
respect in, 78
standing of employer/principal in, maintaining, 78

Duties of professionals toward the profession, 60–65, **65**
breach of of duties toward clients and employers/principals and, 62, 64–65
fairness in, 60, 64
helping profession fulfill its social role in, 63–64
honesty to colleagues, professional organizations, and others in, 62
interpretation of duties and, 61, **61**
mediators' duties toward the profession and, 110
normative basis of, 58–59, **60**
non-professional activity and, 20
personal (private) conduct, limitations on in, 20, 63
profession defined for, 57–58
professional-profession relationship establishing, 58–59, **60**. *See also* Professional-profession relationship
promise-keeping in, 58
public aspect of duties toward clients and employers/principals and, 61, **61**
public trust and, 61–63, **61**, 64, **65**
respect to colleagues, professional organizations, and others in, 62
specification of duties and, 65
standing of the profession in, maintaining, 61–64, **65**
unfair advantage and, 60

Duties of professionals toward the public, 68–72, **72**
abuse of process in, preventing, 68, 71
critical morality and, adherence to, 68, 70
mediators' duties toward the public and, 112–113
non-professional activity and, 20
normative basis of, 66–68, **69**
non-clients and, harm to, 70–71
private conduct and, 20
professional-public relationship establishing, 66–68, **69**. *See also* Professional-public relationship
public defined for, 66, 71
public/social interest in following rules of law and morality, 70
public/social interest in maintaining profession's standing and, 69
public trust and, 20, 69–70
rule of law and, adherence to, 68, 70
standing of the profession in, maintaining, 68–70
substantial process defects in, preventing, 68, 71

Education and training for mediators, 163, 171–173, 179–181
Educational aspects of mediation process, 134
Emotional involvement in outcome, conflicts of interest and, 189
Emotional interrupting parties, case illustration, 390–394
Employers and principals, 72–79, 113–115, 124, 330–340, 409. *See also* Duties of mediators toward

employers/principals; Duties of professionals toward employers/ principals; Mediator–employer/ principal relationship; Professional-employer/principal relationship
Empowerment, 221–222, 370
Equality. *See* Impartiality; Respect and dignity
Ethical bar, 30–31, **31**
Ethical decision-making, 343–363, **346**. *See also* Dilemmas in ethical decision-making
  alternative courses of action, ranking and choosing between, 357–360
  ambiguity of norms' content in, 352–353
  applying norms to facts in, 351
  approaches to, 344–345
  clarifying facts for, 350–352
  competing interpretations of norms in, 352–353
  complexity in, reasons for, 346, 351–354
  creative solutions in, 360–362
  dead-ends in, 360–362
  dilemmas in, 354–362. *See also* Dilemmas in ethical decision-making
  discretion in, 359, 363
  easy cases/questions in, 345, 349–351
  ethical awareness in, 348–349
  ethical dilemmas in, 354–356
  ethical questions arising in, 347–348
  ethical questions vs. technical, practical, or professional questions in, 347–348
  ethical sensitivity in, 348–349
  fairness in, test of, 120–121, 359
  hard cases/questions in, 346, 351–362
  ideals and, 353, 359, 363
  indeterminacy of facts in, 351–352
  integration in, resolving hard cases and dilemmas by, 361–362
  intention to take action in, 348
  interpretation in, 346, 351–356, 359
  intuition in, 344–345, 362
  justification in, 344, 362–363
  meaning of, 344, 362–363
  non-ethical dilemmas in, 356–357
  personal view vs., 362–363
  process of, 345–346, **346**
  Proposed Model Code of Conduct and, familiarity with, 350, 352, 365
  purposive interpretation in, 120, 353, 359
  ranking interpretations or courses of action in, 359
  reconciling competing interpretations of the same norm in, 359
  reconciling competing norms in, 358
  relativity of ethical norms and, 358, 363
  relevant norms in, identification of, 350, 352
  resolving hard cases in, 357–362
  role-morality and, 353
  single "right" solution in, possibility of, 344–345, 360–361
  uncertainty of relevant norms in, 352
Ethical dilemmas, 354–356. *See also* Dilemmas in ethical decision-making
Ethical Guidelines for Mediators (Australia), 91
Ethical norms (norms of professional ethics),
  conflicts between, 2
  conflicts between ethical and moral norms, 21–22
  duty vs. aspiration distinction in, 17–19
  aspirations and, 17, **17**
  duties and, 14, 17–22, **17**, 31, **31**
  ideals and, 13, 16, **17**, 27, 30–31, **31**
  principles and, 14–16, **17**
  ethical relationships and general, 25, 37–81
  rights and, 20
  rules and, 14, 16, **17**
  standards and, 14, 19
  values in, 15–16, **17**
  general ethical norms of professional role in, 25, 37–81
  general moral norms of role in, 25, **27**

justification of, 22, 35–36
legal norms and, 28–29, **29**, 36
mediation practice and, xxiii-xxiv, 105, 114–115, 121
moral norms in, 24–25, **27**
moral norms of role in, 25–26, **27**
particular moral norms of role in, 26, **27**
professional practice and, 8–22, **17**, **27**, **29**, 37, 64, 81
relativity of, 21–22, 37, 117, 345, 358, 363
relativity of duties in, 37, 345
rules–principles–values distinction, 14–16, 19
specification of, 26
standards (or norms) of ethics and, 14, 19
Ethical relationships, xxiv-xxv, 37–81, 105–114, 116–119
Ethics. *See* Professional ethics
Evaluative mediation, 86–87, 94, 175, 238–240
Experience and competence, 171–173
Expertise, subject matter, 174–177

Facilitative mediation, 86–87, 94, 97
Factual appropriateness, 241
Fairness, 15, 102, 104, 108, 109, 114–115, 120–121, 123, 302–310, 411
abuse of process and, 305, 308
case illustration, unacceptable mediation outcomes, 373–384
codes of conduct and, 102, 104
conduct of mediator and, 304–306
conflicts of interest and, 306
consent and, 56, 304–305, 307, 359
disclosure of confidential information and, 304–305
duty of, of mediators toward mediation parties, 307–308
duty of, of mediators toward the mediation profession and public, 109–110, 308–309
duty of, of professionals in professional-client relationship, 40, 55–56
duties of professionals toward the profession and, 58–60, 64
employers/principals and, 79, 308–309, 330
expectations for, 307–308, 309
ethical decision-making and, 359–360
fees and, 306
formal, 303–304, 309
illegal outcome and, 305, 309
impartiality and, 218–223, 303, 307
integrity and, 47, 231–232, 308–309
interpretation of norms and, 56, 120–121, 302, 307, 309–310
law and, adherence to, 303, 305
meaning of, 55–56
meaning of, in mediation, 303–306
morality and, critical, adherence to, 303, 305
narrow approach to, 303–305
norm vs. perception of, 302
normative, 55–56, 303–304, 307, 309
outcome, 304–306, 308–310, 375, 380–383
perception of, 302, 304, 305–306, 309
personal perception of, 304–306
procedural, 143, 234, 306
process, 304–306
Proposed Model Code of Conduct and, 411
proposed standard of, 310
public perception of, 304, 306, 309
public trust and, 306, 308–309
rules and, adherence to, 303
rules of law and, adherence to, 303
self determination and, 138, 142–143, 304–305, 307–308
standing of the profession and, 308–309
subjective perception of, 304
substantive, 55–56, 303–305, 307, 309
unconscionable outcome and, 248–249, 306–307
uninformed outcome and, 304–305
vagueness of, 302
wide approach to, 303, 305, 309

Family Mediation Canada Code, 152, 157, 244, 276, 283, 289–290. *See also* Canadian standards
Family Mediation Model Standards, 144, 193, 224, 250, 289
Favoritism. *See* Impartiality
Federal Employee Mediators Guide, 238, 287
Fees, 103, 114–115, 124, 325–329, 410, 418–419
  appropriateness of, 326–328
  codes of conduct and, 103, 320, 326–327
  conflicts of interest and, 184, 196–197, 326
  contingent on outcome, 326
  disclosure of confidential information in claims for, 285–286, 301, 408
  failure to pay, withdrawal of services and, 327
  fairness and, 306
  honesty in, 325–326
  integrity and, 326–328
  Proposed Model Code of Conduct and, 410
  proposed standard of, 329
  public trust and, 326
  regulation of, purpose of, 325
  rights of professionals and, 20, 80
  role-morality and, 321
  self-determination and, 325–326
  standing of the profession and, 325
  termination of mediation and, non-payment of, 80, 327, 329, 410
  unequal, 328–329
  volunteer services and, 325
  withdrawal from case and, 327
  written agreements for, 327–328
Fiduciary aspect of mediation, 108
Financial involvement in outcome, conflicts of interest and, 189
Flexibility of practice in mediation, 98–101
Florida and *Florida Rules for Certified and Court-Appointed Mediators*, 109, 114, 128, 147, 149, 152, 166, 180, 184–188, 195, 197–198, 202, 210–213, 222, 226, 239, 242–244, 249, 256, 259, 275, 276, 298, 305, 311–312, 321, 323, 332, 337–338
Folger, Joseph P., 228
Fraud, 158, 264, 266
Fuller, Lon L., xxv, 12, 17, 63–64, 68
Function of professional ethics, 33–35, **34**
Fundamental concepts, 3–36
Fundamental social values, 11

Gaines, Michelle D., 214
General norms of professional role ethics, 25
Georgia and *Georgia Ethical Standards for Mediators*, 110, 145, 165, 175, 201, 213–215, 218–219, 221, 222, 231, 248, 256, 262–263, 274, 276, 295, 305, 312, 314, 321, 326, 333
Gert, Bernard, xxv, xxvi, 10, 11, 12, 14, 15, 23, 25, 49–51, 52, 54, 55, 58, 358–361
Gibson, Kevin, 303–304, 306
Goals of mediation, 90–91, 95–98, 184–185, 359
Guidance, provided as function of professional ethics, 33–34
Gunning, Isabelle R., 141

Hart, HLA, 12
Hedeen, Tim, 384
Hierarchy of duties, absence of, 118–119
Honesty, 15, 103, 108, 110, 114–115, 123, 264–270, 407
  advertising, solicitation and, 321–324, 410, 418
  codes of conduct and, 103, 264
  confidence and, 267
  devaluation and, 268
  duty of, of professionals in professional-client relationship, 40, 54
  duty of, toward participants and nonparticipants, 265
  duties of professionals toward the profession and, 62

employers/principals and, 78, 330, 339
exceptions to, 266–269
fairness and, 307
fees and, 325–326
impartiality and, 267
misrepresentation and, 151, 264, 266–268, 270, 407, 417
promoting, among participants, 265–266
Proposed Model Code of Conduct and, 407
proposed standard of, 270
public trust and, 264–267
reframing and, 267–268
self-determination and, 151, 264, 266–267, 269
separate meeting and, 268–269
standing of the profession and, 265, 314
termination of mediation and, 266
trust of parties and, 264, 269
truthfulness and, 264–265, 267, 269–270, 407
Human rights, 9
Hume, David, 66
Humility, 52, 381

Ideals,
ethical, 13, 16, **17**, 27, 30–31, **31**
moral, 13–16, **17**
professional, 23–24, **24**, 26
Ideals, mediation
advancement of the profession in, 317, 319, 410
better society/cooperation in, 96, **97**
communication in, 95
dialogue in, 7, 95, **97**
impartiality in, 212–213, 227
party self-determination in, 95, **97**
professionalization in, 95, 173,236, **97**
professional, 95–98
qualities or traits of the competent mediator and, 173–177
shared professional, 85, 95–97, **97**
narrative mediation in, professional ideals of, 96, 98
problem-solving mediation in, professional ideals of, 96, 97
transformative mediation in, professional ideals of, 96, 98, 359
respect/dignity in, 259
Illegal agreements, abuse of mediation and, 247, 254, 309, 380–383, 406
Illinois standards, 109, 150, 151–159, 214, 248, 250, 289, 290, 298, 312, 314, 336–337
Immoral agreements, abuse of mediation and, 247–248, 254, 380–383, 406
Immoral ethical behavior, possibility of, 21–22
Impairment of mediator, 165
Impartiality, 10, 49–50, 91–92, 101, 103, 108, 114–115, 122, 207–230, 400, 414
abuse of process and, 219
acceptance or refusal of cases based on, 224–227, 230, 376–377
advertising, solicitation and, 323–324
advice or opinion and, 211, 220, 222, 237–239, 380
appearance of partiality, avoiding, 213–217, 224, **225**, 226, 229–230. *See also* perceived partiality
balancing of power and, 221–222
bias and, 209–213, 217–219, 223–224, 229
case illustration for, acceptance or refusal of case, advice, 376–377, 380
case illustration for, uninformed wife in divorce, 365–372
codes of conduct and, 101, 210–212
confidentiality and, disclosure of information, 282, **284**, 288, 291–294, 296, 299
conflicts of interest and, 187–188, **188**, 191–192, **192**, 194, 197, 199, 200–203, 205, 207, 226–227
criticism of, 227–229
definitions of, 209–210
different treatment and, 211

Impartiality (cont.)
different treatment and, justified, 212, 218–224, **225**, 229–230
diligence and, 258
discrimination and, 209–210
duty vs. ideal of, 212–213, 227
duty of, of professionals in professional-client relationship, 40, 49–51
employers/principals and, 77, 330
empowerment and, 221–222
equality and, formal, 218–219, 223–224, 228
equality and, substantive, 218–224, 228–229
equality vs., 209–211, 217–218, 223–224, **225**
equidistance and, 227
expectation of mediation parties and, 208–210, 218–223
expectations of the mediation profession and public and, 208–209, 214, 218, 223–224
external, 212–213, 227, 229
ethical decision-making and, 344
evenhandedness and, 210–211
factual, 213–214, 224, 229–230
fairness and, 303, 307
fairness and, fair process, 218–223
favoritism and, 208–212, 217–220, 223–224, 229
favoritism and, justified, 220–223
formal sense of, 218–219, 223–224, 228
honesty and, 267
ideal of, 212, 227
inaction and, 219
integrity and, 219, 232, 237–239
internal, 212, 227, 229
limitations on mediator interventions and, 222–224, **225**
meaning of, 224, **225**, 229
morality and, 10–11
narrative mediation and, 207, 227–229
neutrality and, 207, 222, 228–229
perceived partiality, avoiding, 213–217, 224, **225**, 226, 229–230
practical source of mediators' duty of, 209
problem-solving mediation and, 227–229
professional ethics and, 22, 35–36, **35**
Proposed Model Code of Conduct and, 400
proposed standard of, 229–230
public trust and, 208–209, 214, 223–224, 226
reasonableness and, test of, vs. subjective (parties') feelings, 216–217
relationship of trust and, 208, 210, 218
respect/dignity and, 261–263
safety-net concept for exercising self-determination and, 222
same treatment and, 210–212, 224, **225**, 230
self-determination and, 210, 219–221, 367–371
separate meeting (caucus) and, 217
sources of mediators' duty of, 208–209
standing of employers/principals and, 209
standing of the profession and, 208–209, 214, 223–224, 229–230, 313–314
substantive sense of, 218–224, 228–229
sympathy and, 212
termination of mediation and, 223–224
transformative mediation and, 207, 227–229
trust of parties and, 208, 214, 219
unequal fees and, 328–329
unequal mediation parties and, 218,
withdrawal from mediation and, 224–227, 230
Incapacitated persons, harm to, 250–251
Incompetence of mediator, 182. *See also* Competence
Indeterminacy of facts and, 351–352
Indiana standards, on mediator qualifications, 164

Information relevant to decision-making, 137–138, 141, 142, 150–159, **151**, 161–162. *See also* Self-determination (autonomy)
Informed consent. *See* Consent of parties to mediation; Self-determination (autonomy)
Institutional enforcement, 17, 34
Integration, in solving dilemmas, 361–362
Integrity, 32, 102, 103, 104, 108, 114–115, 122, 231–254, **234**, 404–406. *See also* Abuse of mediation process
abuse of process and, preventing, 243–251, 253. *See also* Abuse of mediation process
abuse of process by mediators and, 242–243
abuse of process by participants and, preventing, 244–245
accepting/refusing a case based on, 241–243
additional professional role and, exercise of, 237–240, 370, 380
advertising, solicitation and, 321–322, 324
advice vs. provision of information and, 238–239
advice (legal or other) and, 237–240, 370, 380
after mediation, accepting different professional role, 240
after mediation, continuing ethical responsibility of mediators, 240
appropriateness of case to process and, 241–243, 253, 405
appropriateness of participants in process and, 235, 252, 405
authority of mediators to make decisions and, source of, 234–235, 252, 405
authority of representative and, limited, 236
case illustrations for, 370–372, 380–383, 393
codes of conduct and, 102, 231–232
commitment to definition and nature of role and, 231, 233, 237
competence and, 235
concealing vital information and, 244–245
conflicts of interest and, 187, **188**, 191, **192**, 195, 201–202, 231–232, 240
confidentiality and, 274, 294, 296
court's, 333
decision-making and, 233–236, **234**, 252, 372
defects in process and, preventing, 245–251, 380–383
diligence and, 257
discretion and, 233–235, **234**, 248, 252
duty of, defined, 233, 234
duty of, of professionals in professional-client relationship, 40, 46–49
employers/principals and, 330
evaluative mediation and, 238–240
expectations of mediation parties and, 234, 236–237, 241, 243–244,
expectations of the mediation profession and public and, 237, 243, 245–250
fairness and, 47, 308–309
fees and, 326–328
grossly unfair outcome and, 248–249, 380–383, 406
harm to minors or incapacitated persons related to the dispute and, 250–251, 254, 406
harm to nonparticipants and, 249–250, 254, 406
honesty and, 266
ideal of professionalization and, professional, 236
illegal outcome and, 247, 254, 309, 380–383, 406
immoral outcome and, 247–248, 254, 380–383, 406
impartiality and, 219, 232, 237–239
irrelevant considerations and, 234, 372

Integrity (cont.)
likelihood of reaching agreement and, 242, 253, 393, 405
limits to mediator role and, 238–240
loss of business and, 372
meaningful participation in mediation and, 242–243, 253, 393, 405
meanings of, 47
mislabeling a process "mediation" and, 246, 253, 406, 417
misuse of information and, 243–244, 253, 406
personal, 32
process vs. professional, 231–232
professional-client relationship and, 46–49
Proposed Model Code of Conduct and, 404–406
proposed standard of, 252–254
providing information and, 238–239
public trust and, 232–233, 238, 241, 243–251, 254, 312, 406
referring parties to consult outside experts and, 239, 253, 405
respect/dignity and, 260, 262
self-determination and, exercise of, 235–240, 242
self-determination and, limits to 136, **137**, 236–237, 238–239, 246–251, 380–383
separation of professional roles and, 236–240, 252–253, 370, 380, 383, 405
standing of the profession and, 232–233, 238, 241–243, 245–251, 254, 312, 406
termination of mediation and, 241–251, 253, 406
trust of parties and, 241, 243–144
unconscionable outcome, 248–249, 254, 380–383, 406
unruling parties and, 242, 253, 393, 405
withdrawal from mediation and, 241, 244, 246–251
Intention to take action, ethical decision-making and, 348
Interpretation
norms of mediators' ethics and, 115–121, **118**
duties of professionals toward the profession and, 61, **61**
efect of standing of the profession on, 61, 117, 313–314
ethical decision-making and, 346, 351–356, 359
ethical dilemmas and, 355–356
fairness and, 56, 120–121, 302, 307, 309–310
purposive, 120, 353, 359

Justice. *See* Fairness

Kansas and *Kansas Ethical Standards for Mediators*, 246, 325
Kant, Immanuel, 8–9, 52
Kindness, 15
Kiryat-Ono Community Mediation Center, 384, 390
Kohen, Daryl, xxv
Kolb, Deborah, 269
Kovach, Kimberlee, xxiv, 271–272, 349
Kupfer Schneider, Andrea, xxiv

La Caze, Marguerite, 47
Labor mediation, 109, 111, 113, 261, 312, 334
Language, respect in use of, 259–260
Language skills, competence and, 177
Law and ethics, 27–31, **29, 31**
codes of ethics and law in, 28
ethical bar in, 30–31, **31**
ethical status of codes and standards in, 28
ethical threshold in, 13, 30–31, **31**
institutional enforcement of, 31
legal threshold in, 30–31, **31**
professional activities in, application of law to, 28
professional ethics in, 28–30, **29**
professional organizations and law in, 28
standards of conduct and law in, 28
unethical legal conduct in, 29–31, 29

Law and mediation, xxiv–xxv, 85–86. *See also* Courts and mediators
dilemmas arising from conflicting ethical and legal duties, 357
duty of mediators toward the profession to maintain rule of law, 246–247, 309
duty of mediators toward the public to follow law, 112–113, 303
illegal agreements, abuse of mediation and, 247, 254, 380–383, 406
knowledge of law as a matter of competence, 168, 174–177
knowledge of legal rules relating to confidentiality 276, 289, 296, 299
legal advice by mediators, 237–240, 370, 380
legally permitted disclosure of confidential information, vs. ethical duty of confidentiality, 291–292, 299
privileged communications, mediation privilege and, 294–297, 299, 384–390
qualifications for mediators in mediation laws, 163–164
use of mediation to further illegal conduct, preventing, 246, 253, 406
Law Council of Australia, 91
Layers of meaning of ethical duties, 117–119, **118**
Legal norms, 27–31, **29.** *See also* Law and ethics
consistent with morality, 28–29
ethical duty to follow a legally binding code of conduct and, 30
ethical norms and, 28–29, **29**, 36
immoral, 28
unethical, 29
Legitimate expectations and ethical duties, xxiv, 18, 25–26, 30
Levin, Murray S., 87
Levine, Michael P., 47
Licensing of mediators, xxiii–xxv, 163, 171–172
Limits to mediator role, 238–240. *See also* Integrity
Loss of business, integrity and, 372
Luban, David, 52–53
Lukes, Steven, 39

Macfarlane, Julie, xxvi, 345, 347, 361
Maintaining the profession's standing. *See* Standing of the profession
Maute, Judith, 248
McFall, Lynne, 32
Mediation
community, *See* Community mediation centers
definition of, core descriptive, 88–90, 94, **97**
descriptive definition of, 88
diversity of practice in, 98–101
divorce, 91, 163, 176, 185, 201–202, 214–215, 350, 365–384
evaluative, 86–87, 94
facilitative, 86–87, 94, 97
features of, basic (descriptive), 88–90
features of, normative, 91–93
ideals of, professional, 95–98
mandatory, 93–94, 146, 331
narrative. *See* Narrative mediation
normative definition of, 88
norms of, shared set of (based on codes and literature), 85, 101–105
problem-solving. *See* Problem-solving mediation
profession of, 5–6, 108–109
public good and, 7
styles/models of, 86–88, 94–98. *See also* Styles of mediation
transformative. *See* Transformative mediation
Mediation ideals. *See* Ideals, mediation
Mediation outcome
advertising, solicitation and, 322, 324, 410, 418
authority of mediator to impose, lack of, 90
case illustration, unacceptable outcomes, 373–384
coerced, 146–150
conflicts of interest and, 185–186, 189, 204, 377, 401

Mediation outcome (cont.)
contingent fees and, 197, 326, 329, 410
fairness of, 302, 304–306, 308–310, 374, 380–383
as a goal, 87, 184
harmful to minors/incapacitated persons, 250–251, 254, 406
harmful to nonparticipants, 249–250, 254, 406
illegal, 247, 254, 380–383, 406
immoral, 247–248, 254, 380–383, 406
informed, 150–152, 157–158, 162, 371
as a professional ideal, 95
public trust and, 223, 251, 254, 266, 382
self-determination and, 128, 130–135, 143, 147, 150, 158–159, 162, 402, 414
standing of the profession and, 246–251, 254, 316, 372
termination of mediation and, 150, 246–251, 254
unconscionable or grossly unfair, 248–249, 254, 380–383, 406
Mediator Ethics Advisory Committee (MEAC) (New York), 272
Mediator–employer/principal relationship. *See also* Professional-employer/principal relationship
agency relationship in, 113
community mediation center in, 113
courts in, 113
courts' programs in, 113
duties of mediators toward employers/principals in, 113–114, 330–340
employer's/principal's trust in, 113
expectations of employers/principals in, 113
principals in, 113
Mediator–parties relationship. *See also* Professional-client relationship
dependence of parties in, 107
duties of mediators toward mediation parties in, 108
expectations of parties in, 107–108
fiduciary relationship in, 108
power of mediators in, 107
promise to act as a mediator in, 107
relationship of trust in, 107–108
Mediator–profession relationship. *See also* Professional-profession relationship
benefits of mediators in, 109–110
expectations of the profession in, 109–110
duties of mediators toward the mediation profession in, 109–110
fairness in, 109–110
profession of mediation in, definition of, 108–109
public trust in, 110
reciprocity in, 110
unfair advantage in, 109–110
Mediator–public relationship. *See also* Professional-public relationship
benefits of mediators in, 111
court-connected mediators in, 111–112
critical morality in, maintaining of, 112
duties of mediators toward the public in, 112–113
expectations of the public in, 111–112
non-court mediators in, 111–112
power and influence of mediators in, 111–112
public trust in, 112
reciprocity in, 111
rule of law in, maintaining, 112
standing of the profession in, maintaining, 112
Mediators, information about, providing parties with, 153–155, 178–179
Mediators' ethics,
applicability of norms/theory of, to all mediators, 105–106, 115
balancing expectations and their effect on meaning of, 116–117, **118**
balancing duties in, 117–119

codes of conduct and their effect on meaning of, 106, 119–120
content and meaning of, ascertaining, 85, 115–121, **118**
definition of mediation and its effect on meaning of, 115–116
ethical relationships of mediators in, 106–114, 116–117
fairness considerations and their effect on meaning of, 120–121
harm in, minimization of, 119
ideals in. *See* Ideals, mediation
interpretation of norms of, 115–121
layers of meaning of ethical duties in, 117, **118**
mediator–employer/principal relationship in, 113–114
mediator–parties relationship in, 106–108
mediator–profession relationship in, 108–110
mediator–public relationship in, 111–113
norms of (based on theory of,), 114–115
norms of mediation and, shared set of (based on codes and literature), 85, 101–105
perspective-from-above and, 85, 104–105, 106, **106**, 114
perspective-from-below and, 104–105, 106, **106**, 107, 114
professional ethics and, 5–8
Proposed Model Code of Conduct and, 85, 121–122, 397–411
refusal of case in, 118
relativity of norms of, 117
role of mediator and, effect on the meaning of, 116
role-ethics and, 5, 7–8
role-morality and, effect on the meaning of, 85, 116–119
termination of mediation in, 118
theory of, xxv-xxvi, 85, 105–106, **106**, 365
withdrawal from mediation in, 118
Mediators' role. *See* Role of mediators
Members Code of Professional Conduct (Canada), 152. *See also* Canadian standards
Menkel-Meadow, Carrie, xxiv, 327, 373–384
Michigan standards, 193, 261
Millen, Jonathan, 227
Miller, John A., 56
Minimum conception of morality, 10
Minimum criteria of rationality and impartiality, 10
Minnesota standards, 164
Minors, harm to, 250–251
Misrepresentation, 151, 264, 266–268, 270, 407, 417
Missouri standards, 323
Model Standards of Conduct for Mediators, 412–419
abuse of mediation process and, 246
advancement of practice and, 317–319, 410, 419
advertising and solicitation and, 320, 323–324, 418
coercion and, 147, 149
competence and, 165–167, 173, 179, 180, 415–416
confidentiality and, 276–277, 280–281, 283, 287, 297, 416–417
conflicts of interest and, 184–185, 189, 191, 195–197, 200, 203, 414–415
construction and, 118
diligence and, 256
disclosure of confidential information and, 283, 287, 289, 297
ethical dilemmas and, 362
fairness and, 375, 383
fees and, 326, 328, 418–419
honesty and, 266
impartiality and, 211–212, 215–216, 414
integrity and, 231, 234, 235, 237, 238–239, 246
party competency and, 145
quality of the process and, 234–235, 237–239, 246, 256, 261, 266, 417–418
respect and, 261

Model Standards (cont.)
self-determination and, 127–128, 131, 145, 147, 149, 184–185, 375, 413–414
standing of the profession and, 314
Model Standards of Practice for Family and Divorce Mediation, 91
Moffitt, Michael, 88
Monk, Gerald, 227–228
Montana standards, 146
Montana Mediation Association, 146
Moore, Christopher W., xxiv
Moral criterion (Kant), 8–9
Moral norms, 8–12, **17**, 20–22
conflicts between ethical and moral norms, 21–22
conflicting, 21–22
criticism and, 18–19
definition of, 8–12
good reasons and, 10–11
impartiality and, 10–11
minimum criteria of, 10
aspiration in, 12–13, 15, **17**, 17
duty in, 12–15, **17**, 17–19
ideals in, 13–16, **17**
principles in, 14–16, **17**
rights in, 9, 19
rules in, 14, 16, **17**
traits in, 14
values in, 15–16, **17**
virtues in, 14–15
norms of obligation and, 14–17
praise and, 18–19
rationality and, 10–11
relativity of, 21–22
of role, 25
supererogation and, 14, 17–18
Moral relativism, 11–12
Morality
of aspiration, 12–13, 15, 17, 24–25, 27
common, 4, 14, 18
conflicts between professional duties and morality, 21–22
consequentialism and, 9
critical, 12
descriptive, 11–12
of duty, 12–13, 17
ethical demands exceeding, 20–21
ethical demands falling short of, 21–22
ethics and, 3–4
excellence and, 13, 15, 17
fairness and, 303, 305, 309
immoral agreements, abuse of mediation and, 247–248, 254, 380–383, 406
immoral ethical behavior, possibility of, 21–22
impartiality and, 10–11, 28, 35, 344
institutional enforcement and, 17
Kant, Immanuel and, 8–9, 52
legal norms and, 27–31, **29**
legitimate moral exceptions, 22
minimum conception of, 10
moral relativism and, 11–12
norms of ordinary, 24–25
ordinary, **4**, 20–22, 24–25, 130
particular, 3–4
personal, 32, 381
positive, 12, 248–249, 382
professional ethics and, **4**, 8–31
public trust and, 70–71, 112–113
rationality and, 10–11, 28, 35
relativism and, 11–12
respect/dignity and, 52, 259
role and. *See* Role-morality
rules, principles, values, ideals and, 12–19
sanction and, 17
self-determination (autonomy) and, 130
social values and, 11
theories of, 8–12
theories of rights and, 9
theories of virtues and, 9
unethical but moral behavior, possibility of, 20–21
utilitarianism and, 9

N.L.R.B. v. Joseph Macaluso, on disclosure of confidential information, 296
Narrative mediation,
applicability of mediators' ethics norms/theory to, 115

codes of conduct and, 105, 115, 119
common practices and techniques, 100–101, 169–171
culture and, 170, 228
impartiality and, 207, 227–229
meaning of, 87, 94, 98
Proposed Model Code of Conduct and, 121–122
ideals of, professional, 96, 98
role of mediator in, 94, 98, 100–101, 116
National Society of Professional Engineers, 28
Nature of mediation and role of mediators, 85–95
Nebraska standards, 201, 261, 273
Negotiation,
balanced, 151–152
distinguished from mediation, 89–90
of expectations, 116–117
honesty and, 265–267
knowledge of, in basic competence, 168–169
Nesic, Miryana, 87–88, 221, 249, 250, 303
Neutrality, 91–92, 207, 228. *See also* Impartiality
New York standards, 136, 195, 213, 214, 238, 239, 244, 245, 272–273, 297, 335–336
New York State Community Dispute Resolution Center (NY-CDRC), 136
Nolan-Haley, Jacqueline M., 108, 131, 231, 302, 305
Non-ethical dilemmas, 356–357
Non-professional norms, 32–33
Normative appropriateness, 241
Normative fairness, 55–56, 303–304, 307, 309
Norms of mediators' ethics. *See* Mediators' ethics
Norms of professional ethics. *See* Ethical norms
North Carolina standards, 110, 111, 114, 147, 148, 157, 164, 165, 174–175, 184, 187, 202–203, 238, 244–245, 260, 273, 274–275, 280, 290, 337

Obedience, to employers/principals, 76, 79, 113, 314, 330, 338–340, 409
Obligations of . . . *See* Duties of.
Olam v. Cong. Mortgage, on disclosure of confidential information, 296
Ontario Family Mediation Code, on impartiality, 219
Oregon standards, 127, 152, 156, 157, 266, 273–274, 322, 324
Oregon Mediation Association, 127
Outcome of mediation. *See* Mediation outcome

Participation of parties in mediation,
active, 142–143
capacity to participate in, 145, 160
conflicts of interest and, 192
consent to, 93–95
meaningful, 242–243, 253, 393, 405
relevant information for, 155–156
self-determination and, 127–128,131, 134–135, 142–143, 149, 155–156, 159, 191, 205, 275, 277, 325, 401–402
voluntariness in, 146–149
Particular morality, 3–4
Paternalism, 44–45, 54, 269, 379
Permissive norms, 19–20
Personal conduct, 20, 63, 313
Perspective-from-above/below of ethics, 85, 104–105, 106, **106**, 114, 320
Persuasion, 148, 168
Porter Love, Lela, xxiv
Post-mediation issues, conflicts of interest, 199–203, 205, 240, 394–395, 401–402, 415
Pou, Charles, 349, 361
Power
balancing of, 149, 221–222
case illustration for imbalance of, 365–370
empowerment and, 221–222, 370
ethical responsibility and, 25, 39
fairness and, 305
imbalances of, Proposed Model Code of Conduct, 161, 403
impartiality and, 221–222

Power (cont.)
inequality of, in professional-client relationship, 38–39
influence and, in professional-employer/principal relationship, 74
influence and, in professional-public relationship, 65–68
issues of, knowledge and skills in competence, 168
mediators', in mediator–parties relationship, 107
mediators' influence and, in mediator–public relationship, 111–112
of professionals, 8, 25
role-morality and, 8
safety-net concept for exercising self-determination and, 149, 222
supervision of, 34
trust and, 38–40, 57, 67, 107
volunteer mediators and, 336
Practice of mediation, flexibility and diversity in, 98–101
Preemption right to make decisions, self-determination and, 134–136
Prejudice,
abuse of mediation process and, preventing, 244
conflicts of interest and, 185, 199
impartiality and, 211–212, 414
Preparing for mediation, diligence and, 256–257
Pride, professional, 13
Principals. *See* Employers and principals
Principles, 12–19, **17**, 22–24, **24**
Pritchard, Michael S., xxv, 12, 25, 42, 47, 54, 59, 344, 358
Privileged communications, mediation privilege and, 294–297, 299, 384–390
Problem-solving mediation,
court-connected mediation and, 91, 97
definition of, in codes of conduct, 91
common practices and techniques, 99–100, 169–171
competence of mediators and, knowledge and skills required, 116, 169–171
conflicts of interest and, 184
evaluative mediation in, 86–87, 94
facilitative mediation in, 86–87, 94, 97
ideals of, professional, 96–97
impartiality and, 227–229
justice system and, 96
meaning of, 86–87, 94
role of mediator in, 86–87, 94, 97, 171
Process abuse. *See* Abuse of mediation process
Process of mediation. *See* Mediation
Profession,
criteria for, 6
definitions of, 5–6
defined for theory of professional ethics, 57–58
professionals and, defined for theory of professional ethics, 57
social role of, 63–64, 69
Professional integrity. *See* Integrity
Professional-client relationship, 38–57, **40**.
client-centered approach to, 45–46
collaborative approach to, 45
dependence in, 38–39
expectations of clients in, 39, **40**
ethical duties toward clients established by, 40–57, **57**. *See also* Duties of professionals toward clients
ethical standards and, 40–41
features of, 38–39, **40**
fiduciary relationship in, 39
meaning of clients in, 38
mediator-parties relationship, 106–108
paternalistic approach to, 45–46
power inequality in, 38–39
promise to act as a professional in, 38
relationship of trust in, 39, **40**, 56–57
reliance in, 39
rights of professionals, 20, 79–81
trust in, 38–40, 56–57

Professional-employer/principal relationship, 72–75, **75**
agency in, 73
benefits in, 74
control in, 73–74
duties toward clients in, 73–74
ethical duties toward employers/principals established by, 75–79, **80**. *See also* Duties of professionals toward employers/principals
expectations of employer/principal in, 73–75, **75**
fairness in, 79
instructions of employer/principal in, 74
mediator-employer/principal relationship, 113–114
power and influence in, 74
principal in, 73
promise to act as a professional in, 73–74
reciprocity in, 74
relationship of trust in, 74
reliance in, 74
representative in, 73
supervision in, 73–74
trust in, 74
Professional-profession relationship, 57–60, **60**
benefits and, 59
ethical duties toward the profession established by, 60–65, **65**. *See also* Duties of professionals toward the profession
expectations of the profession in, 60, **60**
fairness in, 58–59, **60**
mediator-profession relationship, 108–110
profession defined for, 57–58
promise to act as professionals do in, 50
public trust and, 59
reciprocity in, 58–59, **60**
unfair advantage and, 59
Professional-public relationship, 65–68, **69**
benefits in, 66–67
ethical duties toward the public established by, 68–72, **72**. *See also* Duties of professionals toward the public
expectations of the public in, 66–68, **69**
influence in, 66
leadership in, 66
mediator-public relationship, 111–113
power and influence in, 66
public defined for, 66, 71
promise to act as professionals do in, 66
public interests in, 66–68
public/social interests in, promotion of, 68
public interests vs. private interests in, 66
reciprocity in, 66–67
relationship of trust in, 67
rule of law in, 66–68
social interests in, 67–68
trust in, 67
Professional ethics, xxiii–xxv, 4–8, **4**
commitment to role and, 13
common morality and, 4
conflicts between professional duties and morality, 21–22
critical morality and, 12
discretion and, 44. *See also* Discretion
descriptive morality and, 11–12
duty–aspiration distinction in, 17–19
ethical aspiration in, 17, **17**
ethical bar and, 30–31, **31**
ethical demands exceeding morality and, 20–21
ethical demands falling short of morality and, 21–22
ethical norms, and 8–22, **17**, 24–27, **27**, **29**, 37, 64, 81. *See also* Ethical norms
ethical standards and, 14, 19
ethical threshold and, 13, 30–31, **31**
ethics and, 3–4
ethics of aspiration in, 13
ethics of duty in, 13

Professional ethics (cont.)
excellence and, 13, 18–19, 42, 398
functions of, 33–35
immoral ethical behavior and, possibility of, 21–22
information and guidance provided as function of, 33–34
institutional enforcement and, 17, 34
law and, 27–31, **29**, **31**. *See also* Law and ethics; Legal norms
legal threshold and, 30–31, **31**
legitimate expectations in, xxiv, 18, 25–26, 30
meaning of, 4–5, 22, 35, **35**
mediators'ethics in, 5–8
moral norms in, 8–22, **17**, 24–27, **27**. *See also* Moral norms
moral relativism and, 11–12
morality and, 4, **4**, 8–22
morality of aspiration and, 13, 24–25, 27
morality of duty and, 13, 24–25
non-professional activity and, 20
non-professional norms and, 32–33
norms of, 24–27, **27**. *See also* Ethical norms
norms of obligation and, 16
ordinary morality and, 4, **4**, 24–25
particular activity and, 20, 22–23, 25
particular morality and, 3–4
perspective of, xxiii, xxiv, 81
personal integrity, and 32
personal morality, and 32, 381
positive morality and, 12
private conduct and, 20
professional role and, 4, 22–23. *See also* Professional role
professional (role) norms and, 23–24, **24**, 29–30. *See also* Professional norms
professional pride and, 13
public confidence as function of, 34
religious beliefs and, 33, 189–190, **190**
reputation as function of, 35
rights and, 19–20
rights of professionals and, 20
role and, 4, 20, 22
role-ethics and, 4–5, **4**
role-holders and, 4, 14, 22–25, 35, 105
role-morality and, 4
rules–principles–values distinction in, 14–16, 19
sanction and, 17
standards (or norms) of ethics and, 14, 19
standards of professional conduct and, 5, **5**
supervision as function of, 34
unethical moral behavior and, possibility of, 20–21
unethical legal conduct and, 29–31, **29**
Professional norms, 23–29, **27**, **29**
code of professional conduct and, 29–30
inconsistent with morality, 29–30
law and, 28–30
legal norms and, 28–30
normative force of professional practice and, 24, 26
norms of practice and, 24
ideals in, 23–24, **24**, 26
principles in, 24, **24**
rules in, 24, **24**, 26
values in, 23–24, **24**
Professional role
ethical relationship and, 22
generating expectations beyond those of ordinary person, 20
goals of, 23, 27
identifying/defining, 23
norms of, 23–24, **24**
professional ethics and, 4, 22–23
Professional pride, 13
Professional relationships. *See also* Ethical relationships
with clients, 25
with employers, 25
with the profession and fellow professionals, 25
influence in, 25
legitimate expectations in, 25–26
power in, 25
professional role and, 22

with the public, 25
reliance in, 25
role-morality and, 25
role-ethics and, 25
Professional Standards of Practice for Mediators (Illinois), 109
Professional standing. *See* Standing of the profession
Professionalism, 95, 236
Professions, social role of, 63–64, 69
Programs for mediators, xxiii–xxv, 7, 95, 163
Promise-keeping, 38, 58, 66, 73, 107, 110, 165, 208, 210, 255, 272, 278, 322, 367
Proposed Model Code of Conduct for Mediators, xxvii, 85, 121–122, 343, 365, 397–411
advancement of the profession and, 410–411
advertising and solicitation in, 410
applicable to all mediators, 85, 115, 121–122, 397
case illustrations and, 369, 372, 376–380, 383, 386, 391–392
competence and, 399
confidentiality and, 407–408
conflicts of interest in, 401–402
courts and, 409
decision-making and, familiarity with, 350, 352
diligence and, 406
disclosure of confidential information and, 407–408
employers/principals and, 409
ethical norms and, identifying, 350–351
fairness and, 411
fees and, 410
honesty and, 407
impartiality and, 400
integrity and, 404–406
mediation centers and, 408
normative basis of, 85, 121–122
power imbalances and, 403
purpose of, 397–399
resolving conflicts with other codes and, 121–122, 397
respect/dignity and, 407
self-determination and, 402–404
setting minimum threshold for mediators, 121–122, 397
standing of the profession and, 409
Public confidence. *See* Public trust
Public interests
private interests and, 66
professional-public relationship and, 66–70
rules of critical morality and, maintaining, 70
rule of law and, maintaining, 70
standing of the profession and, maintaining, 69–70
Public trust. *See also* Standing of the profession
abuse of process and, 68, 70–71, 150, 246–251
advancement of the profession and, 317–319
advertising, solicitation and, 321
competence and, 165–167, 181
confidentiality and, 274, 277–278, **279**, 298–299
conflicts of interest and, 193–194, **194**, 197, 200–203, 205–206, 314–315, 377
in courts, maintaining, 232, 332–333
in employers/principals, 332–334, 393–394
diligence and, 255
disclosure of confidential information and, 282, **284**, 288–291, 296, 299–301, 386–387, 407–408
duties of mediators toward the mediation profession and, 110
duties of mediators toward the public and, 112
duties of professionals toward the profession and, 59, **60**, 61–63, **61**, 64, **65**
duties of professionals toward the public and, 20, 68–71, **69, 72**
fairness and, 59, 110, 306, 308–309
fees and, 326

Public trust (cont.)
harmful agreements, abuse of mediation and, 150, 247–251
honesty and, 62, 264–267
impartiality and, 208–209, 214, 223–224, 226, 230, 377
integrity and, 232–233, 238, 241, 243–251, 254, 312, 406
law and, following rule of law, 70–71, 112–113, 247
meaning of, 312–313
in mediation center, maintaining, 336, 339, 393–394
mediation outcome and, 223, 251, 254, 266, 382
morality and, critical, following rules of, 70–71, 112–113, 247–248
personal conduct and, 63
respect/dignity and, 62, 258–259
self-determination and, 136, 145, 152, 158, 358, 372, 377
standing of the profession and, 61–63, **65**, 69–70, 110, 112, 312–313, 315–316
termination of mediation and, 150, 158–159, 194–195, 223–224, 246, 251, 266, 406
volunteer mediators and, 336–337

Qualifications of competent mediator, 163–164, 166–177, 182
Qualities or traits of the competent mediator, 173–174
Quality of the process, 103–104, 134, 136, 232, 234, 238, 244, 255, 264, 312, 318, 391, 394, 417–418

Rachels, James, 10, 344
Rachels, Stuart, 10, 344
Randall, John D., 63–64, 68
Rationality, 9–12, 22, 28, 35
Raz, Joseph, 14, 16
Reamer, Frederic G., 14, 344
Reciprocity,
duties toward the profession and, 58–59, 110
duties toward employers/principals and, 74–75
duties toward the public and, 66–67, 111, 246, 288
Reconciling differences in duties, 117–119, 337–338, 358
Reframing, 168–169, 235, 267–268
Refusing a case. *See* Accepting/refusing a case
Regulation of mediators, xxiii–xxv, 98–99, 101–103, 172, 299, 321, 325
Relationship of trust. *See also* Public trust; Trust of mediation parties
competence and, 167
confidentiality and, 271, 273, 277
impartiality and, 208, 210, 218
with clients/mediation parties, 39, **40**, 56–57, 107–108
with employers/principals, 74, 113, 330, 334, 336
with the public, 67, 111–112
respect/dignity and, 53, 258
Relationships. *See* Ethical relationships; Professional relationships
Relative duties, 37, 117, 132, 218, 229, 345, 398
Relative norms, 21–22, 37, 117, 345, 358, 363
Relativism, moral, 11–12
Religious beliefs, 33, 185, 189–190, **190**, 199
Reporting obligations of mediators, 156, 276, 287–290, 335. *See also* Disclosure of confidential information
Reputation. *See* Standing of the profession
Rescher, Nicholas, 15
Respect and dignity, 104, 108, 110, 114–115, 122, 258–263, 407
abuse of mediation process and, preventing, 261
case illustration for, emotional interrupting party, 390–393
codes of conduct and, 103, 259, 261
court-connected mediators and, 259–260
decorum and, 259–260
duty of, toward mediation parties, 258–260

duty of, toward non-parties, 260–261
duty of, of professionals in professional-client relationship, 40, 52–53
duties of professionals toward the profession and, 62
duties toward employers/principals and, 78, 330
equality and, 262–263
expectations of mediation parties for, 258–259, 263
expectations of the mediation profession and public for, 258–259, 263
ideal of vs. duty, 259
impartiality and, 262–263
language use and, 259–260
meanings of, 52–53
morality and, 52–53, 258–259
other standards and, relationships between, 262–263
promoting, among participants, 261–262
Proposed Model Code of Conduct and, 407
proposed standard of, 263
public trust and, 258–259
self-determination and, 261–262
relationship of trust and, 258
standing of the profession and, 258–260, 262, 314
standing of employer/principal and, standing of court, 260
termination of mediation and, 262, 393

Revised Standards of Professional Conduct for Mediators (North Carolina), 110, 111. *See also* North Carolina standards

Rifkin, Janet, 227

Right and wrong, 3, 32, 361

Rights of clients and mediation parties,
duties and, 19–20
ethical, 20
human rights and, 9
legal, 94, 143, 219, 222
limitations on, 46. *See also* Self-determination (autonomy)
moral rights and, 9, 19–20
to privacy, 55
to respect/dignity, 53
to self-determination (autonomy), 43, 46, 93, 127, 156, 159, 162. *See also* Self-determination (autonomy)
theories of rights and, 9
waiver of, 46, 143–144. *See also* Self-determination (autonomy)

Rights of professionals, 20, 79–81
to accept/refuse cases, 20
to charge fees, 20, 80
duties and, 19–20
limitations on, 80, 327. *See also* Integrity
to withhold services, 20, 80

Rimelspach, Rene L., 127

Risks of mediation, providing information about, 155–156

Role-ethics,
common morality and, 4
expectations of clients, the profession, the public, and employers/principals and, 25
general norms of, 25
mediators' ethics and, 5, 7–8
ordinary morality and, 4
professional ethics and, 4–5, **4**
role-morality and, 4
specification of norms and, 26

Role-morality,
advertising, solicitation and, 321
common morality and, 4
competence and, 164–165, 167, 172
ethical decision-making and, 353
fees and, 321
influence and, 8
ordinary morality and, 4
power and, 8
professional ethics and, 4
providing source of meaning for mediation norms, 85, 116–118
standing of the profession and, 25, 311
theory of professional ethics and, 85, **106**

Role of mediators, xxiii–xxv. *See also* Mediation; Mediators' ethics
  commitment to definition and nature of role and, 231, 233, 237
  communication and, 86–87, 94
  definition of, 88–90, **97**
  dialogue and, 89, 94, 100, 144
  limits to, 238–240. *See also* Integrity
  narrative mediation and, 94, 98, 100–101, 116
  problem-solving mediation and, 86–87, 94, 97, 171
  transformative mediation and, 94, 98, 100, 116
Ross, W. D., on decision-making, 345
Rules, 12–19, **17**, 24, **24**
Ryan Clark, Rebekah, 108

Safety-net concept for exercising self-determination, 149, 222
Schapp, Andrew, 39
Schuwerk, Robert P., 326–327
Self-determination (autonomy), 95, 102, 108, 114–115, 122, 127–162, 377–379, 402–404, 413–414
  active participation and, 142–143
  advertising, solicitation and, 324
  advice and, 157, 160, 238–240, 253, 277, 361, 370–371, 380
  allocation of decision-making powers and, 134–136, **137**
  authority of mediators to make decisions and, 135–136, **137**
  authority of representatives and, limited, 236
  autonomous decision and, 138, 141
  case illustration for, emotional interrupting parties, 390–394
  case illustration for, unacceptable outcomes, 373–384
  case illustration for, uninformed wife in divorce, 365–372
  change of professional role and, 203, 237, 240
  codes of conduct and, 102, 129, 130–131, 137
  coercion and, 129, 137, 140–142, 146–150, **148**, 161, 262, 366–367, 377–379
  competency of mediation parties to make decisions and, 137, 138–140, 142, 145–146, 160–161, 390–392
  conditions for exercise of, 137–143, **142**
  confidentiality and, 273, 275, 277, 281, 283, 290, 298
  conflicts of interest and, 184–185, 188, 191, 198, 204, 205
  duty to respect, of professionals towards clients, 40, 43–46
  duties regarding informed decision-making in, 150–159
  duties regarding party competency in, 145–146
  duties regarding voluntariness and lack of coercion in, 146–148
  duty to prevent coerced decisions in, 148–150
  duty to refrain from undermining voluntariness in, 146–148
  educational aspects of, 134
  elements of, 137–143, **139**
  extent of, 128–136, **137**
  fairness and, 307, 310
  fees and, 325–326
  formal, 138, 141–142, **142**
  honesty and, 264, 266
  impartiality and, 135, 153, 219–221, 367–371
  importance of, according to codes and literature, 127–128
  information about risks of mediation and, 155–156
  information regarding mediation style and, 153–154, 162, 179
  information regarding mediator competence and, 153–154, 178–179
  information relevant to decision-making and, 137–138, 141, 142, 150–159, **151**, 161–162
  informed decision-making and, 138, 141,150–159, 161–162, 178–179,

191, 203, 219–220, 236, 238–239, 250, 321, 325, 367–368, 379
integrity and, 136, 236–237, 238–239, 246, 370–371
justifications for, 132–134
limits to, 135–136, **137**, 143, 150, 194, 237, 314, 372, 377, 386, 393
mandatory mediation and, 93–94, 146, 331
meaning of, 128–129, 137–143
mediation outcome and, 128, 130–135, 143, 147, 150, 158–159, 162
mediators' duties regarding, 144–159
misrepresentation and, 151–152, 264, 266–267, 270, 366, 407
moral right to, 43, 130, 132
normative sources of, 129–132
order of speakers and, 135
participation in mediation and, 127–128,131, 134–135, 142–143, 149, 155–156, 159, 191, 205, 275, 277, 325, 401–402
preemption right to make decisions and, 134–136
pressure and, 147–148, **148**
process vs. outcome distinction and, 132–133
Proposed Model Code of Conduct and, 402–404
proposed standard of, 159–162
psychological welfare and, 134
public trust and, 136, 145, 152, 158, 358, 372, 377
quality of decision and, 138–143, 147, 153
reporting obligations and, 156, 276
respect/dignity and, 262
safety-net concept for exercising, 149, 222
scale and degree of, 138, 140, 142, **142, 148, 151**
selection of mediator and, 131–132, 135, 153, 155, 159, 179, 191–192, 205
separate meeting (caucus) and, 155, 162, 221, 404
shared decision-making and, 134–135
standing of the profession and, 136, 151–152, 158–159
substantive vs. non-substantive decisions and, 128, 130–132
substantive, 138, 140–143, **142**
termination of mediation and, 149–150, 157–159, 161–162, 371, 403–404
therapeutic jurisprudence and, 134
trust and, 130, 153
uncertainty of extent and meaning of, 128–129
undermining of, by other persons, 144, 146, 148–150
voluntariness and lack of coercion and, 129, 137, 140–142, 146–150, **148**, 161, 262, 366–367, 377–379
waiver of, 143–144, 371–372
wide vs. narrow, 121, 131, **131**, 132–136
withdrawal from case and, 93, 128, 131, 149, 159, 371–372
Sensitivity, ethical decision-making and, 348–349
Separate meeting (caucus),
competence and, 169
confidentiality and, 273, 281, 283, 300, 350, 408
conflicts of interest and, changing role and, 203, 240
decision to hold, 129, 235, 370–371, 391, 394
empowerment and, 221
honesty and, 268
impartiality and, 211, 213, 217, 262–263, 371
integrity and, 235, 240
manipulation and, 268
providing information on, 155, 162, 404
respect/dignity and, 262–263
self-determination and, 129, 155, 162, 221, 371, 404
styles of mediation and, 99–100
Separation of professional roles, 49, 62, 77, 233, 236–240, 252–253, 323, 370, 380, 383, 405
Shaw, William H., 29

Skills for mediators, 163, 165, 167–171, 181–182. *See also* Competence
Social interests. *See* Public interests
Social values, 11
Solicitation. *See* Advertising and solicitation
Specifications in norms, 14, 16, 26, 41, 65, 144
Standards. *See* Ethical norms; Law and ethics; Professional ethics
Standards of Conduct for New York State Community Dispute Resolution Center (NY-CDRC), 136. *See also* New York standards
Standards of Practice for California Mediators, 110. *See also* California standards
Standing of the profession, 61–62, **61**, 64, 69–70, 114–115, 122, 311–319, 393–394, 409
  abuse of mediation process and, 243, 245–246
  advertising, solicitation and, 321
  breach of duty and, 60, 65, 314–315
  case illustrations and, 369, 372, 377, 386–390, 393
  codes of conduct and, obligations to the profession in, 311–312
  competence and, 166–167, 180–181, 314
  confidentiality and, 273–274, 277–278, **279**, 298–299
  conflicts of interest and, 193–194, **196**, 200–203, 314–315, 377
  diligence and, 255
  disclosure of confidential information and, 282, **284**, 285, 288–291, 299–301, 386–390, 407–408
  duty of mediators toward the mediation profession to maintain, 110, 311
  duty of mediators toward the public to maintain, 112, 315–316
  duty of professionals toward the profession to maintain, 59, 61–64, **65**
  duty of professionals toward the public to maintain, 68–70
  employers/principals and, 338, 393–394
  employers/principals autonomy and, limits to, 314, 338
  fairness and, 308–309
  fees and, 325
  honesty and, 62, 265, 314
  illegality and, 241, 247
  immoral outcome and, 247, 316
  impartiality and, 208–209, 214, 223–224, 229–230, 313–314, 369, 377, 386
  implications of duty to maintain, 313–315
  integrity and, 232–233 238, 241–243, 245–251, 254, 312, 406
  interpretation of norms and, 61, 117, 313–314
  meaning of maintaining, 312–313
  mediation outcome and, 246–251, 254, 316, 372
  personal conduct and, 20, 313–314
  Proposed Model Code of Conduct and, 398, 400–402, 406, 408–409
  proposed standard of, 316–317
  public interest in maintaining, 69, 315
  public trust and, 61–63, **65**, 69–70, 110, 112, 312–313, 315–316
  respect/dignity and, 62, 258–260, 262, 314
  role-morality and, 25, 311
  self-determination and, limits to, 136, 314, 316
  termination of mediation and, 150, 158–159, 223–224, 242, 246–251, 254, 262, 393–394, 406
  uninformed decision-making and, 152, 158–159
Statement of Principles on Academic Freedom and Tenure, 63
Statman, Daniel, xxvi, 361
Styles of mediation, 86–88, 94–98. *See also* Mediation
  applicability of norms/theory of mediators' ethics to, xxiv, 105–106, 115

competence and, 116, 169–171
core definition of mediation and mediators' role and, xxiv, 94–95
disclosure of, 153–155, 162, 179, 404
flexibility and diversity of practice in, 98–101
impartiality and, 227, 229
meaning of norms and, 105, 115–116, 119, 169–171, 181, 227
norms of mediators' ethics and, 114–115
Proposed Model Code of Conduct and, 121, 404
self-determination and, 153–155, 162, 179, 404
separate professional ideals and, 97–98
shared professional ideals and, 95–96
shared set of mediation norms and, 101–105
Subject matter expertise, competence and, 174–177
Substantive fairness, 55–56, 120–121, 303–305, 307, 309, 359
Supererogation, 14, 17–18
Supervision, as function of professional ethics, 34

Tennessee and *Tennessee Standards of Professional Conduct*, 272, 291–292
Tennessee Alternative Dispute Resolution Commission, 394
Termination of mediation, 104
abuse of mediation process and, 244–245, 248–249, 406
against parties' wishes, 136, 150, 190, 194–195, 246–251
bad faith, fraud, unconscionability and, 158
coercion and, 149–150
conflicts of interest and, 190, 193–196
consent and, 157–158, 162
dishonesty and, 266
duties toward the profession and, 150, 158–159, 194–195, 223–224, 246, 380–381
duties toward the public and, 150, 223–224, 246, 380–381
fairness and, 310
fees and, non-payment of, 80, 327, 329, 410
harmful outcome to minors and, 250–251, 406
harmful outcome to non-participants and, 249–250, 406
illegal outcome and, 247, 406, 418
immoral outcome and, 247–248, 406
impartiality and, 223–224
inability to fulfil ethical obligations and, 118–119, 160, 402
inappropriate case and, 241, 405
incompetency of parties and, 150, 161, 403
integrity and, 232, 241–251, 253, 406
lack of relevant information and, 157–159, 162, 371, 404
as last resort, 149, 151, 159, 242, 246, 327, 399, 406
mediation outcome and, 150, 246–251, 254
no reasonable likelihood of agreement and, 242, 405
public trust and, 150, 158–159, 194–195, 223–224, 246, 251, 266, 406
respect/dignity and, 262, 393
self-determination and, 149–150, 157–159, 161–162, 371, 403–404
standing of the profession and, 150, 158–159, 223–224, 242, 246–251, 254, 262, 393–394, 406
unconscionable, grossly unfair outcome and, 150, 248–249
unruly participants and, 242–243, 391–394, 405
Texas and *Texas Ethical Guidelines for Mediators*, 154, 179, 239, 241, 244
Therapeutic jurisprudence, 134
Thompson, Leigh, 306
Training. *See* Education and training
Traits of the competent mediator, 173–174
Transformative mediation, 86
applicability of mediators' ethics norms/theory to, 115
codes of conduct and, 105, 115, 119

Transformative mediation (cont.)
common practices and techniques, 100, 169–171
competence of mediators and, knowledge and skills required, 116, 169–171
ideals of, professional, 96, 98, 359
impartiality and, 207, 227–229
meaning of, 87, 94, 97–98, 100
Proposed Model Code of Conduct and, 121–122
role of mediator in, 94, 98, 100, 116
Trust of mediation parties. *See also* Public trust; Relationship of trust
confidentiality and, 271–272, 273, 277–278, **279**, 298
conflicts of interest and, 183, 191, **192**, 199, 204
diligence and, 255
disclosure of confidential information and, 287, 296
honesty and, 264, 269
impartiality and, 208, 214, 219
integrity and, 241, 243–144
Truthfulness, 15
advertising, solicitation and, 265, 321–324
communication and, 264–267, 322, 324
honesty and, 54, 264–265, 267, 269–270, 407

Unacceptable outcomes, case illustration, 373–384. *See also* Mediation outcome
Uncertainty of norms, 352, 354
Unconscionable or unfair agreements, abuse of mediation and, 158, 186, 248–249, 254, 306, 380–382, 406
Unethical but moral behavior, possibility of, 20–21
Unfair advantage. *See* Advantage, unfair
Uniform Mediation Act, 280, 285, 296
Utilitarianism, 9, 360

Values
ethical, 15–16, **17**
moral, 15–16, **17**
personal, 32, 185, 199, 226
professional, 23–24, **24**
rules-principles-values distinction, 14–16, 19
Virginia standards, 232, 240, 264, 276, 322
Virtues, 9, 14, 15
Vitakis-Valchine v. Valchine, on obligations of court-connected mediators to court, 331–332
Voluntariness. *See* Self-determination (autonomy)
Volunteer mediators, 7, 113, 325, 330, 334–337. *See also* Community mediation centers

Waiver of self-determination, 143–144, 371–372
Waldman, Ellen, xxiv, 302, 344–345, 364, 373
Wallace, James, 358
Warning others of danger, confidentiality and, 118–119, 289–294
Watkins, Michael, 133
Weidner, Laura E., 127–128
Welsh, Nancy A., 142–143, 306
Whistle-blowing, 78
Wide vs. Narrow self-determination, 121, 131, **131,** 132–136
Win-win solutions, 97, 169
Winslade, John, 227–228
Wisconsin Association Guidelines, 166
Withdrawal from case. *See also* Accepting/refusing a case
competence and, 165, 167
conflicts of interest and, 186, 191–192, **192, 194**, 195–197, **196**, 205
fees and, failure to pay, 327
impartiality and, 216, 224–227, 230
integrity and, 231–232, 241, 244, 245–251, 372
right of professionals to, 80, 327
self-determination and, 93, 128, 131, 149, 159, 371–372
Worldviews, conflicts of interest and, 185, 199, 226, 377
Wueste, Daniel, 4